THE NEW
Whistleblower's
HANDBOOK

A Step-by-Step Guide to Doing
What's Right and Protecting Yourself

STEPHEN MARTIN KOHN

Guilford, Connecticut

An imprint of Globe Pequot

Distributed by NATIONAL BOOK NETWORK

British Library Cataloguing in Publication Information available
Library of Congress Cataloging-in-Publication Data available

ISBN 978-1-4930-2881-8 (paperback)
ISBN 978-1-4930-2882-5 (e-book)

♾️™ The paper used in this publication meets the minimum requirements of American National Standard for Information Sciences—Permanence of Paper for Printed Library Materials, ANSI/NISO Z39.48-1992.

Printed in the United States of America

This book is not a substitute for obtaining advice from an attorney. Every effort has been taken to ensure that the information in this book is accurate as of the date of publication, but legislatures can (and do) change the scope of legal protections, and courts often differ when interpreting legal rights. The circumstances surrounding every person's individual case are unique. If you have a legal issue you should contact an attorney.

This book is dedicated to my six extraordinary teachers: Howard Zinn,
William Worthy, Dennis Brutus, Frederick Brown, Mari Jo Buhle,
and A. Leon Higginbotham Jr.

> *"That it is the duty of all persons in the service of the United States, as well as all other inhabitants thereof, to give the earliest information to Congress or any other proper authority of any misconduct, frauds or misdemeanors committed by any persons in the service of these states, which may come to their knowledge."*
> Resolution of the U.S. Continental Congress unanimously
> passed on the 30th day of July, 1778

Contents

Introduction: What to Do if the Boss Is a Crook?, ix

Rule 1: Use the New Legal Tools, 1

Rule 2: Navigate the Maze, 15

Rule 3: Follow the Money, 19

Rule 4: Find the Best Federal Law, 33

Rule 5: Don't Forget State Laws, 65

Rule 6: Get a Reward! False Claims Act/*Qui Tam*, 71

Rule 7: Get a Reward! Tax Cheats and the IRS *Qui Tam,* 89

Rule 8: Get a Reward! Securities and Commodities Fraud, 103

Rule 9: Get a Reward! Report Foreign Corrupt Practices Worldwide, 119

Rule 10: Get a Reward!: Make Sure Automobiles Are Safe, 129

Rule 11: Get a Reward!: Stop the Pollution of the Oceans, 137

Rule 12: Get a Reward!: End Wildlife Trafficking, 145

Rule 13: If Working for the Government, Use the First Amendment, 151

Rule 14: Federal Employees—Defend Your Jobs!, 155

Rule 15: Make Sure Disclosures Are Protected, 179

Rule 16: Yes, You Are a "Whistleblower", 193

Rule 17: Beware of "Hotlines", 207

Rule 18: Don't Talk to Company Lawyers, 219

Rule 19: Auditors and Compliance Officials: Qualify for Rewards, 227

Rule 20: Cautiously Use "Self-Help" Tactics, 237

Rule 21: Be Prepared for the Lid to Blow, 251

Rule 22: Delay Is Deadly, 257

Rule 23: Conduct Discovery, 263

Rule 24: Get to the Jury, 269

Rule 25: Win the Case: Prove Motive and Pretext, 277

Rule 26: Get Every Penny Deserved, 285

Rule 27: Make the Boss Pay Attorney Fees, 289

Rule 28: Hold Companies Accountable for Paying Hush Money, 293

Rule 29: Politics Is Poisonous, 303

Rule 30: Never Forget: Whistleblowing Works, 315

The Final Rule: Remember July 30, 1778, 327

International Toolkit: Taking the Profits out of Corruption, 339

Checklist 1: Whistleblower Reward Laws (*Qui Tam*), 357

Checklist 2: Whistleblower Protections Under Federal Law, 361

Checklist 3: Whistleblower Protections Under State Common Law, 393

Checklist 4: What to Look for When Blowing the Whistle on
Fraud Against the Government, 410

Checklist 5: Proof of Retaliation, 416

Checklist 6: Discovery in Whistleblower Cases: Obtaining the Evidence
Needed to Win a Case Against an Employer, 431

Checklist 7: Dodd-Frank, Securities Fraud, and FCPA "Q&As", 440

Checklist 8: Foreign Corrupt Practices Act Recoveries 2015–2016, 461

Annotated Chapter Sources, 464

Resources for Whistleblowers, 531

Index, 536

Acknowledgments

Special thanks are owed to my law partners, Michael D. Kohn and David K. Colapinto, who have courageously worked with me for over thirty years fighting for whistleblowers. Additional thanks to Mary Jane Wilmoth and all of the attorneys and staff of the law firm of Kohn, Kohn, and Colapinto, along with the volunteers and staff at the National Whistleblower Center and the numerous students who clerk with us, including Frederic Whitehurst, Jane Turner, Rev. William Yolton, William Sanjour, Mark Toney, Gina Green, Peter Williams, David Lewis, Ashley Binetti, Paul Lyons, Casey Kovarik, Jedd Lewis, Leah Tedesco, and Rebecca Guiterman. Without the support and love from my family, Leslie Rose, Nataleigh Kohn, Max Kohn, Corinne Kohn, Ana Maria Ramos Kohn, Rossie Ramos, Arthur Kohn, and Michael Rose, this book would never have been written. My late sister, Estelle Kohn, deserves special acknowledgment. After interviewing hundreds of whistleblowers seeking help, she was the one who insisted that I write this handbook. Finally, thanks to my agent, Rita Rosenkranz, and Lyons Press editor Keith Wallman for working with me to ensure that this new edition would be published.

Stephen M. Kohn
Washington, DC
July 1, 2017

INTRODUCTION
What to Do if the Boss Is a Crook?

"You can't fix something if you don't know it's broken. That's just common sense."

Senator Charles Grassley, July 30th 2015,
Whistleblower Day Celebration

On August 6, 2012, the U.S. Internal Revenue Service ("IRS") changed whistle-blower law forever. It issued a dramatic ruling on a "reward" claim filed by Bradley Birkenfeld, a whistleblower who successfully exposed illegal secret banking practices by UBS AG (at the time, the world's largest bank). Birkenfeld traveled from Switzerland to the United States and provided detailed information on a twenty-billion-dollar UBS program dedicated to soliciting and managing illegal off-shore Swiss bank accounts on behalf of American tax cheats. He lost his job, was prosecuted for tax violations by the U.S. government, and had spent almost three years in prison. He was a poster child of how whistle-blowers who try to do the right thing can be utterly destroyed. Up until that point it appeared as if his case stood as a warning against others who may dare to hold the most powerful institutions in the world accountable.

But on August 6, 2012, all that would change. The IRS did what many cynics thought was utterly unthinkable. They enforced the whistleblower law designed to protect and encourage the Bradley Birkenfelds of the world who step forward and expose wrongdoing. On that day the IRS issued its ruling on Birkenfeld's case. Mr. Birkenfeld was awarded $104 million under the IRS's whistleblower program. It was the single largest whistleblower reward paid in world history to a single individual. It sent shockwaves not just within American financial institutions but worldwide, especially in Switzerland.

In making its award, the IRS explained not only why Mr. Birkenfeld qualified for such a large reward but also explained the key role whistleblowers play in the detection of otherwise well-hidden frauds:

> *Birkenfeld provided information on taxpayer behavior that the IRS had been unable to detect, provided exceptional cooperation, identified connections between parties to transactions (and the methods used by UBS AG), and the information led to substantial changes in UBS AG business practices and*

commitment to future compliance. . . . The comprehensive information provided by the whistleblower was exceptional in both its breadth and depth. . . . While the IRS was aware of tax compliance issues related to secret bank accounts in Switzerland and elsewhere, the information provided by the whistleblower formed the basis for unprecedented actions against UBS . . .

In Switzerland the fallout from this reward was dramatic and stunning. The leaders of the Swiss banking community, who had prided themselves in keeping offshore banking practices completely secret from international authorities, including the American government, announced that the era of creating illegal bank accounts for American citizens was over. The fear that other Swiss bankers would blow the whistle to U.S. authorities and become multi-millionaires did the trick. Billions upon billions of dollars previously stashed in these hidden accounts has been repatriated to the U.S., resulting in the largest collection of back taxes, fines, and penalties in history ($13.7 billion to date). The whistleblower, Bradley Birkenfeld, had forever changed the course of international banking.

Who are these whistleblowers? Sometimes they are people you read about with admiration in the newspaper. Many others choose to be anonymous or confidential. Whistleblowers are workers performing their jobs. A pipe fitter from Aiken, South Carolina who complained about illegal drug sales at a nuclear weapons plant was fired but won back his job. A technician from Wilmington, North Carolina, who reported radioactive contamination on her workbench. Consequently, she lost her job and never again worked in the nuclear industry. In New Jersey a drug company executive exposed fraud in sales to the federal Medicare program. As a result, he obtained a million-dollar whistleblower reward for "doing the right thing." Whistleblowers are citizens performing their public service. They are your neighbors, your co-workers, your bankers, your bosses. Sometimes they are the highest ranking officials in a company, tired of sitting on the sidelines when witnessing corruption.

The list does not end here. At some point it may even include you, the reader, if not today, then sometime in your career.

In each example cited above, the worker who witnessed wrongdoing or suffered from retaliation did not simply go away, unhappy, impoverished, or dejected. Instead he or she stood up and insisted that "doing the right thing" at work must be protected. In each case a single employee demanded that his company or her government follow the law. This changed the American workplace for the better. These people, and thousands similar to them, changed the laws, protected the taxpayers, exposed frauds, and changed the way we view employees who earn the title "whistleblower."

Whistleblowing is now occurring in every major company in the world, and in every government agency within the United States. Why? The culture of "cover-up" is alive and well. In 2015 the Institute of Internal Auditors, a highly respected trade association of compliance professionals with 180,000 members in 170 countries, published a survey of its members. The numbers speak for themselves. As reflected in **Figure 1**, 55 percent of North American chief audit executives "reported being directed to omit or modify an important audit finding."

Figure 1

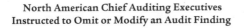

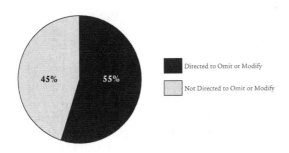

Source: IIA Research Institute, Political Pressure Intense on Internal Audit
(March 10, 2015)

The survey revealed that 49 percent were told "not to perform audit work in high-risk areas," while another 32 percent were "directed to work in low-risk areas so an executive could investigate or retaliate against another individual." The institute's conclusion was most troubling: There were "pervasive efforts" to suppress or improperly influence audit findings. This type of corporate misconduct will give rise to whistleblowers, some of whom will lose their jobs, but others will file claims confidentially and qualify for rewards under the new whistleblower laws.

Based on these findings, it is also not surprising that millions of Americans are aware of misconduct occurring at their jobs. The National Business Ethics Survey found that *62 million American workers have witnessed fraud or misconduct at work.* This survey, conducted by the Ethics Resource Center, was funded by corporate giants such as Walmart, Northrop Grumman, BP, and Raytheon Company, to name a few. This same survey found that an estimated nine million employees who reported misconduct experienced retaliation, and that reports of retaliation were significantly increasing.

Whistleblowing Is More Effective than Regulatory Authorities in Detecting Fraud

Outside of the major headlines, it may be difficult to realize how whistle-blowing works. PricewaterhouseCoopers, among the most well-known and respected corporate auditing firms in the world, conducted "the most comprehensive world-wide" study of corporate fraud. The firm interviewed fifty-four hundred chief executive officers, chief financial officers, and chief compliance officers in nearly every major global corporation, with the goal of detecting the depth of corporate crime in the international economy and the best methods available for combating that crime.

The results of the study were most revealing. It was determined that whistleblowers ("tipsters") are the single most effective source of information in both detecting and rooting out corporate criminal activity. The study showed that some corporate executives privately praised the contributions that whistleblowers made to uncovering fraud and corruption within their companies. In addition, whistleblowers who worked for free uncovered far more fraud than all the government police and regulatory authorities, and they uncovered more fraud than even the paid professional corporate auditors and compliance officers. In other words, worldwide, on a day-to-day basis, whistleblowers detected and exposed more wrongdoing in the corporate world than every investigator and auditor working for every law enforcement and regulator agency combined.

After documenting the immense contributions of the whistleblowers, PricewaterhouseCoopers, speaking for international capitalism itself, concluded that whistleblowers were absolutely essential for the "detection" of corporate crime. The firm urged corporations to change their workplace culture and promote employee disclosures. "Best practice" recommendations for every corporation, the first of which was strong provisions to protect whistleblowers from any form of retaliation, were also established.

The critical role whistleblowers play in detecting fraud was confirmed in all of the annual highly respected Global Fraud Study conducted by the Association of Certified Fraud Examiners. Its 2016 conclusion was clear: "our research has consistently established tips as a major source for detecting fraud."

The internal statistics of the U.S. Department of Justice's Civil Fraud Division confirm these conclusions. Annually, the Civil Fraud Division publishes statistics on the amount of money the federal government recovers from government contractors who commit fraud against taxpayers. Over the past twenty-five years, of the billions of dollars recovered by the government from fraudulent contractors, the majority of money was obtained as a direct result of whistleblowers filing claims under one old whistleblower protection law (the False Claims Act). The Justice Department statistics speak for themselves. Between 1986 and 2016 the government successfully prosecuted fraud cases on its own and recovered $15.347 billion from fraudsters. During the same time period, with the help of whistleblowers the government recovered $37.685 billion. Whistleblowers now uncover 70 percent of the civil frauds recovered by the United States. Whistleblowers were able to detect and report more fraud in government contracting than every government contract officer, inspector general, Justice Department attorney, and other paid government bureaucrat combined.

These findings point to the reality of modern-day whistleblowing—it is widespread, worldwide, and extremely effective. Whistleblowers can create positive change in ways many elected officials can only dream of. At the grassroots level, literally on the factory floors themselves, whistleblowers are changing the way both government and corporations work, and the change is for the better.

The Rewards—Both Personal and Financial

Employees who exposed wrongdoing within their own companies were once universally ridiculed. In the words of U.S. Senator Charles Grassley, they were seen as "skunks at the picnic." However, public opinion has changed. As exemplified by *Time* magazine honoring three whistleblowers as the "Persons of the Year," employees who report wrongdoing are no longer thought of as oddballs or pariahs. In the first truly "scientific" opinion poll testing the public's perception of whistleblowers, an overwhelming majority of those surveyed supported whistleblowers. Furthermore, an overwhelming 79 percent of those surveyed supported increased protection for whistleblowers.

Congress has felt the pressure to act. Over the past fifty years, protections for whistleblowers radically expanded in ways that were unimaginable in the 1960s and 1970s. The federal government mandated that all companies who traded on Wall Street create "employee concern" programs to investigate internal whistleblower allegations. The mandate was expanded to include all large federal contractors. Antiretaliation laws were then passed, covering millions of employees, including those working for federal and state governments and most private-sector corporations. The United States enacted laws designed to financially reward whistleblowers. Initially, these reward laws were focused on protecting employees who exposed fraud in government contracting and procurement. They were based on a percentage of monies recovered by the federal government from fraudulent contractors. Billions have been recovered under this whistleblower law, and (as of September 2016) employees have earned over $6.352 billion in rewards. Congress enacted similar whistleblower reward laws for employees who report large tax frauds, securities or commodities fraud, pollution at sea, auto safety, and illegal wildlife trafficking.

Following this lead, more than half of the states have now enacted whistleblower reward laws for government procurement and contracting. It is only a question of time before all the states also follow the federal lead and expand the scope of whistleblower reward programs. Why? Because they work.

It is difficult to imagine whistleblowers obtaining multimillion dollar rewards for simply doing the right thing, but that is now reality and the law.

Legal Changes in the Workplace

The profound changes in workplace ethics and practices rightly caused by this whistleblower revolution include the following:

- Laws that provide whistleblowers with monetary rewards are now recognized as the most "effective" method to detect fraud.

- The Obama administration's Attorney General and Chair of the Securities and Exchange Commission publicly praised whistleblowers and supported paying large rewards, as have leading Republicans.

- The Foreign Corrupt Practices Act has become the first transnational whistleblower law, permitting workers from foreign countries to obtain rewards in the United States.

- Employees can now blow the whistle confidentially or anonymously on corporate fraud and tax evasion.

- Environmental and public safety laws now include "rewards" provisions, including the auto safety law, the Act to Prevent Pollution from Ships and laws that prohibit wildlife trafficking and illegal logging.

- It is a criminal obstruction of justice for any employer to interfere with the "lawful employment" of any worker who provides law enforcement with "truthful information" relating to the "possible commission of any Federal offense."

- Every publicly traded corporation in the United States is now legally required to operate an "independent" employee concerns program, which must act on confidential whistleblower complaints.

- Forty-nine states now protect workers who are fired for blowing the whistle.

- Congress has enacted numerous laws prohibiting retaliation against workers who blow the whistle on matters as diverse as environmental protection, consumer safety, and corporate fraud.

- Compliance programs and strict quality assurance/auditing requirements are the norm within all government agencies and large corporations.

- Millions of employees must sign oaths that they will report wrongdoing to the appropriate authorities, thus requiring them to "blow the whistle" when necessary.

- Under a Presidential Executive Order, all federal employees are under a mandatory duty to report abuses of power, and this right has allowed for thousands to do so every year.

- "Nondisclosure" agreements that prohibit employees from reporting fraud or violations of law to law enforcement have been struck down as illegal.

- Federal and state laws permit employees to obtain millions of dollars in financial rewards for blowing the whistle. Any business that ignores these new rules faces civil fines, bad press, lost profits, and, in many cases, criminal charges. These reward laws apply to violations of law that occur in foreign countries, and foreign nationals can also qualify for the reward.

- The need to protect whistleblowers has obtained international recognition under international law, including both United Nations and Council of Europe Conventions on fighting corruption.

The Risks and Potential Consequences

Although the laws have matured, workplace culture has not. Difficult choices face employees who uncover wrongdoing. According to a study published in the *New England Journal of Medicine*, even whistleblowers who won their cases had a most difficult time, both at work and at home. While fighting their cases they suffered "devastating" "financial consequences," including being forced to sell their homes, having their cars repossessed, and losing their retirement accounts. Many whistleblowers simply reported that they had "lost everything." The *NEJM* also documented how these "financial difficulties" often caused severe "personal problems," such as "divorces, severe marital strain," and other "family conflicts." Worse still, the whistleblowers suffered "stress-related health problems," including panic attacks, insomnia, migraine headaches, and auto-immune disorders.

"Nobody likes a rat: On the willingness to report lies and the consequences thereof." That was the title of major research findings published in the *Journal of Economic Behavior & Organization*, authored by two professors from the Columbia University Business School. The title speaks for itself. Organizations that could "select their members" fostered a culture where "lying" could be "prevalent." Members of those groups willing to report these lies were "nonexistent."

Most employees who witness wrongdoing understandably fear for their jobs and careers, regardless of whether they have the courage to step forward. But for many employees, their job is more than just a paycheck. Many employees insist that their companies follow the law, and workers for years have been in the vanguard of disclosing health and safety violations. What motivates an employee to become a whistleblower? The *NEJM*'s study identified "four non-mutually exclusive themes" that explain why employees blow the whistle: "integrity," "altruism," a concern for "public safety," and a belief in "justice." A fifth factor also plays a key role among many workers: "self-preservation." These employees do not want to be blamed for the misconduct they witness at work, and they understand their own obligations under applicable policies or laws. The other motivations also center on an employee's basic sense of right and wrong.

The Whistleblower's Handbook

Despite the risks employees take when they blow the whistle, despite the rewards that may be available, despite the long list of laws that may protect those who "do the right thing," almost every American worker, supervisor, and top boss remains unaware of the rules governing whistleblowing. Many employees learn these rules the hard way, through lost cases, public embarrassment, or missed opportunities to create real and meaningful change. Whistleblowers are still fired, managers are still ignorant about employee rights, and the public remains largely unaware of how whistleblowing has changed the face of American democracy, as well as how it can be further changed in the future. Likewise, many managers also learn these rules the hard way—bad press, long and expensive court battles, increased government scrutiny and, in the worst-case scenario, being compelled to pay whistleblowers large financial rewards.

This handbook is designed for honest employees anywhere in the world who need to know the rules for whistleblowing, how to qualify for a whistleblower reward, and how to protect themselves from the retaliation that often follows an honest report of wrongdoing.

Step-by-step *The New Whistleblower's Handbook* explains the rules for whistleblowing. The book provides practical guidance for Americans who must decide whether or not to blow the whistle. For those who choose to move forward, it will guide them on how to not only blow the whistle but also how to win their cases.

The New Whistleblower's Handbook is based on insight gained from thousands of whistleblower cases. It is designed to provide guidance not only to the impacted employee but also to all of those directly involved in the case. Beyond setting forth critical "do's and don'ts," *The New Whistleblower's Handbook* is about individual responsibility, citizen empowerment, and democratic processes within the American workplace.

The changes in whistleblower protections in the American workplace have been nothing short of revolutionary. Every job has been impacted by the transformation. New obligations and responsibilities now govern every major workplace. But the risks facing whistleblowers remain—even strong cases are hotly contested, costly, and hard to win.

The laws protecting whistleblowers are confusing, and many are riddled with loopholes. There is no *one* "National Whistleblower Protection Act." Unlike other areas of employment law, such as the federal laws prohibiting race, sex, or age discrimination, there is no uniform national law creating understandable rules and procedures. Instead, there are over fifty separate federal whistleblower laws and literally hundreds of state statutory or common law protections.

These laws have not been passed in any logical manner. For the most part the laws have been scandal-driven. Only after two Alaska Airline crashes, Congress voted to protect pilots and mechanics who exposed airline safety problems. It was not until the corporate giants Enron and WorldCom collapsed that whistleblower protections prohibiting fraud against shareholders were signed into law. The consumer safety laws were amended to ensure that workers who identified health threats to consumers were protected after "toxic" toys, many containing hazardous lead paint, were discovered being sold across the United States. Each law was a step forward, but each law set forth its own standards for protection.

More than fifty different federal whistleblower protection or financial reward laws mean that there are over fifty unique definitions of protected activity, fifty different statutes of limitation, and fifty separate procedures for filing claims.

Whistleblower protections do not end at the federal level. Whistleblowers are now offered some protection in almost every state. Some state laws are better than their federal counterparts, while others can best be described as pathetic. A majority of states also have financial reward laws.

No one should read this handbook and conclude, "Voilá—I can win my case!" If only life were so simple. Unfortunately, strong cases can be lost, and good people, who tried to serve the public interest, lose their jobs and careers. In today's work environment, however, no employee or employer can afford to remain unaware of the revolution in whistleblower rights.

This handbook is about a new way to look at one's job. Whistleblowing is more than simply winning an employment case or obtaining a financial judgment. It concerns the process of how change occurs at a most fundamental grassroots level—the factory floor. It challenges all employers to make a decision whether honesty and ethics are to be rewarded, or whether outdated notions of loyalty, often demanded at the expense of safety, will govern the contemporary workplace. It is about using the ideals for freedom of speech, fought for by our country's Founding Fathers, to ensure accountability and honesty in government and big business.

RULE 1

Use the New Legal Tools

New legal tools have changed the landscape for whistleblowers and have strengthened the ability of employees to combat fraud in large corporations while incentivizing them to report tax evasion, securities violations, money laundering, fraud in government programs, and bribery of foreign government officials. Under the new laws, whistleblowers can protect their identities and obtain financial rewards if their information helps stop crime and results in a successful prosecution.

What Transformed Whistleblowing?

Forget every preconceived notion you have about whistleblowers and their behavior. To understand how whistleblowing has evolved over the past thirty-five years, you must rethink old assumptions and stereotypes. Even the term "whistleblower" now fails to capture the nature of modern-day whistleblowing.

In the past, whistleblowing came to mean high-profile public exposés calculated to call public attention to major scandals. But the new whistleblowing permits anonymous and confidential filings. Many whistleblowers still make sensational public exposures, but the majority of today's whistleblowers follow a radically different path. The new laws promote anonymous disclosures to shield whistleblowers from retaliation (because their bosses do not know they exposed wrongdoing to federal law enforcement) and permit law enforcement to conduct investigations without revealing their sources. Thousands of whistleblowers are taking advantage of confidentiality protections, and as a consequence, their cases never make the press, and their contributions are not publicly known.

Today, two very different systems governing whistleblowing coexist. One system is made up of old whistleblower laws, based on an antiretaliation model. The whistleblower raises a concern. The boss knows who the whistleblower is. The whistleblower is fired. The antiretaliation law kicks in, and the whistleblower can challenge the termination in court or before an agency like the Department of Labor. The whistleblower is paid compensation commensurate with the damages suffered. These cases are the focus of public attention, often widely publicized.

The second system is a new one, which I lay out below. Understanding how the new whistleblower laws work will allow whistleblowers to avoid many of the pitfalls that have historically made whistleblowing very painful.

The new whistleblower laws are reward-based. You obtain compensation not because you suffer retaliation, but because your information can be used to hold wrongdoers accountable. The focus is on using a whistleblower's insider status to uncover hidden frauds. By protecting a whistleblower's identity, he or she can remain on-the-job and continue to assist in investigations. Compensation is based on being right. The news laws are:

- *False Claims Act* (fraud in government contracting). Cases are filed "under seal" and remain confidential during the first phase of the proceeding. Eligible whistleblowers are entitled to a reward of 15 to 30 percent of collected proceeds obtained by the government. *See* Rule 6.

- *State False Claims Acts* (covering fraud in state and local government spending). More than twenty-six states have such laws, including California and New York. With some notable exceptions, these laws are modeled on the federal FCA.

- *Tax Fraud and Underpayments.* The IRS treats all whistleblower information as strictly confidential. Rewards are 15 to 30 percent of collected proceeds obtained by the government. *See* Rule 7.

- *Securities Exchange Act* (fraud in publicly traded companies). Whistleblowers can file anonymous claims. Rewards are 10 to 30 percent of collected proceeds obtained by the government. *See* Rule 8.

- *Commodity Exchange Act* (fraud in commodities trading, oil, food, electricity, gold, etc.). Whistleblowers can file anonymous claims. Rewards are 10 to 30 percent of collected proceeds obtained by the government. *See* Rule 8.

- *Foreign Corrupt Practices Act* (bribery of foreign government officials). Whistleblowers can file anonymous claims. Rewards are 10 to 30 percent of collected proceeds obtained by the government. *See* Rule 9.

- *Motor Vehicle Safety Act.* Whistleblowers can file confidential claims. Rewards are 10 to 30 percent of collected proceeds obtained by the government. *See* Rule 10.

- *Ocean Pollution* (Act to Prevent Pollution from Ships). No specific rules on confidentiality. Whistleblower is entitled to up to 50 percent of collected proceeds obtained by the government for the APPS violation. *See* Rule 11.

- *Lacey Act* (prohibiting wildlife trafficking in animals, fish, and plants). No minimum or maximum award. No rules on confidentiality. *See* Rule 12.

- *Endangered Species Act*. No minimum or maximum award. No rules on confidentiality. *See* Rule 12.

- *Fish and Wildlife Improvement Act*. Unique rewards law that permits Fish and Wildlife Service and Marine Fisheries to pay rewards for reporting violations, even if no collected proceeds ever obtained. No minimum or maximum reward, and the agencies can use general funds to compensate whistleblowers for valuable information. *See* Rule 12.

- *Financial Institutions Reform, Recovery, and Enforcement Act* (FIRREA). Limited reward provision for banking frauds. *See* Rule 4.

How We Got Here

The change started in 1986 when Congress modernized the False Claims Act. The FCA contained a *qui tam* provision that permitted whistleblowers to file lawsuits alleging that a government contractor had ripped off the taxpayers. If the whistleblower's allegations were proven, the whistleblower would obtain a reward of 15 to 30 percent of the monies collected on behalf of the government. The lawsuits are filed under "seal," and the government would have time to investigate the case. During the investigation the company would not know about the lawsuit or the identity of the whistleblower.

No one knew if this law would work but an experiment was under way. Were whistleblowers simply disgruntled employees, or were they the key to fraud detection in major corporations? For the first time, the effectiveness of whistleblowers could be objectively quantified. Because whistleblowers were entitled to a reward, the government would have to evaluate each fraud case, determine whether the whistleblower's information was the reason the case was successfully prosecuted, and allocate an award based on the whistleblower's contribution. In this manner, the effectiveness of whistleblowing could be calculated to the penny.

The results of this experiment surprised even the strongest whistleblower advocates. They were phenomenal. When the law was initially amended in 1986 to include a modern reward law, the government was having a very difficult time detecting fraud. In 1987, the government collected a total of $86 million in civil penalties from fraudsters nationwide. The amount attributed to whistleblowers was $0. Within six years the total recoveries obtained by the United States dramatically increased. In 1993, the government recovered $372 million from corrupt government contractors. Whistleblowers were *directly responsible* for more than half of those recoveries. The increases continued every year, and the percentage of recoveries directly attributed to the high quality of the whistleblower disclosures skyrocketed. Twenty-nine years after the FCA was amended, whistleblowers were responsible for identifying 70 percent of the civil fraud recoveries from corrupt contractors. **Figure 2** tracks the total sanctions obtained from the U.S. government thanks to whistleblowers from 1985 to 2015, broken down in three-year blocks.

Figure 2

**Sanctions Obtained by the United States
from Whistleblower Disclosures (FCA)**

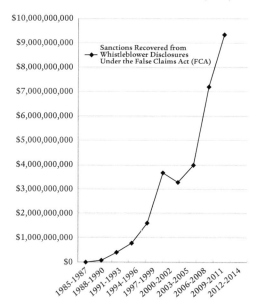

This is why the top officials in the Department of Justice continuously praise the FCA and supported its expansion. Whistleblowing works.

While the FCA was demonstrating, in dollars and cents, the effectiveness of reward-based whistleblowing in government contracting cases, the stock market was being rocked by scandal. In 2002, corporate giants went bankrupt, caused in large part by fraud committed by top executives. Thousands of investors lost their retirements and life savings. Private sector companies and their trade associations started to study the science of fraud detection. They wanted to learn how corporations could prevent meltdowns, as well as protecting themselves from misconduct.

These studies all came to the same conclusion: The largest source of all fraud detections were "tips" from whistleblowers, usually employees of a company. **Figure 3** is a chart of how companies detect fraud. As can be seen, "tips" (i.e., whistleblowers) are the largest source of all fraud detection and constitute 43.5 percent of frauds detected within corporations. "Law enforcement" was able to identify only 1.9 percent of the frauds. Thus, a fraud detection program dependent upon government agents or regulators to uncover fraud is destined to fail. But if whistleblowers can be encouraged to report, the ability to detect fraud will radically increase.

Figure 3

Fraud Detection Methods in Companies with 100 or More Employees

Source: Association of Certified Fraud Examiners, *Report to the Nations on Occupational Fraud and Abuse* (2016)

The next study looked at how employees respond when they uncover misconduct at work. The studies, conducted by the Ethics Resource Center (a corporate-sponsored ethics association) are consistent with every other similar study. As reflected in **Figure 4**, 38 percent of employees told *no one* about the misconduct they witnessed; 60 percent told their supervisors or someone in the company. That accounts for 98 percent of all observed misconduct. Only 2 percent of employees reported the misconduct to "someone outside the company," which would include regulators or law enforcement. But "someone outside the company" could also include a friend, or filings with the Labor Board, OSHA, or the Equal Opportunity Employment Commission, all of which receive numerous employee complaints every year. These studies demonstrated that without some program to encourage and incentivize employee reporting, the vast majority of frauds would not be detected, and the vast majority of misconduct that was detected would not be reported to the government.

Figure 4

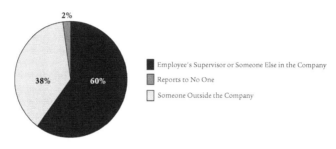

Source: Ethics Resource Center,
"Blowing the Whistle on Workplace Misconduct" (2010)

The most important and comprehensive study on whistleblowing came out of the University of Chicago Booth School of Business. In the wake of the collapse of Enron, leading economists from the University of Chicago and University of Toronto published a groundbreaking article, "Who Blows the Whistle on Corporate Fraud?" Their goal was to "identify the most effective mechanisms for detecting corporate fraud," and their study was based on an "in-depth" analysis of "all reported fraud cases in large U.S. companies between 1996 and 2004." Their conclusions, based on impeccable scientific research, laid the basis for the U.S. Congress to enact new whistleblower reward laws:

- "A strong monetary incentive to blow the whistle does motivate people with information to come forward."

- "[T]here is no evidence that having stronger monetary incentives to blow the whistle leads to more frivolous suits."

- "Monetary incentives seem to work well, without the negative side effects often attributed to them."

The researchers also determined that existing corporate culture was antithetical to employee reporting: *"[E]mployees clearly have the best access to information, [but whistleblowers were] fired, quit under duress, or had significantly altered responsibilities. In addition, many employee whistleblowers report having to move to another industry and often to another town to escape personal harassment."*

Their conclusion was very simple: whistleblowers were the key to fraud detection, but within existing corporate cultures, whistleblowers were punished: "Not only is the honest behavior not rewarded by the market, but it is penalized. . . . Given these costs, however, the surprising part is not that most employees do not talk; it is that some talk at all."

Fraud is committed secretly and privately. Without a whistleblower, it is very hard to detect white-collar corporate crimes. As the False Claims Act recoveries demonstrated, once reporting is incentivized with a monetary reward and a safe reporting procedure, high-quality tips soar and the public benefits.

Based on objective empirical evidence, statistics, and studies, it is not surprising that in 2006 Congress looked toward the False Claims Act to model its IRS tax whistleblower program, and in 2010 looked at both the False Claims Act and IRS laws to model a whistleblower reward program covering the publicly traded economy and foreign bribery. On July 21, 2010 the Dodd-Frank Act was signed into law, which included two new reward-based laws covering securities fraud, commodities trading fraud, and foreign bribery. These laws contained enhanced confidentiality provisions (including, for the first time, a procedure permitting whistleblowers to file anonymous complaints to the government) and set the rewards at 10 to 30 percent.

The Changes

Permitting whistleblowers to proceed confidentially, and basing compensation on a reward for high-quality and useful information, shifted the manner in which employees blow the whistle. The shifts:

Confidentiality: Proceeding anonymously and confidentially is a new way to blow the whistle. This marks a change from the high-profile public disclosures that marked the previous five decades of whistleblowing. Confidentiality is the best safeguard against retaliation. You cannot fire, blacklist, or harass a person whose identity you do not know.

The move toward confidentiality started with the False Claims Act. Under that law the initial whistleblower disclosure is filed in federal court under "seal." This means the complaint remains secret and is neither placed on the public docket nor served on the defendant. Additionally, the complaint and a "disclosure" statement are provided to the U.S. Attorneys Office and the Attorney General. These documents are also kept confidential, and they permit the government to conduct an investigation without the wrongdoer knowing the identity of the whistleblower. These provisions encourage reluctant whistleblowers to step forward, knowing that their bosses will not initially know they filed a charge against the company.

The only problem with the law's confidentiality provision was that it was not permanent. Once the government decides whether or not to prosecute the company, the whistleblower's complaint, under most circumstances, is taken out of seal and becomes a matter of public record. A whistleblower could ask the court to continue the confidentiality requirements, but that was not mandated by law. The discretion on whether to continue a seal is left to the federal judge, to be decided on a case-by-case basis. In practice, cases are simply taken out of seal, making the complaint discoverable.

The Dodd-Frank Act's amendments to the Securities Exchange Act and the Commodity Exchange Act closed this loophole. These laws cover fraud on Wall Street.

Under these laws, any individual can *anonymously* report securities or commodities violations (or violations of the Foreign Corrupt Practices Act) to the Securities and Exchange Commission or the Commodity Futures Trading Commission and *remain* anonymous. Under this provision, the government would not be told who the whistleblower was. This way, employees on Wall Street could be assured that their identity would be protected if they lawfully reported corruption.

The procedure for filing anonymous complaints is very logical. It protects the identity of the whistleblower, but also requires that steps be taken to prevent frivolous or abusive filings. A whistleblower who wants to keep his or her identity secret has to hire an attorney. The attorney has to confirm the whistleblower's identity and make a good-faith effort to ensure that the complaint filed has a sound basis in law and fact. The lawyer has to personally sign the charge filed with the government and affirm under oath that the whistleblower in fact exists and that the information filed with the government was the same information provided by the whistleblower. The lawyer is also required to have a signed statement from the whistleblower, confirming his or her allegations. This statement is kept confidential by the lawyer. If a whistleblower's allegations result in a successful enforcement action and the payment of a reward, the confidential whistleblower must disclose his or her identity in order to assure the government that they qualified for the payment.

The tax whistleblower program also permits whistleblowers to proceed with their cases confidentially. In a major case, entitled simply *Whistleblower 14106 v. Commissioner,* the Tax Court upheld the right of anonymous whistleblowers seeking a monetary reward from the IRS for reporting tax fraud or underpayments to remain anonymous during court proceedings. The Tax Court recognized the "severity" of the "harm" that could befall a whistleblower whose identity was revealed.

Initial reward filings with the IRS Whistleblower Office are required to be signed by the whistleblower, under oath, and thus cannot be anonymous. But the rules governing IRS whistleblower claims require that the IRS keep the whistleblower's information strictly confidential. As mandated in the *Internal Revenue Manual,* the IRS must aggressively protect the confidentiality of its whistleblowers. This includes:

- "Personnel are required to treat the identity of the whistleblower and the whistleblower's information as highly confidential and to exercise the appropriate security precautions."

- "The identity of the whistleblower must not be disclosed to any other Service officials or employees except on a 'need to know' basis in the performance of their official duties."

- "To maintain maximum security, protect documents and screen displays which identify whistleblower information or the whistleblower. Keep all documents, screen displays, and forms secured. This information must be kept concealed from all employees in a locked file cabinet until it is forwarded to the responsible party."

- "Transmit the information in a double-sealed envelope. (Use pink or gray envelopes.)"

The IRS treats whistleblower information under the same legal standards they use to handle other taxpayer information. These rules are among the strictest secrecy rules governing any federal agency.

The confidentiality provisions make it far easier for employees to blow the whistle. In 2016 alone, 13,396 whistleblowers reported tax frauds and underpayments under the IRS's confidential program, and 4,218 whistleblowers filed claims alleging violations of securities laws, almost all of which were confidential. These numbers are staggering, and far greater than the number of employees who expose wrongdoing under the older, more traditional laws that do not provide for a reward and do not facilitate confidential filings.

Compensation: Under employment discrimination laws, whistleblowers are compensated if they suffer retaliation and prevail in a wrongful discharge case. A whistleblower's damages are based on a "make whole" theory (putting the employee back into the position he or she had before blowing the whistle). Damages generally included reinstatement, back pay, compensatory damages (for pain and suffering), and, in some cases, punitive damages. But if the best you can do if you win a traditional whistleblower case is being put in the position you were in prior to blowing the whistle, ultimately the whistleblower always loses. Their career is always damaged and their reputation within their profession is often completely destroyed. You may get your job back, but good luck ever getting another promotion or being placed in an executive position of trust.

The new reward-based laws permit whistleblowers to obtain compensation unrelated to their employment status. Compensation is not based on how much the whistleblower is harmed, but instead on how good the whistleblower's evidence of fraud or corruption is. The premium is on a whistleblower coming forward with good evidence, not on suffering. Compensation is based on a percentage of the fines and penalties paid by the wrongdoer. The better the evidence, the higher the penalties. The higher the penalties, the bigger the reward.

For example, under the False Claims Act, if a whistleblower's evidence was used to successfully prosecute a case, the government is required to pay the whistleblower 15 to 30 percent of the monies collected in fines and penalties. Thus, if a whistleblower reported a hospital for Medicare billing violations and the government collects a $10 million fine, under the False Claims Act, the whistleblower *must* be paid between $1.5 million and $3 million in compensation, even if the company never knew who the whistleblower was and the whistleblower kept his or her job. These mandatory minimum and maximum reward percentages are reflected in other modernized whistleblower laws: Tax (15–30 percent); Securities (10–30 percent); Commodities (10–30 percent); Foreign Corrupt Practices (10–30 percent).

In 2016, the IRS paid out $61 million to whistleblowers, while the SEC paid an additional $57 million in claims. But the False Claims Act, which is the oldest and most established law, still results in the largest payments. The Justice Department (with court approval) paid whistleblowers $519 million in fiscal year 2016.

These new laws successfully align the interests of the whistleblower, the prosecutor, and the public. They all want to bring fraudsters to justice. The prosecutor needs the evidence the whistleblower has, and the public needs the prosecutor to bring the fraudsters to justice—a perfect alliance for achieving accountability.

Emphasis on Being Right: The next fundamental change in whistleblowing relates to the core concept of a protected disclosure. The very first whistle-blower cases created a firm rule: Whistleblowers were protected from retalia-tion even if the issue they disclosed turned out to be harmless or incorrect. A whistleblower's complaint only needed to be "reasonable" or made in "good faith"; it did not have to be proved true. This rule of law, followed by every court, was based on the fact that employees would be very reluctant to ever report fraud or safety violations if they also had to prove their concerns were correct. Who would raise a concern if they could be fired simply because their concern could not be proven?

Reward laws are based on a completely different premise. The heart of the claim is the validity of the whistleblower's allegations. In a reward case, if the issue turns out to be harmless or incorrect, the whistleblower gets nothing. Rewards are based on the usefulness of the information. Whistleblowers can obtain compensation if their allegations prove correct and support a govern-ment prosecution resulting in collection of a sanction from the wrongdoer.

Instead of a whistleblower risking his or her career to report a minor violation, the reward laws encourage potential whistleblowers to objectively evaluate the violation and consider whether the issue could realistically result in a prosecution. This can prevent an employee from being stigmatized as a whistleblower over allegations that can never be fully proved, or that would never result in an enforcement action. Encouraging employees to use a cost-benefit analysis in determining whether to blow the whistle focuses disclosures on issues for which there is strong evidence and/or implicate major violations.

Crimes v. Jobs: Under the old laws, whistleblower cases often became hotly contested employment disputes. The employee would allege that he or she was fired for making a protected disclosure. The company would argue that the worker was fired for just cause, such as insubordination or poor work perfor-mance. Whether or not the underlying whistleblower allegation was proved correct may have been relevant to supporting the whistleblower's credibility, or explaining why the company had a motive to retaliate, but ultimately it was not a required element of the case. A retaliation case is primarily an employ-ment case. Thus the whistleblower's interest in righting a wrong gets folded into an employment dispute, where the employee has to fight for his or her professional career or face economic ruin if the case is lost. Once the whistle-blower becomes embroiled in a hotly contested employment dispute, the focus on the company's wrongdoing fades, and the case centers on whether the whis-tleblower was an incompetent or disgruntled employee.

The reward laws change this. The focus shifts to whether the whistleblow-er's evidence is correct and, if so, what laws were violated and what penalties are owed. The focus is on the company's misconduct, not the employee's work record. This change helps the whistleblower. Instead of facing an embarrassing employment dispute, where the employer has an interest in digging up every piece of dirt against the employee, the goal in a rewards case is to provide the government with enough evidence to prosecute the criminals or hold the company accountable for its violations of law.

Qui Tam: All the reward laws are based on a medieval law enforcement method that empowered citizens to enforce the laws. These old laws were known as *qui tam*, which roughly translates to "in the name of the king." A traditional *qui tam* law permits the citizen to actually file a lawsuit "in the name of the king" and prosecute the wrongdoer as a private attorney general. The longest-standing and most effective reward law contains this mechanism. Under the FCA, the whistleblower files a lawsuit in the name of the United States and has the authority to prosecute the case, even if the government drops the ball. This is the ultimate check against government corruption and collusion with special interests. If government officials are improperly influenced to ignore frauds, "the people," through the whistleblower, are empowered to hold corrupt officials and special interests accountable. Over the past five years (2012–16) whistleblowers used the *qui tam* procedure to recover $1.533 billion for the taxpayers in cases for which the government refused to act.

The SEC, IRS, and other recently enacted reward laws do not have this special *qui tam* provision. In SEC and IRS cases, if the government does not prosecute the alleged fraudster, no reward will be paid. As the reward laws mature, and the importance of *qui tam* becomes more obvious, these citizen empowerment tools most likely will be added to existing laws. But if your case falls under the FCA, you should be fully familiar with the *qui tam* provisions and carefully consider whether you want to litigate against the fraudster, even if the government backs off the case.

How Successful Are These New Laws?

What happens when whistleblowers are empowered, protected, and rewarded under the new reward laws?

As of September 2016, under the False Claims Act alone, the United States has collected $53.032 billion from fraudsters since the law was amended in 1986. The Justice Department confirmed that over $37.685 billion of these recoveries *directly attributed to the "original information" provided by whistleblowers.* These recoveries do not include *billions* in criminal fines, nor do they consider the benefits to the taxpayer from the debarment of corrupt federal contractors, mandatory compliance agreements regularly entered into between the government and the fraudsters to prevent future misconduct, or the imprisonment of some of the worst offenders.

The government has lived up to its end of the bargain. As of September 2016, the federal government paid whistleblowers more than $6.352 billion in rewards for reporting fraud in government contracting since the False Claims Act. These reward payments objectively demonstrate that whistleblowing works, and works remarkably well. The government pays only when the whistleblower's disclosures are correct, result in admissible evidence, and demonstrate that corruption occurred. The whistleblower's information is the key that unlocks the doors to well-hidden fraud. By living up to its end of the bargain, the government not only compensates whistleblowers for taking the *risk* of disclosing violations of law to the government but also provides an incentive to other employees to report similar frauds. That is a true game changer.

The government officials who managed these new whistleblower reward programs universally praised their effectiveness. In their own words:

Chair of the Securities and Exchange Commission: The "whistleblower program . . . has rapidly become a tremendously effective force-multiplier, generating high quality tips, and in some cases virtual blueprints laying out an entire enterprise, directing us to the heart of the alleged fraud."

Attorney General of the United States: The "impact" of the reward laws "has been nothing short of profound. Some of these [cases] may have saved lives. All of them saved money."

Associate Attorney General (responsible for civil fraud prosecutions): "The False Claims Act and its [whistleblower] provisions remain the government's most effective civil tool in protecting vital government programs from fraud. . . . The dollars involved are staggering."

U.S. Attorney, in *U.S. v. Sun Ace Shipping*, "An award to these witnesses . . . encourage[s] those with information about unlawful conduct to come forward and disclose that information to authorities—information otherwise difficult, if not virtually impossible, to obtain."

Chairman of the Senate Judiciary Committee: "One of the smartest things Congress has ever done is to empower whistleblowers to help the government combat fraud. They get results . . . This is not rhetoric . . . The False Claims Act is, hands down, the most effective tool the government has to fight fraud against the taxpayers."

Even the most notorious antiwhistleblower business-lobbying group, the U.S. Chamber of Commerce Institute for Legal Reform, in a 2015 report, lauded the False Claims Act as "the government's most important tool to uncover and punish fraud against the United States."

Conclusion

The new approach to whistleblowing unlocks a most powerful force critical to fighting corruption. It creates procedures that both promote insiders coming forward with high-quality evidence and provides the best protection possible for the whistleblower—compensation for doing the right thing.

These laws now cover much of the U.S. economy. They apply to all federal government procurement, leasing, and contracting. Medicare and Medicaid frauds are covered, as are tax frauds and underpayments. In the private sector, all violations of securities and commodities laws are covered, as are foreign bribery/violations of the Foreign Corrupt Practices Act. Reward laws also exist for auto safety cases, ocean pollution, and wildlife trafficking. Following the lead of the federal government, more than half the states now have reward laws, primarily based on the False Claims Act, covering fraud in state and local government contracting.

Employees who witness fraud or corruption should ask the following questions: Can you file a claim with the government anonymously or confidentially? Are the crimes or frauds you witnessed covered under a reward law? Could the wrongdoer be required to pay a significant fine or penalty if found guilty? If the answer to these three questions is "yes," the modern whistleblower laws may provide you with a safe and effective path to stopping frauds and obtaining rewards. Of course the risk of retaliation is real, and there is no guarantee that the government will investigate or prosecute your case, or that a company will be found guilty. But where they have been properly used, reward laws have worked remarkably well.

─────────────── **PRACTICE TIPS** ───────────────

- The reward-based laws are fully discussed in Rule 3 (overview), Rule 6 (False Claims Act), Rule 7 (Tax Fraud and Underpayments), Rule 8 (Securities and Commodities fraud), Rule 9 (Foreign Corrupt Practices Act), Rule 10 (Auto Safety), Rule 11 (Act to Prevent Pollution from Ships), and Rule 12 (Wildlife Trafficking).

- The Department of Justice's statistics regarding recoveries under the False Claims Act 1987 2016 is located at https://www.justice.gov/opa/press-release/file/918361/download.

RULE 2
Navigate the Maze

On January 28, 1986, the American public watched in horror as space shuttle *Challenger* exploded on national television. Among the seven dead astronauts was Christa McAuliffe, a high school teacher and the first civilian passenger permitted on a space mission.

After the explosion, NASA's top manager for the shuttle program quickly proclaimed that there was "no pressure" to launch the *Challenger* and that "flight safety" was the program's "top priority." Neither was true. The statements were gilded and intended to mislead the public.

The American people soon learned that employees for one of NASA's most important private contractors, Morton-Thiokol, had raised specific safety concerns over the design defects that caused the explosion. However, their internal safety warnings were ignored. High-ranking NASA officials intimidated these engineers, who kept their concerns from the astronauts who boarded that doomed flight and the millions of Americans who would watch the shuttle liftoff on national TV. When the *Challenger* first launched, the engineers actually prayed that the spacecraft would not explode. In less than two minutes after take-off, they and millions of others throughout the world, watched in horror as the *Challenger* exploded on national TV, killing all aboard and subsequently costing the taxpayers billions of dollars.

The *Challenger* disaster occurred at the very time other whistleblowers were exposing corruption in government contracting and absurd cost overruns (for example, the hundred-dollar hammers and thousand-dollar coffee pots). These scandals pointed to the sad reality that corporate managers and government bureaucrats were not capable of policing themselves. Employees with inside information knew of each and every abuse. They needed encouragement and protection if they had the courage to step forward. The status quo was not working.

Change would come. Within a month of the *Challenger* explosion, Congress amended the False Claims Act, an old and ignored Civil War–era statute, in order to protect employees of federal contractors such as Morton-Thiokol and permit these workers to obtain large financial rewards for "doing the right thing." Who could have imagined that in less than twenty-five years thousands of whistleblowers would be using the FCA? Who could have imagined that by 2017 these whistleblowers would force corporations around the world to pay back to the U.S. Treasury more than $50 billion in ill-gotten gains?

New Laws of Protection

At last count over fifty-five different federal laws protect the majority of whistleblowers from retaliation, along with eight others permitting whistleblowers to obtain financial rewards. From truck drivers to airline pilots and from pipeline operators to corporate managers, figuring out the maze of protections is sometimes mind-boggling. Each law is different—some are strong and others weak. Moreover, these protections continue to expand. For example, it was not until 2008, after scandals related to the sale and importation of "toxic toys," that Congress decided to protect workers who exposed safety problems in the products sold to American consumers. A powerful whistleblower protection provision was added to the landmark Consumer Product Safety Reform Act, which provides coverage for over twenty million workers who produce, import, or sell manufactured goods. In 2009 another whistleblower law was attached to the $800 billion stimulus package proposed by President Obama. It covers all federal contractors who expose wrongdoing in stimulus-funded projects.

Then in July 2010 Congress passed the Dodd-Frank Wall Street Reform and Consumer Protection Act. This law took whistleblower protections to a new level. The United States was just starting to recover from one of the worst recessions in modern history—a recession fueled by corporate greed, lax regulations, and multibillion dollar scandals. One of the worst was the revelation that a highly respected Wall Street investor, Bernard Madoff, was a thief. Madoff had created a $20 billion Ponzi scheme. Madoff's fraud went well beyond what anyone could have imagined. But the Madoff scandal was only the beginning. In 2008 and 2009 some of the largest banks, and financial institutions were heavily involved in illegitimate or illegal schemes, went bankrupt, or needed a trillion dollars in government bailouts.

How could such large frauds go undetected year after year? In the Madoff case the answer was simple—a whistleblower, chartered financial analyst Harry Markopolos, uncovered the fraud and tried, on numerous occasions, to get the government to shut down the Ponzi scheme. The regulatory system was completely broken. Only after Madoff's frauds were fully exposed, after thousands of people lost their life savings, and the failures of the government regulators were blasted once again in newspapers across the world, did Congress act.

The Dodd-Frank Act was a game changer for whistleblower protections. The Act contains major whistleblower laws, covering much of the private-sector economy, including two distinct monetary incentive provisions, enabling employees to obtain financial rewards for reporting corrupt corporate practices. It also contains three new antiretaliation laws, one protecting employees who expose fraud in commodities trading, another protecting employees who expose fraud in securities trading, and a third protecting employees who provide information on financial consumer fraud. But the law did not stop there. The Sarbanes-Oxley Act (another major antifraud law enacted in 2002 in the wake of the Enron scandal) was amended to guarantee whistleblowers the right to a jury trial and to expand corporate coverage under the act. Furthermore, the False Claims Act, the premier law that protects employees who expose fraud in government contracting, was strengthened three times in 2009–10, including one amendment tucked into the Dodd-Frank Act. New laws were also enacted improving coverage for federal employees and FBI agents (2016), permitting auto workers to obtain financial rewards (2015) and blocking companies from using "trade secrets" from silencing whistleblowers (2016).

The changes are also international in scope. Although our court system is not designed to protect foreign workers from being fired, the whistleblower reward laws apply across borders. Non-U.S. citizens have shared in major whistleblower reward payments under the Foreign Corrupt Practices Act, the False Claims Act, the Act to Prevent Pollution from Ships, among others. In 2014 the Securities and Exchange Commission sent a loud cross-boarder message in paying a non-U.S. citizen a $30 million reward.

Finding the Law(s) That Protect You

The scandal-driven history behind all whistleblower laws exposes the single greatest problem facing employees trying to figure out "what to do if the boss is a crook." To this day Congress still has not passed a comprehensive national whistleblower protection law. Protections are based on specific issues that workers blow the whistle on: environment, government contracting, fraud against shareholders, defects in manufactured goods, and so on. There are radical differences in the level of protection under each law. Worse still, state legal protections are literally all over the map. Some, like Georgia, pride themselves in being "at-will" and provide their employees with almost no rights. While others, like New Jersey, enacted comprehensive whistleblower reforms. Thus, employees must carefully hunt down the laws that provide adequate coverage, many of which are obscure or even contradictory.

The level of protection you have when you blow the whistle depends on the work you do, what you blew the whistle on, and in what state you reside. If your industry is not covered under a federal whistleblower law, and your state has not recognized whistleblower rights, you are out of luck. The fact that your company broke the law, or endangered someone's life, is not always enough to guarantee protection.

Deciding which law best protects you is, in many ways, the single most important decision affecting the outcome of a case. It will determine whether your disclosures were legally "protected," how much compensation you can obtain if you win your case, whether you can qualify for a reward, and whether you can file a claim confidentially or anonymously. It will determine if your case will be heard by a jury of your peers, or by an appointed "administrative" official. If you are going to blow the whistle, you must understand the complex maze of federal and state laws that govern your conduct, and ensure that you obtain the maximum legal protection. This Handbook walks you through the laws that may protect you, and some of the biggest pitfalls facing whistleblowers.

─────────────── **PRACTICE TIPS** ───────────────

There are checklists included at the end of this handbook to help guide you through the maze of potential protections. The following checklists cover the range of whistleblower laws:

CHECKLIST 1:

Whistleblower Reward Laws: This is a list of federal and state *qui tam* laws that provide protection and monetary rewards for whistleblowers.

CHECKLIST 2:

Whistleblower Protections Under Federal Law: This is a list of federal statutes that protect whistleblowers, along with citations to key cases helpful in understanding the laws.

CHECKLIST 3:

Whistleblower Protections Under State Common Law: This review of whistleblower laws in each state and territory of the United States includes references to state common law and statutory protections, along with citations to key cases in each state.

INTERNATIONAL TOOLKIT:

International Toolkit: Take the Profit out of Corruption: An overview of protections and reward laws afforded non-U.S. whistleblowers and anticorruption NGOs. Additionally, Rules 9, 11, and 12 focus on laws directly applicable to combating international corruption, pollution outside the United States, and wildlife trafficking.

RULE 3

Follow the Money

T he single most important rule for whistleblowers is very simple: Follow the money. Nine federal laws provide for the payment of rewards to whistleblowers who can prove that their employers committed fraud. These rewards can be large. Between 1987 and 2016 the federal government paid out to whistleblowers over $6.7 billion in compensation under five different reward laws. The laws are based on a medieval concept known as *qui tam,* that translates from its Latin roots as "he who brings a case on behalf of our lord King, as well as for himself." Under *qui tam* citizens are encouraged to help the government enforce the law "in the name of the king." The principle behind *qui tam* is simple: If your disclosure results in the recovery of money for the "King," you obtain a portion of the monies recovered.

The *qui tam* or reward laws that provide financial incentives for whistleblowers are:

- The False Claims Act: The oldest of the *qui tam* laws, it covers all federal procurement and contracting. The success of the FCA sparked numerous state governments to enact local versions, providing rewards for persons who blow the whistle on fraud in state and local government contracting.

- Section 406 of the Internal Revenue Code: Enacted in 2006, the IRS *qui tam* covers all major tax frauds and less devious cases of major underpayment of taxes.

- Section 21F of the Securities Exchange Act: The Securities *qui tam* law provides financial rewards for persons who disclose stock fraud and shareholder rip-offs. It also covers violations of laws policed by the Securities and Exchange Commission, including the Foreign Corrupt Practices Act.

- Section 23 of the Commodity Exchange Act: The commodities *qui tam* is modeled directly on the securities law and was enacted in 2010 as part of the Dodd-Frank Act. Whereas the securities whistleblower law covers all trading in stocks and bonds, the commodities *qui tam* covers trades in items such as oil, gas, foreign currency, agricultural products, and other items sold on the commodities futures markets.

- The Foreign Corrupt Practices Act: The Act prohibits American persons or publicly traded companies from paying bribes to foreign officials to obtain a business advantage.

- The Act to Prevent Pollution from Ships: The Act permits U.S. officials to enforce an international treaty prohibiting ships from polluting the ocean.

- Motor Vehicle Safety Whistleblower Act: The Act authorizes the secretary of Transportation to pay rewards to employees who report major safety defects in cars and other motor vehicles.

- The Lacey Act: The Act mandates that the secretaries of Interior, Commerce, Treasury, and Agriculture pay rewards to whistleblowers whose reports documenting illegal international wildlife trafficking result in a sanction. The Act covers animals, plants, fish, and illegal logging.

- The Endangered Species Act (and other wildlife protection laws): The ESA reward provisions are identical to those contained in the Lacey Act.

Together these reward laws encompass the entire federal public sector, the multi-trillion-dollar securities and commodities markets, and businesses that pay bribes in foreign countries. These laws demand that every potential whistleblower carefully "follow the money" and evaluate whether any of the misconduct uncovered by the employee concerns, directly or indirectly, frauds that may be compensable under these *qui tam* laws. Sometimes the fraud is obvious, such as a direct violation of material terms in a federal contract. But other times the frauds are far less obvious, such as the illegal marketing of a drug, which is later purchased by a patient but paid for with Medicare or Medicaid funds.

The critical role *qui tam* laws play in stopping fraud was explained in the 2008 Senate Judiciary Committee Report on the FCA. Quoting from University of Alabama Bainbridge Professor of Law Pamela Bucy's testimony, the committee concluded:

Complex economic wrongdoing cannot be detected or deterred effectively without the help of those who are intimately familiar with it. Law enforcement will always be outsiders to organizations where fraud is occurring. They will not find out about such fraud until it is too late, if at all. . . . Given these facts, insiders who are willing to blow the whistle are the only effective way to learn that wrongdoing has occurred.

Qui tam laws provide an incentive to corporate insiders who are in the best position to learn of frauds and other misconduct for which a *qui tam* reward may be available. They are the only whistleblower laws that both provide on-the-job protection against retaliation and incentives to encourage employees to undertake enormous personal risks.

The False Claims Act

The oldest *qui tam* law, the False Claims Act, was originally enacted in 1863 but was amended in 1943 and 1986. The law was further strengthened by three additional amendments signed into law in 2009 and 2010. Since being modernized in 1986, it has proven to be the most effective antifraud law in the United States (and perhaps the entire world).

How do you know if your disclosures impact the FCA? Ask yourself the following question: Is the taxpayer on the hook for any of the costs that may be incurred for any employer misconduct you have identified? If government funds are involved, the worker who exposes fraud against the taxpayer may find him- or herself covered under this most powerful whistleblower law. The FCA has actually made millionaires out of ordinary workers who did the "right thing." It provides large financial incentives to employees who demand that their companies engage in honest and ethical practices—and who turn them in when they don't stop cheating.

The reasoning behind the law is simple: Reward people for doing the right thing. Under the FCA's *qui tam* procedures, for every dollar the government collects from contractors who abused the system, the whistleblower obtains a reward set at between 15 percent and 30 percent of the monies collected. In an age of multibillion dollar stimulus spending, bulging federal health care costs, and massive defense contracting, the reach of programs or companies obtaining taxpayer monies is staggering.

> *"The False Claims Act has provided ordinary Americans with essential tools to combat fraud, to help recover damages, and to bring accountability to those who would take advantage of the United States government—and of American taxpayers."*
>
> Attorney General Eric Holder

To understand the importance of the FCA, the recent experiences of the powerful drug company Eli Lilly and Company are illuminating. In January 2009 Lilly agreed to pay $1.4 billion in fines and penalties. Whistleblowers caught this company illegally marketing the drug Zyprexa. To increase sales, the company minimized health risks associated with the drug. As it turns out, the taxpayer was a big victim of Lilly's illegal marketing schemes. Doctors were sold on writing prescriptions for Zyprexa. Patients were sold on buying Zyprexa. But the bills were sent to the taxpayer, courtesy of the gigantic Medicare and Medicaid programs. Whistleblowers who worked for Eli Lilly knew of the company's illegal marketing scheme, knew of the problems associated with the drug, and knew of the potential adverse medical effects. They also knew that taxpayers were paying the bill for the illegal marketing scheme, while the company made billions in profits improperly selling Zyprexa.

Under the FCA these Eli Lilly whistleblowers were empowered to directly sue the company. Their lawsuit triggered a Justice Department investigation into the company's wrongdoing. In the Lilly case the investigation resulted in a massive settlement. The company was forced to pay $800 million to the federal and state governments to reimburse the Medicare and Medicaid programs. The company had to pay an additional $615 million in criminal penalties. The whistleblowers used the FCA as a vehicle for a systemic nationwide investigation into illegal drug-marketing practices. The company got caught, and the law forced Eli Lilly to pay the penalty. Thus the big winners were the taxpayers and the safety of all.

Everyday workers had forced one of the world's most powerful drug companies to pay $1.1 billion from its illegal profits back to the American taxpayer. Additionally, the workers who risked their careers to serve the public interest obtained a "whistleblower reward" of over $78.87 million. The nine whistleblowers involved in the case were rewarded for doing the right thing, risking their jobs and careers, and serving the public interest. In the end, they were not the stereotypical whistleblower-martyr. They were the victors.

The Eli Lilly workers followed the first rule for whistleblowers. They followed the money by tracking who profited and who paid. By following the money, they found the best law that would protect and reward their whistleblowing.

How We Got Here: The Birth of
Modern Whistleblower Protections

The mother of all financial reward laws is the False Claims Act. To understand how the False Claims Act works, it is critical to realize that the law was 150 years in the making, from its birth in 1863, during the height of the Civil War, and sweeping amendments, the last of which was passed in 2010.

During the Civil War President Lincoln and his supporters in Congress were disgusted with government contractors, some of whom were selling sawdust as gunpowder and profiting from the terrible costs of the war. Congressional investigations uncovered "waste and squandering" of "public funds." Overcharging was common, and war contracts were given "without any advertising" at "exorbitant rates above market value."

When Congress investigated the frauds, it discovered that insider employees had blown the whistle and were subjected to retaliation. In one case the employee architect of the Benton barracks in Missouri reported that he was "cursed and abused," "terrified," and threatened with imprisonment for blowing the whistle on bribes paid to obtain construction contracts for the barracks.

To encourage citizens to disclose these frauds, Senator Jacob Howard from Michigan introduced into Congress bill number S. 467, what is today referred to as the False Claims Act. As Senator Howard explained, a key provision in the law was a "*qui tam* clause" based on the "old-fashioned idea of holding out a temptation" for persons to step forward and turn in thieves. Howard understood that this *qui tam* mechanism would empower citizens to sue wrongdoers in the name of the United States government (i.e., "in the name of the king") in order to ensure compliance with the law. Senator Howard strongly defended the *qui tam* provisions in the bill as, in his words, the "safest and most expeditious way I have ever discovered of bringing rogues to justice."

Under the law, any person who had knowledge of the fraud—referred to today as "whistleblowers"—were authorized to file a lawsuit on behalf of the United States. If frauds were proven, the wrongdoer had to pay up to twice the amount of the fraud, plus a large fine of $2,000. The whistleblower, known in the law as the "relator," would get half the money, and the United States would collect the other half.

On March 2, 1863, President Lincoln signed into law S. 467, a "bill to prevent and punish frauds upon the Government of the United States." The FCA was visionary legislation. It was passed before the rise of modern industry and before the federal government became a multitrillion-dollar enterprise. Like other visionary civil rights legislation signed into law during the Civil War and Reconstruction, it was progressive, years ahead of its time; its use would remain dormant until the New Deal and the outbreak of World War II, when government procurement would reach a previously unimaginable amount.

In the early 1940s, in the wake of large war-related federal spending, the FCA was dusted off and a handful of *qui tam* suits were filed. By 1943 a mere twenty-eight FCA cases were pending in all the courts in the United States. Although small in number, they targeted some of the most powerful corporations and political machines in the country, including Carnegie–Illinois Steel Corporation (for selling "substandard" steel to the Navy); the Anaconda Wire & Cable Company (for selling "defective wire and cable"); contracts awarded to Hague Machine (led by Frank Hague, Jersey City mayor and the co-chair of the Democratic National Committee); and corrupt contracts awarded to a company owned by Tom Prendergast, the notorious "boss" from Kansas City.

These suits caused panic within the powerful government-contractor community. Before the law was ever really tested, Congress voted to gut the heart of the FCA. On April 1, 1943, Congressman Frances Walter took to the floor of the House of Representatives and obtained, without any real debate, "unanimous consent" to repeal the *qui tam* provision in the FCA. The law would have been repealed, except that William Langer, the controversial populist Republican senator from North Dakota, rose to defend the law.

On July 8, 1943, Senator Langer commenced a filibuster. He recounted President Lincoln's concern that "persons who were willing to make money out of the blood and sufferings of our soldiers" threatened the "very life of our Nation" and "induced" his supporters in the Civil War Congress to take action to stop the abuses. After mentioning this history, Langer concluded: "These far-seeing Senators realized that the most potent weapon to deter these plunderers of our National Treasury, was to make such cheating and defrauding unprofitable."

Senator Langer then warned that the effort to repeal citizen rights under the FCA (i.e., the *qui tam* powers) was an effort to "destroy the most formidable weapon in the hands of the Government" to fight the "fraud practices" that were "inflicted upon our nation." The senator warned that frauds were concocted "in every way" that "human ingenuity could devise." It was the *qui tam* provision of the law, "as old as the common law itself" that "provide[d] the safeguard" and the most "potent weapon to deter" the "plunderers of our National Treasury."

"When President Lincoln enacted this legislation—at the height of the Civil War—he correctly predicted that it would be instrumental in preventing unscrupulous companies from reaping enormous profits at the expense of the Union Army."
Attorney General Eric Holder

But Senator Langer could not hold off his political foes. His filibuster did succeed in blocking the outright repeal of the FCA, but the law was radically weakened. Under the 1943 amendments, whistleblowers were stripped of their practical ability to file *qui tam* claims.

After 1943, attempts by whistleblowers to use the FCA were fruitless. *Qui tam* relators or whistleblowers could not get around the numerous procedural or substantive roadblocks that prevented them from filing claims or collecting recoveries. Consequently, over one hundred attempts to use the law to hold contractors accountable failed in the courts. The law was down and out, but not dead.

Resurrection and the False Claims Reform Act

At the height of the "Reagan Revolution," and its gargantuan increases in defense spending, a freshman senator from Iowa, Senator Chuck Grassley, led the charge to increase oversight and accountability for federal spending by resurrecting the False Claims Act. In 1985 he, along with Congressman Howard Berman, introduced the False Claims Reform Act.

The Senate Judiciary Committee held hearings on the Reform Amendment. The record before the committee was shocking—since 1943 contractor abuses had gotten completely out of control. In fact, things were so bad that the General Accounting Office reached the following conclusion after carefully studying government fraud: "The sad truth is that crime against the Government often *does* pay."

In the middle of the Congressional debate over the Reform Amendment, new scandals rocked the contractor world. When members of Congress took to the floor and exposed that contractors had billed the taxpayers $7,622 for a coffee pot, $435 for a hammer, and $640 for a toilet seat, the media responded. These examples of contractor abuse outraged the public and generated strong support in Congress for the reforms. On October 27, 1986, the False Claims Reform Act was overwhelmingly passed by Congress and signed into law by President Ronald Reagan.

The 1986 False Claims Act Amendments

The False Claims Reform Act reversed the most vicious antiwhistleblower provisions of the 1943 amendments, modernized the law, restored the rights of whistleblowers to file claims, and set mandatory reward levels, regardless of the amount of money collected from the corrupt or abusive contractor.

The 1986 amendments reestablished the rights of whistleblowers to file *qui tam* lawsuits. It permitted whistleblowers to directly litigate their cases against contractors, whether or not the United States joined in the action. In other words, if the United States decided not to file any claim against the contractor, the whistleblower had the right to continue the lawsuit on his or her own, conduct discovery, participate in a trial, and attempt to prove that the contractor had stolen from the taxpayer. If the United States decided to join the lawsuit, the whistleblower was still guaranteed the right to participate in the case, protect his or her rights, and present the case against the contractor.

The 1986 amendments also set mandatory guidelines for monetarily rewarding whistleblowers. If a whistleblower filed a FCA suit and the United States used this information to collect damages from the contractor, the whistleblower was guaranteed between 15 percent and 25 percent of the total monies collected. If the government refused to hold the contractor accountable, the whistleblower could pursue the case "in the name of the United States," even without the intervention or support of the Justice Department. If the whistleblower won the claim, he or she would be entitled to between 25 percent and 30 percent of the amount of money collected by the United States. These provisions held, and the Justice Department did not have the authority or discretion to reduce whistleblower rewards below the statutory minimums.

Other provisions of the law were substantially improved as well. First, Congress no longer simply doubled the amount of money owed by the contractor. The law called for treble damages—the contractor would have to pay three times the amount of the fraud. Second, the amount of the per-violation fine was increased from $2,000 to between $5,000 and $10,000. In 2016 the per-violation sanction was increased to a range of $10,781 to $21,563. The contractor would have to pay the attorney fees and costs incurred by the whistleblower in pursing the claim. An antiretaliation provision was also included in the law. Companies were prohibited from firing or discriminating against employees who filed FCA lawsuits. A worker could file a multimillion-dollar claim against his company and the company was strictly prohibited from firing the employee. If fired, the employee was entitled to reinstatement and double back pay, along with traditional special damages, and attorney fees and costs.

Furthermore, Congress made it easier to prove a fraud. As would be expected, the old law covered any person who "knowingly" filed a "false claim" with the United States or who had "actual knowledge" that information filed with the government was untrue. Despite this acknowledgement, proof of specific intent is very difficult to obtain in fraud cases. Realizing this, in 1986 Congress lowered the threshold for proving a case. The law adopted standards based on the principle that "individuals and contractors receiving public funds have some duty to make a limited inquiry so as to be reasonably certain they are entitled to the money they seek." The standard for proving fraud was lowered, and direct evidence of intent was not necessary to prove a case. The statute specifically states that "proof" of "specific intent to defraud" is no longer required. A person "knowingly" violates the law if he or she "has actual knowledge" that the information is false, "acts in deliberate ignorance of the truth or falsity of the information," or "acts in reckless disregard of the truth or falsity of the information." The statute specifically states that *"no proof of specific intent to defraud is required."*

The "deliberate ignorance" standard is extremely relevant to whistleblowers because, in most cases, employees who uncover wrongdoing disclose these concerns to their supervisors or bosses. Under the 1986 amendments, the failure of a company to reasonably respond to a whistleblower's allegations by conducting a "reasonable and prudent" "inquiry" into the disclosures can trigger liability under the law, even if the top company officials or contracting officers claim they had no specific knowledge of the false claims.

This language was added to the statute in order to prevent companies from escaping liability based on the "ostrich" situation. If a whistleblower raised a concern, and the responsible company official "buried his head in the sand," similar to an ostrich, the company would be held liable, even without proof of specific intent to defraud.

The 1986 amendments also sought to ensure that all recipients of federal monies were covered under the act, not just direct contractors. According to the Senate report accompanying the amendments, this would include "frauds perpetrated on Federal grantees, including States and other recipients of Federal funds." Congress explicitly referenced that payments made under the federal Medicare and Medicaid programs were covered, along with federal contributions for highway grants and housing subsidies.

Employees who blew the whistle on fraud against the government also won job protections under the 1986 amendments. Even if a worker did not have a valid *qui tam*, employers were prohibited from firing employees who filed False Claims Act cases, or who reported frauds to the government. Claims are filed in federal court, and prevailing employees are entitled to double back pay, reinstatement, consequential damages, and attorney fees.

The 2009–2010 False Claims Act Amendments

To be sure, federal contractors fought every inch of the way to avoid liability under the False Claims Act. The biggest and best law firms in the nation turned their powers and intellect into an industry designed to convince courts to weaken the law. They were extremely successful and chipped away at the basic underpinning necessary to defend taxpayer monies under the FCA. Many of the court victories were on the most technical issues, almost impossible for ordinary workers to understand, such as the nature of a "presentment," the definition of an "obligation," and the impact of a "public disclosure" on the jurisdictional standing of an employee to file a *qui tam*. To understand the hypertechnical legal attacks on the law, you would not simply need to be a lawyer; you would literally need to have an entire law firm at your disposal.

By 2008 Congress was completely fed up by these successful legal challenges, and Senator Grassley, with strong bipartisan support, introduced the False Claims Correction Act. At the heart of the effort to fix the law was a recognition that "the effectiveness of the FCA has recently been undermined by court decisions limiting the scope of the law and allowing subcontractors and non-governmental entities to escape responsibility for proven frauds." The urgent need to fix the FCA was further brought home by the increase in federal spending caused by the "economic crisis" of 2008 and 2009, which resulted in more than "$1 trillion" in additional expenditures designed to "stabilize" and "rebuild" the economy.

Consequently, numerous loopholes created by bad judicial decisions were closed by three separate amendments, one enacted in 2009 and two enacted in 2010. The entire False Claims Correction Act was not signed into law, but the major components of the act were.

What was the most effective fraud-fighting law in the United States became even stronger, and the ability of whistleblowers to obtain protection and rewards under the law was strengthened.

The New *Qui Tams:* Taxes, Securities, Commodities, and More

The False Claims Act has worked. Between 1986 and 2016, under this law over $54 billion was paid back into the U.S. Treasury. Countless billions of dollars were saved through better regulations and internal corporate oversight sparked by the fear of FCA cases. During this time period whistleblowers obtained $6.325 billion in payouts. Thousands of wrongdoers were being caught, and it was slowly becoming cost-effective to follow the law.

Based on these successes, Congress enacted new *qui tam* laws, covering taxes (2006), securities fraud (2010), fraud in the commodities futures market (2010), and auto safety (2015). Each of the laws is somewhat different, but given the breadth of coverage, numerous whistleblowers will be covered under their provisions. Taxpayers, honest investors, and contractors who play by the rules will be the big winners.

The ink was hardly dry on the federal tax whistleblower law before billions of dollars in claims were filed with the IRS. Most famous of these were allegations submitted by Bradley Birkenfeld, a banker who had worked for UBS bank in Switzerland. When Birkenfeld blew the whistle, UBS was the largest bank in the world. It had created a "major wealth" section that catered to offshore North American accounts. Over nineteen thousand Americans had stashed their wealth into this UBS program, where their income was hidden and taxes were evaded. Because the accounts were "secret," the stock trades conducted on behalf of these millionaires and billionaires by the UBS bankers were all illegal. The North American program had $20 billion in assets, all in secret "non-disclosed" accounts that violated numerous U.S. tax laws.

Within months of the passage of the new IRS whistleblower law, Birkenfeld walked into the offices of the Department of Justice with thousands of pages of evidence fully documenting the UBS tax scheme. He provided all the details of the accounts, including the fact that the UBS bankers regularly traveled to the United States with encrypted laptops to transact illegal business with their American clients. The scandal that followed shook UBS and Swiss banking to its core.

When the Justice Department confronted UBS with Birkenfeld's information, the bank immediately folded its hand and paid up. UBS agreed to a $780 million settlement with the United States. Moreover, they agreed, for the first time in Swiss history, to turn over the names of more than four thousand U.S. citizens who held illegal accounts with the bank.

Thousands of Americans with Swiss accounts feared being exposed to public shame, heavy fines, and criminal prosecutions. The IRS capitalized on these fears and initiated a one-time "amnesty program," in which U.S. citizens with illegal offshore accounts could confidentially turn themselves in, pay reasonable penalties, and escape criminal prosecution. Over one-hundred thousand Americans took advantage of this program and paid the U.S. Treasury fines and penalties in the billions of dollars. As of January 2017, the United States recovered more than $14 billion in sanctions directly attributable to or triggered by the IRS tax whistleblower law.

What was the role of the whistleblower in the largest ever tax fraud case? That was the very question asked by the federal judge to the prosecutor in the Birkenfeld case:

The Court: Now, you said something that has great significance . . . but for Mr. Birkenfeld this scheme would still be ongoing?

The Prosecutor: I have no reason to believe that we would have had any other means to have disclosed what was going on but for an insider in that scheme providing detailed information, which Mr. Birkenfeld did.

The legendary system of Swiss bank secrecy was cracked wide open by *one* former employee turned whistleblower. *One* whistleblower forced the largest Swiss bank to shut down a $20 billion, highly profitable program and pay the U.S. Treasury a large fine. *One* whistleblower's disclosure triggered widespread voluntary compliance with the tax laws, resulting in additional billions of dollars pouring into the U.S. Treasury. The first publicly known case under the 2006 IRS whistleblower law resulted in the largest tax fraud recoveries in U.S. history.

On August 6, 2012, Birkenfeld's disclosures also led to the largest single payment to a whistleblower under a *qui tam* law ($104 million). *Qui tam* laws work.

The Bottom Line

Why are whistleblower reward laws so important? Worship of the "bottom line" triggers retaliation. Safety costs money. Honesty in contracting costs money. Paying your fair share of taxes costs money. Telling the truth to your investors costs money. Adhering to quality standards costs money. Cutting corners can be enticing and profitable. But in the end, someone pays when rules are violated.

It may take some effort to "follow the money" and determine precisely how your allegations may impact securities, commodities, tax, or government procurement requirements. But that effort is absolutely necessary in order to ensure that you have the best protections offered by Congress and the laws of the United States.

- Checklist 1 offers a list of federal, state, and local *qui tam* laws, along with their official legal citation.

- Checklist 4 contains examples of frauds covered under the False Claims Act.

- Checklist 7 explains in detail the rules for filing reward claims under the Dodd-Frank Act's corporate whistleblower reward laws.

- The **International Toolkit** sets forth the reward laws applicable to whistleblowers who live or work outside the United States.

RULE 4

Find the Best Federal Law

How do you find the best federal law that will actually protect you? If a law has a *qui tam* provision, or lets you file a confidential rewards claim, great. These laws are now the "gold standard" for whistleblowers. They are so important that they are described separately in Rules 6–12. No whistleblower should proceed with either raising a concern at work or filing a case in court without carefully reviewing the reward laws.

But you also need to find the best laws that will protect your job and permit you to obtain justice if you are fired in retaliation for your disclosures. Any whistleblower law worthy of consideration must, at a minimum, reasonably define protected activity, cover your industry, ensure due process procedures, and permit you to obtain a complete "make whole" remedy, including reinstatement to your job, back pay, attorney fees, and reasonable damages.

What follows is a summary of major federal whistleblower protections. A list of federal whistleblower laws, including proper citations and references to important cases decided under those laws, are presented in Checklist 2.

Airline Safety

In 2000, after two Alaska Airlines planes crashed, Congress passed the Aviation Investment and Reform Act. For years airline pilots had testified on Capital Hill about the need for protection. In the wake of the dual airline tragedies, Congress finally acted and passed aviation whistleblower protections on par with the pre-2007 Surface Transportation Act. The law contains a ninety-day statute of limitations and broadly defines protected activity to include internal disclosures to management. Damages include reinstatement, back pay, compensatory damages, and attorney fees and costs. Complaints are filed with the Department of Labor and then investigated. Either party has the right to a full de novo trial on the merits before a DOL judge and two levels of appeal, first to the DOL Administrative Review Board and then to the U.S. Court of Appeals. The law also contains a preliminary reinstatement provision that requires the DOL to order whistleblowers back into their jobs if the initial investigation finds retaliation.

Banking and Financial Institutions

In addition to possible coverage under the Dodd-Frank and Sarbanes-Oxley (SOX) Acts, employees in the banking industry are also covered under three older whistleblower laws that protect employees working for credit unions, "financial institutions, FDIC-insured institutions, federal banking agencies, and the Federal Reserve." The three laws are essentially identical in nature and protect employees who blow the whistle on "gross mismanagement," the "gross waste of funds," an "abuse of authority," "possible" violations of any law or regulation, or specific dangers to the public health or safety. Whistleblowers file their claims directly in federal court. If they prevail they are entitled to reinstatement, compensatory damages, and other "appropriate" remedies. There is a two-year statute of limitations for filing a claim. These laws were enacted years ago; and they do not contain many of the modernized features of the SOX and Dodd-Frank laws, such as *qui tam* provisions. Also, the definition of protected disclosure was not updated to explicitly include internal disclosures. Consequently, a number of courts have narrowly defined protected activity, excluding protection for internal whistleblowing. Because of these issues, if possible, claims filed under the banking laws should be joined with other corporate protection whistleblower laws.

Bank whistleblowers may also be covered under a number of reward laws, including those covering taxes (Rule 7), securities, and commodities fraud (Rule 8), or under the Financial Institutions Reform, Recovery, and Enforcement Act ("FIRREA"). FIRREA is described further on in this Rule.

Consumer Financial Protection Act of 2010

The Dodd-Frank Act did not simply reform the stock and commodities markets. It also contained an entirely new separate provision entitled the Consumer Financial Protection Act. The Act created the Bureau of Consumer Financial Protection within the Federal Reserve System. This bureau has sweeping jurisdiction over numerous federal laws governing consumer financial products and services such as mortgages and credit cards and debt collection. The official report issued by the Senate Committee on Banking described the role of this new consumer protection bureau: "to ensure that consumers are provided with accurate, timely, and understandable information in order to make effective decisions about financial transactions; to protect consumers from unfair, deceptive, or abusive acts and practices and from discrimination . . . to ensure that Federal consumer financial law is enforced consistently in order to promote fair competition. . . ."

The new Bureau wants whistleblowers. On their web page they make a plea for employees to come forward with information: "Do you have information about a company that you think has violated federal consumer financial laws? Are you a current or former employee of such a company, an industry insider who knows about such a company, or even a competitor being unfairly undercut by such a company? If so, the CFPB wants to hear from you. Tipsters and whistleblowers are encouraged to send information about what they know to whistleblower@cfpb.gov."

In order to protect employees who blow the whistle on violations of the Consumer Protection Act, the act contains a strong antiretaliation provision modeled on the Sarbanes-Oxley Act and the Consumer Product Safety Acts. The scope of protected activity is broad, covering employees who blow the whistle on "any violation" of the Consumer Protection Act or other laws designed to prevent fraud in consumer financial products or services. Some of these associated laws are: the Consumer Leasing Act, the Equal Credit Opportunity Act, the Fair Credit Billing Act, the Fair Debt Collection Practices Act, the Federal Deposit Insurance Act, and the Truth in Lending Act.

It permits employees to provide information not only to the newly created Bureau of Consumer Financial Protection, but also to other regulatory authorities and state and federal law enforcement agencies. Like the SOX, it also protects internal disclosures employees make to their managers, and it covers employees who make disclosures in the "ordinary course" of their employment "duties." Similar to other traditional whistleblower laws, the Dodd-Frank Consumer Protection Act prohibits employers from retaliating against employees who file charges, testify, or participate in enforcement proceedings under "any Federal consumer financial law," and also protects employees who "object" to or "refuse to participate in" any violations of "any law, rule, order, standard or prohibition" that is "subject to the jurisdiction" of the newly created Bureau of Consumer Financial Protection.

The law is modeled on the Consumer Product Safety Act and works in the following manner:

- It covers "any individual performing tasks related to the offering or provision of a consumer financial product or service."

- Any employee who believes that he or she was "discharged or otherwise discriminated against" in retaliation for engaging in protected activities must file a complaint with the secretary of the Department of Labor (DOL) within 180 days "after the violation occurs."

- The Secretary of the DOL investigates the complaint. If the Secretary rules in favor of the employee, the Secretary must issue a "preliminary order," which would include a requirement that the employee be reinstated. The reinstatement order would become immediately enforceable. Thus, if the whistleblower had been fired, the DOL can require that the employee be reinstated on the basis of the investigatory findings, and the company would have to reinstate the employee while the case moves forward on appeal.

- The investigation is supposed to be completed within sixty days. The DOL has historically never complied with these tight deadlines.

- Once the DOL completes its investigation and issues its preliminary findings, either the employee or the employer can appeal those findings and request a formal "on the record" hearing before a DOL administrative law judge. The appeal, along with "objections" to the investigatory "findings or preliminary order" must be filed within thirty days.

- DOL hearings are similar to trials conducted before federal judges, but they are tried without a jury. Under the DOL rules, parties can engage in pretrial discovery and have the right to call witnesses at the hearing. The rules of evidence are relaxed in these proceedings, the ability of the DOL to award sanctions against employees are limited, and employers cannot file counterclaims against employees.

- In order to prevail in the case, an employee must demonstrate that his or her protected activity was a "contributing factor" to an adverse action. The company can prevail if it can demonstrate, by "clear and convincing evidence," that it would have taken the same actions against the employee even if the employee had not engaged in any protected activity. This burden of proof is designed to make it easier for employees to prevail.

- A DOL administrative law judge conducts the hearing. After the judge issues a decision, either party can appeal that ruling internally within the DOL to the Administrative Review Board (ARB). These appeals are mandatory if an employee seeks judicial review of a final order of the DOL. The ARB is supposed to issue the final decision of the secretary of the DOL within 120 days. Again, this deadline is rarely followed and internal appeals can take years to decide.

- Once the ARB issues a final order, either party can file an appeal with the U.S. Court of Appeals for the judicial circuit in which the violation arose or the employee resided when the adverse action occurred. Appeals must be filed within sixty days of the "issuance of the final order."

- After filing with the Labor Department, an employee can remove his or her case to an appropriate U.S. District Court. This removal can occur under two circumstances: "[I]f the Secretary of Labor has not issued a final order within 210 days" from the date the complaint was filed, or the employee can file in federal court "within 90 days after the date of receipt of a written determination" from the Secretary of the DOL.

- If a case is removed to federal court, the claim is heard de novo (Latin for "over again"). This means that the federal court is not bound by any of the rulings of the DOL and the employee and employer are entitled to a completely "new" proceeding. Furthermore, either party can request that a jury hear the claim.

- When an employee prevails in his or her claim, he or she is entitled to a complete "make whole" remedy, including injunctive relief, compensatory damages, reinstatement, back pay, compensation for special damages, and attorney fees and costs.

- Employee rights under the whistleblower protection law "may not be waived by any agreement, policy, form, or condition of employment," and mandatory arbitration agreements are void. Although the Consumer Financial Protection Act does not have a rewards provision, cases investigated by the Consumer Bureau may also implicate violations of securities laws. Employees raising concerns with the Bureau should carefully consider whether they should also file a rewards claim under the other provisions of the Dodd-Frank Act, or another *qui tam* law.

Consumer Product Safety

In 2008 the American public was shocked when millions of products were recalled for safety hazards, including lead-laden toys imported from China and toothpaste contaminated with toxic chemicals. In response, Congress enacted strong reforms of safety standards governing consumer product safety. Despite sustained opposition from the National Association of Manufacturers, Congress included strong whistleblower protections in the Consumer Products Safety Act of 2008.

The law was modeled after the Sarbanes-Oxley Act but incorporated significant improvements, including an explicit right to have a case heard by a jury and obtain compensatory damages. A claim must be filed within 180 days with the U.S. Department of Labor. The DOL investigates the claim and provides the employee with preliminary relief if the investigation confirms that a termination was retaliatory. Both the employee and employer can appeal the results of the investigation, and they are entitled to a full evidentiary hearing within the DOL and two levels of appeal. After exhausting administrative remedies, which occurs if the DOL does not issue a final order in 210 days from the filing of the complaint, the employee has the right to file his or her claim in U.S. District Court and have the case decided by a jury. Internal disclosures are fully protected, as are disclosures to regulatory or law enforcement officials.

Corruption in Federal Spending / Enhancement of Contractor Protection Act of 2016

One of the first major laws enacted under President Obama allocated hundreds of billions of dollars for federal spending on countless programs designed to "stimulate" the economy. With that much money at stake, the potential for abuse was evident. Congress recognized that whistleblowers were key to overseeing this enormous spending bill and enacted tough whistleblower protections. The law covered not only private contractors, but also state and local employees whose agencies would obtain billions in aid.

Under this law, employees must file their retaliation claims with a federal inspector general within 180 days of an adverse action. The inspector general is required to conduct an investigation—which could result in early findings in favor of the whistleblower and possible settlement. After exhausting this "administrative remedy," the employee may file his or her lawsuit directly in federal court. A judge can then hear the case. Employees who prevail are entitled to reinstatement, back pay, compensation of damages, as well as attorney fee and costs. A "stimulus" retaliation claim does not preclude an employee from also seeking protection under other state or federal laws, including the False Claims Act. *See* Rule 6.

When the stimulus whistleblower bill was passed, a new push was immediately initiated to extend the scope of this law. Why should employees who expose fraud in stimulus spending be protected, while employees who expose fraud in other taxpayer sponsored programs lack protection? This glaring loophole was partially closed on January 3, 2013, when President Obama approved the Pilot Program for Enhancement of Contractor Protections. This "pilot program" was included as an amendment to the 2013 Defense Authorization Act, and established protections for employees who exposed waste, fraud, and corruption in most federal contracting. The law is similar to the Stimulus Act but only applies to federal contracts or grants approved after the "pilot program" takes effect.

In 2016 the Pilot Program was made permanent. In many cases the False Claims Act will offer federal contractors a better remedy; the 2016 Enhancement of Contractor Protection Act does offer employees tools that can be helpful in protecting one's job. These include a broad definition of protected activity (including internal complaints), a pro-employee burden of proof, and the ability to have a claim investigated by the Office of Inspector General before having to decide whether or not to file a complaint in federal court. The law also provides for reinstatement, back pay, compensatory damages, and attorney fees and costs. Section (c)(7) of the law should prohibit mandatory arbitration of disputes. The Enhancement Act does not cover contractors performing work on behalf of the "intelligence community." The False Claims Act contains no such exception.

Criminal Obstruction of Justice/RICO

In 2002 Congress amended the obstruction of justice laws and prohibited retaliation against whistleblowers. Enacted as part of the Sarbanes-Oxley Wall Street reform legislation, the amendment made it a criminal offense to fire any whistleblower who provided truthful information to any federal law enforcement agency regarding potential violations of federal law. The law was codified as 18 U.S.C. § 1513(e). Retaliation against whistleblowers was criminalized.

The law is very clear: "Whoever knowingly, with the intent to retaliate, takes any action harmful to any person, including interference with the lawful employment or livelihood of any person, for providing to a law enforcement officer any truthful information relating to the commission or possible commission of any Federal offense, shall be fined under this title or imprisoned not more then 10 years, or both."

The law does not permit whistleblowers to sue for damages. Instead, as a criminal law it is the responsibility of the U.S. Attorney's Office to file criminal charges against the retaliator. Whistleblowers who suffer damages as a result of a violation of this law may be entited to restitution under federal victim protection laws.

The federal obstruction statute also reaffirmed old Supreme Court precedent that upheld the right (and duty) of every citizen to report crimes to the police. More than 120 years ago, in *In re Quarles and Butler*, the Court held: "It is the duty and right . . . of every citizen . . . to communicate to the executive officers any information which he has of the commission of an offense against those laws; and such information, given by a private citizen, is privileged."

In 2010, as part of the comprehensive Dodd-Frank Wall Street Reform and Consumer Protection Act, Congress again took a stab at using the criminal obstruction laws to protect whistleblowers. This time they did not leave it up to U.S. attorneys to protect workers. Congress explicitly referenced § 1514(e) as one of the laws an employee could rely on to file a private antiretaliation lawsuit.

In the new antiretaliation law incorporated into section 21F of the Securities Exchange Act, Congress prohibited every "employer" from retaliating against any employee for providing information to federal law enforcement. The law explicitly references disclosures made under the obstruction of justice statute, "section 1513(e) of title 18, United States Code." Under this law employees can file antiretaliation lawsuits directly in federal district court, and if they prevail they are entitled to reinstatement, double back pay, and attorney fees.

In 2011 the U.S. Court of Appeals for the Seventh Circuit considered whether retaliating against a whistleblower in violation of the Obstruction of Justice statute violated the Racketeer Influenced and Corrupt Organizations Act (better known as "Civil RICO"). Michael J. DeGuelle worked in the tax department of S.C. Johnson & Son, Inc. He was fired after reporting millions of dollars in alleged tax fraud schemes to the company and federal law enforcement agencies. Mr. DeGuelle sought protection under the RICO statute because he contacted federal cops and suffered more than two acts of retaliation. The Court ruled that whistleblowers who are retaliated against in violation of § 1514(e) can sue their employer under the Civil RICO statute, provided they meet the other qualifications under that act. The RICO statute provides very strong remedies for victims who suffer a harm caused by a RICO violation, including double damages. Civil RICO cases are filed directly in federal court and a jury trial is available. Although this holding was only adopted by one appeals court, the logic of the ruling was very strong and other courts should follow this precedent.

Discrimination Laws

Every major employment discrimination law contains an antiretaliation provision. They prohibit retaliation against employees who oppose discriminatory practices or who blow the whistle on violations of equal employment opportunity laws, such as Title VII of the Civil Rights Act and the Age Discrimination Act.

Just as a whistleblower in the corporate area plays a key role in protecting shareholders from fraud, employees are also encouraged or expected to report incidents of race, sex, disability, national origin, and other forms of on-the-job discrimination to the proper authorities. These whistleblower-related disclosures are viewed by the courts as key for the proper functioning of civil rights laws.

The employment discrimination laws that include antiretaliation provisions include Titles VII and IX of the Civil Rights Act of 1964, the Americans with Disabilities Act, the Age Discrimination Act, the Fair Labor Standards Act, the National Labor Relations Act, the Family and Medical Leave Act, the Employee Polygraph Protection Act, the Migrant and Seasonal Agricultural Workers Act, and the Employee Retirement Income Security Act.

Dodd-Frank Wall Street Reform and Consumer Protection Act

On July 22, 2010, President Obama signed into law the Dodd-Frank Wall Street Reform and Consumer Protection Act. This two thousand–page law was heralded as the most important overhaul of the rules governing the U.S. economy since the Great Depression of the 1930s. Chairman of the Senate Banking Committee, Senator Christopher Dodd, explained why Congress enacted such sweeping regulatory reforms:

> Over the past two years, America has faced the worst financial crisis since the Great Depression. Millions of Americans have lost their homes, their jobs, their savings and their faith in our economy. The American people have called on us to set clear rules of the road for the financial industry to prevent a repeat of the financial collapse that cost so many so dearly.

The reforms impacted the entire financial sector of the U.S. economy, changing rules governing everything from mortgages, consumer credit, financial products, bailouts, regulatory transparency, hedge funds, "over-the-counter derivatives," and "asset-backed securities," corporate governance, investor protections, enforcement procedures, the operations of the Federal Reserve System, and regulation of foreign exchange transactions.

As Congress debated the law, there was a strong consensus that whistleblower protection was essential for the enforcement of securities laws. Employees would be enlisted to help ensure that investors, consumers, mortgage holders, and taxpayers were not ripped off by sophisticated fraud in the sale of commodities, stocks, and bonds that underpin the American economy. The regulatory safety net designed to prevent fraud on Wall Street was broken. Employees with inside information were needed to "provide a vital early warning system to detect and expose fraud in the financial system."

After months of blocked filibusters, compromises, and legislative horse-trading, the Dodd-Frank Act emerged as one of the most important milestones for protecting corporate whistleblowers ever enacted in the United States. The law did not contain just one whistleblower protection provision. There were eight separate sections creating or enhancing corporate whistleblower rights, including two new *qui tam* laws, new antiretaliation laws attached to the Securities and Commodity Exchange Acts, major reforms of the Sarbanes-Oxley whistleblower law, new whistleblower protections under federal consumer protection laws, an amendment to the False Claims Act antiretaliation law, and a statutory requirement that the Securities and Exchange Commission create a whistleblower protection office. These legislative milestones set the stage for the future of corporate whistleblower protection.

Perhaps the most important whistleblower protections contained in the Dodd-Frank Act created *qui tam* procedures for commodities and securities fraud. They were based on the whistleblower provisions of the FCA and the IRS code. Like these two laws, under the Dodd-Frank Act employees or "relators" can file fraud and misconduct charges against their employers (or other companies or "traders" in the financial services industry) and, if validated, obtain a significant financial reward. Like the FCA, the laws also prohibit retaliation against employees who file these claims. Additionally, like the IRS tax whistleblower law, the SEC is required to establish a new whistleblower protection office dedicated to enforcing whistleblower rights.

The new *qui tam* laws also contained a new, unique feature that for the first time permits whistleblowers to file their claims completely anonymously. The whistleblower can file his or her claim through an attorney, and the government regulators do not even know the name of the employee. Only after the employee actually wins his or her case, and is entitled to a reward, would the government regulators actually learn the identity of the whistleblower. The ability of employees to file anonymous claims is a major breakthrough for whistleblower rights. The Dodd-Frank Act is the first whistleblower protection law that permits anonymous filings.

The *qui tam*–related whistleblower laws include the following:

- A *qui tam* whistleblower incentive law mandating the payment of rewards to whistleblowers who provide inside information on violations of the Security Exchange Act or "SEA." Employees who disclose "original information" to the SEC regarding violations of the securities laws would be entitled to between 10 percent and 30 percent of any monetary sanctions obtained by the United States. These sanctions are not just limited to fines and penalties, but also include "disgorgement" penalties, which force companies to pay to the government the value of all of the benefits it obtained from its wrongful acts. Employees can file their reward claims confidentially, and if a claim is denied, the decision of the SEC can be appealed in court.

- A *qui tam* whistleblower incentive law mandating the payment of rewards to whistleblowers who provide inside information on violations of the Commodity Exchange Act or "CEA." Employees who disclose "original information" to the Commodity Futures Trading Commission (CFTC) regarding violations of the commodities trading laws would be entitled to between 10 percent and 30 percent of any monetary sanctions obtained by the United States, including monies obtained as part of a disgorgement. Employees can file their reward claims confidentially, and if a claim is denied, the decision of the CFTC can be appealed in court.

- The *qui tam* provisions cover not only violations of the SEA and CEA, but also other laws enforced by these agencies, most notably the Foreign Corrupt Practices Act.

- New antiretaliation laws prohibiting discrimination against any person who files a *qui tam* claim under the CEA or SEA. These laws provide direct access to U.S. district court and provide for jury trials. The CEA antiretaliation law permits employees to obtain reinstatement, back pay, special damages, and attorney fees and costs. The law has a two-year statute of limitations and prohibits mandatory arbitration. The SEA antiretaliation law is similar, but it provides for double back pay and has a more liberal statute of limitations. Under the SEA, claims must be filed "three years after the date when facts material to the right of action are known or reasonably should have been known." Because this date is not tied to the date of the adverse action, the law also requires that any employment claim be filed within ten years of the adverse employment action. Neither the CEA nor the SEA whistleblower law are "exclusive," and employees can combine lawsuits under these two new laws with other state or federal protections, such as the Sarbanes-Oxley Act or the newly created whistleblower protections covering the Consumer Financial Protection Bureau.

- A requirement that the SEC establish a whistleblower protection office and implement formal rules ensuring that the rewards program is properly administered. It is critical that any employees who file securities or commodities *qui tam* claims carefully study the rules and regulations of the new SEC whistleblower protection office (and any counterpart established or implemented by the CFTC). Both of the new *qui tam* laws require that all claims filed strictly comply with the regulations issued by these agencies. A whistleblower can be disqualified from obtaining a reward simply for failing to follow these regulations. Thus, before a claim is officially filed, any whistleblower *must* review these rules and file his or her claim accordingly. These requirements are set forth in Checklist 7.

In addition to the *qui tam* provisions, the Dodd-Frank Act also revamped and expanded other antiretaliation laws that apply to corporate America. The most important of these reforms were key enhancements to the 2002 Sarbanes-Oxley Act. The SOX was originally intended to be a "Cadillac" whistleblower protection law, but a series of terrible court rulings created massive confusion as to the scope of the law and effectively undermined its utility. Employee claims were regularly dismissed on narrow technicalities. For example, some courts ruled that the protections only applied to the actual "publicly traded" corporation and did not apply to a subsidiary of a publicly traded corporation. This holding, although not uniformly applied, devastated coverage under the SOX, as many "publicly traded" companies conducted the vast amount of their business through wholly owned subsidiaries.

Responding to these devastating court rulings, the SOX was amended and enhanced in the following manner:

- The right to a trial by jury was made explicit in the law;

- Subsidiaries of publicly held corporations were explicitly added to the type of employers covered under the SOX;

- The statute of limitations was lengthened from 90 days to 180 days;

- Mandatory arbitration was prohibited.

- Corporate rating organizations, such as Moody's and Standard and Poor's, were included in the definition of employers covered under the SOX.

The revamped SOX is *not* an exclusive remedy. Employees can file both *qui tam* claims and SOX retaliation claims. Employees can join state causes of action with their SOX lawsuits, once the SOX claim is removed to federal court. Furthermore, employees can also join the new antiretaliation remedies contained under sections 748 and 922 of the Dodd-Frank Act with claims filed in federal court under the SOX. Joining these multiple causes of action into one large federal suit both expands the remedies available under any one law and expands the scope of activities that may be protected in the lawsuit. For example, state laws often provide for punitive damages that are not available under federal laws. Likewise, section 922 of the Dodd-Frank Act contains a broad definition of protected activity that may encompass disclosures that fall outside of the SOX protection.

The reward laws incorporated through the Dodd-Frank Act are more fully explained in Rules 8 and 9 (commodity and securities fraud and foreign bribery) and Checklist 7 (Dodd-Frank, Wall Street, and FCPA "Q&As").

Employment Contracts, Union Grievance Procedures

Most union contracts protect employees (including government employees) from dismissal unless "good cause" exists. Obviously, firing a worker simply for making a lawful disclosure of misconduct to the appropriate authority would not constitute "good cause." In these cases an employee has the option to seek protection through his or her labor union under contract, grievance, or arbitration procedures. However, utilizing these remedies may result in the waiver of an employee's right to obtain relief under other whistleblower protection laws, and damages available in grievance or arbitration proceedings are limited.

Environmental Laws

Between 1972 and 1980 Congress recognized the importance of workers in exposing violations of environmental law. Employees were in the best position to identify serious environmental violations, as they would be the ones ordered to dump toxic waste, certify compliance with Environmental Protection Agency (EPA) permits, or test the quality of drinking water. Without protecting rank-and-file employees from retaliation, how could local communities learn that they were being polluted, especially before someone died from toxic exposure? The answer was to protect the whistleblowers. Consequently, the environmental whistleblowers were among the first such class of workers protected under law.

Because they were enacted over thirty years ago, these laws are in need of modernization. The major flaw is a radically short statute of limitations (thirty days) and the inability to remove a case to federal court. But despite these significant weaknesses, employees have been able to prevail in cases filed under these older laws.

Six environmental laws contain whistleblower protections that are administered by the U.S. Department of Labor. The first was the 1972 Water Pollution Control Act. Thereafter, Congress used the law as a model for the "employee protection provisions" of the 1974 Safe Drinking Water Act, the 1976 Toxic Substances Control Act, the 1976 Solid Waste Disposal Act, the 1977 Clean Air Act, and the 1980 Comprehensive Environmental Response, Compensation and Liability Act (better known simply as the "Superfund" law). A seventh environmental whistleblower law, attached as an amendment to the Surface Mining Act, is substantially identical to the six DOL-administered laws, except that it is administered by the Department of the Interior. Few cases have been filed under this law, which has been virtually ignored by Interior.

The scope of protected activity under the DOL-administered laws has been broadly defined to include disclosures to government regulators, supervisors, and the news media. The six laws all provide for reinstatement, back pay, compensatory damages, and attorney fees and costs. Punitive damages are available under two of the environmental laws. Claims must be filed with the DOL. Although federal court remedies are considered superior to administrative remedies, the DOL procedures are employee-friendly in that they provide for discovery rights similar to those offered in federal court, and the rules of evidence are relaxed, making it far less formal than federal court proceedings. Claims are first investigated by the Occupational Safety and Health Administration, which issues an initial determination. That ruling is completely nonbinding if either party appeals and requests a hearing. Cases are then tried before DOL administrative law judges, who are knowledgeable about the law and generally permit employees an opportunity to fully present their cases at a hearing.

Cases are subject to two levels of appeal. The first appeal is to a board appointed by the secretary of the DOL (the members whom the secretary can hire or fire at will). The second is to the U.S. Court of Appeals. With the right case these laws can be effective.

These laws have special significance for federal employees. Unlike other laws that cover private sector workers, four of these laws also cover federal employees. *See* Rule 14.

Federal Employees

Protections for federal employees are covered in Rule 14. Additionally, the websites of the Office of Special Counsel and the Merit Systems Protection Board contain extensive information on filing procedures, case precedents, and explanations as to how the Whistleblower Protection Act, the main law protecting federal employees, works. These websites are located at https://osc.gov and www.mspb.gov, respectively.

First Amendment Protections for Public Employees

One of the most important whistleblower protection laws is the First Amendment to the U.S. Constitution. The First Amendment was intended to protect speech critical of government operations or exposing corruption. In 1871, as part of the post–Civil War Reconstruction laws, Congress created a tort-type remedy for persons harmed when "state action" interfered with a constitutional right. Over time this law was applied to public employees and interpreted to protect whistleblowers who work for state and local government from retaliation. The law provides federal court jurisdiction, with the right to have claims heard by a jury. Traditional labor law remedies are available, such as reinstatement and back pay. Public employees are also entitled to compensatory damages, punitive damages, and attorney fees and costs.

The legal protections provided under the First Amendment and the Civil Rights Act of 1871 are explained in Rule 13.

Although the First Amendment should also apply to employees who work in the federal government, a series of Supreme Court cases has radically narrowed its applicability. Federal employees who suffer retaliation for exposing waste, fraud, or abuse are, in almost every circumstance, required to use the Whistleblower Protection Act as their exclusive remedy.

Financial Institutions Reform, Recovery, and Enforcement Act (FIRREA)

In 1989 Congress passed the Financial Institutions Reform, Recovery, and Enforcement Act (FIRREA). The law created civil liability for violations of fourteen underlying criminal laws, mostly as they relate to banks (or, as defined in the statute, "federally insured financial institutions"). These laws include mail and wire fraud, making false statements to government officials, and financial institution fraud. If someone makes a *criminal* false statement to a government official related to fraud in a bank, that person can be criminally indicted under criminal law. But that person can also be held liable for money damages under FIRREA.

Civil lawsuits are far easier to win than criminal cases. The burden of proof is significantly reduced (i.e., from "beyond a reasonable doubt" in a criminal matter to a mere "preponderance of evidence" in a civil case), and constitutional protections against self incrimination do not apply. By using FIRREA to prosecute bankers who engage in criminal fraud, the government can realistically pursue and win a case. Bottom line: The ability of the government to prevail in a bank fraud case under FIRREA is far easier than obtaining a criminal conviction.

In regard to prosecuting the big banks, for twenty-five years the law was ignored. Most of the criminal laws referenced in FIRREA were designed to permit lawsuits against individuals who defrauded a bank, such as a bank teller who embezzled money from a local savings and loan bank. But everything changed in 2013. The United States sued the Bank of New York (BNY) Mellon, one of the world's largest financial institutions. The approach used by the United States was novel: The bank could be sued for defrauding itself. In other words, if bank employees engaged in fraud to enrich the bank, the bank could be held liable. If accepted, this approach would convert FIRREA from a law that simply targeted *people* who violated one of the fourteen identified laws to rip off a bank to one that targeted *banks* for violating one of the fourteen laws to rip off the government, investors, or the American people (such as engaging in illegal loan practices).

In a precedent-setting case, U.S. District Judge Lewis A. Kaplan held that FIRREA was designed to "deter fraudulent conduct that might put federally insured deposits at risk." Thus, banks that harm themselves by engaging in fraudulent financial transactions to increase profits are guilty of placing insured deposits at risk. As explained by Judge Kaplan:

Congress was addressing not only frauds by insiders who were trying to harm their employers, but also frauds by insiders seeking to benefit their employers—perhaps through deception of auditors or regulators.

* * *

Ensuring that taxpayers would not need to bail the industry out again in order to protect the funds of depositors is consistent not only with seeking to prevent fraud perpetrated against the financial institutions, but also with deterring or punishing fraud which occurs as a result of insiders' misguided efforts to benefit their institutions, particularly insofar as those efforts ultimately go on to expose the institutions to new and harmful risks.

* * *

In sum, the essential point is this: the statute permits penalties against "whoever" commits a fraud affecting a federally insured financial institution. The purpose of that provision is to deter frauds that might put federally insured deposits at risk. Here, [BYN Mellon] has been charged with participating in a fraudulent scheme and harming itself in the process. Just as Congress clearly intended to deter bank employees from engaging in fraud that results in harm to these institutions, Congress was entitled to conclude that penalties against financial institutions in cases like this would deter such institutions from similar, harmful, fraudulent conduct.

United States of America vs. The Bank of New York Mellon Corporation unlocked the potential of FIRREA. Since that case, numerous other bank-fraud cases have been filed and billions of dollars recovered from banks that robbed taxpayers by obtaining bailouts, robbed their investors when stocks plummeted, and robbed their customers when they issued bad mortgages and other fraudulent financial instruments.

The BNY Mellon case was settled on March 9, 2015, for a total of $714 million paid to investors, the State of New York, and the federal government. U.S. taxpayers got back $167.5 million, the Department of Labor obtained $84 million to compensate victims who participated in the bank's retirement plans, and the Securities and Exchange Commission obtained $30 million in sanctions to compensate investors.

Eric Schneiderman, Attorney General for the State of New York, explained the importance of the *Mellon* precedent: "Investors count on financial institutions to tell them the truth about how their investments are being managed. The Bank of New York Mellon misled customers and traded at their expense. Today's settlement shows that institutions and individuals responsible for defrauding investors will be held accountable and will face serious consequences for their wrongdoing."

How does all this relate to whistleblowers?

FIRREA is an older law that contains one of the worst federal whistleblower reward statutes. Whistleblower rewards are capped at a maximum of $1.6 million. Even the Attorney General of the United States recognized that this maximum award would not properly incentivize employees to risk their careers to step forward, and in many cases would not even compensate Wall Street bankers for their direct financial losses when they were fired for being whistleblowers. In 2014 the Attorney General called for the law to be amended, consistent with the False Claims Act. Ultimately, in order to promote the detection and prosecution of bank fraud, the FIRREA whistleblower provision will need to be fixed.

Another problem concerns the lack of judicial review. The whistleblower law indicates that the Department of Justice should be required to pay rewards. However, a whistleblower who is denied a reward (or who objects to the amount of a reward) cannot appeal this decision in court.

FIRREA has unique filing provisions that require a whistleblower to execute a detailed "declaration" and confidentially file it with the Attorney General. These provisions are set forth in Title 12 U.S. Code, Sections 4201–23. Declarations must be made under oath and set forth the basis of the whistleblower's knowledge of the underlying facts. The factual assertion should be very specific and must contain "at least one new factual element necessary to establish a prima facie case" of a FIRREA violation that was "unknown to the government."

There is one unique provision in the FIRREA statute that apparently has never been used: If the United States decides not to directly prosecute a FIRREA violation, the Attorney General can appoint a private attorney to bring the case. This private attorney must be approved by the whistleblower, and can be paid on a reasonable contingent fee basis. Additionally, if the Attorney General has not made a decision as to whether to prosecute a FIRREA case, the whistleblower can request the right to appoint a private attorney to pursue the claim. If such a request is made, either the Attorney General "shall" appoint the private counsel identified by the whistleblower to pursue the case or the United States shall file the complaint itself. However, like the reward provision, if the Attorney General refuses to follow this provision of the law, the whistleblower cannot sue in court.

While waiting for FIRREA to be fixed, whistleblowers do have a number of options. The bank frauds that trigger FIRREA liability may also trigger liability under other federal laws with stronger whistleblower provisions, such as the Securities and Exchange Act, the False Claims Act, and the Commodity Exchange Act. These three laws have no caps on reward amounts and permit whistleblowers to challenge denials in federal court.

A review of FIRREA fraud cases demonstrates the potential to use these stronger whistleblower laws. One major FIRREA case was triggered by a whistleblower who filed a False Claims Act lawsuit (due to the false statements issued by the bank). In an unfortunate twist of fate for the whistleblower, the court dismissed the whistleblower's lawsuit due to the statute of limitations (i.e., the case was not filed timely) but permitted the U.S. government to pursue a FIRREA case against the bank.

The SEC has collected billions in sanctions as a result of successful FIRREA prosecutions (including the BNY Mellon case, where the SEC collected $30 million). This is extremely significant. The SEC's whistleblower law has a strong "related action" provision. If the SEC collects at least $1 million in sanctions from a wrongdoer, the whistleblower is entitled to a reward of 10 to 30 percent for monies obtained not only by the SEC but also from any other government agency. Thus, had a whistleblower in the Mellon case filed for a reward under the securities law, he or she could have been entitled to a reward based on the "alternative remedy" provision, which should include not only the $30 million collected by the SEC, but potentially the millions collected from the other government agencies.

The key in bank fraud cases is not to rely solely on FIRREA for a reward but to think outside the box and try to determine whether the bank's misconduct also violated other civil or criminal laws that have real reward provisions.

Food Safety

In December 2008 Clifford Tousignant ate some peanut butter. He was a decorated Korean War veteran and had won three Purple Heart medals for being wounded in combat. He survived the war, but the peanut butter was contaminated with salmonella. Tousignant died from food poisoning on January 12, 2009.

Jacob Hurley had better luck. In early January 2009 he ate his favorite comfort food, Austin Toasty Crackers with Peanut Butter. He became sick and started vomiting. Jacob had diarrhea for eleven days, so much so that blood began to appear in his stool. He became lethargic and his skin sallow. His parents took him to the family doctor, and Jacob tested positive for salmonella poisoning. Jacob's peanut butter crackers were tested and also contained salmonella.

A total of eight people died from this January 2009 outbreak of salmonella. In addition, an estimated nineteen thousand people were sickened in forty-three states. The source of the outbreak: peanut butter sold by the Peanut Corporation of America out of its Blakely, Georgia, processing plant. Jacob Hurley's father asked why no company employees said or did anything. "It sickens me to no end that the majority of a company and its employees could knowingly allow tainted products to go out the door and into the nation's food supply. Does no one have a conscience?"

As reports filtered out from the company's plant, the source of the contamination became obvious. Workers had witnessed rats and cockroaches in the plant and knew about water leaks, surface contamination, and failure to properly clean the facility—all of which potentially contributed to the salmonella outbreak. They knew peanut butter that tested positive for salmonella was shipped out of the plant and sold to customers.

Some workers complained to managers. Most, however, kept silent. None filed a complaint with the government. E-mails later obtained by congressional investigators told the story: Delays caused by trying to stop contaminated shipments were "costing us huge $$$$$." The company even wanted to turn "raw peanuts" found on the factory's "floor into money."

Could this disaster have been prevented?

On December 21, 2010, nearly two years to the day after Clifford Tousignant ate the contaminated peanut butter that killed him, Congress passed the FDA Food Safety Modernization Act. A key provision prohibits retaliation against employees who blow the whistle on contamination and safety risks in the "manufacture, processing, packing, transporting, distribution, reception, holding or importation of food." The peanut butter scandal was the major catalyst for this change in law.

In 2010, responding to the peanut butter scandal, Congress finally approved, as part of the Food Safety Modernization Act, whistleblower protections.

The food safety law included a strong whistleblower antiretaliation provision modeled on the Consumer Product Safety Act's whistleblower laws. The law covers employees "engaged in the manufacture, processing, packing, transportation, distribution, reception, holding or importation of food." Complaints must be filed with the DOL within 180 days of an adverse action, and employees who prevail are entitled to reinstatement, back pay, compensatory damages, and attorney fees. After exhausting DOL procedures, employees can remove their claims to federal court.

Foreign Corrupt Practices Act

The Dodd-Frank Act triggered a critically important breakthrough in the enforcement of the Foreign Corrupt Practices Act (FCPA). Whistleblowers who provide the Securities and Exchange Commission with "original information" regarding violations of the FCPA qualify under the act for large monetary rewards. These rewards are available to U.S. citizens and foreign nationals alike.

For information on the FCPA's whistleblower provision, see Rule 9. Because the FCPA is administered by the SEC's Office of the Whistleblower, individuals filing FCPA claims should also review Rule 8 and Checklists 7 and 8, all of which cover the SEC's Dodd-Frank Act program.

Fraud Against Shareholders

In 2002, after the corporate giants Enron and WorldCom went bankrupt, and shareholders lost billions of dollars in savings, Congress enacted the historic Sarbanes-Oxley Act. The law had a number of provisions directly related to whistleblowers, including the following:

- The requirement that all publicly-traded companies have an independent "audit committee" able to accept, on a confidential basis, whistleblower allegations of corporate fraud;

- A limited disclosure requirement that permits attorneys licensed to appear before the Securities and Exchange Commission to make whistleblower-type disclosures of corporate misconduct;

- An amendment to the criminal obstruction of justice statute, which specifically prohibited any employer from engaging in conduct that interfered with the livelihood of an employee, including terminations, in retaliation for that employee blowing the whistle to federal law enforcement concerning any violation of a federal law, securities related or not.

At the heart of the SOX corporate whistleblower protections is Section 806, the Corporate and Criminal Fraud Accountability Act. This provision created a private right of action for any employee, contractor, or agent of a publicly traded company who blew the whistle on any violation of law related to shareholder fraud and/or any violation of a rule of the SEC. Protected activity was broadly defined to include disclosures to various persons, ranging from supervisors to members of Congress.

"Without . . . accountability, greed can run rampant with devastating results"
Senate Report, Sarbanes-Oxley Whistleblower Act

The law is similar in nature to the Atomic Energy Act, the Surface Transportation Act, and the Airline Safety Act. The SOX has also been used as a model for other whistleblower laws, including the Dodd-Frank Consumer Financial Protection Act and the 2008 Consumer Product Safety Act.

Complaints are initially filed with the Department of Labor, and the law incorporates, by reference, all the procedures set forth in the Airline Safety Act. This includes the right to preliminary reinstatement if the employee prevails during the Occupational Safety and Health Administration (OSHA) investigation, a full hearing before a DOL judge, and two levels of appeal. Damages available under the law are also modeled on the Atomic Energy and Airline Safety Acts and include reinstatement, back pay, special damages, compensatory damages, and attorney fees and costs.

The SOX law permits employees who exhaust their DOL remedies to file their own case directly in federal court. Under the SOX, if the DOL fails to issue a final enforceable order within 180 days, employees can file a de novo claim in federal court.

Since the law was passed in 2002, thousands of whistleblowers have relied on its broad provisions to seek protection. The scope and meaning of most of the core provisions in the law were hotly contested, and corporations took advantage of a number of ambiguities in the law to argue (often successfully) that subsidiary corporations were not covered under the SOX and that employees had no right to a jury trial if a case was removed to federal court. Moreover, employers took advantage of two procedural weaknesses in the law, including a short statute of limitations and mandatory arbitration rules that forced employees to arbitrate disputes utilizing pro-employer procedures, instead of having their claims heard in court.

In 2014 the U.S. Supreme Court, in *Lawson v. FMR, LLC*, further expanded the scope of SOX. Employers had argued that the law narrowly covered only employees of publicly traded companies. The Supreme Court rejected this argument, holding that contractors and agents who perform services for such companies are also protected.

A majority of justices pointed to the Enron scandal, in which outside lawyers and accountants—none of whom were actual employees of Enron—contributed to the multi-billion-dollar frauds. The Court warned that not permitting outside contractors (including "countless professionals" who advise Wall Street firms) to be covered would create a "huge hole" in protections. They also pointed out that most mutual funds are "structured so that they have no employees of their own; they are managed, instead by independent investment advisors." Under *Lawson* mutual fund "advisors" would also be protected.

If employees remove their SOX case to federal court (after exhausting administrative remedies), they may be able to join that case with antiretaliation claims permitted under the Dodd-Frank Act securities whistleblower law and potential state whistleblower laws.

Health Care Entitlement

Because it covers Medicaid and Medicare fraud, the False Claims Act remains the most important law protecting whistleblowers in the health care industry. In 2010, as part of the Patient Protection and Affordable Care Act, the FCA was amended to ensure its continued coverage of health care fraud whenever federal monies or programs are involved, including programs incorporated into President Obama's 2010 health care program.

In addition to the FCA, in enacting the Patient Protection and Affordable Care Act, Congress also incorporated a special antiretaliation provision for employees who blow the whistle on violations of Title I of that act (i.e., the affordability and accountability sections of the law). This law was modeled directly after the Consumer Product Safety Act of 2008 and provides for remedies and procedures identical to that law.

Immigration Law: Political Asylum

Whistleblower coverage under U.S. immigration law is explained in the International Toolkit.

IRS Whistleblower Rewards

In 2006 the Internal Revenue Code was amended to require the payment of monetary rewards for whistleblowers who disclose major tax frauds or the underpayment of taxes. This law is addressed in Rule 7. One major defect in this law is its failure to contain an explicit antiretaliation provision. Unlike other *qui tam* laws, such as the False Claims Act, the Securities Exchange Act, and the Commodity Exchange Act, the IRS law does not explicitly prohibit the termination of employees who file tax *qui tam* claims. But most tax whistleblowers should be able to obtain protection under other federal whistleblower laws or state law. Congress is also considering whether to enact antiretaliation protections for tax whistleblowers, a proposal that has strong bipartisan support.

Military/Armed Services

The Military Whistleblower Protection Act permits members of the armed services to lawfully communicate with Congress, their chain of command,

and military inspectors general. The Act also permits members of the armed services to raise allegations of violations of law, discriminatory conduct and "gross mismanagement, a gross waste of funds, an abuse of authority, or a substantial and specific danger to public health and safety."

Retaliation cases are filed with the Office of Inspector General. There is a sixty-day statute of limitations, but the IG can waive that deadline. Once filed, the IG must "expeditiously" review the claims and determine whether a full investigation is warranted. The IG's report of investigation is filed with the Secretary for the division of the military for which the member served. Appeals of the IG actions can thereafter be filed with the Board for Correction of Military Records. The Board can conduct a full evidentiary hearing. The Board's ruling is provided to the head of the relevant military department for a ruling. That decision is appealable to the Secretary of Defense. If a final decision is not rendered within 180 days, the service member is deemed to have exhausted his or her administrative remedies and should be able to appeal the rulings to court.

Under the law, members of the armed services who prevail in whistleblower cases are entitled to a wide range of relief, including correction of their military records, financial compensation, and remedies related to any courts martial that may have been retaliatory.

Mine Health and Safety

Miners who raise health and safety complaints are protected under the Mine Health and Safety Act. This law is administered by the Department of Labor and protects complaints raised internally with mine management and complaints filed with government officials. There is a sixty-day statute of limitations, and claims are investigated by the DOL. Employees are entitled to preliminary reinstatement pending the outcome of a hearing if the Mine Health and Safety Commission determines that a complaint was not "frivolously brought." Remedies under the act include reinstatement, back pay, and attorney fees.

Although the law contains some progressive features, the statute of limitations is short, damages are limited, and there is no right to a federal court trial. Amendments to strengthen this law were introduced into Congress as a result of continuing mining disasters.

Nuclear Safety

In 1974 nuclear whistleblower Karen Silkwood died in a mysterious "car accident" on her way to provide documentation to a *New York Times* reporter that the Kerr-McGee nuclear plant where she worked was riddled with safety problems. Her case triggered a series of nuclear safety exposés, which led Congress to pass nuclear whistleblower protections in 1978. Originally, the nuclear whistleblower law was identical to the other six environmental whistleblower laws. But Congress did not rest on its laurels and ignore court rulings or the on-the-job reality facing employees.

Congress passed the first major amendments to the whistleblower law in 1992. The thirty-day statute of limitations was abolished and increased to 180 days. The scope of statutorily-protected activity was expanded to conform with the broad interpretation of the law given by the Department of Labor, and it specifically reversed the *Brown and Root* decision of 1984, which had stripped internal whistleblowers from protection. Congress included contacts with managers and other internal company complaints into the rubric of protected activity. A court-made loophole that had prevented workers at nuclear weapons plants from protection was also closed.

Congress again revisited the law in 2004 and updated it with two major changes. Whistleblowers were given the right, after exhausting procedures within the DOL, to file claims de novo in federal court. In other words, if the DOL failed to issue a final ruling in a timely manner (one year), employees would have the opportunity to leave the DOL process and file a new case in federal court.

The scope of coverage was extended so that not only were private-sector employees in the nuclear industry covered under the law, but employees of the two federal agencies responsible for nuclear safety: the Nuclear Regulatory Commission and the Department of Energy. Private-sector and federal employees who exposed nuclear safety problems were given the same protections.

OSHA/Workplace Safety

On-the-job safety is a major concern for workers throughout the United States. An average of fourteen workers die each day from on-the-job accidents, and thousands more are injured. To fix this problem Congress enacted the Occupational Safety and Health Act of 1970. Congress looked to workers as the key on-the-job source of information concerning workplace hazards and established the Occupational Safety and Health Administration as the federal agency designed to investigate worker safety complaints. OSHA also was entrusted with the power to prevent workers from being retaliated against if they exposed workplace hazards.

Under section 11(c) of the act, OSHA was authorized to investigate allegations of retaliation and take strong remedial action to prevent whistleblowers from being fired. The act permitted OSHA to file a lawsuit in federal court against employers who fired health and safety whistleblowers. If victorious, the employee is entitled to "all appropriate relief," which includes reinstatement and back pay. The only Court of Appeals to consider the issue concluded that employees illegally fired under the OSHA law are also entitled to compensatory and punitive damages.

But the law has major flaws that render it impotent. First, a worker must file his or her discrimination claim within thirty days of the adverse action. This short statute of limitations results in numerous claims being automatically denied.

Second, there is no "private right of action" under the federal law. In other words, it is up to OSHA to protect the employee. The employee's complaint triggers an OSHA investigation, but not a lawsuit. Only OSHA can file a lawsuit against the employer. If OSHA declines to defend the employee, the employee cannot sue the company. In other words, if OSHA does not prosecute on your behalf, you have *no federal remedy* if you are fired for exposing workplace hazards that threaten the health and safety of fellow workers. Even if OSHA does file a lawsuit on your behalf (which is very rare), OSHA controls the pace of the lawsuit and is responsible for any settlement.

OSHA's resources are very limited and they cannot file a lawsuit on behalf of every meritorious claim. The vast majority of employees retaliated against in violation of section 11(c) either obtain no relief whatsoever or obtain small, token remedies. When OSHA does act on behalf of a worker (which they do in just a minority of cases), the results are abysmal. According to the most recent statistics available, in 2007 OSHA "settled" 172 occupational safety cases. The average settlement was $5,288. Not one case settled for over $100,000. In other words, if an employer fires a worker who complains about safety, even if OSHA gets involved in the case, the penalty may be token.

For those cases that do not settle, the statistics are even worse. In 2009 OSHA received over twelve hundred retaliation complaints, yet they filed lawsuits on behalf of only *four* workers. The stories of employees abandoned by OSHA are indeed horrific. For example, Roger Wood was fired from his job after he exposed "serious" worker safety problems at the Johnson Atoll Chemical Agent Disposal System, a worksite responsible for the disposal of highly toxic chemicals. After OSHA investigated his safety claims, they found that the company was guilty of "two serious safety violations."

OSHA also looked into Wood's termination. The investigators concluded he had a "valid" section 11(c) complaint and ordered relief. The company ignored the retaliation findings. After *ten years* of administrative delays, the OSHA lawyers decided to reject the investigators' findings and declined to file a lawsuit on behalf of Wood. Wood challenged this decision in court and demanded that either OSHA protect his rights or that he be able to file a lawsuit on his own for reinstatement and back pay. The courts threw out his case. They held that only OSHA can file a lawsuit on behalf of a fired worker and that there was no "private right of action." Despite an administrative finding that he was illegally fired, and despite having exposed two "serious" safety violations, Wood had no remedy, and his company got off scot-free. Similar stories abound.

Congress is seriously considering fixing the OSHA law. But until they muster the wherewithal to fix it, employees fired for exposing safety hazards at work must look elsewhere for protection. The best place to find protection is under state law.

Today, almost every state now provides protections for whistleblowers, either under its common law or under a state whistleblower protection statute. In reaction to the defective federal Occupational Safety and Health Act, workers have sought remedies under alternative state whistleblower laws. To start with, most state courts recognize that the federal Occupational Safety and Health Act is completely ineffective and "inadequate," as a matter of law, to displace state rights over employee safety. A Missouri Court of Appeals decision summarized the weaknesses in the federal law, clearly explaining why it was inadequate and should not displace more powerful state laws:

> OSHA only allows an employee to file a complaint with the Secretary of Labor who then decides whether to bring an action . . . the employee's right to relief is further restricted in that the complaint must be filed within thirty days. . . . The decision to assert a cause of action is in the sole discretion of the Secretary of Labor and the statute affords the employee no appeal if the Secretary declines to file suit.

Consistent with this ruling, the Kansas Supreme Court evaluated the federal Occupational Safety and Health Act and found it to be "inadequate." Consequently, that court allowed Occupational Health and Safety Act–related whistleblowers to file claims in state court under the Kansas "public policy exception." Under this doctrine, the whistleblowers were granted the right to file lawsuits based on state tort (i.e., personal injury) law. If they prevailed, they could request substantial relief from a jury, including back pay and other economic, compensatory, and punitive damages.

Other state courts that have considered the adequacy of the federal Occupational Safety and Health Act have agreed with the holding of the

Kansas Supreme Court and have permitted workers to rely on the state common law public policy exception to obtain relief. These states include Alaska, California, Illinois, Iowa, Minnesota, New Mexico, New Jersey, Nevada, Ohio, and Oklahoma. Employees who allege that companies violate worker safety laws may also be protected under state whistleblower protection statutes. For example, the Maine Whistleblower Protection Act explicitly protects employees who raise concerns regarding "unsafe condition(s)" or practices that "put at risk the health or safety of that employee or any other individual."

Pipeline Safety Act

Congress enacted a special DOL-administered whistleblower law that covers environmental and safety violations at oil and gas pipelines. The pipeline law was modeled on the Energy Reorganization Act, and it follows similar procedures and legal standards as set forth in the nuclear safety law.

Ripping Off the Taxpayer/False Claims Act

President Lincoln signed the first whistleblower protection statute into law on March 2, 1863. This law, today know as the False Claims Act, was conceived at the height of the Civil War, when government contractors were pilfering the U.S. Treasury by selling defective goods to the Union armies (i.e., selling sawdust as gunpowder). The law has been amended five times.

The False Claims Act is the most successful whistleblower law, and its history, procedures, and requirements are spelled out in Rules 2 and 6 and Checklists 1 and 4. Its international application is discussed in the International Toolkit.

Under the modern False Claims Act, whistleblowers file claims with the attorney general and in federal court. If there is a finding that fraud was committed against the government, the whistleblower shares in the proceeds recovered by the United States. In other words, whistleblowers who prove their cases under the FCA are entitled to substantial monetary rewards, often in the millions of dollars. The requirements governing these provisions are detailed in Rule 6.

In addition to the recovery provisions, known as *qui tam*, the 1986 amendments also incorporated a traditional antiretaliation law into the FCA. This provision prohibits termination or on-the-job discrimination against any employee who files a FCA case or assists in an investigation of a false claim against the government.

Whistleblowers who suffer retaliation must file their claims in federal court. They are entitled to reinstatement, double back pay, special damages, and all attorney fees and costs reasonably incurred. The law prevents any employer or other "associated others" from retaliating against employees who undertake any "efforts to stop violations" of the FCA. In 2010 the antiretaliation provision was amended to include a three-year statute of limitations.

Although the FCA is clearly the mother of all antifraud whistleblower laws, there are other federal statutes in which employees can blow the whistle on taxpayer/contract rip-offs. These include the Major Frauds Act (discretionary payments to whistleblowers and an antiretaliation provision similar to the FCA), Public Contractor Employee Protection (inspector general review of retaliation claims), and special antiretaliation protections for defense contractor employees who expose violations of laws related to defense contractors. The Defense Department law permits employees who exhaust their administrative remedies to file claims in federal court and obtain compensatory damages.

Seaman Whistleblower Protection

The Protection of Seaman Against Discrimination law is designed to "encourage employees to aid in the enforcement of maritime laws" by providing information about possible violations of law to the Coast Guard. Court decisions have broadly interpreted the scope of protected activity and permitted employees to obtain back pay, compensatory and punitive damages, along with attorney fees. This law was amended in 2010 and now requires claims to be filed with the Department of Labor according to the procedures utilized under the Surface Transportation Act.

Seamen who provide the government with information on ocean pollution or violations of the MARPOL treaty are eligible for financial rewards. Upon request (usually made by the Department of Justice, which prosecutes ocean pollution cases), courts regularly grant seamen 50 percent of the fines collected under the Act to Prevent Pollution from Ships. This rewards law is explained in Rule 11.

Trade Secrets

On May 11, 2016, President Obama signed the Defend Trade Secrets Act, 18 U.S.C. 1833(b). This law established specific procedures by which employees can disclose information their employers classify as "trade secrets" to government officials, closing a major loophole in protection for whistleblowers.

Before this law was passed, corporations tried, often successfully, to silence whistleblowers by alleging that the concerns they raised included "trade secrets" and that their disclosure outside the company was prohibited by law. To close this loophole Congress included a whistleblower "immunity" provision when it passed the Defend Trade Secrets Act in 2016. Employees who provide trade secret information to federal or state officials, pursuant to the procedures established in the law, are immunized from either civil or criminal liability. The law also preempts state laws that restrict whistleblowers from reporting alleged trade secret information to government authorities.

As explained in Senate Committee on the Judiciary Report 114-220, employees can disclose trade secret information to "a Federal, State, or local government official or to an attorney," if they do so "in confidence" and if the disclosure is "for the purpose of reporting or investigating a suspected violation of law."

Employees can also use trade secret information in a court proceeding, provided the lawsuit is filed "against an employer for retaliation for reporting a suspected violation of law." The litigation-disclosure rule permits trade secret information to be used in court, "provided the individual files any document containing the trade secret under seal and does not disclose the trade secret other than pursuant to a court order." Whistleblowers can confidentially show their attorneys trade secret information.

All employers are required to give their employees notice of this immunity provision. Failure to do so will prevent employers from obtaining exemplary damages or attorney fees from employees who disclose trade secrets in violation of law. Under the law employees are still prohibited from releasing trade secret information to the public.

Transportation (Trucking, Railroads, and Public Transportation)

This is another area in which Congress has made progress. The first transportation safety whistleblower law, incorporated into the Surface Transportation Act, covered employees engaged in commercial motor vehicle safety including truck drivers, freight handlers, and mechanics. The original law was modeled on the environmental protection statutes. Cases are filed within the Department of Labor and subject to full evidentiary hearings similar to those conducted in environmental cases. There are also two levels of appeal: the first within the DOL to the secretary-appointed board and the second to the U.S. Court of Appeals. The statute of limitations is 180 days and the law includes an immediate reinstatement provision. This provision permits employees to be temporarily placed back on the job, with full pay and benefits, while their case is pending in court. Temporary or preliminary reinstatement can be ordered if, on the basis of an investigation by the Occupational Safety and Health Administration, the DOL determines that the employee was fired illegally.

Preliminary reinstatement is an invaluable procedure for employees fired from their jobs. Instead of being out of a job for the years it can take a legal case to move through the courts, the employee is reinstated in the job and stays employed while the case is pending. If the employee loses the case, the company can again remove the employee, but the employee does not have to pay back any of the wages or benefits earned while he or she worked for the company during the "preliminary reinstatement" period.

Preliminary reinstatement provisions are also included in other federal whistleblower laws, including mine safety, airline safety, nuclear safety, consumer product safety, food safety, and corporate shareholder fraud cases. Industry challenged the U.S. Supreme Court regarding the procedures. The U.S. Supreme Court upheld Congress's power to authorize preliminary reinstatement provided that certain basic due process requirements were met. Laws that provide for preliminary reinstatement are very attractive, as the long delay in obtaining a final enforceable ruling in any legal case, including whistleblower cases, can have a disastrous impact on an unemployed worker.

In 2007, based on recommendations issued by the National Commission on Terrorist Attacks Upon the United States (the "9/11 Commission"), Congress further strengthened the transportation whistleblower laws. The Surface Transportation Act was significantly improved, and similar protections were added for railroad workers and employees working for any public transportation agency or contractor. The airline safety law was not covered under these amendments.

The 2007 amendments established uniform protections under three ground-transportation whistleblower laws (i.e., the Surface Transportation Act, the National Transit Systems Security Act, and the Railroad Safety Labor Act). Under the railroad and public transportation laws, the definition of protected activity was not limited to safety violations, but also covered violations of any federal law, any law related to security, and the misuse of any public funds intended to be used for safety or security measures. The definition of "protected activity" under the Surface Transportation Act was expanded to include security matters.

The statute of limitations for all three laws is 180 days, and they all follow the same DOL filing, appeal, and preliminary reinstatement rules. Furthermore, under all three laws punitive damages, capped at $250,000, are permitted. Like the SOX, transportation-safety whistleblowers are granted the right to file de novo claims in federal court. Court filings are permitted only if the employee files his or her initial case within the Department of Labor and utilizes the DOL process for a minimum of 210 days. If the DOL issues a final order within 210 days of a complaint being filed, the employee's right to file a new case in federal court is extinguished.

Witnesses in Federal Court Proceedings

As part of the Civil Rights Act of 1871, Congress also prohibited all conspiracies to deter or harass witnesses who testified in U.S. court proceedings. The procedures and remedies under the witness protection law are identical to those afforded employees under the other portions of the CRA of 1871, and include the right to a trial by jury in federal court and the full array of damages. In 1998 the Supreme Court unanimously permitted an at-will employee to file a CRA claim after he was fired for obeying a federal grand jury subpoena for testimony.

PRACTICE TIP

Checklist 2 offers a comprehensive list of federal whistleblower protection laws, along with citations to major cases.

RULE 5

Don't Forget State Laws

The roots of modern whistleblower protection can also be traced back to a local state court ruling that overturned the one-hundred-year-old "at will" doctrine. That doctrine previously gave employers a near absolute right to fire workers for "any reason or no reason." It was a whistleblower who first put a fatal crack into this old laissez-faire doctrine and ruled that employees could not be fired for reasons that undermined a clear mandate of "public policy."

In October 1955, Peter Petermann was employed as a business agent for the Teamsters Union. He was called to testify before a California State Assembly committee that was looking into corruption. His supervisor demanded that Petermann falsely testify. Petermann refused and was consequently accused of disloyalty for embarrassing his union bosses when he "gave correct and truthful answers to all questions." In consequence, he was summarily fired the very next day.

Petermann challenged his termination in state court. The lawyers representing his bosses argued that under the "at-will" doctrine companies could fire employees for "any reason or no reason" unless they had an employment contract. That was the standard rule governing employment in all fifty states. Breaking with over one hundred years of legal tradition, the California court rejected this argument. It held that the "right to discharge an employee" could be "limited" by "public policy," even when there was no statute protecting the employee.

The court did not use the word *whistleblower* in describing its actions, as that term had not yet entered the vocabulary of employment law. But the Court held that employees could not be fired for testifying about their company's wrongdoing: "It would be obnoxious to the interests of the state and contrary to public policy and sound morality to allow an employer to discharge any employee . . . who declined to commit perjury."

The court recognized Petermann's right to sue the Teamsters Union for damages, and eventually awarded him $50,000.

In the landmark 1959 decision, the court upheld a cause of action by the employee for wrongful discharge based on a violation of "public policy." In other words, a company could not use its economic might to punish an employee who simply wanted to follow the law and tell the truth in court. The whistleblower revolution had started. Within twenty-five years the majority of states agreed with California, and today whistleblowers are protected under the common law in all but a few holdout states.

Under common law, forty-five states and the District of Columbia now protect whistleblowers under a "public policy" exception to the "at will" doctrine. Under this "exception," employers can still fire employees for "any reason or no reason"; they just cannot fire workers for the wrong reason—for a reason that violates public policy. Most states consider this claim a "tort," which means employees file their cases in court, have a right to a jury trial, and the juries can award economic damages (for example, lost wages and benefits), compensatory damages (loss of reputation and emotional distress), and in egregious cases punitive or exemplary damages.

Each state has its own definition of what type of conduct is protected under the "public policy exception," but almost every state protects the following types of disclosures or conduct:

- Refusal to violate a law;

- Performance of job duties required under law;

- The exercising of a legally protected right (such as testifying in court or filing a workers' compensation claim);

- Reporting violations of law for the "public benefit."

If applicable, the "public policy" tort is a great fit for whistleblowers, as it permits an employee to obtain punitive damages and have his or her case heard before a jury. But that is not the only common law remedy employees can use to protect their careers. Whistleblowers have also obtained coverage under more traditional causes of action, such as intentional infliction of emotional distress, defamation, breach of contract, and other similar remedies.

In addition to common law, over twenty-five states and municipalities have enacted their own versions of the False Claims Act, providing for *qui tam* related to fraud in spending state and local tax revenue. In addition to rewards provisions that mirror the federal law, state FCAs almost universally also have antiretaliation provisions that permit employees to file retaliation claims for wrongful discharge. What's more, a growing number of states have also enacted Whistleblower Protection Acts that cover all employees.

Specific State Laws

Listed here is a summary of where the states fall.

COMMON LAW PROTECTION

Many states offer common law protection under this "public policy exception" to the "at-will" doctrine. Under this protection, tort damages are permitted, unless otherwise specified. These states are Alaska (limited to contract damages); Arizona (modified by statute); Arkansas (limited to contract damages); California; Colorado; Connecticut; Delaware; the District of Columbia; Florida (modified by statute); Hawaii; Idaho; Illinois; Indiana; Iowa; Kansas; Kentucky; Maryland; Massachusetts; Michigan (except if covered under a statutory remedy); Minnesota (except where displaced by statutory remedy); Mississippi; Missouri; Nebraska; Nevada; New Hampshire; New Mexico; North Carolina; North Dakota; Ohio (the legislature passed a weak whistleblower law, but the courts still permit common law public policy claims); Oregon; Pennsylvania; South Carolina; South Dakota (contract damages only); Tennessee; Texas; Utah; Vermont; Virginia; Washington; West Virginia; Wisconsin; and Wyoming (except if the employee is covered under another statute or a collective bargaining agreement).

STATES THAT HAVE REJECTED A COMMON LAW PUBLIC
POLICY REMEDY FOR WHISTLEBLOWERS

Alabama; Georgia; Montana (the Montana courts affirmed whistleblower rights under the public policy rule, but the state legislature enacted a law overturning that decision and implementing a very weak state law that provides no real protections for whistleblowers); and New York.

STATES WITH A COMPREHENSIVE WHISTLEBLOWER PROTECTION ACT

Arizona; Connecticut; Florida; Hawaii; Maine; Michigan; Minnesota; New Hampshire; New Jersey; and Rhode Island.

OTHER STATE WHISTLEBLOWER PROTECTION STATUTES

In addition to state Whistleblower Protection Acts, almost every state has narrower whistleblower protection statutes that cover specific claims, such as occupational safety, protection for nurses, and protection for state-employee whistleblowers. Also, many states have recognized whistleblowers' abilities to use other laws to protect themselves, such as libel or intentional interference torts.

STATES AND MAJOR CITIES WITH FALSE CLAIMS ACTS

Most states and some cities have local versions of the False Claims Act. Some are stronger than the federal law; others are weaker. The State of New York also permits whistleblowers to file a *qui tam* lawsuit for tax fraud under its state FCA. A number of states only cover fraud in state Medicaid programs. There is a strong trend for states to enact FCAs, so it is important to check your specific state to determine if a local FCA exists.

The following states and major cities currently have FCAs: California; the City of Chicago; Colorado; Connecticut; Delaware; District of Columbia; Florida; Georgia; Hawaii; Illinois; Indiana; Iowa; Louisiana; Maryland; Massachusetts; Michigan; Minnesota; Montana; Nevada; New Hampshire; New Jersey; New Mexico; New York City; New York; North Carolina; Oklahoma; Philadelphia and Allegheny County, Pennsylvania (the Commonwealth of Pennsylvania has not yet passed an FCA); Rhode Island; Tennessee; Texas; Vermont; Virginia; and Washington.

Preemption and Preclusion

Shortly after states commenced protecting whistleblowers, corporations went on a "counterattack." The first phase was to dispute "federal preemption." Companies argued that federal whistleblower laws, which often were weaker than state laws, should provide an exclusive remedy. In other words, states should be "preempted" from protecting whistleblowers because those protections would somehow interfere with the implementation of the federal whistleblower laws.

This issue came to a head in cases decided under the Energy Reorganization Act's nuclear whistleblower protection law. Corporations aggressively argued that nuclear whistleblowers could only file claims under the federal law. They asserted that because federal nuclear safety laws preempted state nuclear safety laws, whistleblowers who raised nuclear safety concerns were forced to file federally. However, the real reason corporations pushed this argument was not because they were interested in safety—far from it. Instead, before the law was amended in 1992, the federal nuclear whistleblower law had a thirty-day statute of limitations. Many whistleblowers, such as Vera English, who sought protection under state laws, had failed to file claims under the ridiculously short federal statutory deadline.

English worked for the General Electric Company at its Chemet Laboratory near Wilmington, North Carolina. She blew the whistle on major nuclear safety violations. English originally filed a federal claim but lost because she did not meet the thirty-day statute of limitations (the statute of limitations was increased to 180 days in 1992 in large part due to failed claims such as that of English).

Vera English then filed a suit under North Carolina common law, alleging intentional infliction of emotional distress caused by her mistreatment as a whistleblower. General Electric filed a motion to dismiss, claiming that her exclusive remedy was the federal law and that state regulation of nuclear safety matters preempted state involvement. The company won before the district court and the court of appeals. The Supreme Court unanimously reversed the decisions of both courts. The Court held that federal whistleblower laws did not prevent private-sector employees from also seeking relief under state law. After *English* was decided, the federal preemption doctrine was all but dead in whistleblower cases.

One pitfall that must be carefully avoided is the "preclusion" defense. A number of states do not permit employees to pursue the common law public policy exception claim if a statutory remedy exists. These courts require an employee to use a statute, if one exists, arguing that the statute somehow "precludes" the use of a common law remedy. Although this doctrine is illogical, it does have its supporters.

One way to guard against having a case thrown out under the "preclusion" doctrine is to sue under both the common law and a federal or state whistleblower protection statute. If the common law remedy is "precluded," the statutory remedy should prevail.

Additionally, there is a judicial policy of requiring employees to include all potential causes of action in one lawsuit. Courts discourage parties from parceling out various causes of action and filing multiple lawsuits. Indeed, the failure to include all potential causes of action in one lawsuit can result in a waiver of nonincluded claims. Thus, the best tactic is to include all potential causes of action in the one lawsuit, although there may be sound strategic reasons for filing initial claims in multiple forums. If an employee files a claim in U.S. District Court, the Federal Rules of Procedure permit the inclusion of state claims in the federal lawsuit under a doctrine known as "pendant jurisdiction."

PRACTICE TIP

Checklist 1 provides a summary list of states that have enacted False Claims Acts.

Checklist 3 offers a state-by-state list of local protections, including citations to the leading common law "public policy" exception cases and whistleblower protection state laws.

RULE 6

Get a Reward! False Claims Act/*Qui Tam*

"The bill offers . . .a reward to the informer who comes into court and betrays his co-conspirator, if he be such; but it is not confined to that class. . . . I have based the [False Claims Act] upon the old-fashioned idea of holding out a temptation, and 'setting a rogue to catch a rogue,' which is the safest and most expeditious way I have ever discovered of bringing rogues to justice."

Sen. Jacob Howard (Statement upon sponsoring
original False Claims Act in 1863)

Always ask: Is the taxpayer, directly or indirectly, on the hook for any of the costs associated with your disclosure? Do your concerns touch upon federal spending, procurement, or contracting? If you answer "yes," you may be protected under the most effective whistleblower law in the United States: the False Claims Act (FCA).

The False Claims Act is a law that is simply too good to miss. If a whistleblower prevails in an FCA case, the company must pay treble damages based on the contract or procurement fraud. It also has to pay a fine for each false claim, set at no less then $10,781 and no larger then $21,563. The whistleblower reward is between 15 percent and 30 percent of the amount recovered by the government, in addition to attorney fees and costs. Employers cannot retaliate against any employee who takes any "action" under the FCA or who undertakes any effort "to stop 1 or more violations" of the act. The *qui tam* provision can result in large rewards for the whistleblower, and, if fired, the employee is entitled to double back pay, special damages, and fees.

What Is a False Claim?

The scope and reach of government spending is vast and consequently so is the scope for the FCA. The U.S. government is the largest landowner and is the largest employer in the United States. Billions upon billions of federal taxpayer dollars are spent on hiring contractors, allocating grants to state and local governments, buying goods and services, and handing payouts to massive government programs. Federal monies are spent on everything from highway construction to social services to our nation's defense. Federal money is spent in every state, in nearly every nation on earth, and has even been spent on the Moon and Mars, not to mention massive government spending in the Medicare and Medicaid programs. The FCA prohibits fraud in the spending of every penny of taxpayer money.

The FCA also reaches into other programs that do not directly implicate government spending, such as the payment of royalties on government leases (such as oil and gas leases), false statements to obtain benefits from the government, false customs declarations, or statements made to avoid having to pay fines or fees to the United States.

The ways in which government money can be ripped off are as diverse as the imagination. Checklist 4 outlines numerous types of frauds covered under the FCA. Some examples include misrepresentations in grant applications, billing for services not rendered, billing for services not needed, billing for services not properly performed, selling defective merchandise, failure to ensure quality standards, kickbacks to obtain grants or sell products, failure to meet grant requirements, improperly using government property, overcharging for services, billing to the wrong accounts, underpaying on obligations or leases, improper marketing to increase the demand on goods and services paid for by the government, improper denial of required coverage, up coding (false diagnosis to increase payments), obtaining early payments, failure to pay mandatory penalties, fees or customs duties, violation of contracting rules, conflicts of interest, and bill padding. The list is endless and only limited by the creativity of those looking to improperly profit at the taxpayer's expense.

In 2009 and 2010 Congress expanded the scope of the FCA, broadening the definition of *claim* and *obligation*, increasing the reach of the law's conspiracy provisions, and ensuring that subcontractors and government-sponsored corporations or programs were covered under the act. In closing various loopholes in the law, Congress explicitly demanded that the law be interpreted to "protect all Federal funds." Every dime is covered, regardless of who submits the bill or who commits the underlying fraud:

> *[FCA liability] attaches whenever a person knowingly makes a false claim to obtain money or property, any part of which is provided by the Government without regard to whether the wrongdoer deals directly with the Federal Government; with an agent acting on the Government's behalf; or with a third party contractor. . . . The FCA reaches all false claims submitted to State-administered programs.*

On the floor of the House of Representatives, California Congressman Howard Berman, one of the principal sponsors of the FCA, further explained the scope and reach of "our Nation's most effective fraud-fighting tool, the federal False Claims Act." As explained by Congressman Berman, the following conduct "clearly violates the False Claims Act":

- "Charging the government for more than was provided";

- "Seeking payment" when the applicant was "not eligible";

- "Demanding payment for goods or services that do not conform to contractual or regulatory requirements";

- "Attempting to pay the Government less than is owed" for "any goods, services, concession, or other benefits provided by the Government";

- "Fraudulently seeking to obtain a Government contract";

- "Submitting a fraudulent application for a grant of Government funds";

- "Submitting a false application for a Government loan";

- "Requesting payment for goods or services that are defective or of lesser quality than those for which the Government contracted";

- "Submitting a claim that falsely certifies that the defendant has complied with a law, contact term, or regulation";

- "Submitting a claim for payment" if the applicant was violating conditions "material" to the contract or the "conditions of participation."

For years corporations argued for a narrow interpretation of a "false claim." They urged courts to ignore common sense and strictly apply the terms explicitly set forth in the four corners of a contract. If a requirement was not explicitly set forth in a formal contract or a billing statement, there would be no liability.

This dispute came to a head in 2016 before the Supreme Court. The case concerned the death of Yarushka Rivera, who was being treated in a mental health facility owned by Universal Health Services, Inc. Her treatment was paid for by the taxpayers under the Medicaid program. Rivera was prescribed medication by a "doctor." She had an adverse reaction, suffered seizures, and died. She was seventeen years old.

An employee of Universal told Rivera's parents the truth about her treatment. The psychologist who diagnosed Rivera's condition did not have a medical license. Instead, her "PhD" was awarded by an unaccredited Internet college, and her application for a state license had been rejected. The individual who prescribed the medication purported to be a "psychiatrist" but was actually a nurse who "lacked authority to prescribe medications."

The case filed by Rivera's parents alleged that Universal had ripped off taxpayers by billing for services of "unlicensed staff." Universal argued that the billing statements did not explicitly require the persons treating Rivera to be licensed or even qualified. They argued that the FCA did not permit claims to be filed for "implied" requirements. No matter how despicable the treatment, if it was not in the contract, there could be no FCA case.

The Supreme Court, in a decision by Justice Thomas, unanimously rejected these arguments. The Court upheld the theory of "implied certification." If a defendant "knowingly fails to disclose . . . noncompliance" with a material "statutory, regulatory, or contractual requirement," the company can be guilty of violating the law even if that requirement is not explicitly set forth in the agreement entered into between the defendant and the government.

Government contractors or medical facilities charging health care costs to Medicare or Medicaid can be liable even if their noncompliance was "not expressly designated as conditions of payment." A condition of payment can be implied if it was "material" to the services provided: "What matters is not the label the Government attaches to a requirement, but whether the defendant knowingly violated a requirement that the defendant knows is material to the Government's payment decision."

The Court explained that during the Civil War, when the FCA was passed, Congress was concerned about the United States being "billed for nonexistent or worthless goods, charged exorbitant prices for goods delivered, and generally robbed in purchasing the necessities of war." It is not the terms of a contract that are controlling, but whether the goods being sold are "worthless."

The Court defined "materiality" as "having a natural tendency to influence, or be capable of influencing, the payment or receipt of money." The Court warned that "minor or insubstantial" noncompliance is not "material." But material terms do not need to be spelled out in every contract, and can be "implied."

Rivera's case could go forward.

How the Law Works

Unlike standard whistleblower protection laws, the False Claims Act permits whistleblowers to file claims on behalf of the United States and demand that companies, *who have ripped off the taxpayer,* be held fully accountable. The whistleblower can then obtain a reward for this public service. The FCA permits whistleblowers to go to court and show that the government was financially taken advantage of. If the whistleblower's claims are proven to be correct, the whistleblower is entitled to a percentage of the monies recovered for the United States, plus all attorney fees and costs.

The amounts of these rewards can be staggering, sometimes in the multiple millions of dollars. In 2005 the General Accounting Office determined that the average whistleblower reward under the FCA was $1.7 million. In some instances the whistleblowers were able to collect well over $50 million in rewards for a single FCA case. Between 1986 and 2016 the *whistleblower share* of FCA recoveries reached $6.325 billion.

As explained in **Figure 5**, since the FCA was modernized in 1986, whistleblowers account for almost 70 percent of all civil fraud recoveries. Since 1987 taxpayers have recovered $15.14 billion from government investigations, but whistleblower recoveries under the FCA during this same period of time totaled $33.23 billion in civil penalties and fines.

Figure 5

**Total U.S. Civil Recovery: From Whistleblowers and Government Investigation
1987–2016**

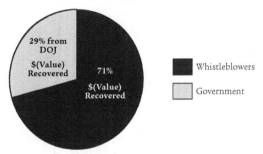

Source: Civil Division, Department of Justice, "Fraud Statistics—Overview"
(Oct. 1, 1987–Sept. 30, 2016)

In remarks given on June 9, 2016, before the American Bar Association, acting Associate Attorney General Bill Baer (who has responsibility over the federal government's efforts to hold federal contractors accountable) confirmed what the statistics prove. The False Claims Act's whistleblower provision "remains the government's most effective civil tool in protecting vital government programs from fraud schemes." The "dollars involved" are "staggering."

The law does not only result in monetary recoveries. Defense attorney John T. Boese, who has extensively written and testified in support of corporate positions on the FCA, conceded in his 2016 paper delivered to the Health Care Compliance Association that the Justice Department uses the law to "encourage adoption" of "best practices" so companies can police themselves. This includes requiring companies to enter into "corporate integrity agreements" when they settle an FCA case.

Given the success of the FCA, over twenty-five states and major municipalities have now enacted local versions. Furthermore, the federal government has established incentives that strongly encourage states to enact FCAs protecting the use of state tax revenue. Every year more states sign FCAs into law, and eventually these remedies should cover local tax revenue in the same manner that federal tax revenues are protected.

Even without a local FCA, state spending is often covered under the federal law. All states and most local governments supply services and sponsor projects in whole or in part through the use of federal monies. If a contractor defrauds a state agency, but federal money is involved, the FCA applies. If a state or local government fails to properly use federal monies, the FCA applies and can be used to hold these local governments accountable.

If government monies are in any manner involved in your whistleblowing allegations, you may be protected under the federal FCA or similar state and local laws.

The FCA is complex, with many pitfalls. But in prosecuting a case under this law, always keep in mind Congress's intent when it enacted this highly effective fraud-fighting tool. One of the first cases ever decided under the FCA contains perhaps the best statement of that original intent. Although decided in 1885 by a district court in Oregon, the decision is not outdated. This holding has been continuously cited by the key authorities, including the U.S. Supreme Court, Senator Langer during his 1943 filibuster to save the law, and in the official Judiciary Committee report accompanying the 1986 amendments, as a true reflection of the purpose behind the FCA:

> *The statute is a remedial one. It is intended to protect the Treasury against the hungry and unscrupulous host that encompasses it on every side and should be construed accordingly. It was passed upon the theory, based on experience as old*

as modern civilization, that one of the least expensive and most effective means of preventing frauds on the Treasury is to make the perpetrators of them liable to actions by private persons acting, if you please, under the strong stimulus of personal ill will or the hope of gain.

The FCA provides employees with an effective tool to protect taxpayer dollars. Every employee who works for government contractors, or who has any knowledge of how government monies are acquired or spent, is a potential relator under the act. The law is designed to encourage, protect, and reward employees who risk their careers to "do the right thing."

Should an employee with information about false claims against federal or state governments blow the whistle? Given the amounts at stake for the whistleblower, the benefits obtained by the taxpayers, and the public interest in holding government contractors fully accountable for how they obtain and spend government money, the question is almost rhetorical. Any employee who believes that he or she has information that the government is being ripped off—that contracts were illegally bid, that kickbacks were paid, that defective products were sold, or that the government was overcharged—should, at a minimum, obtain expert advice as to whether or not he or she may have an FCA case. There is too much at stake to ignore the benefits of this powerful law. No one should simply turn his or her back on a potential multimillion dollar reward, especially when applying for the reward serves overriding public interests.

Twelve Steps to Filing a Successful False Claims Act Case

A number of critical requirements are unique to the False Claims Act. All of the requirements and standards set forth in the law must be strictly followed, regardless of how frustrating these rules may be. Given how whistleblowing actually unfolds in the workplace, unfortunately, it is very easy for whistleblowers to make mistakes. Attorneys defending FCA cases have aggressively jumped on numerous technical requirements, and with some success have convinced some courts to dismiss otherwise legitimate whistleblower cases. Despite Congress's clear intent, given the high stakes in FCA cases, it is imperative that anyone filing a claim strives to conform to a narrow reading of the law. Otherwise he or she risks giving crooked contractors an excuse to throw the case out of court before a jury can hear the facts.

STEP 1: DON'T GO PUBLIC

Unlike almost every other whistleblower law, the FCA does not encourage whistleblowers to publicly disclose their allegations. The opposite is true. When an employee learns that his or her employer is ripping off the government, going to the press may actually prejudice the case. The FCA processes whistleblower claims in two categories. The first are cases for which there has been no "public disclosure." That is the best category for employees. If there has been no public disclosure, almost any person can file a claim and qualify as a "relator," as the term is used under the FCA. Relators do not have to be traditional whistleblowers; they only have to be persons who have knowledge of the underlying fraud and report the fraud to the United States pursuant to the procedures set forth in the FCA. Corporations (including nonprofit public interest groups) have qualified for "relator" status under the FCA.

However, if there has been a "public disclosure," the class of persons who can qualify for obtaining a reward under the FCA is limited. The rationale is simple: If the allegations of fraud are publicly available, anyone could simply read about the fraud in the newspaper and then file a FCA *qui tam* case. The law wants to encourage two types of people to step forward, file FCA cases, and qualify for rewards: First are persons who provide the government with information that is not publicly available. Second, even if some or all of the allegations are publicly available, the government still wants to encourage true "insiders" to step forward and provide the United States with first-hand knowledge about the frauds.

The "public disclosure" rule is counterintuitive to whistleblowing. The very term *whistleblower* indicates someone blowing a whistle—creating a loud, sharp sound in order to call attention to the wrongdoing. Whistleblowers are generally viewed as people who publicly expose wrongdoing in order to force change. But this assumption does not apply to the FCA. Rather than calling public attention to a problem, the goal of the law is to encourage whistleblowers to quietly inform the government of the misconduct, and permit time for the government to conduct a fair and impartial investigation, outside of the public spotlight often caused by a whistleblower disclosure.

The government wants to know what the whistleblower knows before the wrongdoers have an opportunity to hide their crime. If allegations are blasted in the news media, the targets of the fraud investigation can learn that there is a whistleblower on the jobsite, and can learn about the issues being investigated. The government loses not only the element of surprise, but it can also lose access to its most important source of information: the whistleblower. Moreover, the information circulated in the press may aid wrongdoers in coaching or intimidating witnesses, hiding information, "spinning" the problem in a misleading manner, or engaging in an outright cover-up. But if there has been no "public disclosure," there is a stronger possibility that whistleblower's existence will remain confidential, permitting the government to conduct a more thorough investigation. The whistleblower can serve as an undercover informant while still working for the company and provide information on white collar crimes that is often impossible to detect without the assistance of employees willing to risk their careers in order to "do the right thing." In fact, it is not uncommon for government agents to ask the whistleblower to "wear a wire" and secretly record conversations with those involved in the fraud.

What precisely is a public disclosure? This concept is hotly debated in the courts. To resolve some of this confusion, in 2010 Congress amended the FCA and redefined "public disclosure." Currently, a "public disclosure" under the FCA is a disclosure of "allegations or transactions" in a "Federal criminal, civil, or administrative hearing" if the "Government or its agent" was a party to the proceeding. Public disclosures also include "allegations or transactions" disclosed "in a congressional, Government Accountability Office, or other Federal report, hearing, audit, or investigation" or disclosed in the "news media."

STEP 2: TRY TO QUALIFY AS AN "ORIGINAL SOURCE"

As explained in step one, if the basis of your FCA claim was not "publicly disclosed," almost every potential whistleblower will have standing to file an FCA claim and qualify for a reward. But if the basis for your claim was "publicly disclosed," you will most likely have to demonstrate that you were an "original source" of the allegations that form the foundation of the FCA case.

Never assume that there was no "public disclosure." Companies have become infamous for scouring the public record in an attempt to find any release of information that could possibly qualify as a "public disclosure" of the transactions or allegations that form the basis of an FCA case. Thus even if you are not aware of any public disclosure, it is best to prepare for such a defense. When drafting the initial complaint in the case, if possible, set forth the basis for your argument that you are an original source of the allegations.

The definition of an "original source" is as follows: "'original source' means an individual who either (i) prior to a public disclosure. . . has voluntarily disclosed to the Government the information on which allegations or transactions in a claim are based, or (ii) who has knowledge that is independent of and materially adds to the publicly disclosed allegations or transactions, and who has voluntarily provided the information to the Government before filing an action under this section."

In other words, if you file your FCA claim before there is a "public disclosure," you are covered. If you file your claim after a "public disclosure," you must demonstrate that you are a "true whistleblower," i.e., that you were able to obtain knowledge of the underlying wrongdoing independent of any information that may have been published in the press or reported in a government report, and that your information "materially adds" to the information that is in the public domain. Additionally, you must provide this information to the United States prior to filing your FCA case.

In filing a *qui tam*, an employee must always strive to meet the definition of an original source. Congress understood the original source to be the typical whistleblower—an employee with inside information about the fraud.

Word to the wise: If you have an FCA case, don't run to the press, run to the Department of Justice.

STEP 3: CONFIDENTIALLY FILE ALLEGATIONS WITH THE GOVERNMENT

It is best practice to disclose allegations to government regulators *prior* to filing a formal False Claims Act case. Voluntarily providing information to the government before filing the formal complaint satisfies one of the requirements for qualifying as an "original source" whistleblower.

Providing information to the government before filing a formal FCA complaint is very easy. Many whistleblowers, without even understanding the law, contact government agencies before filing a *qui tam*. Employees often initiate contacts with government contracting officials or provide information on government sponsored "hotlines." Every major government agency has an Office of Inspector General. That office has jurisdiction to accept and investigate allegations of contractor fraud and/or any form of procurement abuse. The website for contacting agency inspectors general is set forth in the Resources for Whistleblowers section at the end of the book.

STEP 4: FILE FIRST

Another unique provision in the law is the "first to file" rule. Only the person who files the claim first has the right to pursue the case and collect the reward. If an employee has information on potential false claims, it is imperative that he or she assemble the evidence and file the claim as quickly as possible. An informal disclosure to the government does not count. Additionally, if the government files a claim against the contractor before the whistleblower files his or her claim, the right to file the *qui tam* may also be barred. Whistleblowers cannot delay. Procrastination may prove fatal.

"The False Claims Act works. It works because it is an effective tool to fight fraud across the full spectrum of federal programs and initiatives. The FCA works because it provides powerful incentives for companies to do business the right way."

Stuart Delery, Assistant U.S. Attorney General

STEP 5: CHOOSE THE VENUE

One of the most useful features of the False Claims Act is a very liberal venue rule. A party can file a lawsuit in any jurisdiction in which any of the named defendants "can be found, resides, transacts business, or in which any [false claim] occurred." This often gives an employee a choice of districts in which she or he can file a claim. A claim should be filed in the venue that is most favorable for pursing the case, not necessarily in the judicial district where the company and/or the whistleblower resides. Some of the factors whistleblowers may weigh in deciding which jurisdiction to file a claim are: (a) where you or your lawyers reside (this can reduce litigation costs down the road); (b) the reputation of the local district court judges and U.S. Attorney's Office; and (c) the FCA case law developed by the appeals court in the judicial circuit for which the claim is filed.

STEP 6: PREPARE A DETAILED "DISCLOSURE STATEMENT"

Most civil suits are initiated with the filing of a short, concise complaint that is filed in the local court. Not so with the FCA. The FCA requires that the whistleblower/relator file a detailed "disclosure statement" with the United States at the same time a complaint is served on the government. The rule is fairly simple: "A copy of the complaint *and written disclosure of substantially all material evidence and information the person possesses* shall be served on the Government pursuant to Rule 4(d)(4) of the Rules of Civil Procedure" (emphasis added). The disclosure statement is *only* filed with the United States government. It is *not* filed with the Court and it is *not* served on the defendants. The statement should be kept strictly confidential.

The disclosure statement requirement is consistent with other aspects of the FCA. Essentially all the evidence the whistleblower has to back up his or her allegations of misconduct should be contained in the statement. All documentary evidence that supports the claim should be copied and submitted along with the written statement. This requirement compels the whistleblower to surrender the evidence of wrongdoing to the government as quickly as possible. It also permits the United States to commence its investigation in a timely manner.

Put your best foot forward when filing a disclosure statement. The statement constitutes a documentary record of the nature of your allegations and establishes the scope of your claims. The information set forth in the disclosure can and will play a critical role in determining whether the United States joins in your lawsuit.

STEP 7: FILE THE COMPLAINT "UNDER SEAL" AND KEEP IT CONFIDENTIAL

Unlike a normal lawsuit filed in court, a False Claims Act case must be filed "under seal." Everything about the filing of the complaint is strictly confidential. The defendant is not informed that a lawsuit has been filed. The complaint is kept confidential and only provided to the Justice Department and the court. The whistleblower cannot tell anyone that he or she filed a complaint. The complaint is not "served" on any party, except the United States.

Until the court issues an order lifting the "seal," no one else is provided with a copy of the complaint. When a case is initially filed, secrecy is key. If you tell the news media, the defendants, or anyone else for that matter that you filed the claim, you may lose your case and be subject to sanctions for violating a court-ordered confidentiality requirement.

The specific rule for filing a complaint consists of a two-part process: First, the complaint is filed with the Court. Second, the complaint and the disclosure statement are formally served on the United States.

As for the court filing: "The complaint shall be filed *in camera*, shall remain under seal for at least 60 days, and shall not be served on the defendant until the court so orders." In other words, inform the clerk of the court that the complaint must be filed confidentially, and *never* serve the complaint on the defendant until the court officially lifts the seal and orders that service be completed.

As for the United States, as explained above, both "a copy of the complaint" and the "written disclosure" statement must be "served on the Government pursuant to Rule 4(d)(4) of the Rules of Civil Procedure." This Rule of procedure mandates that the complaint and disclosure statement be served both upon the Attorney General of the United States in Washington, DC, and upon the United States Attorney for the judicial district in which the complaint is filed.

Eventually the complaint will be taken out of seal, and the parties can proceed in a manner consistent with other traditional lawsuits. But the initial complaint must be filed under seal. This rule is based on the theory that the United States needs time to review the complaint and the material filed by the whistleblower and to determine whether or not the government wants to "intervene" and take over the lawsuit. Filing under seal permits the government to investigate the whistleblower allegations before the company knows it is the target of a False Claims Act lawsuit.

Once the government concludes its investigation and determines whether or not to intervene, the court will take the case out of seal, the proceedings will become public, and the complaint must be served upon the defendants. But before this happens, you *must* honor and follow the rules mandating confidentiality of the FCA claims.

STEP 8: THE COMPLAINT FILED IN COURT MUST BE DETAILED

The FCA complaint should contain detailed factual statements setting forth the basis for the complaint. Courts view FCA cases in a manner similar to other fraud cases. Under Federal Rule of Civil Procedure 9(b), fraud cases are subjected to a "heightened pleading" standard. As one court explained, this rule is designed to protect those accused of committing fraud. It requires plaintiffs to "place the defendants on notice of the precise misconduct with which they are charged" in order to "safeguard defendants against spurious charges of immoral or fraudulent behavior."

Courts uniformly have applied this 9(b) standard to FCA cases. Thus, unlike other federal court complaints, which merely require a "plain statement" of the factual basis for the case, FCA cases, under the 9(b) standard, must contain specific information setting forth the grounds for the claim, including "precise information" upon which the FCA violations are based.

Beyond satisfying the technical procedural pleading rules for fraud cases, there are other very good reasons for making sure the complaint (and disclosure statement that is required to be filed with the government) are very detailed. First, because of the "first to file" rule, what happens if your complaint is vague on a key issue of fraud, but another whistleblower files a similar complaint, which provides specific detail of the wrongdoing? Whose complaint meets the "first to file" rule? This is a question every *qui tam* relator should seek to avoid ever having to answer. A properly detailed complaint should go a long way toward resolving such a dispute.

Second, under the Supreme Court's ruling in the *Rockwell International* case, whistleblowers are only entitled to a reward for those frauds properly included within the scope of their complaint. If allegations are vaguely worded, and if the complaint lacks specificity on key issues, the *qui tam* relator risks having their claim denied under *Rockwell*.

Third, the more specificity contained in the complaint (and disclosure statement), the more credibility the whistleblower will have with the government investigators. This will also increase the chance that the government will intervene in the case.

STEP 9: KEEP INVESTIGATING THE CLAIM AFTER THE COMPLAINT IS FILED

After the FCA complaint is filed and the disclosure statement served, do not rest on your laurels. Whistleblowers can and should continue to investigate and collect additional information that backs up their claims. Sometimes this can be done by the employee working on his own (without ever disclosing the existence of the FCA claim to anyone) and sometimes this occurs in conjunction with the government investigation. For example, it is common for government investigators to obtain assistance from the relator after a case is filed.

This can include anything from providing additional documents to government investigators all the way to wearing a "wire" while meeting at work with the managers responsible for the frauds.

Regardless of the method used to obtain additional supporting information, the whistleblower should carefully document his or her post-complaint activities. This documentation can be used to file supplemental disclosure statements with the government or, in the appropriate circumstances, to amend the complaint.

STEP 10: DETERMINE WHETHER STATE FUNDS ARE INVOLVED

A growing number of states and municipalities now have local versions of the False Claims Act. They include California, the City of Chicago, Colorado, Connecticut, Delaware, the District of Columbia, Florida, Georgia, Hawaii, Illinois, Indiana, Louisiana, Maryland, Massachusetts, Michigan, Montana, Nevada, New Hampshire, New Mexico, New Jersey, New York City, New York State, North Carolina, Oklahoma, Philadelphia and Allegheny County, Pennsylvania (not the Commowealth of Pennsylvania), Rhode Island, Tennessee, Texas, Vermont, Virginia, and Washington. Some of these laws are mirror images of the federal FCA, while others contain significant differences. A number of states restrict the scope of their local FCA to fraud in Medicaid spending. The number of states adopting local FCA laws continues to expand. This rapid growth is largely due to the success of the law and federal financial inducements given to states that enact these protections.

When federal and state monies are jointly involved, it is very common to include state claims in the federal complaint. The federal FCA has a special provision that establishes federal jurisdiction "over any action brought under the laws of any State for the recovery of funds paid by a State or local government if the action arises from the same transaction or occurrence as an action brought under [the federal False Claims Act]." In 2009 the FCA was amended to make it easier to join states in the federal action. Relators can serve state government officials copies of the federal complaint and disclosure statement, and the court-ordered seal applies to these filings.

The state FCAs are very similar to the federal law, but most have some statutory differences. Just as with the federal law, if you are using a state FCA, meticulous care must be undertaken to comply with the law's rules and procedures. When including pendent state claims in the federal FCA, it is typical to include a separate count(s) within the complaint for each state and to use this part of the complaint to ensure that any special terms required under state law are met and that additional causes of action are included for states that have more liberal liability or standing procedures than the federal law.

State recoveries can be very large, especially if the defrauded program was a joint federal and state enterprise. A prime example of this is the January 2009 settlement in the Eli Lilly case, where $362 million of the $800 million set aside to compensate for the losses to the Medicare and Medicaid programs was allocated for paying state claims. Joint federal and state settlements such as the Eli Lilly case are common under the FCA.

STEP 11: PREPARE FOR A RETALIATION CASE

If a whistleblower is discriminated against or fired for raising allegations of contract fraud, he or she has the right to include retaliation claims as part of the False Claims Act lawsuit. Subsection (h) of the act prohibits retaliation against employees who engage in protected activities designed to "further" a FCA lawsuit or who engage in "other efforts to stop one or more violations" of the procurement/contracting violations outlawed by the FCA. This law provides for double back pay, reinstatement, special damages, and attorney fees and costs. The statute of limitations for the retaliation claim is three years.

Often subsection (h) retaliation cases are included in the FCA complaint as a "placeholder." The retaliation case is filed and preserved along with the *qui tam* rewards-based claim, but a formal decision whether to actually pursue such a case is left for a later date.

The retaliation claim is handled separate from the contractor-fraud case. The United States generally permits the employee to pursue these claims regardless of whether or not the fraud issues are litigated, dropped, or settled. Even if the United States declines to intervene in the fraud case, and even if upon further investigation the fraud claims appear to have no merit, an employee still has the right to pursue retaliation claims based on discrimination in the workplace.

STEP 12: DECIDE WHETHER TO PROCEED WITH A CIVIL CASE

After the government completes its investigation into the confidential complaint, the United States will inform the court whether or not it will "intervene" in some or all of the claims filed by the relator. This can be the most important decision in a FCA case. Based on raw statistics, if the United States intervenes in a case the odds of prevailing are extremely high. But if the United States declines to intervene, the vast majority of cases are dismissed.

If the United States intervenes in the case, as a matter of law, the government takes over primary control of the litigation. Once this happens, the relator plays a secondary role to the government, and courts often defer to the judgment of the United States. After all, it is the government's money that was defrauded. The FCA defines the role of the government and relator in intervened cases as follows: "If the Government proceeds with the action, it shall have the primary responsibility for prosecuting the action, and shall not be bound by an act of the person bringing the action"; however, the relator "shall have the right to continue as a party to the action."

This provision does not leave the whistleblower out in the cold. The whistleblower has the right to fully participate in the civil proceeding, conduct discovery, file briefs and motions, question witnesses at trial, and otherwise be fully included in every aspect of the case. The relator also must be informed of any settlement agreement and has an opportunity to oppose court approval of a settlement. By actively participating in an intervened case, the whistleblower can help the government prevail on the merits and at the same time protect his or her interests as the relator. Additionally, the relator is also entitled to a payment of attorney fees and costs from the defendant. Thus, even in cases in which the final recovery may be modest, the relator's counsel can still be paid by the defendant pursuant to the statutory attorney fee provision contained in the FCA.

If the United States declines to intervene in the case, the whistleblower must make a major decision of either dropping the case or moving forward with it. Under the *qui tam* provision, the whistleblower is empowered to pursue the case "on behalf of the king." So even if the United States decides that it will not prosecute the claim, a whistleblower can still go forward and prove the merits of the case. If he or she prevails, the United States still collects the lion's share of the award, but the whistleblower is entitled to a minimum 25 percent and maximum 30 percent "relator's share" of any money recovered by the United States, and the whistleblower can also collect a statutory attorney fee.

The FCA contains a section that permits a defendant to seek "reverse attorney fees" from the whistleblower if the United States declines to intervene and the employee-relator continues with the claim. These reverse fees can be awarded only under narrow circumstances: "If the Government does not proceed . . . and the person bringing the action conducts the action, the court may award to the defendant its reasonable attorneys' fees and expenses if the defendant prevails in the action and the court finds that the claim . . . was clearly frivolous, clearly vexatious, or brought primarily for purposes of harassment."

Deciding to pursue a claim if the United States declines intervention is a major decision for a whistleblower, as civil proceedings under the False Claims Act are expensive, time-consuming, and aggressively litigated by the defendant. Most cases are either dropped or dismissed if the United States rejects the case. Regardless of whether or not the United States intervenes in the *qui tam* portion of a case, the whistleblower can pursue his or her retaliation case, if one was filed.

The government's decision not to intervene should not be held against the whistleblower in subsequent litigation. Despite this, courts are unfortunately more skeptical of the merits of a case for which the United States did not join.

No matter how strong you may think your case is, if the United States declines to intervene, it is absolutely imperative that you stop and take a hard look at your claim. You must evaluate why the United States declined to intervene. You must evaluate the costs and risks of going forward. You must evaluate the realistic likelihood of success, especially in light of the controlling case law, how much money is at stake, the facts you actually have at your disposal, whether your complaint can withstand a motion to dismiss, and the various defenses the corporation will aggressively raise.

Despite the complexity of the law, and the numerous procedural and factual hurdles whistleblowers must overcome to file a successful lawsuit, the False Claims Act remains the taxpayer's "primary civil remedy" stopping fraud in government programs. In December 2016 alone whistleblowers recovered $2.9 billion from fraudsters in health care, national security, food safety, mortgage loans, highway funds, small business contracts, agricultural subsidies, disaster assistance, and import tariffs. The top prosecutor in the Justice Department's civil division recognized whistleblowers as being "uniquely positioned to expose fraud" and praised them for their "courage."

PRACTICE TIPS

- Checklist 4 sets forth examples of frauds prosecuted under the False Claims Act. In 2009 and 2010 the definitions of the words *claim* and *obligation* covered under the FCA were significantly expanded.

- All state and local FCAs signed into law as of 2017 are listed in Checklist 1.

- The False Claims Act is codified at 31 U.S.C. §§ 3729-32. Its legislative history is contained in Senate Report No. 99-345 (July 28, 1986) and S. Rep. No. 110-507 (September 17, 2008).

- Recent Supreme Court cases interpreting the FCA are *KBR v. U.S. ex rel. Carter*, 135 S.Ct. 1970 (2015) (clarifying "first to file" rule and statute of limitations); *U.S. ex rel. Escobar v. Universal Health Services*, 136 S.Ct. 1989 (2016) (recognizing implied certification claims) and *State Farm v. U.S. ex rel. Rigsby*, 137 S.Ct 436 (2016) (sanctions for violating seal).

RULE 7

Get a Reward! Tax Cheats and the IRS *Qui Tam*

At a breakfast meeting of one hundred senior "wealth management" leaders held on September 12, 2012, top Swiss bankers and their consultants discussed changes in the infamous secret Swiss banking system—a system that had permitted thousands of millionaires and billionaires to hide their wealth in Swiss banks, escaping taxation and detection from their local governments. The exclusive gathering, held at the Hotel President Wilson in Geneva, Switzerland, occurred just one day after former Swiss banker Bradley Birkenfeld sponsored an international press conference at the National Press Club in Washington, DC, publicly revealing that the U.S. Internal Revenue Service had ruled in his favor and awarded him $104 million as a result of his having blown the whistle on the Swiss banking giant UBS.

According to a report from an *Agence France-Presse* reporter who was able to attend, the mood during this elite meeting was bleak. The attendees were "seething" at Birkenfeld and attacking the whistleblower's "total lack of morality" for having the audacity to blow the whistle on over nineteen thousand secret bank accounts held by wealthy Americans, resulting in numerous criminal prosecutions and the payment of over $13.7 billion in back taxes, fines, and penalties.

Beyond the hatred directed at the whistleblower, the "scandals" he triggered had "driven a nail into the heart of the once seemingly invincible Swiss bank secrecy" system. The head of the Swiss banking group Reyl & Co, Mr. Francois Reyl, described the new reality: "The storm has swept everything away." A respected banking consultant was reported as saying, "Banking secrecy is no longer there. That's gone. It is over."

Whistleblower Bradley Birkenfeld, a former international banker employed at UBS (at the time, the world's largest bank), had blown the lid off the entire Swiss banking empire. As described by the U.S. Internal Revenue Service, in its ruling awarding Mr. Birkenfeld the largest single payment ever given to one whistleblower under U.S. laws, Birkenfeld had provided information that "formed the basis for unprecedented actions against UBS, with collateral impact on other enforcement activities."

The IRS' serious efforts to combat offshore tax evasion, which had long been a problem, began in 2008 with our efforts to address specific situations brought to our attention in part by whistleblowers.

John Koskinen, Commissioner, IRS

The reward given to Mr. Birkenfeld sent shockwaves throughout the international banking community. The effective use of a tax whistleblower law had changed "everything" with the illegal offshore secret banking systems that were estimated to hold trillions of dollars in U.S. assets. The reason was simple. Under a U.S. tax whistleblower law, anyone with "original information" on tax law violations or underpayments could disclose their evidence to the IRS, and if proven true, could qualify for a large cash reward equaling 15 to 30 percent of the proceeds collected by the IRS as a result of the whistleblower's disclosure.

Based on this law, every international banker who turned in American clients who held illegal offshore accounts could potentially qualify for a multimillion-dollar reward. When Birkenfeld first stepped forward the IRS rewards law was brand new. In the beginning of his case Birkenfeld met with disaster. Instead of blowing the whistle to the IRS Whistleblower Office (the office designated with the responsibility of receiving whistleblower claims), Birkenfeld walked into the office of a Justice Department prosecutor and with no immunity dumped his documents at their doorstep. The Justice Department, completely ignoring the new whistleblower law, prosecuted Birkenfeld. The international banking community, which watched with glee the destruction of a whistleblower's career, thought the IRS law was broken and would not work. But when it became public that Mr. Birkenfeld, despite having gone to jail, was still able to file a claim with the IRS, successfully litigate his claim before the agency, and prevail in his request for a $104 million reward, everything changed.

The reality that whistleblowers could effectively report tax fraud and that the U.S. government would follow the law and award whistleblowers (even if the law required payments in the hundreds of millions of dollars) sank in rather quickly to an audience of bankers and private wealth managers. They recognized that any of their colleagues could turn in their institutions and clients and become a multi-millionaires overnight. They also realized that Birkenfeld's rather simple mistake (i.e., giving information to a prosecutor without immunity, as opposed to the lawfully designated IRS Whistleblower Office) could be easily fixed. They recognized the impact whistleblowers could have on their banks and clients under the new IRS whistleblower law. They lamented that their highly profitable secret banking programs for U.S. taxpayers had been "swept away."

How We Got Here

In March 1867 Congress passed a rewards law for people who reported tax crimes. The law was enacted years before there was a federal income tax, and unlike the False Claims Act, there was no *qui tam* provision. Rewards paid to informants were strictly voluntary. The law did not work. Because the IRS was not required to do anything to help would-be whistleblowers, they didn't. The rewards provision remained mostly unused and ignored for years.

One hundred and forty years later, Iowa Senator Chuck Grassley (the principal sponsor of the False Claims Act amendments in 1986) used his position as chairman of the powerful Senate Finance Committee to rectify this problem. The FCA had proven to be the most successful fraud-detection law in U.S. history, but it *excluded* false claims related to tax payments. The FCA only covered government contracting, grants, leases, loans, and purchases; it did not cover the IRS and taxes. That was about to change.

In 2006, the inability of the government to detect massive violations of the tax code was reminiscent of the government's inability to police its contracts twenty years before. Tax frauds were rampant. For example, in illegal offshore accounts alone, it was estimated that over $5 trillion was stashed. For years, millionaires and billionaires had devised sophisticated tax-avoidance schemes, and there was no incentive whatsoever for bankers, accountants, and insiders to blow the whistle. Far from it. If an accountant blew the whistle on his or her client, that accountant would never work again in the industry.

On December 20, 2006, the Tax Relief and Health Care Act was signed into law. Tucked into that bill was a Grassley-sponsored amendment to the archaic and unused 1867 IRS informants rule. Following the lead of the FCA, a *qui tam* law was enacted *requiring* the IRS to pay rewards to whistleblowers who exposed major tax "underpayments," violations of "internal revenue laws," or any actions of persons "conniving" to cheat on their taxes. The IRS was required to establish a Whistleblower Office, and if a claim was denied, the employee could appeal that decision to Tax Court. The law is *not* limited to tax frauds. The ability to obtain rewards for reporting *underpayments* significantly increases the range of claims whistleblowers can file successfully.

The law was not designed to empower ex-husbands and ex-wives to seek revenge by filing tax fraud claims against their former spouses. Instead, the law was specifically designed to target large tax cheats involved in multimillion-dollar frauds. In order to be covered under the Grassley Amendment, an "individual" taxpayer would have to have had a "gross income" in excess of $200,000 for any of the tax years covered under the whistleblower complaint. The total amount of fraud or underpayment of taxes in dispute would have to "exceed $2 million." In other words, the law was designed to encourage detection and reporting of corporate tax fraud schemes, large underpayments of taxes, and schemes that benefited millionaires and billionaires.

In 2009, the inspector general of the Department of Treasury examined the IRS's compliance with the law and determined that the Grassley Amendment "provides the IRS with an opportunity to recover potentially billions." The inspector general also documented the radical growth in claims after the enactment of the Grassley Amendment. For example, in 2007, 83 whistleblower claims were filed, with evidence/allegations documenting $8 billion in tax fraud. The next year, 2008, the number of claims rose to 1,890, and the amount of these claims totaled $65 billion. By September 2016 the number of open submissions under review was over 10,000.

Between December 2006 and August 2012 the IRS was building its whistleblower program. However, hundreds of claims were unpaid and whistleblowers were angry over the snail's pace with which the office was adjudicating claims. That perception changed when the IRS Whistleblower Office issued a ruling on the Birkenfeld case and made the largest award ever paid to a single whistleblower. Remarkably, the IRS's first major ruling was approximately $10 million larger than any reward paid by the Justice Department to an individual whistleblower in twenty-five years. This differential not only sent a message that the IRS was serious about rewarding tax whistleblowers, it also demonstrated how large many of the tax frauds are and the potential that corporate insiders can exploit if they properly use the law.

In the four years following Birkenfeld's historic ruling (2013–16) the IRS paid awards to an additional 751 whistleblowers. Total payments topped $271 million.

Factors Used by the IRS to Judge Awards

When putting together an IRS reward filing, it is important to know the factors applied by the IRS when it evaluates a claim to determine at what percentage to set the award.

The "positive factors" set forth in the IRS's *Internal Revenue Manual* (Part 25, Chapter 2) are:

- Did the whistleblower act "promptly to inform the IRS or the taxpayer of the tax noncompliance"?

- Did the "information provided" identify an "issue or transaction of a type previously unknown to the IRS"?

- Was the "information provided" "particularly difficult to detect through the IRS's exercise of reasonable diligence"?

- Did the whistleblower present his or her information "thoroughly" and present "factual details of tax noncompliance in a clear and organized manner"?

- Did the whistleblower's information save "IRS work and resources"?

- Did the whistleblower provide "exceptional cooperation and assistance during the pendency of the action(s)"?

- Whether "the information provided identified assets of the taxpayer that could be used to pay liabilities, particularly if the assets were not otherwise known to the IRS."

- Whether "the information provided identified connections between transactions, or parties to transactions, that enabled the IRS to understand tax implications that might not otherwise have been understood by the IRS."

- Whether "the information provided had an impact on the behavior of the taxpayer, for example by causing the taxpayer to promptly correct a previously-reported improper position."

The following factors will be used by the IRS to reduce (but not deny) a reward:

- Whether the whistleblower "delayed" reporting the violations;

- Whether the whistleblower's actions "contributed to the underpayment" of taxes;

- Whether the whistleblower interfered or harmed the IRS investigation;

- Whether the whistleblower violated instructions given by the IRS, or violated a confidentiality agreement or other contract entered into with the IRS.

Another ground for reducing an award is whether the whistleblower "profited from the underpayment of tax or tax noncompliance identified." Profiting from the underlying violations is not grounds for denying a reward, but if the whistleblower is found criminally guilty of planning and initiating the violations, there may be grounds for an outright denial.

How the Law Works

The basic rules that govern the IRS whistleblower law are as follows:

1. *Taxes Covered*. As already stated, the tax whistleblower law is not limited to tax fraud. It covers any underpayment of taxes, fraudulent or not. The law provides for whistleblower rewards for information that results in the IRS's "detecting underpayments of tax" *or* "detecting and bringing to trial and punishment persons guilty of violating the internal revenue laws." The law also covers those who conspire to violate the laws. The monetary basis for which a reward is paid includes not just the back taxes, but any "penalties, interest, additions to tax, and additional amounts" obtained by the U.S. government on the basis of the whistleblower's information.

2. *Proceedings Covered*. The whistleblower is eligible for a reward if monies are recovered by the United States "based on" their information, regardless if the money is obtained from an administrative proceeding, a judicial proceeding, a settlement, or "any related action." However, unlike the False Claims Act, the whistleblower does not have the right to initiate legal proceedings against the taxpayer. It is up to the IRS and/or the U.S. government to file the lawsuit, or reach a settlement with the "taxpayer." Once the United States collects the back taxes, interest, penalties, and so on, the whistleblower then becomes entitled to his or her percentage share from the monies recovered by the United States. If the United States does not initiate legal or administrative action against the "taxpayer," the whistleblower cannot file his or her own lawsuit against the "taxpayer."

3. *Who Can File*. Any person can file an IRS whistleblower claim. The applicant for the reward does not have to be an employee of the targeted company. He or she can be an outside contractor,

a banker, a business partner, or any other person who is able to obtain credible information of a major tax fraud or underpayment.

4. *Procedure for Filing.* IRS whistleblower claims are filed directly with the IRS. There is no lawsuit. There is no public filing. Nothing is officially "served" on the employer or the individual who violated the tax laws. You do not have to tell your boss about the tax fraud or file an internal complaint. Doing so could result in your boss retaliating, especially if the IRS were to open an investigation on the very issues you tried to get fixed.

5. *IRS Form 211.* The IRS has created a form to be used for filing a whistleblower claim. The form, entitled "Application for Award for Original Information," is better known simply as "Form 211," named after its official IRS form number. Under IRS rules, Form 211 must be completed in its entirety and should include the following information:

   - Date claim is being submitted;

   - The whistleblower's name and contact information (and name of his or her spouse, if applicable);

   - The whistleblower's date of birth and taxpayer identification number (Social Security number);

   - "Specific and credible information concerning the person(s) that the claimant believes have failed to comply with tax laws and which will lead to the collection of unpaid taxes";

   - A "description of the amount(s) and tax year(s) of Federal tax owed" and "facts supporting the basis for the amount(s) claimed to be owed";

   - All available "documentation to substantiate the claim," including information such as financial records, bank account locations or numbers, "books and records," and documents that contain information concerning the disputed transactions or analyses;

   - An explanation as to "how the information" that forms the basis of the claim "came to the attention of the claimant." This includes details on how the whistleblower "acquired" the information and a "complete description of the claimant's present or former relationship (if any)" to the person accused of failing to pay taxes;

- "Any and all other facts and information pertaining to the claim."

6. *Information Wanted by the IRS.* In the IRS's own words: "The IRS is looking for solid information, not an 'educated guess' or unsupported speculation. We are looking for a significant Federal tax issue—this is not a program for resolving personal problems or disputes about a business relationship." If the whistleblower's allegations cannot be "independently corroborated," a claim will be denied.

7. *Lawful Disclosures/Obtaining Documents.* A whistleblower cannot and should not violate the law in order to obtain information about tax frauds. The IRS's guidance on filing claims states as follows: "Under no circumstances do we expect or condone illegal actions taken to secure documents or supporting evidence." If the whistleblower knows about the existence of supporting evidence, but cannot lawfully obtain that information, the IRS suggests that the whistleblower "should describe these documents and identify their location to the best of his or her ability." In other words, do not steal information. Instead, carefully describe where the documents are hidden so that the IRS can lawfully obtain it through a subpoena or other legal means. In these circumstances, sometimes the whistleblower carefully places supporting documents in a specific location at work and then notifies the government where the document(s) can be found.

8. *Confidentiality.* The IRS Manual requires the Service to "protect the identity" of any person seeking the whistleblower reward "to the fullest extent permitted by law." The Service's rules require the protection of a whistleblower's identity under IRC 6103(h)(4). This provision treats a whistleblower's information on a similar basis as the commission treats other taxpayer information: completely confidential. But the IRS warns that "under some circumstances" the whistleblower's identity may have to be disclosed, such as if the whistleblower "is needed as a witness in a judicial proceeding." But these limited disclosures are covered under special rules. The IRS states that the "circumstances" where such a disclosure is needed

are "rare" and that the "Service will make every effort to notify the whistleblower before deciding whether to proceed in such a case." Furthermore, the Tax Court issued a ruling acknowledging the whistleblower's need for confidentiality and permitting claims to proceed on an anonymous basis.

9. *Anonymous Submissions.* The statute requires that all claims under the Grassley Amendment be filed "under penalty of perjury." In other words, the whistleblower making the claim must personally sign Form 211/written submission and must swear that he or she has "examined" the "application" and any "accompanying statement and supporting documentation" and must affirm that the "application is true, correct and complete, to the best of" his or her "knowledge."

Because the application *must* be filed under the penalty of perjury, the IRS guidance states that claims *cannot* be submitted "anonymously or under an alias." Furthermore, the whistleblower's lawyer cannot simply sign the submission. The whistleblower must personally sign the form. If a joint claim is being filed, all the claimants must personally sign the form and swear to the truthfulness of the information. However, under IRS rules whistleblowers can obtain Confidential Informant status in order to protect their identity.

10. *Where to File/The Whistleblower Office.* The Grassley Amendment also mandated the IRS to create a special "Whistleblower Office." The office is required to "analyze information" received from whistleblowers and has the statutory authority to issue the award to the whistleblower. The decision to make a payment to a whistleblower is made by the director of the Whistleblower Office, not the secretary of Treasury or the head of the IRS. Form 211 is filed with the Whistleblower Office.

The Whistleblower Office is the principal point of contact between the whistleblower and the IRS. It is responsible for both conducting the investigation into the tax violations and deciding whether the whistleblower should receive a reward. However, other offices within the IRS can be assigned investigatory responsibilities. Unlike the False Claims Act, in which the whistleblower can become a party to the litigation against the defendant, under the Internal Revenue Code the investigation into the merits of the whistleblower's claim is conducted solely by the IRS. It is within the "sole discretion" of the IRS as to whether or not to seek any additional "assistance" from the whistleblower after the claim is filed.

11. *Acknowledgment of Claim.* The Whistleblower Office will acknowledge receiving a claim, in writing. Each claim is given a formal claim number. The whistleblower has to be sure that this acknowledgment letter is received, as it is his or her proof that a claim was filed and documents the date the claim was formally received by the Whistleblower Office.

12. *Amount of Reward.* The reward provision is modeled on the FCA. If the IRS collects taxes "based on information" provided by the whistleblower, the whistleblower is entitled to a reward of between 15 percent and 30 percent of any amount recovered by the IRS. These are the same percentages permitted under the FCA; however, they can be reduced if the whistleblower is not an original source of the allegations (for example, if information on the tax fraud was previously disclosed in the news media or other public proceeding) or if he or she initiated and planned the tax fraud. A similar reduction provision exists in the FCA. The law also permits the whistleblower to obtain a reward based on monies collected from "related actions." The scope of a "related action" is currently unclear, but based on strong legal precedent it should be broad.

According to guidance published by the Whistleblower Office, the percentage of a recovery paid by the IRS to the whistleblower is "in proportion to the value of the information furnished voluntarily." Whistleblowers should make a "full disclosure" of all relevant evidence. Rewards are paid when the IRS "determines that the information submitted contributed to the Service's detection and recovery of tax." The law also permits the whistleblower to obtain a reward based on monies collected from "related actions." The scope of a "related action" is currently unclear, but based on strong legal precedent it should be broad.

13. *Judicial Review.* The whistleblower has the right to appeal award-determination decisions of the Whistleblower Office to the U.S. Tax Court. Appeals must be filed within thirty days of the Whistleblower Office's ruling. The Tax Court has issued rules for these appeals (Rule 340-344). They require that the whistleblower file a petition with the Tax Court, setting forth the date the Whistleblower Office made its determination and an explanation

as to why the whistleblower "disagrees with the determination" of the Whistleblower Office, a statement of facts that supports the whistleblower's appeal, and a specific "prayer" for "relief," along with other information.

14. *When Payments Are Due*. Under the law, the IRS will not pay the whistleblower until the IRS actually obtains the money from the delinquent "taxpayer" and the deadline for appealing the payments or obtaining a refund expire. If the delinquent taxpayer challenges the IRS's actions administratively or in court, the payment to the whistleblower will be "delayed until that litigation has been concluded with finality." Given the number of claims being filed by whistleblowers, the small number of employees currently staffing the IRS Whistleblower Office, and the necessity to await final payment to the IRS before any monies are paid to the whistleblower, payments to whistleblowers are taking years to adjudicate and resolve.

15. *Financial Threshold*. The Grassley Amendment targets large taxpayers. Consequently, the IRS rewards program now has two parts. The first part is based on the 1867 law. It covers small tax frauds and underpayments (under $2 million). The amount of any reward paid to informants under this program is strictly discretionary, and there is no appeal of an IRS denial of a claim. The second part of the IRS program was created by the Grassley Amendment. This part of the program mandates that the IRS pay rewards, sets the percentage amounts for such rewards, and provides a judicial review. However, the amount of the tax fraud/underpayment must meet minimum dollar thresholds to be covered.

    The IRS Whistleblower Office describes these thresholds as follows: "To be eligible for an award under [the Grassley Amendment] the tax, penalties, interest, additions to tax, and additional amounts in dispute must exceed in the aggregate $2 million and, if the allegedly noncompliant person is an individual, the individual's gross income must exceed $200,000 for any taxable year at issue in a claim."

16. *No Bar to Recovery If You Participated in the Fraud*. Whistleblowers who participated in the fraud are entitled to a full reward. This aspect of the law dates back to the original False Claims Act signed by President Lincoln. The Civil War Congress that drafted the

original FCA was very clear that the law was designed to encourage "rogues" to step forward and turn in other "rogues." The genius of the law was that it was designed to use greed to fight greed.

17. *"Planning and Initiating" Tax Frauds.* Congress drew a distinction between persons who simply participate in tax frauds and those who actually "plan and initiate" the fraud. This makes sense. For example, if an accountant plans and initiates a tax fraud on behalf of a client and then turns in the very fraud he planned and put into effect, should that accountant be able to profit from the illegal scheme he or she devised?

    Because of this very rare hypothetical possibility, Congress provided for a reduction in any reward owed to a whistleblower who "planned and initiated the actions that led to the underpayment of tax" or who planned and initiated the tax fraud. Under this provision, the IRS can reduce the reward owed to any such person based on the culpability of that person. The reward can be reduced to any level, including zero. The IRS Manual explains that "if the whistleblower participated substantially in the actions that resulted in the underpayment of tax, the Whistleblower Office may deny an award."

18. *Criminal Convictions.* If the whistleblower is criminally convicted of a crime related to his or her role in planning and initiating the tax violations, the whistleblower is disqualified from any reward. This is a very narrow exception.

19. *Persons Not Qualified to File a Claim.* Almost any person is eligible to file a whistleblower claim. The class of excluded persons is very limited. According to IRS regulations, the IRS will not process whistleblower claims filed by: employees of the Department of Treasury; persons working for federal, state, or local governments if they are "acting within the scope of his/her duties as an employee" of the government; persons "required by Federal law or regulation to disclose the information"; and persons "precluded" from disclosing the information under other federal laws.

20. *Power of Attorney.* A whistleblower who wants to be represented by counsel must sign and file a "Power of Attorney," IRS Form 2848. Without this form the IRS will not talk to your attorney or send your attorney any information.

Tax Whistleblowing Comes of Age

The IRS whistleblower law fundamentally changed tax compliance. The reason is simple. A comprehensive fraud detection study by the University of Chicago Booth School of Business confirmed the obvious: "A strong monetary incentive to blow the whistle does motivate people with information to come forward." This was the simple truth recognized by President Abraham Lincoln when he signed America's first whistleblower reward law over 150 years ago.

PRACTICE TIP

The IRS *qui tam* law is codified at 26 U.S.C. § 7623. The internal IRS rules governing the rewards provision is located in Part 25 of the IRS Manual, available at www.irs.gov. Rules for filing claims are also codified at 26 C.F.R. Part 301.7623-1.

- *Whistleblower 14106-10W v. Commissioner of the IRS*, 137 Tax Court No. 15 (December 8, 2011) (decision of the Tax Court permitting whistleblower to remain confidential in Tax Court proceedings).

- *Whistleblower 13412-12W v. Commissioner*, T.C. Memo. 2014-93 (May 20, 2014) (setting forth procedures for requesting anonymity in tax court proceedings).

- *Whistleblower 21276-13W v. Commissioner*, 147 Tax Court No. 4 (August 3, 2016) (broad interpretation of "related action" rule permitting whistleblowers to obtain rewards based on tax-related criminal proceedings).

- *Whistleblower 21276-13W v. Commissioner*, 144 Tax Court No. 15 (June 2, 2015) (whistleblower can qualify for a reward if initially provides information to other government agencies instead of the IRS Whistleblower Office).

- *Whistleblower 11099-13W v. Commissioner*, 147 Tax Court No. 3 (July 28, 2016) (whistleblowers can conduct discovery in tax court as to why the IRS denied a reward).

RULE 8

Get a Reward! Securities and Commodities Fraud

I n the summer of 2010, Congress enacted the Dodd-Frank Wall Street Reform and Consumer Protection Act. The nation was still reeling from the devastating impact of the Great Recession of 2008 and 2009, in which "millions of Americans" lost their jobs, "lost their homes," and "lost their retirement(s)." In large part, the Recession was fueled by misconduct on Wall Street, including outright frauds, the most notorious of which was the Bernard Madoff Ponzi scheme that resulted in over $20 billion in losses to thousands of innocent investors, many of whom lost their life savings.

But as with so many other scandals, it turned out there were whistleblowers with inside information who either tried to call attention to the frauds (and were ignored) or who were too afraid to step forward. The Senate Banking Committee, in devising a long-term fix to the obviously broken Wall Street regulatory system, heard extensive testimony on the role of whistleblowers in detecting and preventing frauds.

The senators listened to the testimony of Harry Markopolos, who had tried for years to expose the Madoff Ponzi scheme. They studied objective statistical data on fraud-detection methods and concluded that "whistleblower tips were 13 times more effective than external audits" in "uncover[ing] fraud schemes." The committee understood that "whistleblowers often face the difficult choice between telling the truth and the risk of committing 'career suicide.'" It was clear that the key to rooting out fraud in the financial services sector of the economy was a strong whistleblower protection program that would financially incentivize employees who had the courage to step forward with information and protect those employees from retaliation. Based on the record, even the Securities and Exchange Commission's own top cop, Inspector General David Kotz, recommended a whistleblower rewards program.

Congress listened. When the final two-thousand-page Dodd-Frank Act was finally passed, a whistleblower incentive program was at the heart of a new enforcement regime. Two new *qui tam* provisions were signed into law.

The two laws cover trillions of dollars in market transactions. One law established a *qui tam* under the Commodity Exchange Act (CEA). The second *qui tam* was attached to the Securities Exchange Act (SEA). In addition, the reward law also covers violations of the Foreign Corrupt Practices Act, as that law is administered in part by the SEC. *See* Rule 9. These two new *qui tam* provisions are sweeping in scope and cover a significant portion of the U.S. economy.

The SEA is the signature law regulating finances in the United States, including all trades conducted on various stock exchanges, such as the New York Stock Exchange and the NASDAQ, and all securities sold in the United States, including stocks, bonds, and debentures.

The CEA is similar to the securities law, but instead of covering the sale of securities, it covers the sale of commodities—the "futures trading" of fungible goods and assets, such as agricultural products (grain, animal products, fruits, coffee, sugar), energy (crude oil, coal, electricity), natural resources (gold, precious gems, plutonium, water), commoditized goods (generic pharmaceuticals), and financial commodities (foreign currencies and securities).

By incorporating *qui tam* incentive provisions into the fabric of these two extremely broad regulatory statutes, Congress sent a clear message: Employees were expected to play a critical role in protecting investors and consumers from financial fraud.

"There have always been mixed feelings about whistleblowers and many companies tolerate, at best, their existence because the law requires it. . . . [I]t is past time to stop wringing our hands about whistleblowers. They provide an invaluable public service, and they should be supported. And, we at the SEC increasingly see ourselves as the whistleblower's advocate."
Mary Jo White, Chair, Securities and Exchange Commission

These two *qui tam* laws are substantially identical. They are modeled on the federal False Claims Act and the 2006 IRS whistleblower rewards law. Under these new *qui tam* laws, qualified whistleblowers are entitled to rewards of "not less than 10 percent" and "not more than 30 percent" of the total amount of money collected by the government as a "monetary sanction" against companies or individuals who violate either of the two laws (and numerous other federal laws that are incorporated by reference into these two laws). Like the IRS *qui tam* provision, the laws only cover major frauds, and the incentives are paid only if the total amount collected by the government exceeds $1 million.

The "monetary sanctions" upon which the reward is based include not only direct fines paid to the Commissions, but interest, penalties, and monies paid as part of a "disgorgement." The disgorgement payments can be massive, as they are the mechanism by which the Commissions require a "wrongdoer" to "disgorge" its "fraudulent enrichment." These sanctions are measured by the amount of a wrongdoer's ill-gotten gains and often are many times larger than actual fines or penalties. Sanctions also include monies placed in the SEC-administered "fair funds," i.e., the funds set aside to benefit investors who were "harmed" by the violations.

Both *qui tam* laws also contain strong antiretaliation provisions, prohibiting employers from firing employees who file *qui tam* actions or engage in other protected activities. Employees can file their retaliation claims directly in federal court. Under the SEA antiretaliation provision, wrongfully discharged workers are entitled to double back pay.

Anonymous Whistleblowing

The Dodd-Frank Act added a new feature, unique in American whistleblower law: Whistleblowers are permitted to file their *qui tam* claims to the government anonymously. This is a major breakthrough and provides extra protection to whistleblowers heretofore unknown under any other employee protection law.

Employees are permitted to act through an attorney intermediary and provide their information to the government without ever having to reveal their names. Thus, there is no risk that the government will inadvertently disclose the identity of the whistleblower to their bosses, and the whistleblower can map out his or her disclosures in confidence with an attorney. Whistleblowers can consciously, carefully, and intelligently figure out, in advance, how to disclose the frauds in a manner that will reduce the risk that the industry will identify the "skunk at the picnic."

Anonymous whistleblowing not only benefits the employee who fears retaliation, but it can be exploited by the commissions as an investigative tool. If the whistleblower remains undetected by management, he or she is in an invaluable position to obtain further information about a possible cover-up or even information that could result in a criminal obstruction of justice charge.

Although the whistleblower can remain anonymous throughout the investigatory process, at the very end of the proceeding, after a decision is made to compensate the whistleblower, the government must verify the whistleblower's eligibility as an original source before the check is placed in the mail. Even then, the disclosure of information on the whistleblower should remain strictly confidential and exempt from public release.

Twenty-Five Steps to Filing a Wall Street *Qui Tam*

It is important to keep in mind that Congress enacted two separate financial *qui tam* laws: one for securities and the other for commodities. Except for the office where a *qui tam* is filed, these laws were drafted by Congress in a virtually identical manner. Here are the basic rules for both laws:

1. *Who Can File:* "Any individual" or "2 or more individuals acting jointly." In addition to the stereotypical whistleblower (i.e., a company insider), the Dodd-Frank Act also permits "analysts" to file reward claims. An analyst is not a traditional original source, but is a person who puts together public or secondary information in a manner that permits the commissions to learn that a violation has occurred.

2. *Where to File:* Claims under the Commodity Exchange Act must be filed with the Commodity Futures Trading Commission. Claims under the Securities Exchange Act must be filed with the Securities and Exchange Commission. Under both *qui tams*, claims must be filed "in a manner established by rule or regulation" by the respective commission. The specific filing procedures of the SEC and CFTC are published on the websites of each of the Commissions. There are very specific forms that must be completed in order to qualify for a reward.

3. *Anonymous Filings:* One of the critical advances in the two Wall Street *qui tam* laws was authorizing whistleblowers to make anonymous filings. When initiating a *qui tam*, an employee or other source of information must decide whether to file the claim in his or her own name or anonymously. If he or she decides to file anonymously, the employee/source must, under the law, hire an attorney to act as his or her intermediary with the SEC and/or the CFTC (referred to collectively as the "Commissions"). Thus, the employee can vet the insider information confidentially with counsel of his or her own choosing and decide what information should be provided to the Commissions. In weighing what (and how) to present information to the Commissions, the employee can seek to simultaneously present the strongest case of fraud (in order to increase the chance that the government investigators will aggressively pursue the claim), while at the same time masking the identity of the source of information. The statute permits a whistleblower to have maximum confidentiality with maximum impact.

4. *Strictly Follow the Commissions' Rules:* The Commissions have the authority to deny whistleblower rewards simply because the applicants failed to file the claim in the manner proscribed by the Commissions. The laws contain the following reward disqualification: "No award" "shall be made" "to any whistleblower who fails to submit information to the Commissions in such form as the Commissions may, by rule or regulation, require." Both Commissions have published extremely detailed rules of procedure governing the whistleblower rewards program. They are published on the Commission websites and codified at 17 C.F.R. Parts 240 and 249 (SEC) and 17 C.F.R. Part 165 (CFTC). Thus, any person seeking to obtain a reward under the CEA *must* review the most recent version of the whistleblower rules published by the CFTC. Any person seeking to obtain a reward under the SEA *must* review the most recent version of the whistleblower rules published by the SEC. Regardless of which *qui tam* is filed, employees *must* ensure strict compliance with these rules. Even if you believe that the rule is inconsistent with the substantive or procedural rights contained in the Dodd-Frank Act, whistleblowers still should file claims as mandated in the Commission rules, and if a claim is denied, challenge the rules in court.

5. *Basis for Qualifying for a Reward:* Rewards are permitted if the individual "voluntarily" files "original information" to the respective Commission that leads to the "successful enforcement" of the SEA or CEA, in a "covered judicial or administrative action" or a "related action" (including a settlement). The enforcement action (or settlement) must result in "monetary sanctions exceeding $1 million." Monetary sanctions include all monies ordered to be paid to the Commissions, including fines, penalties, interest, and monies collected as part of a "disgorgement" of ill-gotten profits.

6. *Disclosures Must Be "Voluntary":* To qualify, whistleblowers must "voluntarily" provide their information to the proper Commission. If the employee is compelled to provide the information, for example if the employee is subpoenaed to testify before a grand jury, the Commission may argue that the disclosure was not voluntary and consequently deny the application for a reward. It is in the best interest of any person who seeks a reward to voluntarily cooperate with government investigators and provide their information in the proper form on a purely voluntary basis.

7. *The Whistleblower's Information Must Be "Original":* In order to qualify for a reward, the information provided to the Commission by the whistleblower must meet the definition of "original information." For information to be considered "original," it must be "derived from the independent knowledge or analysis" of the whistleblower. This requirement is similar to the original source requirement under the False Claims Act.

8. *Public Disclosure Bar:* Like the FCA, the securities and commodities *qui tam* statutes are intended to encourage the disclosure of information to the government that is not already known to the government. The laws consequently prohibit whistleblowers from obtaining a reward under two circumstances. First, rewards are denied if the Commission is already aware of the information provided by the whistleblower, "unless the whistleblower is the original source of the information." Second, if the whistleblower "exclusively" derives his or her information from an "allegation made in a judicial or administrative hearing, in a government report, hearing, audit, or investigation, or from the news media," *unless* the whistleblower is "a source of the information." The *qui tam* law is designed to encourage employees (or other individuals) who have inside information or original analytical skills to step forward and blow the whistle to the Commissions. If information is already known to the government or is already in the public domain, what is the purpose of paying a reward for information that the government knows or can obtain from a Google search?

9. *Amount of Reward:* If the whistleblower's disclosure qualifies for a reward, the individual who filed the claim is entitled to a reward. This payment is required under law, and the refusal of the government to make the payment can be challenged in court. The range of the reward is also set by statute. The whistleblower (either individually or, if more then one, collectively) must receive "not less than 10 percent" and "not more than 30 percent" of the total amount of "monetary sanctions" actually collected by the government as a result of the covered administrative or judicial actions, any monies obtained from "related" actions, and any money recovered as a result of a settlement.

10. *Determination of Amount of Reward:* The Commissions have wide discretion on determining the amount of the reward (i.e., whether to

grant the whistleblower 10 percent, 30 percent, or some percentage in between). In setting the percentage award, the Commissions must weigh the following factors: (a) the "significance of the information provided"; (b) the "degree of assistance provided by the whistleblower" or his or her attorney; (c) the "programmatic interest" of the Commissions in "deterring violations" of law by "making awards to whistleblower"; and (d) other factors that the Commissions may establish by "rule or regulation."

11. *First to File:* Like the FCA, the Dodd-Frank Act *qui tam* contains a "first to file" rule. Rewards are paid to the first whistleblowers to individually or jointly file the claim. If a whistleblower is the second person to file an identical claim, his or her claim could be denied. Claims are considered related under this disqualification if they are "based on the facts underlying the covered action submitted previously by another whistleblower." In practice, the harsh results mandated by the first to file rule are sometimes avoided, as both the original whistleblower and the government often recognize the efficacy of encouraging other employees with additional evidence in support of the initial claim to step forward. The law also permits whistleblowers who "contribute" new information to an ongoing investigation to qualify for a reward. This exception is not contained in the False Claims Act. But the law places a premium on the first employee(s) who files a claim, and the old adage "if you snooze you lose" applies to the Dodd-Frank Act *qui tams*. Bottom line: Don't miss the bus. File first.

But if you are not the first to file, it is still to your advantage to fully cooperate with an ongoing investigation, and provide the government with new information that the original whistleblower could not contribute.

12. *Limitations on Filing Anonymously:* To file an anonymous *qui tam* claim, the whistleblower must be represented by counsel. But "prior to the payment of an award the identity of the whistleblower" must be provided to the Commissions, along with "such other information" the Commissions "may require." Even postjudgment, after the whistleblower's identity has been provided to the Commissions, the Commissions are still prohibited from releasing any information to third parties that may identify the whistleblower, except under very limited circumstances.

13. *Settlement Coverage:* The statute explicitly ensures that *qui tam* rewards are based not only on monies obtained as a result of "judicial or administrative action" but also include monies obtained by the government as a result of "settlement." The basis for rewards also includes actions taken by the Commissions that are in any manner "based upon" the "original information provided by the whistleblower," including indirect "related" actions.

14. *Disqualification of Certain Employees:* Various classes of employees are disqualified by statute from obtaining rewards. The disqualification is primarily applied to employees whose job it is to detect fraud, such as employees of an "appropriate regulatory agency," employees of the Department of Justice, or "law enforcement organization(s)" employees of the "self-regulatory" organizations and the "registered futures association."

15. *Whistleblowers Disqualified from Obtaining Rewards*: Even if a whistleblower is completely eligible to obtain a reward, there are three grounds for disqualification. First, if the whistleblower is "convicted of a criminal violation related to the judicial or administrative action for which the whistleblower otherwise could receive an award." Second, if the whistleblower "knowingly and willfully makes any false, fictitious, or fraudulent statement" when filing his or her *qui tam*. Persons who "knowingly" file false statements in an attempt to obtain a reward can be criminally prosecuted. Third, the failure to file claims in accordance with the rules published by the Commission can, standing alone, result in the denial of a claim.

16. *Antiretaliation:* No employer can terminate or discriminate against any employee who files a *qui tam* claim, who testifies in a *qui tam* case, or who assists in a *qui tam*–related investigation.

    Under the CEA antiretaliation provision, discrimination cases must be filed directly in federal court within two years of the retaliatory adverse action. Employees are entitled to reinstatement, back pay, special damages, and attorney fees and costs. The SEA's protections are broader than the CEA (filing a *qui tam*) and also requires that claims be filed in federal court. The law has a three-year statute of limitations (that can be lengthened up to ten years, depending on when the employee learns of the retaliation). The scope of damages under the two laws are somewhat different. Whereas the CEA directly permits an award of special damages, the SEA is silent on that provision. But the SEA mandates an award of double back pay, whereas the CEA only provides for a straight back pay award. There is no provision in the law for filing retaliation cases confidentially, and an employer will know who the plaintiff is in any such case. The Sarbanes-Oxley corporate reform law also prohibits retaliation against whistleblowers who allege securities fraud. The SOX law has additional protections for which the SEA provisions are silent. Corporate whistleblowers should try to file claims under SOX and if appropriate, join the CEA or SEA claims with the SOX case. The SOX law has a 180-day statute of limitations. See Rule 4.

In a major breakthrough for whistleblower protection, the Securities and Exchange Commission now views retaliation as a securities violation. The logic behind this rule is compelling. The antiretaliation provisions of SOX and Dodd-Frank are both part of the Securities and Exchange Act. Under the law, the SEC can sanction any person who violates *any part* of the SEA. Thus, as a matter of law, firing a whistleblower is a violation of the SEA, just as engaging in insider trading is also a violation. In December 2016 the SEC sanctioned SandRidge Energy Inc. $1.4 million for retaliatory actions.

Because the sanction in the SandRidge Energy retaliation case was over $1 million, the whistleblower who disclosed that violation to the SEC (most likely the victim of the retaliation) would be entitled to a reward of no less than $140,000 and no greater than $420,000. On top of that, the SEC's finding could be admissible in a wrongful discharge lawsuit.

The rewards "create powerful incentives" for informants "to come to the Commission with real evidence of wrongdoing . . . and meaningfully contributes to the efficiency and effectiveness of our enforcement efforts."
Mary Jo White, Chair, Securities and Exchange Commission

---

17. *Confidentiality:* The *qui tams* mandate that the Commissions not disclose any information "which could reasonably be expected to reveal the identity of the whistleblower," except under very

specific circumstances, such as during a grand jury proceeding, or if the Commissions file a lawsuit against a corporation and the corporation is entitled to learn the identity of the informant. The Commissions must also ensure that any information about the whistleblower shared with other law enforcement or regulatory agencies is held in confidence by those agencies.

18. *Access to Information:* The ability of corporations (or the public) to learn the identity of whistleblowers who provide information under the *qui tam* provisions is extremely limited. The statute ensures that the Freedom of Information Act cannot be used by third parties to obtain any information that may identify the whistleblower. However, these documents are not completely shielded from public view, especially if the government prosecutes the wrongdoer and information is used in administrative or court proceedings.

19. *Non-Preemption:* The SEA and CEA whistleblower protection provisions do not preempt states from enacting similar whistle-blower laws and are not exclusive remedies. The Dodd-Frank Act contains an explicit "savings clause" that prevents the law from being interpreted so as to "diminish the rights, privileges, or remedies of any whistleblower under any Federal or State law, or under any collective bargaining agreement."

20. *Rights Cannot Be Waived:* The law prevents any employer from requiring employees to waive their rights to file whistleblower claims under the SEA and CEA *qui tam* laws. The SEC, by regulation, ensured that employers could not interfere with employee communications to the Commission: "No person may take any action to impede an individual from communicating directly with the Commission staff about a possible violation, including enforcing, or threatening to enforce, a confidentiality agreement. . . ." The Commodity Exchange Act has a similar rule, as does the amended version of the Sarbanes-Oxley Act.

The commission has put teeth into these provisions and has sanctioned companies that required employees to sign restrictive nondisclosure agreements, including imposing monetary fines and penalties.

On October 24, 2016 the SEC's Office of Compliance Inspections and Examinations issued a "Risk Alert" carefully setting forth the Commission's policy on restrictive NDAs.

Corporations were advised to review their compliance manuals, codes of ethics, employment agreements, and severance agreements for any policies or rules that could restrict or create a chilling effect on an employee's willingness to contact law enforcement about potential violations, or restrict an employee's right to apply for or obtain a reward.

21. *No Mandatory Arbitration:* Under the Commodity Exchange Act and the Dodd-Frank amendments to the Sarbanes-Oxley Act, whistleblowers cannot be required to have their cases subjected to mandatory arbitration. Even if an employee signs an arbitration agreement that, under federal or state law, would typically require a dispute to be arbitrated, these types of agreements are void under the SOX and CEA.

22. *Follow the Rules:* Both Commissions were granted explicit rule-making authority under the whistleblower provisions. Under the law, whistleblowers are required to follow these rules, and the failure to file a claim in accordance with the specifications set forth by the SEC or CFTC constitute grounds for denying a reward. Any person filing a *qui tam* should obtain the most recent version of any rules published by either Commission and ensure strict compliance with those rules. The SEC also established a separate Whistleblower Office dedicated to administering the rewards program and ensuring SEC compliance with the Dodd-Frank Act. The SEC's whistleblower rules are published at 17 C.F.R. Parts 240 and 249. The CFTC's rules are published at 17 C.F.R. Part 165. The extensive regulatory history justifying these rules is published at 76 *Federal Register* 34300 (June 13, 2011) (SEC rules) and 76 *Federal Register* 53137 (August 25, 2011) (CFTC rules).

23. *File the Second Application:* The SEC's final regulations governing whistleblower rewards established a two-step process for qualifying for rewards. Whistleblowers must initially file a "Form TCR" or a "Tip, Complaint, or Referral" form. This form, available online from the SEC, initiates the reward process. If the SEC issues a sanction against a company for which a reward could be paid, the SEC is required to post notice of this sanction on the SEC's website. Thereafter, in order to obtain a reward, a whistleblower must file a second application—and complete a new form known

as "Form WB-APP." This new application must be filed within ninety days of the SEC's publication of the sanction.

24. *Retroactivity:* The *qui tam* provisions should have retroactive application. Under the law, employees can seek rewards for frauds and violations that occurred *before* the passage of the Dodd-Frank Act. However, the Commission has determined that rewards will only be paid on the basis of information provided to the Commission after July 21, 2010, the date the Dodd-Frank Act was signed into law. This rule was upheld by the U.S. Court of Appeals for the Second Circuit.

25. *Appeals:* Whistleblowers can appeal the denial of their *qui tam* claims. The scope of appeal under the SEA and CEA differ in one material respect. Under the CEA, "any determination" by the Commissions regarding the whistleblower's *qui tam* case is subject to appeal, "including whether, to whom, or in what amount" an award is made. The SEA *qui tam* also permits an appeal of "any determination" made by the SEC, *except* the "amount of an award." In other words, the SEC's discretion as to whether to pay the whistleblower 10 percent, 30 percent, or some amount in between is nonreviewable. Under both laws an appeal must be filed within thirty days "after the determination is issued by the Commission." Appeals are filed with the U.S. Court of Appeals, and the decision of the Commission is reviewed under the Administrative Procedure Act, 5 U.S.C. § 706. Before an appeal can be filed in court, the whistleblower must fully comply with and "exhaust" the administrative procedures mandated under the SEC and CFTC rules.

Dodd-Frank

As of January 2017 the U.S. Securities and Exchange Commission has paid whistleblowers more than $130 million in rewards based on their "unique and useful information" that, in many cases, has permitted the SEC to "move quickly and initiate enforcement action against wrongdoers before they could squander the money." **Figure 6** shows the top ten awards paid by the Commission since the reward laws were approved.

Figure 6

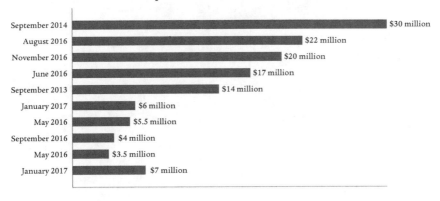

Top Ten SEC Whistleblower Awards

September 2014	$30 million
August 2016	$22 million
November 2016	$20 million
June 2016	$17 million
September 2013	$14 million
January 2017	$6 million
May 2016	$5.5 million
September 2016	$4 million
May 2016	$3.5 million
January 2017	$7 million

Source: SEC Office of the Whistleblower Website

Copies of award decisions are published on the SEC's Office of the Whistleblower website (www.sec.gov/whistleblower). To protect confidentiality, decisions usually do not identify either the company sanctioned or the whistleblower who obtained a reward. For example, in Case No. 2016-02, an "analyst" was awarded $700,000. In Case No. 2015-5, the Commission paid the whistleblower the maximum percentage award (30 percent), in large part due to the "hardships" "suffered" by the employee for making the report. In the same case, the Commission also sanctioned the company for retaliation.

In Case No. 2014-8, the Commission waived a requirement of the rules. This was a significant decision, because the SEC could have used this technicality to deny the reward altogether. But instead it exercised discretion to help a whistleblower. Usually government agencies rule in the opposite direction—if a whistleblower makes a mistake, he or she is denied justice. In this case, however, instead of ignoring the contributions of the whistleblower and blindly following a rule, the Commission rewarded the employee for "diligent efforts to correct and bring to light the underlying misconduct." The Commission also recognized that this whistleblower had tried to protect investors, and had suffered severe "professional injuries" when he or she tried to report the violations internally.

The Commission has also given awards to employees who performed compliance functions and awarded a foreign resident $30 million, noting that the Dodd-Frank Act's whistleblower reward program had extraterritorial reach: "It makes no difference whether, for example, the claimant [whistleblower] was a foreign national, the claimant resides overseas, the information was submitted from overseas, or the misconduct comprising the U.S. securities law violation occurred entirely overseas."

In Case No. 2016-1, the Commission reduced the whistleblower's reward because of a "delay in reporting the violations." When the whistleblower tried to justify the delay by identifying potential "personal and professional" risks associated with making a disclosure, the Commission rejected these arguments, explaining that the Dodd-Frank Act "changed the landscape for whistleblowers, by permitting whistleblowers "the right" to file reports "anonymously and to remain anonymous until the time the award is paid."

In a precedent-setting ruling (*In re KBR*), the Commission sanctioned the multinational defense contracting firm $130,000 for requesting employees to sign restrictive confidentiality agreements concerning disclosures they made to company attorneys, who managed the internal compliance program. Although the confidentiality agreements did not specifically prohibit communications with the SEC, their restrictions were broad enough to cover communications with the Commission: "KBR required witnesses in certain internal investigations interviews to sign confidentiality statements with language warning them that they could face discipline and even be fired if they discussed matters with outside parties without prior approval of KBR's legal department." The SEC found that these terms violated Rule 21F-17, which prohibits companies from taking any action to impede whistleblowers from reporting possible securities violations to the SEC.

Following up on the *KBR* precedent, on December 19, 2016, the Commission sanctioned Virginia-based communications company Neustar, Inc., $180,000 for requiring employees to sign restrictive severance agreements that prohibited communications with the SEC. In its investigation the Commission determined that 246 employees had signed agreements that prohibited them from making any statement that "disparages, denigrates, maligns, or impugns" the company.

Someone Listened!

Someone listened! Study after study documented the key role whistleblowers play in fraud detection. Scientifically sound statistical analyses from organizations ranging from PricewaterhouseCoopers to the Association of Certified Fraud Examiners documented how, even despite the current *disincentives* whistleblowers face, employees still come forward with information and play a central role in successful fraud detection. One such study, published by the University of Chicago Booth School of Business, actually wondered why any employee would ever blow the whistle, given the real risks of financial ruin. Their conclusion was clear: Incentives for employee disclosures were the key for stimulating the single most important source of information on actual frauds.

- The entire Dodd-Frank Wall Street Reform and Consumer Protection Act is printed as House Report No. 111-517 (June 29, 2010). It is available online at www.whistleblowers.org. The sections that relate to whistleblower protections are Section 748 (Commodity Exchange Act) (7 U.S.C. § 26); Sections 922-24 (Securities Exchange Act) (15 U.S.C. § 78u-6); Sections 922 and 929 (Sarbanes-Oxley Act) (amended 18 U.S.C. § 1514A); Section 1057 (Consumer Protection Board) (12 U.S.C. § 5567); and Section 1079B (False Claims Act) (amended 31 U.S.C. § 3730(h)).

- On June 13 and August 25, 2011, the SEC and CFTC published final rules implementing the Dodd-Frank whistleblower reward program. These rules are explained in Checklist 7, Dodd-Frank, Wall Street, and FCPA "Q&As." The SEC's Office of the Whistleblower publishes one of the best websites for whistleblowers: www.sec.gov/whistleblower. It posts all SEC award rulings and copies of the law and regulations.

RULE 9

Get a Reward!
Report Foreign Corrupt
Practices Worldwide

The most important international whistleblower reward law is the Foreign Corrupt Practices Act (FCPA), which targets bribery of foreign government officials. Enacted by the U.S. Congress in 1977, its goal is to stop global corporate bribery. It was amended in 1998 to conform to the Convention on Combating Bribery of Foreign Public Officials in International Business Transactions (Anti-Bribery Convention), of which the United States was a founding party. Since 2010 whistleblowers are covered under the FCPA.

The FCPA is extremely broad in scope, as reflected in the requirements of the Anti-Bribery Convention, which mandates that member countries make it a criminal offense "for any person" to "offer" or "give" money or any other "advantage" to a foreign government official in order to "obtain or retain" a "business advantage." The Convention targets both direct payments and payments made through "intermediaries," and also prohibits the "aiding and abetting" of violations. Furthermore, the Convention requires that all member states "broadly" assert territorial jurisdiction over these crimes so that "extensive physical connection to the bribery act is not required."

Consistent with the requirements of this Convention, the FCPA permits the United States to exercise broad extraterritorial jurisdiction to target bribes paid by non-U.S. citizens to foreign officials in countries outside the United States. This has made the FCPA the most effective transnational anticorruption law in the world.

The law also requires corporations who trade on U.S. stock exchanges, or whose stock is traded on international markets open to investment by U.S. citizens, to have strong internal controls, prohibiting off-the-books accounting. These record-keeping requirements are a key enforcement method; they require an accurate accounting of all assets, thereby forcing a company to admit on paper that it has paid a bribe, or face harsh sanction.

Under the "books and records" provision, publicly traded companies (known in the law as "issuers") must maintain detailed "books, records and accounts" that "accurately and fairly reflect" the company's "transactions" and how it spends its money. Additionally, the law requires publicly traded companies to have a "system of internal accounting controls" capable of accounting for all corporate assets, spending money as intended by company management, and "recorded" in "conformity with generally accepted accounting principles," assuring that monies are lawfully spent as intended.

Wharton School professor Philip M. Nichols aptly described the FCPA as a law designed to regulate "transnational business firms" that operate in the "global market." He warned against viewing the FCPA as a law that applies only to U.S. businesses, instead explaining that "the reality of transnational business activity, often labeled globalization, consists of networks of relationships that take little notice of national borders and which cannot be siloed." He explained that Congress "intended the Act to be part of a global regime to control bribery. . . . [The] Act is concerned with bribery that occurs outside the United States or that relates to a transaction that extends beyond the United States." According to Professor Nichols, those responsible for passing the Foreign Corrupt Practices Act "viewed bribery as presenting an existential threat to international business."

Congress's official report discussing the purpose of the FCPA backed up this view:

> The payment of bribes to influence the acts or decisions of foreign officials, foreign political parties or candidates for foreign political office is unethical. It is counter to the moral expectations and values of the American public. But not only is it unethical, it is bad business as well. It erodes public confidence in the integrity of the free market system. It short-circuits the marketplace by directing business to those companies too inefficient to compete in terms of price, quality or service, or too lazy to engage in honest salesmanship, or too intent upon unloading marginal products. In short, it rewards corruption instead of efficiency and puts pressure on ethical enterprises to lower their standards or risk losing business.

The two agencies with responsibility for prosecuting Foreign Corrupt Practices Act cases, the Department of Justice (DOJ) and the SEC, further explained the important goals of the FCPA and why these agencies have made these prosecutions a priority: "Corruption impedes economic growth . . . it undermines democratic values . . . and weakens the rule of law . . . it threatens stability and security . . . and impedes U.S. efforts to promote freedom and democracy, end poverty, and combat crime and terrorism across the globe. Corruption is also bad for business. Corruption is anti-competitive, leading to distorted prices and disadvantaging honest businesses that do not pay bribes."

For thirty years the Foreign Corrupt Practices Act lacked a whistleblower rewards provision. That changed in 2010, when Congress passed the Dodd-Frank Act. Dodd-Frank required the SEC to establish a Whistleblower Office to accept confidential and anonymous complaints and mandated that the

Commission pay whistleblowers monetary rewards if their "original information" resulted in sanctioning a corporation $1 million or more. Moreover, the law required that the Commission award any qualified whistleblower a minimum of 10 percent and a maximum of 30 percent of the sanctions obtained by the U.S. government as a result of the whistleblower's disclosures. As explained in Rule 8, the SEC has published the criteria it uses in setting the award amount.

These rights are not limited to U.S. citizens. A citizen of any country in the world can provide "original information" and qualify for a reward. The office accepts complaints from non-U.S. citizens alleging violations of the FCPA.

The passage of the Dodd-Frank Act for the first time allowed whistleblowers from foreign countries to report bribes paid to their leaders by foreign corporations and obtain monetary rewards under a U.S. whistleblower law. As of 2015 whistleblowers have obtained well over $30 million in rewards. In granting its first FCPA award, the Commission noted that "it makes no difference whether . . . [the whistleblower] was a foreign national, resides overseas, the information was submitted from overseas, or the misconduct comprising the U.S. securities violation occurred entirely overseas."

The Director of the SEC's Division of Enforcement, Andrew Ceresney, explained the critical role international whistleblowers play in reporting foreign bribery:

[I]nternational whistleblowers can add great value to our investigations. Recognizing the value of international whistleblowers, we have made . . . awards to whistleblowers living in foreign countries. In fact, our largest whistleblower award to date—$30 million—went to a foreign whistleblower who provided us with key original information about an ongoing fraud that would have been very difficult to detect. In making this award, the Commission staked out a clear position that the fact that a whistleblower is a foreign resident does not prevent an award when the whistleblower's information led to a successful Commission enforcement action brought in the United States concerning violations of the U.S. securities laws.

International whistleblowers are required to file their claims under the same rules as those that apply to U.S. citizens. These rules are spelled out in Rule 8. The scope of the FCPA is very broad. As implied by its name, the law covers the bribery of foreign officials in order to obtain a business advantage. Most people think of the FCPA as an antibribery law. Although this is true, the law's other requirements are far broader in scope and coverage. The FCPA requires publicly traded corporations to keep accurate financial records and have proper internal controls over the company's finances. These record-keeping requirements are strict, and violators are subject to large fines and penalties.

> *"In issuing [a $30 million USD] award, the Commission specifically noted that allowing foreign nationals to receive awards under the program best effectuates the clear Congressional purpose underlying the award program."*
> Securities and Exchange Commission Report

The FCPA and whistleblowers are a near-perfect fit. How else could the U.S. government learn about these secret payments, especially when these payments happen in foreign countries? Corporate insiders play a key role in enabling the government to obtain proof of a bribe, proof that a company's books are inaccurate, or proof that a company lacks internal controls over some of its business activities. This point was driven home in a joint publication authored by the DOJ and the SEC. In their *Resource Guide*, these agencies described whistleblowers as "among the most powerful weapons in the law enforcement arsenal." Whistleblower disclosures are used to "swiftly hold accountable those responsible for unlawful conduct."

FCPA cases can be big. The DOJ and SEC have pursued numerous high-profile FCPA cases that have resulted in billions of dollars in fines and "disgorgement" penalties. The list of companies prosecuted under the FCPA, and the amount of monies they paid in fines and penalties, is impressive. It includes corporate giants such as Alcalel-Lucent ($137 million), BAE Systems ($400 million), Chevron Corp. ($30 million), ENI, S.p.A./Snamprogetti Netherlands ($125 million), Kellogg Brown & Root (now KBR) and three other companies (collectively paid $1.28 billion in fines and penalties), and Siemens ($800 million). As reflected in **Checklist 8**, some of the successful prosecutions in 2016 include:

- **VimpelCom.** The Dutch-based telecommunications provider agreed to a $795 million global settlement to resolve its violations of the FCPA to win business in Uzbekistan.

- **GlaxoSmithKline.** The U.K.-based pharmaceutical company agreed to pay a $20 million penalty to settle charges that it violated the FCPA when its China-based subsidiaries engaged in pay-to-prescribe schemes to increase sales.

- **Och-Ziff.** The hedge fund and two executives settled charges related to the use of intermediaries, agents, and business partners to pay bribes to high-level government officials in Africa. Och-Ziff agreed to pay $412 million in civil and criminal penalties.

- **Anheuser-Busch InBev.** The Belgium-based global brewery agreed to pay $6 million to settle charges that it violated the FCPA by using third-party sales promoters to make improper payments to government officials in India and chilled a whistleblower who reported the misconduct.

- **LAN Airlines.** The South American–based airline agreed to pay more than $22 million to settle parallel civil and criminal cases related to improper payments authorized during a dispute between the company and union employees in Argentina.

- **Novartis AG.** The Swiss-based pharmaceutical company agreed to pay $25 million to settle charges that it violated the FCPA when its China-based subsidiaries engaged in pay-to-prescribe schemes to increase sales.

FCPA whistleblowers (who may face particularly harsh treatment in their home countries) can file their reward claims with the SEC both confidentially and anonymously. Rules governing Dodd-Frank rewards are set forth in Rule 8 and **Checklist 7**.

Here is an overview of the FCPA's major provisions:

Who is covered? First, "issuers" (companies that sell stock to U.S. citizens) and their officers, directors, employees, and agents are subject to prosecution under the FCPA. An issuer does not have to be a U.S. company. Issuers are broadly defined to include companies that trade on U.S. stock exchanges and foreign companies that trade in American Depository Receipts (ADRs). Most foreign corporations that sell securities to U.S. investors use ADRs and are thus covered under the statute. Persons acting on behalf of an issuer are also personally liable under the FCPA, including corporate officers, directors, employees, agents, or "coconspirators." Between companies that trade on Wall Street and foreign companies that utilize ADRs, most major corporations in the world are subject to the FCPA, and their employees are eligible for rewards under the Dodd-Frank Act. The SEC publishes lists of these companies on its website.

Second, all "domestic concerns" are also covered. A domestic concern is defined as any citizen, national, or resident of the United States or any corporation, partnership, association, business trust, sole proprietorship, or other association "organized" under the laws of the United States. The law also covers foreign nationals who, directly or indirectly, commit "any act in furtherance of a corrupt payment" while in the United States.

Third, issuers or domestic concerns that work with foreign companies in joint ventures are also covered. Joint ventures can be particularly high risk.

Daniel Grimm, an attorney with a major FCPA defense firm (Sullivan & Cromwell), explained that companies can be liable for FCPA violations under a "willful blindness, deliberate ignorance," or "conscious disregard" standard. Thus the failure to exercise "due diligence" over the actions of a non-U.S. joint venture partner can trigger liability, even if the U.S. partner did not pay or authorize any bribes.

To determine whether your company is an issuer subject to the FCPA, you should determine whether it is listed on a national securities exchange in the United States (either stock or American Depository Receipts) or whether the company's stock trades on the "over-the-counter market." The SEC publishes the reports filed by issuers, which can be accessed at www.sec.gov/edgar/searchedgar/webusers.htm. If a company is listed, it is covered under the FCPA.

Jurisdictional triggers: The FCPA covers conduct that occurs inside the United States or in a foreign country. The Act broadly defines the interstate commerce necessary to trigger jurisdiction for foreign nationals or companies under the law. The DOJ/SEC *Resource Guide* puts it this way: "Placing a phone call or sending an e-mail, text message, or fax from, to, or through the United States involves interstate commerce—as does sending a wire transfer from or to a U.S. bank or otherwise using the U.S. banking system, or travelling across state borders or internationally to or from the United States." As for U.S. persons and corporations, the interstate commerce requirement was removed in the 1998 amendments, and such persons are subject to the FCPA "even if they act outside the United States."

What is a prohibited bribe? The law covers payments intended to influence foreign officials to use their positions "in order to assist . . . in obtaining or retaining business for or with, or directing business to, any person." The FCPA prohibits paying a bribe to gain a business advantage. The DOJ/SEC *Resource Guide* lists the following actions as prime examples of when corporations are often induced to pay bribes to foreign officials: (1) "winning a contract"; (2) "influencing the procurement process"; (3) violating "rules for importation of products"; (4) "gaining access to non-public tender information"; (5) "obtaining exceptions to regulations"; and (6) "avoiding contract termination."

What types of payments constitute a bribe? Paying "anything of value" to a foreign official in order to obtain a business advantage can constitute a bribe. The law is very broad and, as explained in the DOJ/SEC *Resource Guide*, "bribes come in many shapes and sizes." This would include any corrupt "offer, payment, promise to pay, or authorization of the payment of any money, or offer, gift, promise to give, or authorization of the giving of anything of value" to a foreign official, such as "consulting fees," "commissions," "travel expenses," and "expensive gifts."

These payments must be made with "corrupt intent" (i.e., the purpose behind the payment is to secure an improper business advantage or improperly influence foreign government officials in order to gain such an advantage). In determining what constitutes a bribe, whistleblowers need to apply common sense. Small gifts or paying something of nominal value, such as covering a taxi ride, will not be actionable. However, as DOJ/SEC warns in their *Resource Guide*, "the larger or more extravagant the gift, . . . the more likely it was given with an improper purpose." DOJ and SEC enforcement cases have "involved single instances of large, extravagant gift-giving (such as sports cars, fur coats, and other luxury items)." Companies can pay "reasonable expenses associated with the promotion of their products" and can make payments to facilitate "routine governmental action."

What is "aiding and abetting"? Persons or companies that aid or abet in a bribery scheme are guilty under the law to the same degree as those who pay a bribe. As explained in the DOC/SEC *Resource Guide*, "a foreign company or individual may be held liable for aiding and abetting an FCPA violation . . . even if the foreign company or individual did not take any act in furtherance of the corrupt payment while in the territory of the United States." Both Japanese and European companies have been charged with FCPA violations, despite having no contacts with U.S. territory.

What is a business purpose? Like other provisions in the law, the "business purpose" test is very broad and includes payments to obtain or keep a contract or lease, influence the procurement process, eliminate customs duties, prevent competitors from entering the market, avoid permit requirements, circumvent importation rules, gain access to nonpublic information to help obtain a contract or government tender, evade taxes, or obtain exemptions for regulations.

Who is a public official? The foreign officials covered under the Act include "any officer or employee of a foreign government, or any department, agency, or instrumentality." Instrumentalities include state-owned or state-controlled entities. Foreign political parties are also included in the definition, as are candidates for foreign political office. In 1998 the FCPA was amended to include "public international organizations" within the definition of foreign officials, including entities such as the World Bank, International Monetary Fund, and the Organization of American States.

Books and records violations: The "books and records" provision prohibits off-the-books accounting. Companies can be prosecuted for books and records violations independent of a prosecution for paying a bribe. The law requires publicly traded companies to accurately account for all assets, and forms the "backbone" of most SEC and DOJ accounting fraud cases. In the context of the FCPA, its significance is obvious. Bribes are not accurately recorded in corporate books. When a company pays a bribe, it does not admit the purpose of the payment in its financial records.

Congress included the bookkeeping requirements in the FCPA, recognizing that "corporate bribery has been concealed by the falsification of corporate books and records." By mandating large civil and criminal penalties for falsifying financial records, Congress intended to "strengthen the accuracy of the corporate books and records and the reliability of the audit process, which constitute the foundations of our system of corporate disclosure."

The accounting provisions of the FCPA have two major requirements. The first mandates that issuers "keep books, records, and accounts that, in reasonable detail, accurately and fairly reflect an issuer's transactions and dispositions of an issuer's assets." The second provision requires that issuers "devise and maintain a system of internal accounting controls sufficient to assure management's control, authority, and responsibility over the firm's assets."

Although these requirements are not strictly tied to foreign bribery, it is evident how the accounting provisions can be used to prove violations of the Act. As explained in the DOJ/SEC *Resource Guide*, "Bribes, both foreign and domestic, are often mischaracterized in books and records. . . . Bribes are often concealed under the guise of legitimate payments, such as commissions or consulting fees." If, for a technical reason, the government cannot meet the standard to prove a bribe, companies can still be held liable under the books and records provision if the improper payments were not accurately recorded in the company's books. Given the large fines associated with an internal controls violation, this prosecutorial tool can be used to close potential loopholes in the bribery provisions.

In FCPA cases, companies have been found guilty of books and records violations when they recorded a bribe in the corporate books as a "commission," a "consulting fee," "sales and marketing expenses," "travel and entertainment expenses," "rebates and discounts," "service fees," "miscellaneous expenses," "petty cash" payments, and "write-offs," among other obfuscations.

The accounting provisions do not apply to privately held companies but do apply to all issuers, including companies that trade securities on the national securities exchanges in the United States and foreign issuers that trade in ADRs. The requirements also apply to subsidiaries of publicly traded companies.

Third-party liability: The FCPA prohibits the practice of using "third parties or intermediaries" to pay the bribes. Companies cannot deny knowledge that a bribe was paid simply by using intermediaries to make the payments. The fact that a company may hire a foreign "agent" or attorney to conduct its business affairs does not insulate the company from liability for the actions of these agents or intermediaries. In order to demonstrate that the company knew or should have known that the third party was paying bribes, the DOJ/SEC look at various "red flags" to determine third-party liability, such as (1) "excessive commissions" paid to "agents or consultants"; (2) "unreasonably large discounts"; (3) "consulting agreements" that include "vaguely described services"; (4) use of a third party who is "related to or closely associated with the foreign official"; or (5) if a third party "requests payment to offshore bank accounts."

Knowledge requirement: Corporations can be held liable under the FCPA under the "willful blindness" standard. As explained in the DOJ/SEC *Resource Guide*, "Because Congress anticipated the use of third-party agents in bribery schemes—for example, to avoid actual knowledge of a bribe—it defined the term 'knowing' in a way that prevents individuals and businesses from avoiding liability by putting 'any person' between themselves and foreign officials. ... [I]t's meant to impose liability not only on those with actual knowledge of wrongdoing, but also on those who purposefully avoid actual knowledge." In its 1988 legislative history on the FCPA, Congress described the firm's knowledge requirements as prohibiting "the so-called 'head-in the sand'" defense, which would include "willful blindness," "deliberate ignorance," or other "unwarranted obliviousness" that should have alerted them to a "high probability" that the FCPA could be violated.

Red flags: According to the DOJ/SEC, the following "red flags" can trigger corporate liability for the actions of third parties, even if the corporation did not have any direct knowledge of a bribe: (1) excessive commissions to third-party agents or consultants; (2) unreasonably large discounts; (3) third-party "consulting agreements" that are vague; (4) close associations between consultants and foreign officials (especially if the consultant becomes part of the transaction at the request of the foreign official); (5) shell companies as third parties; and (6) payments made to the consultant or third party to offshore bank accounts.

Sanctions and fines: The amount of the sanction or fine paid under the FCPA is very important for whistleblowers, as the Dodd-Frank reward provisions only kick in if the government (or the SEC) obtains a total of $1 million or more in collected proceeds. The penalties for FCPA violations include fines up to $2 million for each violation committed by corporations or business entities and fines up to $100,000 for each violation committed by an individual.

The accounting laws have far higher penalty provisions. Corporations can be fined up to $25 million and individuals fined up to $5 million for these violations. Moreover, under the Alternative Fines Act, courts can impose "up to twice the benefit that the defendant sought to obtain by making the corrupt payment" as a penalty in an FCPA case. Even larger sanctions can be recovered under the accounting provisions of the Act, which permit the SEC to obtain "disgorgement" penalties equal to "the gross amount of the pecuniary gain to the defendant as a result of the violations." There is no upper limit on a disgorgement penalty. The more profits a company made from paying a bribe, the higher the disgorgement penalty.

Statute of limitations: There is a five-year statute of limitations for the criminal violations of the FCPA, but acts committed beyond the five-year period may be still be actionable under a "conspiracy" theory if one or more of the actions were timely. Civil cases filed by the SEC also have a five-year statute of limitations, but, as explained in the DOJ/SEC *Resource Guide*, the five-year statute of limitations "does not prevent SEC from seeking equitable remedies, such as an injunction or the disgorgement of ill-gotten gains for conduct pre-dating the five-year period."

Other violations: An FCPA violation may also result in prosecution for other related crimes, including obstruction of justice, mail and wire fraud, tax violations based on how the bribes were reported to the IRS, securities violations related to the accuracy of corporate books, and the failure to disclosure liabilities to shareholders.

Under the whistleblower reward law, an original source is eligible for a reward based on all monies obtained in an FCPA case, including penalties obtained from "alternative remedies" and all criminal or civil proceedings prosecuted by any branch of the U.S. government. Reward claims under the FCPA follow the same procedures as those for filing securities claims with the SEC. *See* Rule 8 and Checklist 7.

────────────────── **PRACTICE TIPS** ──────────────────

- The Foreign Corrupt Practices Act, 15 U.S.C. § 78m and § 78dd-1, et seq.

- The Department of Justice (DOJ) resource page on the FCPA is located at www.justice.gov/criminal-fraud/foreign-corrupt-practices-act.

- The best source of information explaining the requirements of the FCPA is the *Resource Guide to the U.S. Foreign Corrupt Practices Act,* available at https://www.globalwhistleblower.org or from the Department of Justice.

RULE 10

Get a Reward!
Make Sure Automobiles Are Safe

On December 27, 1994, the Chrysler Corporation fired safety executive Paul Sheridan. His discharge commenced a twenty-one-year battle to pass whistleblower protections for autoworkers. It wasn't until 2012 that autoworkers obtained federal protections against being fired for simply raising safety concerns. Three years after passing these on-the-job protections, and in the wake of some of the worst auto safety scandals, including deadly airbags and malfunctioning ignition switches, Congress passed the first whistleblower law designed to pay rewards when employees exposed safety hazards.

Antiretaliation

Before anyone died from a defective liftgate latch used in the newly developed Chrysler minivans, Paul Sheridan reported the problems and risks they posed. He raised concerns with management (they were ignored). He filed an anonymous "tip" with an auto safety public interest group, and ultimately some of his concerns were reported in an industry newspaper. Sheridan told his bosses that he was going to report the defect to the National Highway Transportation Safety Administration (NHTSA). Chrysler's reaction was brutal.

During the Christmas holiday season, Sheridan's office was "raided." Shortly thereafter, he was fired. Next Chrysler went to court "without notice and obtained an *ex parte* 'muzzle order' which threatened him with arrest if he disclosed what he knew about Chrysler safety defects." Despite these attacks, Sheridan testified before NHTSA, which investigated his concerns and found them to be true.

Sheridan's safety allegations were vindicated, but not in time to save some of the lives for which he risked his career. The liftgate latch defect was eventually linked to thirty-seven deaths.

During the NHTSA investigation, Chrysler increased its pressure to shut Sheridan up. The company amended its state law lawsuit against him, demanding money in addition to simply gagging him. Under pressure from the company's lawsuit, Sheridan was forced to settle his own state whistleblower claims in exchange for Chrysler's dropping its lawsuit. As the U.S. Senate investigation revealed, for trying to save lives, Sheridan "suffered untold sums in legal expenses and personal trauma."

Sheridan's mistreatment prompted Congress to pass the first whistle-blower protections for autoworkers. In 2012 the Moving Ahead for Progress in the 21st Century Act, known simply as "MAP-21," was signed into law. It should have been named "Sheridan's Law." Modeled on the Sarbanes-Oxley Act and the airline and trucker safety laws, it utilizes the DOL procedures outlined in the beginning of this Rule. It covers employees working for "motor vehicle manufacturer(s), part supplier(s) or dealership(s)" who are "discriminate(d) against" for reporting "motor vehicle" defects or "noncompliance" with auto safety laws to their employer or the Department of Transportation. The process is as follows:

- MAP-21 has a 180-day statute of limitations. This means that employees filing a whistleblower retaliation complaint must file their charge with the U.S. Department of Labor within *180 days* of any discriminatory action.

- After a complaint is filed with the Occupational Safety and Health Administration, OSHA conducts an investigation. If the employee prevails, OSHA can order the employer to immediately reinstate the worker and pay back pay, economic and compensatory damages, and reasonable attorney fees and costs.

- Anyone losing before OSHA has a right to request a full trial on the merits of his or her case before a Department of Labor judge. A ruling by the Labor judge can be appealed within the Department of Labor to the Administrative Review Board, an agency body appointed by the Secretary of Labor. Only the review board has the authority to issue a final order, which is subject to appeal before the U.S. Court of Appeals.

- The law has a "kick-out" provision. If the Labor Department fails to issue a final order in a case within 210 days from the filing of the complaint (i.e., fully complete the three-step process outlined above), the employee (not the employer) can have the case removed to federal court, where it will be heard de novo before a U.S. District Court judge. The federal court process is completely independent of the Labor Department proceedings, which are automatically terminated once the case is moved to federal court. Either party can request the federal judge to have the case heard by a jury.

- A complainant who loses either before the Department of Labor or in federal court has the right to file an appeal with the U.S. Court of Appeals that has jurisdiction over the case.

Whistleblower Rewards

MAP21 helped with retaliation, but it wasn't the solution to ending misconduct in the auto industry. Employees who suffered brutal retaliation, like Sheridan, could get relief, but the law did nothing to incentivize workers to blow the whistle. Scandals continued to plague the auto industry. Who would want to suffer as Mr. Sheridan had, even if you could eventually prevail in a wrongful discharge lawsuit? The antiretaliation law also had a major loophole: It did not cover employees who worked outside the United States, where many cars are designed and built. U.S. employment laws could not protect auto workers in Mexico, Japan, Korea, or Germany.

The solution: Create a rewards law. That is precisely what Congress did. Legislators took the language from the Dodd-Frank Act and IRS rewards law and crafted an auto safety reward law. Senator John Thune explained that his legislation was "modeled after existing statutory whistleblower protections that encourage individuals to share information with the Internal Revenue Service and the Securities and Exchange Commission."

In 2014, the year before the auto safety rewards law was passed, the NHTSA recalled 63 million vehicles for safety problems, including GM cars that had faulty ignition switches and numerous models that used the deadly Takata air bags. Auto companies and suppliers paid $126 million in fines. Based on this record, which included "numerous injuries and deaths," Congress looked towards the highly effective reward laws as a model. As stated in the Senate report, the law would "incentivize" workers to "provide information about defects, instances of noncompliance, and motor vehicle safety reporting violations as early as possible to help improve automobile safety."

The auto safety rewards law tracks the Dodd-Frank Act but is somewhat weaker. Here are the major provisions:

First, to qualify for the reward the whistleblower must be an employee or contractor in the auto industry and the sanction obtained by the U.S. government must be at least $1 million. The reward range was set between 10 and 30 percent of the sanction. Thus, a $1 million fine would trigger a whistleblower reward of $100,000 to $300,000.

Second, whistleblowers must voluntarily provide "original information" to the Department of Transportation. Original information is explicitly defined in the statute, and a whistleblower seeking a reward should carefully review this definition and make sure the "disclosures" described in a claim conforms with this definition. The definition provides that the "information" must be "derived from the independent knowledge or analysis of an individual" and that this information [or analysis] was "not known to the Secretary [of Transportation] from any other source, unless the individual is the original source of the information."

Third, the information must relate to a "motor vehicle defect, noncompliance, or any violation" (including reporting violations) that is "likely to cause unreasonable risk of death or serious physical injury."

In determining the amount of a reward (if any) to give to a whistleblower, the Department of Transportation was mandated to consider the following factors:

Factors that can *increase* reward:

- Reporting the safety concern internally first.

- "Significance" of the original information.

- High "degree of assistance" provided by the whistleblower (or his/her lawyer) in the government investigation.

- Other factors identified by the Secretary of Transportation when the final rule on this law is published. The Department of Transportation has not yet published these rules.

Factors that will result in a reward being *denied*:

- Being convicted of a criminal violation related to the enforcement action he or she triggered.

- "Knowingly and intentionally makes any false, fictitious, or fraudulent statement" to the government.

- The same information was previously filed with the Secretary of Transportation. This is similar to the False Claims Act's "first to file" rule.

- Failing to follow the procedures required by the Secretary of Transportation. The Secretary has not yet published these procedures, but Congress has mandated that the rules be published on or before June 3, 2017. Thus, it is critically important that *before filing a claim under the auto rewards law you check to see if the Department of Transportation has published the whistleblower reward law rules.* Once these rules are published, make sure that any claim is filed precisely how the Department of Transportation requires.

- If acting without orders from his or her boss, deliberately causing the violation he or she reported. This provision is fairly technical. The disqualification applies "to any whistleblower who, acting without direction from an applicable motor vehicle manufacturer, part supplier, or dealership, or agent thereof, deliberately causes or substantially contributes to the alleged violation of a requirement of this chapter."

Internal Compliance Requirements

Unlike any other whistleblower reward law, the auto safety law requires that, under some circumstances, an employee first report his or her concerns within the company to be eligible for a reward. This provision conflicts with the right of whistleblowers to file confidential claims with the government, which is also protected under the law. It is very common for the boss to suspect that the employee who raised concerns internally became the person who later reported the company to the government. Additionally, the mandate could be highly problematic for whistleblowers outside the United States, where most countries lack any effective legal protections for whistleblowers.

The simple truth is that in whistleblowing, "no good deed goes unpunished." Employees who have to let their company know about problems sometimes get fired before they have the time or wherewithal to report their concerns to the government. If they do eventually report to an authority outside the factory gates, they become the primary suspect for snitching on the company. This places employees in a difficult position: Risk being disqualified for a reward, or potentially give up your confidentiality.

Under the rewards law, if the auto company/supplier/dealership has "an internal reporting mechanism in place to protect employees from retaliation," a whistleblower must use that mechanism in order to qualify for a reward. The provision sets a dangerous precedent. Historically, many companies have used internal reporting programs as a trap for whistleblowers. For example, many corporations delegate responsibility for internal compliance with the company's general counsel. In doing so, the company can use attorney-client privilege to hide information from the government (*see* Rules 17 and 18) and use the program to put pressure on the employee to keep quiet.

The requirement to use internal corporate reporting mechanisms has important exceptions that demonstrate Congress was aware that many company compliance programs are problematic. These exceptions apply if:

- A whistleblower "reasonably" believes he or she would be subject to retaliation if the issues were reported internally through the company's "mechanism";

- The whistleblower "reasonably" believes the safety concern was already reported internally, was the subject of a company investigation or inquiry, or was "already known" to the employer;

- The Department of Transportation has "good cause to waive" the requirement. This "good cause" will be defined in the rules the Department of Transportation is required to publish.

Confidentiality

The reward law has strong confidentiality protections. As a general matter, the Department of Transportation cannot disclose information that would reveal the whistleblower's identity or that "could reasonably be expected to reveal the identity of a whistleblower." This statutorily mandated confidentiality requirement has a number of carefully defined exceptions.

The main exception to the confidentiality requirement is if the whistleblower's identity is "required to be disclosed to a defendant" in "connection with a public proceeding instituted" by the Secretary of Transportation. Most enforcement actions are resolved through a settlement. But, if there is a public proceeding, there is a strong chance that the amount of penalty assessed will be large; this could help mitigate the potential negative impact of a whistleblower being identified in the legal proceedings.

The law states that the identity of the whistleblower can only be revealed in conformance with the Privacy Act. This helps the whistleblower. The Privacy Act is designed to permit disclosure of government documents to the individual requestor, in this case the whistleblower. The law permits whistleblowers to use this provision to obtain government records about themselves. It does not permit public disclosure of the whistleblower's identity, and the Department of Transportation could be sued under the Privacy Act for any improper disclosure.

However, even when such a disclosure may be required under law, the Secretary of Transportation must still take "reasonable measures to not reveal the identity of the whistleblower." There are a number of legal procedures that can be used to protect a whistleblower's identity, even in a public proceeding. For example, a protective order can be issued prohibiting parties from publicly disclosing the name of the whistleblower.

If criminal proceedings are initiated, the statute also permits the Secretary of Transportation to share evidence obtained from the whistleblower with a grand jury or with witnesses or defendants in ongoing criminal investigations. Because of this exception, whistleblowers should consider obtaining "confidential informant" status from the Justice Department if federal prosecutors indicate an interest in using the whistleblower's information in a criminal case.

Information may also be shared with other federal agencies. But when information is shared, the agencies obtaining the information must also agree to honor confidentiality consistent with law.

Appeals

A whistleblower can appeal a reward decision issued by the Department of Transportation to the U.S. Court of Appeals, pursuant to the Administrative Procedure Act, 5 U.S.C. § 706. Appeals must be filed within thirty days of the denial.

PRACTICE TIPS

- The auto worker's antiretaliation law is codified at 49 U.S.C. § 30171, and its implementing rule are located at 29 C.F.R. § 1988.

- The rewards law is codified at 49 U.S.C. § 30172.

- Legislative history of the reward statute: Senate Report 114-13, "Motor Vehicle Safety Whistleblower Act, Report of the Committee on Commerce, Science, and Transportation on S. 304" (April 13, 2015).

RULE 11

Get a Reward!
Stop the Pollution of the Oceans

Panic is spreading among shipowners and their corporate attorneys. There is a new "secret weapon" in the war against shipowners who pollute the oceans: whistleblowers! According to the shipping industry publication *Officer of the Watch,* shipowners need to establish a "whistleblower *prevention* program," to prevent "greedy seamen" and other "liars" from qualifying as whistleblowers.

Why this near hysteria in the shipowning community? Seamen have been remarkably successful in documenting illegal ocean pollution. Incentivized by a whistleblower reward law, crewmembers are providing documentation to U.S. officials, testifying against shipowners, and obtaining protection and rewards as whistleblowers. Currently, most, if not all Act to Prevent Pollution from Ships (APPS) ocean pollution cases are brought to the government's attention by whistleblowers, and these sources are now the key to the successful prosecution of ocean polluters. APPS includes a whistleblower reward provision that, over time, has proved vital to enforcing laws preventing pollution on the high seas.

How can the United States obtain jurisdiction over pollution that is dumped into the high seas, outside U.S. territorial waters? Jurisdiction is based on how the United States implements the International Convention for Prevention of Pollution from Ships, as modified by the protocol of 1978, better known simply as the MARPOL Protocol, the leading international treaty protecting the oceans from pollution. Signed by more than 150 countries including the U.S., the convention prohibits, among other things, dumping oil or garbage on the high seas. Most ships covered under this convention are not U.S.-flag ships, nor are they owned by U.S. companies. Almost all ocean pollution occurs outside U.S. jurisdictional waters. Moreover, most of these vessels have non-U.S. crews. So despite all these impediments, how has the United States become the number-one country enforcing the MARPOL Protocol? The answer is simple: whistleblowers.

This leads us to a second question: How are seamen, almost all of whom are non-U.S. citizens, able to successfully blow the whistle?

APPS requires every ship entering U.S. territorial waters to have an accurate log of all discharges. If a ship from a foreign country, owned by a foreign company, and staffed by a foreign crew enters U.S. territorial waters, the U.S. Coast Guard can ask to inspect the discharge log. If the log does not record all discharges accurately, the ship is in violation of the APPS. The ship's owners and captain can be charged with not having an accurate log. The predicate for prosecution is not the dumping of oil or garbage on the high seas but the failure to record that dumping in the oil record book. Most ship captains who violate MARPOL and illegally pollute the oceans do not accurately record their criminal actions in the discharge log because doing so would be an admission of a MARPOL violation. Catching a ship captain's failure to keep an accurate log is like catching Al Capone on tax evasion.

To prosecute a case under APPS, the U.S. government needs proof that an illegal discharge was not accurately recorded in the ship's log. Whistleblowers are the key to unlocking this door. Crewmembers are in a position to witness the discharges and gather evidence to prove that a ship illegally dumped. This evidence often consists of photos taken on crewmembers' cell phones and the ability of crewmembers to show Coast Guard inspectors where the equipment used to discharge oil is hidden onboard.

Why would crewmembers who reside outside the United States, and who would have little or no protection in their native lands from retaliation, risk their jobs to report ocean pollution? The answer is simple: large whistleblower rewards, paid by the United States regardless of country of citizenship.

APPS also has prosecutorial teeth. Sanctions and fines under the law are steep. Once the Coast Guard obtains credible evidence of an APPS violation, the ship can be impounded, the captain arrested, and the shipowners sanctioned millions of dollars. The "knowing violation" of MARPOL is a Class D felony, punishable by a maximum six years in jail and heavy fines for individual violators. For a corporation the maximum fine is $500,000 per day for each day the ship is in violation.

The prosecution of the Efploia and Aquarosa shipping companies is a case in point. Efploia, a Marshall Islands corporation based in Greece and registered in Malta, operated the ship accused of polluting. Aquarosa, a Danish company, was the shipowner. The ship sailed from China, with stops in Singapore, Brazil, and the Netherlands, but eventually arrived in a Baltimore, Maryland, harbor. During the ship's travels, crewmember Salvador Lopez (a Philippine national) took photos of the illegal dumping with his cell phone. When the ship arrived in Baltimore, he handed Coast Guard inspectors a note that stated, "I have something to till (sic) you but secret." He met with the inspectors, provided more than three hundred photographs depicting the discharges, drew diagrams for the government, showed them the location of tools and equipment used in the discharges, and provided them with a notebook.

The United States was able to use Mr. Lopez's information to successfully prosecute the ship's operator and owner, as well as the ship's chief engineer (who was sentenced to three months in prison), for having an inaccurate discharge log. A total of $1.85 million in fines and community service payments were awarded. The DOJ, with court approval, earmarked more than $500,000 of the collected penalties for projects to improve the Chesapeake Bay. Salvador Lopez, the whistleblower, was awarded $550,000.

"The availability of the APPS award aptly reflects the realities of life at sea and the pollution of the oceans. A monetary award both rewards the crew member for taking that risk and may provide an incentive for other crew members on other vessels to alert inspectors and investigators regarding similar crimes."
Department of Justice in *U.S. v. Odfjell*

When the plea agreement was approved, DOJ reiterated its policy to "vigorously prosecute" APPS cases: "the intentional dumping of oil and plastic from ships and falsification of ship records because they are serious crimes that threaten our precious ocean resources." In approving the whistleblower reward, the court stated: "[T]he APPS whistleblower provision reflects a congressional intent to encourage seafarers to come forward with information regarding illegal pollution activities, which otherwise would be difficult to detect. . . . The Court finds it appropriate to render a total award that is sufficient to provide incentive for seamen to inform the United States of violations of the MARPOL protocol."

APPS permits the U.S. government to ask a court to award whistleblowers up to 50 percent of the criminal penalties obtained by the government for APPS prosecutions. DOJ now regularly asks the courts to pay these international whistleblowers the maximum award, and courts consistently approve the request. The result demonstrates again how whistleblower reward laws can have a transnational impact, both by preventing pollution outside the United States and by rewarding whistleblowers who are non-U.S. citizens. The rewards have incentivized reporting and protected witnesses who otherwise would be at extreme risk of retaliation and resultant economic devastation.

As reflected in **Figure 7**, the track record under the APPS speaks for itself:

- **Fines collected.** Over the past ten years the U.S. government has collected approximately $279 million in fines and penalties from APPS violators in whistleblower-originated cases.

- **Public interest.** From all fines and penalties collected, $65 million was paid directly to environmental organizations as part of "community service" or "restitution" payments. The monies were used directly to benefit the environment and oceans, such as the payments directed to the Chesapeake Bay in the Efploia and Aquarosa prosecution.

- **Incentivizing and protecting whistleblowers.** From APPS fines collected, courts approved $34.1 million in compensation to the whistleblowers. In 80 percent of the cases, the court approved a maximum whistleblower reward (50 percent of the fines collected). The largest reward paid to an individual whistleblower was $2,100,000 in *USA v. Omi Corporation*. The largest total compensation set aside in one case for payment to whistleblowers was $5,250,000, awarded to twelve whistleblowers from the Philippines in *USA v. Overseas Shipholding Group*. The average reward paid per whistleblower in the seventy most recent identified cases was $455,668.

Figure 7

**Chart of Revenue Distribution from APPS Cases
Involving Whistleblowers**

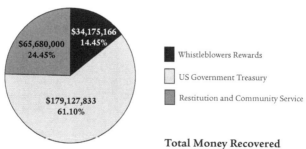

Total Money Recovered

When the DOJ Environment and Natural Resources Division (the DOJ unit with jurisdiction over APPS) asks a court to approve rewards at the maximum 50 percent level, the DOJ carefully explains the importance of paying "significant whistleblower awards" as a matter of "routine practice." DOJ's rationalization for paying maximum rewards says it all:

> The APPS award provision serves a valuable law enforcement purpose by encouraging those most likely to know of the illegal conduct to report it and cooperate with law enforcement. Because the discharge of oily waste typically takes place in the middle of the ocean in international waters, the only persons likely to know about the conduct and the falsification of the ORB [the discharge log] are the crewmembers. Absent crewmembers with firsthand knowledge of the illegal conduct coming forward, APPS violations are otherwise extremely difficult to uncover. The government's success in detecting the illegal activity and obtaining sufficient evidence to support investigations and prosecutions is dependent upon the willingness of a crewmember to step forward. In turn, a crewmember must assess the risks associated with coming forward, such as the possibility that the crew member will lose relatively lucrative employment and be blacklisted and barred from working in the marine shipping industry in the future.
>
> "A substantial monetary award, as provided by APPS, both rewards the crewmember for taking those risks and provides an incentive for other crewmembers to come forward and report illegal conduct on vessels in the future.

In the above ocean pollution case, the DOJ outlined the essence of why whistleblower reward laws work on an international scale to the district court.

First, the DOJ recognizes that the reward provides an incentive to those "likely to know" about illegal conduct to both report the criminal activity and cooperate with law enforcement. In other words, because the reward is dependent on the success of the prosecution, the whistleblower has a strong motive to provide the government with the best possible evidence of wrongdoing, and cooperate as a witness throughout the investigatory process and/or at trial.

Second, the DOJ recognizes that the criminal activity in these cases originates outside U.S. jurisdiction (i.e., in the "middle of the ocean" and in "international waters"). Most of these crimes are initiated outside the United States, so the ability of the U.S. government to obtain evidence of this type of crime is almost completely dependent upon witnesses who reside or work outside the United States.

Third, the DOJ explains that the whistleblowers have "firsthand knowledge." This type of witness is key to any successful criminal or civil enforcement action. In order to successfully prosecute, the government needs a witness who can provide competent, non-hearsay testimony.

Fourth, the DOJ frankly admits that the success of their cases is dependent on whistleblowers. This type of admission is a breath of fresh air, as it gives whistleblowers their fair share of the credit.

Fifth, the DOJ recognized the stressful and difficult decision whistleblowers face when they decide to step forward. When a whistleblower makes a disclosure, he or she does not know if a reward will be paid. But whistleblowers are fully aware that whenever they disclose illegal activity to law enforcement, they are taking a big risk and may lose "lucrative employment," face blacklisting, or worse. Thus the DOJ has explained to the court in APPS cases that a reward must be large and that there must be a reasonable guarantee that a reward will be paid if the whistleblower's information is used successfully.

Finally, the DOJ acknowledged how paying a reward can serve both to encourage others to come forward and to make boat owners aware that if they decide to break the laws, there is a strong chance they will be caught, heavily fined, and held accountable in a court of law.

The DOJ's Environment and Natural Resources Division not only uses the APPS fines to reward whistleblowers; it also uses the monies generated from whistleblower-originated cases for the public good. Under the law, fines and penalties collected in criminal cases can be set aside for restitution or community service payments. These public interest payments can be agreed to by the parties to the proceedings and included in the formal plea agreement. That plea agreement must be approved by the court. The DOJ has used the criminal penalties derived from APPS whistleblower cases to address pressing environmental needs, especially in regard to waterways and the oceans. Based on a review of the past seventy APPS whistleblower cases, courts have approved plea agreements that have set aside more than $45 million for beneficial purposes. **Figure 8** lists five of the organizations that have obtained monies from

Figure 8

Beneficial Purposes of Sanctions Obtained in Whistleblower Cases	
Samples of Groups Who Obtained Restitution	**Examples of Projects Funded**
Smithsonian Environmental Research	Restoring U.S. water ecosystems
Florida National Keys Marine Sanctuary	Conservation of wildlife resources for U.S. coastline
Alaska Sea Life Center	Protection of coral reefs
Puget Sound Marine Conservation Fund	Scientific research of marine habitats
Columbia River Conservation Fund	Education on protecting marine environment from pollution

Source: APPS prosecution plea agreements published on PACER

court-ordered restitution or community service payments, along with examples of the projects funded with these funds.

The DOJ used whistleblowers to successfully prosecute ships owned by or registered in Turkey, Jordan, Portugal, South Korea, Denmark, Liberia, Germany, Cyprus, Greece, Panama, Italy, Japan, Bahamas, Malta, Egypt, Bermuda, Singapore, China, Spain, Norway, New Zealand, Sweden, and the Philippines. Court records confirm that whistleblowers from the Philippines, Greece, Honduras, Venezuela, Korea, and the United States have all obtained payments.

The procedures used to investigate whistleblower tips are unique. Tips are supposed to be filed at the U.S. Coast Guard National Response Center, which offers a toll-free number (800-424-8802) and a web page that contains an online spill report form (www.nrc.uscg.mil). The Coast Guard does not automatically offer whistleblowers confidential informant status, so seamen who wish to proceed confidentially should obtain counsel.

Once the Coast Guard gets a tip, they have powerful tools to hold shipowners accountable. The Coast Guard can board the ship, investigate the vessel, and interview crewmembers. They can withhold a ship's departure authority, forcing it to remain in the United States or compel the ship owner to sign a Security Agreement and post a bond, agreeing to pay the hotel costs, wages, and travel expenses of crewmembers who stay in the United States as witnesses or potential criminal defendants.

A challenge to the Coast Guard's authorities under APPS was rejected by the Court of Appeals for the D.C. Circuit in *Watervale Marine Co. v. U.S. Dept. of Homeland Security*, where the Court upheld the legality of holding a ship indefinitely while civil or criminal proceedings were commenced or, alternatively, requiring the shipowners to pay for housing and meals and continue to pay the crew's wages as a condition to release the ship from port. These conditions were "reasonable" in order to ensure that the civil or criminal proceedings could be successfully completed, even if the ship was foreign owned and staffed.

Courts also carefully scrutinize the conduct of counsel for the seamen. The seamen are often indigent foreign nationals who do not speak fluent English and are unfamiliar with the U.S. legal system. Under maritime law, seamen are given "special status" and are considered a "ward of the Admiralty," and contracts they enter (including a fee agreement) are subject to "rigid scrutiny." Attorneys representing the seamen are sometimes paid for by the shipowners or are court-appointed criminal attorneys unfamiliar with whistleblower law or more concerned with defending potential criminal charges. Some contingency fee agreements have been struck down as "excessive." Lawyers who undertake representation of seamen must be able to document their work and the reasonableness of their fees.

Enforcement of APPS is having impact. The Carnival Corporation was prosecuted under APPS for illegal discharges from one of its cruise ships and paid an $18 million fine. Thereafter, Carnival made a public presentation to the American Association of Port Authorities, noting that other cruise lines were also prosecuted under APPS for illegal discharges, including Royal Caribbean ($27 million in fines based on two violations), Holland America ($2 million in fines), and Princess and the Norwegian Cruise Lines ($1 million fine). Based on these prosecutions, Carnival's recommendation for the cruise line industry was very clear:

What gets reported? Everything—when in doubt report even the slightest pollution.

Don't shoot the messenger.

────────────── **PRACTICE TIPS** ──────────────

- The Act to Prevent Pollution from Ships whistleblower reward provision is codified at 33 U.S.C. § 1908(a).

- A detailed listing of APPS cases for which rewards were paid is posted at www.kkc.com/resources/APPS.

- The Marine Defenders handbook designed to help seamen involved in government investigations is available at www.marinedefenders.com/commercial/rewards.php.

- A major case explaining the reward provision is *U.S. v. Efploia Shipping Co. S.A.*, Case 1:11-cr-00652-MJG, Bench Decision *Re: Whistleblower Award* (ECF Doc. 80) (D. Maryland) (April 25, 2016).

RULE 12

Get a Reward!
End Wildlife Trafficking

Thirty-five years ago, with no fanfare or publicity, the U.S. Congress enacted whistleblower reward laws in the form of amendments to two of the most important wildlife protection laws in the United States: the Lacey Act and the Endangered Species Act. The problem the laws targeted was of exceptional public importance: Prevent the extinction of iconic and endangered species and protect their habitat (worldwide). The strategy to be used was simple: Incentivize informants to report violations of the laws protecting endangered species and prohibiting illegal wildlife trafficking by paying monetary rewards to whistleblowers.

Wildlife whistleblower reward laws remained dormant for more than thirty-five years. Between 1981 and 2016 there is nothing in the public record to indicate that a whistleblower ever applied for a reward. The laws were unknown to wildlife protection non-government organizations (NGOs), and none of the responsible federal agencies posted notice of these laws on any public websites. Although money was required to be set aside to pay whistleblowers, three of the four agencies empowered to pay rewards have never paid one penny to a whistleblower. It is not an exaggeration to state that the laws had been forgotten. But they remain on the books, and the agencies entrusted to reward whistleblowers have a legal duty to pay rewards.

"Powerful tools are needed to combat and control the massive illegal trade in wildlife which threatens the survival of numerous species, threatens the welfare of our agricultural and pet industries, and imposes untold costs upon the American taxpayers."

The House Report No. 97-276

Illegal trafficking in plants, fish, and animals did not disappear after 1981. Extinctions continue, and the illegal trade has grown exponentially. A 2014 report issued by the international police organization INTERPOL and the United Nations Environment Program estimated that total losses worldwide due to illegal trafficking in plants, fish, and animals and illegal logging ranges from $48 to $153 billion annually. The growing threat of extinctions caused President Barack Obama, on July 5, 2013, to issue Executive Order 13648, calling for systemic federal action to prevent extinctions:

> *The poaching of protected species and the illegal trade in wildlife and their derivative parts and products (together known as "wildlife trafficking") represent an international crisis that continues to escalate. . . . The survival of protected wildlife species such as elephants, rhinos, great apes, tigers, sharks, tuna, and turtles has beneficial economic, social, and environmental impacts that are important to all nations.*

Illegal wildlife trafficking also promotes organized crime and undermines the rule of law in numerous countries. On April 22, 2015, John Cruden, the Assistant Attorney General responsible for the Environment and Natural Resources Division of the DOJ, described the problem in testimony before Congress: "Wildlife trafficking . . . has become one of the most profitable types of transnational organized crime. Illegal trade at this scale has devastating impacts: It threatens security, hinders sustainable economic development, and undermines the rule of law. The illicit trade in wildlife is decimating many species worldwide."

WHISTLEBLOWER REWARDS UNDER THE LACEY AND ENDANGERED SPECIES ACTS

The principal law enforcement mechanism for stopping wildlife trafficking is the Lacey Act. Originally passed in 1900, it has been amended over time to become the premier antitrafficking law. Under the Act, it is "unlawful for any person to import, export, transport, sell, receive, acquire, or purchase in interstate or foreign commerce" any fish, wildlife, or plant "taken, possessed, transported, or sold in violation of any law or regulation of any State or in violation of any foreign law." The Lacey Act's scope includes trafficking in violation of the Convention on International Trade in Endangered Species of Wild Fauna and Flora (CITES), the international convention designed to protect endangered species and forests.

In 1981 Congress amended the Lacey Act to include whistleblower rewards. Its intent was clear—increase the ability of the U.S. government to detect and prosecute wildlife crimes: "Powerful tools are needed to combat and control the massive illegal trade in wildlife which threatens the survival of numerous species, threatens the welfare of our agriculture and pet industries, and imposes untold costs upon the American taxpayers."

Whistleblowers were one of the "powerful tools" Congress envisioned enlisting in the war against traffickers. The powerful tool would be effectuated by paying rewards to informants whose testimony resulted in successful prosecutions: "[The whistleblower reward provision] directs the Secretary to pay rewards to persons who furnish information leading to an arrest, conviction, assessment or forfeiture from sums received as penalties, fines or forfeitures."

Under the Act, the "Secretary" is defined as the Secretaries of Commerce, Interior, and Treasury. They are given joint authority to pay rewards. The Department of Agriculture is also given authority to pay awards under the "plants" provision of the Act, which includes illegal logging. These agencies have broad discretion to reward whistleblowers and, unlike most other whistleblower reward laws, there is no cap on the amount of award or percentage of collected proceeds that may be given to a whistleblower. By contrast, under the whistleblower provisions of the Commodity Exchange Act, False Claims Act, Foreign Corrupt Practices Act, Internal Revenue Act, and Securities Exchange Act, rewards are capped at a maximum of 30 percent of collected proceeds. The Act to Prevent Pollution from Ships caps rewards at 50 percent. By declining to cap whistleblower awards in the 1981 Lacey Act amendments, Congress provided agencies with tremendous power to aggressively use the reward law and to ensure that in cases where a monetary sanction may be small, the whistleblower reward can still be significant.

The 1981 Lacey Act amendments also contained a "miscellaneous" section that included an identical reward provision for whistleblowers who report violations of the Endangered Species Act. Over the next few years, Congress included whistleblower reward provisions identical to the Lacey Act in four other wildlife protection laws: the Rhinoceros and Tiger Conservation Act, the Antarctic Conservation Act, the Fish and Wildlife Improvement Act, and the Wild Bird Conservation Act.

On December 31, 1982, Congress went even further in strengthening the authority of the government to pay awards for whistleblowers who report wildlife crimes. A little-noticed appropriations act for conservation programs on military reservations contained a provision "for other purposes," amending the Fish and Wildlife Improvement Act. One of these "other purposes" was the grant of sweeping authority to the Departments of Interior and Commerce to pay whistleblower rewards from "appropriations." Unlike other whistleblower reward laws, payments would not have to be based on the amount of funds recovered in a specific enforcement action. Instead, these Departments can use appropriated funds to compensate whistleblowers who report violations. Rewards can be paid even if no "collected proceeds" are ever obtained. The goal of the Fish and Wildlife Improvement Act's whistleblower provision was to incentivize the reporting of violations, regardless of whether or not the United States could ever successful prosecute the case.

The 1982 amendment also broadened the scope of laws for which rewards could be paid. Under the amended Fish and Wildlife Improvement Act, *all* wildlife laws administered by the Fish and Wildlife Service or the National Marine Fisheries Service (the Department of Commerce's National Oceanic and Atmospheric Administration [NOAA] division) were covered. The law explicitly ensures that rewards can be paid to whistleblowers who report violations of "any laws administered by the United States Fish and Wildlife Service or the National Marine Fisheries Service relating to fish, wildlife, or plants." The amendment now covers more than *forty* major wildlife laws, effectively closing any loopholes in coverage.

During the House floor debate on the amendment, Congress understood the importance of paying rewards in order to detect crimes. Then-congressman John Breaux (D-LA) explained that "undercover activities," which implicitly included almost all whistleblower cases, were always "difficult and dangerous but highly successful." Additionally, the amendment was designed to draw out insiders who could help "apprehend large-scale commercial violators of wildlife laws."

For thirty-five years the federal agencies entrusted to protect endangered species and stop illegal wildlife trafficking never implemented these most powerful laws. There are no published rules, no application procedures, and no publicly available guidelines on how to use the laws. Unlike with the SEC or the IRS, there is no "whistleblower office" or web portal where informants can safely provide information about violations of law and register for a potential reward should their information result in a successful prosecution.

The public's renewed attention to these forgotten endangered species and wildlife trafficking laws was sparked by *"Monetary Rewards for Wildlife Whistleblowers: A Game-Changer in Wildlife Trafficking Detection and Deterrence,"* published in the January 2016 edition of the *Environmental Law Reporter.* In September 2016 the U.S. Agency for International Development, in partnership with the Smithsonian Institution, the National Geographic Society, and TRAFFIC (the wildlife trade monitoring network), awarded the nonprofit National Whistleblower Center a "Grand Prize" for an international program to educate whistleblowers and antitrafficking organizations worldwide about the wildlife whistleblower laws. That program is being administered at www. whistleblowers.org/wildlife.

Although the laws have not been fully implemented, whistleblowers who provide information to the federal government should protect their right to a reward. First, they must carefully document the information they provide to U.S. (or other) law enforcement officials that is used to trigger an investigation or contribute to a successful prosecution. Second, whistleblowers must monitor any civil or criminal prosecution that is triggered by their information, or for which their information is used. Finally, whistleblowers must be prepared to file a formal application, similar to the reward applications filed under other laws, to justify a maximum reward. Until rules are published, these applications should be directed to the four cabinet officials with responsibility to pay rewards: Treasury, Commerce, Interior, and, in the case of illegal logging or importation of protected plants, Agriculture.

Typically, when a judgment or plea agreement is entered in a Lacey Act or Endangered Species Act prosecution, monies obtained in fines and penalties will be carefully explained in the judgment. These monies are often allocated to a special fund administered by the Fish and Wildlife Service known as the Lacey Act Reward Fund. Monies obtained from various wildlife prosecutions are required to be deposited into this account and should be used to reward whistleblowers. If possible, whistleblowers should follow any prosecutions triggered by their disclosures and be aware whenever a court is planning to enter a plea agreement or make restitution payments in order to request a reward. Also if money has been deposited into the Lacey Act Reward Fund, the whistleblower should request a reward.

In addition to permitting traditional whistleblowers to qualify for a monetary reward, the Lacey Act specifically permits any "person" defined under the Act to obtain a reward. "Person" under the Lacey Act "includes any individual, partnership, association, corporation, [or] trust. . . ." Because corporations are persons under the Act, non-government and nonprofit wildlife advocacy groups (often referred to as NGOs), which often play a critical role in obtaining information from local sources concerning illegal hunting, fishing, or lumbering, can also file a reward application under the law. The ability of NGOs to work with local whistleblowers (who may reside in very dangerous areas) and qualify for a reward has the potential to expand the use and effectiveness of these laws.

When fully implemented, the wildlife whistleblower laws will have significant worldwide impact.

- The three main wildlife whistleblower reward laws are: Lacey Act, 16 U.S.C. § 3375(d); Endangered Species Act, 16 U.S.C. §1540(d); and Fish and Wildlife Improvement Act, 16 U.S.C. §7421(c)(3).

- The Congressional history behind the original 1981 amendments to the Lacey Act and the 1982 Fish and Wildlife Improvement Act are located in House Report No. 97-276 (Oct. 19, 1981) (Lacey); 128 CONG. REC. H10207 and H31972 (Dec. 17, 1982) (Improvement).

- The wildlife whistleblower laws and program are fully explained in Kohn, *Monetary Rewards for Wildlife Whistleblowers: A Game-Changer in Wildlife Trafficking Detection and Deterrence*, 46 *Environmental Law Reporter* 10054 (January 2016), available at www.whistleblowers .org/wildlife.

RULE 13

If Working for the Government, Use the First Amendment

For government workers the major breakthrough in whistleblower protection occurred in 1968, when the Supreme Court decided whether the First Amendment guarantee of "freedom of speech" applied to public employees who blew the whistle on "matters of public concern."

The case started after Marvin Pickering, a high school teacher from Will County, Illinois, wrote a letter to the local newspaper. He strongly criticized his school system for practicing "totalitarianism" and accused the school's administration of taking the "taxpayers" to the "cleaners" by mismanaging the high school. Pickering alleged that the school board was misleading voters in a hotly contested bond issue referendum and identified serious shortcomings at the school, including classrooms that lacked doors, the failure to have running water in the first aid treatment room, and overcharging children in the cafeteria.

The board's reaction was typical. Pickering was accused of making "false statements," impugning the "motives, honesty, integrity, truthfulness, responsibility and competence" of the board and of damaging the "professional reputations" of the school's administrators. His letter was labeled as "disruptive of faculty discipline." The board fired Pickering with the claim that the "publication of [his] letter was detrimental to the best interests of the school," and because it would foment "controversy, conflict and dissension" within the school system.

In *Pickering v. Board of Education* the Supreme Court decided the case. Writing for the Court, Justice Thurgood Marshall held that the First Amendment prohibited government officials from using the power of the paycheck to cover up their own wrongdoing. Government workers who blew the whistle on matters of "public concern" were therefore protected from discrimination and wrongful discharge under the First Amendment's guarantee of freedom of speech.

The *Pickering* decision spelled out precisely why whistleblowers needed legal protections. Millions of government workers—from schoolteachers to police—could not afford to be fired from their jobs or lose their pensions simply for engaging in constitutionally protected speech. Without protecting the job, the underlying right to blow the whistle would be meaningless. Justice

Marshall recognized that the "threat of dismissal" from a job constitutes a "potent means of inhibiting speech."

The Supreme Court affirmed that public employees did not give up their constitutional rights when they took on a job with the government. "[F]ree and unhindered debate on matters of public importance" is part of the "core value" standing behind the "Free Speech Clauses of the First Amendment." Government workers were in a position to learn about official misconduct, and they often had specialized knowledge on matters of public concern that the people needed to know about in order to make informed decisions within a democratic society.

"The public interest in having free and unhindered debate on matters of public importance [is] the core value of the Free Speech Clause of the First Amendment . . the threat of dismissal from public employment is [a] potent means of inhibiting speech."

Justice Thurgood Marshall, *Pickering v. Board of Education*

However, these rights had limits. Whistleblowers were not immune from termination simply because they engaged in protected speech. Not all workplace grievances would rise to a constitutionally protected status. The Supreme Court balanced the needs of employers to maintain discipline in their workplace with the right of free speech. "The problem in any case is to arrive at a balance between the interests of the teacher, as a citizen, in commenting upon matters of public concern and the interest of the State, as an employer, in promoting the efficiency of the public services it performs through its employees."

State and Local Government Workers and the Civil Rights Act of 1871

The 1968 Supreme Court ruling in *Pickering* recognized that government whistleblowers were protected under the First Amendment. These newly established rights were given significant teeth by a once obscure Reconstruction Era civil rights law that provided for a tort remedy whenever state and local government officials violated constitutional rights. Once the Supreme Court applied First Amendment protections to public-sector employees, the tort remedies contained in this old civil rights law also became available to public-sector workers.

Six years after the Civil War, Congress enacted the Civil Rights Act of 1871, better known today simply as 42 U.S.C. section 1983. This act created a private cause of action for any person alleging that, under the "color of law," they were deprived of a "right" "secured by the Constitution and laws" of the United States. As a result of the 1968 *Pickering* decision, state and local government workers who were fired for blowing the whistle could collect damages under the 1871 act.

The remedies in the Civil Rights Act are broad. Employees can file claims in federal court and can request a trial by jury. Whistleblowers who prevail are entitled to a full range of damages and injunctive relief, including compensatory damages, punitive damages, and attorney fees and costs.

The Civil Rights Act of 1871 only covers violations committed under color of state law, and does not apply to the federal government or private sector jobs.

The law has a number of pitfalls, including a prohibition of directly suing a state government—the law permits lawsuits against "persons," not the state. Thus, whenever a state government is responsible for the retaliation, it is imperative to name all the individual managers responsible for the termination, the governor of the state, and the head of the relevant state agency. Additionally, the Supreme Court decision in *Garcetti v. Ceballos* narrowed the rights of employees to obtain constitutional protection for speech performed as part of their "official duties," even when exposing wrongdoing.

Injunctive Relief Under the First Amendment

State and federal government employees can also directly use the First Amendment to challenge workplace rules that harass, restrict, or prevent employee whistleblowing. For example, in 1992 the Environmental Protection Agency implemented "outside speaking" rules that restricted its own employees from speaking publicly about problems with the agency. In *Sanjour v. EPA*, the rules were challenged under the First Amendment and the U.S. courts issued a nationwide injunction preventing all federal agencies from using the rule to restrict whistleblowing speech. The whistleblower did not win damages, but rules that could have been used to discipline him and others were struck down as unconstitutional. The *Sanjour* precedent has been applied to state and local government. In 2002, Justice Samuel Alito, while still an appeals court judge, applied *Sanjour* and other precedents to strike down as unconstitutional a Philadelphia police department rule that limited the right of policemen to testify against their department.

Federal Employees

The *Sanjour* precedent was limited to cases in which employees used the First Amendment to obtain nonmonetary injunctive relief prohibiting agencies from instituting unconstitutional conditions of employment, such as illegal gag orders or restrictions on outside speaking and writing activities. That precedent does not permit federal employees to file claims in court for damages.

In the case of *Bush v. Lukas,* the Supreme Court ruled that federal employees who sought monetary damages had to "exhaust" their administrative remedies. Instead of filing First Amendment challenges to adverse employment decisions in federal court, they had to first file their claim before the Merit Systems Protection Board under the procedures set forth in the Civil Service Reform Act and a 1989 amendment to that law known as the Whistleblower Protection Act or WPA.

As explained in Rule 14, the WPA is now the primary law covering federal employee whistleblowers. Employees must file their cases with the Merit Systems Protection Board or the Office of Special Counsel.

PRACTICE TIP

Checklist 2 includes citations to the major cases under the First Amendment, the Civil Rights Act of 1871, and the Civil Rights Attorney Fee Act.

- *Pickering v. Board of Education*, 391 U.S. 563 (1968) (landmark case establishing First Amendment protection for public employee whistleblowers).

- *Garcetti v. Ceballos*, 547 U.S. 410 (2006) (affirming and explaining *Pickering*, but limiting protections for internal disclosures).

RULE 14

Federal Employees—Defend Your Jobs!

---

*"In the vast federal bureaucracy it is not difficult to conceal wrongdoing pro-
vided that no one summons the courage to disclose the truth."*
Senate Report, Whistleblower Protection Enhancement Act (2012)

Federal employees are on the front lines of controversy. They witness abuses
highly political in nature, and embarrassing to those who live or work in
the White House. Their expertise is called upon to address the hottest top-
ics that divide the country, such as how to best combat terrorism, the science
behind global warming, and the safety of offshore oil drilling. Given the sensitive
nature of the work performed by these civil servants, federal employees are regularly caught in the middle of special interest lobbyists and political opportunists.
They become whistleblowers, either by choice or just plain bad luck.

Laws protecting federal employee whistleblowers have been subject to
intense debate for many years. The main law covering federal employees, the
Whistleblower Protection Act; (WPA), was originally passed in 1978 as part of
the Civil Service Reform Act, it has been amended three times—in 1989, 1994,
and 2012. The law is complex, technical, and problematic. There are some alternatives to the WPA, such as Title VII of the Civil Rights Act (discrimination),
the Privacy Act (improper leaks of private information), and environmental
whistleblower laws. Also, rules governing employee speech outside of work
can provide an outlet for effective whistleblowing. But on a whole the whistleblower laws protecting federal workers are not as strong as those protecting
most corporate employees. They lack rewards, and access to federal court jury
trials is almost impossible.

The Whistleblower Protection Act (WPA)

The WPA is the main law protecting federal employee whistleblowers. It covers applicants, employees, and former employees working in the federal civil
service. The Act was originally passed as part of the Civil Service Reform Act of
1978. The Senate Report accompanying that law spelled out the intent of the
new whistleblower law:

Often, the whistleblower's reward for dedication to the highest moral principles is harassment and abuse. Whistleblowers frequently encounter severe damage to their careers and substantial economic loss. Protecting employees who disclose government illegality, waste, and corruption is a major step toward a more effective civil service. In the vast federal bureaucracy, it is not difficult to conceal wrongdoing provided that no one summons the courage to disclose the truth. Whenever misdeeds take place in a federal agency, there are employees who know that it has occurred, and who are outraged by it. What is needed is a means to assure them that they will not suffer if they help uncover and correct administrative abuses.

After its initial enactment in 1978, the law proved to be weak and ineffective. It was amended in 1989, but still did not function properly. Amended again in 1994, it still was plagued with problems. In 2012 it was amended for the last time. Its most glaring defects were fixed, but unlike with many modern laws, employees are required to have an administrative agency, the Merit Systems Protection Board (MSPB), decide their cases. The board is supposed to act independently, but its composition undermines its independence. The Board consists of three presidential appointees. Two of these Members are required to be members of the political party that holds the White House, and one Member is required to be a member of the opposition party; for example, President Donald Trump would appoint the three members, two would be Republicans, and one a Democrat. Senate approval is needed for these appointments. Federal employees cannot have their retaliation cases heard by a jury in federal court, but there is judicial review of final orders issued by the MSPB.

PROTECTED ACTIVITY UNDER THE WPA

The Whistleblower Protection Act broadly describes what conduct is protected:

> ***any disclosure*** *of information by an employee or applicant which the employee or applicant reasonably believes evidences—(i) any violation of any law, rule, or regulation; or (ii) gross mismanagement, a gross waste of funds, an abuse of authority, or a substantial and specific danger to public health or safety, if such disclosure is not specifically prohibited by law . . . or Executive order [emphasis added].*

The "any disclosure" provision is deceptively broad. Information that federal employees have, which may form the basis of their whistleblowing, may be prohibited by law from being revealed to the public.

In addition to the "any disclosure" provision, the WPA also explicitly protects disclosures to certain receiving offices. This enables whistleblowers to make disclosures that may otherwise be prohibited from public release. These receiving offices are the safest place to make a disclosure:

- The Office of Special Counsel (a special office established to accept whistleblower allegations, even if those disclosures are filed confidentially or anonymously).

- The Office of Inspector General. Every executive agency has an Inspector General and is also permitted to accept complaints on a confidential or anonymous basis.

The WPA also protects disclosures to Congress.

Finally, the WPA protects employees who "refuse to obey an order that would require the individual to violate a law" or who participate as witnesses or informants to any investigation of the Inspector General or Special Counsel.

Protected disclosures do not include arguments over policy.

Given confusion as to the meaning of "any disclosure," in the 2012 amendments to the WPA that term was explicitly defined to include the following:

- Disclosure to a supervisor.

- You do not have to be the first person to raise the concern.

- An employee's motive for making a disclosure is not relevant.

- Disclosures do not need to be in writing.

- A disclosure can be informal or formal.

- Disclosures can be made while the employee is off duty.

- A disclosure can be made during the normal course of an employee's duties.

- Disclosures of information that has been "previously disclosed" and the amount of time that has transpired between the time an employee makes the disclosure and the time the alleged wrongful act happened are irrelevant.

ADVERSE ACTION

Consistent with most other employment discrimination laws, the WPA broadly defines the adverse actions from which whistleblowers are to be shielded. Adverse "personnel actions are actions that impact the following areas of an employee's job or pay: (i) an appointment; (ii) a promotion; (iii) disciplinary or corrective action; (iv) a detail, transfer, or reassignment; (v) a reinstatement; (vi) a restoration; (vii) a reemployment; (viii) a performance evaluation; (ix) a decision concerning pay, benefits, or awards, or concerning education or training if the education or training may reasonably be expected to lead to an appointment, promotion, performance evaluation, or other action described in this subparagraph; (x) a decision to order psychiatric testing or examination; (xi) the implementation or enforcement of any nondisclosure policy, form, or agreement; and (xii) any other significant change in duties, responsibilities, or working conditions.

FILING A RETALIATION COMPLAINT

The WPA permits employees to initially seek protection from the Office of Special Counsel or the Merit Systems Protection Board (MSPB), depending on the type of adverse action at issue in the case and the status of the employee victimized by the retaliation. Employees can also choose to file a grievance under their union contract. These options are mutually exclusive. Whichever option you choose will likely waive your right to file under the other two options.

The primary procedure used by federal employees to adjudicate their whistleblower cases starts with filing a complaint before the Office of Special Counsel (OSC). Complaints can be confidentially filed, and the OSC is required to protect the whistleblower's privacy. Any whistleblower case filed with the OSC triggers specific due process rights, cumulating with the right to a hearing before an administrative judge and judicial review before the U.S. Court of Appeals for the Federal Circuit (or another appeals court, if permitted).

The OSC process begins with an independent investigation by the OSC into the allegation that the agency committed a prohibited personnel practice when it took adverse action against the whistleblower. If the OSC backs up the worker, the OSC can file administrative complaints on behalf of the employee, seeking a "stay" of an adverse action. The OSC also has a mediation program, which it can employ to try to resolve a case.

If the OSC issues a finding in support of the employee, and the agency appeals the OSC finding, the OSC can represent the worker in an administrative hearing, seeking damages or reinstatement. The whistleblower also has a right to intervenc in this action and participate with his or her own counsel, or pro se. If the OSC supports the employee, there is a very high likelihood that the case will be favorably settled or resolved to the advantage of the whistle-blower, as OSC backing sends a strong message that the agency involved most likely violated the law. Unfortunately, the OSC has very limited resources and simply cannot come close to representing all whistleblowers who have valid cases. As a result, the OSC often does not rule in the employee's favor or even conduct a thorough investigation.

If the OSC decides to take no action on behalf of the employee, delays issuing a finding, or makes a finding adverse to the employee, the whistle-blower can request a hearing before an "administrative judge" appointed by the MSPB. Employees can request a full hearing before the MSPB judge either within 65 days of receiving an adverse determination from the OSC or within 120 days of filing the complaint with the OSC. Employees do not have to wait for a final ruling by the OSC in order to request a hearing. One-hundred-and-twenty-days after filing a complaint with the OSC, employees can abandon the OSC process and directly request a hearing on the merits before an MSBP judge.

Once a case is filed with an MSPB judge, the parties have the right to conduct discovery. This includes questioning witnesses at depositions, sub-poenaing records, submitting document requests, and requiring under oath responses to written interrogatory questions. The time limits for filing and completing discovery are strict. If employees fail to take immediate advantage of the discovery rules, they may miss strict deadlines contained in the MSPB rules, and inadvertently waive their right to discovery. One of the major criti-cisms of the hearing process concerns the quality and temperament of the judges. MSPB administrative judges do not need to be licensed attorneys. Unlike federal court judges or statutory "administrative law judges," MSPB judges are not subject to a formal confirmation process and their appoint-ments are not for life. They are civil servants and there are no mandatory quali-fications for holding one of these "judgeships."

After the hearing, the MSPB judge must issue a written decision, which either party can appeal to the three-member MSPB. The Board then issues the final agency decision, which either party can appeal to the U.S. Court of Appeals for the Federal Circuit. Under the 2012 amendments, appeals can also be heard in other appeals courts, but this right was provided on a temporary basis.

Some federal employees have the option to skip the OSC process and request an immediate hearing before an MSPB judge. There are two bene-fits to this option. First, the case will move very quickly, as the MSPB judges are required to expedite discovery and conduct the hearing on the merits in a fairly short time period. Second, the employee can raise issues beyond the whistleblower issue. If you are a tenured civil servant, the government can fire you only if it has "just cause." The government has the burden of proof to demonstrate just cause and also must demonstrate that it afforded you the proper procedural due process available to tenured federal employees. By filing a case directly with the MSPB, and bypassing the OSC, an employee can enjoy the full benefits of civil service protection. A direct appeal to the MSPB permits the federal employee to raise both civil service issues, and he or she can raise the whistleblower issues as an affirmative defense.

Although confusing, it is important to remember that if you file your case directly to the OSC, the only issue that can be addressed is whether your adverse action violated the Whistleblower Protection Act. Even if the case is appealed to an MSPB judge, the only issue is the WPA issue. But if you are able to file directly with the MSPB judges, the MSPB and Court of Appeals also can decide whether your adverse action complied with the rules governing the civil service.

Another major distinction between filing your case with the OSC and filing it directly with an MSPB judge concerns the statute of limitations. The WPA has *no* statute of limitations; a complaint can be filed at any time with the OSC. However, if you are able to file a case directly with the MSPB, there is a thirty-day statute of limitations. The WPA is available to federal employees who missed the deadline, for whatever reason, for filing a direct case with the MSPB. There is no logic to these rules, and in some ways they defy common sense. That is the result of patchwork legislation, covering large groups of employees, enacted over a forty-year time period.

WHO CAN FILE A CASE DIRECTLY WITH THE MSPB?

Generally, employees in the competitive service who have completed a probationary period and those in the excepted service (other than the Postal Service) with at least two years of continuous service may appeal certain adverse actions directly to the MSPB. A rule of thumb is that in order to appeal directly to the Board you must suffer a suspension of over 14 days. All other lesser adverse actions are only subject to OSC jurisdiction. The following adverse actions can be appealed directly to the MSPB: removals, suspensions that exceed fourteen days, reductions in grade or pay, furloughs for thirty days or less, denials of within-grade salary increases, reduction-in-force actions, and denials of restoration or reemployment rights. Thus, if you are given a poor performance review or forced to undergo a psychiatric examination in retaliation for whistleblowing, you must file your case with the OSC. But if you are fired, you have an option of appealing the termination directly to the board or filing with the OSC.

Because a fully tenured federal civil servant has employment rights above and beyond the rights afforded employees under the WPA, it is generally to the employee's advantage to file a wrongful discharge case directly with the MSPB so that a hearing concerning those rights can be incorporated into the whistle-blower case. It is possible to lose a whistleblower case but prevail on issues related to your status as a tenured civil servant, or vice versa.

If you file your case directly with the MSPB, or appeal a denial by the OSC to the Board, be aware that the Board operates on a rocket-docket. All dead-lines are short, and discovery must be immediately commenced or it will be waived. Be prepared to complete discovery, respond to pretrial motions, and participate in a full evidentiary hearing within a matter of months. It is the official policy of the MSPB to have their judges complete the entire pretrial and hearing proceedings and issue their initial decisions within 120 days of a case being docketed. Extensions of time can be obtained, but the case will proceed far faster than any typical federal or state lawsuit.

DISCOVERY

One of the major traps in the MSPB process concerns discovery. Discovery permits employees to question managers and obtain agency documents. Whistleblowers can learn all the justifications for the adverse action and try to obtain evidence that supports a finding that the discipline was not justified but motivated by retaliatory animus. But, as set forth in **Figure 9,** the MSPB's regulations concerning the timing of discovery requests are very tricky and can result in a waiver of discovery rights. Here are the rules:

- All initial discovery must be filed within thirty days of the administrative judge issuing the initial docketing order. In other words, it is best to have your discovery prepared and served at the time you file your request for a hearing.

- Responses to discovery must be served by the agency within twenty days. If the agency does not answer your discovery, or if the answers are incomplete, you must file a motion to compel within ten days. Failure to file a motion to compel waives all your objections to the answers (or non-answers) of the agency.

- If you are intending to file a second round of discovery, it must be filed within ten days of the agency's responses to your initial discovery (or within ten days of the agency's failure to respond) or else discovery is considered completed.

Figure 9

Discovery in MSPB Employment Cases	
Initial Disclosures	Filed within 10 days of the administrative judge's acknowledgement order.
Initial Discovery Requests (e.g., depositions, documents, interrogatories)	All initial disclosures filed within 25 days after the date the judge issues an order to the respondent agency to produce the agency file (which is usually contained in the acknowledgement order).
Response to Discovery Request	Filed within 20 days after the date of service of the request.
Additional Discovery Requests	Must be served within 10 days of the date of service of the prior response.
Motion to Compel	Must be filed within 10 days of the date of service of objections or, if no response is received, within 10 days after the time limit for response has expired.
Motion to Dispose a Non-party (third-party discovery requests)	Submitted to the judge within 25 days after the date on which the judge issues an order to the respondent agency to produce the agency file.
Opposition to Motion to Compel	Filed with the judge within 10 days of the date of service of the motion.

Source: 5 C.F.R. §§ 1201.73 & 1201.74 (2016)

BURDEN OF PROOF AND REMEDIES

Regardless of whether you initially file a case with the MSPB or the OSC, the substantive law governing a whistleblower case is the same. The scope of protected activity is identical regardless of which forum in which your case is filed, as are the burdens of proof and the remedies available to a prevailing employee.

Congress created a pro-whistleblower standard of proof under the WPA. The first step to prevailing in a WPA case is for the whistleblower to demonstrate that his or her protected disclosure was a "contributing factor" in the adverse personnel action. The proof necessary to demonstrate a "contributing factor" was intended to be very low. The WPA specifically authorized the use of "circumstantial evidence" alone to meet this burden, and codified "timing" test. Thus, if the employee can demonstrate that the manager who took or approved the adverse action knew of the protected activity, and the discipline "occurred within a period of time such that a reasonable person could conclude that the disclosure or protected activity was a contributing factor in the personnel action," the timing sequence alone satisfied this element of the case.

If the employee can meet the low "contributing factor" threshold, the actual burden of proof shifts to the agency. Thereafter, the agency must demonstrate by "clear and convincing evidence that it would have taken the same personnel action in the absence" of the protected disclosures. The "clear and convincing" standard is a high burden of proof. These shifting burdens were designed by Congress to make it easier for whistleblowers to win their cases.

If the whistleblower prevails, the MSPB must order "corrective action," which may include the following relief: (i) placing the whistleblower "as nearly as possible, in the position the individual would have been in had the prohibited personnel practice not occurred"; (ii) back pay and related benefits, medical costs incurred, travel expenses, any other reasonable and foreseeable consequential damages, and compensatory damages (including interest, reasonable expert witness fees, and costs); (iii) attorney fees and costs for the WPA case; (iv) attorney fees and costs incurred as a result of any investigation conducted by the agency in retaliation for the protected disclosures.

Contacting Congress

In the early 1900s Presidents Theodore Roosevelt and William Taft battled with Congress over whistleblower rights. Federal workers were providing information to Congress, and Roosevelt and Taft wanted to silence them. The implemented "gag" rules restricting federal employees from communicating to Congress and triggered a major dispute between Congress and the president. After strenuous debate, in 1912 Congress exercised its authority and passed the Lloyd-LaFollette Act. This law prohibits retaliation against federal employees who provide information to any member or committee of Congress. Additionally, any nondisclosure agreement that restricts a federal employee's right to communicate with Congress is unenforceable.

Communications with Congress are often a key to successful whistleblowing by federal employees. A supportive member of Congress can exert significant pressure on the federal bureaucracy to prevent or stop retaliation. The law remains in effect today and is commonly relied upon by federal whistleblowers.

The Alternative to Blowing the Whistle at Work: Outside Speaking and Writing (including talking to the Press)

One of the most effective avenues for public employees to expose wrongdoing is by speaking or writing outside of work. In 1968 the Supreme Court held that public employees had a First Amendment constitutional right to directly attack the policies and priorities of their government-employer in the press. That case remains good law and has been expanded over time. Today, court precedents support the right of federal employees, acting outside of work and in their capacity as private citizens, to blow the whistle. These rights would include talking to the news media, communicating on social media, and speaking at conferences.

But like all constitutional rights, freedom of speech has its limits. Not all outside speech is protected.

The basic rules governing the right of public employees, on their own time, to criticize their government agencies was established in the 1968 landmark case of *Pickering v. Board of Education*. Simply said, the Supreme Court held: "Individuals do not automatically relinquish their rights under the First Amendment by accepting government employment" and consequently, "it is essential that" government employees "be able to speak out freely on [matters of public concern] without fear of retaliatory dismissal." This speech is protected even though the government employee is attacking his superiors: "Statements by public officials on matters of public concern must be accorded First Amendment protection despite the fact that the statements are directed at their nominal superiors." The *Pickering* case and the scope of its protection is also discussed in Rule 13.

Although *Pickering* was authored fifty-years ago by liberal Supreme Court Justice Thurgood Marshall, it was reaffirmed by the Supreme Court in 2006 in a decision by Justice Anthony Kennedy, joined by all of the so-called "conservative" members of the Court: "a citizen who works for the government is nonetheless a citizen. The First Amendment limits the ability of a public employer to leverage the employment relationship to restrict, incidentally or intentionally, the liberties employees enjoy in their capacities as private citizens." In the *Garcetti v. Ceballos* case Justice Kennedy explained:

> *The Court's employee-speech jurisprudence protects, of course, the constitutional rights of public employees. Yet the First Amendment interests at stake extend beyond the individual speaker. The Court has acknowledged the importance of promoting the public's interest in receiving the well-informed views of government employees engaging in civic discussion. . . . Were [public employees] not able to speak on [the operation of their employers], the community would be deprived of informed opinions on important public issues. The interest at stake is as much the public's interest in receiving informed opinion as it is the employee's own right to disseminate it.*

Although *Pickering* and *Garcetti* concerned the rights to state and municipal government workers, the U.S. Supreme Court and D.C. Circuit Court of Appeals applied these principles to federal employees. In *United States v. National Employees Treasury Union*, the Supreme Court ruled that restricting the right of federal employees to engage in outside speaking and writing activities was unconstitutional. The *NTEU* decision was further clarified in the case of William Sanjour, a Policy Analyst for the Environmental Protection Agency, who sought permission to publicly criticize the Agency's decision to permit toxic waste incinerators in poor and predominantly minority communities. The EPA argued that an official government regulation limited Sanjour's rights. Sanjour challenged the constitutionality of that rule, and won. In *Sanjour v. EPA*, the D.C. Court of Appeals held that government regulations that empower officials to restrict outside-employee speech based on the content or viewpoint of the speaker were unconstitutional:

> *[A] law or policy permitting communication in a certain way for some but not for others raises the specter of content and viewpoint censorship. This danger is at its zenith when the determination of who may speak and who may not is left to the unbridled discretion of a government official. . . . [W]e have often and uniformly held that such statutes or policies impose censorship on the public or press, and hence are unconstitutional.*

Both *NTEU* and *Sanjour* concerned challenges to government regulations that placed restrictions on outside speaking, writing or teaching. In each case the employees did not seek money damages, or relief from individual retaliatory actions. Instead the cases requested broad injunctive relief, finding the challenged laws and regulation unconstitutional and unenforceable.

In 2015 the U.S. Supreme Court decided a more typical whistleblower-retaliation case filed by Robert J. MacLean. MacLean was a federal Air Marshal, assigned to protect passenger flights from potential hijackings. In 2003 the Department of Homeland Security warned that *al Qaeda* may be planning other "suicide hijackings" with the intent to "destroy aircraft in flight, as well as to strike ground targets." MacLean was personally informed by his managers that terrorists planned to "smuggle weapons in camera equipment or children's toys through foreign security," and then "fly into the United States . . . overpower the crew or the Air Marshals and . . . fly the planes into East Coast targets."

Just days after this briefing MacLean learned that Air Marshals were being *removed* from airplanes. MacLean was shocked, and "believed that cancelling those missions during a hijacking alert was dangerous." MacLean went to his bosses to try to change the policy, but they refused, and told him that the Air Marshals were grounded "to save money on hotel costs because there was no more money in the budget."

Frustrated, MacLean leaked the story to an MSNBC reporter, and NBC ran a story titled "Air Marshals pulled from key flights." After the press exposed the scandal, the Department of Homeland Security/TSA reversed its decision, and placed Marshals back on flights. MacLean's disclosures served the public interest. But DHS wanted to take revenge on the whistleblower who embarrassed the agency. Eventually DHS investigated the press leaks and MacLean admitted he was the source. He was fired.

MacLean sought protection under the Whistleblower Protection Act. MacLean argued that his leaks to NBC were protected disclosures. But the Department of Homeland Security claimed that his disclosures were not permitted, as they were "specifically prohibited by law." Significantly, in MacLean's case there was no law that prohibited his communications with the press. Instead, he violated regulations issued by his employer. The case dragged on in the courts and administrative agencies for over ten years and eventually landed in the U.S. Supreme Court. In *Department of Homeland Security v. MacLean* Chief Justice John Roberts ruled that MacLean was illegally fired. MacLean's disclosures to NBC were not "specifically prohibited by law." Thus, he had the right to expose the threat to public safety caused by the government's irresponsible decision to withdraw Air Marshals from transnational flights during a major terrorist alert. MacLean prevailed in the case even though this disclosure of information violated an agency rule. Justice Roberts did not buy off on the agency's argument that its internal rule should have the force of law, writing, "Congress passed the whistleblower statute precisely because it did not trust agencies to regulate whistleblowers within their ranks." MacLean eventually returned to his job as an Air Marshal.

Limits on Outside Speaking and Writing

The right of government employees to speak out on matters of public concern is broad, but not without limits. Federal employees should try to ensure that their outside disclosures are covered under the definition of a protected disclosure under the Whistleblower Protection Act. Other cautionary steps include:

- Make sure that you clearly indicate that you are not representing the official position of the U.S. government. Employees have been sanctioned for not giving a "disclaimer" when speaking out on their own time;

- Do not release information that must be held in confidence as a matter of law, or which is classified;

- Do not release information protected under the Privacy Act;

- Do not use government property when speaking out as a citizen.

- Do not use government laptops or cell phones or utilize government-owned servers when blowing the whistle or communicating with counsel;

- If your agency has a prepublication clearance policy, follow those rules;

- Exercise common sense. Be aware that your managers or those in higher positions may be listening/reading. You should strongly consider obtaining confidential legal advice before you engage in controversial outside speaking or writing, to make sure you do not make an easily correctable mistake when exercising your constitutional rights as a citizen.

Major cases and laws establishing the right of government employees to engage in outside speaking, writing, and teaching critical of their employing agency:

- *United States v. Treasury Employees*, 513 U. S. 454 (1995) (applying *Pickering* to federal employees).

- *Department of Homeland Security v. MacLean*, 135 S.Ct. 913 (2015) (permitted disclosures to the press).

- *Sanjour v. Environmental Protection Agency*, 56 F.3d 85 (1995) (en banc) (viewpoint based restrictions on employee speech made on their own time is unconstitutional).

- *Whistleblower Protection Act*, 5 U.S.C. § 2302(a)(2)(D), (b)(8) and (9), and (f).

Options outside a WPA Case

In addition to the WPA, there are a few other laws federal employees can utilize. The nuclear whistleblower law covers employees of the Nuclear Regulatory Commission and Department of Energy, if the disclosures relate to nuclear safety.

Federal employees who raise concerns about violations of environmental laws may also be protected under regulations implemented by the U.S. Department of Labor. Banking whistleblower laws cover employees at the Federal Reserve, the Comptroller of the Currency, and other federal banking offices.

Federal employees can file discrimination and retaliation cases under Title VII of the Civil Rights Act (covering cases of discrimination based on race, sex, religion, national origin, age, and disability). Under the controlling rules, employees must seek "counselling" from their employing agency within 45 days of a discriminatory or retaliatory action. The failure to timely seek "counselling" can result in a waiver of the right to pursue a discrimination case. After exhausting administrative remedies, the Title VII case can be adjudicated either before a EEOC judge or in federal court (with the right to a jury trial). Remedies include reinstatement, back pay, compensatory damages, and attorney fees.

If an employee has both a whistleblower case and a discrimination case, the two causes of action can be consolidated into one lawsuit filed in U.S. District Court. This is an extremely important procedural right. After an employee exhausts his or her administrative remedies under Title VII and the Whistleblower Protection Act, the two causes of action can be joined. This procedure is known as a "mixed case." The rules governing mixed cases are complex, and were explained in detail in the case of *Bonds v. Leavitt* decided by the U.S. Court of Appeals for the Fourth Circuit. The "mixed case" process is the only way a federal employee can have his or her whistleblower case heard in federal court. All other whistleblower cases must be pursued through the Office of Special Counsel/Merit Systems Protection Board process. For employees who suffer retaliation or discrimination based on both whistleblowing and their protected status, the mixed case procedure provides these workers with the strongest whistleblower protections (i.e., access to federal court).

ENVIRONMENTAL WHISTLEBLOWERS

The environmental whistleblower laws have been successfully used by employees at the Environmental Protection Agency and other government departments as an alternative to the Whistleblower Protection Act. The scope of a protected disclosure can be broader under the environmental laws than under the WPA. Additionally, the procedures used to adjudicate environmental whistleblower cases are more employee-friendly then those used by the Merit Systems Protection Board. The decision to use environmental whistleblower laws to defend jobs and careers is a viable option for employees who may raise concerns over hot-button environmental issues, such as global warming, environmental risks associated with energy production, or lead in drinking water.

Federal employees successfully used the environmental laws as far back as the early 1990s. But it was not until 2006 that the issue of federal-employee coverage was finally decided. In *Erickson v. EPA*, the U.S. Office of Legal Counsel, that provides binding guidance to administrative agencies on legal matters, informed the U.S. Department of Labor that federal employees could file cases under the Clean Air Act, Safe Drinking Water Act, Superfund, and the Solid Waste Disposal Act. All of these laws are administered by the U.S. Department of Labor and are discussed in Rule 4. These laws permit federal employees to have their cases investigated by OSHA (as opposed to the Office of Special Counsel) and have their cased tried by a statutory Administrative Law Judge. These ALJ's have job protection similar to federal judges, and have a reputation for competence and independence. Final decisions of the Labor Department are subject to judicial review in the Courts of Appeal. Remedies include reinstatement, back pay, compensatory damages, punitive damages under the Safe Drinking Water Act, and attorney fees and costs. The biggest drawback to the environmental laws is their short statute of limitations — a mere 30 days.

National Security and Intelligence Agency Whistleblowers

In 1978, when Congress was on the verge of passing the comprehensive whistleblower law covering all federal employees, powerful intelligence agencies wanted to exclude their employees from any protection. They wanted to silence their whistleblowers. Compromises were made in the final version of the Civil Service Reform Act, and the bill that was presented to President Jimmy Carter to sign on October 13, 1978, contained a glaring exemption.

The law covered all federal agencies *except* the Federal Bureau of Investigation (FBI), the Central Intelligence Agency (CIA), the Defense Intelligence Agency (DIA), the National Security Agency (NSA), the National Geospatial Intelligence Agency, the Office of the Director of National Intelligence, and the National Reconnaissance Office. The president was also given the authority to exempt from the WPA "any agency or department" whose "principal function" concerns "the conduct of foreign intelligence or counterintelligence activities."

This exemption had, and continues to have, a terrible impact both on national security whistleblowers and the public's right to know about abuses within these excluded agencies.

After 1978 the nonintelligence federal agencies slowly started to adjust their management practices and workplace culture to accommodate whistleblower rights. The intelligence arms of the government did not. Because would-be whistleblowers at intelligence agencies had no rights, the agencies covered under the exemption had no reason to become whistleblower-friendly.

In addition to not having legal protections, national security whistleblowers also risk losing their security clearances. Losing clearance renders future employment in law enforcement impossible.

The first well-known national security whistleblower was Daniel Ellsberg, who worked for a government contractor (the Rand Corporation) and had access to top-secret government documents regarding the Vietnam War. After month of reflection over whether to release these highly explosive documents, he eventually leaked the "secret history" of the Vietnam War to the press. He provided the *New York Times* and *Washington Post* more than seven thousand pages of classified documents known as the Pentagon Papers. Although these papers exposed systemic abuses of authority that surrounded the United States' involvement in the Vietnam War, Ellsberg was indicted for leaking confidential information and faced criminal charges that could have resulted in a 117-year prison sentence. But his case was dismissed because of prosecutorial misconduct. In other words, no judge or jury ever weighed in on the legality of Ellsberg's actions, or the consequences he would face if found guilty. In the middle of his trial, some of the worst abuses of the Watergate era surfaced, resulting in a dismissal of all criminal charges. Ellsberg was a free man.

Oddly enough, Ellsberg would become one of the first beneficiaries of the Watergate scandal. During Ellsberg's criminal case, the Court learned that officials working for President Richard Nixon had engaged in gross misconduct in a covert campaign to discredit Ellsberg. The White House had established a clandestine "plumber's unit" designed to "plug leaks," and their first illegal operation was to break into Ellsberg's psychiatrist's office to obtain information that could discredit him in the eyes of the public. They wanted to find dirt, and they figured the best place to start was with his psychiatrist, where they might learn his most private and embarrassing secrets. Once the break-in was exposed, the government's case collapsed. It was this misconduct that would result in the dismissal of the criminal charges against him.

The Ellsberg case did not set legal precedent protecting future national security whistleblowers. In the *Pentagon Papers* case, which arose directly out of Ellsberg's disclosures, the Supreme Court weighed in on whether the Nixon administration could obtain an order halting two newspapers from publishing the classified documents Ellsberg had released. The Court sided with the newspapers, refused to halt the presses, and permitted the *New York Times* and *Washington Post* to print the classified material. In that case a number of Supreme Court justices wrote concurring opinions addressing the potential liability of the leaker. These justices sent a clear warning that the United States could use criminal laws to prosecute anyone involved in releasing classified information. They warned that although the newspapers could publish the material, the person who leaked the information could be prosecuted.

Justice Potter Stewart (who joined with the Court majority in permitting the *New York Times* to publish the Pentagon Papers) drew a sharp distinction between the right of the news media to publish information and the right of a whistleblower to disclose information. The government could not obtain a court order stopping the *New York Times* from publishing the Pentagon Papers, but the executive could prosecute the "leaker" for violating government secrecy laws. Justice Stewart wrote: "Congress has the power to enact specific and appropriate criminal laws to protect government property and preserve government secrets. Congress has passed such laws, and several of them are of very colorable relevance to the apparent circumstances of these cases."

Ellsberg escaped conviction only because of prosecutorial misconduct. Other whistleblowers have not been so lucky. More recently there have been numerous indictments and convictions of intelligence agency employees who illegally released classified top secret information, including Edward Snowden, who was indicted under the Espionage Act, and Thomas Drake and John Kiriakou, who were convicted of illegally releasing classified information when they tried to expose official misconduct in the NSA and CIA.

"Secrecy in government is fundamentally anti-democratic, perpetuating bureaucratic errors. Open debate and discussion of public issues are vital to our national health. On public questions, there should be 'uninhibited, robust, and wide-open' debate."

Justice William Douglas, *U.S. v. New York Times*
(Pentagon Papers case)

The Ellsberg case highlighted the lack of legal protections for national security whistleblowers. When Ellsberg wanted to expose the scandal he uncovered, there was literally no government agency equipped to address his concerns. The government itself had committed the misconduct, and there was no one in the government able or willing to confront the scandal he had uncovered. Many other whistleblowers who work in intelligence agencies feel the same way and, like Ellsberg, turn to the news media as their best outlet for revealing the "truth." The stakes in these cases are immense. When the government lies to justify a military action, innocent lives and the credibility of U.S. foreign policy are risked. When the government hides behind its power to classify information as "secret" to violate the law outside public view, it is nearly impossible for citizens to know what their government is doing, and to properly exercise their right to vote as an informed citizenry. Yet there is a strong legal consensus supporting the government's ability to classify information and prevent it from unauthorized release.

When Edward Snowden released classified information on the National Security Agency's illegal domestic spying program, a national debate erupted as to whether his actions were justified. Some argued that he was a whistleblower, others labeled him a "leaker," while yet others considered him a traitor. But one part of this debate was clear. The legal protections afforded employees like Snowden, who wanted to expose illegal government actions, were grossly deficient. It was brutally clear that honest employees working in agencies like the CIA or NSA faced a terrible dilemma if they witnessed misconduct. Without adequate legal protections, blowing the whistle could have catastrophic repercussions. Whistleblowers could lose their jobs, security clearances, and possibly even their freedom.

But whistleblowers were not the only losers. By not establishing a safe and protected channel for employees to blow the whistle, it was only a matter of time before an employee would engage in "self-help" and make disclosures with the intent of exposing wrongdoing but that also harmed national security. The legal protections in place at the time Snowden released his documents to the press were a lose-lose-lose situation. Snowden lost because his disclosures were illegal, and he faces years in prison or a prolonged exile from his homeland. The public loses because most employees will remain silent, even if they know of abuses the public should learn about. The agencies lose, as it was only a question of time before an employee like Snowden would become upset with abuses he or she witnessed and engage in self-help whistleblowing—taking his concerns outside any proper channel and giving them directly to the press.

The Protection of Intelligence Community Whistleblowers Act of 2014

In the wake of the Snowden case, Congress took some basic steps to fix the problem. Tucked into the Intelligence Authorization Act for Fiscal Year 2014 was the first federal law providing a semblance of protection for national security whistleblowers. The law, entitled Protection of Intelligence Community Whistleblowers, codified at 50 U.S.C. Section 3234, is very simple (and very weak).

First, the law covers the intelligence community, including employees who work with such highly secretive agencies as the CIA and NSA.

Second, it contains a very narrow definition of protected activity. Employees are given the right to blow the whistle (make a "lawful disclosure") to the following organizations or people: (1) the Director of National Intelligence; (2) an employee designated by the Director of National Intelligence to receive whistleblower complaints; (3) the Inspector General of the Intelligence Community; (4) the head of the employing agency (e.g., the Director of the CIA); (5) an employee designated by the head of an intelligence agency to receive whistleblower complaints; (6) the Inspector General of the agency that employs the whistleblower; (7) a congressional intelligence committee; and (8) a member of a congressional intelligence committee.

Third, to be protected under this law, a whistleblower *must* make a disclosure to one or more of these eight entities. Generally speaking, it is best to go to the top—and make sure the head of your agency knows you are a whistleblower. As a practical matter, the more top agency officials or members of Congress learn of a whistleblower's allegations, the harder it is for an agency to cover up misconduct.

The law defines a protected disclosure as any information "the employee reasonably believes evidences (1) a violation of any Federal law, rule, or regulation; or (2) mismanagement, a gross waste of funds, an abuse of authority, or a substantial and specific danger to public health or safety."

Fourth, the law prohibits an agency from retaliating against the employee and prohibits a broad number of adverse actions, including an appointment, promotion, or any disciplinary action; a detail, transfer, or reassignment; a demotion, suspension, or termination; a negative performance evaluation; a decision concerning pay, benefits, or awards; or any other significant change in duties, responsibilities, or working conditions.

This sounds pretty good . . . but:

Unlike every other whistleblower law enacted over the past three decades, the intelligence agency law does not permit the employee to seek judicial review of an adverse determination. National security whistleblowers cannot get access to court in order to ensure that the minimum rights afforded them under the Protection of Intelligence Community Whistleblowers Act are enforced. The president of the United States is given the authority to approve the procedures that will be made available to whistleblowers. The law simply states: "The President shall provide for the enforcement of this section." The failure to include in the law the specific procedures national security whistleblowers can utilize to protect their rights, in combination with the lack of judicial review, renders the law seriously defective, to say the least.

Another defect in the law is equally glaring. It does not stipulate the remedies available to the whistleblower. There is no statutory right to reinstatement, back pay, compensatory damages, or attorney fees. The relief available under this law is up to the president or the intelligence agencies delegated with authority to rule on these cases. The lack of independent or judicial review permits the fox to guard the chickens. The law sets a very low bar for whistleblower protection. The Intelligence Community Whistleblower Protection Act is among the weakest whistleblower laws passed by Congress in the past fifty years.

In addition to the Intelligence Community Whistleblower Protection Act, there are a few other options available to national security whistleblowers. Courts have long recognized that the freedom of speech protected under the U.S. Constitution was intended to protect citizens who exposed government misconduct and crimes committed by those holding political power. However, these same courts recognized the right of the executive power to keep national security–related information secret. In the Pentagon Papers case, Supreme Court Justice Thurgood Marshall echoed the warning: "In these cases, there is no problem concerning the President's power to classify information as 'secret.' . . . Nor is there any issue here regarding the President's power as Chief Executive and Commander-in-Chief to protect national security by disciplining employees who disclose information and by taking precautions to prevent leaks."

In other words, under Supreme Court precedent, the First Amendment rights of national security whistleblowers will always be balanced against the government's need to maintain secrecy in its military, counterterrorism, and counterintelligence programs.

PREPUBLICATION REVIEW

After the *Pentagon Papers* rulings, the next major intelligence agency whistleblower case to come before the U.S. Supreme Court was *Snepp v. United States*. Frank W. Snepp III was a former CIA employee who published a book exposing problems within that agency. Even though Snepp's book did not contain classified information, the Court upheld the right of intelligence agencies to review, prior to publication, its employees' (and former employees') publications. In *Snepp* the Court affirmed the constitutionality of a prepublication clearance process utilized by various national security institutions, including the FBI and CIA. Although the Court ruled against Snepp, it did affirm that the U.S. Constitution and the Bill of Rights applied to federal employees working at the CIA and other intelligence agencies, although those rights could be limited. The *Snepp* decision established procedures employees who have access to classified information can use to make their whistleblower concerns public.

Under these clearance rules, intelligence agents may publish nonclassified information about their agencies (including information concerning official misconduct), but first they must provide a copy of their publications to their employer and permit their employer reasonable time to ensure that classified information is not revealed. If an employee disagrees with the classification decision, he or she can obtain judicial review. Once in court, the whistleblower can ask a federal judge to review the censored material and make a decision as to what information can be publicly released. The judge has the authority to review the information in camera (i.e., secretly) and can then independently rule whether, in light of the First Amendment, the government can censor the whistleblower's disclosure. The burden of proof is on the government, not the whistleblower. Both the executive agencies and the courts are required to expedite the adjudication of these cases. This procedure can be used by both current and former employees.

This process gives employees a "safe harbor" for making disclosures, and the right to challenge, in court, the government's attempt to keep its misconduct secret.

The FBI WPA

The FBI also has a special law that covers its whistleblowers. This law is stronger than the Intelligence Community Whistleblowers Protection Act, but it's still riddled with problems. Like NSA and CIA employees, FBI agents were also excluded from protection under the 1978 Civil Service Reform Act. However, the FBI Whistleblower Protection Act required the president of the United States to ensure that FBI agents have rights "consistent with" the rights of other federal employees. This mandate was not included in the Intelligence Agency law, and has resulted in much stronger remedies for FBI agents than their counterparts working in the CIA or NSA.

The FBI WPA was originally passed in 1978 and amended in 1989 and 2016. Between 1978 and 1998, all presidents ignored the law until FBI Supervisory Special Agent Frederic Whitehurst sued President Clinton and demanded that it be implemented. Whitehurst had been removed from his position as the FBI's top explosives expert after he exposed widespread abuses in the Bureau's crime lab, including misconduct in the first World Trade Center and the Oklahoma City bombing cases. As a result of the lawsuit, President Bill Clinton issued a directive requiring the Attorney General to implement the FBI WPA and publish administrative protections for FBI employees. These procedures, published as Title 28 CFR Part 27, permit FBI employees to make disclosures to the Justice Department's Inspector General or the Office of Professional Responsibility, the Director of the FBI, his or her supervisor, and other designated offices. If they are retaliated against, the DOJ Inspector General must investigate their claims, and they can request an administrative hearing. Remedies include reinstatement, back pay, and attorney fees and costs.

Title VII and Privacy Act Remedies for National Security Whistleblowers

Federal antidiscrimination laws also provide all federal employees, including intelligence agency employees, an avenue for protection. Intelligence agency employees can file complaints under Title VII of the Civil Rights Act (prohibition against discrimination/retaliation on the basis of race, sex, color, national origin, age, disability, or religion) and have the same basic rights as all employees, including the right to a jury trial in federal court, compensatory damages, reinstatement, and attorney fees.

Finally, all national security employees are also covered under the Privacy Act and can file administrative and judicial complaints if an agency improperly maintains files or discloses records in retaliation for protected speech. When Congress debated the Privacy Act, sponsors of the bill pointed to the Daniel Ellsberg case as a major justification for enacting the law. They wanted to make sure that whenever the government creates records on its citizens (such as creating records based on information learned from the illegal break-in at Ellsberg's psychiatrist's office), the citizens have a means to obtain copies of those records, file a lawsuit to have the records corrected, and obtain damages if the records caused them economic harm. The Act also prohibits the government from creating records describing a citizen's exercise of his or her First Amendment rights. The Privacy Act is available to all Americans, including persons who work at intelligence agencies.

In 2012 the Supreme Court narrowed damages available to victims of Privacy Act violations to "economic" harm caused by the privacy breaches. Damages for emotional distress or punitive damages are not available under the Act. The law can still be used to obtain access to documents and require an agency to "correct" inaccurate records, but the ability to obtain monetary relief for violations of privacy is extremely limited.

National security whistleblowers have limited rights. Compared with the protections afforded other government employees, or employees who work in the private sector, they are working in the Dark Ages of whistleblower law.

PRACTICE TIPS

- The major laws governing federal employees are the Whistleblower Protection Act, at 5 U.S.C. §§ 2302 (general law), 1214–15 (OSC procedures), and 1221; the Protection of Intelligence Community Whistleblowers Act, 50 U.S.C. § 3234; and the FBI Whistleblower Protection Act, 28 CFR Part 27.

- Under 50 U.S.C. 33412(b)(7), whistleblowers have a limited right to challenge denial of a security clearance.

- The Merit Systems Protection Board website (www.mspb.gov) has special Q&As on the Whistleblower Protection Act and links to the regulations that govern discovery, hearings, filing requirements, and how to participate in MSPB proceedings.

- The website for the U.S. Office of Special Counsel (https://osc.gov) has detailed information on filing a whistleblower complaint and how to make a confidential whistleblower disclosure about government abuse.

- The Office of the Director of National Intelligence publishes on its website a notice, "Making Lawful Disclosures," with information on how intelligence community whistleblowers can report violations of law. *See* www.dni.gov/index.php/about-this-site/contact-the-ig/making-lawful-disclosures.

- The Equal Employment Opportunity Commission (EEOC) has a comprehensive website that fully explains rules governing federal employee discrimination or retaliation cases. See, https://www.eeoc.gov.

- How to pursue a "mixed case" combining a discrimination claim with a whistleblower claim (and obtaining the right to have a whistleblower claim heard in federal court) is explained in the case of *Bonds v. Leavitt*, 629 F.3d 369 (4th Cir 2011).

- *Erickson v. EPA*, 1999-Clean Air Act Case No. 2 (U.S. Department of Labor, Office of Administrative Review Board, May 31, 2006) (discussing the right of federal employees to use environmental whistleblower laws).

RULE 15

Make Sure Disclosures Are Protected

What if an employee tells the boss about a problem, but nothing is fixed? What if an employee is asked to violate a law? What if an employee thinks the company will cover up wrongdoing? When is it time to tell the government—or the press—about the allegations? Will these disclosures be protected?

Before looking at the specific legal authorities that may provide protection for an employee's whistleblowing, remember that Freedom of Speech is part of the American *credo*. The fundamental right to expose wrongdoing, criminality, or corruption was imbedded into the heart of the Constitution as one of the foundations of the American Way.

On June 8, 1789, James Madison stood before the First Congress of the United States of America and proposed that the Constitution be amended to include a Bill of Rights. His words were clear, and the intent behind what would eventually be incorporated into the Constitution as the First Amendment was unmistakable:

> *The people shall not be deprived or abridged of their right to speak, to write, or to publish their sentiments; and freedom of the press, as one of the great bulwarks of liberty, shall be inviolable. The people shall not be restrained from peaceably assembling and consulting for their common good; nor from applying to the Legislature by petitions, or remonstrates, for redress of their grievances.*

But Madison does not currently sit in the House of Representatives, and many judges have never even read these words. Madison's vision of "freedom of speech" is not part of modern-day corporate culture. The schism between whistleblowing celebrated in Hollywood movies and the reality of the legal protections for this speech is deep and wide.

Understanding Protected Disclosures

A shortcoming of the piecemeal approach to whistleblower protection is the confusion surrounding what is a protected disclosure. There is no uniform definition of a "protected disclosure." Each statute contains its own unique rules defining protected activities, and courts have not been consistent in applying these rules. The judicial confusion over whether or not to protect employees whose disclosures were made to their managers, or were part of their "official duties," simply highlights this legal headache facing employees who must decide whether or not to "do the right thing."

"It is the right, as well as the duty, of every citizen . . . to communicate to the executive officers any information which he has of the commission of an offense against those laws. . . . The right does not depend upon any of the amendments to the Constitution, but arises out of the creation and establishment by the Constitution itself of a national government."
—*In re Quarles and Butler* U.S. Supreme Court (1895)

The basic rule for ensuring that disclosures are protected seems simple on its face: When preparing to make a whistleblower disclosure always check the requirements of the law to determine whether there are specific disclosure rules or limitations that must be met in order to be protected. But in practice, this rule is not so simple. Most employees engage in protected activities *first* and ask questions about the law only when they suspect retaliation. Most employees utilize common sense when making a disclosure, but the law does not always conform to common sense and can be unforgiving to an employee who raised concerns in good faith, but to the wrong office.

FOLLOW STATUTORY MANDATES

Some laws contain specific requirements on how to make a disclosure that will be protected. The four laws that are directly implicated in this rule are the *qui tam* provisions of the False Claims Act, the Internal Revenue Code, the Securities Exchange Act, and the Commodity Exchange Act. Each of these four very powerful whistleblower protection laws, either by statute or regulation, contains very specific rules on how to file a claim in order to qualify for a reward. These rules *must* be strictly followed.

Not only do these laws specify filing procedures, they also contain confidentiality rules and other rules of conduct to which a whistleblower must adhere. For example, once a FCA claim is filed in court, the claim is under a court-ordered "seal." While the case is under seal, the whistleblower cannot publicly discuss the case. The law requires the whistleblower to keep the FCA claim confidential. By choosing this remedy, the whistleblower also chooses to follow the filing requirements of that law.

REPORTS TO FEDERAL LAW ENFORCEMENT

Most whistleblower laws explicitly protect filing claims with federal law enforcement agencies. Reasonable doubt that existed on this matter was cleared up in 2002, when Congress amended the obstruction of justice statute and criminalized retaliation against any person who provided truthful information to federal law enforcement concerning the "possible" violation of any federal law.

The terms of the 2002 amendment to the obstruction of justice law are clear, broad, and applicable to all Americans:

> *Whoever knowingly, with the intent to retaliate takes any action harmful to any person, including interference with the lawful employment or livelihood of any person, for providing to a law enforcement officer any truthful information relating to the commission or possible commission of any Federal offense, shall be fined under this title or imprisoned for not more than 10 years, or both.*

In 2010, as part of the Dodd-Frank Wall Street Reform and Consumer Protection Act, Congress permitted employees retaliated against for making disclosures protected under this obstruction of justice law to file a civil claim for damages. In addition to the generalized protection in the Dodd-Frank Act, every federal whistleblower law also should be interpreted as protecting disclosures made to federal law enforcement agencies.

REPORTS TO CONGRESS OR A LEGISLATIVE BODY

The earliest whistleblowers in American history risked their careers, reputations, and even their freedom by disclosing abuses of the commander of the American Navy to the Continental Congress. Their spokesperson testified before a committee of the Congress in 1777. This subsequently triggered the enactment of America's first whistleblower law one year later.

The right to "petition" Congress for a redress of grievances was unquestionably recognized as a fundamental human right by the Founding Fathers, and it was explicitly incorporated into the First Amendment of the U.S. Constitution.

Years later, in the early 1900s Presidents Theodore Roosevelt and William Taft battled with Congress over whistleblower rights. In this instance federal workers were providing information to Congress regarding abuses of power. Roosevelt and Taft wanted to silence them and implemented various "gag" rules prohibiting federal employees from blowing the whistle to Congress. These gag rules triggered a major dispute between the two branches of government. After strenuous debates on Capital Hill, in 1912 Congress exercised its authority and rebuked President Taft. Congress passed the Lloyd-LaFollette Act, which prohibited the president from retaliating against federal employees who provided information to any member or committee of Congress. The law remains in effect today and is commonly relied upon by federal whistleblowers.

Other whistleblower laws explicitly reference an employee's right to provide information to Congress, such as the Sarbanes-Oxley Act. However, even without these specific statutory references, there are no known modern cases under either federal or state whistleblower laws in which the firing of an employee for lawfully providing information to Congress (or a State Legislature) was upheld.

Disclosures to Congress often provide whistleblowers with a key ally. Perhaps the elected representative is willing to investigate the legitimacy of an employee's allegations and demand that an agency not fire the whistleblower? It is one thing for an employee to personally stand up for his or her rights; it is an entirely separate matter when a company learns of a formal congressional investigation or gets a letter from a member of Congress warning them against retaliation.

DISCLOSURES TO THE UNITED STATES ATTORNEY GENERAL

In 1863 Congress enacted the False Claims Act. Amended in 1986, this act is the premier whistleblower law. The law requires whistleblowers to make a formal disclosure of substantially all their allegations with the U.S. attorney general. These disclosures are protected. Unlike other whistleblower laws, the FCA mandates that employees disclose their concerns to the government before filing a lawsuit. They must make a disclosure to the attorney general at the time they file their lawsuit.

Regardless of whether you file an FCA claim or not, raising allegations of wrongdoing with the attorney general is always a safe bet as to a protected agency for blowing the whistle. The attorney general has a responsibility to enforce federal laws, so why not file a claim with the top cop?

TESTIFYING IN COURT

During the post–Civil War Reconstruction period, Congress was concerned about citizens' ability, especially those from the South, to protect their federal rights. Among the laws enacted, in an effort to address this concern, was the Civil Rights Act of 1871. This law contained numerous provisions applicable to modern-day whistleblowing, including a provision known as Section 1985. This provision prohibited retaliation against witnesses in federal court proceedings. In 1996 the U.S. Supreme Court applied this provision to whistleblowers, permitting an employee to file a damages lawsuit for wrongful termination after being fired for testifying. Court testimony is also covered under most (if not all) other federal and state whistleblower laws, provided the testimony concerns the subject matters protected under the specific statute.

FILING A CLAIM OR INITIATING A PROCEEDING

The act of filing a whistleblower claim in court, with a regulatory agency or with a labor-rights department, such as the Department of Labor or the Equal Employment Opportunity Commission, is considered protected activity. Courts recognize that without the right to freely allege retaliation by filing a claim, no employee could or would ever blow the whistle. Additionally, federal whistleblower laws protect employees who "initiate proceedings" to enforce regulatory requirements.

REFUSING TO VIOLATE A LAW

Most, if not all, state courts recognize the common law "public policy exception" to the "termination at will" doctrine that prohibits firing workers who reasonably refuse to violate a law. Similar protections are also found under the majority of federal whistleblower laws.

The reason for this tie-in between a refusal to perform illegal work and whistleblower protections is simple. Many whistleblower cases originate with a refusal. For example, if an employee complains about pressure from management to falsely certify an audit report or quality assurance certifications, this complaint should be protected. Most occupational health and safety laws, including the federal Occupational Safety and Health Adminstration, also provide protection for employees who refuse to engage in hazardous work.

There is, however, one very important caveat regarding work refusals. Should management demonstrate that the requested conduct is legal or safe, the right to refuse to perform that work terminates, and an employee can thereafter be disciplined for failing to perform the task.

DISCLOSING A VIOLATION OF LAW

Most, if not all, federal and state whistleblower laws protect employees who disclose violations of law to the proper authorities. But four major whistleblower laws require such disclosures to the government before an employee can qualify for a reward. The *qui tam* provisions of the False Claims Act, the Internal Revenue Code, Commodity Exchange Act, and the Securities Exchange Act all require specific and detailed disclosures to the government to qualify for a reward. Each law sets forth the specific disclosure requirements, i.e., who a disclosure must be filed with and what type of information must be disclosed to qualify as a "whistleblower." The FCA, Commodity, and Securities *qui tam* laws all prohibit retaliation against employees who file such claims.

CONTACTING OR PROVIDING INFORMATION TO A FEDERAL REGULATORY AGENT/INSPECTOR

Federal whistleblower laws permit employees to provide information to inspectors or regulatory agents. These laws allow for a wide range of formal and informal communications with federal investigators/regulators, including oral and written communications, formal testimony, and the filing of a complaint.

THE NEWS MEDIA

From the day Deep Throat secretly met with *Washington Post* reporter Bob Woodward in a Washington, DC parking garage, the potential impact of whistleblowing was seared into the American psyche. A whistleblower could play a key role in preserving Democratic institutions and force a corrupt president out of office. Going to the press—be it *60 Minutes* or a local newspaper—is a quintessential act of whistleblowing. But obtaining protection for going to the news media can be very difficult. Ask Michael Andrew.

After thirty-one years on the Baltimore Police Department, Major Michael Andrew was very troubled. He had witnessed a police-shooting incident in which officers had killed an old man who had barricaded himself in his apartment. He wrote an internal memorandum expressing concerns over the misuse of deadly force. When upper management tried to cover up the potential misconduct surrounding the killing, Major Andrew took his concerns to the *Baltimore Sun*. For that crime he was fired. As in most whistleblower cases, loyalty trumps truth—even if someone was wrongfully shot to death.

Was providing his memorandum to the newspaper protected? The district court said no and left Major Andrew without a job. The U.S. Court of Appeals for the Fourth Circuit disagreed. A concurring Judge, J. Harvie Wilkinson, eloquently explained why: To "throw out" a case because an employee "took his concerns to the press" would have "profound adverse effects on accountability in government." Without such protection, "scrutiny of the inner workings of massive public bureaucracies charged with major public responsibilities" would be "in deep trouble." The "First Amendment should never countenance the gamble that informed scrutiny of the workings of government will be left to wither on the vine. That scrutiny is impossible without some assistance from inside sources such as Michael Andrew." In conclusion, Judge Wilkinson warned: "[A]s the state grows more layered and impacts lives more profoundly, it seems inimical to First Amendment principles to treat too summarily those who bring, often at some personal risk, its operations into public view. It is vital to the health of our polity that the functioning of the ever more complex and powerful machinery of government not become democracy's dark lagoon."

Although no whistleblower statute explicitly states that employee reports to the news media are covered, courts have historically protected them. The news media is widely understood to be the "Fourth Estate" in American politics, wielding significant influence over the actions of both government and its regulators. Most judges who have written on this issue have expressed an understanding that many workers would view the press as an effective means to alert the public and government to potential wrongdoing, and actually place pressure on the elite to fix a problem.

In cases of public employment, there is no question that lawful and reasonable contacts with the press are constitutionally protected under the First Amendment and the Civil Rights Act of 1871 (42 U.S.C. § 1983). The leading First Amendment whistleblower case, *Pickering v. Board of Education*, protected a schoolteacher who wrote a letter to the editor of his local newspaper.

Administrative agencies have also protected disclosures to the news media. The U.S. Department of Labor has longstanding rules that protect whistleblower disclosures to the press, including well-established precedent under Occupational Health and Safety Administration and the environmental and nuclear whistleblower laws.

Employees must be very careful when talking to the press. First, many courts still have not made definitive rulings concerning whether communications with the press are covered under various federal or state laws. Second, news reporters, like everyone else, have their own reputations. Some will religiously protect sources; others are not so careful and are more interested in a good story than in making sure a whistleblower is protected. Third, it is not uncommon for employers to initiate press "leak" investigations, on the pretext that confidential information may have been improperly disclosed to the press. Fourth, under the False Claims Act, and other reward-based anti-fraud laws, there are compelling reasons to confidentially provide information to government agencies, and avoid any contact with the press. Fifth, in the area of national security, federal employees have been criminally prosecuted for "leaking" confidential or "secret" information to the press. Sixth, in private sector whistleblower cases, there is no clear precedent that contacting the news media is protected. Seventh, under the laws protecting corporate trade secrets, communications with the news media are not protected, whereas whistleblowers can confidentially disclose such secrets to government investigators.

If done carefully and properly, the news media can be a critical catalyst for positive change. With some significant exceptions, especially when trade secrets or confidential information is at issue, most courts have recognized this reality.

DISCLOSURES TO SUPERVISORS

As mentioned in Rules 16 and 17, nearly all whistleblower laws should explicitly or implicitly protect employees who raise concerns directly with their supervisors. Some state whistleblower statutes actually require employees to inform supervisors of problems as a prerequisite for obtaining protection under local law. However, unless such disclosures are unequivocally covered in the statutory definitions of a whistleblower law, employees must be very careful in simply relying upon the assumption that a court exercise common sense and rule that internal protections are covered.

The *Garcetti* and Dodd-Frank Act cases stand as reminders that relying solely on internal whistleblower disclosures as the foundation of a legal case, in the absence of explicit statutory protection, is dangerous and may result in a whistleblower losing his or her case.

"WHISTLEBLOWER" WEB SITES/WIKILEAKS

Various organizations sponsor websites or other online services that solicit whistleblowers to disclose confidential information anonymously. These sites often claim that they can protect the identify of their sources. But leaking information through these services is extremely risky and can be counterproductive. There are numerous reasons whistleblowers should be very wary of these sites. Here are a few:

First, there is no legal privilege associated with communications to web sites such as Wikileaks. They are not covered under the attorney-client privilege or a law enforcement privilege. The website that sponsors the "whistleblowing" service can be subjected to subpoena, civil discovery or various high-tech searches conducted under the U.S. Patriot Act and other legal authorities. If a whistleblower is questioned under oath (such as in a deposition) whether they were a source to the website, they either must admit to the leak, plead the 5th Amendment against self-incrimination, or commit perjury. It puts the whistleblower in a lose-lose-lose situation.

Second, the Chelsea Manning case should be a lesson to any whistleblower thinking of doing an online document dump. Manning leaked information to Wikileaks. He was discovered and sentenced to 35 years in prison. His mistreatment resulted in two suicide attempts while in military jails. Although Manning wanted to expose wrongdoing, the method he used to disclose his information stripped him of the rights he potentially had as a whistleblower under the military whistleblower law, and opened him to criminal prosecution.

Third, you may be harming legitimate law enforcement investigations. If law enforcement obtained the information confidentially from the whistleblower, and opened an investigation, the online document dump could tip-off the company about the evidence that could be used against it, and permit the company to create a strong defense. The company could also claim that any investigation was tainted by the improper theft of its documents.

Fourth, courts have been unkind to whistleblowers who "steal" information from the government or their employer and then have it published online. This type of prejudice can result and has resulted in the dismissal of an otherwise strong case.

Fifth, you could be prejudicing an otherwise strong reward case under the False Claims Act and other related laws.

Finally, the online site is under no legal obligation to protect you. They can profit from your information, even if you go to jail. The law views publishers of information differently from those who leak information. It is rare for a news organization to be prosecuted from publishing classified information, whereas sources of classified information have been investigated, fired, and prosecuted.

Before using an online "whistleblower" website to make a disclosure, contact an attorney. Learn the risks associated with such a document-dump, how you may release materials lawfully, and alternatives that may exist to using these services.

DISCLOSURES THAT BYPASS THE CHAIN OF COMMAND

It is common for whistleblowers to bypass their formal chain of command when they raise concerns within their company. If an immediate supervisor is the perceived problem, employees may decide that this level of management should be ignored and that they should therefore inform higher-level officials of the concern. Likewise, some companies have established complaint processes that employees are either required or urged to follow.

When the U.S. Department of Labor reviewed this issue it held that employees could not be disciplined simply for failing to follow the chain of command when making protected disclosures. Moreover, the DOL ruled that if an employer fired a worker for refusing to follow the chain of command when making a protected disclosure that discharge was, per se, illegal.

TRADE UNIONS AND PUBLIC INTEREST GROUPS

Working directly with union officials to report illegal or unsafe conditions should be protected activity under the National Labor Relations Act and most federal whistleblower laws. The nuclear and environmental whistleblower laws, either in their statutory text or legislative history, make clear that working with union representatives is protected activity. In a 1982 decision, the U.S. Court of Appeals for the Second Circuit agreed and found an employee's reports to a union safety committee to be protected under the Atomic Energy Act.

In a 1987 case filed under the nuclear whistleblower law, the secretary of the DOL held that employee communications with public interest groups may constitute protected activity. An employee's decision to work with an advocacy group to ensure that his or her concerns were properly investigated was considered a reasonable response to the discovery of safety problems.

In a water pollution case, the DOL reasoned that bringing "sludge discharge information to the attention" of an "environmental activist" who could be "expected to act on the information" was protected activity. The DOL judge recognized that "while the [employee] did not himself ask" for a government investigation by government officials, there was a "causal nexus" between his disclosure to an environmental activist, the news media, and the fact that an investigation was started.

CORPORATE COMPLIANCE PROGRAMS

Since the passage of the Sarbanes-Oxley Act, every publicly traded corporation in the United States is mandated to have an internal employee-concerns program, which is required to provide confidentiality to employees who blow the whistle internally. The SOX whistleblower protection law specifically protects employees who contact this type of internal department. The federal rules for government procurement and the federal sentencing guidelines also contain provisions that strongly encourage or require companies to establish internal corporate compliance programs.

As explained in Rules 16–18, before using one of these programs, you should try to find out its reputation for independence, honesty, and objectivity. Do the corporate managers truly support employees who utilize these company-controlled systems? Is the program controlled by the company attorneys? More important, you must determine whether contacting compliance officials will be legally protected. Under the Sarbanes-Oxley Act, SOX disclosures to an internal corporate compliance department are protected, but if a law does not explicitly protect such intercorporate reporting, you may share the fate of the employees discussed in Rules 16 and 17, who lost their jobs because they raised internal complaints.

DISCLOSURES BY ATTORNEYS

It is extremely tricky for attorneys to become whistleblowers. Under well-established rules governing attorney-client privilege, lawyers must keep the secrets of their clients. But under whistleblower laws, all employees have the right to report violations of law to appropriate authorities. What happens when these two principles collide?

The U.S. Courts of Appeals have recognized that lawyers can sue for wrongful discharge if they are fired for blowing the whistle inside their companies.

In one such case, Shawn and Lena Van Asdale worked as in-house counsel for a publicly traded company. They reported "possible shareholder fraud in connection with a merger" to the company's general counsel and were subsequently fired. They sued the company under the Sarbanes-Oxley Act. The company asked the Court to throw out the lawsuit on the basis of their status as attorneys. This argument was completely rejected by the Court. Looking at the text of the Sarbanes-Oxley Act, the Court held that attorneys could be protected under the law, reasoning that "Congress plainly considered the role attorneys might play in reporting possible securities fraud." The Court further explained that procedures could be employed, such as issuing a protective order, to protect a company's legitimate interests if the case went to trial and confidential matters become relevant to the case.

In a second case, the U.S. Court of Appeals for the Fifth Circuit summed up the status of lawyers: "[T]he attorney-client privilege" is *not* a "per se bar to retaliation claims under the federal whistleblower statutes." In other words, being an attorney does not automatically forfeit your whistleblower rights.

Although the courts have been amenable to attorneys filing wrongful discharge lawsuits, the issue of when, how, and to whom an attorney can make a protected disclosure is complex and often contested. It is imperative that attorneys take special care to ensure that any disclosures they make conform to state or federal law. Put another way, be cautious what you report and to whom so that you do not end up fired or disbarred for trying to do the right thing.

Federal and state courts have applied local bar rules to attorney-whistleblower disclosures. In one such case, *Quest Diagnostics*, the U.S. Court of Appeals for the Second Circuit dismissed the whistleblower's case, even though the Court recognized that the dismissal could result in the dismissal of a legitimate whistleblower claim. The Court determined that protecting the attorney-client privilege may, in some cases, "impede the pursuit of meritorious litigation to the detriment of the justice system."

The U.S. Securities and Exchange Commission has special rules on attorney conduct. Attorneys who "appear" or "practice" before the Commission can (and in some circumstances, must) raise securities fraud issues to the "client" or to his or her supervisors at a law firm. Under federal law (which should trump state bar rules), there are specific circumstances under which a corporate attorney can provide privileged information to the SEC. An article published by Latham & Watkins (a large corporate law firm that does *not* represent whistleblowers), explained that if an attorney reasonably believes his or her SEC-regulated corporate client is continuing to commit a "material violation" of law that is "likely to cause a substantial injury to the financial interests" of investors, he or she can disclosure privileged information to the SEC. These reports are limited to three circumstances: (1) "to prevent a material violation" of law "that is likely to cause substantial injury to the financial interest" of the company or its investors; (2) to prevent the company from "committing perjury, suborning perjury," or committing a fraud on the SEC; or (3) to "rectify the consequences of a material violation" caused by the company that is likely to cause a "substantial injury" to the financial interests of investors, if the "attorney's services were used." If an attorney meets one of these strict requirements, he or she should also be able to qualify for a financial reward from the SEC under the Dodd-Frank Act, although no court has specifically addressed this issue.

The case law has gone in two directions. Corporations have hidden behind attorney-client privilege to keep information about fraud and their criminal conduct from the public. They have filed disciplinary actions against attorneys whom they have accused of improperly blowing the whistle. But attorney-whistleblowers have pursued their cases and prevailed. The law in this area is still developing, and there are no easy answers for attorneys who want to blow the whistle.

DON'T BE INSUBORDINATE

Blowing the whistle does not give an employee license to be insubordinate. The courts recognize that in the context of protected activities, emotions may run high, and consequently they acknowledge "some leeway for impulsive behavior." The key issue in these types of cases is "whether an employee's actions are indefensible under the circumstances." This analysis often is conducted on a case-by-case basis and is based on the type of work an employee performs and what type of "unduly disruptive" behavior is involved.

BEWARE OF TRAPS

Remember that each whistleblower protection law is different. The laws all have their own definitions of protected activity, and there is no judicial consensus defining even the most basic parameters of employee rights of speech. Often an employee blows the whistle first and then tries to figure out if the disclosures were protected. Before you sound the alarm, find out what law may protect you.

- Checklist 2 lists federal whistleblower laws, with citations to important cases, including cases defining the scope of protected activity. The references for this Rule also cite specific court rulings on the scope of protected activities.

- Rules 16 and 17 explain the pitfalls that an employee faces when he or she reports misconduct only internally to the bosses.

- An excellent critique of court decisions that narrowly define protected activity is contained in the Senate Report on the Whistleblower Protection Enhancement Act, S. Rep. 112-155, pp. 4-8.

RULE 16

Yes, You Are a "Whistleblower"

"I am not a whistleblower! I was only doing my job!"

No one takes a job intending to become a whistleblower. Picking a career-ending fight with one's boss is never the initial intent of an employee with legitimate concerns. No one starts cherishing the idea of being a "whistleblower." No one courts that label.

In almost every instance, employees tagged as "whistleblowers" started out simply doing their jobs. A truck driver tells a dispatcher that his brakes need maintenance, a teacher questions why new textbooks never arrived, an engineer refuses to certify that bolts can stand up to reasonable stress, a nurse tells a physician that the hospital failed to review an X-ray; the list is nearly endless. Before employees ever think they are whistleblowers, they usually believe they are doing a good job to help the employer follow the rules. But as one judge described it, perhaps they were doing their job "too well."

Instead of following a Hollywood script, where a young, idealist professional stumbles upon an evil scientific plot, these cases confront issues that arise in the typical workplace. Outside of major nationally reported scandals, the real impact of whistleblowing has been documented in numerous objective corporate-sponsored studies. A 2007 PricewaterhouseCoopers study of corporate behavior within fifty-four hundred major corporations found that professional auditors were able to uncover only 19 percent of the fraud/misconduct, while law enforcement detected only 3 percent of corporate fraud. The real heroes in uncovering fraud were ordinary employees just doing their jobs. The PricewaterhouseCoopers study credited "tipsters" or whistleblowers with uncovering 43 percent of frauds. These findings remain consistent year after year. In a 2016 report published by the Association of Certified Fraud Examiners (based on a survey opened to 41,788 certified fraud examiners), "tips were the most common" fraud "detection method by a large margin." For companies with one hundred or more employees, "tips" were the source of 43.5% of frauds detected, as compared to 1.9% from "law enforcement." The majority of tips come from employees. Of all the classes of workers in corporate America, whistleblowers contributed the most in protecting investors and honest corporations from fraud.

When should an employee begin to suspect that she or he may be a whistleblower? The answer is simple: as soon as possible. Without accepting this change of status, employees cannot begin to take the crucial steps to protect their careers. In the infamous 2002 Enron corporate meltdown, the whistleblower, Sherron Watkins, sent a "heads-up" memo to her boss, Kenneth Lay. Watkins believed she was doing the right thing by alerting her boss to accounting problems, which just so happened to be the very problems that would land Enron officials in jail and cause the company to collapse. Her boss did not appreciate these disclosures and asked the corporate attorneys what whistleblower rights Watkins enjoyed. At the time, publicly traded companies were not covered under the federal whistleblower laws. She also was not covered under Texas law.

Given the lack of protection, Enron's president was given a green light to fire the whistleblower. Before Watkins even knew she was a whistleblower, the company had already labeled her as such, reviewed its legal options, and commenced a strategy to "shoot the messenger."

This scenario is not unique. For years the Georgia Power Company assumed that any employee who contacted its internal "hotline" was a potential litigation risk. In addition, any employee who filed a "hotline" concern had his or her concerns forwarded to in-house attorneys for their review. While the worker was manipulated into thinking he or she was doing a good job, the company feared the employee was a potential whistleblower and started to build a case that could justify disciplinary action.

It is important for employees who raise concerns about potential misconduct in the workplace to see themselves as whistleblowers, even if they have no intention of ever dropping the dime on their employer to a government agency. Most whistleblower cases begin with a straightforward report to a supervisor concerning a potential problem. Hence, it is never too early to take steps to protect oneself from retaliation. Throughout, it is crucial to ensure that disclosures, regardless of how informally they are raised (or even if such reports are encouraged or required under company policy), are protected under law.

A company's attorneys will carefully review a whistleblower's exposé and will later determine whether those disclosures constituted legally protected whistleblowing. Shouldn't the whistleblower undergo the same type of analysis *before* putting one's job at risk? Unfortunately the majority of whistleblowers do not. Most whistleblowers initially raise their concerns, without thinking they may be targeting themselves as the "skunk at the picnic."

Internal Whistleblowing

The fact remains that most employees initially disclose potential misconduct before reviewing their legal rights. When employees suspect that their companies may have violated the law, they typically report the issues to their first-line supervisor. They naively expect their chain of command to be appreciative. With this assumption the employees believe that their concerns will be taken seriously and investigated accordingly. If wrongdoing is proven, they believe that their company will fix the problem immediately.

Despite employee hopefulness, the reaction of managers is typically not to sing the employees' praise. No one likes to be told that he made a mistake, let alone from a subordinate. No one likes to be told that she may have violated a law. Corporate or political "loyalty" is often synonymous with a culture that warns employees to "mind their own business" and in doing so not to question upper-level decisions. The PricewaterhouseCoopers study understood this cultural problem and lamented that companies have all too often instilled fear and have not given "employees the confidence to do the right thing."

With this background, it is not surprising that one of the first major issues in whistleblower law concerned whether or not employees who did nothing more than disclose misconduct to their immediate supervisor were protected. These cases have been hard fought and concluded with mixed results. Nearly everyone has weighed in on the argument—from regulatory agencies, to Congress, to the Supreme Court.

Kentucky Coal Dust

The first case that wrestled with this issue involved Frank Phillips, a miner working at the Kencar Mine in Phelps, Kentucky. The mine was plagued with harmfully "excessive coal dust" and "defective electrical wiring." These conditions resulted in "serious problems of both health and safety" for the employees. Phillips, who operated a shuttle car at the mine, informed his foreman about these dangers. Angered, his foreman called Phillips a "troublemaker," and on April 28, 1971, after an argument over the conditions at the mine, told Phillips that he was fired. Within days upper management approved his firing for the offense of "interfering with the operation of the mine," "abridging the rights of management," and "refusing to obey" an order to continue working in the hazardous conditions.

The case was heard under the 1969 Federal Mine Health and Safety Act. This law contained one of the first federal whistleblower protection provisions and would later be used as a model for numerous other federal laws covering environmental, transportation, and nuclear whistleblowers. The 1969 act explicitly protected employees who exposed safety concerns to the government but was silent about internal complaints to management. The mine owners argued that Phillips was not covered because he never raised his concerns with a federal safety inspector, had not initiated a formal proceeding, and did not testify in any case before the Mine Health and Safety Commission. In complaining to his foreman, Phillips was merely doing his job, not blowing the whistle.

If the mine had an accident, people could have died and millions of dollars would have been lost. Even without an accident, the excessive coal dust was a bomb waiting to go off, for it had the potential to make miners extremely sick. No one accused Phillips of being a bad worker. He never "ratted out" the company to any inspectors. Philips only wanted to ensure that his foreman followed mandatory safety rules. His case was no different than that of any employee, working for any company, who simply asked his or her boss to follow the necessary rules. However, the question is: Was the complaint to his foreman protected under law?

The legal showdown occurred before the U.S. Court of Appeals for the District of Columbia Circuit, a court with significant authority, directly under the Supreme Court. Phillips stood alone against the company, who had fired him; the Bituminous Coal Operators Association (which represented the entire coal industry); and the U.S. government. The Nixon Administration supported industry and directly opposed the miner. The Department of Interior ruled that Phillips's firing was legal. The Department of Justice defended that ruling in court.

A three-judge panel in Washington, DC, heard the case. Judge Malcolm Wilkey wrote the majority opinion on behalf of the court. Before being named to the federal appeals court by President Nixon, Wilkey had served for years as general counsel of the Kennecott Copper Corporation. Given his background, Wilkey was no liberal activist judge.

After painstakingly reviewing the facts of the case, on June 20, 1974, Wilkey ruled that the "answer is clear." Miners are protected if they report "safety violations," if only to their foreman. There was no need for an employee to contact the government and file a formal complaint. This decision was made based on the understanding that "safety costs money" and there is always a "temptation to minimize compliance with safety regulations" in order to "shave costs." Workers at the shop-floor level are "in the best position to observe the compliance or noncompliance with safety laws." In addition, reliance upon federal inspections "can never be frequent or thorough enough to ensure compliance."

Wilkey recognized that any worker who "insist(s)" that health and safety rules be "followed" could adversely impact profits by "slowing down production." These employee whistleblowers "are not likely to be popular" with management. However, "only if" workers are "given a realistically effective channel" to raise or communicate their concerns could the safety laws of the nation be enforced. Wilkey held that raising concerns with a supervisor was the most reasonable first step in any compliance activity, and consequently it was critical that miners such as Phillips have full "protection from reprisal" upon "making complaints" to their supervisors.

Informing the foreman of the "possible dangers" in the mine was an "essential preliminary stage" in the notification process. It was imperative that the courts and administrative agencies responsible for ensuring compliance with the laws understand the "practicalities of the situation" the average worker faces. Without protecting the method and manner used by the typical worker to report concerns, the safety law would be rendered "completely ineffective."

The impact of the *Phillips* decision was immediate and widespread. Courts adopted the resulting logic in other whistleblower contexts. Also, Congress amended the 1969 Mine Safety Act to explicitly protect internal complaints raised by miners to their supervisors. In doing so, Congress issued a formal report adopting the *Phillips* decision and clarifying its intent to cover internal complaints.

The Debate Over Internal Reporting Did Not End

Although this ruling should have ended the debate, the battle over whether concerns raised to managers were protected under whistleblower laws had only just begun. The issue was next disputed in the area of nuclear safety. In 1984 two federal appeals courts, one in Washington State and the other in Texas, issued two diametrically opposite opinions.

The first case concerned Robert Mackowiak, a sheet metal worker at Washington Public Power Supply System (WPPS). WPPS was a nuclear plant under construction in Richland, Washington. As a certified welding inspector, Mackowiak's job was to review the heating, ventilation, and air-conditioning systems at WPPS; and if the work on these systems failed to meet federal specifications, he was to place a "red tag" on the improperly installed items and file a "Non-Conformance Report."

Mackowiak was fired because he was an "overly zealous inspector." In other words, although he had "excellent" "qualifications" and "expertise," and was a "good inspector," he did his job "too well" because each time he "red tagged" an item and filed a "Non-Conformance Report," the work on those specific systems was delayed and the costs of the project increased.

His employer complained that Mackowiak had "attitudinal problems" and would not accept "management directives." The U.S. Court of Appeals for the Ninth Circuit explained, "[A]t times, the inspector may come into conflict with his employer by identifying problems that might cause added expense and delay." The bottom line was simple: "[I]nspectors must be free from the threat of retaliatory discharge for identifying safety and quality problems." Mackowiak could not be fired simply because of his "competent and aggressive inspection work." Mackowiak was simply doing his job, and, as acknowledged by the court, doing his job well. Guided by the logic of *Phillips*, the court ruled that Mackowiak was protected under the federal nuclear whistleblower laws.

Despite the ruling of the court, employers did not get the message and continued to aggressively fight the *Phillips* precedent. It was abundantly apparent that if employers had the ability to fire employees for making disclosures to their supervisors, management could win the majority of whistleblower legal cases on the basis of this technicality. Under this assumption, management would have the upper hand because the vast majority of employees who exposed safety hazards or violations of law did so initially to their supervisors. If employees were fired before they made a report to the government, the company would win the case. With this, corporate lawyers saw an easy path to victory, regardless of whether such decisions made any sense whatsoever.

Winning was paramount in the context of fighting a whistleblower case, even if the ability of workers to simply report misconduct to a supervisor was stifled. Instead of following the practical advice of PricewaterhouseCoopers by promoting internal mechanisms that would effectively provide workers with the "confidence to do the right thing," the ground war against whistleblowers continued to be fought on the shop floor.

Although the motive for having *Phillips* overturned was clear, the logic behind the corporate arguments was not. What company would not want a reasonable "heads-up" so they could fix a problem before it became a major federal case? The answer: Brown & Root/Halliburton. That company took it upon themselves to lead the corporate charge against the *Phillips* decision by arguing a seemingly ridiculous position. Employees who had the courtesy or good sense to report problems to their supervisors could be fired, at will, and have no protection. If an employee wanted to be protected, he or she was required to go to the government and file a complaint. In other words, under the Brown & Root/Halliburton vision of corporate compliance, the only method available to employees seeking protection under whistleblower laws was to file reports with government law enforcement agencies.

In the same year that the Ninth Circuit decided *Mackowiak*, Brown & Root finally "got its way" in another appeals court, the U.S. Court of Appeals for the Fifth Circuit. Chuck Atchison, a quality control inspector at the Comanche Peak nuclear power plant construction site, had been fired for raising safety concerns to his supervisor. The Department of Labor found that Atchison was fired in retaliation for raising these concerns, and ordered his reinstatement into his position. In the case of *Brown & Root v. Donovan*, the Fifth Circuit became the first appeals court to reject the *Phillips* holding. It ruled that without direct contact with the federal regulatory agency, the Nuclear Regulatory Commission, Atchison could not be protected under the nuclear whistleblower law. Atchison was out of a job and out of a career simply for doing his job too well. How could he possibly be identifying and disclosing nuclear safety violations too well?

For the next twenty years after that decision, no employee prevailed in a federal court nuclear whistleblower case within the jurisdiction of the Fifth Circuit. Essentially the ruling gutted the law. Employees are not lawyers, they do not know the intricacies of what is, or is not, "protected activity." An employee would therefore never guess that disclosing violations to one's employer, even within the context of a formal corporate "hotline" complaint, would not be protected.

The DOL understood the devastating impact of the *Brown & Root* decision and argued vigorously against it in court after court. Congress ended the argument in 1992, amending the nuclear whistleblower law such that internal reports to management were explicitly included as protected activity under the law.

Congress took further steps after 1992 to ensure that internal, job-related whistleblowing was protected under law. For example, the Sarbanes-Oxley Act, a landmark corporate reform law, mandated that all publicly traded companies establish internal procedures for accepting whistleblower complaints. The Act specifically protected complaints raised with supervisors in the statutory definition of protected whistleblowing. Other laws contained similar protections, including the transportation, food safety, defense-contracting, stimulus spending, consumer products safety, armed services, and airline safety whistleblower laws.

After thirty years of legal disputes over the basic core meaning of "whistle-blowing," it finally appeared as if the dispute over protecting internal complaints to management was over. It seemed as if the "common sense" approach of Judge Wilkey had finally prevailed. If only we were so lucky.

Supreme Confusion

In 2006, the Bush Administration's Department of Justice and the Los Angeles County District Attorney's Office joined forces in an attempt to narrow the scope of protected whistleblowing under the First Amendment.

In the *Garcetti v. Ceballos* case, an employee within the Los Angeles District Attorney's Office, Richard Ceballos, had once again done his job all too well. He disclosed "[i]naccuracies in an affidavit used to obtain a critical search warrant." The affidavit filed by his office contained "serious misrepresentations," and Ceballos reported those violations to his supervisors. In retaliation Ceballos was transferred and denied a promotion. He sought protection under the First Amendment.

The Supreme Court initially heard arguments in 2005. However, due to a vacancy in the Court, no decision was rendered. This was an indication that the Court was deeply divided on the issue, perhaps four to four. After Justice John Roberts was installed as the new chief justice, the case was reargued in 2006. The *Garcetti* decision would be the first major First Amendment case decided by the Roberts Court.

In a five-to-four decision written by Justice Anthony Kennedy and joined by Chief Justice Roberts and Justices Antonin Scalia, Clarence Thomas, and Samuel Alito, the Court reopened the *Phillips* debate. Ceballos's case was thrown out of court. The decision, although very narrow in scope, was a remarkable step backward.

Initially, the majority opinion recognized the importance of protecting public employees' speech under the First Amendment: "The Court has acknowledged the importance of promoting the public's interest in receiving the well-informed views of government employees." It realized that there could be "widespread costs" if government-employee whistleblowing was "repressed" and that "exposing governmental inefficiency and misconduct is a matter of considerable significance." The Court recognized that First Amendment protections could apply to purely internal whistleblowing speech. In other words, public employees "may receive First Amendment protection for expressions made at work." The Court also stated that public employee speech concerning the subject matter of an employee's job can, under some circumstances, be protected under the Constitution: "The First Amendment protects some expressions related to the speaker's job." So far, so good—if the Court had only stopped here, and simply continued to apply its past precedent, Ceballos would have been protected under the law. Unfortunately that is not what happened.

Instead of continuing to move forward, the Court carved out an exception to the First Amendment based on an employee's "official duties." If the whistleblower's concern was voiced "pursuant to official duties," a public employee's report to management would not be protected, the Court ruled: "We hold that when public employees make statements pursuant to their official duties, the employees are not speaking as citizens for First Amendment purposes, and the Constitution does not insulate their communications from employer discipline."

According to the five-justice majority, the "controlling factor" turned out to be the contents of Ceballos's job description. If the whistleblower concerns were part of Ceballos's "official duties," or were part of the work required under his position description, his memorandum to management was not protected. Despite being disciplined in retaliation for communicating allegations that an illegal or improper search warrant had been issued in violation of law, Ceballos's case was dismissed.

The dissent immediately picked up on the absurdity of the majority holding. Justice Stevens remarked that it was "senseless" to permit "constitutional protection(s) for exactly the same words to hinge on whether they fall within a job description."

Justice Stevens also recognized the catch-22 nature of the ruling. If reporting a concern related to "official duties" to a supervisor was not considered a protected activity, employees would be compelled to file official complaints to the news media, the state legislature, or another law enforcement agency or others outside of the internal chain of command, in order to obtain protection. In other words, had Ceballos reported the misconduct to the press, his allegations would have been constitutionally protected. Instead, he was punished and left without legal protection, simply for doing his job too well.

Referring to this outcome as "perverse," Justice Stevens warned: "Moreover, it seems perverse to fashion a new rule that provides employees with an incentive to voice their concerns publicly before talking frankly to their superiors."

The *Garcetti* holding can be interpreted narrowly. The Court's five-member majority also held that government agencies could not expand the scope of an employee's "official duties" by drafting overly broad job descriptions. The Court reasoned that descriptions needed to be carefully reviewed in order to prevent "excessively broad job descriptions" from interfering with free speech.

Congress did not ignore the consequences of *Garcetti* and similarly decided cases. On November 27, 2012, President Obama signed into law the Whistleblower Protection Enhancement Act of 2012, protecting most federal employee whistleblowers. Not one senator or congressman had voted against this law.

The Enhancement Act explicitly rejected the *Garcetti* line of cases. The Senate Report had harsh words for the court precedents that handcuffed whistleblower disclosures, stating that these decisions had "undermined" Congressional intent and were "wrongly" decided. Congress used the act to "overturn several court decisions that narrowed the scope of protected activities." The Enhancement Act removed any ambiguity whatsoever as to whether or not internal whistleblowing was protected. The act explicitly protected disclosures "made to a supervisor" or made "during the normal course" of an employee's "duties." Just to make sure that the courts did not continue to emasculate the scope of protected disclosures, Congress also stated that an employee's "motive for making" a "disclosure" was irrelevant, and that both "formal or informal communications" would be protected. Although the Enhancement Act is limited to the scope of protected activities enjoyed by federal employees, it sends a strong message that the hypertechnical approach defining precisely what is a protected whistleblower disclosure should be firmly rejected.

Although the Enhancement Act solved the problem faced by internal whistleblowers working for the federal government, it had no impact on the scope of protected activity for state and local employees. *Garcetti* is still the law under the First Amendment.

Back to the Future: Internal Whistleblower Protections Under Dodd-Frank

As part of the historic financial reforms enacted after the 2008 financial crisis, Congress added an antiretaliation law to the legal arsenal available to Wall Street whistleblowers. The Securities Exchange Act was amended to provide employees with direct access to federal court and award them double back pay, among other damages. When initially proposed, this law contained a narrow definition of a protected activity, reminiscent of the type of language used in the 1969 Mine Health and Safety Act at issue in the *Phillips* case. Both the Senate and House bills defined whistleblowing as disclosing information to the *Commission* (i.e., the government). Neither bill explicitly protected internal whistleblowers.

While Congress was reconciling the House and Senate versions of the Dodd-Frank Act, the Senate Banking Committee became concerned that internal whistleblowers might not be protected under the Act. An eleventh-hour change was made.

Here is the history behind this change. On April 23–24, 2010, while the bill was being finalized in conference, the Senate Banking Committee showed the final (and approved) draft of the Securities and Exchange Act's whistleblower law to the National Whistleblower Center (NWC). The committee staff wanted to make doubly sure that the whistleblower law would work. On April 24 the NWC staff, fully familiar with the historic disputes over the scope of protected activities under the Mine Health and Safety Act and similar laws, proposed adding a new provision to the Act to ensure that internal whistleblowers were protected.

The NWC recommended expanding the definition to forestall any debate as to the scope of protected activities. As reflected in the e-mail to the Senate Banking Committee by the NWC on April 24, the NWC proposed incorporating by reference two provisions in the 2002 Sarbanes-Oxley Act (SOX). The first provision, Section 301, explicitly protected employees who raised concerns with their managers or compliance officials. The second provision, Section 1107, also protected employees who provided information to the Department of Justice or other federal law enforcement agencies, other than the SEC.

The NWC's proposal recommended adding a new subsection (iii) to the definition of protected activity, covering "disclosures" that were "required, authorized or protected" under these two sections of SOX, as well as protecting employees who made disclosures under "any other law, rule or regulation subject to the jurisdiction of the Securities and Exchange Commission." The reason for this recommendation was to make sure that certain disclosures frequently made by employees did not fall through the cracks. Internal disclosures to management through the "audit committee" process were one such "crack." With this change, Congress could avoid the frustrating judicial debates that had occurred under prior laws and ensure that a common sense approach toward whistleblowing would be followed.

The Senate Banking Committee approved this change, and it was incorporated, nearly word for word, into the final bill.

One might assume that this would end the argument. Not only did congressional and case-law precedent support the "common sense" interpretation given to these types of laws, but statutory langue was added that should have foreclosed any debate. But in whistleblower law, things are never easy.

The very first Court of Appeals case to address whistleblower protections under the Dodd-Frank Act was *Asadi v. G.E. Energy*. Corporate giant General Electric argued that internal whistleblowers were not protected under the new law, and it prevailed with this argument in federal district court. The employee pleaded his case before the U.S. Court of Appeals for the Fifth Circuit. The Court threw out the whistleblower's case at the request of G.E., ignoring years of case law protecting internal whistleblowers. The Court held that the law "only" protected "individuals who provide information relating to a violation of securities law to the SEC."

The argument raised by General Electric (and other corporations), and adopted by the Fifth Circuit Court of Appeals, sent a powerful message to whistleblowers: Beware of blowing the whistle to the boss. Beware of raising concerns to company compliance programs. Regardless of all the glowing praise highlighting the importance of internal compliance, corporate culture was still at war with whistleblowers. Raising concerns inside the company placed employees at risk of being fired, with no remedy under the Dodd-Frank Act's antiretaliation law.

The second appellate court to weigh whether internal whistleblowing would be protected under Dodd-Frank was the U.S. Court of Appeals for the Second Circuit in *Berman v. Neo@Ogilvy*. In a 2-1 decision, the Second Circuit sided with the whistleblower and affirmed a common sense reading of the law. The Court rejected the reasoning of the Fifth Circuit and held that employees who report their concerns within the company *are* protected under the law.

Whistleblowers must be aware of these inconsistent judicial decisions. They are a warning that corporations such as General Electric and their Wall Street supporters will use any trick in the book to make sure whistleblowers lose their case. Regardless of which interpretation eventually prevails, these cases further demonstrate that most companies remain hostile to whistleblowers, even to the detriment of their own internal compliance programs.

Why would companies consistently seek judicial findings that undermine their own internal compliance programs? Perhaps the answer can be found in the comprehensive 2015 study by the Institute of Internal Auditors. After surveying five hundred chief audit executives in North America, the institute found that a majority of auditors were directed to suppress valid complaints, and another 49 percent were directed "not to perform audit work in high-risk areas." The source of these troubling instructions was the companies' top management, including the chief executive officer (38 percent of requests) and the chief financial officer (24 percent). Even corporate officials responsible for oversight and accountability of the company, such as the audit committee, legal counsel, board of directors, and chief risk officer, accounted for 30 percent of these improper requests.

Auditors who questioned these demands found themselves in the same position as other whistleblowers. The Institute of Internal Auditors surveyed more than fourteen thousand auditors and found that "internal auditors who resist pressure to change their findings are at times subjected to negative consequences such as pay cuts, involuntary transfers to other positions, or even termination of employment." This study demonstrates that corporate executives are fully aware that auditors are being pressured to change their findings, and that auditors suffer retaliation when they resist. By arguing that internal whistleblowers, like the auditors surveyed by the institute, should be denied protection, these corporations are promoting bad corporate citizenship and undermining years of effort to create stronger internal controls within major corporations.

Where to Go?

The controversy surrounding Ceballos's whistleblowing is a harsh reminder that employees should think of themselves as whistleblowers long before they are fired. Only after he or she has accepted the label is an employee in a position to think about precisely to whom he or she is going to blow the whistle, and ensure that this disclosure right is fully protected under the law.

Employees such as Ceballos who want to disclose wrongdoing can go about the process in several ways. Ceballos, like most workers, probably didn't think that management's reaction to constructive criticism would be as hostile as it was. Lesson learned. This is why it is so important for employees to understand that their constructive criticisms may be interpreted as disloyalty, and they may be tagged, sooner than they could ever imagine, with the "whistle-blower" label.

Most workers act just like Ceballos or Phillips. The key is to find out whether reporting to the boss is protected—hopefully before raising a concern. But no matter what, employees must figure out whether their act of blowing the whistle is protected at the earliest possible moment—it will make the difference in what law covers them, *if any*.

Leading cases on internal whistleblowing are cited as:

- *Phillips v. Interior Board,* 500 F.2d 772 (D.C. Cir. 1974) (landmark case explaining why internal whistleblowing must be protected)

- *Mackowiak v. University Nuclear Systems,* 735 F.2d 1159 (9th Cir. 1984) (following *Phillips* and protecting internal whistleblowers under nuclear safety law)

- *Brown & Root v. Donovan,* 747 F.2d 1029 (5th Cir. 1984) (first court to reject *Phillips*)

- *Kansas Gas & Electric v. Brock,* 780 F.2d 1505 (10th Cir. 1985) (nuclear safety) (affirming *Phillips*)

- *Passaic Valley v. DOL,* 992 F.2d 474 (3rd Cir. 1993) (Clean Air Act) (affirming *Phillips*)

- *Garcetti v. Ceballos,* 547 U.S. 410 (2006) (First Amendment)

- *Berman v. Neo@Ogilvy LLC,* 801 F.3d 145 (2nd Cir. 2015) (explaining dispute in courts over scope of protected activity under the Dodd-Frank Act)

In 2011 the SEC issued landmark rules implementing the Dodd-Frank Act's corporate whistleblower rewards program. As part of those rules, the SEC acknowledged the importance of employee internal reports, and provided financial incentives to employees who utilize internal reporting systems. These rules are fully explained in Checklist 7, Dodd-Frank, Wall Street, and FCPA "Q&As."

The legislative history of the Whistleblower Protection Enhancement Act is set forth on pages 1-2 and 4-8 of Senate Report No. 112-155. Congress's explanation of what should be considered a protected disclosure is set forth in § 101 of Public Law 112-199, codified at 5 U.S.C. § 2302(f).

RULE 17

Beware of "Hotlines"

D o not blindly trust corporate-sponsored "hotlines" or corporate-sponsored compliance programs.

Every major employer—be it a publicly traded corporation or a government agency—must deal with a basic fact: Love them or hate them, employee whistleblowers are the single most important source of information uncovering fraud and abuse in the workplace. If you want to know what is really going on in your company, you need reasonable and effective channels for information to be disclosed and investigated.

As a consequence, there has been a worldwide proliferation of internal reporting programs. They usually start with a "hotline," for example a toll-free phone number, publicized on a poster, that urges employees who witness misconduct to place a confidential phone call to a responsible company agent. Thereafter, a compliance department supposedly independently investigates the "concern."

There's just one hitch. Is the hotline truly independent? Can it keep callers' identities confidential? Will there be a proper investigation? Is contacting the internal compliance group really the "right thing" to do?

The bottom line on using such programs is not simple. Even poorly run programs can help a would-be whistleblower. First, contacts with hotline programs document the fact that an employee legitimately raised a concern through channels approved by the employer. Second, they can demonstrate that the employer had "knowledge" of the employee's whistleblowing. Finally, they can create a documentary record related to the company's investigation of the claim. Demonstrating that a company or government agency covered up a legitimate concern can be important evidence of motive. On the other hand, if the hotline investigation vindicates the employee's concern, a company may never retaliate against the employee.

Consequently, whether or not an employee should contact a hotline should be carefully planned, monitored, and independently judged. These programs are inherently conflicted. They empower the fox to police the chickens. But they also can put the company on the spot. On the one hand they can force the company to live up to its commitment to transparency and accountability; on the other hand they can be used as a tool to cover up misconduct and gather evidence to destroy a whistleblower. The burden is on a company to demonstrate that its internal compliance program is truly independent, and that it will aggressively protect the employee. Today, most programs do not meet this standard. Programs managed by a company's general counsel cannot meet this standard. The burden is on the company to establish corporate governance procedures that are truly independent and will work, not just on paper but also in practice.

The Traps

But can a company properly investigate its own wrongdoing? What is the cost of compliance? What happens when it is cheaper to violate the law than to adhere to unpopular or overly burdensome regulations? What if the top managers are responsible for the crimes?

Case in point, Houston Lighting and Power Company and its subcontractor, EBASCO Constructors, Inc. In the 1980s Houston Lighting was investing millions in the construction of two nuclear power plants, known as the South Texas Project. One of the main companies hired to actually build the plant was EBASCO. The South Texas Project was plagued by regulatory violations, building delays, and cost overruns. They were under heightened regulatory scrutiny. In response to these pressures, Houston Lighting established an "independent" internal compliance program known as SAFETEAM. SAFETEAM was given the authority to receive and investigate safety complaints filed by employees. Houston Lighting and EBASCO heavily promoted the program. As a Department of Labor review concluded, "postings about SAFETEAM" were "quite visible" throughout the plant, and employees were strongly encouraged to contact this "independent" safety program.

On its face, the SAFETEAM program was very reasonable and operated in a manner consistent with most "hotlines" and corporate employee concern programs. It offered employees a safe haven to raise concerns, and it promised a full and objective investigation into safety violations. What company would not want to promote safety and compliance with regulatory rules? What company would want its nuclear power plant to have an accident?

Just ask Ronald J. Goldstein. He would know. Goldstein was hired by EBASCO as a craft supervisor at the South Texas Project. In the summer of 1985 he identified serious safety problems onsite, including the failure of project managers to follow "correct safety inspection procedure(s)," the "falsification of documents," the failure of employees to "issue non-conformance reports on safety problems," and "serious" quality control violations that impacted systems "critical" for the safe construction of the plant. Consistent with company policy, Goldstein reported his concerns to SAFETEAM, the "independent safety organization."

But what Houston Lighting and EBASCO did not tell their employees was that the company did not believe reports to its SAFETEAM program were legally protected. In other words, they believed they could fire employees who raised safety concerns with SAFETEAM. Goldstein learned the hard way. After raising his concerns with SAFETEAM, he was fired.

In the beginning everything went according to plan. He filed a whistle-blower complaint under federal law with the U.S. Department of Labor. After a hearing the DOL ruled that Goldstein's termination was illegal. The DOL found that Goldstein's reports to SAFETEAM were protected activities. How could they not be? He raised safety concerns to a responsible "independent" organization designed to investigate and fix problems in order to ensure that the nuclear plant was safe. The judge ordered that Goldstein be reinstated with full back pay. He also awarded compensatory damages for emotional distress and attorney fees and costs. His employment record was cleared up, and references to his termination were expunged.

Lynn Martin, President George W. Bush's secretary of the DOL, affirmed the judge's ruling. She ruled that SAFETEAM was "an organization established by Houston Lighting and Power Company to receive and investigate allegations of safety and quality violations" and that "reporting violations" to SAFETEAM was therefore "protected activity."

The company appealed to the U.S. Court of Appeals for the Fifth Circuit, arguing that SAFETEAM was simply an internal management program and that in order to be legally protected, employees had to contact government regulators. According to the company, Goldstein's case had to be dismissed because his complaints to SAFETEAM were not covered under the federal nuclear whistleblower law. Obviously this limitation was not presented in any of the literature or "posters" that encouraged employees to report safety concerns to SAFETEAM. Who would contact a hotline program if the propaganda encouraging such contacts also told employees they could be fired simply for making a hotline disclosure!?! Indeed, reading the company propaganda, one would readily expect that employees who filed such allegations would be rewarded, not punished.

Incredibly, the appeals court agreed with the company. The court reversed Secretary Martin's ruling and concluded that the federal nuclear safety whistleblower law did *not* protect employees who made disclosures to SAFETEAM. According to the court, whistleblowers had to contact a government agency to be protected, and SAFETEAM, although marketed to employees as an independent safety program designed to investigate complaints, was, legally speaking, a sham. Contacts with the program offered no protection whatsoever, and companies were free to use these programs to identify whistleblowers and fire them.

Goldstein lost his right to back pay, compensatory damages, and attorney fees. He lost his right to work at the South Texas Project. His termination was upheld.

In the wake of the Goldstein decision, and other similar rulings stripping protection from employees who raised nuclear safety concerns with corporate-run programs, Congress amended the nuclear whistleblower law to explicitly protect such internal reports. But the precedent was set, and even today it is still uncertain whether reports to internal hotlines or compliance programs are fully protected. Where a statute explicitly protects such disclosures, the law is clear. But in the absence of such rules, contacting an internal hotline may result in retaliation that is outside the law's protection.

In a sense, Houston Lighting and its contractor EBASCO won the legal battle. But ultimately they lost the war, as employee confidence in "hotlines" and compliance programs was seriously eroded.

At the Tennessee Valley Authority (TVA) another problem with hotline programs arose. TVA hired an outside corporation, the Quality Technology Company, to develop and operate an on-site "employee concerns program" that would investigate employee safety concerns and protect the confidentiality of any worker who filed charges with the program. The program worked, and the number of employees who filed credible safety issues "far exceeded the expectations" of TVA. Instead of welcoming this development, TVA upper management became concerned, and officials for the company actually complained that the Quality Technology Company was "finding too many problems." One official went so far as to call the Quality Technology program a "cancer" that had to be "dealt with." The solution: TVA terminated its contract with Quality Technology. All Quality Technology investigators lost their jobs, and TVA's independent employee concerns program was ended. Quality Technology's investigators filed a lawsuit claiming they lost their jobs in retaliation for performing a critical safety function for TVA, but their case was dismissed on legal technicalities.

Hotline programs are under no duty to help whistleblowers. They are voluntary programs, and the nature and extent of their "investigations" are outside of the control of the employee. There is no requirement that these programs offer employees complete or accurate information about their legal rights. In other words, the programs exist for the benefit of the government/corporation; they are not "legal service" programs for whistleblowers.

As an example, in 2010 a federal inspector general's office published a brochure entitled "Fraud, Waste, and Abuse." The pamphlet accurately set forth examples of how workers can identify fraud and had a section entitled "Common Fraud Schemes—What to Look for from Your Suppliers, Vendors, Contractors, or Subcontractors." The flier had specific advice on how to report fraud allegations: "Contact" the Inspector General's "Hotline." It also had a page entitled "Whistleblower Protection" that set forth two laws designed to protect whistleblowers.

What was wrong with the flier? There was nothing wrong with what it said. The problem was what it did not say. The flier failed to mention the most powerful federal antifraud law, the False Claims Act. Under this law, whistleblowers not only can obtain protection from retaliatory discharge, they are also entitled to a reward based on any financial recovery obtained by the United States. In other words, if a whistleblower provided proof of a fraud to an Office of the Inspector General hotline, and the inspector general investigated the fraud and collected $10 million from the contractor in fines, what would the whistleblower obtain? Nothing, except maybe a pink slip and the "right" to try to get your job back.

But under the FCA, the very same whistleblower (if he or she had properly filed the claim) would be entitled to 15 percent to 30 percent of the monies collected by the government as a reward for having the courage to "do the right thing." The inspector general's information materials failed to mention this most important law. The office wanted the information from the employee, but did not want the employee to file a proper claim for a reward.

Legislative Reforms

Government or corporate sponsored "hotlines" sometimes work as intended. For example, in 2008 *Compliance Week* published the results of a study of hotline calls made over a five-year period in 650 various companies (small and large businesses engaged in various industries and services). The hotline programs handled 280,000 calls, determined that 65 percent of the allegations submitted warranted investigation, and concluded that in 45 percent of the investigated cases the whistleblowers' claims were valid and corrective action was warranted. As these statistics and other studies demonstrate, hotline-initiated investigations of whistleblower complaints can be instrumental in weeding out fraud and vindicating the whistleblower.

But the failure of internal compliance programs became evident in 2001 and 2002. Wall Street was shocked by the overnight disintegration of two highly respected, multinational corporations that employed tens of thousands of workers and supposedly were worth billions upon billions of dollars. These two companies, Enron and WorldCom, imploded, literally, overnight. Their highly rated and expensive blue-chip stocks crashed in value, and the companies went bankrupt. What were once highly respected and powerful corporations became worthless; shareholders lost fortunes, including billions in retirement accounts. The losses were caused by good old-fashioned fraud—both criminal and civil. The managers of the companies were able to hide behind numerous complex financial transactions to deceive their investors and the public.

In each case there were whistleblowers who tried to identify and fix the problems in-house: Sherron Watkins at Enron and Cynthia Cooper at WorldCom. As in other cases, employees were in the best position to see what was happening and uncover potential violations. But in each case, after the frauds had their devastating impact on investors, it was painfully obvious that the companies lacked any reliable in-house compliance program capable of responding to legitimate employee concerns. In each case the entire network of internal and external auditors had failed to detect or report massive civil and criminal fraud. The whistleblowers were either ignored or harassed. In the case of Watkins, the company's lawyers started to plot her termination—and like the lawyers who prevailed against Goldstein at the South Texas Project, they delighted in the fact that the law did not protect Watkins because she had only availed herself of internal reporting mechanisms.

As the Senate Judiciary Committee noted during its investigation of the scandals, there were no reliable "gatekeepers" who could "detect and deter fraud." Instead, the company managers, lawyers, and accountants "brought all their skills and knowledge to bear" "covering up" the frauds. These shortfalls prompted Congress, in 2002, to enact the historic Sarbanes-Oxley Act. Key aspects of the reform legislation were statutory mandates for internal compliance programs.

Although a modest start, for the first time Congress enacted mandatory rules governing internal compliance programs. First, every publicly traded corporation was required to establish, by law, an independent "audit committee." The committee was required to create procedures for the "receipt, retention, and treatment of complaints" filed by employees with the audit committee.

Second, the audit committee was also required to establish internal employee concerns programs that would permit any employee to file "confidential" or "anonymous" complaints "regarding questionable accounting or auditing matters." In other words, every publicly traded corporation was mandated to create procedures that would protect the identity of employees who reported allegations of stock or accounting fraud to the audit committee. Because it is often easy to identify a whistleblower based on the nature of the allegations filed (often a supervisor knows which employee reported him or her to the authorities based on the nature of the concerns and which employees would have knowledge of those concerns), companies were required to create safeguards to prevent the identification of employee whistleblowers.

Third, Congress also enacted an antiretaliation law that specifically ensured that employee complaints raised with an audit committee would have the same legal protections as complaints raised directly with government regulators. In the context of corporate whistleblower disclosures protected under the SOX law, the dilemma faced by Goldstein based on his contacts with SAFETEAM were statutorily fixed. Internal disclosures were explicitly included in the legal definition of a protected disclosure.

But the SOX law did not go far enough. Corporate law firms worked endlessly to find loopholes in the law, and some companies even fired their chief compliance officers after they identified too many problems. In the end, it is often impossible for a company to balance the legal requirement to encourage (and protect) internal disclosures of misconduct, while at the same time trying to promote the stock value of a company. The pressure to hide bad news from investors is often impossible to overcome, and firing a whistleblower may be a much cheaper alternative than risking the fallout from the investor community.

On June 30, 2008, the "Close the Contractor Fraud Loophole Act" was signed into law. The act—just a few sentences added onto a large appropriations bill—barely scratched the surface of attacking fraud in U.S. government contracting. Its main purpose was to require the Federal Acquisition Regulatory Council to enact new rules that would require government contractors to create truly effective internal compliance programs. This time the target was large government contractors (companies that obtained government grants or contracts of $5 million or more).

Five months later the Council amended the Federal Acquisitions Regulations (FAR) and published new rules for corporate internal compliance programs designed to finally close the loopholes in the sentencing guidelines and SOX.

These rules, although only mandatory in the context of corporations that engage in large government contracting, ultimately set forth the framework for an effective internal compliance program. The main requirements included the following:

- *Mandatory Disclosures.* All contractors and grant recipients (regardless of the $5 million threshold that applies to other parts of the act) can be debarred or suspended from all government contracting if they fail to "timely disclose" to an inspector general "credible evidence" of a "violation of Federal criminal law involving fraud, conflict of interest, bribery, or gratuity violations" or any violation of the "civil False Claims Act."

- *Code of Ethics.* Contractors are required to have a "written code of business ethics and conduct" made available to every employee who works under a government contract.

- *Culture of Compliance.* Contractors must "exercise due diligence" in order to "detect" and "prevent" criminal conduct and must "promote an organizational culture that encourages ethical conduct and a commitment to compliance with the law."

- *Internal Compliance Program.* Contractors must establish a compliance and an ethics program. All employees, contractors, and subcontractors must obtain training in these programs.

- *Internal Control System.* The government contractors must establish procedures to "facilitate" the "timely discovery of improper conduct in connection with Government contracts" and procedures that "ensure corrective measures are promptly instituted."

- *Employee Hotline.* The rule mandates an "internal reporting mechanism, such as a hotline, which allows for anonymity or confidentiality by which employees may report suspected instances of improper conduct."

Unfortunately, even these aggressive new rules did not fully fix the problems. They continue to parcel out compliance. Government contractors do not need to report all criminal violations—just those that immediately impact their contract. The ethics code only needs to be provided to employees working under the government contract. The mandate for an "ethical" work "culture" only applies when employees are performing work under a federal contract. The "internal control system" only monitors misconduct and violations of law related to the contract. The compliance rules do not apply to violations of other federal laws, such as federal environmental statutes, federal worker safety statutes, or consumer safety laws. Thus, a company can have two compliance programs—a substandard program filled with loopholes and conflicts governing violations of federal law and public safety, and another program, narrowly tailored just to monitor government spending. Workers who contact the hotline would bear the risk that they call the right phone number.

Should Employees Avoid Hotlines?

Question: "Are corporate compliance and ethics programs just window-dressing?"
Answer: "In many companies, probably yes."
                      Donna Boehme, Former Chief Compliance Officer, BP

A corporate compliance program is not a substitute for a strategy to protect the whistleblower. Employees must take steps to defend themselves, and not simply rely upon the goodwill of an in-house compliance program, regardless of the best intentions of the compliance officers. There is no hard-and-fast rule concerning hotline communications. It depends on the quality of the in-house program and the nature of the employee's concerns. However, before contacting any hotline, whether a corporation or the government runs it, an employee should take the following steps.

STEP 1: ENSURE THE CONTACT IS PROTECTED UNDER LAW

Employees need to be sure that their disclosures to compliance are protected under law. If the contact to the hotline is not fully protected, whistleblowers should find another method to report the misconduct.

STEP 2: THE FALSE CLAIMS ACT AND OTHER *QUI TAM* PROCEDURES ARE SUPERIOR TO THE BEST INTERNAL COMPLIANCE PROCEDURES

If employees want to complain about fraud in government contracting, large-scale tax fraud, or violations of the securities and commodities exchange laws, they may want to consider utilizing the respective *qui tam* laws applicable to their case. The False Claims Act is the most powerful antifraud law; it contains provisions that help protect an employee's identity, and it requires the government to conduct an investigation. It is the best mechanism to force a company to fix a problem. It also provides for substantial rewards for whistleblowers who risk their careers in order to expose wrongdoing.

STEP 3: RESEARCH THE IN-HOUSE PROGRAM

Before using an in-house program, employees should do some research into the program. Is the program required under the Sarbanes-Oxley Act or Federal Acquisitions Regulations? Employees should try to find out if other workers have alleged retaliation after using an in-house program (that information may be online). An attorney should be able to conduct more detailed reviews of an in-house program, including a review of materials published by the corporation in order to determine whether the company is contractually bound to follow its own in-house compliance procedures and whether the company procedures comply with acceptable "best practices."

STEP 4: DOCUMENT EVERYTHING

Whistleblowers need to create a detailed paper trial. If a lawsuit were to develop, contacts with the hotline program will be very relevant. Employees can also conduct civil discovery into the company's hotline records after a lawsuit is filed. These records can be extremely helpful in demonstrating protected activity, employer knowledge, retaliation, or pretext.

STEP 5: DON'T REST ON LAURELS

Whistleblowers cannot assume the system will work. The contact with a hotline often is just the first step in a series of disclosures. It is common for workers to first raise a concern with a supervisor, then elevate the concern to an internal compliance department, and finally file a concern with a government agency. But simply relying on a hotline investigation to fix a problem or provide protection is naive.

STEP 6: DON'T TAKE LEGAL ADVICE FROM A COMPLIANCE OFFICER

Compliance officers and hotline investigators work for the company; they do not work for the employees. They are under no obligation to provide employees with complete or accurate advice. They are under no obligation to inform employees of their rights or the laws that may protect them. Even if whistleblowers contact a government inspector general, the government official need not tell them of their right to obtain a financial reward, and they have no obligation to advise them to file a proper claim to obtain a reward.

STEP 7: DETERMINE WHETHER CONTACTING THE HOTLINE IS NECESSARY

If a whistleblower has already attempted to solve a problem internally within a company, contacting the hotline may be futile.

STEP 8: BE SKEPTICAL ABOUT CONFIDENTIALITY

Many hotline programs promise confidentiality. Under the Sarbanes-Oxley Act and Federal Acquisitions Regulations, companies are required to grant confidentiality to employees. However, it is well-known that the very nature of an employee's complaint can act to "fingerprint" the worker. Often, only a small group of workers are aware of the details concerning a regulatory violation. When the hotline investigator commences his or her review of the complaint, it is often not difficult for the employer to figure out the identity of the whistleblower.

STEP 9: AVOID PROGRAMS MANAGED BY CORPORATE ATTORNEYS

Whistleblowers should investigate who manages the compliance program. Some compliance programs report directly to a company's chief executive officer or to an independent audit committee. These programs tend to have more integrity than compliance programs that report to, or are managed by, the company's general counsel. Not surprisingly, company attorneys focus on protecting employers from lawsuits, not fixing problems. As is more fully explained in Rule 18, compliance programs that report to the office of general counsel (or other company attorneys) should be avoided or approached with extreme caution.

STEP 10: GIVE THEM ROPE TO HANG THEMSELVES

The failure of a corporation to properly investigate a hotline concern can constitute evidence of a cover-up and evidence that a company was hostile to the whistleblower. The hotline records can be obtained as part of pretrial discovery. These files may contain significant information that could help prove retaliation, including statements by various managers and factual findings related to the underlying allegations of misconduct. Under the False Claims Act, the failure of a company to properly investigate a hotline allegation can be essential in helping an employee prove his or her case. The hotline allegation can demonstrate that a company was aware of the fraud against the government and failed to take reasonable action to prevent or correct the fraud. Even when a company tries to use its hotline investigation to demonstrate that an employee's concern had no basis, an employee can still muster additional facts that the compliance officers failed to consider and impeach the company's conduct.

Given the sensitivity of internal compliance programs, and the pressure that is sometimes placed on compliance officers to cover up problems, it is not uncommon for compliance officers themselves to become whistleblowers and/ or witnesses in an employee's case.

Thus, pursued thoughtfully and carefully, a disclosure to a hotline can be an important part of a successful whistleblower case.

STEP 11: BLOWING THE WHISTLE ON THE LACK OF PROPER "INTERNAL CONTROLS"

A publicly traded company that lacks effective "internal controls" necessary to detect securities fraud, ensure accurate corporate disclosures, and detect improper payments (such as paying bribes) may be in violation of the "bookkeeping" and accounting requirements of the Foreign Corrupt Practices Act and other securities laws. These failures can result in large fines, and under the Dodd-Frank Act a whistleblower (including, in the appropriate circumstances, a whistleblower who works directly in a company's compliance program) can qualify for a large financial reward by exposing these defects. Recent cases have held that employees who blow the whistle on corporate violations of "internal control standards" engage in protected activity under the Sarbanes-Oxley Act.

The New Dodd-Frank Rules

On June 13, 2011, the Securities and Exchange Commission published new rules implementing the whistleblower rewards provisions of the Dodd-Frank Act. These rules contained two provisions that would enhance internal whistleblower protections and corporate compliance. See Rule 19.

───────────── **PRACTICE TIPS** ─────────────

- The Sarbanes-Oxley Act requirement mandating that audit committees include a confidential employee concerns program is codified at 15 U.S.C. § 78(f)(4). The Federal Acquisition Regulations mandating compliance and ethics programs are located at 48 C.F.R. Chapter 1 and Subpart 3.900.

- In 2011 the Securities and Exchange Commission and the Commodity Futures Trading Commission implemented whistleblower reward rules mandated under the Dodd-Frank Act. These rules created incentives for employees to report potential violations to corporate compliance programs. These new incentives are codified at SEC Final Rules 17 C.F.R. §§ 240.21F-4(b)(7) and F-6(a)(4) and CFTC Final Rules 17 C.F.R. §§ 165.2(i)(3) and 165.9(b)(4).

- Rule 19 fully explains the circumstances when compliance officials, auditors, and corporate directors can qualify for rewards under Dodd-Frank. It also explains how employees can qualify for rewards if they intentionally report fraud to their managers or to a company's compliance department.

RULE 18

Don't Talk to Company Lawyers

At the height of the war in Iraq, employees from the U.S. government's largest defense contractor, Kellogg Brown & Root, Inc. (better known as KBR), witnessed gross frauds and reported them to the company's compliance investigators stationed in Iraq. They provided highly credible information that KBR employees were involved in bribery and "presented inflated and fraudulent bills" for "terrible" work paid for by the taxpayers. They did not know that the "compliance" program was managed by the company's general counsel, whose primary goal was to protect the company, not combat corruption. The compliance investigators (none of whom were attorneys) sent the investigatory reports that confirmed the frauds up the chain of command and, ultimately, to the company lawyers in Houston, Texas. The lawyers' job was not to disclose misconduct to the government but to advise the company on how to escape liability. None of the information disclosed by the whistleblowers was ever provided to the government. Instead the information collected could be used to help KBR defend against a government investigation, or a whistleblower claim if one was ever to be filed.

Years later, one of these KBR employees, frustrated that the company had gotten away with the frauds, filed a complaint under the False Claims Act. The whistleblower, Harry Barko, had worked for KBR and suspected that other employees would confirm what he saw: widespread fraud in KBR's contracting practices that cost U.S. taxpayers millions. He subpoenaed the compliance department. KBR objected to the release of the investigatory files, claiming the documents were protected under corporate attorney–client privilege. Their basis for objecting was simple. KBR's compliance program, known as the Code of Business Conduct (COBC), ultimately reported to the company's general counsel; therefore all its documents, including direct evidence of fraud provided to the company internal whistleblowers, were confidential.

The trial judge reviewed the contested documents in camera (privately), without giving a copy to Mr. Barko's counsel. After looking at the materials, he ordered KBR to produce the documents for Mr. Barko's review. The judge noted that the documents contained no legal advice, were not written by lawyers, and the employees who were interviewed were never directly advised that their interviews were covered under an attorney-client or attorney-work product privilege. Moreover, because the interviews were conducted as part of the company's standard compliance program—a program all large government contractors were required to have under federal law—the judge determined that the primary purpose of the investigation was business related and not part of a protected attorney investigation.

The judge looked at the interviews and called the material "eye-openers." Clearly, KBR wanted to keep the material secret because it was damaging and supported findings that KBR committed serious fraud while profiting from its war contracts. Describing the contents of the COBC reports, the court spelled out the direct evidence of contract fraud the company had uncovered as part of its internal compliance review:

- "Preferential treatment" to a favored subcontractor;

- KBR employees accepting payoffs to illegally steer business to an unqualified subcontractor;

- Permitting the less-qualified subcontractor to improperly undercut bids submitted by companies that were not paying bribes by giving them inside information;

- Approving contracts that were more expensive to the United States, with "terrible completion performance" and "regular attempts to double bill";

- Awarding a contract despite the "bid being twice another bid from a competent contractor" (the bid was twice as expensive as a more competent competitor);

- Paying the full bills from a favored subcontractor (which had given payoffs to KBR employees), despite the work being "incomplete and late" and "substandard";

- Paying "ballooned" costs (three times the contract price) for work, even when performance was terrible.

The trial judge ordered the reports to be produced.

KBR, with strong support from the U.S. Chamber of Commerce, filed an emergency appeal to the U.S. Court of Appeals District of Columbia Circuit. The basis of their appeal was simple: KBR's COBC program was ultimately managed by the company's law department. Thus, all the investigatory files and interview notes were protected from disclosure under attorney-client privilege. According to KBR, it did not matter that the employees were misled about the nature of the program they were reporting to.

The U.S. Court of Appeals sided with KBR. The documents would remain secret, despite the fact that they proved that taxpayers had been robbed. Nor did it matter that none of the persons interviewed at KBR were directly told that the interviews were covered under company's attorney-client privilege.

The Court of Appeals justified its holding by reasoning that "[t]he attorney-client privilege protects confidential employee communications made during a business's internal investigation led by company lawyers." Corporate compliance reviews managed by general counsel are such internal investigations. Because the privilege applied not only to the lawyers themselves but also to "agents and subordinates" working under the "direction or control of the lawyer," everyone working within compliance can fall under the privilege. In the case of KBR, this included its entire compliance program. In this way a company can choose to hide the results of an internal investigation (if the results are harmful), release the results (if they do not vindicate the whistleblower), or use some (or all) of the investigatory materials to build a defense against a government sanction or a whistleblower case.

One of the justifications used by the Court of Appeals to justify its broad holding was that it did not want to "inject uncertainty into the application of the attorney-client and work product protection to internal investigations." The Court effectively protected KBR's COBC compliance program by defining it as an arm of the company's Office of Legal Counsel. The Code of Conduct, designed in theory to promote ethical behavior, became a tool for the lawyers. Instead of supporting a rule that would promote independent compliance programs, the Appeals Court went in the opposite direction. They provided legal support for keeping compliance programs under the tight control of lawyers primarily tasked with protecting companies from liability and defending against whistleblower lawsuits, undermining the trust and transparency necessary to change corporate culture.

The incriminating KBR documents remained secret. The evidence of fraud, which the employees wanted to report, was suppressed. Mr. Barko, the U.S. government, and the American public were denied access to these materials.

The main lesson from KBR is to be aware of for whom compliance officials work before talking with them. In Mr. Barko's case, KBR used its compliance program to find out who the whistleblowers were, learn what evidence they had against the company, and prepare legal defenses should the government learn about the allegations and initiate its own investigation.

> *"It doesn't take a pig farmer from Iowa to smell the stench of conflict in that arrangement."*
>
> Senator Charles Grassley on General Counsels
> running compliance programs

But the ability for companies like KBR to twist compliance programs to serve their self-interest is far greater them simply hiding information. KBR, the corporate client, can always decide to "waive" the privilege and release the attorney-client information any time it is to their advantage. If the documents had been critical of Mr. Barko, KBR could have used them to attack his credibility. If the reports demonstrated that the company was a good corporate citizen, they could be released to impeach the "good faith" of the whistleblower or to demonstrate to a court how thorough and objective its program is. Under the KBR precedent, the purported goals of a lawyer-run compliance program can be twisted and, instead of promoting ethical corporate behavior, become a prime enabler for corporate crime.

Before you speak with company lawyers or compliance officials who report to lawyers, beware of their incentives. They may be hired to protect the company and not you. In reality, they may be part of a cover-up, like in the KBR case. The company may use your own words against you and actually try to blame you for the problems you report. As a number of courts have recognized, these lawyer-run compliance programs are legally permitted to throw any employee "under the bus" if it is in the company's interest.

The division between compliance programs that report to the general counsel and compliance programs that are independent (reporting directly to the CEO or board of directors) is the biggest disputed issue within the compliance profession. Leading experts in this area, along with a majority of compliance professionals, all oppose general counsel controlled compliance programs. They strongly argue that for compliance to work, the programs must be transparent, trustworthy, and independent. Employees do not, and should not, trust lawyer-run compliance programs. Always remember that the company's lawyer is only required to act in the company's best interest, not yours. Unlike other company officials who can be compelled to release their e-mails or other documents if a case is ever filed, lawyers can use attorney-client privilege to hide evidence that may help your case.

Compliance officials are not to blame; they often speak out against lawyer-controlled program and even become whistleblowers. This is why, as explained in Rule 15, the Securities and Exchange Commission created a specific rule permitting auditors, directors, and all employees who perform compliance functions to blow the whistle on the company and obtain a reward. The SEC has paid rewards to compliance officials.

Most compliance professionals, whether or not they ultimately report to the general counsel, want their programs to be independent. A March 2013 survey of ten thousand compliance professionals, conducted by the Society of Corporate Compliance and Ethics and the Health Care Compliance Association, demonstrated this point. The question was simple: Should corporate compliance officials report to the company's general counsel? The response was overwhelming—"88.5% of the surveyed compliance professionals were opposed to the corporate counsel serving as the compliance officer." According to the survey, employees who worked in compliance understand there is an inherent conflict of interest between a compliance function ("encouraging reports") and the job performed by a company attorney ("defending the company").

Senator Charles Grassley, as chairman of the Senate Finance Committee, also weighed in on this issue. He pointed out that the roles of general counsel and chief compliance officer were distinct, and that merging these two functions created a conflict of interest. As an Iowan, his words were blunt: "It doesn't take a pig farmer from Iowa to smell the stench of conflict in that arrangement."

New York Ethics Opinion 650

Should there be any doubt as to where a lawyer-run compliance program's loyalties lie, the cautions approved by Opinion 650 of the New York State Bar Association Committee on Professional Ethics settle the issue. The Committee looked at the corporate attorney's conflicts of interest and explained the nature of the warning that must be given to employees who contact an attorney-managed compliance program. These warnings, which are almost never given, are designed to ensure that an employee who contacts an attorney-managed program clearly knows that the program is designed to protect the company, not the worker or whistleblower.

In its opinion, the committee addressed the question of whether a corporate attorney could participate in a "compliance" program under which employees are required to report illegal or unethical behavior. The Committee determined that lawyers, as well as those individuals operating under the attorneys (such as paralegals or investigators), could participate in such programs only if certain precautionary measures were taken. The Committee approved an adverse-interest script, drafted by the company seeking the ethics opinion.

The company mandated that this script be read to all persons who called into the company's compliance program:

When it appears that a caller's interests may differ from or there is a reasonable possibility that such interests may be "in conflict" with the Company's interests:

1. *Determine whether the caller is represented by counsel. If yes, make the following statement: "The Company's policy requires that you report non-compliance with the law or other unethical behavior. However, as you are represented by counsel, I can only talk to you through your counsel. Please have him/her call me or give me his/her name and I would be happy to call him/him."*

2. *If the caller is unrepresented by counsel, please make the following statement: "I want to caution you that I am an attorney for the Company and not for you or other employees. Therefore, while I can record your complaint, I cannot and will not give you legal advice, and you should not understand our conversation to consist of such advice. I do advise you to seek your own counsel, however, as your interests and the Company's may differ. Having said this, I would be happy to listen to your complaint," etc.*

The Committee also noted that although the Code of Professional Conduct is addressed to lawyers, the lawyers must diligently supervise *non-lawyers* to ensure that the rules of professional responsibility are not violated. In other words, the non-lawyers also have to provide these warnings to the employees who call into the compliance hotline. The New York rule is consistent with the general ABA rules governing attorney conduct.

What to Do If the Company's Attorneys Knock on Your Door

The key advice for any potential whistleblowers who may find themselves in the middle of a compliance investigation (or whose concerns may have triggered the investigation) is to contact your own attorney before you make any disclosures. Whether or not to meet with or provide information to a company lawyer (or compliance personnel who work for the lawyer) must be made on a case-by-case basis. You must understand that the company lawyer does not represent you, and may use any information you provide (or don't provide) against you.

Various hypothetical situations call for differing responses. For example, assume you are already giving information confidentially to the government. Your allegations trigger a DOJ investigation. The company's lawyers (or outside counsel), not knowing that you were the source, ask to interview you as part of their defense to the DOJ review. If you refuse to be interviewed, you may tag yourself as a whistleblower or, at a minimum, not a "team player." Refusal to be interviewed will raise suspicion. On the other hand, assume you agree to the interview but withhold information. The company may use your statement to impeach you in the future, stating that either you did not really know the facts or were holding information back for nefarious reasons. The decision whether to be interviewed, and what to say during the interview, is highly strategic and must be well thought out. It is highly recommended that any such decision be made after consulting with your own attorney, an attorney whose allegiance is to you and you alone.

Another frequent issue arises when the company informs you that you are a witness in an investigation and then offers to pay for an attorney to represent you personally due to a potential conflict of interest. This is very common, especially in Foreign Corrupt Practices Act cases, where individuals can be held personally accountable, along with the company itself. Don't be fooled by this offer. You get what you pay for. When companies hire outside attorneys to represent their employees, these outside lawyers are almost always beholden to the company that pays their fee. In most every case these attorneys will work hand in hand with the company lawyers, share your information with the company, and give you bad advice.

The decision whether to let the company hire a lawyer for you and what you say to that lawyer is another strategic decision. If all the other company witnesses are letting the company hire and pay for their attorneys, you will stick out like a sore thumb if you refuse. When you talk with a company-sponsored outside attorney, regardless of what the lawyer says, understand that he or she cannot be trusted. The attorney was picked by the company, is paid for by the company, and knows where his or her next (very large) paycheck is coming from.

In each of these circumstances, you need a lawyer who understands the law, can advise you as to whether you could qualify for a reward, and who has undivided loyalty to your best interests. Working with your own counsel is the best way to navigate these extremely treacherous waters. Bad decisions can undermine your credibility, arm the company with defenses against your whistleblowing, or even lead you to becoming a scapegoat for the problems. Good decisions can give you a door into the company's strategies and help you and the government understand how the company may be manipulating witnesses or trying to cover up wrongdoing.

- *Upjohn Co. v. United States*, 449 U.S. 383 (1981) (the Supreme Court decision discussing when attorney-client privilege applies to a compliance investigation).

- *In re: KBR*, 756 F.3d 754 (D.C. Cir. 2014) (broadly defining corporate attorney-client privilege in the context of compliance investigations).

- *U.S. ex rel. Barko v. Halliburton Co.*, No. 1:05-cv-2276, Opinion and Order dated March 6, 2014 (D.D.C.) (district court docket in the *KBR* cases).

- New York State Bar Association Committee on Professional Ethics Opinion 650, July 30, 1993; available at http://old.nysba. org/Content/ContentFolders/EthicsOpinions/Opinions601675/ EO_650.pdf (ethical rule discussing the duties attorneys are supposed to follow when participating in compliance programs and investigations).

- The RAND Center for Corporate Ethics and Governance, *"Transforming Compliance: Emerging Paradigms for Boards, Management, Compliance Officers, and Government"*; published at www.rand. org/pubs/conf_proceedings/CF322.html (presents an excellent discussion of the policy issues facing compliance programs, especially those run by general counsel).

RULE 19

Auditors and Compliance Officials: Qualify for Rewards

Almost all large corporations in the United States (and worldwide), including most banks, hospitals, government contractors, and every publicly-traded company, are required to have compliance programs, auditing departments, and strong procedures for "internal controls." All companies that trade on the U.S. Stock Exchanges are required to have employee concern programs capable of accepting and investigating confidential or anonymous internal employee allegations regarding "questionable" accounting or auditing practices. Thousands of compliance professionals (including auditors, accountants, and lawyers) work within these programs. The work they do is inextricably linked to whistleblowing.

These compliance professionals are on the front line of uncovering and reporting fraud. In 2015 the Institute of Internal Auditors, a trade association of more than 180,000 members in 170 countries, published its study *Politics of Internal Auditing*. As part of the study five hundred North American chief audit executives (CAEs) were questioned as to the pressures confronting auditors. A majority of CAEs reported that they had been directed to suppress important audit findings.

- 55 percent of the CAEs were directed to omit important findings from their audit reports;

- 49 percent were directed "not to perform audit work in high-risk areas";

- 32 percent were instructed to audit "low-risk" areas, in part so that executives could "retaliate against another individual."

The pressure to change audit reports came from the top (see **Figure 10**). When asked who "directed" them "to suppress or significantly modify a valid internal audit finding," the CAEs reported that 38 percent of these requests came from a company's Chief Executive Officer, 24 percent came from a Chief Financial Officer, and 12 percent came from the Board of Directors. Significantly, 18 percent of the requests came from persons with significant oversight responsibility (the Chief Compliance Officer, legal or general counsel, the Chief Risk Officer, or the company's Audit Committee).

Figure 10

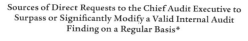

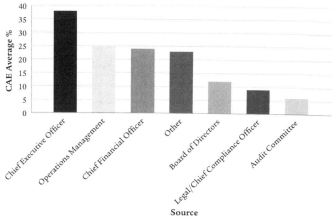

Sources of Direct Requests to the Chief Audit Executive to Surpass or Significantly Modify a Valid Internal Audit Finding on a Regular Basis*

Source

Source: IIA Research Foundation Survey (2015)
*Total percentage is greater than 100 because more than one person can make a request.

A comprehensive survey of 14,518 auditors from 166 countries reported vicious retaliation when the auditors refused to change their findings. Forms of retaliation included pay cuts, transfers to other positions, terminations, being eased into retirement, budget cuts, exclusion from important meetings, being ostracized, audit department outsourcing, and hostile working conditions.

After Congress enacted the Dodd-Frank Act, authorizing corporate whistleblowers to obtain monetary rewards for reporting violations of securities and commodity trading laws, and the Foreign Corrupt Practices Act, the U.S. Chamber of Commerce worked overtime to block auditors and compliance officials from obtaining whistleblower protection. The group vigorously argued that employees paid by the company to uncover, report, or correct problems should not be afforded an opportunity to obtain a whistleblower reward. The Chamber advocated for a strict rule prohibiting all workers who had corporate oversight duties from collecting rewards.

The whistleblower advocacy community quickly spoke up about the injustices suffered by compliance officials for doing their job "too well," and the Securities and Exchange Commission was provided with examples of compliance officials being fired in retaliation for their audit findings. Directors, auditors, and compliance officials are often the first to see or understand the nature of a company's illegal actions, and whistleblower advocates argued that prohibiting them from qualifying for rewards would seriously undermine the ability of the government to learn about major frauds.

In 2010–2011 the SEC, after conducting public rulemaking proceedings, made a historic compromise on this issue. The SEC approved a creative approach that promoted honest and independent compliance programs, while at the same time recognizing whistleblower rights. Shortly thereafter, the Commodity Futures Trading Commission adopted an identical rule.

The Chair of the SEC explained the basis for her compromise:

> *No issue received more focus during this process than the role of internal compliance programs. As I have often said, internal compliance programs play an extremely valuable role in the fraud prevention arena. And we have sought to leverage compliance officers who can help protect investors by keeping companies on the straight path. . . . I believe that the final recommendation strikes the correct balance—a balance between encouraging whistleblowers to pursue the route of internal compliance when appropriate—while providing them the option of heading directly to the SEC.*

The final rule is tricky. The bottom line is that in almost every case, employees performing compliance functions who learn about violations of law as part of their official duties can qualify for rewards. However, they must pay careful attention to the fine procedural details of the SEC's final reward rules.

At first glance, the rules appear to disqualify employees who perform compliance functions. The rules state: "An employee whose principal duties involve compliance or internal audit responsibilities" cannot obtain a whistleblower reward. Additionally, any employee who "learned" of the violations "in connection with the entity's processes for identifying, reporting, and addressing possible violations of law" is also exempt from obtaining a reward. This exemption also applies to employees from any outside "firm retained to perform compliance or internal audit functions."

Based on this prohibition, it would appear that Wall Street won the day, and that thousands of employees were excluded from the rewards available under the Dodd-Frank Act.

But that isn't the whole story. The regulations contained *three* exceptions that effectively circumvented the rule:

First, if "you [the compliance officer, director, attorney, auditor, etc.] have a reasonable basis to believe that disclosure of the information to the Commission is necessary to prevent the relevant entity from engaging in conduct that is likely to cause substantial injury to the financial interest or property of the entity or investors," you can immediately report your concerns to the SEC and qualify for a reward.

Second, if "you have a reasonable basis to believe that the relevant entity is engaging in conduct that will impede an investigation of the misconduct," you can immediately report your concerns to the SEC and qualify for a reward.

Third, if "at least 120 days have elapsed since you provided the information to the relevant entity's audit committee, chief legal officer, chief compliance officer (or their equivalents), or your supervisor, or since you received the information, if you received it under circumstances indicating that the entity's audit committee, chief legal officer, chief compliance officer (or their equivalents), or your supervisor was already aware of the information," you can thereafter report to the SEC and qualify for a reward.

The third exception—"120-day rule"—is the easiest and safest exception to qualify under. The rule sets tangible, quantitative criteria. Comply with the deadline and you can qualify for the rule. It is that simple. If the company does not make a full and complete self-report to the government within the given time frame, the 120-day rule kicks in, and every employee who performs compliance-related functions can now file a whistleblower claim and qualify for a reward. In this regard, the safest method for compliance-related employees to qualify for a reward is to count the days the company is aware of the fraud allegations. If the company does the right thing, aggressively investigates and self-reports the violations to the government, then the matter is resolved and there is no need for an SEC filing. But if the company obfuscates, delays, covers up, retaliates, or ignores the bad news, after 120 days all employees, including those working in compliance and audit functions, can file a claim with the SEC.

In addition to the 120-day rule, compliance-related employees can file claims at any time if the underlying fraud is large and could cause "substantial injury" to investors, or if the company is engaging in a cover-up (i.e., impeding an internal investigation). The main problem with these two exceptions is their subjective nature. What evidence does an employee need to produce to demonstrate a potential cover-up? When is an employee's concern about a "substantial injury" reasonable in the eyes of the SEC? These exemptions involve subjective judgments. The 120-day rule eliminates the discretion the SEC has to deny or reduce a reward because it disagrees with the employee's opinion that the company was impeding the investigation or that investors were about to suffer "substantial injury."

These exceptions will permit compliance officials to obtain financial rewards, except in cases in which companies with extremely well-structured, independent, and accountable compliance programs are willing and able to conduct aggressive investigations and top management will react properly to the bad news they often try to avoid. Moreover, these companies must also be willing and able to honestly and completely self-report their misconduct to the government within 120 days of their initial receipt of an internal whistleblower complaint or negative audit finding.

The SEC's intent was explicit: Wall Street must stop trying to rig the system and start playing by the rules. Companies need to establish effective compliance programs, capable of identifying problems within 120 days of being reported, with sufficient authority and independence to ensure that companies self-report violations before they get caught. That day has not yet come.

The SEC wasted no time in granting monetary rewards to compliance-related employees. The ninth whistleblower to receive a financial reward from the SEC worked as a compliance official. In the SEC's press release announcing this award, it explained its policy behind permitting compliance officials to qualify for a reward: "Individuals who perform internal audit, compliance, and legal functions for companies are on the front lines in the battle against fraud and corruption. They often are privy to the very kinds of specific, timely, and credible information that can prevent an imminent fraud or stop an ongoing one."

The Chief of the SEC's Office of the Whistleblower explained how the 120-day rule works:

> [Compliance officials] may be eligible for an SEC whistleblower award if their companies fail to take appropriate, timely action on information they first reported internally. . . . This particular whistleblower award recipient reported concerns of wrongdoing to appropriate personnel within the company, including a supervisor. But when the company took no action on the information within 120 days, the whistleblower reported the same information to the SEC. The information provided by the whistleblower led directly to an SEC enforcement action.

Thereafter, the Commission also awarded a "compliance professional" a $1.5 million award for reporting information for which the employee had a "reasonable basis to believe that disclosure to the SEC was necessary to prevent imminent misconduct from causing substantial financial harm to the company or investors." The SEC explained that the company "failed to take steps" to prevent financial harm to investors after the whistleblower had disclosed the concerns. The Commission's message was clear. The goal of the whistleblower reward program was to protect investors, not prevent employees from becoming whistleblowers simply because they are auditors, attorneys, compliance professionals, or even members of the company's Board of Directors who sit on the official Audit Committee.

If you perform a compliance function for a publicly traded company—whether you are an intake officer answering a company hotline, the Chief Compliance Officer, or the Chair of the Board of Director's Audit Committee, you can qualify for whistleblower financial rewards so long as you follow SEC protocol.

One last note: There are no restrictions whatsoever on auditors or compliance officials qualifying for rewards under other programs, including the False Claims Act, the IRS tax whistleblower law, the Act to Prevent Pollution from Ships, and wildlife protection laws.

The SEC Rule Covering Employees Who Voluntarily Report to Compliance Officials, Supervisors, or Auditors before Making a Report to the SEC

The existence of corporate compliance programs raised an entirely different issue during the debate over whistleblower protections for corporate employees. Should employees be required to disclose fraud or misconduct internally before they reported these issues to the SEC? Should the SEC take steps to encourage internal reporting as a means to incentivize companies to create truly effective programs? These issues do not concern the rights of compliance professionals, but instead impact the procedures rank-and-file employees would use to report concerns

During the SEC's Dodd-Frank Act's rulemaking process, the U.S. Chamber of Commerce tried to persuade the Commission to require all employees to first report allegations of fraud internally in order to qualify for a reward. The Chamber depicted corporations as honest and willing to listen to their employees and claimed that financial rewards for whistleblowing would undermine good corporate governance. They alleged, with no empirical evidence, that by permitting employees to report allegations directly to the SEC and obtain a reward, employees would skip internal reporting. This argument had no credibility. As explained in Rule 17 (Beware of Hotlines), many companies had a history of firing employees who reported concerns internally and thereafter defending those terminations in court. Moreover, the nonprofit advocacy group National Whistleblower Center provided the Commission with detailed studies explaining how other reward laws (the False Claims Act) did not negatively impact corporate compliance programs.

The SEC rejected the Chamber's argument that employees must report their concerns internally before they can qualify for a reward. The Commission reiterated that no employee would be required to report his or her concerns to the company first as a condition of obtaining a reward. The decision on where to report would be left up to the employee. If the employee trusted the company's managers, they could report internally, if the employee feared retaliation or wanted complete confidentiality, they could go directly to the SEC.

As explained by the Chair of the Commission:

I believe that the final [rule] strikes the correct balance—a balance between encouraging whistleblowers to pursue the route of internal compliance when appropriate—while providing them the option of heading directly to the SEC. This makes sense as well, because it is the whistleblower who is in the best position to know which route is best to pursue. . . . I believe that incentivizing—rather than requiring—internal reporting is more likely to encourage a strong internal compliance culture. Our rules create incentives for people to report misconduct to their employers, but only if those companies have created an environment where employees feel comfortable that management will take them seriously— and where they are free from possible retaliation.

Under the SEC's rules, employees can either report internally *or* go directly to the SEC. When they report to the SEC, they can qualify for a reward. But the SEC understood that many (or most) employees will report internally before approaching the government. The Commission crafted a rule that fully protected employees who initially reported their concerns internally to a compliance official or their supervisor, as long as they also report to the government in a timely manner.

Under the SEC's whistleblower rules, if an employee discloses misconduct to his or her supervisor or the company's internal compliance program, that employee enjoys the same rights as if he or she reported the allegations directly to the SEC. However, the employee is still required to file a claim with the SEC within 120 days of his or her internal report in order to fully qualify for a reward.

This rule is extremely significant, but it's also confusing. It concerns how the SEC interprets the requirement that information provided to the Commission be "original" in order to qualify for a reward. The following scenarios should help explain the rule:

- An employee personally witnesses fraud and reports it to the SEC. S/he is the original source of that report.

- What if the same employee, instead of reporting the fraud to the SEC, reported the fraud to the company's compliance department? The employee is given credit for the internal report. Even if others make the same report to the SEC, the employee is still the "original source" for purposes of qualifying for the reward, if s/he eventually reports the issue to the SEC within the 120-day grace period.

- What rights do the compliance officials for whom the report was made have? These officials cannot blow the whistle for 120 days. But if the employee who filed the original concern has not contacted the SEC, after 120 days expires, the compliance official can contact the SEC and be considered the original source.

The SEC rules implement the "first to file" rules that exist in all whistleblower-reward programs. If two whistleblowers give the same information to the government, the whistleblower who *first* provided the information gets credit for providing the "original" information for which the Commission is not aware. The whistleblower who is second in line gets no credit, as his or her information is already known to the SEC and is no longer "original." The Commission already knows about the allegations from the first whistleblower. The "first to file" rule encourages early reporting. [*Note:* Under the Commission rules, if the second whistleblower "contributes" to an ongoing investigation, or provides information the first whistleblower did not have, he or she can still qualify for a reward.]

The SEC's 120-day rule permits a whistleblower to give information to internal compliance or a supervisor and still be the first to file, as long as he or she reports the concern to the SEC within 120 days of reporting the concern internally. Even if another employee went to the SEC during this 120-day period, the employee who initially raised his or her concerns with the company would still be the first to file and would qualify for the reward. This provides employees an opportunity to try to work out issues with their employer before taking the risky step of going outside the company and filing a claim with the government. The SEC's goal was simple: Provide strong incentives for companies to establish independent and ethical compliance programs or risk an army of whistleblowers flooding directly to the SEC with allegations of corporate misconduct.

The SEC rules provide an additional benefit to reporting a concern internally. If an employee reported his or her concerns internally, and thereafter the company self-reported the violation, the employee could still qualify as the original source of the information provided he or she also reported the information within the 120-day grace period. In this scenario, if the information a company self-reports to the government results in a fine or penalty, the whistleblower who provided the information to the company that led to the self-reporting can still qualify for a reward. This is so, even if the penalty imposed on the company was triggered by the company's self-reporting. Thus, if the employee was the original source of the fraud allegation, and the company acted on the employee's allegation and self-reported the violation, the employee could still qualify for a reward.

This is the first time under any regulatory scheme that an employee could qualify for a reward even if the company self-reported the violation before the employee officially filed the fraud allegation with the government. The key to qualifying for the reward is to make sure that whatever information an employee provides to his or her supervisor or a compliance official is also disclosed to the SEC within 120 days of the initial report.

The Commodity Futures Trading Commission has an identical rule covering employees who report violations of the Commodity Exchange Act.

PRACTICE TIPS

- The SEC rule on compliance and director eligibility for rewards is set forth at 17 C.F.R. § 240.21F-4(b)(4)(iii) and (v).

- The SEC rule permitting employees to qualify as the original source for purposes of obtaining a reward if they report their concerns to the Commission within 120 days of providing information to a compliance officer is set forth at 17 C.F.R. § 240.21F-4(b)(7).

- The Commodity Futures Trading Commission's rule on compliance and director eligibility is set forth at 17 C.F.R. § 165.2(g)(4), (5), and (7).

- The Commodity Futures Trading Commission's rule permitting employees to qualify as the original source for purposes of obtaining a reward if they report their concerns to the Commission within 120 days of providing information to a compliance officer is set forth at 17 C.F.R. § 165.2(i)(3).

- To learn the origin of the SEC's rules governing compliance departments, see *The SEC's Final Whistleblower Rules & Their Impact on Internal Compliance* (West Law Publishing, October 2011).

- *Ethics and Pressure, Balancing the Internal Audit Profession*, an overview of the pressures facing auditors, was written by Dr. Larry Rittenberg for the Institute of Internal Auditors (IIA Research Foundation, 2016).

RULE 20

Cautiously Use "Self-Help" Tactics

W histleblowers have no choice but to engage in "self-help" tactics. They have to obtain evidence to prove their cases. But this can be extremely tricky. There are privacy rules, "trade secret" rules, rules governing the use of company computers, telephones, e-mail accounts, and even the use of copying machines. How does an employee balance the need to collect supporting information with various workplace rules that limit or prohibit evidence gathering?

When engaging in self-help tactics, whistleblowers have to be extremely careful. Judges will not sympathize with their plight simply because it is difficult for whistleblowers to obtain supporting witnesses, or because the company has an overwhelming advantage regarding access to documents. No matter how hard it is to obtain evidence of wrongdoing, courts continuously warn employees "not to engage in dubious self-help tactics or workplace espionage in order to gather evidence." The law is clear on this issue: Engaging in protected activity does not immunize employees from being accused of "inappropriate workplace activities," even if they are engaged in that conduct simply to document corporate wrongdoing.

To further complicate the matter, there is no clear rule on self-help tactics. The leading cases all apply a "balancing test" for determining whether an employee's evidence-gathering tactics are protected. In one case widely followed by other courts, the U.S. Court of Appeals for the Fifth Circuit explained: "Courts have required that the employee conduct be reasonable in light of the circumstances, and have held that the employer's right to run his business must be balanced against the rights of the employee to . . . promote his own welfare."

Here are basic guidelines to follow when using self-help tactics, such as taping conversations or removing company documents.

Don't Break the Law

Do not break the law. This is a basic rule that must be followed. If a court determines that an employee broke a criminal law in order to obtain evidence in the case, the employee will suffer a sanction. The case may be dismissed, the employee's credibility will be attacked, and there may even be a referral for criminal prosecution. Even if dismissal is not imposed, the employee's ability to introduce illegally obtained evidence in court may be blocked, and the defendants will capitalize on this conduct at every phase of the case: They will use it as grounds to have a case dismissed, they will use it to cross examine the employee at trial, and they will use it on appeal to justify having the case thrown out.

One-Party Taping of Conversations

Whistleblowers often tape conversations with their supervisors or coworkers. In numerous cases employees have testified regarding their fear that no one will believe their story, and that they need to document the oral admissions of witnesses or wrongdoers in order to prove their case. Without a doubt these fears are well-founded. Taped conversations have often proven to be key evidence in a whistleblower's case. They can be the difference between winning and losing a case.

Also, tapes can be powerful evidence proving wrongdoing. When Linda Tripp taped her coworker at the Pentagon, she obtained admissions that directly led to unprecedented sanctions against a sitting president of the United States, including a contempt citation, disbarment, an adverse finding in a sexual harassment case, and a vote by the House of Representatives for impeachment (only the second time in history). The tapes provided irrefutable evidence. They documented oral admissions that would have been denied under oath by all the other witnesses.

The Tripp case is not without precedent. Many other whistleblowers have successfully used taped conversations to document serious wrongdoing. But is taping legal or ethical?

The rule on one-party taping traces back to a 1961 incident on which IRS agent Roger S. Davis interviewed German Lopez, the owner of Clauson's Inn in North Falmouth, Massachusetts. Lopez paid Davis a bribe. Davis promptly reported the pay-off to his supervisors and returned to Clauson's Inn to collect more evidence. But when he returned to the inn, he had a pocket tape recorder and another taping device on his body. This time he taped the conversation with the inn's owner, and the tape was key evidence in convicting Lopez. However, Davis never obtained a search warrant.

Davis's taping would become the landmark federal decision on the legality of "one-party" taping (when one party to a conversation tapes the conversation without telling the other party), whether done by federal agents or private persons. When the case of *Lopez v. the United States* wound its way up to the Supreme Court three years later, Justice John Harlan upheld the legality of one-party taping. He reasoned that the "electronic device" was not used to document "conversations" the IRS agent "could not otherwise have heard. Instead, the device was used only to obtain the most reliable evidence possible of a conversation" in which the person using the hidden tape recorder "was a participant" and was "fully entitled to disclose."

The IRS agent was a party to the conversation and the person making the criminal admissions knew that the agent could hear him. The court drew a strict distinction between using a tape recorder when you are a party to a conversation and planting a listening device (that would have been illegal if a search warrant for the device had not been obtained).

Chief Justice Earl Warren, one of the Supreme Court's most vocal supporters of a right to privacy, supported the decision. But to ensure that there was no misunderstanding as to why he fully joined in a ruling that may appear counter to his strong support of an individual's right to privacy, Justice Warren wrote a separate concurring opinion. For Chief Justice Warren, permitting one-party taping was a simple matter of fairness. It would be wrong for the court to render Davis "defenseless" against attacks on his own "credibility." How else could someone defend themselves against countercharges that during the conversation they attempted to obtain a bribe or they acted to illegally entrap a defendant? Chief Justice Warren understood that no matter what the outcome of the court trial may be, the IRS agent had his reputation to defend. As he explained:

> [When] faced with situations where proof of an attempted bribe will be a matter of their word against that of the tax evader and perhaps some of his associates [IRS agents such as Mr. Davis] should not be defenseless against outright denials or claims of entrapment, claims which, if not open to conclusive refutation, will undermine the reputation of the individual agent for honesty and the public's confidence in his work. Where confronted with such a situation, it is only fair that an agent be permitted to support his credibility with a recording as Agent Davis did in this case.

In 1968, five years after the *Lopez* decision, Congress enacted the federal wiretapping law governing citizen one-party taping. The law memorialized the rules set forth in Justice Harlan's and Chief Justice Warren's opinions. One-party taping by both private citizens and government agents was explicitly permitted under the federal act, but surreptitious taping was outlawed, unless a search warrant was obtained. Thus, under federal law, if you personally tape a conversation for which you are a party, your actions are legal. But if you plant the tape recorder in a room, and taped a conversation for which you are not a party, that conduct is strictly prohibited. This is the critical distinction in the law governing taping of conversations. If you are a party to the conversation, under federal law you can tape. But if you plant a listening device to record conversations for which you are not a party, you are violating the law.

The fact that your taping may be permitted under federal law does not end the issue. States are also permitted to regulate privacy matters and the legality of one-party taping. Although most states follow the federal model, a number of states specifically outlaw one-party taping and require that all persons participating in a private conversation consent before any one person is permitted to tape. Specifically, twelve states do not permit one-party taping. If an employee's taping of a conversation violates state law, he or she may be fired and even referred to state prosecutors to face possible criminal charges.

The Lawyers Committee for Freedom of the Press published a highly useful booklet online entitled, "A Practical Guide to Taping Phone Calls and In-Person Conversations in the 50 States and D.C." (2008, printed at www .rcfp.org). The committee conducted a careful state-by-state analysis of the law governing one-party taping, and summarized the current status of the law as follows:

> *Federal law allows recording of phone calls and other electronic communications with the consent of at least one party to the call. A majority of the states and territories have adopted wiretapping statutes based on the federal law. . . . Thirty-eight states and the District of Columbia permit individuals to record conversations to which they are a party without informing the other parties that they are doing so. . . . Twelve states require, under most circumstances, the consent of all parties to a conversation. Those jurisdictions are California, Connecticut, Florida, Illinois, Maryland, Massachusetts, Michigan, Montana, Nevada, New Hampshire, Pennsylvania and Washington. . . . Regardless of the state, it is almost always illegal to record a conversation to which you are not a party, do not have consent to tape, and could not naturally overhear. Federal law and most state laws also make it illegal to disclose the contents of an illegally intercepted call or communication.*

Ensuring that taping is legal is just the first step in weighing whether or not to surreptitiously record a conversation. Even if a taping is legal, an employee still must be concerned with a variety of questions that could impact the taping, such as:

- Does the company have a rule that prohibits such conduct?

- Will a decision to tape appear credible? In the *Lopez* case no one could doubt the reasonableness of the agent's decision to tape. He had been offered a bribe, and he wanted to document the next offer, which he reasonably expected would occur during the meeting for which he taped.

- What if the taped conversation contains no evidence that is helpful to the employee's case? If the taped conversation contains a "smoking gun," the decision to tape the conversation will most likely appear reasonable to an objective observer (such as a judge or juror). But what if the supervisor suspects the employee may be "documenting" the conversation and decides to make statements that make the employee look bad? Taping carries risks. Once a record of the conversation is created, for better or worse, that record will have an impact on the outcome of a case.

- Will the company learn of the taping? Most probably, yes. In civil discovery the company's attorneys can ask whether or not the employee taped any conversations and can require that the employee produce copies of the tape(s).

- If an employee tapes conversations, can he or she destroy tapes that do not help the case? No. The failure to preserve evidence (for example, erasing the contents of the tapes) can be considered a serious discovery abuse and result in sanctions.

- Can an employee take steps to increase the chances that the tapes will be used in evidence? Yes. If an employee is taping, he or she should try to have the case heard in a forum that is most sympathetic to using tapes as evidence. It may be possible to research how courts in the specific jurisdiction have resolved issues related to one-party taping. The U.S. Department of Labor, which has jurisdiction over numerous federal whistleblower laws, has permitted the use of one-party tapes in whistleblower cases, when such taping is legal under state law. In one case the DOL found that taping itself could be a statutorily protected activity, if conducted in order to document safety violations. In other words, the Labor Department ruled that not only was one-party taping permissible, employees had a right to tape conversations if necessary to demonstrate violations of law.

- What if a government official asks an employee to tape? In such circumstances the taping will almost always be found reasonable. If the government wants the whistleblower to tape, it usually means there is strong evidence of misconduct, which can significantly support the employee's case.

- How can an employee demonstrate that a taping was reasonable? In a decision by the U.S. Court of Appeals for the Second Circuit, the court recognized that "a range of factors" could justify taping, including an employee's "belief that he was gathering evidence" to support his discrimination claim. But there is no better way to demonstrate reasonableness of taping than the contents of the tapes themselves. For example, in a case filed under the Clean Water Act's whistleblower provision, the employee's one-party recording of a taped meeting of Eastern Ohio Regional Wastewater Authority, the key manager admitted that the violations committed at the plant could harm his political career. When the court rendered its decision, this taped admission was critical: "The best indication that [the employee's] dismissal was motivated by his protected activity is contained in the tape recorded comments of the Board members . . . [who were] obviously aghast at [the employee's] whistleblower letter and were fearful of the effect the disclosure of environmental violations would have on their reputations and careers."

One-party taping has been instrumental in exposing government misconduct, protecting the public's health and safety, and enabling whistleblowers to win their cases. But whether or not to tape always raises complex questions that should be carefully weighed before an employee decides to put a recorder in his or her pocket and have at it.

Removing Documents from Work

To prevail in any case, whistleblowers must obtain documentation. Often documents from the employer are the best evidence for proving a case. But employees do not have an unlimited right to obtain documents from work.

First, an employee cannot sneak into a supervisor's office and copy information. Courts draw a sharp distinction between information that an employee has access to at work as part of his or her job and confidential or private information that may be in the possession of a supervisor. As one court bluntly stated: "[R]ummaging through his supervisor's office for confidential documents" is not permitted.

Second, if a company has a "legitimate and substantial interest" in keeping certain documents confidential, such as "personnel records," an employee cannot, without very, very good cause, "surreptitiously" copy the data. Courts that have sanctioned employees for copying confidential documents have noted that if an employee can demonstrate that the copied materials would have been "destroyed," and their conduct was undertaken to "preserve evidence," its decision may have been different. But outside such circumstances, copying and disseminating otherwise confidential materials may be highly problematic.

Some employers have become very aggressive in enforcing confidentiality agreements that prohibit employees from removing documents from work, including filing "counterclaims" or seeking injunctions against the employees, demanding the return of information or other sanctions.

In one case, a registered nurse reported numerous violations, including fraudulent billing, the improper treatment of suicidal patients, and the unlawful discharge of other psychiatric patients. After she filed her whistleblower suit, the medical center filed a counterclaim, alleging illegal "conversion" and "theft" of hospital records. The court threw out the counterclaim, holding that the employee had not taken the documents for illegal purposes, such as using them to "compete" against the medical center. The court recognized that as a registered nurse, the employee was obligated to refer issues of patient care to "licensing authorities." Also, the court cited an exception to the federal law on medical confidentiality that permitted whistleblowers to disclose "protected health information" to an attorney or "public health authority." If she had a "good faith belief" that the medical center had violated "professional standards" or had placed patients "at risk," then her activity was protected.

In this case the nurse was able to explain to the court why her removal of documents was reasonable. Many employees are not able to meet that level of proof.

Beware: The Boss Will Monitor E-mails and Computers

Do not think work e-mails are private. Do not think that any computer or cellphone owned by the company (including laptops they let you bring home) is safe from a complete search of the hard drive, including searches for deleted documents. It is now standard operating procedure for a company to seize a whistleblower's computer, especially when the employee is about to be fired. It is also becoming standard for the company to aggressively search hard drives and e-mails for any document it can use to impeach the whistleblower.

The "open season" on employee's e-mails and hard drives was made easier by a June 17, 2010, Supreme Court case, *City of Ontario v. Quon*. The case concerned the search of an employee's text messages, which were sent on a cell phone owned by the city. Because the government conducted the search, the employee challenged it on the basis of the U.S. Constitution's restrictions on warrantless searches. The Supreme Court held that government agencies can, under certain conditions, search the computer files of its employees without a warrant. The holding was broad: "[W]hen conducted . . . for the investigation of work-related misconduct, a government employer's warrantless search is reasonable if it is justified at its inception and if the measures adopted are reasonably related to the objectives of the search and not excessively intrusive . . ."

The authority of private-sector employers to search company-owned computers is even broader. In warning employees of this management power, the Privacy Rights Clearinghouse summarized the current state of the law as follows:

> *New technologies make it possible for employers to monitor many aspects of their employees' jobs, especially on telephones, computer terminals, through electronic and voice mail, and when employees are using the Internet. Such monitoring is virtually unregulated. Therefore, unless company policy specifically states otherwise (and even this is not assured), your employer may listen, watch, and read most of your workplace communications.*

The ability of employers to search company-owned computers is extremely significant in whistleblower cases. First, courts have held that evidence of misconduct obtained during the search of an employee's computer can be used against that employee in a subsequent discrimination case. Second, employees sometimes include private information on their company-owned computers, including legal documents and communications with counsel. At a minimum, placing these types of materials on company computers can provide the company with a treasure trove of information that would otherwise be unavailable to the company. At worst, the employee will be accused of doing personal business on company time.

Bottom line: An employee should not use company property to "blow the whistle." He or she needs to keep protected activities private. Do not give the company the rope it will need for the hanging.

Do Not Destroy Evidence

An employee should not destroy documentary evidence. Once evidence is created, an employee cannot destroy it simply because it does not support his or her claim or may be embarrassing. For example, if an employee uses a company-owned computer, he or she cannot simply wipe out the hard drive, especially if he or she is afraid that the computer contains files that the company may use against him or her in an upcoming legal case. The rule is fairly clear and applies in the context of any civil lawsuit, not just whistleblower cases: "A litigant or potential litigant is under a duty to preserve evidence in his possession that he knows or should have known is relevant to the litigation or which might lead to the discovery of admissible evidence." Stated another way: "Willful spoliation occurs when a party has clear notice of an obligation to preserve evidence and proceeds to intentionally destroy evidence in spite of its obligation not to."

In one unfortunate case filed under the False Claims Act and the Sarbanes-Oxley Act, the employee used a "wiping program" to erase data from the "hard drive of his company-issued computer." When trying to justify the destruction of evidence, the employee's explanations only made matters worse. He admitted to having highly embarrassing personal materials on the computer. This did nothing to further his claims, except to undercut his credibility even more. The issues of retaliation and corporate wrongdoing were lost in the dispute over the computer files, what he wiped off the hard drive, and how those materials may have helped the company. Because the documents were gone forever, the company was able to speculate as to what "might have" been located in the employee's "personal directories" and what "could have" been used by the company to bolster its case. As a direct result of the "spoliation" of evidence, the employee lost his case and had to pay the company a sanction.

Given the new rules on management access to employee information stored on company-owned computers (including e-mails, text messages, and documents stored on hard drives), it is extremely important that employees be aware that they lack basic rights of privacy when using company equipment—even company equipment that they are permitted to take home and use on their own time. Employees should avoid using company property while engaging in protected activities.

On the other hand, spoliation cuts both ways. There are far more examples of companies and government agencies destroying evidence than there are of employees doing so. The government is under strict obligations to preserve all types of records due to the mandates of various laws, including the Freedom of Information and Privacy Acts. Corporations must maintain accurate records under audit, tax, and government contracting rules. The spoliation rules have been successfully used by employees and have likewise resulted in default judgments in favor of employees, when their employers have willfully destroyed evidence.

Do Not Let the Boss Abuse the "After-Acquired Evidence" Rule

What happens in a case where the employee proves that he or she was fired in retaliation for blowing the whistle? In this hypothetical, assume there is no doubt that employee engaged in protected activities and the termination was illegal. But what happens if *after* the termination, the employer learns that the employee engaged in misconduct that *would have* resulted in a termination, regardless of the protected activity? For example, what happens if during the course of the employee's deposition she or he admits to lying on the job application and did not have the professional licensing required for the job? It is under these circumstances that the "after-acquired evidence" rule applies.

The rule is simple. If the termination was illegal, the employee can still win the case. But damages are cut off, effective the date upon which the company learned of the offensive conduct and can show that it would have fired the employee, even if she or he had not engaged in protected activity.

Once an employer learns of this disqualifying conduct, the employer no longer is required to reinstate the employee. Requiring the reinstatement of a worker who could have and should have been fired would be rather odd, and the rules simply do not permit it. Furthermore, under the after-acquired evidence rule, damages are cut off from the date the company learned of the disqualifying misconduct. Thus, if an employee is fired, but thirty days later the company learns of the disqualifying conduct, the employee is only entitled to thirty days' back pay.

When debating the merits of the after-acquired evidence defense, there was a three-hundred-pound gorilla in the room. Could an employer use pretrial discovery to snoop around an employee's background in order to obtain information about potentially disqualifying conduct? The potential for abusing this practice was evident. If companies could use the fact that an employee filed a whistleblower case to engage in extensive discovery to try to dig up dirt, these tactics would have a strong chilling effect on the willingness of anyone to blow the whistle or file retaliation claims. No one wants to invite such a wide-ranging review of his or her past conduct.

In permitting the use of after-acquired evidence, the U.S. Supreme Court warned against this type of discovery abuse and prohibited its use. As stated by the Court in *McKennon v. Nashville Banner Publishing*: "The concern that employers might as a routine matter undertake extensive discovery into an employee's background or performance on the job to resist claims under the Act is not an insubstantial one, but we think the authority of courts to [sanction discovery abuses] will deter most abuses."

This warning to company attorneys in *McKennon* is of critical importance to employees. Assuming that an employee did engage in some workplace misconduct that the company does not know about, the employee should not freely *admit* to engaging in such violations. It is up to the company to learn these facts through legitimate and relevant discovery. Questions by employers such as, "Did you rummage through your supervisor's office?" or "Did you improperly remove company documents before you were fired?" should be objected to, and if necessary should be the focus of a motion for protective order or sanctions.

Self Help

GUNTHER V. DELTEK: CASE STUDY IN TAPING AND REMOVING DOCUMENTS

Dinah Gunther worked as a financial analyst for a technology company, Deltek, Inc. She was fired after reporting suspected financial frauds to her bosses and the SEC. She fought Deltek for years and eventually prevailed in a showdown at the U.S. Court of Appeals for the Fourth Circuit. Hers is a textbook case on why employees have to tape conversations and obtain documents to win their cases.

The central dispute concerned a meeting between Gunther, the company's director of Human Resources, and another management employee. Deltek accused Gunther of being "confrontational," "demanding," and "challenging" toward the director at the meeting and used her so-called unprofessional conduct as the main justification for firing her. Thus, what happened at that meeting was the key to whether Gunther's termination would be sustained.

The company had the word of its HR director and a witness who would attest to her aggressive and inappropriate behavior. Two against one; alone, Gunther did not stand a chance. But Gunther had a secret weapon. She had surreptitiously taped the meeting (which is legal in the state of Virginia, where she was employed).

The tape was proof that the meeting didn't go as Deltek claimed. The judge listened to what actually happened during that meeting and ruled in Gunther's favor: "Based upon my listening to the recording, I find there was no basis for asserting that [Gunther] was confrontational. . . . Having listened to the tape more than once, I do not agree with [the HR director's] characterization of [Gunther's] actions. . . . At all times [Gunther] was calm, quiet, and polite."

The judge also explained that Gunther's taping was reasonable in the context of her employment. The taping "was done in furtherance of [Gunther's] case, and it was these tapes which revealed that [Deltek's] reasons for terminating [Gunther] were pretext. . . . [Gunther's] recordings were all made in furtherance of her whistleblower claims and therefore constitute protected activity."

Without that tape, it is almost certain Gunther would have lost her case. But with the tape she could demonstrate that the company lacked credibility, was doctoring testimony, that a witness apparently lied on the stand, and that the reasons given for her termination were a pretext. The tape ensured that Gunther would eventually win her case, and obtain more than $500,000 in back pay, front pay, and damages.

The company also attacked Gunther for removing company documents (i.e., sending company information to her home e-mail account) in contravention of her confidentiality agreement and company policy. They sought to use the "after-acquired evidence" defense to deny damages to Gunther. Under that defense, Deltek could argue that once it learned Gunther had removed documents in violation of company policy, it had the right to deny her reinstatement and cut off her ability to collect damages. Deltek cited cases holding that "Sarbanes-Oxley is not a license to steal documents or break contracts."

The Department of Labor judge carefully reviewed the law on document removal, recognizing "the inherent tension between a company's legitimate business policies that protect confidential information and the whistleblower programs created by Congress." The cases cited by Deltek were not black and white. None of them prohibited the removal of documents under all circumstances. An employee's conduct had to be reviewed on a case-by-case basis. The judge concluded that Gunther "forwarded these documents in an effort to support her Sarbanes-Oxley Act [SOX] allegations." She also noted that Gunther "only took documents relevant to her SOX complaint and did so for fear that they would be shredded," and that there were "strong policy reasons for permitting whistleblowers in SOX cases to take necessary actions to protect relevant documents from being destroyed, as long as the employee's actions are necessary, reasonable, and not overbroad."

The judge also understood that the legality of an employee's removal of confidential business documents in violation of company policy "would depend on the facts of each case" and that the "indiscriminate misappropriation of proprietary documents would not be protected." But in this case, Gunther "took these documents for the sole purpose of preserving evidence relevant to her whistleblower complaint and alleged violations under SOX." Thus Gunther's actions were not only permitted but also constituted protected activity; "her collection, retention and forwarding of the documents constitute protected activity."

Gunther's case is a lesson learned. If you are careful using self-help tactics, you can prevail. But if you indiscriminately take company documents or engage in other unprofessional activity, you may find yourself out of luck.

Be Careful

Employees sometimes make mistakes when they are trying to collect evidence to support their claims. Thus, when responding to company discovery questions, it is important to ask whether this question is material to the whistleblower case, or whether the company is engaging in a "fishing expedition" to dig up dirt on the whistleblower. If the company learns of an employee's mistakes through legitimate means, that is fair game. But if the company uses the civil discovery process to obtain after-acquired evidence of employee misconduct (including self-help tactics that may have gone over the line), such questioning must be vigorously opposed.

PRACTICE TIP

- The Supreme Court decision on the after-acquired evidence rule: *McKennon v. Nashville Banner Publishing*, 513 U.S. 352 (1995).

- The Department of Labor case of *Gunther v. Deltek, Inc.*, 2010-SOX-49, affirmed *Deltek v. Department of Labor*, 2016 U.S. App. LEXIS 9274 (4th Cir. 2016), provides analysis of both document removal and one-party taping.

- The best one-party taping case is *Mosbaugh v. Georgia Power Co.*, 91-ERA-1/11 (November 20, 1995), where the Secretary of Labor ruled that one-party taping constituted a protected activity for which an employee could not be fired. See www.oalj.dol.gov (DOL whistleblower cases are published on this site).

RULE 21

Be Prepared for the Lid to Blow

"Our President has gone on a rampage about news leaks on Watergate. He told the appropriate people, 'go to any length to stop them' . . . Internal investigations, plus he wants to use the courts . . . Nixon was wild, shouting and hollering that 'we can't have it and we're going to stop it, I don't care how much it costs . . .'"

Bob Woodward, quoting the whistleblower "Deep Throat"

Whistleblowers need to be prepared. If they think blowing the whistle will automatically win them a grand prize, they should think again. They need to understand the serious nature of whistleblowing, the impact it may have on their career and family, and the necessary steps that they may take to protect themselves.

One of the biggest mistakes shared by most whistleblowers at the onset of a case is the belief that somehow doing the "right thing" will be rewarded, and that the system will naturally work. Although a nice thought, that is the exception, not the rule. Regardless of the reputation of one's boss, it is simply not possible to predict how a company will respond to a report of wrongdoing by one of its own employees.

The company's reaction to disclosures may be very subtle, but it may also reflect emotion. In rare cases employers go far overboard, beyond the pale of acceptable conduct—so much so that even the Supreme Court held that outrageous conduct, such as turning in employees who engage in protected activity to the immigration authorities, constitutes an unfair labor practice.

It is absolutely critical that whistleblowers know what steps to take to protect their job. If an employee is tagged as a whistleblower for trying to fix a problem in-house, there is no choice but to prepare a defense for his or her career and reputation. If an employee is so lucky, in that he or she understands the potential for retaliation before blowing the whistle, following are some questions that must be carefully considered:

- Have I accepted the whistleblower label? Am I prepared for a fight?

- Are there laws that would let me blow the whistle confidentially?

- Does my family support me? If so, how much do they support me?

- Do I have the resources necessary for either hiring a lawyer or weathering a termination? If I don't, do I have an alternative plan?

- Is the concern I am raising worth the risks that I will potentially face? Do the benefits outweigh the costs?

- How good is my employment record? Could I win a wrongful discharge suit or are there enough past problems within the workplace to make my case questionable to a judge or jury? Whistleblowers have to be prepared to defend their performance and conduct at work. There is a strong likelihood that a company will defend its adverse action by pointing to so-called performance problems. The company cannot admit that the reason it wants to get rid of an employee is because he or she blew the whistle. The company must therefore find an excuse, and it will dig deep.

- Am I prepared to be treated poorly? Whistleblowers should not think they will be treated like other employees or as they were treated in the past. One of the most common issues in a whistleblower case is "disparate treatment." The concept is self-explanatory. Whistleblowers may be treated differently than others and held to a higher standard.

- Is there anything in my background that my employer could use to smear me? Whistleblowers must think of all of the little things that they could be nabbed for.

- What evidence do I have to support my allegations that the company or agency engaged in misconduct? Do I have tapes, written documents, or pictures? It is also important to obtain expert advice before making a final decision as to whether or not to blow the whistle.

- If I risk my job, can I qualify for a reward? Can I file an anonymous claim under laws such as the Dodd-Frank Act?

Depending on the state and situation, some whistleblower laws are very powerful while others are weak and virtually nonexistent. Each whistleblower must understand where his or her situation falls, and an expert can help with that.

One of the tragedies in whistleblower cases is having to tell an employee who "did the right thing," who saved lives or saved consumers millions of dollars, that there are not any good laws to protect him or her, or that a deadline was missed. These employees are in the unfortunate position of having put their jobs and careers at risk to help the public interest, yet finding themselves deserted by the courts due to their failure to comply with vagaries of the law. Given the numerous options now available to employees under state and federal laws, if an employee takes the time to ensure that his or her disclosures are fully protected, this tragic pitfall usually can be avoided. Whistleblowers must do due diligence.

Collecting evidence while still an employee is critical. If you are considering filing a False Claims Act, the law requires that you file, with the Attorney General, "substantially" all of the evidence you have proving your allegations of contractor fraud. Hence it is to your advantage to make this disclosure as comprehensive as possible. The better your evidence, the greater the probability that the Justice Department will join your team and join in your False Claims Act case, significantly increasing the likelihood that you will win the claim.

Employees with the foresight to legally collect e-mails, reports, and other internal documents before the first incident of retaliation are better prepared to defend a case, should it arise.

An employee who is contemplating blowing the whistle should understand that his or her social standing at work may change radically. For example, prior management tolerance for minor workplace infractions have the potential to end and may suddenly become grounds for attacking an employee's performance. Management may scrutinize an employee's conduct with a fine-tuned microscope, searching for any justifications to downgrade, transfer, or even terminate the employee. One government agency notorious for retaliating against whistleblowers coined a phrase for these practices: "keeping book." When asked under oath, the agency's top manager frankly admitted that "keeping book" was a method of documenting minor infractions, in order to build a paper trail that could be used against an employee. In this particular case, the supervisor's "keeping book" included documenting derogatory workplace gossip, without any attempt to verify its truthfulness, monitoring whom an employee ate lunch with, and carefully noting typographical errors in inter-office memoranda prepared by the whistleblower. All of the minor issues were eventually bundled together to paint a highly negative and completely misleading picture of the employee.

Employees make a mistake if they embark on a yellow brick road to whistleblowing, initially expecting that their employer will reward them for helping identify and fix major problems. They believe that someone at the top will "see the light" and recognize the exemplary contributions the employee made to safety, the public interest, or the company's long-term best interest. But you aren't in Kansas anymore. No company presents an annual "whistleblower award" for the employee who filed the most effective complaint with a federal law enforcement agency.

Rather than praise and acknowledgement, the usual scenario is as follows: An employee's careful attention to detail is re-interpreted as "nitpicking," the act of raising safety concerns is characterized as "disrupting" overall production and threatening jobs within the company, and identifying illegal work practices becomes an automatic mark of disloyalty. In the end, it is far more realistic to expect a pink termination slip for failure to be a "team player" than a gold embossed plaque for "employee of year."

To reiterate, it is essential for any employee who is considering blowing the whistle to understand that these types of changes in the workplace are very likely to occur. Perhaps management will welcome the information. Perhaps the culture of the company is such that whistleblowing is welcomed. The aforementioned are rare. Most likely, your manager simply cannot live up to the laudatory goals of the company. It is essential to determine whether you are covered under a reward law and thus can avoid many of the pitfalls that whistleblowers have endured over the years.

Some employees will be pigeonholed as "whistleblowers" simply because they did their job honestly or aggressively. Other workers may be forced into becoming "whistleblowers" because they either answered a government investigator truthfully or refused to sign-off on shoddy work. These employees may have no choice but to accept that they are now "whistleblowers," even if they never intended to be. Other workers do have a clear decision to make.

Regardless of how you are confronted with the reality of whistleblowing, the worst mistake you can make is to brush it under the carpet and to simply ignore the issue. The ostrich approach does not work, especially when reputations, careers, money, and jobs are on the line. Weigh the pros and cons, the benefits and the costs. Carefully consider whether you can blow the whistle anonymously. Search your conscience. Seek out advice. Know your rights. Follow the law. Do not lie. Be prepared.

An excellent book discussing what employees face after they blow the whistle: Myron and Penina Glazer, *The Whistleblowers: Exposing Corruption in Government and Industry* (New York: Basic Books, 1989).

- Aaron Kesselheim, et al., "Whistle-Blowers' Experiences in Fraud Litigation against Pharmaceutical Companies," *New England Journal of Medicine* (2010) ("Special Report").

- Ernesto Reuben and Matt Stephenson, "Nobody likes a rat: On the willingness to report lies and the consequences thereof," 93 *Journal of Economic Behavior & Organization* 384 (Sept. 2013).

RULE 22
Delay Is Deadly

D elay is deadly. Don't miss the deadline for filing the case!
As explained in Rule 2, there is no single comprehensive national whistleblower protection law. The laws vary from state to state, and the federal government has enacted numerous other laws and regulations that offer protection for whistleblowers. Each law has its own unique statutes of limitation (i.e., filing deadline) and its own unique procedure for properly filing a claim or lawsuit.

Some laws require claims to be filed within thirty days, while others permit years to pass before a case is filed. Other laws are filed with an administrative agency, such as the Department of Labor, while several are filed directly in court. Once an employee identifies the best legal protections that apply to his or her case, compliance with each and every technical requirement of the law is absolutely required. The strictest of these requirements is known as the "statute of limitations," which sets forth the deadline for filing a claim. Miss the deadline, lose the case. It is that simple. **Figure 11** is a summary of the filing deadlines for cases that must be originally filed in federal court. **Figure 12** summarizes the deadlines for filing complaints under major DOL laws.

Complying with the statute of limitations is particularly relevant in whistleblower cases. First, some of the limitations periods are very short. The periods are measured in days, not years. For example, the federal environmental and occupational safety whistleblower laws say claims must be filed within thirty days of the adverse action. Also the Sarbanes-Oxley corporate whistleblower law requires that claims be filed within 180 days of the adverse action. The deadlines start running on the day an employee is given notice of the termination or discipline, not the last day of work. With very few exceptions, the failure to comply with these statutes of limitation spells doom.

Second, figuring out the filing deadlines for qualifying for a reward is somewhat tricky. All of the reward laws place an emphasis on being the "first to file." This means, whoever files a reward claim first may be the only person who qualifies to obtain compensation. The False Claims Act has a strict "first to file" rule. Whoever raises a claim first is the only person who has standing to pursue that claim. Thus, regardless of the actual statute of limitations for filing a case, you may lose your rights if you do not act quickly and secure your position as "first to file." Whether or not you are the "first to file," False

Claims Act cases generally must be filed within six years after the fraud is committed. Securities cases generally need to be filed within five years of the violation.

Take the case of Vera English. For twelve years English worked as an hourly employee at the General Electric (GE) Chemet Laboratory in Wilmington, North Carolina. She was responsible for the quality control of dangerous radioactive materials. After witnessing, time and again, hazardous practices within the laboratory, English began to document and report various improper practices. These hazards included contamination, defective equipment, the failure of employees to be tested for radiation before leaving the "controlled" areas, leaks of radioactive materials, employee exposure to dangerous fumes, and spills of radioactive materials left unmarked by the responsible parties. Her complaints led to a work stoppage in the contaminated areas. They also caused the Nuclear Regulatory Commission to cite GE for a number of nuclear safety violations, including a "Severity Level IV violation" due to the failure of employees to use radiation-detection equipment to monitor their exposures and/or to prevent radioactive materials from escaping without detection from the controlled areas.

Figure 11

Statute of Limitations for Retaliation Cases Filed in Federal Court		
Name of Law	Citation	Amount of Time to File
Banking Fraud (Credit Unions, FDIC Insured Institutions, & Monetary Transactions)	12 U.S.C. § 1790b 12 U.S.C. § 1831j 31 U.S.C. § 5328	2 years
Commodity Exchange Act (Retaliation)	7 U.S.C. § 26 (h)(1)(B)(iii)	2 years
False Claims Act (Retaliation)	31 U.S.C. § 3730(h)(3)	3 years
First Amendment 42 U.S.C. § 1983 (State, Municipal, & County Employee Speech on Matters of Public Concern)	*Owens v. Okure*, 488 U.S. 235, 240-241 (1989).	Federal Court: No uniform statute of limitations. Follow relevant statute of limitations in state where claim is filed.
Securities Exchange Act (Retaliation)	15 U.S.C. § 78u-6(h)(1) (B)(iii)	6 years after the violation occurred or 3 years after the date when facts material to the right of action are known or reasonably should have been known by the employee. Required action within 10 years .

Figure 12

Statute of Limitations for Retaliation Claims Initially Filed with the Department of Labor		
Name of Law	Citation	Amount of Time to File with the Department of Labor
Airline Safety	29 Code of Federal Regulations § 1979	90 days
Consumer Financial Fraud	29 Code of Federal Regulations § 1985	180 days
Consumer Product Safety	16 Code of Federal Regulations § 1102	180 days
Environmental Safety (Clean Air, Superfund, Clean Water, Safe Drinking, Waste Disposal, and Toxic Substances)	29 Code of Federal Regulations § 24	30 days
Food Safety	29 Code of Federal Regulations § 1987	180 days
Nuclear Safety	29 Code of Federal Regulations § 24	180 days
Occupational Safety and Health Act (OSHA)	29 Code of Federal Regulations § 1977	30 days
Sarbanes Oxley Act (Securities Fraud)	18 U.S.C. § 1514A(b)(2) (D); 29 Code of Federal Regulations § 1980	180 days
Transportation Safety Laws (Railroad, Automobile, Transit, Maritime, & Trucks)	29 Code of Federal Regulations § 1982 & 1978	180 days

English's reward for exposing these violations and unsafe conditions could have been predicted: GE barred her from the lab and gave her ninety days to find a new position within the GE facility. When she could not find another position, she lost her job. Under the federal nuclear whistleblower law in existence at the time, she was required to file her wrongful discharge claim within thirty days of the adverse action. She filed her claim within thirty days of her termination—her last day of work. Her case went to trial, and GE was found guilty of illegal retaliation. She was ordered reinstated with full back pay and benefits, she was awarded $70,000 for emotional distress damages, and she was awarded compensation to cover her attorney fees and costs. English's case seemed to have a fairy-tale ending.

However, GE was not finished, and they had not given up. GE fought English's case every step of the way, hiring major corporate law firms to carry its water. Numerous legal technicalities were raised, and they were finally able to get one to stick: failure to file a timely complaint. They argued that English had failed to file her claim under the thirty-day statute of limitations.

How could this be? She filed her claim within thirty days of losing her job. GE argued that because she was told that she had ninety days to find a new position within the company, her thirty-day filing period commenced to run even before her last day of work. The courts agreed, and her case was thrown out. GE got away with violating the nuclear whistleblower law based on this technicality. English lost her job and career. She collected not one dime in damages. The fairy-tale ending was not to be.

The courts created precedents for strictly interpreting the statutes of limitations, even those as short as thirty days. Somehow courts have reasoned that employees such as English should know, right from the start, that GE's offer to permit her to find a new position in the company was bogus, and that her mandatory obligation to file a claim within thirty short days commenced when she was told her position was being eliminated, not when GE actually terminated her employment. With few exceptions, these interpretations remain the law of the land.

A few years after English's case was thrown out, Congress amended the nuclear whistleblower law and increased the statute of limitations under that law to 180 days. Unfortunately, other laws (most notably the federal environmental whistleblower protection laws) still have radically short thirty-day limitations periods.

Timing is also very important under whistleblower reward laws. Laws such as the False Claims Act have a "first to file" rule that awards monetary benefits to the whistleblower who is the "first" to file a rewards claim. Likewise, the Dodd-Frank Act's corporate rewards program has a similar incentive for being the first to file a claim, as do all other reward laws. Under the rules of the Securities and Exchange Commission, delaying filing a claim can result in the SEC's lowering the amount of reward for which you may be entitled, or even disqualifying you from a reward if another whistleblower files the same claim before you filed yours.

The bottom line? Don't delay. Deadlines are easily missed but rarely forgiven.

Major Court rulings on how to determine when a statute of limitations commences to run:

- *Nat'l R.R. Passenger Corp. v. Morgan*, 536 U.S. 101 (2003); *Lewis v. City of Chicago*, 130 S.Ct. 2191 (2010) (continuing violations) (must show present violation within statutory filing period)

- *Delaware State College v. Ricks*, 449 U.S. 250 (1982) (when the clock starts ticking on your filing deadline)

- *Turgeau v. Administrative Review Board*, 446 F.3d 1052 (10th Cir. 2006); *School District of Allentown v. Marshall*, 657 F.2d 16 (3rd Cir. 1981); *Bonham v. Dresser Indus.*, 569 F.2d 187 (3rd. Cir. 1977) (cases explaining potential "equitable" justifications for enlarging the statute of limitations)

- *KBR v. U.S. ex rel. Carter*, 135 S.Ct. 1970 (2015) (clarifying "first to file" rule and statute of limitations under the False Claims Act)

The SEC rule on qualifying for a reward if you contribute to an ongoing investigation for which you are not the original source is located at 17 Code of Federal Regulations § 240.21F-4(c)(2).

The SEC rules explaining the benefits of being the "first to file" are published at 17 C.F.R. Part 240.21F-4(b)(5) and (c) and are explained at 76 *Federal Register* 34300, 34321-23. Handbook Rule 6 sets forth the "first to file" rule under the False Claims Act.

RULE 23

Conduct Discovery

Don't be fooled; modern civil lawsuits have nothing in common with the courthouse dramas portrayed on television shows such as *Law & Order*. The case is not won as a result of a dramatic admission during a trial. There are no sobbing confessions, nor are there admissions of guilt. Friends forget, coworkers get scared, and witnesses lie. Jurors can be skeptical, and judges can be cynical. Whistleblowers' motives will be under scrutiny, and their performance will be challenged.

Whistleblowers do not win cases because justice is on their side, and they do not win because of luck. Cases are won and lost on hard evidence, usually obtained through the extraordinary efforts of the whistleblower before he or she is fired or his or her attorneys during the pretrial discovery process.

In other words, simply being right is not enough. Whistleblowers have to prove they are right. Contemporaneous documentation is key. If a report was falsified, where is the original? If a quality assurance standard was not met, where are the test evaluations? If a concern is raised with a supervisor, where is the e-mail documenting these disclosures? Was a log kept? Were incriminating conversations lawfully taped? The hard and often tedious work of collecting evidence, saving documents, and engaging in extensive discovery is the foundation of a good case. The foundation must be strong, and there are no shortcuts.

Begin "Discovery" Ahead of Time and Be Thorough

Discovery can and should start well before a lawsuit is filed, because documentary evidence makes or breaks a case. When someone is lying, a simple e-mail can prove a claim or demonstrate the pretext used to justify the discharge.

As important as collecting documentation is, be sure efforts at "self-help" do not cross the line. As explained more fully in Rule 20, an employee should not sneak into his or her boss's office at night and steal company documents. Stealing confidential personnel files about other employees usually results in a severe sanction against the whistleblower. If an employee breaks the law to prove a case, he or she probably has already lost. In extraordinary circumstances there may be some plausible justification for violating rules (such as removing company documents in violation of policy if *and only if* it can be proven that they would have been destroyed). However, generally speaking, whistleblowers will be held to higher performance and higher conduct standards than other employees.

When companies learn that an employee may have stolen "confidential" information from work, their high-priced attorneys often jump with glee, not out of concern for the previous but out of joy, as they may have stumbled upon a way to discredit the whistleblower. They sometimes use that fact to justify a termination (if the employee still works for the company) or to severely limit damages (if the employee was already fired). In evaluating how to deal with improper document removals, courts apply a "balancing test." One federal district court described the test as follows: "Employee conduct must be reasonable in light of the circumstances and must be balanced against the employer's right to run his business."

Another court set forth six factors that should be considered when weighing this balance:

1. How were the documents obtained? Did the employee have proper access to the documents, or did the employee obtain them in an innocent manner? Did the employee rifle through company files and surreptitiously copy the material?

2. To whom did the employee show the documents? Were they shown to coworkers and friends, or were the documents just provided to government investigators?

3. What was in the documents? Was the information the type that should be kept strictly confidential and that clearly should not have been copied?

4. Why were the documents obtained and why were they produced?

5. What was the employer's privacy or confidentiality policy?

6. Could the employee have obtained the material in a manner that did not violate company policy?

The best practice clearly is very simple: Don't break the law to expose the boss.

Documentary Evidence Is Vital

Examples of the critical role the right documents play in any whistleblower case are endless. Performance records of the whistleblower are crucial in establishing the employee's credibility. E-mails can substantiate employer knowledge of protected activity and document animus against the whistleblower. Safety records can prove that the company lied. Applications for government contracts can demonstrate false statements used to illegally obtain a grant or contract, and financial records can prove tax fraud. The list goes on and on, and the need for the records is obvious.

If a case enters active litigation, the company must respond to informational requests filed by the whistleblower. Under the rules of Federal Civil Procedure (which are consistent with the rules of practice under state laws and within the Department of Labor), a party to a lawsuit can engage in "discovery." This permits a whistleblower to submit broad document requests, requiring the company to produce thousands of pages of potentially relevant documents, such as performance records, personnel records of other comparable employees, internal investigative reports and audits, e-mails, and records related to the whistleblower allegations. In addition to document requests, witnesses can be questioned, under oath, in pretrial depositions, and subpoenas can be served on persons who have information relevant to the case.

Discovery is the single most important part of the pre-trial process. It creates the factual record necessary to defeat a motion for summary judgment (an attempt by the employer to have a case thrown out of court by a judge) and permits the whistleblower to "test" all the material evidence prior to trial. There are major tools at the disposal of a whistleblower during the discovery process.

DEPOSITIONS

Attorneys from each side can question relevant witnesses under oath prior to the trial. This gives an employee the opportunity to question all the company employees identified as having participated in the adverse action. These employees may confirm that the whistleblower engaged in protected activity and that the company knew of these activities. They may have information about causation, hostility against the employee's whistleblowing, or pretext. All the deciding officials can be questioned about the case.

DOCUMENT REQUESTS

A company can be required to produce documents relevant to a whistleblower case, including e-mails, personnel files, and internal investigatory files. To prevent companies from destroying evidence, it is a good practice to compile a detailed list of materials that should be subpoenaed while still working. If a company obtains a detailed request for documents, it may suspect that you already have the materials and consequently will produce them, without a big argument, or you may be able to find evidence that it improperly destroyed documents, and use these facts as a basis to seek sanctions.

INTERROGATORIES AND REQUESTS FOR ADMISSIONS

Interrogatories are written questions that the company must answer under oath. Admissions are similar to interrogatories in that the company must admit or deny various facts, under oath. These can be used to force a company to explain specific actions in order to eliminate surprise at trial. For example, if an employee is fired, the company may be asked to explain the precise grounds for the termination and identify all persons responsible for the adverse action. In this manner an employee can conduct further discovery in order to disprove the justifications for the firing. Furthermore, the employee can act without the worry that the company will change its story at trial once the weaknesses in the case are documented.

THIRD-PARTY SUBPOENAS

If evidence is not in the control or possession of the employer, third party subpoenas can be filed. These subpoenas permit a party to conduct discovery (such as depositions and requests for production of documents) on former employees, government investigators, and other nonparty witnesses.

Discovery tends to be far more important for the employee than the employer. The company usually possesses most of the relevant records, such as the employment files of other employees (to determine whether the whistle-blower was subjected to "disparate treatment") and documentation related to the underlying whistleblower allegations. However, the company can conduct discovery against the employee as well.

Common areas of company discovery are: psychological records if the employee is alleging emotional distress; an employee's prior work history (in an attempt to either argue that the employee engaged in résumé fraud to get his or her job, or argue that the employee had a history of poor performance); and a fishing expedition in an attempt to find derogatory information to use in cross examination.

What to Look for in Discovery

There are a number of important goals of discovery that an employee whistle-blower needs to identify in planning. Many of these goals are unique to a specific case, but some are predictable, such as:

- Learn precisely what the company's case is against the employee to prevent any "surprises" at trial.

- Start building a defense. Learn the company's case, both its strengths and weaknesses. If the whistleblower doesn't know what the company witnesses are going to say, how can he or she prepare a solid impeachment?

- Prove that the underlying whistleblower allegations were true. This can bolster an employee's credibility, while impeaching the company's motives. Although the company may argue that evidence of misconduct is irrelevant, this is simply not the case. If the company did in fact engage in misconduct, that misconduct is highly relevant to proving the true reason for retaliation.

- In a False Claims Act case, prove the fraud.

- Verify "disparate treatment." Disciplining a whistleblower for offenses for which other employees are regularly given a "pass" constitutes strong evidence of discrimination and pretext. Under a disparate treatment analysis, even if the whistleblower did have performance problems, the employee can prevail in the case if the employee experienced harsher treatment than other workers who never engaged in protected activity. That is the classic definition of discrimination: treating two similarly situated employees differently solely because one engaged in protected activities and the other did not. The primary method for proving disparate treatment is to engage in discovery concerning how other employees are treated, including obtaining access to disciplinary records and personnel files.

- Obtain e-mails and other computer-generated files. This type of contemporaneous documentation is often highly relevant to a case, as it contains confirmation that various managers knew or suspected that an employee was a whistleblower and often documents how these managers reacted to the protected activities of their subordinate.

- Obtain evidence of pretext. In order to demonstrate weaknesses in the company's case against the employee, each manager responsible for the adverse action can be questioned under oath.

Did the company thoroughly investigate the allegations against the employee? Did the company give the employee a fair shot in disproving those allegations? Are there conflicts regarding the reasons given by the managers for taking the adverse action? Did anyone lie about the employee? Is the oral testimony of the managers consistent with the documentary evidence? Proving that a company lied about an employee is never an easy task, but without discovery it is usually an impossible one.

During the discovery process a whistleblower should gather all the evidence that may help prove his or her case, or disprove the company's case. Discovery is an opportunity to find out the other team's weaknesses and adjust strategy accordingly. Hunting for weaknesses in the company's case, contradictory testimony, harmful admissions, and incriminating documents are all examples of weaknesses that a whistleblower can use to his or her advantage.

PRACTICE TIP

Checklist 6 sets forth the common areas for which employees seek discovery in retaliation cases, along with supporting case authority.

RULE 24

Get to the Jury

Every law sets forth a series of elements that must be met; otherwise a case is subject to summary dismissal. In other words, whenever a whistleblower case is filed, the very first thing an employer does is pull out a checklist. The checklist begins with a set of mandatory requirements under law for setting forth a valid case. One by one the skilled and highly paid company lawyer examines each element to find any technicality to have a court throw out the case. It will not matter if the whistleblower saved lives or saved money. To the company, winning is the single objective from the start. If you do not meet the criteria for each element in that checklist, the employer will file a motion to dismiss your case, and a court most likely will grant that motion. You will lose your case before it even starts.

Know the Checklist of Mandatory Requirements Under Law

Whistleblowers need to study the checklist first. They need to make sure they cover all their bases before filing a claim. The basic elements universally applicable to almost all whistleblower employment retaliation cases include the following:

1. The whistleblower must be an employee covered under the law.

2. The company must be an employer covered under the law.

3. The employee must have engaged in protected activity.

4. The management must have known of the protected disclosures.

5. The whistleblower must have suffered an adverse action.

6. There must be some proof of a connection between the adverse action and the protected conduct.

Although not a formal "element" of a claim, many whistleblower laws require employees to "exhaust" their administrative remedies before they can file cases in court.

THE EMPLOYEE AND EMPLOYER MUST BE SUBJECT TO THE LAW

This is usually not a major issue. However, some laws narrowly define whom they cover, and some employment situations are inherently problematic. For example, are employees who work in a foreign country for an American corporation protected? What happens if a person works for a subcontractor and the contractor retaliates? What liability does a parent corporation have for a subsidiary? These types of issues are complicated, and there are no simple answers. It is best for whistleblowers to find laws that explicitly cover their job and their employer.

There is a distinction between public and private employment in the majority of whistleblower laws. For employees who work in the private sector, certain laws, such as the Sarbanes-Oxley corporate whistleblower law, apply to them. Similarly, employees who work for the government are protected under specialized whistleblower protection laws. Protections under the First Amendment generally apply only to public-sector employees. Most federal statutes only apply to private-sector employees, although some apply exclusively to government workers, or both sectors of the economy.

Under federal law, employees can include former employees, job applicants, contractors, and agents. Employers can include companies that control access to job sites. Attorneys can also be protected employees. The SOX Act covers "agents" of employers and explicitly requires certain attorneys to blow the whistle if they witness securities fraud. Other whistleblower laws have also protected in-house counsel from retaliation, even when the information disclosed may be covered under the attorney-client privilege.

Most statutes explicitly define which employees are covered under which laws. Where there is a gray area, case law must be carefully reviewed.

ENSURE THAT YOUR DISCLOSURES ARE PROTECTED

Before blowing the whistle, an employee needs to decipher what type of "whistleblowing" is protected by law. He or she should ask questions: Does the law protect disclosures to supervisors? Does the law protect disclosures to hotlines? Does the law protect disclosures to the news media? Are there specific government agencies identified in the law for which disclosures are encouraged or permitted?

Protected activity is defined within the text of the statute. But these definitions tend to be very general in nature. Thus it is important to review judicial interpretations of the law. The risks are immense for employees who blow the whistle before knowing what disclosures were protected under law.

Sometimes common sense does not apply and laws are interpreted in a highly technical manner that undermines the intent behind protecting whistleblowers. For example, if an employee works for the FBI and exposes illegal conduct to Congress, he or she is not protected under the Department of Justice FBI whistleblower law. However, if the employee exposes the exact same illegal conduct to the Department of Justice inspector general, he or she is fully protected. No law is perfect. It may appear logical that certain disclosures should be protected, but it is absolutely imperative to confirm that they are protected before stepping into the water with the sharks.

The safest course of action is to blow the whistle to an agency explicitly protected under the statute or under controlling judicial decisions. Conducting this research before a disclosure is made can significantly strengthen an employee's case, by ensuring that the disclosure is protected under the most powerful law available to the employee.

IF FILING A RETALIATION CASE, MAKE SURE THE BOSS KNOWS WHO BLEW THE WHISTLE

A critical element in proving a whistleblower retaliation case is employer "knowledge" about who engaged in protected activity. The manager responsible for the adverse employment action must either know or suspect that the employee was a whistleblower. In other words, if an employee reports violations, but the boss never knew who blew the whistle, how can that employee be fired in retaliation for something the boss did not know he or she did? It is a perfect management defense. A boss cannot fire an employee in retaliation for conduct of which the boss was unaware.

An "innocent party" can actually be protected under whistleblower laws. This can happen when an employee never engaged in protected activity but was fired by "mistake" because that unlucky worker was a "suspected culprit" in the disclosures.

The "knowledge" element has caused significant problems. For instance, some employees want to blow the whistle anonymously because it makes sense to make a confidential disclosure for job protection. But what happens if the boss figures out who made the exposure? If an employee cannot prove that the boss knew who blew the whistle, he or she risks losing the case. Most courts permit employees to prove knowledge by direct or "circumstantial" evidence. In other words, if an employee was a confidential whistleblower, he or she can use circumstantial evidence, such as off-hand comments, or the nature of the allegations themselves (for example, he or she was one of the few persons who spoke out against the violation) to demonstrate that the employer thought that employee was the informer.

Employees who blow the whistle to their immediate supervisor usually can meet the knowledge requirement. A boss will have great difficulty denying knowing that an employee engaged in protected activity when the disclosure was made directly to him or her. Moreover, once an employee complains internally about a violation, that employee is always the number one suspect if a government regulatory agency becomes involved.

The major exception to this rule is the False Claims Act and other similar rewards-based whistleblower laws, including the Dodd-Frank Act and the IRS whistleblower rewards law. Under the FCA, whistleblowers must file confidential disclosures to the attorney general, and the initial lawsuit is filed under seal with the courts. In other words, the whistleblower is not permitted to tell the company that he or she has filed an FCA lawsuit. The case must remain confidential in order to give the Department of Justice time to investigate the merits of the claim. The confidential nature of the FCA disclosures can benefit employees. Filing a claim is statutorily protected. In other words, the law protects the filing of a confidential complaint and disclosure statement with the DOJ, even though the company cannot be served copies of these documents. Under the Dodd-Frank Act, employees can obtain whistleblower rewards if they file their claims anonymously with the government.

PROTECTED ACTIVITY MUST BE CONDUCTED IN "GOOD FAITH"

This is a confusing element. The "good faith" standard does not mean that an employee who blows the whistle must be an angel, or must be strictly serving the public interest. Most laws, and nearly every court, understand that the subjective motive of an employee for blowing the whistle may be less then honorable (for example, an employee who is upset he or she did not get a promotion). The good faith element looks at whether an employee has a reasonable belief that what he or she is disclosing constitutes a violation of law/threat to public safety/fraud.

The good faith standard does not relate to an employee's subjective motivation for becoming a whistleblower. Take a case in which an engineer blows the whistle on defective welds. The engineer believes that the defect in the welds could cause a bridge to collapse and files a complaint with the Department of Transportation. The government investigates the complaint, and the welds are found to be in fine shape. Should the employee be protected under a whistleblower law?

Almost universally, courts addressing this issue have held that if an employee's concerns over the safety of the welds had a reasonable basis in fact, the whistleblower must be protected. In other words, courts seek to determine whether a "reasonable" person could have a good faith belief that the welds could fail and cause harm. If the factual predicates for the claims are reasonable, courts will find that the whistleblowing was in good faith and those disclosures will normally be fully protected. But in cases in which no reasonable person could, in good faith, have suspected that the welds were faulty, the employee may lose protection. How much proof must an employee put forward to demonstrate to a court that his or her concerns were objectively reasonable? That is decided on a case-by-case basis, and different standards can be applied to different laws. Consequently, even though employees do not have to prove that their allegations were correct, it is important to ensure that they are based on objective facts.

No federal antiretaliation law requires that the employee's allegations of misconduct be verified. For example, when Congress debated the Sarbanes-Oxley corporate whistleblower law, they cited with approval to an environmental whistleblower case decided by the U.S. Court of Appeals that clearly set forth this rule:

> [A]n employee's non-frivolous complaint should not have to be guaranteed to withstand the scrutiny of in-house or external review in order to merit protection . . . for the obvious reason that such a standard would chill employee initiatives for bringing to light perceived discrepancies in the workings of their agency.

The key feature of whistleblower laws is to encourage employees to *report* suspected wrongdoing.

All whistleblower laws are meant to encourage employees to step forward and provide information about wrongdoing to the proper authorities. These employees are often motivated by a desire to serve the public good; however, angelic motives are not required in whistleblower law.

AN EMPLOYEE MUST SUFFER ADVERSE ACTION

Merely calling oneself a "whistleblower" does not mean a person can file a suit. With the exception of the False Claims Act (and other rewards-based laws), all whistleblower protection laws require that the employee suffer some form of adverse action. A termination is universally accepted as an adverse employment action. Conduct short of a firing, such as a demotion, a suspension, or placing an employee on probation may also be considered adverse actions. There are numerous court decisions evaluating nearly every type of potential adverse action, ranging from "hostile work environment" to "constructive discharge" (i.e., when the working conditions become so intolerable that an employee is permitted to quit and then sue for being terminated).

What constitutes adverse action differs from state to state, law to law, and court to court. On one hand, some states require an actual discharge in order to file a public policy tort. On the other hand, under federal law, a "hostile work environment" can constitute adverse action, even if no direct negative action was ever taken against the whistleblower. Adverse action can include: transfer to a dead-end position, blacklisting, bad evaluations (that could impact pay or benefits) or bad references, denial of a promotion or benefits afforded other workers, retaliatory layoff, refusal to hire, a hostile work environment, reprimands or suspensions, and constructive discharge.

In *Burlington Northern & Santa Fe Railway Co. v. White* the Supreme Court wrestled with the issue of whether employer action that did not result in an employee losing money or benefits constituted adverse action. The Court held that it did if the harassment was "likely to deter" a reasonable employee from exercising protected whistleblower activities. This was a big win for whistleblowers, as it recognized the "chilling effect" employer harassment has on the willingness of any employee to risk a job to report misconduct.

But it is equally well settled in law that "not everything that makes an employee unhappy is actionable adverse action." Although it is very important to document changes in working conditions that followed the whistleblowing (as these changes may constitute evidence of retaliation), an employee should not necessarily file a lawsuit over every minor action taken by an employer. If the judge or jury does not think that the mentioned conduct rose to the level of a true adverse action, the case will be thrown out. But sometimes it is important to send a message that any act of retaliation will be strongly challenged. You should not wait until you are fired, or until the boss builds a strong case against you, to file a lawsuit.

Take-home message: Don't pick a fight over any minor slight. Wait until the fight is both winnable and worth the effort.

Exhaust Administrative Procedures

The final technicality companies often use to have cases thrown out of court is referred to as the "exhaustion" doctrine. This rule applies to the numerous statutes that require employees to file a claim with a designated administrative agency before a case can be filed in court. For example, under the Sarbanes-Oxley Act, a complaint must be filed with the Department of Labor (DOL). Only after the case has been before the DOL for 180 days can the case be removed to federal court. Even if the DOL has taken no action, the employee must still wait until he or she has "exhausted" administrative remedies. If the claim was filed directly in federal court, the case would be dismissed due to the failure to "exhaust."

Numerous employment laws require exhaustion of administrative remedies, including Title VII of the Civil Rights Act (sex- and race-based discrimination). Others, like the Clean Air Act or the Mine Health and Safety Act, only allow for administrative proceedings.

Because so many whistleblower laws require complainants to be initially filed with the U.S. Department of Labor (DOL), that agency has developed an expertise in whistleblower law. Consequently, even when employees are permitted to remove their cases to federal court, many employees choose not to, and have their cases heard by DOL judges. Among the whistleblower laws that require initial filings within the DOL are: the Sarbanes-Oxley Act; the Consumer Products Safety Act; the Railroad, Airline, Trucking, and Public Transportation laws; and the Atomic Energy Act.

Regardless of whether you want to pursue your case in court or in an agency, it is absolutely imperative to carefully review the filing and appeal procedures to ensure that you fully "exhaust" all administrative requirements at each step of the game.

PRACTICE TIPS

Federal Rules of Civil Procedure 12 and 56 set forth the standards for having a case dismissed (and conversely, what is needed to avoid dismissal).

- *NLRB v. Scrivener*, 405 U.S. 117 (1972) (premier case on broad scope of protected activity)

- *Passaic Valley Sewerage Commissioners v. U.S. Dept. of Labor*, 992 F.2d 474 (3rd. Cir. 1993) (premier case on "good faith")

- *Fraizer v. MSPB*, 672 F.2d 150 (D.C. Cir. 1982) (premier case on employer "knowledge")

- *Burlington Northern & Santa Fe Railway Co. v. White*, 548 U.S. 53 (2006) (premier case defining adverse action)

- *Halliburton v. ARB*, 771 F.3d 254 (5th Cir. 2014) (applying Burlington to corporate whistleblower cases)

RULE 25

Win the Case: Prove Motive and Pretext

The penultimate question in every whistleblower retaliation case revolves around proving "causation." The employee must prove that he or she was fired or retaliated against because of a protected disclosure. In other words, employees must prove that protected activity was a "contributing" or "motivating" cause for the adverse employment action. Employees must show that the act of blowing the whistle played a part in the decision-making process. There must be some form of causal relationship between the whistleblowing and the adverse action.

The reason for this requirement is simple: Whistleblowing does not grant employees immunity to engage in misconduct or fail to perform their job. Companies can always discipline an employee for a legitimate business reason. However, a company cannot treat a whistleblower more harshly than they treat other employees (this is known as "disparate treatment").

Typical Arguments the Company Will Use to Defend Actions

The main difficulty in proving causation is simple. Employers do not admit that they fired an employee because he or she blew the whistle. In almost every case, regardless of how outrageously an employee was treated, a company will formulate a "pretext" or a so-called "legitimate" justification for terminating an employee. And sometimes this pretext is benign.

For example, a company may state that it simply "loved" the employee and greatly "appreciated" the fact that the employee's whistleblowing cost them millions of dollars, but unfortunately, the company had no alternative but to "lay off" the employee due to "lack of work."

Sometimes the justification for firing a whistleblower is malignant. A company uses allegations of serious performance failures to justify firing the worker. Often the employee is confronted with a choice at the time of his or her discharge—if he or she "voluntarily resigns" and signs various releases (which will prevent the whistleblower from suing the company), the company will keep the so-called performance-based reasons for the firing confidential and may even provide a reference for finding another job. The gun is put to the employee's head: Quit and drop any cases, or the company will fire you for misconduct. Meanwhile the company is very aware of the fact that firing the employee for "cause" can make it difficult for the whistleblower to find another job.

The risks for whistleblowers attacked in this manner are enormous. Given the resources available to a company, including ready access to witnesses and documentation, how does an employee defeat a company's performance-based allegations?

Sometimes you can get lucky and the proof of causation is self-evident. In a rare case the company admits that the reason it fired the employee was retaliatory. This usually occurs in circumstances in which the company does not understand that the employee's conduct is legally protected, and thus its admission as to why the employee was fired becomes legally damning. For example, many laws protect employees who blow the whistle outside of the "chain of command." Under these laws, if management admits that the employee was fired because he or she violated the "chain of command," the company indirectly admits to the wrongdoing. Direct evidence that an employer was angry with a worker who tipped off a government inspector or raised a concern to upper management without the "courtesy" of telling his or her immediate boss can be key to proving causation. But in most cases the proof of causation will be far more subtle.

An Iowa federal court judge explained how difficult it can be for employees to prove that their protected activities caused their termination:

> Employment discrimination and retaliation, except in the rarest cases, is difficult to prove. . . . Today's employers, even those with only a scintilla of sophistication, will neither admit discriminatory or retaliatory intent, nor leave a well-developed trail demonstrating it. Because adverse employment actions almost always involve a high degree of discretion, and most plaintiffs in employment discrimination cases are at will, it is a simple task for employers to concoct plausible reasons for virtually any adverse employment action ranging from failure to hire to discharge.

One important method an employee can use to prove causation is by demonstrating that an employer's justification for an adverse action was not truthful. If a company lies about an employee's performance, that lie can constitute "persuasive" circumstantial evidence of "intentional discrimination." Writing for the U.S. Supreme Court, Justice Sandra Day O'Conner put it this way:

> The fact finders disbelief of the reasons put forward by the defendant (particularly if disbelief is accompanied by a suspicion of mendacity) may,

together with the elements of the prima facie case, suffice to show intentional discrimination. Thus, rejection of the defendant's proffered reasons will permit the trier of fact to infer the ultimate fact of intentional discrimination.

If a company lies about an employee's alleged poor performance, or fails to properly credit an employee's good performance, an employee is in a strong position to prove pretext.

Disparate Treatment and Circumstantial Evidence

The U.S. Supreme Court recognized that there rarely is direct proof of causation. Few employers will admit that they fired an employee for blowing the whistle. Consequently, the Court has ruled that employees can rely solely on circumstantial evidence to prove causation. No "smoking gun" is necessary to win a case, and the employer never has to admit that whistleblowing played any part of the decision to fire the employee. Of course such admissions can make a case much stronger, but they are not required (and most often never exist).

"[E]vidence that a defendant's explanation for an employment practice is 'unworthy of credence' is one form of circumstantial evidence that is probative of intentional discrimination."
Justice Clarence Thomas, *Desert Palace v. Costa* (2003)

Although the types of circumstantial evidence an employee can rely on to prove causation are case specific, the timing of an adverse action is another factor heavily relied on in whistleblower cases. How did the boss view the employee before he or she became a whistleblower? How was the employee viewed after the whistleblower incident? Other than becoming a whistleblower, did anything else happen within the employment context that could rationally explain why there was a change in attitude toward the employee after the whistleblowing?

Both the timing of an adverse action and demonstrating pretext can be key to demonstrating the link between the protected activity and the adverse action. Other factors can also come into play. The following list is not exhaustive, but it sets forth some of the factors courts have considered to sustain a finding of causation or pretext:

- Excellent performance rating before the whistleblowing, and performance problems after the protected disclosure;

- The failure of an employer to follow routine procedures, such as adequately investigating the charges against the employee or failure to seek an employee's input prior to making a decision to downgrade or terminate the employee;

- Absence of previous complaints against the employee;

- Disparate treatment between the way the whistleblower was treated and the manner in which other employees who did not blow the whistle were treated;

- A determination that an employee was not guilty of the alleged violations and the failure of the employer to adequately look into the charges and/or follow procedures generally afforded other employees to prove their innocence;

- Statements that an employee's protected activity was "disloyal" or somehow wrong. Any remarks whatsoever that indicate that the employer was upset or displeased with an employee's protected activities, including statements indicating that the employee was a troublemaker or failed to follow the chain of command;

- A pay increase shortly before the whistleblower disclosure was made and adverse action shortly after the disclosure;

- Hostility or anger directed toward an employee's protected activities;

- Shifting explanations for the reason(s) given for the adverse action;

- Advising employees not to report safety problems or to talk with government inspectors;

- Any dishonesty by an employer regarding facts material to a case, including knowledge of protected activity, reasons given for taking adverse action against an employee, or statements about the validity of the underlying whistleblower disclosure.

The nature of the whistleblowing may, unto itself, provide evidence of improper motive by the employer, especially when the company actually engaged in misconduct and has a reason for keeping it secret. As explained in a nuclear safety case:

> Antagonism toward activity that is protected . . . may manifest itself in many ways, e.g., ridicule, openly hostile actions, or threatening statements, or, in the case of a whistleblower who contacts the NRC, simply questioning why the whistleblower did not pursue corrective action through the usual internal channels. In addition, deliberate violations of NRC regulations suggest antagonism toward the [government] regulatory scheme and thus may provide support for an inference of retaliatory intent.

In some cases, employers inadvertently admit to facts that prove causation, such as when managers testify that they are upset that employees went above them to raise a concern. Who would not be upset that a subordinate ignored them and went over their head in raising a concern? Who would not be upset that a lower-level employee did not have the courtesy of pointing out errors and giving time to fix the problem before making a "federal case"? Who would not be embarrassed by such acts of disloyalty? These may appear to be simply honest feelings or reasonable reactions from a manager to a whistleblower. The only problem with these admissions is that they constitute direct evidence of guilt. An admission that a supervisor was upset or troubled by an employee's whistleblowing constitutes evidence of discriminatory motive.

The "Contributing Factor" Test

Under most state and federal laws, employees have the burden of demonstrating both causation and pretext. Employees must prove these two elements by a preponderance of evidence. However, starting in 1989, Congress came to understand that this burden was often difficult for an employee to meet. Companies generally control information about employment practices, thus proving that a company deviated from procedures or covered up misconduct was very difficult. Likewise, witnesses are often under the control of the employer because of fear, a mistaken sense of loyalty, or concerns over their own jobs.

In the Whistleblower Protection Act of 1989 (the law covering most federal employees), Congress overruled the judge-made precedent regarding the proof necessary to win a whistleblower case. It created a brand-new standard designed to make it easier for employees to win their cases. This standard is commonly referred to as the "contributing factor" test.

In enacting the "contributing factor" test, Congress explained its intent:

The bill makes it easier . . . to prove that a whistleblower reprisal has taken place. To establish a prima facie case, an individual must prove that whistleblowing was a factor in the personnel action. This supersedes the existing requirement that whistleblowing was a substantial, motivating or predominant factor in the personnel action. One of the many possible ways to show that the whistleblowing was a factor . . . is to show that the official taking the action knew (or had constructive knowledge) of the disclosure and acted within such a period of time that a reasonable person could conduce that the disclosure was a factor in the personnel action. The bill establishes an affirmative defense for an agency. [C]orrective action would not be ordered if the agency demonstrates by clear and convincing evidence that it would have taken the same personnel action in the absence of the disclosure.

Instead of having to prove hostility toward the whistleblowing as the main motivating factor in an adverse action, the employee need only prove that the hostility was "a factor," regardless of how small. As explained by the Federal Circuit Court of Appeals, "contributing factor . . . mean(s) any factor which, alone or in connection with other facts, tends to affect in any way the outcome of the decision."

Just as the burden of proving causation was decreased for the employee, the burden for proving a legitimate business reason was significantly increased for management. Instead of the employee having the burden of proving pretext, the burden shifted to the employer. The employer had to demonstrate a legitimate reason for the discipline or discharge. This burden was increased from preponderance of evidence to "clear and convincing" evidence, a much higher standard.

Evidence of causation and pretext are normally the most important elements in proving a whistleblower case and Congress's intervention made it easier for whistleblowers to win their cases under laws that apply the contributing factor test. Today these laws include the following: the Consumer Product Safety Act, the Whistleblower Protection Act, the Automobile Safety Whistleblower Act, the Contractor Whistleblower Act, the Affordable Care Act, Seamen Whistleblower Protection Act, the Sarbanes-Oxley Act, the Food Safety Modernization Act, the Atomic Energy Act, the Consumer Financial Protection Act, the Airline Safety Act, the Surface Transportation Act, the Railroad Safety Act, the Pipeline Safety Improvement Act, and the Stimulus Spending Act. Some states are also following this precedent, including the public employee whistleblower law enacted by the District of Columbia.

The *Qui Tam* Alternative

Proving retaliation is not easy. This is why many whistleblowers, when they can, shift the focus of their claim from a wrongful discharge case to a False Claims Act case. If an employee's whistleblowing concerns misuse of taxpayer monies, and he or she has strong proof that the employer engaged in contracting or procurement abuses, shifting the focus of the case from proving employment discrimination to proving a false claim may be a good tactic.

When proving a false claim, issues such as an employee's performance or proof of retaliation are normally not material to the case. The issue is completely different: Regardless of whether or not the whistleblower was a "good employee," did the company rip off the taxpayer? If the answer is yes, the whistleblower prevails on his or her *qui tam* whistleblower case. It is often in the employee's best interest to focus his or her limited resources on proving fraud against the government. The ability of whistleblowers to focus their energy on rewards-based laws was significantly enhanced when Congress amended the Internal Revenue Code in 2006 and enacted the Dodd-Frank Act in 2010. These laws expanded the scope of potential *qui tam* claims from just government contracting to tax, securities, and commodities fraud. In every case, it is essential to determine whether the whistleblower's case is just an employment retaliation case or whether the whistleblower can prove frauds covered under the *qui tam* laws. An employee can pursue both a retaliation case and a claim for a whistleblower reward, but that decision should be made before any lawsuit is filed.

Animus, Pretext, and Corporate Culture

Some day customs and attitudes within the workplace will change. Raising allegations that a company is threatening public safety, ripping off taxpayers, or violating the law will be accepted within corporate culture. Some day large institutions will recognize that responsiveness in the face of credible allegations of wrongdoing serves both the public interest and the long-term interest of the institution. That day is not at hand. Sometimes Congress has stepped in, and new whistleblower laws enacted after 1989 have often made the job of proving retaliation easier for whistleblowers by including the contributing factor test in modern whistleblower protection statutes. Even with this modification, winning a whistleblower retaliation case is still very difficult, and it requires careful attention to necessary facts that prove causation and motive in every case (regardless of who has the burden of proof).

Checklist 5 provides a list of factors used to demonstrate discriminatory motive and pretext in retaliation cases.

RULE 26

Get Every Penny Deserved

Many attorneys and their clients focus their efforts on winning a case and do not spend the time and effort putting forward a proof of damages. It is easy to focus on the battle to save whistleblowers' jobs and reputations and prove that the whistleblowers were right. But in doing so, it is also equally important to stay focused on ensuring that if whistleblowers win the case, they will get all the relief they deserve.

The basic approach to setting damages in whistleblower employment discrimination cases is known as the "make whole" rule. Damages are designed to place the wrongfully discharged whistleblower in the precise place he or she would occupy if the discrimination never occurred. The bottom-line standard for obtaining relief was set forth in an 1867 U.S. Supreme Court case, which stated that "compensation" awarded to a victim must be "equal to the injury ... the injured party is to be placed, as near as may be, in the situation he would have occupied if the wrong had not been committed."

Just as the scope of protected activity is different under every whistleblower law, so is the scope of relief. Each statute generally sets forth the relief that can be granted. In deciding which law or laws a claim should be filed under, it is very important to carefully review the scope of relief available.

The major categories of damages relevant in whistleblower cases include the following:

- *Reinstatement.* Employees are entitled not just to reinstatement to a job, but reinstatement to their old job, or if not possible, a comparable job. This includes a position with the same status and promotional opportunities as the one they lost.

- *Front pay.* Front pay is an alternative to reinstatement. It is available in cases when an "irreparable animosity" exists between the company and the whistleblower. The amount of front pay is calculated to compensate employees for lost future earnings if they are not reinstated. However, employees are not automatically entitled to front pay, and the authority to award this form of relief is vested with a judge or jury. In order to be entitled to front pay in lieu of reinstatement employees must demonstrate that a "productive and amicable working relationship" between the parties "would be impossible."

- *Back pay and benefits.* Employees are entitled to an award of back pay and lost benefits. However, employees need to be fully aware that companies can escape large back-pay awards by alleging that the employee failed to "mitigate" damages. This means that an employee cannot simply be fired and await the outcome of the legal case. They are under an obligation to look for new employment. If an employee does not look for work, the amount of damages for which he or she may be entitled can be reduced if the employee "did not exercise reasonable diligence" in trying to find a new job. A company has the burden of proving that an employee did not exercise reasonable diligence.

- *Compensatory damages.* Compensatory damages are awarded for pain and suffering, humiliation, emotional distress, and loss of reputation. Although not required, expert psychological testimony is often relied upon to justify major emotional distress damages. Sometimes referred to as "special damages," compensatory damages are available under state public policy tort claims and most federal statutes. A request for compensatory or special damages should be pleaded in the initial complaint, as this is sometimes a requirement for obtaining a jury trial.

- *Punitive or exemplary damages.* Punitive damages are available under state public policy tort claims and some federal statutes (including First Amendment or witness retaliation claims filed under the Civil Rights Act of 1871). Even if available under law, punitive damages are not automatically awarded. According to U.S. Supreme Court precedent, employees must demonstrate that the employer's "conduct" was "motivated by evil motive or intent" or that the employer acted with "reckless or callous indifference to the federally protected rights of others." The Supreme Court of Mississippi upheld a punitive damage award of $1.5 million because "people" should not be fired because they report "illegal acts."

- *Other relief.* Outside of the big-ticket items listed above, the "make whole" remedy available under federal law can be aggressively and creatively applied in order to ensure that whistleblowers are truly made whole. An important question to ask is how can this very general rule be molded to ensure that any particular worker gets all the benefits necessary to be truly made whole? This includes relief related to the loss of status and career opportunities, which always flow from a termination or other adverse action. The types of relief awarded under this rule include the following:

- Monetary compensation for lost overtime pay that an employee would have earned but for the discharge;

- Restoration of vacation time;

- Interest on all damages;

- Restoration of seniority;

- Restoration and/or compensation for all lost benefits, such as parking privileges and financial compensation for having lost access to a company car;

- Positive recommendations from the employer;

- Back pay awards to take anticipated salary increases into consideration;

- Compensation for forced sale of assets due to a prolonged unemployment;

- All job search expenses (including the use of a "headhunter");

- Removal of negative information from a personnel file;

- Reinstatement of stock options and employee savings plans;

- Restoration of lost retirement benefits;

- Medical expenses (including future expenses);

- A letter of apology from the company president to all employees;

- A notification from the company to all employees that it violated the law when it fired the whistleblower;

- Company-wide training for managers about the rights of whistleblowers.

- *Qui tam* damages. Proof of damages in a False Claims Act and other *qui tam* cases are totally different than the proof necessary in an employment retaliation case. Under the rewards provision of the False Claims Act, damages are not tied to the harm suffered by an employee. Instead, they are set by the economic harm experienced by taxpayers. If the whistleblower can prove a violation of the False Claims Act, the wrongdoer must pay the government three times the amount of any fraud/wrongful billing (in addition to a fine for each violation), and the whistleblower is entitled to a percentage of the monies obtained by the government (15 percent to 30 percent).

This same formulation holds true for all *qui tam* claims. The statute sets the percentage reward: Internal Revenue Code (15 percent to 30 percent); Securities Exchange Act (10 percent to 30 percent); Commodity Exchange Act (10 percent to 30 percent).

PRACTICE TIP

Before filing a claim review, read the actual text of the federal whistleblower protections laws cited in Checklist 2, as the statutes themselves usually set forth the relief available under each law. The sources for this rule cite case precedents setting forth the specific types of damage awards available in retaliation cases.

RULE 27

Make the Boss Pay Attorney Fees

One of the first major problems encountered by any whistleblower is the ability to locate and retain competent legal counsel. Whistleblower cases are complex and often hard fought. The defendant may be a powerful or well-connected special interest and cases can go on for years. Without an attorney, most whistleblowers will lose their cases.

Under the "American Rule," absent a statute, parties to civil lawsuits are responsible for paying their own attorney fees, regardless of who wins or loses a lawsuit. Often, attorneys work for clients on a "contingency fee" basis and accept a percentage of a recovery as compensation for their fees. Contingency fee agreements are typical in whistleblower-reward cases. However, in employment cases this arrangement can be highly problematic. For example, assume an employee had an income of $50,000 per year. He or she was wrongfully fired, and after a two-year battle won the case and obtained a $100,000 judgment. A 40 percent contingency payment would only provide the attorney who represented the client with a $40,000 fee, an amount that could not adequately compensate an attorney who had to litigate a whistleblower case.

Moreover, in cases in which an employee suffered harm but was not fired (such as a hostile work environment case or a denial of a promotion), the amount of monetary damages may be very low.

To resolve this problem and encourage attorneys to represent whistleblowers, Congress included attorney fee provisions in almost every federal whistleblower law. The reason for including the payment of fees and costs as part of the damages in employment cases was explained by Congress in the Senate Report on Civil Rights Attorney Fee Awards Act of 1976, codified as 42 U.S.C. § 1988: "If private citizens are able to assert their civil rights, and if those who violate the nation's fundamental laws are not to proceed with impunity, then citizens must have the opportunity to recover what it costs them to vindicate these rights in Court."

Section 1988 permits employees who win their cases to obtain fees in civil rights cases, including retaliation cases filed under Title VII of the Civil Rights Act of 1964 and First Amendment cases filed under the Civil Rights Act of 1871. The statutory attorney's fee provisions in whistleblower laws are all modeled on this Section 1988.

The U.S. Supreme Court recognized that fee-shifting statutes were intended by Congress to "ensure effective access to the judicial process" by properly compensating attorneys in order to ensure that employees had the ability to "attract competent counsel" to represent their claims. As Justice Alito held in the 2010 case of *Perdue v. Kenny*: The statutory fee provisions are intended "to ensure that federal rights are adequately enforced."

Under these provisions, if the employee wins the case, the company must pay the employee's counsel at reasonable market rates. Attorneys can be paid fees in the hundreds of thousands of dollars (or even millions of dollars), and the payment of attorney fees is not directly tied to the amount of money awarded to the employee, or the sum the employee was able to pay an attorney as part of a retainer agreement. As explained in the *Perdue* case, a "reasonable fee is a fee sufficient to induce a capable attorney to undertake the representation of a meritorious civil rights case . . . but that does not produce windfalls to attorneys."

When determining which law should be used to pursue a whistleblower case, it is absolutely necessary to check and make sure the law has an attorney's fee provision. Most federal whistleblower protection laws do, including the FCA, the Consumer Products Safety Act, the Dodd-Frank Act antiretaliation provisions, and the environmental and nuclear safety laws.

The amount of attorney fees can and often do exceed the amount of damages awarded to the employee. This permits an attorney to spend the time necessary to carefully litigate a whistleblower case. It enables a whistleblower's counsel to compete with big firms, afford aggressive discovery, and fight a case as hard as the most obstinate employer.

The following are the basic rules governing awarding attorney fees and costs to employees who win a whistleblower case:

- Properly document all costs incurred and the amount of time an attorney spends working on every aspect of the case. If the whistleblower wins, the attorney will be required to submit a detailed statement of all hours worked on the case and all costs incurred. Without proper documentation a client may not be able to obtain reimbursement for all costs, and a court may refuse to require a defendant to pay for attorney fees that are not adequately documented.

- In setting a reasonable fee, the court will apply a "lodestar" calculation in which the reasonable amount of time spent working on the case is multiplied by the "reasonable" market rate for the attorney's services. The market rate is not tied to the amount of fees actually charged by the attorney, but is established by the general market rates governing "complex civil litigation." In other words, fees are not limited due to the inability of a client to pay and/or the fact that an attorney may charge public interest clients a reduced hourly fee. The "market rate" is governed by the rates charged by attorneys engaged in non-public interest work, such as antitrust litigation. Often the market rate is pegged to the amount of fees charged by large for-profit law firms that represent paying defendants. Attorneys should not be penalized because they choose to represent whistleblowers or other public interest clients at a reduced rate.

- Reasonable market rates vary from location to location and from court to court. Some of the factors taken into consideration in setting a fee include the "novelty and difficulty of questions presented" in the case, the "results obtained" by the attorney, the "undesirability" of the case, and the "customary fee" charged for similar types of cases.

- There is no proportionality rule. The amount of attorney fees is not conditioned by the size of the judgment obtained. The Supreme Court confirmed this rule in 1986, when it upheld an award of $245,456.26 in attorney fees in a case in which the damages awarded to the victim of the discrimination were limited to $33,350.00. If an employee obtains injunctive relief only (no monetary judgment), there is still no cap on attorney fees and costs.

- Prevailing employees can obtain compensation for expert witness costs only if the statute permits payment for expert witnesses.

- The attorney fee provisions also permit payment for paralegal and law clerk fees.

- Attorney fees are permitted for work performed during every phase of a case, including administrative proceedings.

- Applications for attorney fees and costs are generally submitted after the court issues a judgment for the employee.

- The rates of attorney fees are not determined by the fee agreement entered between the attorney and the client, but are established by the controlling market rates. This is very important because many clients cannot afford full-market rates and their day-to-day billings reduced.

- Attorney fees are permitted even if an employee is only partially successful in his or her case.

- Reasonable costs incurred by the client or the attorney are compensable, including travel costs, meals, hotel and airline expenses, deposition costs, arbitration costs, telephone fees, copy costs, subpoena fees, and filing fees.

PRACTICE TIPS

Each whistleblower statute must be checked to ensure that attorney fees are either covered explicitly under the law, or eligibility for fees are included in the Civil Rights Attorney Fee Act, 42 U.S.C. § 1988. Here are key Supreme Court decisions on how to calculate statutory fee awards:

- *Perdue v. Kenny*, 559 U.S. (2010) (fee enhancements)

- *Hensley v. Eckerhart*, 461 U.S. 429 (1983) ("lodestar" method)

- *Blum v. Stenson*, 465 U.S. 886 (1984) (determining fee rate)

- *Missouri v. Jenkins*, 491 U.S. 274 (1989) (use of current rates; paralegals)

- *City of Riverside v. Rivera*, 477 U.S. 561 (1986) (no proportionality)

- *Blanchard v. Bergeron*, 489 U.S. 87 (1989) (fee not controlled by agreement)

RULE 28

Hold Companies Accountable for Paying Hush Money

"This corporate code of silence . . . creates a climate where ongoing wrongdoing can occur with virtual impunity."

Senate Report, Sarbanes-Oxley Whistleblower Act

In 1987 in Stevensville, Texas, attorneys for the powerful multinational corporation Brown & Root/Halliburton pressured a journeyman electrician, Joseph J. Macktal Jr., to accept a settlement of his whistleblower case. Macktal had been fired from the Comanche Peak nuclear power construction site after raising safety concerns. The Nuclear Regulatory Commission (NRC) had validated many of his allegations, and he had a case pending with the U.S. Department of Labor under the federal nuclear safety whistleblower law.

Brown & Root wanted his silence and was willing to pay. Macktal's attorneys wanted their fees and strongly urged him to accept the company's offer. His attorneys even threatened to quit his case if he did not sign the deal. Macktal was mad. He felt trapped. He documented his opposition to the settlement, and even recorded his lawyers delivering a threat: If you do not remain silent, Brown & Root will "follow you to the ends of the earth." Macktal thought he had no choice. He signed the deal.

As part of the settlement, he agreed not to testify about any of his nuclear safety concerns. If subpoenaed, he would do his best to "resist" service. He agreed to keep the entire deal "strictly confidential," and if he ever told anyone about the secret settlement, Brown & Root could sue him, retrieve all their settlement money, and force Macktal to pay all the company's attorney fees and costs. Disclosure meant bankruptcy.

The settlement ate at Macktal's conscience. He knew it was wrong. He was a whistleblower; he had safety concerns. In September 1988 Macktal did something that no other whistleblower had ever done. He hired new attorneys who were willing to challenge the legality of the settlement. He filed motions with the NRC and the DOL seeking to have his agreement declared void. He went further. He released his "strictly confidential" agreement to the press and demanded that the government regulators protect the public interest. Macktal placed everything at risk to do the "right thing." If the agreement's legality was sustained, he all but admitted to massive liability, risking a Brown & Root counter-lawsuit for breach of contract.

Macktal's actions were unprecedented. No one knew how the NRC or DOL would rule. The NRC acted first, and blew it. It issued a decision finding that paying witnesses *not* to provide testimony to the NRC was *not* a safety violation. The NRC refused to take action against Brown & Root. The ruling set Macktal up for a counterclaim.

Backed against the wall, Macktal and his attorneys went to Congress and found a sympathetic ear with the staff of the U.S. Senate Subcommittee on Nuclear Regulation. The committee staff (and their bosses) were outraged by the settlement agreement. They understood the insidiousness of the agreement and how paying witnesses not to testify could threaten the integrity of the entire nuclear regulatory scheme. The subcommittee took action. They subpoenaed Brown & Root and their high-priced corporate attorneys, demanding documents related to the Macktal agreement and other "hush money" deals the nuclear power industry had demanded from its workers. They called the NRC officials on the carpet and grilled them on the Macktal agreement.

The chair of the subcommittee, John Breaux from Louisiana, did not hold back: "It is shocking to me that we should even have to hold a hearing on such questions. It seems self-evident that it is wrong to pay witnesses not to testify, regardless of context. Yet we find that in the area of nuclear regulation the practice may be common."

Senator Alan K. Simpson from Wyoming was slightly more blunt: "This stinks!"

Under pressure, the NRC reversed its ruling. It issued a new decision finding that such agreements violated public policy. And then it went further. The NRC sent a letter to every nuclear utility in the United States, demanding that every such "hush money" settlement be turned over to the NRC. Additionally, every worker who ever signed such an agreement be notified, in writing, that the agreement could not be enforced and that all workers were free to contact the NRC and disclose safety concerns. Numerous Macktal-style agreements became public, and the nuclear industry was given a big black eye.

The DOL initially balked, but then issued a series of decisions outlawing restrictive settlements under the federal nuclear and environmental whistleblower laws it administered. The first *Macktal* decision ruled that the settlement as a whole could be enforced, but the specific clause in the agreement restricting Macktal's right to blow the whistle to government agencies was void. Macktal challenged that ruling in the U.S. Court of Appeals for the Fifth Circuit. He demanded that the DOL void the entire deal and reinstitute his labor case.

The Fifth Circuit agreed with Macktal and held that it was all or nothing—the DOL could not effectively rewrite the agreement by striking one clause. They sent the case back to the DOL. Following the Fifth Circuit's ruling, the DOL issued a series of *Macktal* decisions, holding:

- The DOL had the authority to review all settlements and approve each and every term;

- If a settlement contained restrictions on an employee's right to blow the whistle, testify, provide information to government regulators, or engage in any statutorily protected activity, the *entire agreement* was void;

- If the settlement was voided, the employee had the right to continue his or her labor case, as if no settlement had ever been issued;

- If the company had paid money to the worker, the employee could *keep the settlement money* and still pursue his or her case.

On the basis of the *Macktal* precedent, the DOL ruled that inserting "gag provisions" in a settlement was an adverse action, permitting an employee to sue his or her employer for retaliation, and obtain damages and attorney fees. The U.S. Court of Appeals upheld that ruling.

Consistent with *Macktal*, on August 23, 2016 the Director of the Department of Labor's Whistleblower Protection Program issued policy guidelines instructing OSHA to reject any settlement agreement that contained restrictions on employee whistleblower rights. OSHA investigators were asked to keep an eye out for any settlement agreements that contained a provision that:

- Restricts an employee's "ability to provide information to the government, participate in investigations, file a complaint, or testify in proceedings";

- Requires an employee "to notify his or her employer before filing a complaint or voluntarily communicating with the government";

- Requires an employee "to affirm that he or she has not previously provided information to the government or engaged in other protected activity, or to disclaim any knowledge that the employer has violated the law";

- Requires an employee "to waive his or her right to receive a monetary award from a government-administered whistleblower award program for providing information to a government agency."

The SEC Follows *Macktal*

On August 12, 2010, just weeks after the president signed the Dodd-Frank Act, representatives of the Securities and Exchange Commission met with the National Whistleblower Center (NWC) to discuss whistleblower rules being drafted by the Commission. The NWC explained how the Commission had the legal authority to ban retaliation against whistleblowers and prohibit restrictive nondisclosure agreements. At the heart of the NWC's argument was legal precedent that treated retaliation not simply as an employment matter, but as a major regulatory concern. If companies could restrict or intimidate employees from providing information to regulatory authorities like the SEC, the government would not be able to do its job: protecting the public.

The SEC agreed. In its final rules it affirmed its authority to police corporations that tried to use their economic power to threaten or punish whistleblowers. One of the key SEC rules outlawed restrictive nondisclosure agreements. The SEC adopted the *Macktal* rule. Known as Title 17 C.F.R. § 240.21F-17, the rule states: "No person may take any action to impede an individual from communicating directly with the Commission staff about a possible securities law violation, including enforcing, or threatening to enforce, a confidentiality agreement."

The Commission put teeth into this regulation. On April 1, 2015, the SEC ruled that any publicly traded company that requires employees to sign nondisclosure agreements in violation of Rule 240.21F-17 is also in violation of the Securities and Exchange Act and is subject to fines and penalties. In a paradox of history, Kellogg Brown & Root (or KBR), the same company that had forced Mr. Macktal to sign a restrictive settlement agreement back in the 1980s, had once again resorted to using illegal nondisclosure agreements. This time the company compelled employees who had information that KBR was cheating on its Iraq war contracts to sign restrictive nondisclosure agreements, prohibiting employees from discussing their concerns about bribery and fraud in its lucrative war contracts with "anyone" without the approval of corporate attorneys. When a whistleblower asked the SEC to protect employees from these types of abusive contracts, the Commission did not hesitate to strike down the KBR agreement. The Commission not only ruled that the agreement was illegal but also fined KBR $130,000 for making an employee sign it. KBR paid the fine. This precedent triggered numerous companies to change their severance and settlement agreement terms to specifically permit communications to the SEC and other government agencies. Companies that fail to follow the KBR ruling have been subsequently fined.

Restrictive Settlements and Public Policy

The *Macktal* rulings remain good law and based on the actions of the Securities and Exchange Commission, among other government agencies; it is now widely accepted. However, in the past, some courts have not been as aggressive in policing settlement abuses. Employees have been targeted with countersuits for settlement violations, and companies have gone into court for injunctions prohibiting employees from releasing embarrassing information.

For example, the Brown & Williamson Tobacco Corporation used a confidentiality agreement signed by its former vice president for research and development, Jeffrey Wigand, to file lawsuits against him in a pro-Tobacco local circuit court in Kentucky. Brown & Williamson "legally" harassed Wigand through this lawsuit and threatened him with ruin in order to stop his truthful disclosures. The company wanted to stop Wigand from talking to the news media and testifying in court concerning his former employer's misconduct in adding dangerous chemicals to tobacco and then lying about the health risks of its products.

The Wigand agreement was not unique. There are numerous other instances where wrongdoers hid serious abuses from the public eye, sometimes for years, through the misuse of secrecy agreements, including "sexual abuse by Catholic priests, Bridgestone/Firestone tires failing on Ford SUVs, health risks from the Dalkon Shield and silicone breast implants, exploding fuel tanks on General Motors pickup trucks, and hazardous chemical spills."

Whether a restrictive settlement agreement is enforceable requires a court to determine if the agreement violates "public policy." The U.S. Supreme Court, in *Town of Newton v. Rumery*, held that a contract may be "unenforceable if the interest in its enforcement is outweighed" by "public policy." Precisely what restrictions may violate "public policy" is an open question in most jurisdictions. However, the precedent in federal court weighs heavily against enforcing overly restrictive employment contracts, or settlements that restrict the ability of an employee to provide information to federal regulatory or law enforcement agencies.

Under the False Claims Act, a number of courts have prevented (or limited) companies from using private agreements to interfere with the ability of the government to learn about contracting fraud. As one court explained:

It is in the Government's best interest to gain full information from the relator. To enforce the release . . . would ignore the public policy objectives spelled out by Congress in the FCA and would provide disincentives to future relators. . . . [E]nforcing the release and indemnification clauses would encourage individuals guilty of defrauding the United States to insulate themselves from the reach of the FCA by simply forcing potential relators to sign general agreements invoking release and indemnification from future suit.

But even in the context of the FCA, courts have upheld broad general releases that have prohibited employees from filing *qui tam* cases. These courts have ruled that if the government had prior knowledge of the frauds, and did not need the information from the relator, private contractual releases of FCA claims could be enforced. Although this rule appears fair on its face, how can the United States or a court ever be sure that the employee has in fact provided all of his or her information to the government before such materials are actually provided to the United States?

Mandatory Arbitration Agreements

The use of settlement agreements to directly prevent employees from testifying or blowing the whistle to government agencies has been severely criticized; and based on the sustained legal attack on this process, the ability of a corporation to enforce such agreements is in doubt. But less obvious methods of using private contractual agreements to restrict employee rights are still widely used, and some with great success.

The most common such contracts are preemployment arbitration agreements. These agreements are, on their face, neutral. They do not require employees to waive rights, but they do require employees to utilize arbitration procedures to litigate their claims. Mandatory arbitration agreements can block employee access to courts, requiring employees to forgo litigation in favor of arbitration proceedings. Many employers require prospective employees to sign mandatory arbitration agreements as a condition of employment.

If a claim is subjected to arbitration, many basic due process rights available in court proceedings simply do not exist. There is never a jury, and an employee does not have his or her case heard by a professional judge. Instead, only an arbitrator decides the case, and the proceedings are often conducted under confidentiality rules. The rules of procedure are also determined by the terms of the private contract and can be extremely tilted in favor of the employer. These agreements are very hard on whistleblowers, as corporate arbitrators may not be sympathetic to the very notion that employees should be blowing the whistle.

The U.S. Supreme Court has upheld the use of mandatory arbitration agreements under most circumstances. Many of the landmark Supreme Court rulings requiring employees to use these nonjudicial proceedings to enforce labor laws were based on highly divisive five-to-four rulings. The dissenting judges readily understood how blocking access to court would, in practice, undermine the ability of employees to have their cases fairly decided.

Congress has recently responded to the abusive use of arbitration agreements and employment contracts. The Dodd-Frank Wall Street Reform and Consumer Protection Act contains a number of provisions that prohibit the use of contracts to undermine whistleblower rights, and it specifically prevents companies from using preemployment arbitration agreements to block court access. Both the commodities whistleblower law and the Sarbanes-Oxley Act make it crystal clear that abusive private contracts, including mandatory arbitration agreements, cannot be used to thwart an employee's right to blow the whistle: "The rights and remedies provided for in this section [the securities whistleblower law] may not be waived by any agreement, policy, form, or condition of employment, including a predispute arbitration agreement."

If an employee whistleblower signed a mandatory arbitration agreement, it is imperative that he or she carefully review the terms of the agreement to determine what causes of action are required to be arbitrated and whether or not his or her whistleblower claim is covered. Also, the employee should do a careful check of the language of the federal laws to see if they contain provisions, such as those found in the Dodd-Frank Act and the Sarbanes-Oxley Act, that prohibit employers from enforcing mandatory arbitration agreements.

Mandatory arbitration agreements do not work in the context of *qui tam* filings. If an employee files an IRS, securities, or commodities *qui tam*, the employer may never even learn the identity of the employee, and there is simply no court proceeding for the company to block. Even the Supreme Court recognized that private arbitration agreements cannot be used to prevent federal agencies from filing lawsuits in U.S. district court to benefit the public interest, even if an employee will directly benefit financially from that lawsuit.

What Is the Best Response to Restrictive Employment Contracts or Settlement Proposals?

In weighing whether or not to blow the whistle, it is imperative not only to review the laws that provide protection, but also any signed agreements that may restrict these rights. These contractual agreements may require arbitration of disputes and contain other restrictions on the use of corporate property or the confidentiality of "trade secrets." Employment agreements that may impact a whistleblower case are typically contained in the following document groups:

- Agreements and waivers contained in an employee's application packet or in the materials companies request new employees to sign as a condition of being hired;

- Special confidentiality agreements or agreements to protect trade secrets (Note: Under the Protect Trade Secrets Act, Congress created specific procedures permitting employees to blow the whistle on trade secret information. This law is explained in Rule 4.);

- Employee handbooks;

- Company compliance materials and ethics handbooks;

- Waivers contained in a severance agreement;

- An agreement to arbitrate employment disputes;

- The terms set forth in a settlement agreement.

Agreements between the employee and the employer must be carefully weighed in deciding the best forum to use in trying to vindicate the employee's rights. Some of these agreements may be enforceable, others not. Some of these agreements may actually violate federal law. Under the new SEC rule, employees can file a formal charge against publicly traded companies that require employees to sign restrictive agreements. The safest approach is to understand how the employer may use these agreements to undermine a whistleblower's case and how best to defend (or avoid) against any such attack long before it is launched.

Beware of Waivers

The reasons an employee accepts a settlement agreement, signs a mandatory arbitration agreement, or enters into other contractual agreements with his or her employer are simply too complex to evaluate in any general analysis. Employees often have good reasons for entering into agreements that, on their face, appear very restrictive. Without a doubt, reaching a fair settlement in a whistleblower case should be a major goal of any reasonable employee advocate. Even if an employee accepts a highly restrictive agreement, the odds are it may not be enforceable if the employee needed to provide law enforcement authorities additional information on wrongdoing. Settlements are normally very good and bring to a close a very painful episode in an employee's life. But employers will use their superior economic bargaining position to try to gain whatever short-term benefits they can. When companies overreach, it is up to the courts, the Department of Labor, or the SEC to do their job and protect the public interest.

But there is good news concerning restrictive employment agreements. Any employer who requires an employee to sign an agreement not to disclose potential crimes to the government is in violation of numerous laws, including the Securities Exchange Act and the federal obstruction of justice laws. Paradoxically, if an employer asks you to sign away your rights to blow the whistle to the government, such an offer (or agreement) may actually strengthen your whistleblower claims. Restrictive waivers will be an eye-opener for federal investigators and could result in sanctions against the company that offered the hush money deal.

PRACTICE TIPS

The following are key cases on enforcement of settlement and arbitration agreements:

- *Town of Newton v. Rumery,* 480 U.S. 386 (1987) (defining "public policy")

- *EEOC v. Astra,* 94 F.3d 738 (1st Cir. 1996) (agreement cannot bar filing charge)

- *CL&P v. SOL,* 85 F.3d 89 (2nd Cir. 1996) (restrictive agreement as adverse action)

- *Macktal v. Brown & Root,* U.S. Department of Labor Case File 86-ERA-23

- *U.S. v. Purdue Pharma,* 600 F.3d 319 (2010) (releases under False Claims Act)

- *Gilmer v. Interstate,* 500 U.S. 20 (1991) (leading case requiring mandatory arbitration of employment claims)

- *In the Matter of KBR, Inc.*, Securities and Exchange Commission File No. 3-16466 (April 1, 2015) (SEC decision sanctioning company for restrictive nondisclosure agreement)

- Federal Acquisition Regulation prohibiting use of federal funds for restrictive NDAs. 82 *Federal Register* 4717 (January 13, 2017)

- Rules prohibiting restrictions on the right of federal employees to communicate with Congress or file whistleblower claims. Public Law No. 114-113 § 713 (2015); Public Law No. 112-199 § 115(a)(1) (2012)

RULE 29

Politics Is Poisonous

Whistleblower cases are politically charged. Allegations raised by employees often embarrass elected officials, political appointees, or well-connected special interests. Whistleblowers are individuals who lack the influence or financial resources comparable to those to whom they are reporting. When evaluating laws that protect whistleblowers, it is critical to ask whether the available procedures are sufficient to mitigate the potential adverse consequences of political interference.

Whistleblowers need to identify and use laws that are as independent as possible. Some of the early whistleblower statutes, such as the Occupational Health and Safety Act (1970), the six environmental whistleblower laws (passed between 1971 and 1980), and the Civil Service Reform Act (1978) are susceptible to political pressure. These laws are administered by executive agencies and ultimately report to either a Cabinet Secretary or a Board appointed by the President. The right to judicial review is limited, and none of these laws allow whistleblowers to file a case in federal district court. Their deficiencies gave federal whistleblower protection a bad name. Cases were delayed within hostile agencies for years, and prosecutors refused to file claims on behalf of the employees they were supposed to defend. In some cases, the officials responsible for "protecting" whistleblowers turned against them and used their positions to retaliate.

Given that politicians and special interests often view whistleblowers as a threat, it is important for whistleblowers to determine which laws are best shielded from political pressure. The following is an overview of potential traps for whistleblowers and laws that provide maximum independence.

Executive Agencies

Under U.S. law, various agencies are required to appoint persons whose job it is to implement whistleblower protections. By definition, these executive-appointed employees can be biased or political. Some of these appointed officials have done a good job protecting employees; others have disgraced their positions.

Office of Special Counsel. This is the most controversial whistleblower-watchdog position. The Special Counsel is appointed by the president for a five-year term and has authority to enforce the Whistleblower Protection Act (the law covering most federal employees). The Counsel can prosecute federal agencies that retaliate against employees. The Special Counsel has the discretion to do nothing to help a whistleblower, and some persons who have held this office have used it to undermine the law. The most notorious case concerned Mr. Peter Bloch, the Special Counsel appointed by President George W. Bush. He was criminally indicted and convicted of contempt of Congress and destroying evidence concerning his misconduct as Special Counsel. The criminal destruction of documents occurred after Mr. Bloch, was accused of engaging in retaliation.

President Obama's appointment as Special Counsel took steps to rehabilitate the reputation of the office and initiated various actions to protect whistleblowers. President Trump will appoint the next Special Counsel, subject to confirmation by the Senate.

Merit System Protection Board. This three-member Board is appointed and confirmed by the Senate to serve seven-year terms. The MSPB hears most federal employee whistleblower cases. Whistleblowers come before the MSPB if they object to the findings of the Office of Special Counsel or request a hearing on the merits of a retaliation case. Whistleblowers have a narrow right to appeal a final order of the MSPB to the Court of Appeals, but federal employees cannot have their cases directly heard in U.S. District Court and have no right to a jury trial. The MSPB acts as the trial court, creates the evidentiary record, and issues the final agency decision on behalf of the United States.

The composition of the Board is political. Two are from the President's political party, and one position is set aside for the opposition party. In other words, the political party that holds the White House dominates the composition of the MSPB. Because the White House often has an interest in squashing exposure of wrongdoing within the agencies it controls, the composition of the MSPB has always been controversial and heavily weighted to benefit the President.

Office of the Inspector General. All federal agencies have an Inspector General, who acts as the internal watchdog for that agency. Inspectors General are traditionally more independent than the Special Counsel. The law permits them to receive confidential whistleblower disclosures and prohibits retaliation against whistleblowers who provide the IGs with information. The IGs often investigate cases of fraud against the government committed by contractors and consequently are involved with many False Claims Act cases. IGs are appointed by the president of the United States, and confirmed by the Senate.

Over time IGs have obtained a mixed reputation. Many IGs take their role as whistleblower protectors seriously. Favorable IG reports have resulted in the reinstatement or vindication of numerous whistleblowers. But other IGs have not acted in good faith. Some have been accused of retaliating against whistleblowers and have left office in disgrace. Others have used their offices to investigate whistleblowers at the request of agency officials intent on quashing dissent within their programs.

One notorious case of IG abuse occurred within the Environmental Protection Agency. Large multinational chemical corporations covertly worked with IG agents to destroy the reputation of an EPA scientist who regularly served as an expert witness against these companies in toxic tort cases. What better way to discredit your critics than to get the EPA to fire the star witness who testified on behalf of victims of toxic chemical exposures? The IG's target was Dr. William Marcus, the EPA's Senior Science Advisor and the only certified toxicologist employed by the agency. He was an expert on the adverse health effects of numerous deadly chemicals. The chemical companies wanted to silence him. They almost succeeded.

At the request of counsel for these companies, the EPA's Office of Inspector General commenced a prolonged and secret investigation of Dr. Marcus. The evidence assembled by the IG was gathered almost exclusively by attorneys for the very companies Dr. Marcus had accused of selling unsafe products. The company attorneys spent countless hours poring over Dr. Marcus's court testimony where he had provided scientific evidence demonstrating adverse health consequences caused by human exposure to various chemicals. They put packets of information together, fed the evidence to the IG agents, who ultimately used it as the basis for getting the EPA to fire him. Dr. Marcus faced the loss of his job and the complete destruction of his reputation as a world-renowned toxicologist.

Dr. Marcus used the environmental whistleblowers laws to fight back. During his hearing the misconduct of the IG, and its covert relationship with the chemical companies, was exposed. Among the facts confirmed was that the IG had unlawfully destroyed evidence. Dr. Marcus had filed discovery requests to obtain access to the notes of all of the communications between the chemical company attorneys and the Office of Inspector General. But the notes had been shredded. One IG agent testified that after Congress had made a request to obtain documents related to Dr. Marcus, and after a Freedom of Information request had been filed for these records, the agent systematically went into the case file and shredded all investigatory notes. Despite this misconduct, other evidence still confirmed that the chemical companies were the source of most of the information used to fire Dr. Marcus. Dr. Marcus won his case and was reinstated with back pay.

Department of Labor. Two appointed offices within the DOL have significant authority over whistleblowers. The first is the OSHA division. This division investigates numerous whistleblower cases, including those filed under the Occupational Safety and Health Act, the Sarbanes-Oxley Act, environmental and nuclear protection laws, transportation safety laws, auto safety laws, food safety laws, and consumer protection laws. In most cases the results of these investigations can be appealed and a hearing requested. Unfortunately, under the Occupational Health and Safety Act, if OSHA administratively denies the claim, the whistleblower has no right to a hearing and cannot file a case in federal court.

But under almost all other DOL-administered laws, whistleblowers can request a hearing (with full discovery) before an administrative law judge. These DOL ALJs have independence, and their positions are protected under law. The reputation of these judges can be gleaned from reading their decisions, which the DOL publishes online. ALJs issue a "recommended order," which is reviewed by a five-member Administrative Review Board (ARB). The ARB has the authority to issue final enforceable orders.

Unlike the ALJs, the ARB is not independent. The Secretary of Labor has complete authority to appoint ARB members. There are no controls on who can be an ARB member. There is no confirmation process, and there is no requirement that the composition of the ARB be balanced, let alone have a track record of being fair to whistleblowers. In other words, the U.S. Chamber of Commerce can call the Secretary of Labor on the phone and ask the Secretary to fire a pro-whistleblower ARB member and appoint a business-friendly attorney to that position (although there is no evidence that this type of blatant interference has ever happened).

Needless to say, if a whistleblower has a case before the ARB, it is important to determine the reputation of the current ARB members.

Over the years, whistleblowers complained about extensive delays in OSHA investigations and the ARB's decision-making process. Congress responded to these long-standing and well-documented concerns. Approximately 15 years ago Congress started permitting whistleblowers caught up in DOL proceedings to remove their cases to federal court and have a full trial on the merits before a federal jury. This removal process was de novo. If the whistleblower law you were suing under permitted removal, you could move your case to federal court, and your case would not be biased by any negative findings issued by OSHA or an ALJ. Instead, the federal courts were required to start your case from the beginning, allow you to engage in discovery, and permit a new trial on the merits. But in order to remove your case to federal court you still have to "exhaust" your administrative remedy at the DOL (usually waiting 210 days).

Removal to federal court is *not* permitted under several environmental whistleblower laws (Clean Air, Pipeline Safety, Clean Water, Toxic Substances, Superfund violations, Solid Waste Disposal, and Safe Drinking Water) and the airline safety law. But whistleblowers who file initial claims within the Department of Labor and exhaust their administrative proceedings can obtain de novo trials in federal court under the following laws:

- Affordable Care Act; access to federal court after waiting 210 days;

- Consumer Financial Protection; access to federal court after waiting 210 days;

- Consumer Product Safety; access to federal court after waiting 210 days;

- Energy Reorganization Act/Nuclear Safety (both private sector and federal); access to federal court after waiting one year;

- Food Safety Act; access to federal court after waiting 210 days;

- Railroad Safety Act; access to federal court after waiting 210 days;

- MAP-21 (auto safety); access to federal court after waiting 210 days;

- National Transit Systems Security Act; access to federal court after waiting 210 days;

- Sarbanes-Oxley Act (corporate fraud); access to federal court after waiting 180 days;

- Seaman's Protection Act; access to federal court after waiting 210 days;

- Surface Transportation Act (truck driver safety); access to federal court after waiting 210 days;

There are three exceptions to the right of whistleblowers to remove their cases from the Department of Labor to federal court: First, if the whistleblower intentionally delays the case in order to run out the clock. There are no reported cases in which a whistleblower has been found guilty of this violation, but it is important to follow procedures and meet all deadlines. Second, if the whistleblower fails to exhaust the DOL administrative procedures. For example, even though the whistleblower may eventually have the right to file a case in federal court, he or she must first file the claim with the DOL, cooperate with the OSHA investigation, and potentially request a hearing with an ALJ. You must continue to pursue the case within the DOL and meet all deadlines until your time limit expires. Third, you can file to remove your case anytime after the 210-day (or 180-day/1-year) requirement has expired. But if the DOL's Administrative Review Board issues a final order before you remove your case, you may lose your right to have a federal court trial and instead be limited to appealing the final decision of the ARB to the U.S. Court of Appeals.

All of these deadlines are carefully set out in the published regulations of the Department of Labor, available online. Any decision to remove a case from the DOL to federal court should be carefully weighed, as is more fully explained in Rule 4.

Whistleblower Reward Laws

A number of federal agencies have responsibility for paying or facilitating the payment of whistleblower rewards. The amount of political pressure each of these offices is subjected to varies depending on the type of rewards law. These laws can be broken down into three categories:

False Claims Act. This is the best whistleblower law. First, its antiretaliation provision can be filed directly in federal court. There is no administrative procedure to exhaust, and the Department of Justice has no control whatsoever over a retaliation case.

Second, the False Claims Act's reward provision has a *qui tam* process. *Qui tam* is a Latin phrase, roughly translated as "in the name of the king." Consequently, if a whistleblower files a fraud case under the False Claims Act and the Department of Justice refuses to enforce the law (or prosecute the wrongdoer), the whistleblower can proceed with the lawsuit. The whistleblower can stand in for the United States and pursue the case on behalf of the United States. This is one of the most important citizen-empowerment laws enacted by Congress. It permits citizens to act as "private attorneys general" and hold corrupt government contractors accountable. Even if the Justice Department is not doing its job, or has been compromised by politics and lobbyists, a whistleblower can pursue his or her False Claims Act case in court without Justice Department intervention. If the whistleblower wins, the United States still collects the majority of the damages awarded against the contractor, but the whistleblower is entitled to a reward of 25 to 30 percent, and the corrupt contractor must pay the whistleblower's attorney fees and costs.

If a whistleblower wants to pursue the case without the help of the Justice Department, all cases still must be first filed under "seal" and served on the Justice Department before they are served on a defendant. The government has the right to "intervene" in the case and become the lead prosecutor against the fraudster. But even in these circumstances, the False Claims Act permits the whistleblower to actively participate in the lawsuit and obtain a reward. Furthermore, if the government tries to deny or reduce a reward, the whistleblower can object and ask a court to approve his or her compensation.

Non-*Qui Tam* Reward Laws. The second group of reward laws offers a hybrid approach. Once the whistleblower alerts the appropriate agency as to the suspected violation, the agency has the discretion whether to investigate or prosecute. Even if the agency prosecutes the wrongdoers, the agency has the sole right to settle the case and set the amount of damages paid to the government. Only after the government collects fines, penalties, or sanctions from the wrongdoer does the right of the whistleblower to collect a reward kick in. There is no *qui tam* provision. If the government fails to act, the whistleblower cannot independently sue the wrongdoer, as is permitted under the False Claims Act. Likewise, if the government does prosecute, but sets the damage levels at a very low level (thereby lowering the amount of any reward), the whistleblower cannot object. Under the False Claims Act the whistleblower can object to a settlement between the government and the wrongdoer.

On the bright side, these hybrid laws require that whistleblowers who meet the criteria for a reward obtain payment. Agencies that fail to pay the whistleblower can be appealed to in federal court or Tax Court. Most of these laws also set a mandatory minimum percentage a whistleblower must be paid. For example, under the IRS reward law, if the IRS collects $1 million in sanctions as a result of a whistleblower disclosure, the whistleblower is entitled, *as a matter of law*, to a minimum 15 percent recovery ($150,000). If the IRS does not pay that reward, the whistleblower can sue the IRS in Tax Court and enforce his or her right to a payment. Tax Court decisions can be thereafter appealed to federal court.

Under these hybrid laws, the whistleblower has no right to force the government to investigate or prosecute, but once there is a recovery based on the whistleblower's information, he or she can enforce that recovery in court. The impact of political appointees on the enforcement programs administered by these agencies will have a dramatic impact as to whether sanctions are obtained. But if a reward is wrongfully denied by a biased political appointee or bureaucrat, the whistleblower can appeal the ruling in court.

The main reward laws that follow the hybrid model are the Securities Exchange Act (minimum reward of 10 percent enforceable in court); Foreign Corrupt Practices Act (minimum reward of 10 percent enforceable in court);

IRS tax whistleblowers (minimum reward of 15 percent enforceable in court); Commodity Exchange Act (minimum reward of 10 percent enforceable in court); and Auto Safety Act (no minimum set by regulation at this time, but rewards are enforceable in court).

The Act to Prevent Pollution from Ships grants federal courts the discretion to award up to 50 percent of any monies recovered as a result of a whistleblower's providing information to the United States that results in a successful prosecution of the APPS claim. There is no mandatory minimum award. Requests for a reward in APPS cases are filed directly with the Court at the time a plea agreement is entered or at sentencing. In most cases the Department of Justice asks the Court to pay the reward, but the statute does not require this.

In each of these cases, a federal agency is responsible for investigating and prosecuting the misconduct. However, once monies are collected from fines, penalties, or sanctions, the ability of the whistleblower to be paid is subject to judicial oversight or review.

Discretionary Reward Laws. Another class of reward laws that are more susceptible to political pressure are those that do not set a mandatory minimum for a reward and/or do not explicitly authorize judicial review. These laws grant administrative agencies the right to pay a reward, but they lack the punch necessary to keep federal agencies honest. One such law *prohibits* judicial review if a reward is denied, even if the denial is prejudicial.

These discretionary reward laws include the wildlife trafficking reward laws (Lacey Act), the Endangered Species Act, and the Fish and Wildlife Improvement Act. The worst of these reward laws is the Financial Institutions Reform, Recovery and Enforcement Act (FIRREA). This law not only caps the maximum amount of a reward but also explicitly prohibits whistleblowers from contesting the reward amount or the denial of a reward in federal court. Under FIRREA, if the Attorney General denies you a reward, or your reward is set at just one penny, you cannot challenge that decision in court.

Other Independent Remedies

First Amendment/42 U.S.C. § 1983. The First Amendment to the Constitution is the quintessential whistleblower law. It protects freedom of speech (whistleblower disclosures are "speech") and the right to petition Congress. In 1871 Congress passed a Civil Rights Act permitting all persons to file tort lawsuits in federal court if their constitutional rights were violated by persons acting under "color of state law." Over the years this old civil rights law, now known primarily by its federal code designation, "§ 1983," permits whistleblowers to sue state, county, and municipal governments and supervisors who retaliate against them for making whistleblower disclosures on matters of "public concern." These First Amendment lawsuits are filed directly in federal court and permit the whistleblower to have a jury trial, seek compensatory and punitive damages, and obtain injunctive relief and attorney fees paid by the retaliator. Because of the right to go directly to federal court, state and local government employees can avoid various political traps and have their whistleblower cases decided by a jury.

National Security and Intelligence Agency Protections

One area where Congress has failed to provide independent remedies for whistleblowers is national security. Since the Edward Snowden controversy, Congress enacted a law covering federal employees who work for the CIA, National Security Agency, and other intelligence agencies. This law fails to provide any independent remedy. Enforcement authority is delegated to the President of the United States or other executive officials.

National Security Agency, CIA, and other intelligence employees are subject to Presidential Policy Directive PPD/19. Signed by President Obama in 2012, it established in-house procedures for "protecting" national security whistleblowers within the "Intelligence Community." PPD/19 lacked any enforceable substantive rights and left intelligence agency whistleblowers at the mercy of their employing agencies. To make matters perfectly clear to these intelligence community employees, the last paragraph of PPD/19 states: "This directive is not intended to, and does not create any right or benefit, substantive or procedural, enforceable at law or in equity by any party against the United States." PPD/19 vested complete power over intelligence agency whistleblowers to political presidential appointees.

The Inspector General for the Intelligence Community approved procedures for adjudicating whistleblower complaints under PPD/19. Issued on May 15, 2014, the "IC IG External Review Panel Procedures Pursuant to Presidential Policy Directive-19 vest the "department or agency head" with authority for making all final decisions in whistleblower cases. In other words, the head of the agency that retaliated against the whistleblower is the final judge and jury over the whistleblower case, with no rights to appeal. Finally, someone in the federal bureaucracy read Franz Kafka and Lewis Carroll.

Two years later Congress passed the Intelligence Community Whistleblower Protection Act, covering the CIA, Defense Intelligence Agency, National Geospatial-Intelligence Agency, National Security Agency, Office of the Director of National Intelligence, National Reconnaissance Office, and "any executive agency or unit thereof," "determined by the President," to "have as its principal function the conduct of foreign intelligence or counterintelligence activities." This law established whistleblower rights that are controlled by presidential appointees, and mirrors the procedures in PPD/19. The post-Snowden legal protections for national security whistleblowers flatly states that the President of the United States "shall provide for the enforcement" of this law. So much for independence.

The FBI Whistleblower Protection Act is somewhat stronger than the intelligence agency law. Judicial review is not explicitly prohibited (although the few courts to consider the issue have denied any review) and the statute requires the President or Attorney General to establish procedures consistent with those afforded other federal employee whistleblowers — including a confidential investigation into the merits of a case, and an opportunity for a hearing. FBI whistleblowers must file their cases with the Department of Justice Office of Inspector General or Office of Professional Responsibility. The hearings are conducted within the Justice Department, and the authority to issue final decisions was delegated to the Deputy Attorney General, a political appointee.

As explained in Rule 14, using the prepublication review process to have an agency (and thereafter a federal court) approve the public release of whistleblower disclosures is still the best method for intelligence agency employees to make the public aware of abuses within these agencies.

Federal Laws that Permit Access to Federal Court. A number of federal laws covering whistleblowers provide for direct filings in federal court and/or permit whistleblowers to have their cases independently heard by a judge and jury after they exhaust administrative remedies. The antiretaliation provisions of the Securities Exchange Act and Commodity Exchange Act permit whistleblowers to file directly in federal court, without having to make any filings before the Department of Labor or the SEC. Title VII of the Civil Rights Act permits employees who claim retaliation because they opposed discriminatory practices (or disclosed evidence that their employers engaged in discrimination) can file claims in federal court after exhausting remedies before the Equal Employment Opportunity Commission. Other antiretaliation laws that permit direct access to federal court (or access to court after exhausting administrative remedies) are the Fair Labor Standards Act, the DOL-administered laws referenced above, banking sector antiretaliation laws, and laws covering government contractors who expose waste, fraud, or abuse. All Americans can also use the Privacy Act to obtain access to federal court. The Privacy Act also prohibits federal agencies from collecting information on the First Amendment activities of Americans.

State Laws. More than one-half of the states have *qui tam* laws modeled on the federal False Claims Act. In these jurisdictions, if state or local taxpayer monies are being ripped off by corrupt contractors, whistleblowers can use the state *qui tam* laws to obtain independent access to the courts. This permits whistleblowers who use the state laws to avoid or minimize federal political interference with their cases.

In addition to the state False Claims Acts, most states permit whistleblowers to challenge a wrongful discharge under their local laws. As explained in Rule 5 and Checklist 3, some states have enacted Whistleblower Protection Acts that usually permit employees to file cases in court. Also, a large majority of states recognize a "public policy" exception to the termination-at-will doctrine, permitting whistleblowers to file common law breach of contract or tort (personal injury) cases in state courts.

Conclusion

When deciding whether to take the risk and blow the whistle it is important not only to learn whether or not you are protected by law, but also who has been delegated the authority to protect you. Is it a judge or jury? Is it a federal bureaucrat? Is it the President of the United States or one of his/her appointees? Is the process independent, or is it subject to overt political pressure?

RULE 30

Never Forget: Whistleblowing Works

One of the hardest dilemmas facing employees who want to blow the whistle is a nagging doubt that they are powerless. Why blow the whistle if nothing will get better?

It is impossible to judge the actual impact of the thousands of employees who blow the whistle every year. How can one quantify the environmental protections obtained from the numerous whistleblowers who exposed violations of the Clean Air Act? Or the health and safety benefits obtained for workers under the OSHA, Surface Transportation, and Mine Safety whistleblower laws? Or the savings to investors that have been, or will be, achieved under the Dodd-Frank and Sarbanes-Oxley whistleblower laws?

But one area of whistleblower law can be objectively judged. The False Claims Act has been actively used by whistleblowers since 1986. Because the United States must pay whistleblowers who prevail in these claims a percentage of the monies *actually recovered* by the government from dishonest contractors, the U.S. Department of Justice keeps accurate statistics of *every FCA recovery*. The DOJ, down to the penny, has calculated the monies obtained as a direct result of whistleblower disclosures. The results are stunning. Whistleblowing does work.

Proof by Dollars and Cents

The FCA is the only law that has been actively used by employee whistleblowers for over thirty years and for which actual hard data exists that can quantify the impact of whistleblowers.

The statistics on False Claims Act recoveries published by the U.S. Department of Justice Civil Fraud Division speak for themselves. Between October 1, 1987, and September 30, 2016, the following recoveries have been obtained:

- By the DOJ Civil Fraud Division *without* the help of whistleblowers under the FCA: $15.347 billion;

- By the DOJ Civil Fraud Division based on FCA cases *filed by whistleblowers*: $37.685 billion;

- Rewards *actually paid* to whistleblowers under FCA: $6.352 billion;

- Since the False Claims Act was amended in 1986, whistleblowers are the direct source of 70 percent of civil fraud recoveries obtained by the United States.

"Most [civil fraud cases that result] in recoveries were brought to the government by whistleblowers" under the False Claims Act.

–U.S. Assistant Attorney General

The following are examples of the amounts of money actually recovered by the taxpayer under the federal or state FCA due to the risks taken by employees who blew the whistle:

- Amerigroup Insurance: $225 million for illegally denying Medicaid coverage to pregnant women;

- Armor Holdings, Inc., and Hexcel Corporation: $45 million for manufacturing and selling defective body armor;

- Bank of America: $1 billion for banking/mortgage fraud;

- Beverly Enterprises, Inc.: $170 million for charging to Medicare the salaries paid to nurses who worked on non-Medicare patients;

- Bristol-Myers Squibb: $515 million for illegal pricing and marketing of over fifty different types of drugs;

- Ciena Capital, LLC: $26.3 million for false certification of small business loan requirements;

- Cisco Systems: $48 million for overcharging and defective pricing;

- Citigroup: $158 million for mortgage fraud;

- Conoco Phillips: $97.5 million for underpayment of natural gas royalties on public lands;

- CVS Corporation: $37 million for overcharging Medicaid;

- Deutsche Bank: $202 million for defrauding HUD and the FHA;

- Eli Lilly & Co.: $1.415 billion for promoting drugs for uses not approved by the Food and Drug Administration;

- GlaxoSmithKline: $750 million for selling adulterated drugs;

- Hospital Corporation of America: $840 million for performing medically unnecessary tests, overbilling, "up coding" (using false diagnosis codes to increase payments), and billing for nonreimbursable costs;

- Lockheed Martin: $10.5 million for filing false invoices to obtain early payments;

- Los Angeles Department of Water and Power: $160 million for overcharging customers;

- Merck: $650 million for kickbacks and Medicaid Best Practice violations;

- Northrop Grumman: $191 million for fraudulent overcharging and selling defective equipment;

- Oracle: $200 million for price-gouging on computers;

- Pfizer, Inc.: $2.3 billion for illegal kickbacks and illegal marketing of numerous drugs, including Lipitor, Viagra, and Celebrex;

- Pratt & Whitney: $52 million for defective turbines used in fighter jets;

- Purdue Frederick Co.: $634.5 million for misbranding the painkiller Oxycontin;

- Schering Plough: $435 million for illegal sales and marketing of brain tumor, cancer, and hepatitis drugs;

- Science Applications International Corporation: $5.9 million for violations of conflict of interest rules in contract with the Nuclear Regulatory Commission;

- Shell Oil Company: $110 million for underreporting and underpaying royalties;

- Smithkline Beecham Clinical Laboratories: $325 million for charging government for tests that were not performed, "adding on" additional unnecessary tests to increase billable costs, paying kickbacks to obtain a doctor's medical business, and double billing for dialysis tests;

- Tenet Healthcare: $900 million for Medicare billing violations, kickbacks, and bill padding;

- University of Phoenix: $67.5 million for violations of student loan regulations;

- Walgreens: $120 million for improper drug switching.

The list goes on and on and on: Abbott Labs ($400 million recovery for taxpayers); Bank of America ($187 million recovery for taxpayers); Bayer Corporation ($257 million recovery for taxpayers); Boeing ($54 million recovery for taxpayers); BP/Amoco ($32 million recovery); Chevron ($95 million recovery for taxpayers); ConocoPhillips ($97 million recovery); General Electric ($59.5 million recovery); Harvard University ($31 million recovery); Hercules, Inc. ($26 million recovery); Ingersoll-Rand ($3 million recovery); MCI/WorldCom ($27 million recovery); Mellon Bank ($16.5 million recovery); Office Depot ($4.75 million recovery); OfficeMax ($9.8 million recovery); Princeton Review ($10 million recovery); Roche Biomedical Laboratories ($325 million recovery); Rockwell International ($27 million recovery); State of California ($73 million recovery); Texaco Oil ($43 million recovery); the Scooter Store ($4 million recovery); United Technologies ($150 million recovery); University of Pennsylvania ($30 million recovery).

The "whistleblower program . . . has rapidly become a tremendously effective force-multiplier, generating high quality tips, and in some cases virtual blueprints laying out an entire enterprise, directing us to the heart of the alleged fraud."

–Chairman, Securities and Exchange Commission

Of the $37.685 billion recovered as a result of whistleblower-initiated FCA cases resolved as of 2016, whistleblowers themselves obtained $6.352 billion in rewards. The government only pays these rewards because the whistleblowers, who risked their careers to expose the frauds, were the key to the successful prosecution. Some examples of extraordinarily large whistleblower rewards include the share relators obtained in cases against Medco Health Solutions, United Technologies Corporation, and Northrop Grumman, where the whistleblowers obtained rewards of $23 million, $22.5 million, and $27.2 million, respectfully. In the massive case against Hospital Corporation of America, Inc., the whistleblowers collectively obtained $154 million in rewards.

None of these rewards were paid for by the taxpayer. The company that fired or harassed the whistleblowers had to pay the bill. Although the average reward paid is approximately $1.5 million, the astronomically large rewards create a powerful incentive both for employees to blow the whistle and for companies to ensure that they are impeccably honest in their use of taxpayer money.

These numbers are simply staggering.

From the shop floor straight into the highest corporate offices and into the courts, whistleblowers make real change.

The size of FCA judgments sends the shockwaves necessary for entrenched corporate traditions to change. These judgments create the most powerful incentive known under law for ensuring honesty in the use of government monies. The large rewards grab headlines, advertise the existence of the FCA within the government-contractor community, and encourage an extremely reluctant workforce to come forward and protect taxpayers. These recoveries directly result from the contribution that whistleblowers made to the public interest. These whistleblowers placed their careers and reputations on the line. They won their cases. Taxpayers obtained billions of dollars in recoveries, and the whistleblowers were rewarded for having the courage and integrity to stick their necks out (using the ostrich metaphor) to serve the public interest.

The FCA simply offers the best concrete example of the power behind employee whistleblowing. Under this law, the impact of whistleblowing is measured in dollars and cents. Now that Congress has created four new *qui tam* laws, for the Internal Revenue Code, the Securities Exchange Act, auto safety, and the Commodity Exchange Act, the massive savings and recoveries obtained under the FCA are being duplicated. Additionally, older whistleblower reward laws that have received minimum publicity, such as the Act to Prevent Pollution from Ships, the Lacey Act, and the Endangered Species Act, are now being used to hold polluters and people who traffic in endangered species accountable.

A great example of how the new rewards laws are being used is the Bradley Birkenfeld case. The IRS has admitted that the information provided by Birkenfeld concerning illegal U.S. taxpayer accounts held in secret Swiss banks has already led to unprecedented monetary recoveries and the crippling of the entire "undeclared" offshore Swiss-U.S. banking industry. How the Birkenfeld disclosures triggered more than $13.7 billion in recoveries for the taxpayers is explained in the Anticorruption Toolkit. As the first major whistleblower to obtain a reward under the 2006 IRS whistleblower law, Birkenfeld's case made international headlines. After some initial mishaps the IRS paid Mr. Birkenfeld $104 million as a result of his successfully filing a proper whistleblower claim under the IRS tax laws. Given the critical role whistleblowers play in holding large institutions accountable, over time many more such awards will be paid. The long-term benefits to the public interest will be incalculable. Whistleblowing does work.

Beyond the False Claims Act

Outside of corruption in government contracting, the anecdotal evidence of how whistleblowers have saved lives, held government officials accountable, or accurately warned of disasters that would rock the largest institutions in the world provides additional ample evidence that whistleblowing works. Whistleblowers have rightly embarrassed (and consequently changed) many cherished institutions. Highly popular elected officials from both major political parties have been exposed by truthful whistleblower disclosures.

Whistleblowers tried to warn the officials about the financial, security, and safety concerns that led to the collapse of the corporate giant Enron, the tragic explosion of the Space Shuttle *Challenger,* and even the early detection of the terrorists who would fly jetliners into the World Trade Center towers. Whistleblowers exposed the illegal beatings of inmates in Iraq's Abu-Ghraib prison and the massive illegal domestic searches of U.S. citizens by the National Security Agency. Indeed, two presidents were held accountable by whistleblowers: President Richard Nixon resigned from office in large measure due to the disclosures of a whistleblower code-named "Deep Throat." President Bill Clinton was debarred from the practice of law due to the secret tape recordings of Pentagon employee whistleblower Linda Tripp. Supervisory Special Agent

Frederic Whitehurst forced the FBI to admit that its internationally respected crime lab was contaminated. His allegations compelled the FBI to agree to outside oversight for the first time in its seventy-year history, and resulted in freeing innocent people from jail. Environmental Protection Agency scientist David Lewis singlehandedly took on an entrenched EPA bureaucracy and forced the agency to abandon its policy of promoting the use of human waste byproducts on farmland. This list could go on for pages.

The Power of the Truth in a Whistleblower Case

The final rule for whistleblowers is to fully understand the power of the truth. Whistleblowers should never underestimate the impact of their initial disclosures. They cannot lose sight of why they placed their job on the line. Obviously in a *qui tam* case, the truthfulness and provability of the whistleblower allegations are all-important. If an employee can prove fraud against the government or violations of the securities or tax laws, the employee can win his or her case.

But what about in retaliation cases? Although the "black letter" law holds that employees are under no obligation whatsoever to prove the accuracy of their whistleblower allegations, this standard of proof can be somewhat misleading. The law on "good faith" holds that as long as whistleblower disclosures were objectively reasonable—made with a good faith belief that wrongdoing had occurred—the whistleblowing is protected and there is no need to ever prove that misconduct actually occurred. If proving the validity of a disclosure is not required, why bother?

If you know that the underlying allegations were not verified and/or were relatively insignificant in nature, there is no reason to make them central to your case. The courts are absolutely correct in demanding that whistleblower laws be interpreted as "freedom to disclose" laws, and their analysis of the detrimental impact of forcing an employee to demonstrate the accuracy basis in the allegations is completely on point.

Many attorneys reviewing the whistleblower cases reasonably stop their analysis here. The law does not require that the whistleblower prove the accuracy of his or her allegations of misconduct. So why prove the accuracy? It will delay the proceeding, cost money (in terms of discovery and litigation costs), and may not even be admissible in the hearing (especially if the company enters into a stipulation or does not contest the fact that the employee engaged in protected activity). This can be a big mistake. The accuracy of the underlying allegations can be the train that moves the entire proceeding forward.

First, a smart company does not want a regulatory agency to find that the company violated the law. It's very bad public relations to say the least. Such findings can trigger further investigations, spark criminal or civil enforcement proceedings, and undermine the credibility of the company with its government regulators and the public. A smart employer will admit that problems exist and try to resolve the dispute with the whistleblower. An intransigent employer will fight on, often with devastating results (including, in some cases, bankruptcy).

Second, it is important to ask why a whistleblower risked his or her career in the first place. It surely wasn't to obtain a "make whole" remedy. Proving the truthfulness of the whistleblower allegations provides the vindication many whistleblowers need to make things right, not to mention providing the company a strong motive to settle a case on reasonable terms.

Third, even if the employer does concede that the employee's protected activity was reasonable or conducted in good faith, an employee can still pursue discovery into the underlying concerns in order to obtain evidence of motive. Companies that violate safety standards, cheat on government contracts, or manipulate stock prices have a *motive* to fire a whistleblower. Proving that motive not only satisfies a critical element of an employee's retaliation case but also impeaches the credibility of the employer's "legitimate business reason" for firing the whistleblower. An unbiased juror or judge will understand that a company would want to suppress an employee whose complaints were accurate. What better reason to retaliate against an employee than to cover up a mistake or regulatory violation?

Getting the Facts Out: The Turner Trial

On a frozen February morning in 2007, ten Minnesota jurors returned from their deliberations to announce their verdict in a nine-year legal battle between Jane Turner and her former employer, the FBI. During the two weeks of trial, three government lawyers, two from the Justice Department and one from the FBI, called witness after witness to attack Turner. The witnesses included the top official from the FBI's powerful Criminal Division and the former special agent in charge of the FBI's Minneapolis division. A high-ranking former "inspector," who led an "independent" review of Turner's performance was one of the government's star witnesses. Turner, who had worked as an agent for twenty-five years, listened to these managers tear apart her career, and she was not at all surprised at what they had to say.

Turner had challenged one of the most tight-knit and insular agencies in the county—an employer with an authoritarian history and a motto proclaiming: "Thou Shall Not Embarrass the Bureau." Turner had directly taken on the FBI's "old boy network." She had accused respected and high-level G-men of incompetence and misconduct in handling horrendous child-crime cases. She accused her bosses of ignoring the brutal rape of a five-year-old Indian child. Shocking allegations.

As a technical matter, Turner was not obligated to prove that the FBI had botched child-crime cases. Like most retaliation cases, she only needed to demonstrate the reasonableness of her concerns, not their truth. At first blush, the issue at trial appeared typical of any employment case. Turner claimed she was an excellent agent with years of strong performance. Her FBI managers claimed her performance had radically dropped, that she botched cases, and that she no longer could perform her job. The scenario was typical. Like almost every company bent on retaliation, the FBI built a "case" against Turner—documenting every minor infraction, monitoring her every movement, and placing her on endless "performance improvement plans" whose essence was creating a mechanism to document performance failures.

Turner challenged the FBI head-on. She put on evidence documenting her main whistleblower concern: that the FBI had botched child-crime cases. If she was right, her managers would be discredited. If she was wrong, the performance failures would appear credible. The truth of her serious allegations of misconduct became the centerpiece of the trial.

Turner subpoenaed two assistant U.S. attorneys with whom she worked during the five months her alleged performance collapsed. She questioned them about a case she worked over the summer and fall of 1999. Turner was very lucky. Although they were still employed as prosecutors for the United States, and regularly interacted with their FBI investigators, both told the truth without hesitation. They explained what happened in a controversial child-crime case Turner had worked, over the objection of her immediate supervisor.

On the July 4 weekend in 1999, a five-year-old boy from the Turtle Mountain Indian Reservation was hospitalized. The child suffered from severe rectal tearing, injuries that were consistent with having been brutally raped. Nurses in the emergency room were traumatized over the injury. The parents, who acted cold and detached while at the hospital, said that the injury resulted from a car accident. The treating emergency room doctor found the explanation absurd. However, the Bureau of Indian Affairs policeman accepted the story. The FBI agent responsible for Turtle Mountain reviewed the file and decided that no charges would be pursued. Case closed.

Weeks later Turner visited the local hospital. The medical staff accosted her, including the doctor who worked on the child in the emergency room. They were angry and upset. Why were no charges filed? Why was the child sent back to the family—where the stepfather (the most likely suspect) would have access to him?

Turner reviewed the case file and immediately contacted the U.S. attorney's office. She relayed what had occurred. Based on the file, it was clear that her fellow agent had completely botched the case. Just as her management was hammering her over so-called performance issues, she now was confronted once again with another example of FBI mishaps, another example of the FBI turning its back on a child victim on an Indian reservation. She could turn her back and support the decision of her fellow agent, or she could pursue the matter and potentially once again "embarrass the Bureau."

She reopened the case. It did not take long for Turner to rule out the ridiculous story initially credited by the FBI. The auto-accident theory forensically fell apart, and the one witness who initially backed up the suspected rapist recanted his testimony. An objective review of the medical information left only one explanation for the injuries. Now it was only a question of time. The suspect was the stepfather. On the day of the crime his conduct in the emergency room was consistent with that of a child molester. Turner knew the profile well, as she had successfully cracked other cases and was a certified psychological profiler, trained by the FBI's top experts.

Turner recommended that the stepfather be asked to undergo a voluntary polygraph and questioned about the incident. After significant delays, at the request of the federal prosecutors, Turner's recommendation was followed. A confession was obtained. The stepfather pleaded guilty to the sexual assault.

Instead of greeting Turner's superb gumshoe work on the child-rape case with gratitude, her managers grew even more upset. How dare Turner second-guess a fellow agent? How dare she embarrass the FBI by reopening a closed case—after the FBI had made a determination that the child had not been raped? The FBI's reaction to Turner was typical of how mid-level and upper-level managers often react to whistleblowers. Circle the wagons, defend the line supervisor implicated in the retaliation, and "shoot the messenger." Turner was given another terrible performance review. She was a pariah—an agent to be avoided at all costs.

But Turner could prove she was right. A child had been brutally raped. The FBI had accepted a patently absurd alibi, without any investigation. It had closed the case. As confirmed by the federal prosecutors who worked the case, but for Jane Turner's tenacity, a child rapist would have been walking the streets.

The managers who tried to justify the FBI's handling of the case lost their credibility before the court. How could a juror believe the testimony of FBI supervisors who attacked Turner's performance, when these same managers had backed up the agent who closed the child-rape case? The truth of Turner's allegations that the FBI botched child-crime cases at the Turtle Mountain Indian Reservation impeached every FBI witness who tried to smear her.

The *Minneapolis Star Tribune* reported on the jury's verdict:

> *Federal jurors hugged former FBI agent Jane Turner. "I think you were the very best FBI agent," juror Mashima Dickens told Turner, who investigated child sex-abuse crimes.*
>
> *"Looking at the way you were treated, I just said you were screwed left and right," Dickens said, tears rolling down her cheeks.*
>
> *"I just want to tell you I have nothing but the utmost respect for you," juror Renee Anderle said as she hugged Turner in the hallway outside Chief U.S. District Judge James Rosenbaum's courtroom in Minneapolis.*
>
> *"This is vindication," said Turner, 55, of St. Paul. "We spoke truth to power, and we won."*

"The Truth Shall Set You Free"

The "truth" behind a whistleblower's cause can be the engine that drives a case, pushing it forward while placing the company on the defense, establishing strong credibility for the whistleblower, and eventually enabling an employee to triumph against a far stronger and well-funded foe. In the end, the hardest part of a case is to make the whistleblowing work—both to fix a problem and save a job.

PRACTICE TIPS

The U.S. Department of Labor's Administrative Review Board has issued a number of rulings explaining how proof of employer violations constitutes important evidence of retaliatory motive:

- *Khandelwal v. Southern Cal. Ed.*, 97-ERA-6 (ARB, March 31, 1998)

- *Seater v. Southern Cal. Ed.*, 95-ERA-13 (ARB, September 27, 1996)

THE FINAL RULE
Remember July 30, 1778

One thing is certain: The roots of whistleblowing can be found deep in the American Dream. They are not based on wealth or opportunity, but on service and a Democratic Ideal that can be traced directly back to the earliest days of the American Republic and the very first whistleblowers in the newly independent United States.

On February 19, 1777, just six months after the Declaration of Independence was signed by our Founding Fathers, the warship *Warren* was anchored outside of Providence, Rhode Island. On board, ten sailors and marines who had joined the U.S. Navy to fight for independence from Great Britain, met, not to plot a battle against the King's armies, but rather to vet their concerns about the incompetence and lack of moral integrity of the commander in chief of the Continental Navy, Commodore Esek Hopkins. Their boss not only held the top Navy job, but came from a powerful colonial family; his brother was a governor of Rhode Island and one of the original signers of the Declaration of Independence.

These sailors were devoted to fighting and winning the War for Independence. They were revolutionaries, risking their lives to build a free and independent America; they wanted nothing more than to fight and defeat their British foes. However, they feared that their commander could not successfully lead any such effort, for his tactics foreshadowed doom for the new American Navy. They blew the whistle on the mistreatment of prisoners almost 250 years before other whistleblowers exposed mistreatment of prisoners in the modern "war on terror."

The American Republic was not yet one year old. There was no First Amendment protection for freedom of speech. There were no legal protections for any whistleblowers, let alone sailors and marines who intended to expose misconduct by their commander in the middle of a war. Yet these ten men agreed to send a petition to Congress to expose misconduct by the Navy's highest officer. They became the first whistleblowers of the newly independent United States of America: Captain of the Marines John Grannis, First Lieutenant of the Marines George Stillman, Second Lieutenant of the Marines Barnabas Lothrop, First Lieutenant Roger Haddock, Second Lieutenant James Sellers, Third Lieutenant Richard Marvin, Chaplain John Reed, midshipman Samuel Shaw, ship's gunner John Truman, and ship's carpenter James Brewer.

Their petition, straightforward and written from their hearts, is found below:

On Board the Ship 'Warren'

Feb 19, 1777

Much Respected Gentlemen: "We who present this petition engaged on board the ship 'Warren' with an earnest desire and fixed expectation of doing our country some service. . . . We are ready to hazard every thing that is dear & if necessary, sacrifice our lives for the welfare of our country, we are desirous of being active in the defense of our constitutional liberties and privileges against the unjust cruel claims of tyranny & oppression; but as things are now circumstanced on board this frigate, there seems to be no prospect of our being serviceable in our present situation. . . . We are personally well acquainted with the real character & conduct of our commander, commodore Hopkins & we take this method not having a more convenient opportunity of sincerely & humbly petitioning, the honorable Marine Committee that they would inquire into his character & conduct, for we suppose that his character is such & that he has been guilty of such crimes as render him quite unfit for the public department he now occupies, which crimes, we the subscribers can sufficiently attest.

Each sailor also signed personal affidavits to Congress setting forth specific instances of misconduct committed by the commander in chief that they had witnessed. These included allegations that commodore Hopkins "treated prisoners in the most inhuman & barbarous manner," failed to attack a British frigate that had run aground (thereby permitting the enemy to escape), and stated that he would "not obey the Congress" of the United States.

Captain John Grannis agreed to secretly leave the *Warren* and present the whistleblower allegations to the Continental Congress's Marine Committee. Grannis traveled from Rhode Island to Philadelphia, presented the petitions to the Congress and testified before a special congressional subcommittee appointed to hear the whistleblower's concerns:

Q: Are you the man who signed the petition against Esek Hopkins, Esq. by the name of John Grannis?

A: Yes . . .

Q: Commodore Hopkins is charged with being a hindrance to the proper manning of the fleet, what circumstances do you know relative to this charge?

A: For my part his conduct and conversation are such that I am not willing to be under his command. I think him unfit to command . . . his conversation is at times so wild & orders so unsteady that I have sometimes thought he was not in his senses & I have heard others say the same. . . .

Q: Had you liberty from Commodore Hopkins . . . to leave the frigate you belong to?

A: No. I came to Philadelphia at the request of the officers who signed the petition against Commodore Hopkins & from a Zeal for the American cause.

Q: Have you, or to your knowledge either of the signers aforesaid any difference or dispute with Commodore Hopkins since you or their entering into service?

A: I never had, nor do I believe that either of them ever had. I have been moved to do & say what I have done & said from love to my country . . .

On March 26, 1777, the Marine Committee concluded its investigation and presented the matter to the full Continental Congress, including all the papers signed by the officers of the *Warren*. After considering the matter, Congress backed up its whistleblowing sailors and passed the following resolution: "Resolved, That Esek Hopkins, be immediately and he is hereby, suspended from his command in the American Navy."

Congress listened to the voices of the whistleblowers and suspended the highest-ranking naval officer. John Hancock, the president of the Continental Congress, and the most famous signer of the Declaration of Independence, certified the resolution and ordered that it be served on Hopkins. Hopkins remained under suspension for over nine months. He never appeared before Congress to refute the allegations. On January 2, 1778, Congress voted to fully terminate Hopkins's service, and he was subsequently removed from the U.S. Navy.

Unfortunately, the incident did not end with the commodore's removal from office. Hopkins sought revenge against the whistleblowers—both during his short remaining stint as commodore and after he was stripped of his command. Upon learning of the letters signed by the ten sailors and the fact that the information was being delivered to the Continental Congress, Hopkins sprung into action during his last days as commander. He used his authority to pressure the sailors to change their testimony, and he organized a rump military prosecution for one of the petitioners, Lieutenant Marvin. Marvin, a follower of Thomas Paine, was accused of being the "prime mover in circulating" the petition. Hopkins ordered Marvin arrested and tried by a court-martial.

The military court consisted only of Hopkins' supporters, including his own son. Hopkins was permitted to personally question the accused. If found guilty, Marvin's only appeal would be to Hopkins himself. Marvin's sole crime: having "signed" "scurrilous papers" "against his Commander in Chief."

At his court-martial Marvin stood strong. He did not plead for mercy or back down from his actions. Indeed, he readily admitted to his crime of signing the petition against Hopkins. He told the prosecutors that the accusations brought forth against the commander "were of such a nature that we thought it was our duty to our Country to lay them before Congress."

Hopkins grilled Marvin as to who else had signed the petition and what specific information was provided to Congress. Marvin would not turn in his fellow sailors or tip off Hopkins as to the allegations provided to Congress. Instead, he stated, "I refuse answering to that until such time as I appear before Congress or a Committee authorized by them to inquire into the affair."

It was no surprise when Marvin was found guilty of treating the commander with the "greatest indignity" by "signing and sending to the Honorable Continental Congress several unjust and false complaints." Commodore Hopkins immediately affirmed the findings of the court-martial and ordered Marvin expelled from the Navy. America's first whistleblower was fired from his job.

"Your petitioners, not being persons of affluent fortunes, but young men who have spent most of their time in the service of their country . . . finding themselves arrested for doing what they then believed and still believe was nothing but their duty . . . do most humbly implore the interposition of Congress in their behalf."
Richard Marvin and Samuel Shaw, Letter to Congress sent from jail
(1778)

Hopkins was not satisfied with merely firing the ringleader of the whistleblowers. On January 13, 1778, the former commodore sued the ten whistleblowers for conspiracy and criminal libel. Hopkins demanded ten thousand pounds in retribution, and the whistleblowers could be jailed if found guilty. Hopkins hired a well-known Rhode Island attorney, Rouse J. Helme, and filed his "writ of attachment" in the Rhode Island Inferior Court of Common Pleas. Only two of the ten sailors, Shaw and Marvin, were actually served with the complaint. The others resided outside of the jurisdiction of the Rhode Island court. Therefore, they escaped the retaliatory lawsuit.

Even though the United States was still in the middle of its War for Independence, Hopkins used his resources and connections in an attempt to destroy the lives of two sailors who had the courage to file allegations of serious wrongdoing with the Continental Congress. Shaw and Marvin were both arrested, held in jail, and forced to post an "enormous bail."

Shaw and Marvin were not men of means. They had nowhere to turn, except to plead for help from the Continental Congress. On July 8, 1778, the two whistleblowers wrote an impassioned letter to the Congress:

> *Your petitioners, not being persons of affluent fortunes but young men who have spent most of their time in the service of their country in arms against its cruel enemies since the commencement of the present war, finding themselves arrested for doing what they then believed and still believe was nothing but their duty, held to bail in a state where they were strangers, without connections that can assist them in defending themselves . . . against a powerful as well as artful person who by the advantages of his officers and of the present war hath amassed great wealth—do most humbly implore the interposition of Congress in their behalf in such way and manner as the wisdom of that most august body shall direct and order . . .*

The petition was read to Congress on July 23, 1778. A special "Committee of Three" was appointed to review the matter. After a seven-day review, the committee reported back to the Continental Congress. History was made.

On July 30, 1778, the Continental Congress came to the defense of Marvin and Shaw. The Congress, without any recorded dissent, passed a resolution that encouraged all citizens to blow the whistle on official misconduct. Perhaps for the first time in world history—and unquestionably for the first time in the history of the United States—a government recognized the importance of whistleblowers in exposing official misconduct of high-ranking officials working for the government itself. The act of Congress could have been written today:

> *That it is the duty of all persons in the service of the United States, as well as all other inhabitants thereof, to give the earliest information to Congress or any other proper authority of any misconduct, frauds or misdemeanors committed by any persons in the service of these states, which may come to their knowledge.*

The Continental Congress was also sympathetic to the personal plight of Shaw and Marvin. The Founding Fathers understood that finding whistleblowers guilty of criminal libel was counter to the framework of the new Republic. Congress authorized the government to pay the legal costs and attorney fees for Shaw and Marvin so that the two men would have excellent lawyers and be able to fully defend themselves in the Rhode Island courts.

Moreover, the Congress did not hide behind government secrecy edicts, even during time of war. Instead, the Congress authorized the full release of government records related to the appointment and removal of Hopkins as commander in chief, as well as the various papers of the Marine Committee as related to the information provided by the ten sailors. No "state secret" privilege was invoked, and Marvin and Shaw did not even need to use a Freedom of Information Act to obtain documents necessary to vindicate their whistleblowing.

Just like in modern whistleblower cases, documentary evidence can make or break a case. In 1778, the Founding Fathers understood this simple fact and made sure that Marvin and Shaw had the necessary evidence to defend their actions before a jury of their peers. The Founding Fathers went beyond passing a law endorsing whistleblowers. They spent scarce federal monies to defend and protect the sailors who had the courage to blow the whistle to the Congress.

With the help of the Congress, Shaw and Marvin were able to retain top-notch legal assistance. Their main lawyer at the trial was William Channing—a distinguished Rhode Island attorney who had been recently elected as the attorney general for the state. His father-in-law was William Ellery, one of the signers of the Declaration of Independence. Interestingly, Ellery had attended the initial examination of Grannis when he testified before the Marine Committee and was the member of the Congress responsible for transcribing Grannis's testimony.

The criminal libel trial lasted five days. Shaw and Marvin "relied almost entirely for their case upon" the information provided to them by the Congress, including "copies of letters from President John Hancock and others" to Commodore Hopkins, along with the "depositions of the officers and men on the *Warren* who had signed the petition to Congress against Hopkins."

The jury ruled for the whistleblowers. The defendants were vindicated and Hopkins was ordered to pay their court costs.

In May 1779, the Congress "examined the accounts of Samuel Shaw and Richard Marvin for expenses incurred in defending an action at law brought against them by Esek Hopkins" authorized the payment of "fourteen hundred and eighteen dollars and 7/90 to be paid to Mr. Sam. Adams," of which $500 was set aside for William Channing.

Despite his so-called "court-martial," Marvin also received his full sailor's pension for his service during the Revolutionary War.

Whistleblower Day

The Founding Fathers' endorsement of whistleblowers during the height of the American Revolution is a profound testimony to American Democracy and the responsibility citizens have to report abuses of authority and violations of law. Since this history was "rediscovered" with the initial publication of the *Whistleblower's Handbook* in 2011, the U.S. Senate has repeatedly passed resolutions honoring July 30 as "National Whistleblower Appreciation Day."

On July 7, 2016, the Senate unanimously passed the following resolution:

Whereas, in 1777, before the passage of the Bill of Rights, 10 sailors and marines blew the whistle on fraud and misconduct harmful to the United States;

Whereas the Founding Fathers unanimously supported the whistleblowers in words and deeds, including by releasing government records and providing monetary assistance for reasonable legal expenses necessary to prevent retaliation against the whistleblowers;

Whereas, on July 30, 1778, in demonstration of their full support for whistleblowers, the members of the Continental Congress unanimously enacted the first whistleblower legislation in the United States . . .;

Whereas whistleblowers risk their careers, jobs, and reputations by reporting waste, fraud, and abuse to the proper authorities;

Whereas, when providing proper authorities with lawful disclosures, whistleblowers save taxpayers in the United States billions of dollars each year and serve the public interest by ensuring that the United States remains an ethical and safe place . . . .

Now, therefore, be it

That the Senate—

(1) designates July 30, 2016, as "National Whistleblower Appreciation Day"; and

(2) ensures that the Federal Government implements the intent of the Founding Fathers, as reflected in the legislation enacted on July 30, 1778, by encouraging each executive agency to recognize National Whistleblower Appreciation Day by—

> (A)*informing employees, contractors working on behalf of United States taxpayers, and members of the public about the legal rights of citizens of the United States to "blow the whistle" by honest and good faith reporting of misconduct, fraud, misdemeanors, or other crimes to the appropriate authorities; and*
>
> (B)*acknowledging the contributions of whistleblowers to combating waste, fraud, abuse, and violations of laws and regulations in the United States.*

As equally remarkable as the historic 1778 whistleblower resolution are the actions taken by the First Congress of the United States. Numerous drafters of the U.S. Constitution were prominent members of the First Congress, including Elbridge Gerry, Rufus King, Robert Morris, and James Madison, and its actions are often cited as evidence of the vision our Founding Fathers had of American Democracy. At the heart of this vision were whistleblowers.

In 1999–2000, when the U.S. Chamber of Commerce and its government-contractor allies raised a Supreme Court challenge to the constitutionality of the False Claims Act (the most effective whistleblower law in the United States), Supreme Court Justice Antonin Scalia rebuked their attack, extensively citing the actions of the First Congress. He pointed out that on July 31, 1789, our Founding Fathers enacted the first of eighteen *qui tam* laws mandating that whistleblowers (informants) whose original information resulted in a successful enforcement action be entitled to a percentage of the collected proceeds. This is the precise model used in the False Claims Act and the other very successful whistleblower reward laws today.

The Founding Fathers looked toward the People to be a full partner in enforcement of law—and included whistleblower reward provisions in the major revenue-producing and government accountability laws enacted by the First Congress. The eighteen *qui tam* laws established the right of whistleblowers to obtain monetary rewards for disclosing violations of customs laws (still covered under the False Claims Act), reports of bribery, disclosure of illegal conflicts of interest, reporting criminal larceny and the receipt of stolen goods, and providing evidence of improper lending by the Bank of the United States. These rewards generally were set at 25 to 50 percent of the monies collected from the wrongdoer.

Whistleblowers and the Birth of the First Amendment

It was not by accident that the Founding Fathers, some of the very people who voted to defend the *Warren* whistleblowers, enshrined "freedom of speech" and the "right to petition" as the first governing principle of the Bill of Rights: "Congress shall make no law . . . abridging the freedom of speech . . . or the right of the people . . . to petition the government for a redress of grievances."

Whistleblowing embodies the heart and soul of the First Amendment. It establishes the right of the people to expose wrongdoing and empowers them with the right to demand that powerful leaders remain accountable. The *Warren* incident demonstrates that the Founding Fathers were not only aware of "whistleblowing," but that they strongly supported it.

Former Supreme Court Justice Louis Brandeis hit the nail on the head when he described the early American political culture and influential personalities whose struggles led to the passage of the First Amendment: "Those who won our independence by revolution were not cowards. They did not fear political change. They did not exalt order at the cost of liberty."

Justice Brandeis went on to describe those who fought for the First Amendment as: "[C]ourageous, self-reliant men" whose "confidence in the power of free and fearless reasoning" rested at the heart of "popular government. . . . They valued liberty both as an end and as a means. They believed liberty to be the secret of happiness and courage to be the secret of liberty. They believed that freedom to think as you will and speak as you think are means indispensable to the discovery and spread of political truth . . . they knew that order cannot be secured merely through fear of punishment . . . that the path of safety lies in the opportunity to discuss freely supposed grievances and proposed remedies. . . . They eschewed silence coerced by law . . ."

Justice Brandeis could well have been referencing the sailors and marines on the *Warren*, who risked courts martial and criminal libel charges to blow the whistle on their commander in chief. His description seems to fit the personality of the courageous whistleblowers far more than the nameless and faceless bureaucrats who harass or make decisions to fire these employees.

As understood by the Founding Fathers, the First Amendment established a credo at the very heart of American politics that valued the contributions of whistleblowers: "The dominant purpose of the First Amendment was to prohibit the widespread practice of government suppression of embarrassing information."

If whistleblowers are silenced, if voters cannot learn about the corruption of their leaders, if investors cannot learn the truth about companies they rely upon for their retirement security or their child's education, what then is the future of the American Dream? On the reverse side, if ordinary workers are empowered to do their job honestly, even when they are faced with pressure to cut corners on safety, sell defective products, or lie to obtain lucrative government contracts, what then of the American Dream? Is it one to be proud of—to aspire toward?

In Conclusion

Corruption is a cancer on all Democratic institutions. It converts the "rule of law" to the "rule of backdoor influence." Greed trumps justice.

When the United States was born, the Founding Fathers believed, almost religiously, that freedom of speech would protect the people from corruption. So much so that in the middle of the Revolution they protected whistleblowers who exposed malfeasance in the top leadership of the newly created Continental Navy. After the Revolutionary War they incorporated the right to criticize the government and expose wrongdoing into the heart of the First Amendment to the Constitution and enacted numerous *qui tam* laws. During the Civil War, when the existence of the United States was again under attack, the leaders of the Union enacted the first modern whistleblower law (the False Claims Act) to empower citizens to defend key laws in court, use these legal proceedings to expose and defeat corruption in public contracting, and obtain monetary rewards for taking the risk to expose wrongdoing. The role of the people in defending democratic institutions from the destructive impact of corruption was clearly recognized, endorsed, and encouraged by the founders and saviors of American democracy.

Over the past fifty years, a national framework for protecting people who courageously step forward and report corruption has developed. The framework is extremely complex and consists of numerous federal and state laws, but is also plagued by loopholes and technicalities that cause unnecessary hardship to many employees.

But despite many personal hardships, change has come for whistleblowers. There are now *qui tam* and reward laws covering a sizable segment of society. The False Claims Act and IRS whistleblower law now cover fraud in the public-sector economy. The Dodd-Frank Act now covers fraud in trading securities and commodities. With the auto safety law, the Act to Prevent Pollution from Ships, and the Lacey Act, whistleblower reward laws are also covering areas of public heath and safety and the environment. State governments are slowly following the federal lead, and a majority of states now have *qui tams* covering public procurement.

Slowly, antiretaliation laws are being modernized. The new laws passing through Congress almost uniformly permit employees access to federal court proceedings and reasonable damages. Reforms are slowly fixing infamous tricks and technicalities used to undermine whistleblowers—such as mandatory arbitration agreements and the failure to protect internal disclosures.

Today the key to obtaining protection as a whistleblower is navigating the maze: finding the best laws, becoming fully aware of the traps and pitfalls facing any whistleblower, and ultimately using these laws effectively to ensure real protection. At some point there will be a change in corporate culture. At some point corporations, government agencies, and most judges will acknowledge the benefits of strongly promoting employee disclosures of wrongdoing. We are not there yet—not even close. But the legal framework for changing this culture is coming into place, and a growing number of whistleblowers are landing on their feet.

INTERNATIONAL TOOLKIT
Taking the Profits Out of Corruption

Corruption is an insidious plague that has a wide range of corrosive effects on societies. It undermines democracy and the rule of law, leads to violations of human rights, distorts markets, erodes the quality of life and allows organized crime, terrorism, and other threats to human security to flourish.

So wrote the UN Secretary-General in the official introduction to the United Nations Convention against Corruption. Since the Convention's approval by the UN General Assembly in 2002, it has been ratified by more than 140 countries, including the United States, South Africa, India, the United Kingdom, and Russia. The Convention not only mandates that each signatory take strong steps to combat corruption but also explicitly recognizes the importance of protecting whistleblowers as a tool in fighting corruption.

Article 32 of the Convention calls on member states to take action to prevent "retaliation" against witnesses or persons who give testimony against corrupt officials. Article 33 urges all nations to enact "domestic" legislation to "provide protection" against "unjust treatment" for any person who reports evidence of corruption to "competent authorities." Similar conventions have been approved by other international bodies, most notably the Council of Europe. Article 9 of the Council's Civil Law Convention on Corruption mandates that all European nations protect whistleblowers: "Each Party shall provide in its internal law for appropriate protection against any unjustified sanction for employees who have reasonable grounds to suspect corruption and who report in good faith their suspicion to responsible persons or authorities."

But the reality facing international whistleblowers does not resemble the protections called for in these treaties. For example, in South Africa, Jimmy Mohlala documented millions of dollars in fraudulent payments during the construction of a stadium built for the 2010 South Africa–hosted World Cup. A masked gunman murdered him the day before he was scheduled to testify in court exposing the fraud. In India, Shehla Masood was shot dead after reporting corruption in government contracts. According to a Bloomberg investigation, she was just one of twelve whistleblowers murdered in India since 2010. In Russia, Sergei Magnitsky died in prison after exposing large-scale business fraud committed with the help of government officials. His death triggered worldwide outrage. The U.S. Congress took an unprecedented step and passed the Sergei Magnitsky Rule of Law Accountability Act, sanctioning Russian officials who participated in Magnitsky's imprisonment and the corruption he died trying to expose. Most recently, a comprehensive report on the United Kingdom's whistleblower law (often cited as a model for other nations to follow) ripped the law apart as being completely ineffectual, providing minimal compensation and failing to protect most whistleblowers.

"Very few other countries have any track record of prosecuting deliberate . . . violations, let alone a legal process that would protect witnesses from obstruction of justice . . ."

U.S. Department of Justice, in *United States v. Efploia*

What effective options are available to international whistleblowers who want to expose fraud or corruption?

Transnational Reward Laws on a Worldwide Stage

On September 22, 2014, the U.S. Securities and Exchange Commission (SEC), the top cop on Wall Street, issued a historic ruling in a case under the Foreign Corrupt Practices Act. The Commission awarded a non-U.S. citizen $30 million for turning in a corporation that paid bribes to foreign government officials. In making this award, the Commission sent a message to whistleblowers worldwide: The rewards program was open to anyone.

In issuing the $30 million award, the Commission stated:

> In our view, there is a sufficient U.S. territorial nexus whenever a claimant's information leads to the successful enforcement of a covered action brought in the United States. . . . When these key territorial connections exist, it makes no difference whether, for example, the claimant was a foreign national, the claimant resides overseas, the information was submitted from overseas, or the misconduct comprising the U.S. securities law violation occurred entirely overseas.

The Commission's payment had its intended impact. By September 2016 more than nineteen hundred whistleblowers from ninety-seven countries had filed corruption claims in the United States. **Figure 13** indicates the countries from which international whistleblowers have filed claims in the United States.

Figure 13

Countries from Which Whistleblowers Have
Filed Reward Claims under U.S. Law
2012–2016

Source: U.S. Securities and Exchange Commission, 2012–2016 Annual
Report on the Dodd-Frank Whistleblower Program

After making its first payment to a foreign national, the Commission continued paying rewards to other non-U.S. citizens, including paying an Australian whistleblower $3.75 million for reporting illegal payments made to Chinese officials by an Australian company. Australians took notice. One local senator told the *Sydney Morning Herald*: "Whistleblowers in the United States get rewarded and protected, but here they get punished and ruined."

Rule 9 details how the FCPA works.

The Foreign Corrupt Practices Act is not the only U.S. law with transnational application. The Act to Prevent Pollution from Ships (APPS), discussed in detail in Rule 11, implements an international treaty prohibiting ships from polluting the oceans. Other U.S. whistleblower reward laws applicable to foreign nationals include the False Claims Act, the Lacey Act/Endangered

Species Act, the Internal Revenue Act, the Securities Exchange Act, and the Commodity Exchange Act.

The bottom line is simple: The best bet for whistleblowers worldwide is to try to find a U.S. whistleblower law under which the misconduct they have witnessed may be covered. Next, worldwide whistleblowers must use the law's reporting procedures (which often protect confidentiality), provide information that could result in a successful prosecution, and apply for a reward.

Foreign Corrupt Practices Act (FCPA)

The Foreign Corrupt Practices Act (FCPA) targets bribery of foreign government officials by publicly traded corporations or U.S. persons. It is the most powerful and effective transnational anticorruption law in the world. In 2010, when Congress passed the Dodd-Frank Act's securities reward law, whistleblowers from around the world became eligible for a reward if they provided original information about bribery or other violations of the FCPA. The FCPA whistleblower law is explained in Rule 9. Additionally, Rule 8 and Checklists 7 and 8 provide additional information on the FCPA and the securities whistleblower law for which the FCPA provisions are a part.

Offshore Banking or Tax Fraud

Bankers from any nation in the world can now turn in their U.S. clients who hold illegal offshore bank accounts or are evading taxes. Under the Internal Revenue Service (IRS) program, whistleblowers can confidentially disclose any violation of U.S. tax laws, including violations that are perpetrated by foreign banks.

In discussing the role of whistleblowers in exposing illegal conduct in foreign banks, the Commissioner of the IRS explained how one Swiss banker's disclosures were critical in triggering the IRS's successful multibillion-dollar campaign to eliminate illegal offshore banking:

> The IRS's serious efforts to combat offshore tax evasion . . . [were] brought to our attention . . . by whistleblowers. . . . A turning point in our enforcement efforts came in 2009 with the agreement reached with UBS. This agreement represented a major step toward global tax transparency and helped build a foundation for our future enforcement efforts.

Under the U.S. tax whistleblower law, employees who risk their jobs to report tax frauds or underpayments are eligible for a mandatory reward. The range for the reward is 15 to 30 percent of any monies recovered by the IRS based on the whistleblower's "original" information. The IRS treats all whistleblower submissions under strict confidentiality rules. The IRS program is explained in Rule 7.

In June 2007 the first major whistleblower to use this law stepped forward. Bradley Birkenfeld was a Swiss banker with inside information as to how the largest bank in the world, the Zurich-based UBS, had an illegal program of more than nineteen thousand Americans, all of whom held nondisclosed and secret accounts in Switzerland for which they did not pay U.S. taxes. Although Mr. Birkenfeld was a U.S. citizen, there is nothing in the law that requires whistleblowers to be U.S. citizens. Any "individual" can provide information to the IRS, regardless of his or her country of citizenship.

Birkenfeld's disclosures triggered the largest successful tax fraud prosecutions in world history. The results were staggering, and the power of whistleblowers to change the world was affirmed. Here is the story.

It all started when Bradley Birkenfeld, a banker from UBS, turned over documents proving that UBS served approximately twenty thousand U.S. clients, all of whom had illegal and undeclared bank accounts designed to hide assets from government review and thus avoid paying taxes. Based on this disclosure, UBS was forced to enter into a deferred prosecution agreement with the United States. In exchange for avoiding criminal charges, UBS paid a $780 million fine and turned over information on 4,450 U.S. clients.

This sanction triggered the largest individual reward given to a whistleblower. The IRS awarded Mr. Birkenfeld $104 million under the whistleblower reward law. That award had worldwide ramifications, as taxpayers with illegal offshore accounts realized that their own bankers could become multimillionaires by turning them in to U.S. authorities. The "trust" needed to make an international secret banking program work was undermined. Any participant in that illegal program could become a whistleblower—regardless of the participant's own country's domestic laws (or lack thereof) and despite the fact that he or she may have personally participated in the secret banking system.

Mr. Birkenfeld's whistleblowing not only forced UBS to pay a large fine but also forced UBS to agree to turn over the names of the U.S. citizens who held illegal bank accounts in Switzerland. This concession radically undermined the concept of Swiss banking secrecy. Switzerland had boasted for decades that its domestic laws protected the identity of U.S. account holders, but because of Mr. Birkenfeld's disclosures, secrecy could no longer be guaranteed. As explained in the publication swissinro.ch, "The U.S. had long suspected Swiss banks of harboring U.S. tax cheats. But Swiss banking secrecy made this impossible to prove. That changed when former UBS employee Bradley Birkenfeld came to the Department of Justice with strong documentary evidence in 2007."

What happened next was simply amazing.

The $104 million reward, in combination with the mandatory disclosure of account-holder names and significant sanctions imposed on the banks, caused U.S. tax cheats with assets hidden around the world to panic and rush to take advantage of a tax amnesty program established by the IRS. The amnesty program was simple: Turn yourself in; pay fines, penalties, and back taxes; and in exchange you could escape criminal prosecution and keep your identity secret. If you did not turn yourself in, the IRS promised to aggressively prosecute everyone who did not turn themselves in—and seek far higher fines and penalties.

More than 100,000 Americans have taken advantage of the amnesty program. As the Government Accountability Office (GAO) explained, Switzerland's agreement to name names "created uncertainty among UBS account holders as to whether their names were on the list." To escape prosecution, tens of thousands of millionaires and billionaires turned themselves in. As of October 2016, the United States had collected more than $13.7 billion in fines and penalties from these tax cheats and the offshore banks that hide their wealth, with thousands of cases still awaiting processing.

The IRS and DOJ also used whistleblowers' information to indict other Swiss banks. After the UBS case was resolved, fifteen other Swiss banks were indicted for tax fraud. The prosecutions are ongoing, but as of 2016 Credit Suisse had pleaded guilty to criminal conspiracy and paid $2.811 billion in fines and penalties, Bank Leumin group had paid $270 million in fines, and the Julius Baer Group Ltd. had paid $547 million in fines and penalties. Moreover, a whistleblower turned in the oldest bank in Switzerland, Wegelin & Co., which pleaded guilty to tax fraud, paid $74 million in fines, and was forced into bankruptcy. Wegelin's bankruptcy sent additional shockwaves throughout the Swiss banking system, and, for the most part, all known U.S. illegal accounts were closed.

After indicting the fifteen banks, the DOJ cut deals with eighty smaller Swiss banks, which agreed to pay a total of $1.36 billion in penalties. In addition, these banks were forced to "make a complete disclosure of their cross-border activities; provide detailed information on an account-by-account basis for accounts in which U.S. taxpayers have a direct or indirect interest." They also agreed to close all illegally held U.S. accounts and "provide detailed information as to other banks" that hold illegal U.S. accounts.

By 2015 the United States had successfully criminally prosecuted 45 American-UBS account holders, resulting in $224 million in recoveries. By 2016 the DOJ announced that more than one hundred U.S. account holders had been found guilty in federal court. By the end of 2016, well over $13.7 billion had been collected from the Swiss banks and their U.S. account holders.

When issuing its reward to the whistleblower, UBS Swiss banker Bradley Birkenfeld, the IRS stated that he had "provided information on taxpayer behavior that the IRS had been unable to detect." His "comprehensive information . . . was exceptional in both its breadth and depth" and "formed the basis for unprecedented actions against UBS, with collateral impact on other enforcement actions." This was not an overstatement. Even DOJ conceded that the initial UBS case was "the centerpiece of the Division's current efforts" that "resulted in an historic agreement" that "dealt the fabled Swiss bank secrecy a devastating blow."

International bankers and the numerous support employees who establish the illegal structures used to hide money in secret foreign banks accounts (such as those identified in the "Panama Papers") hold the key to policing all illegal U.S. offshore accounts. These bankers, lawyers, accountants, and trustees are potentially eligible for large rewards under the U.S. program.

Employees who work for international banks, and who want to file a confidential whistleblower reward claim, must follow the rules governing IRS tax whistleblowers. These steps are spelled out in Rule 7.

Wildlife Trafficking, Protection of Endangered Species, and Illegal Logging

The U.S. Congress enacted whistleblower reward laws in key laws prohibiting wildlife trafficking and protecting endangered species. Whistleblowers can obtain rewards under the Lacey Act, the Endangered Species Act, and the Fish and Wildlife Improvement Act when they disclose violations of laws protecting plants, fish, and animals under the major international treaty banning trade in endangered species (the CITES Convention). These laws cover illegal logging, which destroys the habitat for many critically threatened species.

These reward laws have international application and permit any "person" to qualify for a reward. Under the Lacey Act, a "person" includes a corporation. Consequently, international organizations committed to fighting illegal trafficking can also qualify for a reward, provided they submit original information that documents violations of the antitrafficking laws and/or information that results in a successful prosecution of criminal traffickers.

Rule 12 explains how these wildlife trafficking laws work.

False Claims Act

The oldest whistleblower reward law, the False Claims Act (FCA), also has extraterritorial application. As explained in Rule 6, the FCA is America's premier whistleblower reward law. It broadly covers frauds against the United States taxpayer/government. Many schemes that are hatched by foreign companies are covered under the Act, and whistleblowers that are non-U.S. citizens are fully qualified to file claims under the law and collect rewards. Because the False Claims Act is such a powerful law (allowing treble damages and recovery of attorney fees and including a private right of action and mandatory rewards for qualified whistleblowers), employees who work outside the United States should be fully aware of the types of misconduct covered under this law. Following are some examples of the misconduct for which foreign companies have been held liable:

- Failure to pay customs or "anti-dumping" duties and violation of tariff obligations: Toyo, Inc. (Japan); CMAI (China)

- Improper relocation of employees in the United States (B-1 visa violations): India-based Infosys Technologies

- Sale or importation of defective products for use in government contracts: Lincoln Fabrics (Canada); Barrday (Canada); Itochu (Japan)

- Kickbacks or illegal marketing of drugs paid for by Medicaid, Medicare, or the Veterans Administration: Valeant Pharmaceuticals (Canada); Serono (Switzerland); Organon International (Netherlands); B. Braun Melsungen AG (Germany),

- Fraud in obtaining gas or oil leases or underpayment of royalties owed on such leases: Louis Dreyfus Group (France), Royal Dutch Shell (Netherlands)

- Fraud in providing food and water to U.S. troops in Afghanistan: Supreme Foodservice FZE (United Arab Emirates)

- Phony claims submitted to the U.S. government for payment: BNP Paribas (France)

- Violation of terms in fixed price contract: Hesco Bastion Limited (U.K.)

- Using misleading testing certificates in selling products to the U.S. Army: Alcatl Lucent (France)

- Improper billing of defense contracts: Securitas Gmblt Werkschutz (Germany)

- Selling adulterated drugs: Ranbaxy Laboratories (India)

Employees working for foreign companies are often unaware of whistleblower rewards available under U.S. law. Employees who work for companies that import products to the United States, sell goods or services to the American government (including state governments), or obtain U.S. government contracts are all potentially eligible for whistleblower rewards.

The procedures for filing claims under the False Claims Act are explained in Rule 6.

Preventing Ocean Pollution: The Act to Prevent Pollution from Ships/MARPOL

The Act to Prevent Pollution from Ships (APPS) permits whistleblowers from any country in the world to report ocean pollution committed on the high seas and obtain a financial reward. This whistleblower provision has proven, over time, to be the key to the successful prosecution of ship owners who dump oil and other waste into the oceans in violation of the International Convention for Prevention of Pollution from Ships, as modified by the protocol of 1978, better known simply as the MARPOL Protocol. The APPS law has enabled the United States to use whistleblower information as the basis for successfully prosecuting ships registered outside the United States, including those whose flagship nation is Turkey, Jordan, Portugal, South Korea, Denmark, Liberia, Germany, Cyprus, Greece, Panama, Italy, Japan, Bahamas, Malta, Egypt, Bermuda, Singapore, China, Spain, Norway, New Zealand, Sweden, and the Philippines, among others.

How the law works, and how whistleblowers from outside the United States can qualify for rewards, is spelled out in Rule 9.

Motor Vehicle Safety

As set forth in detail in Rule 10, in December 2015 the U.S. Congress passed a reward law covering motor vehicle safety. This law should have transnational application, as numerous automobiles and their parts (such as airbags) are manufactured outside the United States. Whistleblowers from countries such as Korea, Japan, Mexico, and Germany who report safety concerns in accordance with this law should fully qualify for rewards.

The Role of Non-Government Organizations or "Analysts"

Internationally there are numerous NGOs, often nonprofit groups, dedicated to working on issues for which U.S. whistleblower laws apply, such as anticorruption or wildlife protection. The U.S. whistleblower reward laws are ingeniously structured to permit or encourage these international NGOs to act as a bridge between whistleblowers who may not speak English or have access to information about reward laws and don't have the ability to effectively blow the whistle under the U.S. laws. For example, in 2016 the nonprofit Natural Resources Defense Council qualified as a relator under the False Claims Act and shared in a $920,000 reward in an environmental clean-up case.

The Lacey Act, the premier wildlife trafficking law, contains a specific definition of who is eligible for a reward. The law uses the term "person" as the class of people who qualify for monetary rewards. This definition may cause some to think that you have to be an actual "person" to be a whistleblower. Although individuals are covered under the law, the Lacey Act also classes corporations and partnerships as "persons": "The term 'person' includes any individual, partnership, association, corporation, trust. . . ." Obviously it makes no difference if the corporation is a for-profit news outlet or a not-for-profit wildlife advocacy organization.

Consequently, there is no legal impediment to an NGO filing a reward claim under the Lacey Act.

The Foreign Corrupt Practices Act's definition of "whistleblower" follows this pattern, but requires that claims be filed by an individual, not a corporation. When the U.S. Congress enacted the Dodd-Frank Act (which included the FCPA coverage), Congress understood that a whistleblower often did not meet the traditional definition of an "insider." Consequently, Congress defined the term "whistleblower" to include both "individuals" (i.e., the classic whistleblower) and "analysts."

The analyst concept was a radical departure from the historical understanding of who is a whistleblower. Under the "analyst" provision, persons without any firsthand knowledge of potential violations can qualify as whistleblowers if they can evaluate information (public or nonpublic) and present an "independent analysis" documenting the criminal activity. If the information from this analysis is used to trigger or assist in a prosecution, the analyst is a covered whistleblower. Although it may be hard to understand how an analyst can obtain access to unique information necessary to quality for a reward, as explained below, persons who work for NGOs have access to witnesses or potential whistleblowers who do not speak English or may not understand how they can file a claim in the United States. The NGO, which is active on-the-ground in a foreign country, can act as the intermediary, collecting information, doing translations, and communicating with attorneys in the United States concerning how to file an effective reward case. The NGO, acting through one of its employees/representatives, can serve as the "analyst," explaining the importance of the various witness statements or other materials obtained from witnesses and sources outside the United States.

The SEC's definition of the type of "independent analysis" necessary to justify a reward to an analyst (such as an employee of an anticorruption NGO) is as follows:

> *Independent analysis means your own analysis, whether done alone or in combination with others. Analysis means your examination and evaluation of information that may be publicly available, but which reveals information that is not generally known or available to the public.*

The analyst brings together evidence from other sources (including public sources) and presents the U.S. government with an analysis of facts that can demonstrate a violation of law. For example, there would be no legal reason an analyst working for an African-based NGO could not work with various confidential sources and "analyze" that source information. Thereafter, the analyst could create a report incorporating the source information and file a reward claim under U.S. law.

The use of NGOs as intermediaries for "insiders," or "sources on the ground," to facilitate the transmittal of high-quality information about bribes, corruption, or illegal wildlife trafficking can assist in the protection of whistleblowers. The traditional whistleblower can work with attorneys or respected NGOs in raising concerns but remain one step removed from the actual process of blowing the whistle.

Immigration Law: Political Asylum

Whistleblowers have been granted political asylum in the United States. This is in recognition that citizens outside the United States who report fraud and corruption within their own countries can face life-threatening retaliation. The process for obtaining asylum is dictated by U.S. immigration law. Court rulings interpreting these laws recognize some whistleblowers as a protected class.

The landmark case concerned Dionesio Grava, who worked for the Philippine government's Bureau of Customs where he witnessed corrupt supervisors profiting from smuggling schemes. He blew the whistle. At first he was falsely accused of work-related misconduct but was completely "cleared" after a review. He was then transferred to an "outlying post" in an attempt to shut him up. That did not work. In defiance of his direct supervisor's wishes, he filed charges and testified against a customs official in a corruption case. Unfortunately for Mr. Grava, the official had "family ties to the Philippine Congress and the National Bureau of Investigations." The retaliation got dark and personal. His pet dog was poisoned, his car tires were slashed, and he received direct death threats. Fearing for his life, Mr. Grava fled his homeland and entered the United States. Upon arrival, he applied for political asylum.

The U.S. immigration authorities (the Immigration and Naturalization Service, or INS) initially ruled that he must be deported. The INS refused to recognize whistleblowers as a group that could qualify for political asylum. This logic was not sustained. In a landmark ruling from the U.S. Court of Appeals for the Ninth Circuit, the INS decision was reversed. The Court noted that Grava's "tormentors" were not "mere criminals or guerrilla forces," but rather they were "instruments of the government itself."

Not every whistleblower can obtain asylum. Courts have ruled that whistleblowing against government corruption can constitute protected speech under immigration laws: "[W]here the whistle blows against corrupt government officials, it may constitute political activity sufficient to form the basis of persecution. . . . Thus official retaliation against those who expose and prosecute governmental corruption may, in appropriate circumstances, amount to persecution on account of political opinion."

Whistleblowers seeking asylum must contact immigration attorneys, as the process for obtaining asylum is completely distinct from the process of applying for rewards or filing cases under the Foreign Corrupt Practices Act. Furthermore, because being granted asylum as a whistleblower is unusual, and the rules governing these decisions are controlled by the courts, whistleblowers seeking political asylum in the United States are strongly urged to obtain counsel with expertise in immigration.

International Efforts

Numerous other countries have enacted whistleblower legislation, mostly prohibiting domestic retaliation. These laws are almost universally weak, and fail to meet the standards endorsed by Transparency International. On January 26, 2017 the European Commission, the executive arm of the European Union, published a formal "Inception, Impact Assessment" on the state of whistleblowing in Europe. The Commission expressed "strong concerns about the lack of effective whistleblower protection across the different Member States," and recognized that the "lack of adequate whistleblower protection may discourage the disclosure of wrongdoing and illegal activities," with "negative effects on compliance with rules on procurement, state aid, implementation of structural funds, environmental protection, and competition and investment."

The European Commission's Assessment concluded that "whistleblower protection would contribute to preventing and tackling corruption, enhancing corporate social responsibility and legal compliance, ensuring healthier competition and greater investor confidence in the internal market," and endorsed efforts to ensure "effective whistleblower protection across the European Union."

The United Kingdom's Public Interest Disclosure Act of 1998 was long considered one of the best whistleblower protection laws outside of the United States. In 2016 the international NGO Blueprint for Free Speech and the Thomson Reuters Foundation published *Protecting Whistleblowers in the UK: A New Blueprint*. The report reviewed each element of the Public Interest Disclosure Act and evaluated it relative to international best practices. The highly critical report explained that the average whistleblower received only about £17,000 equivalent to approximately $21,000 in compensation, hardly enough to encourage people to blow the whistle, let alone lose their job, damage their career, and harm their reputation. The report is available at https://blueprintforfreespeech.net/wp-content/uploads/2016/05/Report-Protecting-Whistleblowers-In-The-UK.pdf. The report provides twenty recommendations to fix the U.K. law and is also a blueprint for other nations to follow when drafting whistleblower legislation.

Despite weaknesses, some international whistleblowers have used their nation's laws to obtain reinstatement and other relief, including high profile cases in Ireland, Serbia, Bosnia, and Herzegovina. Before trusting that any law will prove effective, the protections afforded employees under the law must be carefully reviewed. Does it provide adequate due process rights? What compensation is available? What agency will investigate the whistleblower's claims or provide protection to the whistleblower? Can you obtain an attorney to help? Is there an anticorruption NGO available to help and provide support?

Canadian Whistleblower Laws

Canada has gone the farthest in establishing reward-based procedures that have potential transnational application for whistleblowers. One of the Canadian administrative procedures permits rewards for whistleblowers who report major violations of international tax laws. The second was established by the Ontario Securities Office and is modeled closely on the U.S. Dodd-Frank Act's securities whistleblower reward law.

Canadian Tax Whistleblower Law

Canada started to modernize its whistleblower laws by adopting a limited rewards program for whistleblowers who report illegal and undeclared offshore bank accounts held by Canadian citizens. Established by the Canada Revenue Agency in January 2014, the Offshore Tax Informant Program permits the government to provide financial awards "to individuals who provide sufficient, specific and credible details related to major international tax non-compliance which lead to the assessment and collection of more than $100,000 (CAD) of additional federal tax (excluding penalties and interest)." The awards offered are significantly lower than those in the United States, with a range between 5 and 15 percent (compared to the award range in the United States between 15 and 30 percent). Rewards are only paid on the amount of federal taxes paid based on international violations. If the back tax payment is less than $100,000 (CAD), no reward is paid. The reward is not based on criminal fines and penalties, and it appears that rewards are not paid on interest collected.

According to the Canada Revenue Agency, the law permits rewards for information about the following international violations:

- Undeclared Canadian taxable income that has been transferred outside Canada

- Undeclared foreign taxable income

- Undeclared foreign property

- Offshore transactions and undeclared trusts held offshore

The Revenue Agency's Offshore Compliance Division manages the program, accepts tips, screens the cases, and has responsibility for paying rewards. Paying rewards is completely discretionary, and the Revenue Agency "will determine whether a payment will be made under the contract and what that amount will be." There is no judicial review if the Authority denies a reward or fails to pay a proper amount.

The administrative procedures approved by the Canada Tax Agency are weak and need to be significantly strengthened. After two years the Agency had only entered into approximately twelve contracts with whistleblowers, and no rewards had been paid. The website for the program is www.cra-arc. gc.ca/gncy/cmplnc/otip-pdife/menu-eng.html.

CANADIAN SECURITIES WHISTLEBLOWER LAW

The Ontario Securities Commission (OSC) has also taken the first step to institute a Dodd-Frank–style whistleblower reward law for securities fraud. The program contains many of the features of the U.S. securities whistleblower reward law, but it has three serious drawbacks: It has a low cap on the maximum amount of rewards, no judicial review, and the Commission has complete discretion whether or not to pay a reward.

The program's rules are detailed and many are modeled, almost word for word, on the SEC's reward program. This includes rules on how compliance officials can obtain a reward, the criteria used by the Ontario Securities Commission to determine eligibility, and specific procedures for applying for a reward. Anyone providing information to the OSC should carefully review OSC Policy 15-601 (Whistleblower Program) before providing any information to the Commission. The rules are available at www.osc.gov.on.ca/documents/en/ Securities-Category1/20160714_15-601_policy-whistleblower-program.pdf.

The Commission is actively publicizing its new reward program, encouraging whistleblowers to risk their careers and provide information. Their page starts with the following promotion: "Do you have inside knowledge of, or suspect, a possible violation of Ontario securities law that could harm investors? We want to hear from you." Their website goes on to describe the program:

A whistleblower can be an individual, or a group of individuals acting jointly, who voluntarily provide high quality information that contains timely, specific and credible facts regarding potential misconduct. Whistleblowers who report information that leads to an OSC administrative proceeding resulting in monetary sanctions and/or voluntary payments of $1 million or more may be eligible for a financial award of up to $5 million. We will make all reasonable efforts to protect the identity of whistleblowers. Under the Ontario Securities Act, the OSC may take enforcement action against employers who take reprisals against whistleblowers. Whistleblowers can choose to report anonymously if they are represented by a lawyer.

The $5 million payment cap may seem reasonable, but it will discourage high-level informants and act as a disincentive for whistleblowers. In the United States, although most rewards are less than $5 million, the prospect of obtaining a large award motivates whistleblowers afraid of retaliation. Also, whistleblowers who have high-placed jobs and large incomes are in the best position to know about the massive frauds that can rock markets or cause a company and its investors to suffer large losses. These executives or directors will not be effectively incentivized by such a cap.

In addition to the cap, the percentage range permitted under the law is lower than any of the U.S. programs. The Ontario program's reward range is between 5 and 15 percent, whereas the minimum payment for securities violations under U.S. law is 10 percent, with a maximum payment of 30 percent.

Another problem with the Canadian law is that whistleblowers have no guarantee that they will ever be paid, or that the OSC will honor any of the requirements set forth in its policy. The Commission explicitly cut off the rights of a whistleblower to challenge either a denial of reward or the amount of a reward. OSC Policy 15-601 is clear: "The Commission's determination whether or not to grant a whistleblower award and any amount awarded to a whistleblower are not subject to appeal. No private right of action is conferred on a whistleblower to seek a whistleblower award."

The OSC's whistleblower program website is located at www.osc.gov.on.ca/en/whistleblower.htm.

CONCLUSION

Both the OSC's and the Canada Revenue Agency's reward programs are steps forward for international whistleblowers. Other countries have also implemented weak reward programs, offering low amounts of compensation for whistleblowers, and vesting the government with the discretion to deny rewards. These laws fail to acknowledge the tremendous risks whistleblowers take and the catastrophic impact being a whistleblower can have on one's job, career, and quality of life. Without realistic incentives and due process guarantees capable of both encouraging employees to step forward and fully compensating them (especially those who hold high-level and well-compensated positions), these programs will not achieve their goals, and may completely fail. If a government is serious about using a rewards program to fight corruption, the program must have the following features:

- Confidentiality and anonymity must be realistically protected.

- The agency must pay a mandatory minimum award (no less than 10 to 15 percent) to qualified whistleblowers.

- There must be an "alternative remedy" provision that permits whistleblowers to obtain rewards based on all enforcement actions taken based on their disclosures.

- The decision to make an award cannot be discretionary. If a whistleblower provides information pursuant to the program's rules, the reward must be paid.

- Whistleblowers must be able to review the record upon which a reward determination was made and be able to challenge any denial of a reward in court.

- The agency for which a whistleblower provides information, and which has the obligation to review the claim and pay the reward, must be highly specialized, trusted, and capable of protecting the identity of the whistleblower and advocating on his or her behalf.

Until other nations implement effective whistleblower programs, the U.S. laws offer the best opportunity for international whistleblowers to effectively expose fraud or pollution and then obtain fair compensation.

The U.S. laws for which international whistleblowers can obtain a reward are discussed in Rule 1 and 3 (overviews), Rule 4 (Financial/banking frauds), Rule 6 (False Claims), Rule 7 (tax and offshore banking), Rules 8 and 9 (securities fraud and Foreign Corrupt Practices Act), Rule 10 (Auto Safety), Rule 11 (Ocean Pollution/Act to Prevent Pollution from Ships) and Rule 12 (wildlife trafficking).

- Online resource page for international whistleblowers: https://www.globalwhistleblower.org. This site has links to major international treaties and information on the FCPA translated into various languages.

- Information on the Canadian whistleblower laws: The Ontario Securities Commission Whistleblower Office is located at http://www.osc.gov.on.ca/en/whistleblower.htm.

- The University of Toronto held a seminar on whistleblower reward laws, with a focus on the new Canadian rewards law on January 26, 2017. The presentations, along with valuable links, is available here: http://www.rotman.utoronto.ca/FacultyAndResearch/ResearchCentres/CapitalMarketsInstitute/Events/Past-Events.

- A detailed report by Transparency International on the status of whistleblower laws in Europe is located here: http://www.transparency.org/whatwedo/publication/whistleblowing_in_europe_legal_protections_for_whistleblowers_in_the_eu.

CHECKLIST 1

Whistleblower Reward Laws (*Qui Tam*)

Federal Qui Tam *Laws*

False Claims Act	**31 U.S.C. § 3729–3732** Rewards for employees who file *qui tam* actions in U.S. district court concerning federal contractor fraud or other frauds that result in a financial loss to the federal government.
Internal Revenue Code	**26 U.S.C. § 7623** Requires awards to qualified persons who provide information to the IRS relating to the underpayment of federal taxes or violations of the Internal Revenue Code, if the information leads to the recovery of monies to the United States. Whistleblowers are entitled to a percentage recovery ranging from 15–30% of recovered tax revenues, interest, civil penalties, and other fines.
Securities Exchange Act	**15 U.S.C. § 78u-6** Requires awards to qualified persons who provide information to the Securities and Exchange Commission relating to violations of the Securities Exchange Act, if the information leads to the recovery of monetary sanctions exceeding $1 million. Whistleblowers are entitled to a percentage recovery ranging from 10–30% of collected sanctions. To qualify for a reward, claims must be filed in accordance with the rules published by the SEC. 17 C.F.R. § 240 and 249.
Commodity Exchange Act	**7 U.S.C. § 26** Requires awards to qualified persons who provide information to the Commodity Futures Trading Commission relating to violations of the Commodity Exchange Act, if the information leads to the recovery of monetary sanctions exceeding $1 million. Whistleblowers are entitled to a percentage recovery ranging from 10-30% of collected sanctions. To qualify for a reward, claims must be filed in accordance with the rules published by the CFTC. 17 C.F.R. Part 165.

Financial Institution Reform, Recovery, and Enforcement Act (FIRREA)	12 U.S.C. §§ 4201-10 Permits the payment of rewards to informants who provide original information on fraud committed by (or to) federally insured banks or other institutions insured by the FDIC. Rewards paid at discretion of Attorney General.
Foreign Corrupt Practices Act	15 U.S.C. §§ 78m, 78dd, 78ff Requires the Securities and Exchange Commission to pay whistleblowers 10-30% of sanctions obtained for violations of the FCPA. This includes sanctions obtained directly from the SEC or sanctions obtained from the Department of Justice as a result of a "related action." The files and filing procedures for FCPA cases are identical to other securities law violations filed with the SEC. Those rules are published at 17 C.F.R. Parts 240, 241, and 249.
Motor Vehicle Safety Act	49 U.S.C. § 30172 Permits the Department of Transportation to pay whistleblowers 10-30% of sanctions obtained from motor vehicle manufacturers, contractors, and dealerships for reporting safety violations that result in a sanction of at least $1 million.
Act to Prevent Pollution from Ships (APPS)	33 U.S.C. § 1908(a) Permits federal courts to grant a whistleblower a reward of up to 50% of sanctions obtained for providing information that results in a successful prosecution for violations of the APPS.
Lacey Act	716 U.S.C. § 3375(d) Permits the Departments of Interior, Treasury, and Commerce (for lumber or plants, the Department of Agriculture) to reward whistleblowers who disclose violations of the Lacey Act (illegal international trafficking in protected animals, fish, or plants and other violations of the CITES Convention).
Endangered Species Act	16 U.S.C. § 1540(d) Permits the Departments of Interior, Treasury, and Commerce (for lumber or plants, the Department of Agriculture) to reward whistleblowers who disclose violations of the Endangered Species Act.
Fish and Wildlife Improvement Act	16 U.S.C. § 742l(k) Permits the Departments of Interior and Commerce to pay rewards for reporting violations of any wildlife protection law (plants, fish, or animals) enforced by the U.S. Fish and Wildlife Service or the National Marine Fisheries Service.

State and Municipal False Claims Acts

California	California False Claims Act § 12650, et seq.
Colorado	Colorado Medicaid Fraud False Claims Act, C.R.S. § 25.5-304, et seq.
Connecticut	Connecticut False Claims Act § 17b-301a.
Delaware	Delaware False Claims and Reporting Act § 1201, et seq.
District of Columbia	District of Columbia False Claims Act § 2-308.03, 2-308.13-2-308.21, et seq.
Florida	Florida False Claims Act § 68.081-68.093. Miami Dade County False Claims Ordinance (Ord. No. 99-152, § 1, 11-2-99) § 21-256-266.
Georgia	State False Medicaid Claims Act § 49-4-168-§ 49-4-168.8, et seq.
Hawaii	False Claims to the State § 661-21-§ 661-29, et seq. *Qui Tam* Actions or Recovery of False Claims to the Counties § 46-171-§ 46-179, et seq.
Illinois	Illinois Whistleblower Reward and Protection Act § 175-1-§175-8, et seq.
Indiana	Indiana False Claims and Whistleblower Protection IC 5-11-5.5-IC 5-11-5.5-18.
Iowa	Iowa False Claims Act, Title XV, Subtitle 5, Ch. 685.
Louisiana	Louisiana False Claims Act § 46:437.1-46:437.14, 438.1-438.8, 439.1-439.2, 439.3-439.4, 440.1-440.3.
Maryland	Maryland False Health Claims Act § 2-601-2-611.
Massachusetts	Massachusetts False Claims Act Ch 12 § 5A-12 § 5O, et seq.
Michigan	The Medicaid False Claims Act MCL 400.611.
Minnesota	Minnesota False Claims Act Minn. Stat. § 15C.01, et seq.
Montana	Montana False Claims Act § 17-8-401-§ 17-8-403, et seq.
Nevada	Nevada Submission of False Claims to State or Local Government § 357.010-§ 357.250, et seq.
New Hampshire	Medicaid Fraud and False Claims § 167:61-b-§ 167:61-e, et seq.

New Jersey	Supplementing Title 2A of the New Jersey Statutes and amending 2 P.L. 1968, c.413 (N.J.S.A. 2A:32C-1).
New Mexico	Medicaid False Claims Act § 27-14-1, et seq.
	Fraud Against Taxpayers Act § 44-9-1–§ 44-9-14, et seq.
New York	New York State False Claims Act § 187–§ 194, et seq.
	New York City False Claims Act § 7-801–§ 7-810.
	Rule Governing the Protocol for Processing Proposed Civil Complaints Pursuant to the New York City False Claims Act § 3-01–§3-03, et seq.
North Carolina	North Carolina False Claims Act § 1-605–§ 108A-63.
Oklahoma	Oklahoma Medicaid False Claims Act Title 63 § 5053, et seq.
Rhode Island	Rhode Island False Claims Act § 9-1.1-1–§ 9-1.1-8.
Tennessee	Tennessee Medical False Claims Act § 71-5-181–§ 71-5-186.
Texas	Texas False Claims Act § 32.039.
	Medicaid Fraud Prevention § 36.001–36.008, § 36.051–§36.055, § 36.101–§ 36.117, § 36.131–§ 36.132.
	Health and Human Services Commission § 531.101–§ 531.108, § 531.1061–§ 531.1062, et seq.
Vermont	Vermont False Claims Act, 32 V.S.A. §§ 630-6423.
Virginia	Virginia Fraud Against Taxpayers Act § 8.01-216.1–§ 8.01-216.19, et seq.
Washington	Washington False Claims Act, RCW 43.131; 74.09.
Deficit Reduction Act of 2005	42 U.S.C. § 1396(h) Provides extra financial incentives for states to enact False Claims Acts.
	Statute has stimulated numerous states to enact such laws covering misuse of state taxpayer monies.

CHECKLIST 2

Whistleblower Protections Under Federal Law

(Laws that have been effectively used to protect whistleblowers are marked with an *.)

A. *Constitutional Protection: First Amendment "Freedom of Speech"*

*U.S. Constitution First Amendment (*Also see* discussion below on 42 U.S.C. § 1983, which applied the First Amendment to state and local government employees.)	Protection for Public Employees who Blow the Whistle on Matters of Public Concern.
	Pickering v. Board of Education, 391 U.S. 563 (1968) (First Amendment protected teacher who complained about school budget to newspaper).
	Lane v. Franks, 134 S.Ct. 2369 (2014) (public employee's grand jury testimony, which concerned his job duties, protected).
	Sanjour v. United States EPA, 56 F.3d 85 (D.C. Cir. 1995) (en banc); *Swartzwelder v. McNeill,* 297 F.3d 228 (3rd Cir. 2002) (injunctive relief blocking implementation of antiwhistleblower rules).
	Harlow v. Fitzgerald, 457 U.S. 800 (1982) (immunity defense).
	Bush v. Lucas, 462 U.S. 367 (1983) and *Weaver v. USIA,* 87 F.3d 1429 (D.C. Cir.) (requirement to use administrative remedies in federal cases).
	Garcetti v. Ceballos, 547 U.S. 410 (2006) (limiting application of First Amendment protections when speech is part of "official duties").
	The holding in *Garcetti* was clarified in *Lane v. Franks,* 134 S.Ct. 2369 (2014), where the Court held that the "critical question . . . is whether the speech at issue it itself ordinarily within the scope of an employee's duties, not whether it merely concerns those duties."
	Flora v. County of Luzerne, 776 F.3d 169 (3rd Cir. 2015) (protected activity includes blowing the whistle on matters within an employee's official duties, provided the speech itself is not part of those duties).
	Howell v. Town of Ball (2016) U.S. App. LEXIS 12171 (5th Cir. 2016) (police officers cooperating with FBI investigation protected).
	Posey v. Lake Pend, 546 F.3d 1121 (9th Cir. 2008) (discussion of conflicting judicial interpretations of rules mandated by *Garcetti*).

	Marable v. Mark, 511 F.3d 924 (9th Cir. 2007) (determination whether speech is part of "official duties" and therefore not protected under First Amendment is a "practical one") (post-*Garcetti* analysis).*Thomas v. City of Blanchard*, 548 F.3d 1317 (10th Cir. 2008) (fact that employee "threatened to go outside his usual chain of command and report" "suspected criminal activity" "leads us to believe that he was not acting pursuant to his official duties") (post-*Garcetti* analysis). *Walker v. City of Moline Acres*, 2009 U.S. Dist. LEXIS 11022 (E.D. Missouri) ("fact that employee learns" of the misconduct "though his employment" "does not preclude him" from also speaking as a citizen and obtaining constitutional protection) (post-*Garcetti* analysis).
*Civil Rights Act of 1871, 42 U.S.C. § 1983 [Applying First Amendment Protection to State and Municipal Employees]	Statutory protection for state and local government employee whistleblowers whose speech is protected under First Amendment. Law permits federal court lawsuit for damages and other relief. Compensatory and punitive damages permitted. Cases heard by jury trial. *Carey v. Piphus*, 435 U.S. 247, 253 (1978) (§ 1983 creates tort-like liability). *Mt Healthy v. Doyle*, 429 U.S. 274 (1977) (burden of proof). *Will v. Michigan*, 491 U.S. 58 (1989) (immunity defenses and requirement to name individual government managers as defendants). *Orange v. District of Columbia*, 59 F.3d 1267 (D.C. Cir. 1995); *Parks v. City of Brewer*, 56 F. Supp. 2d 89, 98–99 (D. Maine 1999) (collecting cases concerning disclosures of government misconduct protected under § 1983). *Heck v. Humphrey*, 512 U.S. 477, 483 (1994) (no requirement to exhaust state administrative remedies when filing claim under § 1983). *Robinson v. York*, 566 F.3d 817 (9th Cir. 2009); *McGreevy v. Stroup*, 413 F.3d 359 (3rd Cir. 2005); *Kinney v. Weaver*, 367 F.3d 337 (5th Cir. 2004) (rejecting immunity defense in First Amendment cases). *Catletti v. Rampe*, 334 F.3d 225 (2nd Cir. 2003) (court testimony protected) (truthful testimony provided at trial is *per se* a matter of public concern). *Owens v. Okure*, 488 U.S. 235 (1989) (because § 1983 does not have a statute of limitations, the deadline for filing claims is controlled by the local states statute of limitations for personal injury cases). *Andrew v. Clark*, 561 F.3d 261 (4th Cir. 2009) (providing memorandum created at work to press constituted protected activity).

Civil Rights Attorney Fee Act, 42 U.S.C. § 1988(b) and (c)	Provision in law permitting award of statutory attorney fees in employment discrimination and retaliation cases filed under Title VII of the Civil Rights Act and the Civil Rights Act of 1871, 42 U.S.C. §§ 1983 and 1985.
	Perdue v. Kenny, 130 S. Ct. 1662 (2010) (awarding attorney fees "serves important public purpose of making it possible for persons without means to bring suit to vindicate their rights) (permitting enhancement of fee award under "extraordinary circumstances").
	Hensley v. Eckerhart, 461 U.S. 424 (1983) (fees paid at market rates to ensure the enforcement of federal rights)(fees paid even if employee was only partially successful).
	Missouri v. Jenkins, 491 U.S. 274 (1989) (fees paid at current rates to compensate for delay in payment).
	Blanchard v. Bergeron, 489 U.S. 87, 96 (1989) (attorney fees are not limited by contractual fee agreement or controlled by a contingency fee agreement. The standard for determining the fee is the reasonable market rate for similar services).
	City of Riverside v. Rivera, 477 U.S. 561 (1986) (attorney fee payment may be larger than judgment obtained by client).
	Pennsylvania v. Delaware Valley, 478 U.S. 546 (1986) ("lodestar" method basis for calculating reasonable fee). *Blum v. Stenson*, 465 U.S. 886 (1984) (attorneys paid at market rates).
	Johnson v. Georgia Highway, 488 F.2d 714, 717-19 (5th Cir. 1974) (setting forth twelve factors used in setting reasonable attorney fee rate).
	Salazar v. District of Columbia, 809 F.3d 58 (D.C. Cir. 2015) (method to calculate reasonable market rate).

B. Consumer Product Safety Whistleblower Protections

*Consumer Product Safety Act of 2008	Protection for employees who blow the whistle on covered consumer safety hazards and violations. This is a DOL case with similar procedures and law as found under the Energy Reorganization and Sarbanes-Oxley Acts.
15 U.S.C. § 2087	Claims filed with U.S. Department of Labor/OSHA within 180 days of adverse action. Claims can be removed to federal court for jury trial.
	Reinstatement, back pay, compensatory damages, and attorney fees permitted. 29 C.F.R. § 1983 (U.S. Department of Labor rules for adjudicating administrative complaint).

C. Corporate Whistleblower Protection

*Dodd-Frank Wall Street Reform and Consumer Protection Act of 2010 Public Law No. 111-203	The Dodd-Frank Act of 2010 contained three new whistleblower protection provisions and amended the Sarbanes-Oxley and False Claims Act whistleblower laws. The new statutory protections are contained in the following sections of the Dodd-Frank Act:
Section 748 (creating a new section 21 of the Commodity Exchange Act (7 U.S.C. § 26))	Section 748 (creating a new section 23F of the Commodity Exchange Act): • *Qui tam* rewards for whistleblowers who provide "original information" to the commission "relating to a violation" of the Commodity Exchange Act or "CEA." • Antiretaliation provision for employees who file *qui tam* claims or assist in *qui tam* actions. • Retaliation claims filed in federal court within two years of adverse action. Relief includes reinstatement, back pay, special damages, and attorney fees. • Mandatory arbitration prohibited.
Section 922 (creating a new section 21F of the Securities Exchange Act (15 U.S.C. § 78u-6))	Section 922 (creating a new section 21F of the Securities Exchange Act): • *Qui tam* rewards for whistleblowers who provide "original information" to the SEC "relating to a violation" of the Securities Exchange Act. • Antiretaliation provision for employees who file *qui tam* claims or assist in *qui tam* actions. • Antiretaliation protections for employees who make disclosures "required or protected" under the SOX Act, SEA, federal Obstruction of Justice Act, and other laws, rules or regulations under the jurisdiction of the SEC. • Retaliation claims filed in federal court. Relief includes reinstatement, double back pay, and attorney fees. • Statute of limitations: Three years after learning "facts material to the right of action," but not later than six years from date of violation. *Caution:* Claims should be filed within three years of the adverse action.

Section 924 (requiring SEC to establish a whistleblower protection office)	Section 924 (SEC must establish a whistleblower protection office and issue regulations on whistleblower rewards program).
Section 1057 (creating whistleblower protections under the Consumer Financial Protection Act of 2010)	Section 1057 (whistleblower protections for disclosures to newly created Bureau of Consumer Financial Protection): · Antiretaliation protections for employees who perform "tasks related to the offering or provision of a consumer financial product or service." · Broad definition of protected activity, including protection for employees who provide information to their employers in the "ordinary course" of their job and disclosures to state or federal law enforcement or regulatory agencies. · Complaints must be filed with the secretary of the DOL within 180 days of an adverse action. Procedures utilized are similar to the SOX Act. · Employees may remove claims to federal court, for de novo review and with the right to a jury trial, if DOL does not issue a final order within 210 days or within 90 days "of receipt of a written determination." · Relief includes reinstatement, back pay, compensation for special or compensatory damages, and attorney fees. · Mandatory arbitration prohibited.

*Publicly Traded Corporations and Their Subsidiaries Contractors and Agents Sec. 806, Sarbanes-Oxley Act of 2002, 18 U.S.C. § 1514A Department of Labor Rules at 29 C.F.R. Part 1980.	Protection for Employees who blow the whistle on fraud against shareholders and violations of securities laws. Complaint filed with U.S. Department of Labor within 180 days of adverse action. Reinstatement, back pay, special damages, and attorney fees permitted. *Lawson v. FMR LLC,* 134 S.Ct. 1158 (2014) (broad interpretation of employers covered under SOX). *Sylvester v. Parexel International,* 2007-SOX-39/42 (DOL ARB 2011) (major decision establishing broad definition of protected disclosure and "good faith" requirements; liberal rules for filing initial complaints). *Sylvester*'s holding on the issue of good faith whistleblowing was affirmed in *Wiest v. Lynch,* 710 F.3d 121 (3rd Cir. 2013). Thereafter, every appeals court to review the issue has affirmed *Sylvester. See Beacom v. Oracle,* 2016 U.S. App. LEXIS 10183 (8th Cir. 2016). *Halliburton v. ARB,* 771 F.3d 254 (5th Cir. 2014) (broad interpretation of adverse action) (disclosing identity of whistleblower to coworkers can constitute adverse action). *Johnson v. Siemens,* 2005-SOX-15 (DOL ARB 2011) (broad definition of employers covered under SOX, including subsidiaries); *Spinner v. Landau and Associates,* 2010-SOX-29 (DOL ARB 2012) (employee of private accounting firm protected as a contractor for publicly held company). *Stone v. Instrumentation Laboratory,* 591 F.3d 239 (4th Cir. 2009) (claims can be removed to federal court after pending in Labor Department for 180 days). *Van Asdale v. International Game Tech.,* 577 F.3d 989 (9th Cir. 2009) (scope of protected activity). *Collins v. Beazer Homes,* 334 F.Supp.2d 1365 (N.D. Georgia 2004) (burden of proof; inclusion of state claim; protected activity). *Jordan v. Sprint,* 2006-SOX-41 (DOL ARB, September 30, 2009) (attorneys protected under statute). *Welch v. Chao,* 536 F.3d 269 (4th Cir. 2008) (narrow definition of protected activity); *Harp v. Charter,* 558 F.3d 722 (7th Cir. 2009) (dissenting opinion discussing "dilemma" facing employees due to narrow construction of Sarbanes-Oxley Act). *Smith v. Corning,* 496 S.Supp.2d 244 (W.D. N.Y 2007) (broader definition of protected activity).

	O'Mahony v. Accenture LTD, 537 F.Supp.2d 506 (S.D.N.Y. 2008) (broad definition of protected activity) (explains when SOX can be applied to international corporations).
	Solis v. Tennessee Commerce Bancorp 713 F.Supp.2d 701 (M.D. Tenn. 2010) (employee right to preliminary reinstatement after OSHA findings).
	Deltek, Inc. v. Department of Labor, 2016 U.S. App. LEXIS 9274 (4th Cir. 2016) (standard for employee conducting one-party taping and removing company documents).
	Palmer v. Canadian National Railway, 2014-FRS-154 (ARB, Sept. 30, 2016) (en banc) (demonstrating a "contributing factor").
	Sections 922(b) and (c) and section 929(A) of the Dodd-Frank Wall Street Reform and Consumer Protection Act: SOX statute of limitations increased from 90 to 180 days; right to jury trial guaranteed; mandatory arbitration prohibited; subsidiaries of publicly traded corporations covered; definition of employer expanded to include "nationally recognized statistical rating organizations," such as Moody's and Standard and Poor's.
Sarbanes-Oxley Act Audit Committee 15 U.S.C. § 78j-1(m)(4)	Requirement that publicly traded corporations have independent audit committee that can accept employee concerns on a confidential basis. *Menendez v. Halliburton,* 2007-SOX-05 (DOL ARB, Sept. 13 2011), affirmed *Halliburton v. ARB,* 771 F.3d 254 (5th Cir. 2014) (violation of audit committee confidentiality rule is an adverse action).
Sarbanes-Oxley Act Rules of Professional Responsibility for Attorneys 15 U.S.C. § 7245	Requirement that attorneys disclose wrongdoing and limitations on attorney-client privilege. SEC Rules implementing law: 17 C.F.R. 205.1, et seq. *Van Asdale v. International Game Tech.,* 577 F.3d 989 (9th Cir. 2009) (in-house attorney could file whistleblower retaliation suit).
*Banking Industry 12 U.S.C. § 1790b (Credit Unions) 12 U.S.C. § 1831j (FDIC Insured Institutions) 31 U.S.C. § 5328 (Monetary Transactions)	Federal Court remedies for employees in banking industry, including the Federal Reserve, any "insured depository institution," and other private and federal financial institutions. Two-year statute of limitations. *Haley v. Retsinas,* 138 F.3d 1245 (8th Cir. 1998); *Frobose v. American Savings and Loan,* 152 F.3d 602 (7th Cir. 1998); *Rouse v. Farmers State Bank,* 866 F. Supp. 1191 (N.D. Iowa 1994) (interpreting law broadly to protect whistleblowers); *Hill v. Mr. Money Finance,* 2009 U.S. App. LEXIS 2228 (6th Cir.) (interpreting protected activity narrowly).

Protection for Whistleblowers Who Disclose Trade Secrets Defend Trade Secrets Act 18 U.S.C. § 1833(b)	Whistleblowers can disclose trade secrets when they confidentially report suspected violations of law to federal or state law enforcement authorities. Disclosures can also be filed confidentially in court cases concerning whistleblower retaliation. The Defend Trade Secrets Act sets forth specific procedures for disclosing trade secrets and requires employers to notify employees concerning their rights under this law.

D. Criminal Prohibition Against Retaliation

Obstruction of Justice, Retaliation Against Whistleblowers 18 U.S.C. § 1513(e) * 15 U.S.C. § 78u-6 (h)(1)(A)(iii) Dodd-Frank Wall Street Reform and Consumer Protection Act of 2010 (establishing a civil action for wrongful discharge based on violation of 18 U.S.C. § 1513(e))	Federal felony to harm an employee's livelihood in retaliation for providing truthful information about potential crimes to federal law enforcement. The Dodd-Frank Act creates civil remedy for wrongful discharge based on disclosures protected under the criminal obstruction of justice statute.
Racketeer Influenced and Corrupt Organizations Act 18 U.S.C. § 1961, 1962 and 1964	*Beck v. Prupis,* 529 U.S. 494 (2000) (limiting availability of RICO under the pre–Sarbanes-Oxley version of the federal obstruction of justice law). *DeGuelle v. Camilli,* 664 F.3d 192 (7th Cir. 2011) (permitting whistleblower to file a Civil RICO case based on violations of § 1514(e); the post-SOX federal obstruction of justice statute).

E. Environmental Protection, Ocean Pollution, and Wildlife Trafficking

*Environmental Whistleblower Protections 42 U.S.C. § 7622 (Clean Air Act) 42 U.S.C. § 300j-9(i) (Safe Drinking Water) 42 U.S.C. § 6971 (Solid Waste Disposal) 42 U.S.C. § 9610 (Superfund) 15 U.S.C. § 2622 (Toxic Substances) 33 U.S.C. § 1367 (Water Pollution)	Broad coverage for environmental whistleblowers, but law has short statute of limitations (thirty days) and must be filed with the Department of Labor. Remedies include reinstatement, back pay, compensatory damages, and attorney fees. Safe Drinking Water and Toxic Substances also permit exemplary damages. *DeKalb County v. U.S. DOL*, 812 F.3d 1015 (3rd Cir. 2016) (burdens of proof and standard of review in environmental cases) (employee must show whistleblowing was a "motivating factor" in discharge, but risk that legal and illegal reasons for discharge cannot be separated falls on employer). *Passaic Valley Sewerage v. DOL*, 992 F.2d 474 (3rd Cir. 1993) (good faith allegations protected, even if "ill-informed"). *Willy v. ARB*, 423 F.3d 483 (5th Cir. 2005) (internal complaints within the company protected) (company attorney could pursue whistleblower claim). *Wedderspoon v. Milligan*, 81-WPC-1 (DOL ALJ 1980), adopted by secretary of the DOL (July 28, 1980) (disclosures to news media and environmental organization protected). *Williams v. Dallas Independent School District*, 2008-TSC-1 (DOL ARB) (December 28, 2012) (reasonable belief test for protected activity). 29 C.F.R. Parts 18 and 24 (DOL rules implementing the environmental whistleblower protection provisions).
*Pipeline Safety Improvement Act 49 U.S.C. § 60129	Similar protections and rules as contained under the Atomic Energy Act and Sarbanes-Oxley Act. Department of Labor rules implementing the act are codified at 29 C.F.R. Parts 18 and 1981. *Donahue v. Exelon*, 2008-PSI-1 (DOL ALJ 2008) (setting forth elements of pipeline safety claim). There is a 90-day statute of limitations for filing a complaint with the DOL.
Surface Mining Act 30 U.S.C. § 1293	Legal protections similar to other environmental statutes, but administered by the Department of Interior, not the Department of Labor. Department of Interior rules codified at 30 C.F.R. § 865.
Reward Laws for Ocean Pollution and Wildlife Trafficking Act to Prevent Pollution from Ships (APPS) 33 U.S.C. § 1908(a)	Court can award whistleblowers up to 50% of monies obtained from criminal and civil penalties collected for violations of the APPS. *U.S. v. Efploia Shipping Co. S.A.*, Case 1:11-cr-00652-MJG, Bench Decision Re: Whistleblower Award (D. Md.) (April 25, 2016). This case discusses criteria for granting rewards under the APPS.

Endangered Species Act (ESA)	Secretaries of Commerce, Interior, and Treasury (and for plants, Agriculture) can pay rewards based on monies obtained from fines and penalties in ESA cases.
16 U.S.C. § 1540(d)	
Fish and Wildlife Improvement Act	The U.S. Fish and Wildlife Service and the National Marine Fisheries Service can pay rewards under all wildlife protection laws (plants, fish, and animals) administered by these two agencies to whistleblowers who report violations, even if no final enforcement action is undertaken.
16 U.S.C. § 742l(k)(2)	
Lacey Act	Secretaries of Commerce, Interior, and Treasury (and for plants, Agriculture) can pay rewards based on monies obtained from fines and penalties in Lacey Act cases.
16 U.S.C. § 3375(d	
	The article "Monetary Rewards for Wildlife Whistleblowers: A Game Changer in Wildlife Trafficking Detection and Deterrence," 46 *Environmental Law Reporter* 10054 (January 2016), explains these wildlife trafficking reward laws, and also identifies the more than 40 other fish and wildlife protection laws covered under the reward laws.

F. Federal Contractor Fraud

*American Recovery and Reinvestment Act of 2007 Public Law No. 111-5 (February 7, 2009), 48 C.F.R. 3.907-1. Also see 41 U.S.C. § 4712	Strong whistleblower protections concerning allegations of misconduct or misspending in the use of stimulus spending monies. A cause of action under the False Claims Act may also be available in cases of stimulus spending fraud. In 2016 this law was made applicable to most government contractors. 41 U.S.C. § 4712.
*Department of Defense Contractor Fraud Antiretaliation	Misuse of Department of Defense (DOD) monies by a contractor. Complaints filed with the DOD (or NASA) inspector general. After exhausting administrative remedy, employee can file a claim in federal court and request a trial by jury. Compensatory damages available. This statute is substantially identical to the Enhancement of Whistleblower Protection for Contractor and Grantee Employees Act, codified at 41 U.S.C. § 4712.
10 U.S.C. § 2409	
	Employees who state a claim under this law may also have a claim under the False Claims Act, both for wrongful discharge and for a monetary reward pursuant to 31 U.S.C. § 3729-32.
	On January 3, 2013, this law was amended, but the amendments were made applicable only to contracts awarded or "task orders" entered into after July 2013 (i.e., 180 days after January 3). Public Law 112-239 § 827.

Federal Acquisition Regulations; Contractor Business Ethics Compliance and Contractor Whistleblower Protection Rules 48 C.F.R. Ch. 1 48 C.F.R. Subpart 3.900 73 *Federal Register* 67064	Regulations mandating that federal contractors not retaliate against whistleblowers and establish ethics/compliance programs. Under this regulation employees suffering retaliation by a federal contractor may file a complaint with the Inspector General from the agency that awarded the grant. The definition of a protected activity is narrow (disclosures to Congress, an "authorized official of an agency" or the Department of Justice), and must relate to a "substantial violation of law" related to the contract at issue. Employees who raise concerns over federal spending under the American Recovery and Reinvestment Act of 2009 have additional rights codified at 48 C.F.R. § 3.907. Federal contractors are prohibited from using confidentiality agreements to restrict an employee's right to report "waste, fraud, or abuse" to an appropriate law enforcement officer. See 48 C.F.R. § 3.909. This rule is set forth in Public Law 113-235 § 743.
*False Claims Act, Whistleblower Antiretaliation 31 U.S.C. § 3730(h)	Strong protections for employees who disclose violations of the False Claims Act (fraud in federal contracts). Claims filed in federal court, employees entitled to reinstatement, double back pay, special damages, and attorney fees. Cases under this subsection are often filed as part of a *qui tam* lawsuit under the FCA in order to obtain a financial reward pursuant to 31 U.S.C. §§ 3729-32. *U.S. ex rel. Yesudian v. Howard University,* 153 F.3d 731 (D.C. Cir. 1998) (broad definition of protected activity). *U.S. ex rel. Williams v. Martin-Baker Aircraft Co.,* 389 F.3d 1251 (D.C. Cir. 2004) (setting forth prima facie case and pleading requirements). *Neal v. Honeywell,* 191 F.3d 827 (7th Cir. 1999) (emotional distress damages included in special damage award) (affirming double back pay award and attorney fees). In 2009-10, the FCA antiretaliation provisions were strengthened as follows: Statute of limitations set at three years; definition of employer expanded to include traditional employers and "associated others"; definition of protected activity clarified to include filing FCA claims and any other "efforts to stop violations of FCA."

Major Frauds Act, Whistleblower Antiretaliation Provision 18 U.S.C. § 1031(h)	Similar remedy as contained under the False Claims Act, 30 U.S.C. § 3730(h). *Moore v. California Institute of Technology*, 275 F.3d 838 (9th Cir. 2002) (setting forth elements of Major Frauds Act claim). Because statute does not contain a filing deadline, the statute of limitations would be controlled by "most closely analogous state statute of limitations." See, *Graham County v. U.S. ex rel. Wilson*, 545 U.S. 409 (2005).
Public Contracts–Procurement Provisions, Contractor Employees: Protection from Reprisal for Disclosure of Certain Information 41 U.S.C. § 265	Note: Employees who state a claim under this law may also have a claim under the False Claims Act, 31 U.S.C. § 3729-32.

Enhancement of Whistleblower Protection for Contractor and Grantee Employees 41 U.S.C. § 4712	On January 3, 2013, a four-year "pilot program" was signed into law that provides all employees of government contractors, subcontractors, personal services contractors, subgrantees, or grantees with a private right of action for making protected disclosures to Congress, Inspectors General, law enforcement agencies, courts, federal contract administrators, or management officials, among others. On December 14, 2016 the "pilot program" was made permanent. See Public Law 114-261, § 1(a)(2), (3)(A). Protected disclosures include information evidencing the "gross mismanagement of a Federal contract or grant, a gross waste of Federal funds, an abuse of authority relating to a Federal contract or grant, a substantial and specific danger to the public health or safety, or a violation of law, rule, or regulation related to a Federal contract or grant." Initial complaints must be filed with the Office of Inspector General of the agency involved with the contract or grant within three years of any adverse action. The Inspector General is required to keep the identity of the whistleblower confidential, except as necessary to conduct the investigation into the reprisal. The burdens of proof under this law are those set forth in 5 U.S.C. § 1221(e), which are favorable to the employee. Whistleblowers only need to demonstrate that retaliation was a "contributing factor" to an adverse action, and thereafter the burden of proof shifts to the employer to justify the adverse action by "clear and convincing evidence." This is a more pro-employee burden of proof than exists under the False Claims Act. Mandatory arbitration agreements should not be enforceable. The statute provides that "the rights and remedies" "may not be waived by any agreement, policy, form, or condition of employment." Contractors who work on projects related to the U.S. intelligence community are exempt from this law. If the executive agency involved with the grant has not issued appropriate corrective action within 210 days of the filing of the complaint, the employee may file a complaint in federal court and seek a trial by jury. A federal court action must be filed no later than two years after the expiration of the 210-day time period.

	Remedies under this provision include reinstatement, back pay, compensatory damages, and attorney fees and costs.
	This law only applies to contracts, grants, or task orders entered into 180 days from January 3 (or if an existing contract or grant is modified to require compliance with this provision).
	Employees covered under this provision may also be protected under the False Claims Act.

G. Federal *Whistleblower Reward and* qui tam *Statutes*

*False Claims Act, Whistleblower Rewards Provision (*qui tam*) (contractor fraud) 31 U.S.C. §§ 3729–3732	Whistleblowers (known as "relators") can obtain major rewards for disclosing fraud in government contracting, sales, or loans. Claims filed under seal in federal court and served on U.S. Government. Relators permitted to recover 15–30% of the monies recovered by the federal government from contractors who defrauded the United States. Law originally enacted in 1863 and was subject to major amendments in 1943, 1986, 2009, and 2010. *Vermont Agency of Natural Resources v. U.S. ex rel. Stevens,* 529 U.S. 765 (2000) (holding that permitting whistleblowers to file claims on behalf of the United States to recover monies obtained fraudulently by contractors is constitutional). *Rockwell International v. U.S.,* 549 U.S. 457 (2007) (standing requirements for whistleblower to qualify for reward) (FCA amendments enacted in 2010 modified this ruling). *Kellogg Brown & Root v. U.S. ex rel. Carter,* 135 S.Ct. 1970 (2015) (statute of limitations on filing fraud cases defined; "first to file" rule liberally construed to prevent dismissals of whistleblower claims). *Universal Health Servs. v. U.S. ex rel. Escobar,* 136 S.Ct.1980 (2016) (permitting "implied certification" claims, i.e., claims based on violations not specifically set forth in contract). *State Farm Ins. v. U.S. ex rel. Rigsby,* 136 S.Ct. 2386 (2016) (no automatic dismissal of seal violated; sanction determined by Court on case-by-case basis) *U.S. ex rel. Davis v. District of Columbia,* 679 F.3d 832 (D.C. Cir. 2012) (rejecting narrow interpretation of "original source"). Filing a *qui tam* lawsuit is considered a protected activity.

*Commodity Exchange Act, Section 748 of the Dodd-Frank Wall Street Reform and Consumer Protection Act of 2010 7 U.S.C. § 26	*Qui tam* rewards for whistleblowers who provide "original information" to the Commodity Futures Exchange Commission "relating to a violation" of the Commodity Exchange Act, 7 U.S.C. § 1 et seq. Claims must be filed in conformance to the rules published by the CFTC. 17 C.F.R. Part 165.
	Rewards structure is modeled on *qui tam* provisions of the False Claims Act and the Securities Exchange Act and permits most whistleblowers to obtain a reward of 10–30% of monies collected by commission for violations of commodities law. Rewards are only paid if the total fines, penalties and other recoveries exceed $1 million.
	Whistleblowers can anonymously file reward requests with the commission. Filing claims considered a protected activity.
*Securities Exchange Act, Section 922 of the Dodd-Frank Wall Street Reform and Consumer Protection Act of 2010 15 U.S.C. § 78u-6	*Qui tam* rewards for whistleblowers who provide "original information" to the Securities and Exchange Commission "relating to a violation" of the SEA, 15 U.S.C. 78a et seq. Claims must be filed in accordance with the rules published by the SEC. 17 C.F.R. Parts 240 and 249.
	Law creates an SEC whistleblower office. Rewards structure is modeled on False Claims Act and the Commodity Exchange Act and permits most whistleblowers to obtain a reward of 10–30% of monies collected by SEC for violations of securities law. Rewards are only paid if the total fines, penalties, and other recoveries exceed $1 million.
	Whistleblowers can anonymously file reward requests with the commission. Filing claims considered a protected activity.
*IRS Payment for Detection of Fraud and Underpayment of Taxes 26 U.S.C.A. § 7623	Law creates an IRS whistleblower rewards program that entitles whistleblowers who disclose cases of major tax fraud or underpayment of taxes to apply for a reward from the Whistleblower Office of the IRS. Rewards structure is modeled on the False Claims Act and permits most whistleblowers to obtain a reward of 15–30% of monies collected by IRS from the delinquent or fraudulent taxpayer.
Major Frauds Act 18 U.S.C. § 1031(h)	Attorney general, in "his or her sole discretion" can authorize a reward not to "exceed $250,000" to employees who disclose information on federal contracting fraud. False Claims Act is stronger law.

H. Federal Court Witness Protection

*Civil Rights Act of 1871 42 U.S.C. § 1985(2)	Conspiracy to interfere with the administration of justice in U.S. courts by retaliating against witnesses in federal court proceedings. *Haddle v. Garrison,* 525 U.S. 121 (1998) ("at-will" employees fired for obeying a grand jury subpoena stated claim). *Kinney v. Weaver,* 367 F.3d 337 (5th Cir. 2004); 301 F.3d 253 (5th Cir. 2002) (applying § 1985 to government employees and expert witnesses in federal court proceedings). *Irizarry v. Quiros,* 722 F.2d 869 (1st Cir. 1983) (denial of reemployment actionable under § 1985, clause 2) (employee permitted to obtain full tort-style damages, including punitive damages, and statutory attorney fees under § 1988). *McAndrew v. Lockheed Martin,* 206 F.3d 1031 (11th Cir. 2000) and *Bowie v. Maddox,* 642 F.3d 1122 (D.C. Cir. 2011) (scope of "conspiracies" covered under § 1985 clause 2 remains open to question). *Lenard v. Argento,* 699 F.2d 874, 882-83 (7th Cir. 1983); *Powell v. Pittsfield,* 221 F. Supp. 2d 119 (D. Mass. 2002) (proof necessary to prove civil conspiracy and violations of §§ 1983 and 1985). *Odum v. Rayonier, Inc.,* 2008 U.S. App. LEXIS 16884 (11th Cir.) and 2007 U.S. Dist. LEXIS 48551 (S.D. Georgia) (affirming $2.3 million dollar jury verdict for violation of §1985 clause 2).

I. Federal Employee Whistleblower Protections

Restrictions on Federal Non-disclosure Agreements P.L. 112-199 § 115, 5 U.S.C. § 2302 note and 5 U.S.C. §§ 2302(a)(2)(A)(xi) and 2302(b)(12)	Amendment to Appropriations Act that prevents the Executive Branch from utilizing overly broad nondisclosure agreements that prevent federal employees from reporting violations of law. As part of the Whistleblower Protection Enhancement Act of 2012, this antigag provision was incorporated into the federal civil service laws. Nondisclosure agreements used by the U.S. government must inform employees and government contractors of their right to provide information about serious misconduct to Congress, Inspectors General, and other appropriate law enforcement agencies.
Civil Service Reform Act, Whistleblower Protection Act 5 U.S.C. § 2302	Major law protecting most federal employee whistleblowers. Employees can file retaliation complaints with Office of Special Counsel and appeals with the Merit Systems Protection Board.
5 U.S.C. § 1211-1215, 1218-1219, 1221-1222	*Marano v. DOJ,* 2 F.3d 1137, 1140 (Fed. Cir. 1993) and *Whitmore v. Department of Labor,* 680 F.3d 1353 (Fed. Cir. 2012) (standard of proof). *Chambers v. Department of Interior,* 602 F.3d 1370 (Fed. Cir. 2010) (application of "Carr" factors to mitigate level of punishment in whistleblower cases). *Elgin v. Department of Treasury,* 132 S.Ct. 2126 (2012) (Civil Service Reform Act the exclusive remedy for most federal employees, even if constitutional issues raised). *Department of Homeland Security v. MacLean,* 135 S.Ct. 913 (2015) (legal exclusions for a protected disclosure "prohibited by law" must be explicit). *Navy v. Egan,* 484 U.S. 518 (1988) (challenge to security clearance decision cannot be raised under CSRA). The Whistleblower Protection Enhancement Act of 2012 expanded the definition of protected activities, authorized the payment of compensatory damages, and prohibited scientific censorship, among other major reforms. P.L. 112-199; U.S. Senate Report of the Committee on Homeland Security and Government Affairs, *Whistleblower Protection Enhancement Act of 2012,* S. Rep. 112-155.

Principles of Ethical Conduct for Government Officers and Employees	*Chambers v. Department of Interior,* 2011-MSPB-7 (January 11, 2011) (key decision of MSPB applying retaliation analysis and ordering reinstatement of whistleblower).
Executive Order 12731, §101(k)	Requires federal employees to report waste, fraud, abuse and corruption to appropriate authorities.
5 C.F.R. § 2635.101	
57 *Federal Register* 35006	
Inspector General Act	Inspectors General can receive allegations of misconduct and investigate retaliation.
5 U.S.C. Appendix, §§ 3 and 7	On November 27, 2012, Congress established a five-year experimental program requiring all Inspectors General to establish a Whistleblower Protection Ombudsman office. P.L. 112-199 § 117.
Lloyd-LaFollette Act, Employees' Right to Petition Congress	Federal employees permitted to contact Members of Congress.
5 U.S.C. § 7211	
No Fear Act	Requires federal agencies to notify and train federal employees concerning their rights under whistleblower protection and antidiscrimination laws.
5 U.S.C. § 2301 (Note)	
P.L 107-174	
Congressional Accountability Act	Protections for Congressional offices under traditional employment discrimination laws, such as Title VII and OSHA. Law establishes special office and procedures for employees. Whistleblower protected only if covered under specific laws referenced in Act.
2 U.S.C. § 1301, et seq.	

J. Food Safety Whistleblower Protections

Food Safety Modernization Act of 2010 21 U.S.C. § 399d	Covers all employers "engaged in the manufacture, processing, packing, transportation, distribution, reception, holding or importation of food." § 1012(a). This is a DOL case with similar procedures and law as found under the Energy Reorganization and Sarbanes-Oxley Acts.
	Claims must be filed with the U.S. Department of Labor within 180 days of a discriminatory action. § 1012(b)(1).
	After exhausting administrative remedies, employees have a right to remove their cases to federal court and have a jury determine liability and damages. § 1012(b)(4).
	Employees who prevail are entitled to reinstatement, back pay, attorney fees and costs and compensatory damages. §§ 1012(b)(3) and (b)(4)(B).

K. Health Care Whistleblower Protections

Patient Protection and Affordable Care Act § 1558 of Public Law No. 111-148 29, U.S.C. 218C	Employees who disclose violations of Title I of the Patient Protection and Affordable Care Act or section 2706 of the Public Health Service Act obtain protections modeled on protections contained in the Consumer Product Safety Act of 2008, 15 U.S.C. § 2087. These provisions relate to the "affordability and accountability" sections of the act. This is a DOL case with similar procedures and law as found under the Energy Reorganization and Sarbanes-Oxley Acts.
	Patient Protection Act also enhanced False Claims Act, and ensured that its whistleblower rewards provisions would apply to fraud under applicable provisions of the new health care law. Public Law No. 111-48 §§ 1558, 1754, 6703(b)(3), and 6105.
	On Feb. 27, 2013, OSHA published Interim rules and regulations administering this act that will be codified at 29 C.F.R. Part 1984.

L. IRS Tax Whistleblower Reward (Qui tam)

*IRS Payment for Detection of Fraud 26 U.S.C.A. § 7623	Law creates an IRS whistleblower rewards program that entitles whistleblowers who disclose cases of major tax fraud or underpayment of taxes to apply for a reward from the Whistleblower Office of the IRS. Rewards structure is modeled on the False Claims Act and permits most whistleblowers to obtain a reward of 15–30% of monies collected by IRS from the delinquent or fraudulent taxpayer. This law does not have an antiretaliation provision. Employees who suffer retaliation for reporting tax fraud must seek protection under other federal corporate whistleblower laws or state law.

M. Military Whistleblower Protection, Department of Defense Components (Including Military Departments, Combatant Commands, Secretary of Defense, and All Other Department of Defense Agencies)

Coast Guard Whistleblower Protection 33 C.F.R. Part 53 56 *Federal Register* 13404 (April 2, 1991)	This regulation implements the statutory protections afforded to members of the armed services, codified in 10 U.S.C. § 1034 for members of the Coast Guard. This is a DOL case with similar procedures and law as found under the Energy Reorganization and Sarbanes-Oxley Acts.
Department of Defense Employees of Non-appropriated Fund Instrumentalities 10 U.S.C. § 1587	Department of Defense Directive No. 1401.03 (April 23, 2008).
Department of Defense Office of Inspector General Rules and Procedures Governing Department of Defense Component and Contractor Complaints	Department of Defense Directive No. 7050.6 (July 23, 2007). Defense Hotline Program, Department of Defense Directive No. 7050.01 (December 17, 2007).
Armed Forces/Prohibition Against Retaliation (Reemployment Rights) 38 U.S.C. § 4311 38 U.S.C. § 4322–24 (procedures)	Retaliation for invoking reemployment rights. *Staub v. Proctor Hospital,* 131 S.Ct. 1186 (2011) (retaliation law created tort-like remedy and permitted court to hold hospital liable based on animus of supervisor who did not make the ultimate decision to fire employee).

Armed Forces/Prohibition Against Retaliation (Active Duty Military)	Permits members of the armed services to contact members of Congress, the Office of Inspector General, DoD auditors, and other military officials designated to receive complaints.
10 U.S.C. § 1034	Retaliation complaints are filed with DoD or military agency inspectors general. Appeals can be adjudicated through the Board for Correction of Military Records pursuant to 10 U.S.C. § 1552. Members of armed services may not file their claim directly in federal court. *Acquisto v. U.S.*, 70 F.3d 1010 (8th Cir. 1995).

N. National Security Whistleblower Protection

CIA Employee Disclosures to Inspector General 50 U.S.C. 403q	CIA Inspector General Act authorized to accept complaints and investigate retaliation against employees of the agency.
Homeland Security Act of 2002 6 U.S.C. § 463	Provides protection for Homeland Security employees pursuant to the Civil Service Reform Act, 5 U.S.C. § 2302(b)(1) and§ 2303 (b)(8) and (b)(9).
Department of Defense Intelligence Agencies (National Security Agency, Defense Intelligence Agency and other Department of Defense Intelligence-Related Components) 96 Stat. 751 § 8	DOD inspector general authorized to accept complaints from DOD intelligence-related components, including those excluded from coverage under the Civil Service Reform Act.
Title VII Whistleblower Protection for Intelligence Community; Employees Reporting Urgent Concerns to Congress 4 U.S.C.A. App. Sec. 3 § 8H note: Public Law 105-277, Title VII, § 701(b)	Procedures for national security/intelligence agency employees to obtain protection for contacting Congress concerning classified matters.

Federal Bureau of Investigation Whistleblower Protection Act 5 U.S.C.A. § 2303 28 C.F.R. Part 27 (implementing regulations)	Retaliation claims for FBI employees filed with Department of Justice Office of Inspector General. On December 16, 2016 the FBI whistleblower law was amended to cover employees who make disclosures to their supervisors, the FBI and DOJ Offices of Professional Responsibility, Members of Congress, the Office of Special Counsel, and the "head of the employment agency." Under the controlling regulations, initial complaints are filed with the Department of Justice IG or OPR. Thereafter, an employee may request a hearing before the DOJ Office of Attorney Recruitment and Management, and an appeal may be filed to the Deputy Attorney General. Currently the Justice Department has taken the position that there is no judicial review from a final order issued by the Deputy Attorney General.
Inspector General of the Intelligence Community Whistleblower Protection Act Public Law § 405, 111-259, 50 U.S.C. § 403-3h.	Prohibits reprisals against intelligence community employees who disclose waste, fraud, or abuse to the Intelligence Community Inspector General. The Act also provides a procedure for intelligence community employees to report serious abuses to Congress.
Presidential Policy Directive/ PPD-19 (Signed by President Obama on October 10, 2012)	The Presidential Directive requires that intelligence agencies, including the Central Intelligence Agency, the National Security Agency and the Defense Intelligence Agency, establish procedures to protect employees who make disclosures covered under the directive. The rights under the directive cannot be enforced in court, and the ultimate decision-making authority under the directive is vested with the head of the agency for which the employee works.

O. Nuclear Safety Whistleblower Protection

*Atomic Energy Act/Energy Reorganization Act 42 U.S.C. § 5851	Broad protection for employees who disclose safety and regulatory violations at civilian nuclear facilities and nuclear weapons facilities. Complaints must be filed with Department of Labor within 180 days. Claims can be removed to federal court only after employee exhausts administrative remedies. Employees entitled to reinstatement, back pay, compensatory damages, and attorney fees. Private-sector employees covered, along with employees of the Nuclear Regulatory Commission and Department of Energy. Case law under the Sarbanes-Oxley Act and other DOL administered cases is applicable to this law. *Mackowiak v. University Nuclear,* 735 F.2d 1159 (9th Cir. 1984); *Kansas Gas and Electric v. Brock,* 780 F.2d 1505 (10th Cir. 1985); *Bechtel Constr. v. DOL,* 50 F.3d 926 (11th Cir. 1995) (broad definition of protected activity). *Macktal v. SOL,* 923 F.2d 1150 (5th Cir. 1991); *Connecticut Light & Power v. SOL,* 85 F.3d 89, 95 (2nd Cir. 1996) (secretary of the DOL must approve settlement agreements) (settlement agreements that restrict employee's right to blow the whistle are void and presenting such an agreement to an employee may constitute a separate actionable adverse action). *Hobby v. Georgia Power,* 90-ERA-30 (DOL judge decision dated September 17, 1998, and Administrative Review Board decision dated Feb. 9, 2001) (setting forth damages available under nuclear whistleblower law). 29 C.F.R. Parts 18 and 24 (Department of Labor rules implementing nuclear safety protections). The Nuclear Regulatory Commission also has rules prohibiting retaliation against employees who raise safety concerns. 10 C.F.R. § 50.7.
Department of Energy, Defense Activities, Whistleblower Protection Program 50 U.S.C. § 2702	This law is weak and the Atomic Energy Act, 42 U.S.C. § 5851 should be used, if possible.

P. Occupational Health and Safety

Asbestos School Hazard Abatement, Employee Protection Provision, 20 U.S.C. § 4018	No cases have been filed under this law.
Asbestos School Hazard Detection and Control, Employee Protection Provision, 15 U.S.C. § 2651	Claims filed with Department of Labor within ninety days of adverse action. The DOL conducts review and litigation under the Occupational Safety and Health Administration law, 29 U.S.C. § 660(c).
*Mine Health and Safety Act, Nonretaliation Act

30 U.S.C. § 815(c) | Retaliation complaints must be filed with the U.S. Department of Labor's Mine Safety and Health Administration within sixty days of an adverse action. Employees are entitled to preliminary reinstatement if an initial review determines that the complaint was not "frivolously brought." Damages include reinstatement, back pay, and attorney fees.

Secretary of Labor v. Mullins, 888 F.2d 1448 (D.C. Cir. 1989); *Hays v. Leeco, Inc.,* 965 F.2d 1081 (D.C. Cir. 1992); *National Cement v. FMSHC,* 27 F.3d 526 (11th Cir. 1994) (qualified right to refuse to perform hazardous work).

Phillips v. Interior Bd. Mine Op., 500 F.2d 772 (D.C. Cir. 1974) (broad definition of protected activity). |
| Occupational Safety and Health Act (OSHA), Nonretaliation Provision

29 U.S.C. § 660(c) | Claims must be filed with the Department of Labor within thirty days of an adverse action. There is no private right of action under the federal law. It is up to the DOL to file a suit against the employer on the employee's behalf. If the DOL does not litigate the case on behalf of the employee, the case is closed. Because of the weaknesses in this federal law, many employees have utilized state laws that prohibit retaliation against employees who blow the whistle on unsafe or unhealthy working conditions.

Scope of protected activity under OSHA is broad, and includes complaints filed with the government, a union, management, and newspapers. *Donovan v. Diplomat Envelope Corp.,* 587 F. Supp. 1417, 1424–25 (E.D.N.Y. 1984); *Marshall v. Springville Poultry,* 445 F. Supp. 2 (M.D. Pa 1977); *Donovan v. R.D. Andersen,* 552 F. Supp. 249 (D. Kan. 1982).

Reich v. Cambridgeport Air, 26 F.3d 1187 (1st Cir. 1994) (prevailing employees permitted to full scope of tort-style damages, including reinstatement, back pay, and compensatory and punitive damages).

Whirlpool Corp. v. Marshall, 445 U.S. 1 (1980) (refusal to perform hazardous work in limited situations is protected activity).

Reich v. Hoy Shoe Co., 32 F.3d 361 (8th Cir. 1994) (setting forth requirements to prove causal connection between protected disclosure and adverse action). |

Q. Privacy Act

*Privacy Act 5 U.S.C. § 552a	Prevents federal government from "leaking" confidential information; permits persons to obtain copies of their government records and request a correction of record to ensure they are accurate. Damages available from the U.S. government for willful violations of the act. However, these damages are limited to actual economic harm caused by the leaks. Damages for emotional distress are not available under current Supreme Court case law. *FAA v. Cooper,* 132 S.Ct. 1441 (2012). *Alexander v. FBI,* 971 F. Supp. 603 (D.D.C. 1997) (Privacy Act permits claims for damages resulting from "leaks" of confidential information). *Tripp v. Department of Defense,* 193 F.Supp.2d 229 and 219 F.Supp. 2d 85 (D.D.C. 2002) (cause of action for leaking documents concerning whistleblower).

R. Transportation Whistleblower Protection

*Airline Safety 49 U.S.C § 42121	Department of Labor rules implementing the act are codified at 29 C.F.R. Parts 18 and 1979. There is a 90-day statute of limitations under this law. This is a DOL case with similar procedures and law as found under the Energy Reorganization and Sarbanes-Oxley Acts. *Gary v. The Air Group*, 397 F.3d 183 (3rd Cir. 2005) (New Jersey whistleblower law not preempted by federal airline whistleblower law). *Contra., Botz v. Omni Air*, 286 F.3d 488 (8th Cir. 2002) (finding preemption of state law).
Automobile Safety 49 U.S.C. § 30171 (antiretaliation) 49 U.S.C. § § 30172 (rewards)	Employees working for automobile manufacturers, part suppliers, and dealerships protected if they raise safety concerns with their employers or the Department of Transportation. Complaints must be filed with the DOL within 180 days of an adverse action. Procedures are consistent with those contained in the Food and Safety Act and the Consumer Products Safety Act. This is a DOL case with similar procedures and law as found under the Energy Reorganization and Sarbanes-Oxley Acts. Damages available under the law include reinstatement, back pay, compensatory damages, and attorney fees. The Motor Vehicle Safety Whistleblower Act authorizes the Secretary of Transportation to pay rewards to employees who disclose safety violations in accordance with the procedures set forth in the Act and regulations issued by the Department of Transportation.

*Public Transportation (National Transit System Security Act) 6 U.S.C. § 1142	Protections for public transportation workers are substantially identical to those contained in the Surface Transportation Act, 49 U.S.C. § 31105. *Nichik v. New York City Transit Authority*, No. 1:10-cv-05260 (E.D.N.Y. Jan. 11, 2013) (setting forth standards of proof under the act).
*Truck Safety 49 U.S.C. § 31101 49 U.S.C. § 31105	Protection for employees who file complaints concerning commercial motor vehicle safety or who refuse to operate the vehicle due to safety or security concerns. Complaints must be filed with U.S. Department of Labor within 180 days of adverse action. The DOL rules implementing the law are located at 29 C.F.R. § 1988. The procedures are similar to those under the Energy Reorganization, Surface Transportation, and Sarbanes-Oxley Acts. Reinstatement, back pay, compensatory damages, and attorney fees permitted. Punitive damages capped at $250,000 also permitted. If DOL does not issue final decision in 210 days after claim is filed, the employee can file a claim in federal court and request a trial by jury. *Brock v. Roadway Express*, 481 U.S. 252 (1987) (upheld the right of Congress to require the reinstatement of whistleblowers as a result of an Occupational Safety and Health Administration investigation, but prior to a hearing or trial) (precedent used to establish the right of preliminary reinstatement in other federal whistleblower laws, including the Sarbanes-Oxley Act and the Atomic Energy Act). *Clean Harbors v. Herman*, 146 F.3d 12 (1st Cir. 1998) (broad definition of protected activity). *Manske v. UPS*, 870 F.Supp.2d 185 (D. Maine 2012) (performing ordinary and routine job duties can be protected). DOL rules implementing the act are codified at 29 C.F.R. Parts 18 and 1978.

*Railroad Safety Act 49 U.S.C. § 20109	Protections for railroad workers are substantially identical to those contained in the Surface Transportation Act, 49 U.S.C. § 31105. See *Anderson v. Amtrak,* 2009-FRS-3 (DOL ALJ 2010). *BNSF Ry. Co. v. U.S. DOL,* 816 F.3d 628 (10 Cir. 2016) (standards applied in railroad safety case) (standards applied in awarding punitive damages). *Worcester v. Springfield Terminal,* 2016 U.S. App. LEXIS 11941 (1st Cir. 2016) (upholding $250,000 punitive damage award). *Rudolph v. National Railroad,* 2009-FRS-15, Final Decision and Order of DOL ARB (April 5, 2016) (proof of causation).
Safe Containers for International Cargo Act, Employee Protection Provision 46 U.S.C. § 80507	Complaints filed with Department of Labor within sixty days of adverse action. DOL must file claim in court on behalf of employee. There are no reported cases of the DOL ever seeking to protect an employee under this law. Employees should consider filing claims under other federal or state whistleblower laws.
Seamen Whistleblower Protection 46 U.S.C. § 2114	Department of Labor and Federal Court jurisdiction over complaints filed by seamen alleging retaliation for raising concerns with the Coast Guard. Back pay, attorney fees, and compensatory and punitive damages available. The seamen's whistleblower law was amended in 2010 as part of the Coast Guard Authorization Act, § 611 of Public Law No. 111-281. The 2010 amendment requires initial complaints to be filed with the Department of Labor and bases the new procedures for the law on those applicable to Surface Transportation, 49 U.S.C. § 31105(b)-(d). On Feb. 6, 2013, the Department of Labor published rules for administering this. See Interior Final Rule, Seamen's Protection Act, 78 Fed. Reg. 8390 (Feb. 6, 2013). *Gaffney v. Riverboat Services,* 451 F.3d 424 (7th Cir. 2006) (broad definition of protected disclosure and "good faith" in order to "encourage employees to aid in the enforcement of maritime laws") (upholding award of compensatory damages). *Gwin v. Am. River Transp.,* 482 F.3d 969 (7th Cir. 2007) (upholding jury verdict in favor of employee). *Robinson v. Alter Barge Line,* 513 F.3d 668 (7th Cir. 2008) (holding that the district court erroneously found state claims were pre-empted by the Seaman's Protection Act and admiralty law). *Dady v. Harle Marine,* 2012-SPA-2 (DOL ARB) (July 31, 2015) (upholding administrative finding for seamen, awarding punitive damages).

S. *Workplace Discrimination: EEO Retaliation*

Age Discrimination in Employment Act, Nonretaliation Provision 29 U.S.C. § 623(d)	*See* Title VII–similar rights and procedures.
Americans with Disabilities Act 42 U.S.C. § 12203	*See* Title VII–similar rights and procedures.
*Civil Rights Act of 1964, Title VII 42 U.S.C. 2000e-3(a)	Title VII contains a broad antiretaliation provision protecting from retaliation employees who oppose discriminatory practices or who participate in Title VII proceedings. Similar antiretaliation provisions exist in the other major antidiscrimination laws, including the Age Discrimination Act, the Americans with Disabilities Act, and the Family and Medical Leave Act. Claims initially filed with Equal Employment Opportunity Commission (EEOC). After exhaustion of administrative remedies, cases can be filed in federal court, with access to a jury trial when compensatory damages are requested as part of the damage. Reinstatement, front pay, back pay, and attorney fees are also available. *St. Mary's Honor Center v. Hicks,* 509 U.S. 502 (1993) (burden of proof for employee). *McDonnell Douglas v. Green,* 411 U.S. 792 (1973) (burden-shifting framework for presenting evidence in Title VII cases). *Desert Palace, Inc. v. Costa,* 539 U.S. 90 (2003) (circumstantial evidence used to prove discrimination). *Burlington Northern v. White,* 548 U.S. 53, 68 (2006) (leading case defining adverse employment action) (adverse action includes employer conduct that would dissuade a reasonable employee from engaging in protected activity). *Pettway v. American Cast Iron,* 411 F.2d 998 (5th Cir. 1969) (broad interpretation of protected activity). *Hochstadt v. Worcester Foundation,* 545 F.2d 222 (1st Cir. 1976); *EEOC v. Crown Zellerbach,* 720 F.2d 1008 (9th Cir. 1983) (leading cases discussing scope of protected opposition).

Civil Rights Act of 1871, Conspiracy to interfere with civil rights 42 U.S.C. 1985(3)	Claims filed in U.S. district court. Remedies similar to 42 U.S.C. § 1983. [Note: Both § 1983 and § 1985 are part of the original Civil Rights Act of 1871.]
Reporting discrimination in sale or lease of property 42 U.S.C. 1982	*Sullivan v. Little Hunting Park,* 396 U.S. 229 (1969) (implied cause of action prohibiting retaliation).
Family and Medical Leave Act 29 U.S.C. 2615(a)&(b), & 261	*See* Title VII–similar rights and procedures.
Reporting/Opposing discrimination in contracts 42 U.S.C. 1981(a)	*CBOCS West, Inc. v. Humphries,* 553 U.S. 442 (2008) (implied cause of action prohibiting retaliation).
Reporting/Opposing discrimination under Title IX (women's athletic programs) 20 U.S.C. 1681, et. seq.	*Jackson v. Birmingham Bd. of Ed.,* 544 U.S. 167 (2005) (implied cause of action prohibiting retaliation).

T. *Workplace Discrimination: Labor Rights*

Employee Polygraph Protection 29 U.S.C. § 2002 (defining protected activity) 29 U.S.C. § 2005 (enforcement procedures)	Antiretaliation provision protecting employees who object to illegal polygraph examinations. Claims filed in federal court.
*Fair Labor Standards Act (FLSA)/Equal Pay Act, Nonretaliation Provisions 29 U.S.C. § 215(a)(3) 29 U.S.C. § 216 (penalties and damages) 29 U.S.C. § 255 (statute of limitations)	Employees who suffer retaliation for filing FLSA complaints may file claims either in federal court or with the Department of Labor within two years of an adverse action. *Kasten v. Saint-Gobain,* 131 S.Ct. 1325 (2011) (oral complaints covered) *Soto v. Adams Elevator,* 941 F.2d 543 (7th Cir. 1991) (damages under the statute include reinstatement, back pay, liquidated damages, attorney fees, and compensatory and punitive damages). *Lambert v. Ackerley,* 180 F.3d 997 (9th Cir. 1999) (interpreting scope of protected activity). *Bailey v. Gulf Coast,* 280 F.3d 1333 (11th Cir. 2002) (preliminary injunction reinstating employee).
Longshore and Harbor Workers' Compensation Act 33 U.S.C. § 948a	Antiretaliation law under maritime workers' compensation law (protecting employees who testify in proceedings or file claims). Complaints filed with the U.S. Department of Labor. 20 C.F.R. §§ 702.271-274. See U.S. Dept. of Labor, Benefits Review Board, Longshore Deskbook, Part XXXV (section 49) (cases and procedures for retaliation cases).
Migrant and Seasonal Agricultural Workers Protection Act, Nonretaliation Provision 29 U.S.C. § 1855	*Centeno-Bernuy v. Perry,* 302 F. Supp.2d 128 (W.D.N.Y. 2003) (injunctive relief).

National Labor Relations Act (NLRA), Nonretaliation Provision, Unfair Labor Practices	*NLRB v. Scrivener,* 405 U.S. 117 (1972) and *John Hancock v. NLRB,* 191 F.2d 483 (D.C. Cir. 1951) (broad interpretation to scope of protected activity) (precedent followed in other federal whistleblower laws).
29 U.S.C. § 158(a)(4)	*Linn v. United Plant Guard,* 383 U.S. 53, 62 (1966) (applying First Amendment principles to definition of protected speech under NLRA).
	Gateway Coal v. UMWA, 414 U.S. 368 (1974); *NLRB v. Washington Aluminum,* 370 U.S. 9 (1962) (work stoppage to protest dangerous working conditions protected activity under Labor Management Relations Act and NLRA).
	Sure-Tan v. NLRB, 467 U.S. 883 (1984) (broad coverage under act/reporting undocumented workers to Immigration and Naturalization Service constituted unfair labor practice). *International Union of Op. Eng.,* NLRB Case 14-CB-10424 (April 19, 2010) (unfair labor practice for union to discipline members for blowing the whistle on safety violations caused by other employees).
Employment Retirement Income Security Act (ERISA)	Prohibition against retaliation for participating in an ERISA retirement plan or blowing the whistle on ERISA violations.
29 U.S.C. § 1140 29 U.S.C. § 1132 29 C.F.R. § 2560	*Hashimoto v. Bank of Hawaii,* 999 F.2d 408 (9th Cir. 1993) and *Momchilov v. McIlvaine Trucking,* 2010 U.S. Dist. LEXIS 27620 (N.D. Ohio) (broad definition of protected disclosure) (finding preemption of state claims); *Edwards v. A.H. Cornell,* 2009 U.S. Dist. LEXIS 63720 (E.D. Pa. 2009) (narrow definition of protected activity).
	Donatellis v. Unumprovident Corp., 2004 U.S. Dist. LEXIS 25866 (U.S. Dist. Maine) (no federal preemption of state claim); *Hashimoto v. Bank of Hawaii,* 999 F.2d 408 (9th Cir. 1993) (finding federal preemption); *Zipf v. ATT,* 799 F.2d 889 (3rd Cir. 1986) (procedures for filing complaint).
	Dunn v. Elco Enterprises, 2006 U.S. Dist. LEXIS 26169 (E.D. Mich.) (prima facie case and proving causation).

CHECKLIST 3

Whistleblower Protections Under State Common Law

Alabama	Does not recognize common law tort remedy for wrongful discharge of employees. State protections currently limited to traditional common law remedies, such as libel laws, or statutory protections.
	Court Decisions: *Hinrichs v. Tranquilaire,* 352 So. 2d 1130. (Ala. 1977); *La Roche v. Campbell,* 512 So. 2d 725. (Ala. 1987).
	Statute: 36-25-24 and 36-26a-1-7 (public employees).
Alaska	Whistleblowers protected under common law "public policy" tort.
	Court Decisions: *Alaska Housing Finance Corporation v. Sulvucci,* 950 P.2d 1116 (Alas. 1997); *Ruest v. Alaska Petroleum Contractors, Inc.,* 127 P.3d 807 (Alas. 2005); *Kinzel v. Discovery Drilling,* 93 P.3d 427 (Alas. 2004); *Hammond v. Department of Transportation & Public Facilities,* 107 P.3d 871 (Alas. 2005); *Bernard v. Alaska Airlines,* 367 P.3d 1156 (Alas. 2016) and *Lingley v. Alaska Airlines,* 2016 LEXIS 66 (Alas. 2016) (no preemption).
	Statute: 39.90.100 (public employees); 08.68.279 (nurses).
Arizona	Whistleblowers protected under common law "public policy" tort, as modified by Employment Protection Act.
	Court Decisions: *Wagenseller v. Scottsdale Memorial Hospital,* 710 P.2d 1025 (Ariz. 1985); *Logan v. Forever Living Products International, Inc., et al.,* 52 P.3d 760 (Ariz. 2002) (clarification on scope of law); *Higgins v. Assmann Electronics, Inc.,* 173 P.3d 453 (Ariz. App. 2007) (sustaining jury verdict and damages); *Revitt v. First Advantage,* 2012 W.L. 1230841 (D.Ariz. 2012) (federal court discussion of Arizona law).
	Statutes: Employment Protection Act, A.R.S. §23-1501 (in general); A.R.S. 38.531-533 (public employees); A.R.S. 36-2282 (health and safety); A.R.S. 41-1492.10 (prohibition against retaliation and coercion).

Arkansas	Whistleblowers protected under common law "public policy" claim under breach of contract theory. Court Decisions: *Sterling Drug Inc. v. Oxford,* 747 S.W.2d 579 (Ark. 1988); *Crawford County v. Jones,* 232 S.W.3d 433 (Ark. 2006); *Lynn v. Wal-Mart Stores, Inc.,* 102 Ark. App. 65 (Ark. 2008); *Northport Health Services Inc. v. Owens,* 356 Ark. 630 (Ark. 2004); *TFS of Gurdon v. Hook,* 474 S.W.3d 897 (Ark. App. 2015 ("the public exception presents an exclusive contract cause of action"). Statute: 21-1-601–608 (public employees).
California	Whistleblowers protected under common law "public policy" tort, but statutory remedy may impact scope of remedy. Court Decisions: *Tameny v. Atlantic Richfield Company et. al.,* 610 P.2d 1330 (Cal. 1980); *Silo v. CHW Medical Foundation et. al.,* 45 P.3d 1162 (Cal. 2002); *State Board of Chiropractic Examiners et. al v. The Superior Court of Sacramento County,* 201 P.3d 457 (Cal. 2009); *Silo v. CHW Medical Foundation et. al.,* 45 P.3d 1162 (Cal. 2002); *Cabesuela v. Browning-Ferris Industries,* 68 Cal. App. 4th 101 (1998) (Occupational Safety and Health Adminstration remedy not exclusive); *Boston v. Penny Lane Centers Inc.,* 170 Cal. App. 4th 936 (2009); *Petermann v. International Brotherhood of Teamsters, et. al.,* 174 Cal. App. 2d 184 (1959). Statutes: California Labor Code § 1102.5; Whistleblower Protection Act 9149.20–.23; California Whistleblower Protection Act §8547.1–.12; Cal. Gov. Code 8548.1–.5 (whistleblower information); Whistleblower Protection, Health and Safety Code Sec. 1278.5; 53298 (health and safety); 1102.5 (right to disclose). Employees need not exhaust administrative remedies under Labor Code §§ 98.7 and 6310. *Sheridan v. Touchstone TV,* 241 Cal.App. 4th 508 (2015).
Colorado	Whistleblowers protected under common law "public policy" tort. Court Decisions: *Martin Marietta Corporation v Lorenz,* 823 P.2d 100 (Col 1992); *Kearl v. Portage Environmental, Inc.,* 205 P.3d 496 (Col App. 2008). Statute: C.R.S. 24-50.5.-101–107 (public employees).

Connecticut	Whistleblowers protected under common law "public policy" tort, but other statutory remedies may preclude use of the common law remedy. Court Decisions: *Sheets v. Teddy's Frosted Foods*, 427 A.2d 385 (Conn. 1980); *Arnone v. Town of Enfield et. al.*, 79 Conn. App. 501 (2003); *Burnham v. Karl and Gelb PC*, 745 A.2d 178 (Conn. 2000); *Thibodeau v. Design Group One Architects*, 802 A.2d 731 (Conn. 2002). In particularly egregious cases, employee may have a "negligent infliction of emotional distress" claim based on the manner the employee is terminated. *Forgione v. Skybox Barber Lounge*, 2016 Conn. Super, LEXIS 467 (2016). Statutes: Conn. Gen. Stat. § 31–51q and § 31–51m; Conn. Gen. Stat. Sec. 33-1336 (whistleblower protection); Sec. 4-61dd (whistleblowing, state agencies); Conn. Gen. Stat. Sec. 16-8a (Nuclear Regulatory Commission protection).
Delaware	Whistleblower protection was recognized as a breach of contract/covenant of good faith and fair dealing. However, the state legislature called into question this precedent when it amended the Delaware Discrimination Employment Statute, making that law the sole remedy for violations of the act. Prior to filing a common law claim for wrongful discharge in Delaware, it is important to review the scope of the exemption set forth in 19 Del. C. § 712. *Crawford v. George & Lynch, Inc.*, 2012 W.L. 2674546 (D. Del. 2012). Court Decisions: *Merrill v. Crothall-American, Inc.*, 606 A.2d 96 (Del. 1992); *Rizzitiello v. McDonald's Corp.*, 868 A.2d 825 (Del. 2005); *E.I. Dupont De Nemours and Co. v. Pressman*, 679 A.2d 436 (Del. 1996); *Town of Cheswold v. Vann*, 9 A.3d 467 (Del. 2010 (compensatory damages available in good faith and fair dealing case); *Kelsall v. Bayhealth*, 2015 Del. Super. LEXIS 1045 (2015) (requirements under Delaware WPA). Statutes: Delaware Whistleblower Protection Act § 1702-1708; 29 Del.C. § 5115 (public employees). The Delaware Whistleblower Protection Act covers public and private employees, has a three-year statute of limitations, and permits whistleblowers to obtain reinstatement, back pay, and attorney fees.

District of Columbia	Whistleblowers protected under common law "public policy" tort.
	Court Decisions: *Carl v. Children's Hospital,* 702 A.2d 159 (D.C. App. 1997); *Lerner v. District of Columbia, et al.,* 362 F. Supp.2d 149 (D.C. 2005); *Williams v. Johnson,* 776 F.3d 865 (D.C. Cir. 2015)(interpreting DC WPA).
	Statutes: D.C. Code Sec. 2-223.01–.07 (public employees); D.C. Code Sec. 1-615.51–.59 (contractors).
Florida	Florida courts primarily rely on the Florida Whistleblower Protection Act in providing a remedy for wrongful discharge.
	Court Decisions: *Rodriguez v. Casson Mark Corp.,* 2008 U.S. Dist. LEXIS 60754 (jury trials are permitted under the Florida Whistleblower Act); *Fox v. City of Pompano Beach,* 984 So. 2d 664 (Fla. App. 2008); *Tracey-Meddoff v. J. Altman Hair & Beauty Centre, Inc.,* 899 So. 2d 1167 (Fla. App. 2005); *Kearns v. Farmer Acquisition,* 157 So.3d 458 (Fla. App 2015) (upholding whistleblower claim under WPA).
	Statutes: Florida Whistleblower Act, Fla. Stat. ch. 448.101–105 (private sector); ch 112.3187 (public sector); Fla. Stat. § 68.088-089 (lawful act); Investigative Procedure, Fla. Stat. § 112.3189 (public employees).
Georgia	Does not currently recognize a "public policy" wrongful discharge claim for whistleblowers.
	Court Decision: *Reilly v. Alcan Aluminum Corp.,* 528 S.E.2d 238 (Ga. 2000). Filing a retaliation case under the Georgia False Claims Act requires the consent of the state attorney general. *McKinney v. Fuciarelli,* 2016 Ga LEXIS 313 (2016).
	Statute: O.C.G.A. § 45-1-4 (public employees). See *Albers v. Georgia Board of Regents,* 766 S.E.2d 520 (Ga. App. 2014) (sustaining whistleblower claim).
Hawaii	Whistleblowers protected under "public policy" tort, but other statutory remedies may preclude use of the common law remedy.
	Court Decisions: *Parnar v. Americana Hotels,* 652 P.2d 625 (Haw. 1982); *Ross v. Stouffer Hotel Company Ltd, Inc.,* 879 P.2d 1037 (Haw. 1994); *Fa v. Brigham Young University,* 98 P.3d 246 (Haw. 2004).
	Statute: Whistleblower Protection Act, HRS Sec. 378.61–69.

Idaho	Whistleblowers protected under common law, but other statutory remedies may preclude use of the remedy. Court Decisions: *Hummer v. Evans*, 923 P.2d 981 (Idaho 1996); *Van v. Portneuf Medical Center*, 212 P.3d 982 (Idaho 2009); *Curlee v. Kootenai County Fire & Rescue*, 224 P.3d 458 (Idaho 2008); *Stout v. Key Training Corp.*, 144 Idaho 195 (2007). Statute: Idaho Whistleblower Act, §§ 6-2101–2109 (public employees).
Illinois	Whistleblowers protected under common law "public policy" tort. Court Decisions: *Kelsay v. Motorola*, 384 N.E.2d 353 (Ill. 1978); *Palmateer v. International Harvester Company*, 421 N.E.2d 876 (Ill. 1981); *Wheeler v. Caterpillar*, 485 N.E.2d 372 (Ill. 1985); *Blount v. Stroud*, 904 N.E.2d 1 (Ill. 2009); *Callahan v. Edgewater Care & Rehabilitation Center, Inc.*, 374 Ill. App. 3d 630 (Ill. App. 2007). Statutes: Whistleblower Act, 740 ILCS 174 1, 5, 10, 15, 20, 25, 30, and 35 (public and private employees); 820 ILCS 130-11b (discharge/retaliation of whistleblowers prohibited); 5 ILCS 430/15-5, 10, 20, 35, and 40 (state officials); 105 ILCS 5-34-2.4c (education); 210 ILCS 86-35 (health care); 20 ILCS 415-19c.1 (disclosure of prohibited activity protection–whistleblowers); 30 ILCS 105-5.317 (state finances); 415 ILCS 5-52 (Environmental Protection Act–Whistleblower Provision).
Indiana	Whistleblowers protected under common law "public policy" tort. Court Decisions: *Frampton v. Central Indiana Gas Company*, 297 N.E.2d 425 (Ind. 1973); *Meyers v. Meyers*, 861 N.E.2d 704 (Ind. 2007); *Baker v. Tremco*, 917 N.E.2d 650 (Ind. 2009). Statutes: Burns Ind. Code Ann., § 22-5-3-3 (public contracting); Burns Ind. Code Ann., §36-1-8-8 (public resources).
Iowa	Whistleblowers protected under common law "public policy" tort. Court Decisions: *Jasper v. Nizam*, 764 N.W.2d 751 (Iowa 2009); *George v. Zinser Company* 762 N.W. 2d 865 (Iowa 2009) (Occupational Safety and Health Administration statute does not preclude employees from obtaining a common law remedy); *Dorshkind v. Oak Park Place*, 835 N.W.2d 293 (Iowa 2013) (internal whistleblowing protected under public policy exception). Statute: 70A.28–29 (public employees).

Kansas	Recognizes a public policy exception to the at-will employment doctrine in tort.
	Court Decisions: *Palmer v. Brown*, 752 P.2d 685 (Kan. 1988); *Hysten v. Burlington Northern Santa Fe*, 108 P.3d 437 (Kan. 2004) (Occupational Safety and Health Administration statute does not preclude employees from seeking protection under common law). *Campbell v. Husky Hogs*, 255 P.3d 1 (Kan. 2011) (adequate statute must provide tort remedies); *Shaw v. Southwest Kansas Groundwater Management*, 219 P3d 857 (Kan. App. 2010) (internal reports protected).
	Statutes: Kansas Whistleblower Act, K.S.A. Art. 75-2973 (public employees); Kansas False Claims Act, K.S.A. Art. 75-7506; K.S.A. Art. 44-615 (witness protection).
Kentucky	Whistleblowers protected under common law "public policy" tort.
	Court Decisions: *Berrier v. Bizer*, 57 S.W.3d 271 (Ky. 2001); *Firestone v. Meadow*, 666 S.W.2d 730 (Ky. 1983).
	Statute: 61.102 (public employees). *Cope v. Gateway Area*, 2015 U.S. App LEXIS 15240 (6th Cir. 2015) (explaining § 61.102).
Louisiana	Civil Law State–whistleblowers protected under statutes.
	Court Decisions: *Hale v. Touro*, 886 So. 2d 1210 (La. 2004); *Ray v. City of Bossier City*, 859 So.2d 264 (La. 2003). To be protected under the state's main whistleblower law an employee must first notify his or her employer of the alleged violation. *Thomas v. ITT Educational Services*, 2012 W.L. 1964501 (E.D. La. 2012). The law provides coverage for employees who report illegal work practices and object to or refuse to participate in these practices. There is no requirement that the employee make a disclosure to the government. *Danna v. Ritz-Carlton Hotel*, 2016 La. App. LEXIS 902 (LaApp. 4 Cir. 2016).
	Statutes: La. R.S. 23:967 (general whistleblower protection law) (strict definition of protected disclosures and provisions permit employees who use law to be sanctioned); La. R.S. 39:2163 (Hurricane Relief); La. R.S. 23:967 (workers' compensation); La. R.S. 30:2027 (environmental whistleblowers); La. R.S. 42:1169 (public employees). *Richardson v. Axion Logistics*, 780 F.3d 304 (5th Cir. 2015) (sustaining cause of action under § 23:967).

Maine	Whistleblowers protected under state Whistleblower Protection Act. Court Decisions: *Stanley v. Hancock County*, 864 A.2d 169 (Me. 2004) (discussing statutory remedy); *Pooler v. Maine*, 532 A.2d 1026 (Me. 1987); *Levitt v. Sonardyne, Inc.*, 2013 W.L. 159928 (D.Me. 2013) (reports to federal officials not protected under Maine WPA) (internal safety complaints protected); *Cormier v. Genesis Helathcare*, 129 A.3d 944 (Me. 2015) (nurse's health care complaint protected; timing used to demonstrate causation); *Brady v. Cumberland Cnty.*, 126 A.3d 1145 (Me. 2015) (burden of proof under Maine WPA). Statute: Whistleblower Protection Act, 26 M.R.S. § 831–833; § 836–840.
Maryland	Whistleblowers protected under a narrow common law "public policy" tort. Court Decisions: *Adler v. American Standard Corporation*, 432 A.2d 464 (Md. 1981); *Porterfield v. Mascari II, Inc.*, 823 A.2d 590 (Md. 2003); *Wholey v. Sears, Roebuck and Co.*, 803 A.2d 482, (Md. 2002); *Lark v. Montgomery Hospice*, 994 A.2d 968 (Md. 2010) (internal reporting protected under the Health Care Worker Whistleblower Protection Act); *Parks v. Alpharma*, Inc., 25 A.3d 200 (Md. 2011) (narrow definition of public policy). Statutes: Code Ann. § 5-301-313 (executive branch of state government); Code Ann. § 1-501-506 (health care worker); Code Ann. § 11-301-306 (State Contractor Employees).
Massachusetts	Whistleblowers protected under common law "public policy" tort. Court Decisions: *Fortune v. National Cash Register*, 364 N.E.2d 1251 (Mass. 1977); *Upton v. JWP Businessland*, 682 N.E.2d 1357 (Mass. 1997). Statues: ALM GL ch.12, Section 5J (attorney general); ALM GL ch. 149, Section 185 (public employees); ALM GL ch. 111F, Section 13 (hazardous substances); ALM GL ch. 149, Section 187 (health care facilities).

Michigan	Whistleblowers protected under common law "public policy" tort, but coverage under the Michigan Whistleblower Protection Act may be exclusive. Court Decisions: *Suchodolski v. Michigan Consolidated Gas Company*, 316 N.W.2d 710 (Mich. 1982); *Pace v. Edel-Harrelson*, Supreme Court Docket No. 151374 (Mich. 2016); *Dudewicz v. Norris-Schmid, Inc.* 503 N.W.2d 645 (Mich. 1993) (common law claims covered under Michigan's whistleblower law are pre-empted); *Kimmelman v. Heather Downs*, 753 N.W.2d 265 (Mich. App. 2008) (claim barred under Michigan WPA's ninety-day statute of limitations); *Sventko v. Kroger Company*, 245 N.W.2d 151 (Mich. App. 1976). Statutes: Whistleblower Protection Act, MCL Section 15.361–15.369 (general law); MCL Section 333.16244 (public health).
Minnesota	Whistleblowers protected under common law "public policy" tort. Court Decisions: *Phipps v. Clark Oil & Refining Corporation*, 396 N.W.2d 588 (Minn. App. 1986); *Nelson v. Productive Alternatives, Inc.*, 715 N.W. 2d 452 (Minn. 2006); *Brevik v. Kite Painting*, 416 N.W. 2d 714 (Minn. 1987) (Occupational Safety and Health Administration statute does not preclude use of the common law remedy); *Larson v. New Richland Care*, 538 N.W.2d 915 (Minn. App. 1995) (whistleblower claims filed under the Whistleblower Protection Act statute of tort claims subject to two-year statute of limitations). Statutes: Minn. Stat. 181.931–181.937 (Minnesota Notice of Termination and Disclosure Protection); Minn. Stat. 363A.15 (Minnesota Unfair Discrimination Practices).
Mississippi	Whistleblowers protected under a narrow common law "public policy" tort. Court Decisions: *McArn v. Allied Bruce-Terminix Company, Inc.*, 626 So.2d 603 (Miss. 1993); *DeCarlo v. Bonus Stores, Inc.*, 989 So.2d 351 (Miss. 2008); *Zeigler v. University of Mississippi*, 877 F.Supp.2d 454 (S.D. Miss. 2012) (federal court held that employee must show that he or she reported actual violation of law to obtain protection under state common law). *Galle v. Isle of Capri Casinos*, 180 So.3d 619 (Miss. 2015) (public policy exception is narrow). Statute: M.C.A. 25-9-171 (public employees); M.C.A. 7-5-307 (investigations).

Missouri	Whistleblowers protected under common law "public policy" tort. Court Decisions: *Smith v. Baue Funeral Home,* 370 S.W.2d 249 (Mo. 1963); *Entwistle v. Missouri Youth Soccer,* 259 S.W.3d 558 (Mo. App. 2008). Statutes: 105.055 R.S.Mo. (state employees); 191.908 R.S.Mo. (whistleblower protection); 198.301 R.S.Mo. (whistleblower protection).
Montana	Common law remedy repealed by statute. *Wrongful Discharge from Employment,* Mont. Code Anno. 39-2-911-915 (statute creating very limited rights).
Nebraska	Whistleblowers protected under common law "public policy" tort. Court Decisions: *Schriner v. Meginnis Ford Company,* 421 N.W.2d 755 (Neb. 1988); *Wendeln v. Beatrice Manor, Inc.,* 712 N.W.2d 226 (Neb. 2006); *Simonsen v. Hendricks Sodding & Landscaping, Inc.,* 558 N.W.2d 825 (Neb. App. 1997). Statutes: R.R.S. Neb 81-2702-2711 (public employees); R.R.S. Neb. 48-1114 (opposition to unlawful practice, participation in investigation, discrimination prohibited).
Nevada	Whistleblowers protected under common law "public policy" tort. Court Decisions: *Hansen v. Harrah's,* 675 P.2d 394 (Nev. 1984); *Dillard Department Stores, Inc. v. Beckwith,* 989 P.2d 882 (Nev. 1999). Statutes: N.R.S.A. Sec. 613.340 (equal employment); N.R.S.A. 281.611-.671 (disclosure of improper governmental action); N.R.S.A. 433.536 (retaliation by officer); N.R.S.A. 618.445 (employee protection).

New Hampshire	Whistleblowers protected under common law "public policy" tort, but remedy may be impacted by statute.
	Court Decisions: *Monge v. Beebe Rubber Company*, 316 A.2d 549 (N.H. 1974); *Lacasse v. Spaulding Youth Center*, 910 A.2d 1262 (N.H. 2006); *MacKenzie v. Linehan*, 969 A.2d 385 (N.H. 2009); *Porter v. City of Manchester*, 849 A.2d 103 (N.H. 2004).
	Employees filing a claim under the New Hampshire Whistleblowers' Protection Act must first notify the employer of any violation before making the claim. *Appeal of Bio Energy Corp.* 135 N.H. 517 (N.H. 1992).
	Statutes: RSA 170-E:48 (Retaliation Prohibited); Whistleblowers' Protection Act, RSA 275-E:1 to :7.
New Jersey	Whistleblowers protected under common law "public policy" tort. New Jersey also enacted strong whistleblower protection statute. Employees must elect remedy.
	Court Decisions: *Pierce v. Ortho Pharmaceutical Corporation*, 417 A.2d 505 (N.J. 1980); *Tartaglia v. UBS Painewebber, Inc.*, 961 A.2d 1167 (N.J. 2008); *Donelson v. Dupont*, 20 A.3d 384 (N.J. 2011) (damages for mental injury); *Winters v. North Hudson*, 50 A.3d 649 (N.J. 2012) (whistleblower claim denied based on collateral estoppel doctrine); *D'Annunzio v. Prudential Ins. Co.*, 192 N.J. 110 (N.J. 2007).
	Statute: The Conscientious Employees Protection Act, N.J.S.A. 34:19-1-8.
New Mexico	Whistleblowers protected under common law "public policy" tort.
	Court Decisions: *Silva v. American Fed'n of State, County, and Mun. Employees*, 37 P.3d 81 (N.M. 2001).

New York	Does not currently recognize a public policy exception to the at-will employment doctrine. Employees must obtain protection under a statute or a traditional common law remedy, such as libel. However, a company compliance program that encourages employees to report misconduct and promises no retaliation may be enforced under contract law. Court Decisions: *Horn v. N.Y. Times,* 790 N.E.2d 753 (N.Y. 2003); *Murphy v. American Home Products Corp.,* 58 N.Y.2d 293 (N.Y. 1983); *Brady v. Calyon Securities,* 406 F. Supp. 2d 307 (S.D. N.Y. 2005); *Villarin v. Rabbi Haskel Lookstein School,* 96 A.D.3d 1 (N.Y.S. 2012) (upholding claim based on reporting child abuse). Statutes: NY CLS Civ. Serv. 75-b (retaliatory action by public employees); NY CLS Lab. 740 (retaliatory personnel action by employers: prohibition); NY CLS Lab. 741 (retaliatory action by employers: health care). The New York State False Claims Act is a state-of-the-art FCA and contains antiretaliation provisions.
North Carolina	Recognizes a public policy exception to the at-will employment doctrine in tort. Court Decisions: *Sides v. Duke,* 328 S.E.2d 818 (N.C. App. 1985); *Coman v. Thomas Mfg. Co., Inc.,* 381 S.E.2d 445 (N.C. 1989); *McDonnell v. Tradewind Airlines, Inc.,* 670 S.E.2d 302 (N.C. 2009). Statutes: 95-240-245 (retaliatory employment discrimination); 126-34.1 and 36 (public employees); 126-84-88 (Reporting Improper Government Activities).
North Dakota	Whistleblowers protected under common law "public policy" tort, but statutory remedies may impact claim. Court Decisions: *Krien v. Marian Manor Nursing Home,* 415 N.W. 2d 793 (N.D. 1987); *Vandall v. Trinity Hospitals,* 676 N.W. 2d 88 (N.D. 2004); *Long v. Samson,* 568 N.W. 2d 602 (N.D. 1997). Statutes: 34-01-20 (private employees); 34-11.1-04–08 (public employees).

Ohio	Whistleblowers protected under common law "public policy" tort, but statutory remedies may impact or preclude claim. Court Decisions: *Leininger v. Pioneer Nat'l Latex*, 875 N.E.2d 36 (Ohio 2007); *Painter v. Graley*, 639 N.E.2d 51 (Ohio 1994); *Klopfenstein v. NK Parts Industries, Inc.*, 870 N.E.2d 741 (Ohio App. 2007); *Kulch v. Structural Fibers, Inc.*, 677 N.E.2d 308 (Ohio 1997); *McGowan v. Medpace*, 42 N.E.3d 256 (Ohio Appeals 2015). Statute: Whistleblower Protections, ORC Ann. 4113.51 to 53, 61, 62, 71, and 99.
Oklahoma	Prior to 2011 whistleblowers were protected under common law "public policy" tort. In 2011 the State Legislature enacted the Oklahoma Anti-Discrimination Act, OKLA. STAT. tit. 25 § 1101, 1350, and "abolished" common law employment claims. In *Moore v. Warr Acres Nursing Center*, 2016 OK 28 (March 8, 2016), the Oklahoma Supreme Court affirmed the use of a narrow public policy exception. Court Decisions: *Burk v. K-Mart Corp.*, 770 P.2d 24 (Okla. 1989); *Darrow v. Integris Health, Inc.*, 176 P.3d 1204 (Okla. 2008); *Shepard v. Compsource Oklahoma*, 209 P.3d 288 (Okla. 2009); *Vasek v. Board of County Commissioners of Noble County;* 186 P.3d 928 (Okla. 2008) (Occupational Safety and Health Administration statute is not an exclusive remedy and common law tort is applicable); *Hall v. Davis H. Elliot*, 2012 W.L. 3583017 (N.D. Ok. 2012) (the Anti-Discrimination Act abolished the prior-existing common law remedies for wrongful discharge). Statutes: Oklahoma Anti-Discrimination Act, OKLA. STAT. tit. 25 § 1101, *et seq.*; Oklahoma Whistleblower Act, 74 O.S. Supp. 2008 § 840-2.5 (statutory remedy for state employees); 403 (health and safety); 74-840-1.2–1.3 (state employees).

Oregon	Whistleblowers protected under common law "public policy" tort, but an adequate statutory remedy may preclude common law claim. Court Decisions: *Nees v. Hocks,* 536 P.2d 512 (Ore. 1975); *Delaney v. Taco Time,* 681 P.2d 114 (Ore. 1984); *Babick v. Oregon Arena,* 40 P.3d 1059 (Ore. 2002); *Lamson v. Crater Lake Motors,* 216 P.3d 346 (Ore. 2009) (narrow view of internal complaints to management). *Chouinard v. Grape Expectations,* 2009 U.S. Dist. LEXIS 2569 (Ore. 2009) (Oregon Safe Employment Act does not preclude common law claim); *Lucas v. Lake County,* 289 P3d 320 (Ore.App. 2012) (public policy tort used by public employee). Statutes: 659A.200 to 224 (Public Employees); 659A.230 and 233 (Testimony and Cooperation); 659A.236 (Whistleblowing: Legislative Testimony); 659A.885 (Civil Rights).
Pennsylvania	Whistleblowers protected under a limited common law "public policy" tort, and this right may be precluded based on a state statutory remedy. Court Decisions: *Geary v. United States Steel Corp.,* 319 A.2d 174 (Pa. 1974); *Rothrock v. Rothrock Motor Sales,* 883 A.2d 511 (Pa. 2005); *Weaver v. Harpster,* 975 A.2d 555 (Pa. 2009); *Oliveri v. U.S. Food Service,* 2010 U.S. Dist. LEXIS 11199 (M.D. Pa.); *Morton v. Stryker Medical,* 2012 W.L. 3617399 (M.D. Pa. 2012); *Roman v. McGuire Memorial,* 127 A.3d 26 (Pa. Super. 2015). Statutes: 43 P.S. § 1421-28 (public employees or employees working for companies funded by the state); 65 P.S. Sec. 67.708 (right-to-know law, public employees); 63 P.S. Sec. 1015.1 (water and wastewater systems); 40 P.S. Sec. 1303.307 (medical); 66 Pa.C.S. Sec. 3316 (public utility); 53 P.S. Sec. 4000.1714 (waste and recycling); 27 Pa.C.S. Sec. 4112 (environmental lab employees); 35 P.S. Sec. 6020.1112 (hazardous sites); 35 P.S. Sec. 7130.509 (radioactive waste); 4 Pa. Code Sec. 1.295 (public employees).
Rhode Island	Whistleblower protections based on state statute. Court Decision: *New England Stone, LLC v. Conte et al,* 962 A.2d 30 (R.I. 2009). Statutes: Rhode Island Whistleblower Protection Act, R.I. Gen. Laws § 28-50-1-9 (general protection); R.I. Gen. Laws, Sec. 23-17.11-11 (nurses); R.I. Gen. Laws Sec. 27-18-45 (health services); R.I. Gen. Laws Sec. 27-20-32 (nonprofit medical); R.I. Gen. Laws Sec. 27-54-7 (insurance fraud); R.I. Gen. Laws Sec. 36-14-5 (public officers).

South Carolina	Whistleblowers protected under common law "public policy" tort, but an adequate statutory remedy may preclude common law claim. Court Decisions: *Barron v. Labor Finders*, 2011 W.L. 3273596 (S.C. 2011); *Dockins v. Ingles Markets, Inc.*, 413 S.E.2d 18 (S.C. 1992); *Lawson v. South Carolina Department of Corrections*, 532 S.E.2d 259 (S.C. 2000); *Ludwick v. This Minute of Carolina, Inc.*, 337 S.E.2d 213 (S.C. 1985); *Fisher v. City of North Myrtle Beach*, 2012 W.L. 3638769 (D.S.C. 2012); *Donevant v. Town of Surfside Beach*, 778 S.E.2d 320 (S.C. App.2015) (upholding $300,000 jury verdict for whistleblower). Statutes: S.C. Code Ann. Sec. 8-27-10–50 (public employees); S.C. Code Ann. Sec. 41-15-510 and 520 (health and safety).
South Dakota	Whistleblowers protected under public policy tort. Court Decisions: *Tiede v. Cortrust Bank*, 748 N.W. 2d 748 (S.D. 2008); *Dahl v. Combined Insurance Co.*, 621 N.W.2d 163 (S.D. 2001). Statute: S.D. Codified Laws Sec. 3-6A-52 (Public Employees).
Tennessee	Recognizes a public policy exception to the at-will employment doctrine in tort. Court Decisions: *Clanton v. Cain-Sloan Co.*, 677 S.W.2d 441 (Tenn. 1984); *Chism v. Mid-South Milling*, 762 S.W.2d 552 (Tenn. 1988); *Hodges v. S.C. Toof & Company*, 833 S.W. 2d 896 (Tenn. 1992); *Gager v. River Park Hospital*, 2009 Tenn. App. LEXIS 43 (2009); *Guy v. Mutual of Omaha Ins. Co.*, 79 S.W.3d 528 (Tenn. 2002); *Williams v. Greater Chattanooga Public Television*, 349 S.W.3d 501 (Tenn. App. 2011); *Williams v. City of Burns*, 465 S.W.3d 96 (Tenn. 2015) (upholding cause of action). Statutes: Tennessee Public Protection Act, Tenn. Code Ann. § 50-1-304; 68-11-903 (nursing homes); 8-50-116 (public employees).

Texas	Under common law it is unlawful to terminate employees if the sole reason is their refusal to perform an illegal act.
	Court Decisions: *Sabine Pilot Service Inc. v. Michael Andrew Hauck*, 687 S.W.2d 733 (Tex. 1985); *Texas v. Lueck*, 290 S.W.3d 876 (Tex. 2009); *The Ed Rachal Found. v. D'Unger*, 207 S.W.3d 330 (Tex. 2006); *Safeshred v. Martinez*, 365 S.W.2d 655 (Tex. 2012); *Peine v. Hit Sers. LP*, 479 S.W.3d 445 (Tex. App. 2015).
	Statutes: Tex. Health & Safety Code Sec. 161.134, 135 (health care); Tex. Health & Safety Code Sec. 242.133 (nursing homes); Tex. Occ. Code Sec. 301.413 (nurses); Tex. Gov't Code Sec. 554.001–.010 (public employees); 502.017 (health and safety).
Utah	Recognizes a public policy exception to the at-will employment doctrine in tort.
	Court Decision: *Touchard v. La-Z-Boy Inc.*, 148 P.3d 945 (Ut. 2006).
	Statute: Utah Code Ann. Sec. 67-21-1–9 (public employees).
Vermont	Whistleblowers protected under common law "public policy" tort.
	Court Decisions: *Payne v. Rozendaal et al.* 520 A.2d 586 (Vt. 1986); *LoPriesti, MD v. Rutland Regional Health Services*, 865 A.2d 1102 (Vt. 2004).
	Statutes: 3 V.S.A. Sec. 971 to 978 (state employees); 21 V.S.A. Sec. 507–509 (health-care employees); 21 V.S.A. Sec. 495 (Civil Rights); 21 V.S.A. Sec. 231 (Employee rights, Health and Safety).
Virginia	Recognizes a public policy exception to the at-will employment doctrine in tort.
	Court Decisions: *Rowan v. Tractor Supply Company*, 559 S.E.2d 709 (Va. 2002); *VanBuren v. Grugg*, 733 S.E.2d 919 (Va. 2012); *Bowman v. State Bank of Keysville*, 331 S.E.2d 797 (Va. 1985).

Washington	Whistleblowers protected under narrow common law "public policy" tort. Court Decisions: *Thompson v. St. Regis Paper Company*, 685 P.2d 1081 (Wash. 1984); *Wilmot v. Kaiser Aluminum and Chemical*, 821 P.2d 18 (Wash. 1991); *Danny v. Laidlaw Transit*, 193 P.3d 128 (Wash. 2008); *Cudney v. Alsco*, 259 P.2d 244 (Wash. 2011); *Rose v. Anderson Hay & Grain Co.*, 358 P.3d 1139 (Wash. 2015) (statutory remedies do not preclude state remedy). Statutes: Rev. Code Wash. Sec. 42.41.010–.902 (local government); Rev. Code Wash. Sec. 34.12.038–.039 (local government); Rev. Code Wash. Sec. 43.70.075 (health care); Rev. Code Wash. Sec. 70.124.100 (state hospitals); Rev. Code Wash. Sec. 74.34.180 (health care).
West Virginia	Whistleblowers protected under common law "public policy" tort. Court Decisions: *Harless v. First National Bank*, 246 S.E.2d 270 (W.Va. 1978); *Kanagy v. Fiesta Saloons, Inc.*, 541 S.E.2d 616 (W. Va. 2000); *Kalany v. Herman Campbell*, 640 S.E.2d 113 (W. Va. 2006); *Wiggins v. Eastern Associated Coal*, 357 S.E.2d 745 (W.Va. 1987) (Mine Health and Safety Act not an exclusive remedy). Statute: W. Va. Code Sec. 6C-1-1–8 (public employees).
Wisconsin	Whistleblowers protected under public policy tort. However, remedy may be precluded if statutory remedy available. Court Decisions: *Brockmeyer v. Dun & Broadstreet*, 335 N.W.2d 834 (Wis. 1983); *Bammert v. Don's Super Valu Inc.*, 646 N.W.2d 365 (Wis. 2002). Statutes: Wis. Stat. Sec. 230.80–90 (state employees); Wis. Stat. Sec. 146.997 (health care).
Wyoming	Whistleblowers protected under public policy tort. However, remedy may be precluded if statutory remedy available. Court Decisions: *Hermreck v. UPS Inc.*, 938 P.2d 863 (Wyo. 1997); *McLean v. Hyland Enterprises, Inc.*, 34 P.3d 1262 (Wyo. 2001). Statute: Wyo. Stat. Sec. 9-11-101–103 (state employees).
Guam	Federal court recognizes common law protections for whistleblowers under local law. Court Decisions: *Hill v. Booz Allen Hamilton, Inc.*, 2009 U.S. Dist. LEXIS 50193 (Guam 2009).

Puerto Rico	Whistleblowers protected under Labor Code against Unjust Dismissal. Court Decisions: *Asociacion de Empleasdos del Estado Libre Asociado de Puerto Rico v. Union Internacional de Trabajadores de la Industria de Automoviles*, 515 F. Supp. 2d 209 (D.P.R. 2007). Statutes: Labor Code Against Unjust Dismissals, 29 L.P.R.A. Sec. 185a; Whistleblowers Protection Act, 1 L.P.R.A. Sec. 601 to 606 (public employees).
Virgin Islands	Statutory protection against unjust dismissal. Court Decisions: *Johnson v. Government of the Virgin Islands*, 35 V.I. 27 (V.I. 1996). Statutes: Law Prohibiting Unjust Dismissal, V.I. Code Ann. Title 24 § 76–79; Whistleblower Protection Act, 10 V.I.C. Sec. 121 to 126 (public employees).

CHECKLIST 4

What to Look for When Blowing the Whistle on Fraud Against the Government

Examples Of Frauds Covered Under False Claims Act 31 U.S.C. § 3729

Type of Fraud Legal Authority/Source

"All types of fraud, without qualification, that might result in a financial loss to the government" or improperly "inducing the government" to "part with money."	*United States v. Neifert-White Co.,* 390 U.S. 228, 232 (1968), cited in S. Report No. 99-345.
Altering export certificates to avoid paying a fee.	*United States ex rel. Bahrani v. Conagra, Inc.,* 465 F.3d 1189 (10th Cir. 2006).
Assisting others to defraud the government.	*U.S. ex rel. Marcus v. Hess,* 317 U.S. 537 (1943).
Billing government for training services not provided.	"Learning Tree International Inc. Agrees to Pay $4.5 Million to Settle Allegations of Improper Billing" (Department of Justice Press Release, April 7, 2010).
Billing Medicare and Medicaid for services not performed.	*U.S. ex rel. Grubbs v. Kanneganti,* 2009 W.L. 930071 (5th Cir. April 8, 2009).
Billing Medicaid for services provided to ineligible persons.	"California & Los Angeles County to Pay U.S. $73 Million For Overbilling Medicaid Program" (DOJ Press Release, June 20, 2002).
Billing Medicare for services not performed by required licensed professional.	*United States v. Mackby,* 339 F.3d 1013 (9th Cir. 2003).
Billing Medicare for unnecessary ambulance services.	"U.S. Settles False Claims Allegations With Hartford Area Ambulance Companies" (DOJ Press Release, December 18, 1996).
Charging for research costs unrelated to government grant.	"Mayo Clinic Pays U.S. $6.5 Million" (DOJ Press Release, May 26, 2005).
Claims for services that were not reimbursable (false statements regarding the patient's eligibility for Medicare).	"Tenet Hospital in Florida Pays U.S. $29 Million to Resolve False Claims Act Allegations" (DOJ Press Release, July 17, 2002).
"Conflict of interest" (false certification).	*Harrison v. Westinghouse Savannah River Co.,* 176 F.3d 776 (4th Cir. 1999).
"Conflict of interest" (failure to disclose).	*U.S. ex rel. Davis v. District of Columbia,* 679 F.3d 832 (D.C. Cir. 2012)
Collusive bidding.	*Murray & Sorrenson, Inc. v. United States,* 207 F.2d 119 (1st Cir. 1953), cited in S. Report No. 99-345.

Conspiracy to defraud government	*U.S. ex rel. Westrick v. Second Chance*, 2010 West Law 623466 (D.D.C. 2010).
Customs duty violation	*U.S. ex rel. Customs Fraud Investigators LLC v. Victaulic Co.*, 839 F.3d 242 (3rd Cir. 2016).
"Defective pricing" in violation of the Truth in Negotiations Act.	*U.S. ex rel. Campbell v. Lockheed Martin*, 282 F. Supp. 2d 1324 (M.D. Fla. 2003).
Delivering defective transmission parts that caused two Chinook helicopters to crash.	"United States Settles False Claims Act Lawsuit For $7.2 Million Allowed Claim With Ohio Company" (DOJ Press Release March 7, 1997).
Environmental compliance false certification.	*U.S. ex rel. Fallon v. Accudyne Corp.*, 921 F. Supp. 611 (W.D. Wis. 1995).
Environmental violations (failure to handle and dispose of dangerous waste for work under U.S. contract).	DOJ press release dated February 29, 2016 (Lockheed Martin Corp. fined $5 million).
Failure to adhere to the "quality assurance requirements" required in contract.	*Varljen v. Cleveland Gear Co.*, 250 F.3d 426 (6th Cir. 2001).
Failure to comply with "best pricing" for Medicaid-sponsored drugs.	"Aventis Pharmaceutical to Pay U.S. $95.5 Million to Settle False Claims Act Allegations" (DOJ Press Release, May 28, 2009).
Failure to comply with the reporting requirements of the Vietnam Era Veterans Readjustment Act.	*United States ex rel. Kirk v. Schindler Elevator Corp.*, 601 F.3d 94 (2nd Cir. 2010).
Failure to enroll pregnant women and unhealthy patients in managed care Medicaid-sponsored program.	"Amerigroup Settles Federal & State Medicaid Fraud Claims for $225 Million" (DOJ Press Release, August 14, 2008).
Failure to meet quality requirements in sale of goods or services to Government.	*United States v. Bornstein et al.*, 423 U.S. 303 (1976), cited in S. Report No. 99-345.
Failure to perform required testing.	"U.S. Settles False Claims Case Involving Teledyne for $500,000" (DOJ Press Release December 6, 1994).
Failure to perform tests of air, soil samples, and water as required by its contracts.	"Environmental Testing Company to Pay U.S. Nearly $9 Million to Settle Claims of Contractual Violations" (DOJ Press Release, March 25, 2002).
Failure to provide adequate construction management and quality assurance service concerning the "Big Dig" in Boston.	"Bechtel Infrastructure Corp., Pb Americas Inc., and Consultants Agree to Pay $458 Million to Settle Federal & State Claims" (DOJ Press Release, January 23, 2008).
Failure to record illegal discharges of hazardous substances on required log.	*Pickens v. Kanawha River Towing*, 916 F. Supp. 702 (S.D. Ohio 1996).
Fair Housing Act false certification.	*U.S. v. Incorporated Village*, 888 F. Supp. 419 (E.D.N.Y. 1995).

False claim for payment under Medicare or Medicaid.	*Peterson v. Weinberger,* 508 F.2d 45 (5th Cir. 1975), cited in S. Report No. 99-345.
False claim in government financed housing sales.	*United States v. De Witt et al.,* 265 F.2d 393 (5th Cir. 1959), cited in S. Report No. 99-345.
False claims to federal agencies for travel reimbursements.	"PricewaterhouseCoopers, LLP to Pay U.S. $41.9 Million to Settle False Claims Involving Claims for Travel" (DOJ Press Release July 11, 2005).
False statements in a grant proposal.	*United States ex rel. Longhi v. Lithium Power,* 575 F.3d 458 (5th Cir. 2009).
False statements on application for a government loan.	*United States v. Neifert-White Co.,* 390 U.S. 228 (1968), cited in S. Report No. 99-345.
False statements to obtain Housing and Urban Development loan insurance.	*United States v. Eghbal,* 548 F.3d 1281 (9th Cir. 2008).
Falsely certifying compliance with Small Business Administration minority contracting program.	*Ab-Tech Construction v. U.S.,* 31 Fed. Cl. 429 (1994).
Falsely certifying compliance with statute, regulation, or contract term that is a "prerequisite to payment."	*U.S. ex rel. Mikes v. Straus,* 274 F.3d 687 (2nd Cir. 2001).
Falsely certifying that company paid "prevailing wage" required under Davis-Bacon Act.	*U. S. ex rel. Plumbers and Steamfitters Local Union v. C.W. Roen Construction Co.,* 183 F.3d 1088 (9th Cir. 1999).
Falsely stating eligibility to participate in government program.	*Alperstein v. United States,* 291 F.2d 455 (5th Cir. 1961), cited in S. Report No. 99-345.
Falsified expiration dates.	"Whistleblower's Complaint Leads American Grocers to Pay $13.2 Million," NASDAQ OMX/ Newswire (Nov. 19, 2010).
Falsified test results at clinical laboratory (paid for by Medicare).	*United States ex rel. Lee v. Smithkline Beecham, Inc.,* 245 F.3d 1048, 1053 (9th Cir. 2001).
Fraudulent mortgage origination activities.	"United States Settles False Claims Act Allegations Against National Home Builder and Mortgage Lender" (DOJ Press Release, July 1, 2009).
Fraudulent pricing.	*U.S. ex rel. Hagood v. Sonoma Co. Water Agency,* 929 F.2d 1416 (9th Cir. 1991).
Implied false certification concerning compliance with legal requirements for grant.	*Mikes v. Straus,* 274 F.3d 687 (2nd Cir. 2001).
Improper student recruitment practices (pay incentives for recruiters in violation of federal regulations).	"University of Phoenix Settles False Claims Act Lawsuit for $67.5 Million" (DOJ Press Release, December 15, 2009).
Inflated cost estimates.	*U.S. v. General Dynamics,* 19 F. 3d 770 (2nd Cir. 1994).

Kickbacks to obtain business.	"Heart Device Manufacturer to Pay Nearly $4 Million to Resolve Fraud Allegations" (DOJ Press Release, June 4, 2010).
Knowing failure to perform a material requirement of contract without disclosing the nonperformance.	*U.S. ex rel. Fallon v. Accudyne Corp.*, 921 F. Supp. 611 (W.D. Wis. 1995).
Media campaign to entice sales of unneeded wheel chairs purchased with Medicare and Medicaid funds.	"The Scooter Store to Pay United States $4 Million to Resolve False Claims Act Allegations" (DOJ Press Release, May 11, 2007).
Misrepresenting costs of a subcontractor.	*Harrison v. Westinghouse Savannah River Co.*, 176 F.3d 776 (4th Cir. 1999).
Noncompetitive bidding practices.	"New Mexico–Based Computer Assets Inc. Agrees to Settle False Claims Allegation Involving the E-Rate Program" (DOJ Press Release, July 30, 2009).
Obtaining contract based on false information.	*U.S. ex rel. Schwedt v. Planning Research Group*, 59 F.3d 196 (D.C. Cir. 1995).
"Off-label" promotion of drugs.	"Eli Lilly and Company Agrees to Pay $1.415 Billion to Resolve Allegations of Off-Label Promotion of Zyprexa" (DOJ Press Release, January 15, 2009).
Overcharging for books sold to public libraries and educational institutions funded by government grants.	*United States ex rel. Costa v. Baker & Taylor, Inc.*, 1998 U.S. Dist. Lexis 23509 (N.D. Cal. 1998).
Overcharging rent payments on "Section 8" sponsored housing.	*Coleman v. Hernandez*, 490 F. Supp. 2d 278 (D. Conn. 2007).
Overcharging under a government contract.	*United States ex rel. Green v. Northrop Corp.*, 59 F.3d 953 (9th Cir.1995).
Paying "kickbacks" to health care providers to induce prescriptions.	"Justice Department Announces Largest Health Care Fraud Settlement in Its History" (DOJ Press Release, September 2, 2009).
Performing unnecessary medical treatments.	"Intercare Health Systems Agrees to $10 Million" (DOJ Press Release, May 27, 2010).
Recalled beef sold to National School Lunch Program.	"U.S. Intervenes in Suit Against Former Beef Suppliers to National School Lunch Program" (DOJ Press Release, May 1, 2009).
"Reverse False Claim": Material misrepresentations to avoid paying money owed to the government.	*United States v. Bourseau*, 531 F.3d 1159 (9th Cir. 2008).
Sale of adulterated drugs.	"GlaxoSmithKline to Plead Guilty and Pay $750 Million to Resolve Criminal and Civil Liability Regarding Manufacturing Deficiencies" (DOJ Press Release, Oct. 26, 2010).

Sale of defective bullet-proof vests.	"Canadian Firm Pays $4 Million to Settle Lawsuit in Connection with Sale of Defective Bullet-Proof Vests" (DOJ Press Release, February 12, 2010).
Sale of defective or inferior products.	*Henry v. United States*, 424 F.2d 677 (5th Cir. 1970), cited in S. Report No. 99-345.
Self-referral false certification.	*U.S. ex rel. Thompson v. Columbia/HCA*, 125 F.3d 899 (5th Cir. 1997).
Selling office supplies to government agencies manufactured in countries ineligible under the Trade Agreements Act.	"Office Depot Pays United States $4.75 Million to Resolve False Claims Act Allegations" (DOJ Press Release, September 19, 2005).
Small Business Administration loan (false certification).	"New York Small Business Lender to Pay U.S. $26.3 Million to Resolve False Claims Act Allegations" (DOJ Press Release, May 6, 2010).
Stark Act violations (42 U.S.C. § 1395nn) (i.e., prohibition on certain physician referrals to entities/hospitals with which they have a financial relationship).	*U.S. ex rel. Kosenske v. Carlisle HMA*, 554 F.3d 88 (3rd Cir. 2004); *U.S. ex rel. Drakeford v. Tuomey Healthcare System*, 675 F.3d 394 (4th Cir. 2012).
Steering contracts toward companies owned by themselves, their spouses, and others, resulting in kickbacks and inflated contract prices.	"Dynamics Research Corporation to Pay $15 Million to Resolve Allegations of Kickbacks and False Claims Related to Air Force Contracts" (DOJ Press Release, August 13, 2009).
Subcontractor causes a prime contractor to submit a false claim to the government.	*United States ex rel. Drescher v. Highmark, Inc.*, 305 F. Supp. 2d 451 (E.D. Pa. 2004).
Submitting fraudulent cost reports.	*U.S. ex rel. Augustine v. Century Health*, 136 F. Supp. 2d 876 (M.D. Tenn. 2000).
Submitting inflated claims for insurance payments.	"Pacificare Health Systems to Pay U.S. More Than $87 Million to Resolve False Claims Act Allegations" (DOJ Press Release, April 12, 2002).
Submitting an "inventory sheet with false information" causing the government to "undervalue the purchase price" paid by the company.	*U.S. v. Pemco Aeroplex, Inc.*, 195 F.3d 1234 (11th Cir. 1999) (en banc).
Submitting false progress reports stating that computer software was compliant with contract requirements.	*United States ex rel. Schwedt v. Planning Research Corp.*, 59 F.3d 196 (D.C. Cir. 1995).
Substandard products (sold to government).	*U.S. v. Aerodex*, 469 F.2d 1003 (5th Cir. 1972).
Switching patients from the tablet to capsule version of a drug to increase Medicare reimbursements.	"CVS Caremark Corp. to Pay $36.7 Million to U.S." (DOJ Press Release, March 18, 2008).
Unauthorized venting and flaring of gas (failure to disclose and pay royalties).	"Shell Oil Agrees to Pay U.S. $49 Million for Unauthorized Venting and Flaring of Gas (DOJ Press Release, August 5, 2003).

Underpaying royalties.	"Chevron to Pay U.S. More Than $45 Million to Resolve Allegations of False Claims for Royalties Underpayment" (DOJ Press Release, December 23, 2009); *In re: Natural Gas Royalties Qui Tam Litigation,* 2010 U.S. Dist. LEXIS 64525 (D. Wy. 2010).
Underwriting mortgage loans insured by HUD that did not meet federal standards.	DOJ press release dated May 13, 2016 ($64 million penalty paid by M&T Bank).
Violation of Anti-Kickback Act (42 U.S.C. § 1320a-7b).	*U.S. ex rel. Thompson v. Columbia/HCA,* 125 F.3d 899 (5th Cir. 1997).
Violation of Best Prices Statute (sale of drugs).	*In re Pharmaceutical Industry Average Wholesale Price Litigation,* 685 F.Supp.2d 186 (D. Mass. 2010).
Violation of contract terms (even when final product was of "equal quality").	*United States v. National Wholesalers,* 236 F.2d 944 (9th Cir. 1956), cited in S. Report No. 99-345.
Violation of cost provisions set forth in statute governing government contract.	*United States ex rel. Hagood v. Sonoma County Water Agency,* 929 F.2d 1416 (9th Cir. 1991).
Violations of Federal Truth in Negotiations Act.	"SAIC to Pay $2.5 Million to Settle False Claims at Kelly Air Force Base" (DOJ Press Release, May 27, 2005).

CHECKLIST 5

Proof of Retaliation

Facts Used to Demonstrate "Pretext" And "Causation"

A. Allegation of Disloyalty/Vague and Subjective Personality Issues

Statement by decision maker that employee was not loyal.	*Decaire v. Mukasey*, 530 F.3d 1 (1st Cir. 2008) (protesting illegalities "cannot be a basis for a loyalty test") ("As a matter of law, the filing of an EEO complaint cannot be an act of disloyalty . . . which would justify taking adverse action."). *Mandell v. County of Suffolk*, 316 F.3d 368 (2nd Cir. 2003) (viewing protected activities as a "betrayal of the department").
Statement that person providing information to investigators was a "rat."	*Raniola v. Police Commissioner*, 243 F.3d 610 (2nd Cir. 2001) ("There is an investigation going on in the precinct and there is a rat here . . . so everyone watch what you are doing").
Vague and subjective personality issues.	*Bobreski v. J. Givoo Consultants*, 2008-ERA-3 (DOL ARB, June 24, 2011) (citing cases).

B. Antagonistic or Derogatory Remarks Concerning Protected Activity

"Antagonistic statements concerning the protected activity provide circumstantial evidence of a retaliatory motive."	*Douglas v. Skywest Airlines,* 2006-AIR-14 (DOL ALJ, Airline Safety Whistleblower Case) (October 3, 2007).
Derogatory comments by decision makers.	*Santiago-Ramos v. Centennial P.R. Wireless Corp.,* 217 F.3d 46 (1st Cir. 2000) (comments made by key decision maker to employee and coworkers).
Discriminatory comments made by decision maker.	*Ashe v. Aronov Homes, Inc.,* 354 F. Supp. 2d. 1251 (M.D. Ala. 2004) ("comments or remarks that suggest discriminatory animus can be sufficient circumstantial evidence to establish pretext").
Referring to protected activity as "baggage."	*Mandell v. County of Suffolk,* 316 F.3d 368 (2nd Cir. 2003) (referring to past protected activity as "baggage" that could harm career).
Employer "irritated" by protected activities.	*Fasold v. Justice,* 409 F.3d 178 (3rd Cir. 2005) (statement that employee's complaint "irritated" the supervisor).
Statement by supervisor to employee critical of employee's protected activity.	*Fierros v. Texas Dept. of Health,* 274 F.3d 187 (5th Cir. 2001) (statement by manager to employee admitting to retaliatory motive).
Threat to fire employee for "stirring up" regulatory concern.	*Simas v. First Citizen,* 170 F.3d 37 (1st Cir. 1999) (stating whistleblower should be fired for "stirring up" regulatory issue).
Manager "upset" with allegation he was "stealing."	*Dunn v. ELCO Enterprises,* 2006 U.S. Dist. LEXIS 26169 (E.D. Mich. 2006).
Supervisor "frustrated" over safety concerns.	*Testa v. Consolidated Edison,* 2007-STA-27 (DOL ALJ decision) (December 4, 2007), *affirmed,* Administrative Review Board (March 19, 2010).
Supervisor statement that employee could not "keep his mouth shut."	*Cecil v. Flour Hanford,* 2004-ERA-11 (Labor Department Judge) (August 16, 2006) (manager's statement that employee laid off "because he did not 'keep his mouth shut'" constituted "direct evidence of discrimination").
Manager pointing to fact that employee had filed an "unsubstantiated" complaint as evidence employee was a "problem employee."	*Fabela v. Socorro Independent School District,* 329 F.3d 409 (5th Cir. 2003) (statement constituted direct evidence of causation).

C. Change in Conduct After Protected Disclosures

Long record of positive performance, bad performance findings after engaging in protected activity.	*Fierros v. Texas Dept. of Health*, 274 F.3d 187 (5th Cir. 2001); *Thomas v. Texas Dept. of Criminal Justice*, 220 F.3d 389, 394 (5th Cir. 2000) (evidence that employee had eighteen-year record of no prior complaints, but disciplined after filing EEO complaint).
Change in demeanor.	*Abramson v. William Paterson College*, 260 F.3d 265 (3rd Cir. 2001) ("change in demeanor" after employee made protected disclosure).
Change in behavior toward employee after protected activity.	*Che v. Massachussetts Bay Transportation Authority*, 342 F.3d 31 (1st Cir. 2003) ("evidence of a pattern of antagonism following protected conduct"). *Hite v. Vermeer*, 446 F.3d 858 (8th Cir. 2006) ("escalating adverse and retaliatory action" after protected disclosures). *Brammer-Hoelter v. Twin Peaks*, 492 F.3d 1192 (10th Cir. 2007) (obtaining "poor performance evaluations" that "differed materially" from prior evaluations "during the period in which they exercised their First Amendment rights") ("very positive" opinion of employee prior to protected activity).
Making unfounded allegations against plaintiffs after they engaged in protected activity.	*Centeno-Bernuy v. Perry*, 302 F. Supp. 2d 128 (W.D. N.Y. 2003).
Satisfactory performance/no criticism for year before protected activity/fired shortly after blowing whistle.	*Fleeman v. Nebraska Pork*, 2008-STA-15 (DOL judge) (February 9, 2009), *affirmed* Administrative Review Board (May 28, 2010) (truck-safety case).

D. Conflicting Reasons/Shifting Explanations

"An employer's shifting explanations for its adverse action may be considered evidence of pretext, that is, a false cover for a discriminatory reason."	*Douglas v. Skywest Airlines,* 2006-AIR-14 (DOL ARB Airline Safety Whistleblower Case) (September 30, 2009) (citing other cases); *Clemmons v. Ameristar,* 2004-AIR-11 (DOL ARB 2010).
Shifting explanations evidence of motive and pretext.	*Wallace v. DTG Operations,* 442 F.3d 1112 (8th Cir. 2006) ("shifting explanations" for adverse action evidence of pretext) timing part of overall record justifying finding of retaliation.
Conflicting reasons as to why disciplinary actions were administered.	*Waddel v. Small Tube,* 799 F.2d 69, 73 (3rd Cir. 1986) (inconsistent reasons for discharge). *Bechtel Construction v. SOL,* 50 F.3d 926, 935 (11th Cir. 1995) ("pretextual nature" of termination "demonstrated" by employer's "shifting explanations for its actions").
Conflicting justifications evidence of post hoc rationalizations.	*Gaffney v. Riverboat Services,* 451 F.3d 424 (7th Cir. 2006).

E. Deviation from Procedure

Failure to follow disciplinary procedures.	*Smith v. Xerox*, 584 F. Supp. 2d 905 (N.D. Tex. 2008).
Disregarding termination procedures in manual.	*Florek v. Eastern Air Central*, 2006-AIR-9 (DOL ARB) (May 21, 2009).
Deviation from policy or practice evidence of pretext.	*Hite v. Vermeer*, 446 F.3d 858 (8th Cir. 2006) ("employee can prove pretext by showing that the employer varied from its normal policy or procedure to address the employee's situation"). *Dietz v. Cypress Semiconductor*, 2014-SOX-2 (DOL ARB) (March 30, 2016) (failure to follow "Global Whistleblower Policy").
Conducting "superficial investigation."	*Lawson v. United Airlines*, 2002-AIR-6 (DOL judge) (December 20, 2002).
Swift use of "progressive disciplinary procedures."	*Pierce v. U.S. Enrichment Corp.*, 2004-ERA-1 (Department of Labor Administrative Review Board) (August 29, 2008).
Failure to seek input from employee's immediate supervisor.	*Diaz-Robainas v. FP&L* 92-ERA-10 (January 19, 1996); *Donovan v. Peter Zimmer America, Inc.*, 557 F. Supp. 642 (D. S.C. 1982) (employee's immediate foreman did not want employee fired).
Failure to provide employees an opportunity to explain their version of the events.	*Donovan v. Peter Zimmer America, Inc.*, 557 F. Supp. 642 (D.S.C. 1982).
No oral or written warnings before termination.	*Clean Harbors v. Herman*, 146 F.3d 12 (1st Cir. 1998).

F. Direct Evidence/Charges of Disloyalty

Supervisor upset over employee's protected activity.	*Bechtel Construction v. SOL*, 50 F.3d 926, 935 (11th Cir. 1995) (supervisor "admitted that he was 'a little upset'" when employee raised safety issue).
Protected activity described as "disruptive."	*Donahue v. Exelon*, 2008-PSI-1, DOL (ALJ order under Pipeline Safety Act) (December 4, 2008).
Reference to employee as troublemaker.	*Stone & Webster v. Herman* 115 F.3d 1568 at 1574 (11th Cir. 1997).
Anger, antagonism, or hostility toward complainant's protected activity.	*Lewis Grocer Co. v. Holloway*, 874 F.2d 1008 (5th Cir. 1989).

G. Disparate Treatment

"Disparate treatment of similarly situated employees may also provide evidence of pretext. 'Similarly situated' employees are those involved in or accused of the same or similar conduct but disciplined in different ways."	*Douglas v. Skywest Airlines,* 2006-AIR-14 (DOL ARB Airline Safety Whistleblower Case) (September 30, 2009). *Kowaleski v. New York State Dept. of Correctional Services,* 942 N.E.2d 291, 295 (N.Y. 2010) ("whistleblower protections . . . must shield employees from being retaliated against by an employer's selective application of theoretically neutral rules."
Disciplinary rules applied against whistleblower in uneven or selective manner.	*M&S Steel Co.,* 148 NLRB 789, 795 (1964), enforced, 353 F.2d 80 (5th Cir. 1965). *Vieques Air v. DOL,* 437 F.3d 102 (1st Cir. 2006) ("less severe sanction imposed" on nonprotected employee). *EEOC v. Thomas Dodge Corp.,* 2009 U.S. Dist. LEXIS 24838 (E.D.N.Y.) (other employee with low sales figures not fired) (not obligated to show disparate treatment regarding "identically situated employees"). *Miller v. Fairchild Industries,* 885 F.2d 498 (9th Cir. 1989) (laying off protected employee, while offering other employees opportunity to transfer to other department). *Donovan v. Zimmer America, Inc.,* 557 F. Supp. 642, 652 (D.S.C. 1982) (no prior enforcement of rule) (actions taken against employees were "selective and unevenly applied"). *Donovan on Behalf of Chacon v. Phelps Dodge Corp.,* 709 F.2d 86, 93 (D.C. Cir. 1983). *NLRB v. Heck's Inc.,* 386 F.2d 317, 320 (4th Cir. 1967). *Che v. Massachusetts Bay Transportation Authority,* 342 F.3d 31 (1st Cir. 2003) (discrimination demonstrated when employer did not punish other employees who engaged in the same actions). *Reich v. Hoy Shoe,* 32 F.3d 361 (8th Cir. 1994) (employees with "equivalent or worse records" were "not discharged").
Disciplinary response clearly does not fit with the type of infraction at issue.	*Conley v. Yellow Freight,* 521 F.Supp. 2d 713 (E.D. Tenn. 2007) ("no employee" other than whistleblower had "ever been terminated" for violating policy; no training in policy).
Substantially disproportionate discipline is evidence of retaliation.	*Pogue v. U.S. DOL,* 940 F.2d 1287, 1291 (9th Cir. 1991). *Borel Restaurant Corp. v. NLRB,* 676 F.2d 190, 192-193 (6th Cir. 1982).

Anger, antagonism, or hostility toward complainant's protected conduct.	*NLRB v. Faulkner*, 691 F.2d 51, 56 (1st Cir. 1982). *Lewis Grocer Co. v. Holloway*, 874 F.2d 1008 (5th Cir. 1989).
Disparate treatment of hiring process.	*Dartey v. Zack Co.*, 82-ERA-2, D&O of SOL, at 10 (April 25, 1983).

H. Evidence of Violations/Antagonism Regarding Protected Activity or Safety

Antagonism toward protected activity.	*Timmons v. Mattingly Testing Services*, 95-ERA-40, D&O of Remand by ARB, at 12, 14-15 (June 21, 1996) ("antagonism toward activity that is protected . . . may manifest itself in many ways, e.g., ridicule, openly hostile action, or threatening statements, or in the case of a whistleblower who contacts the NRC, simply questioning why the whistleblower did not pursue corrective action through the usual internal channels").
Making employees perform work "at expense" of safety.	*Bechtel Construction v. SOL*, 50 F.3d 926, 935 (11th Cir. 1995) (supervisor was "preoccupied with getting work started quickly at the expense of proper safety procedures").
Hiding evidence of wrongdoing from whistleblower.	*Jayaraj v. Pro-Pharmaceuticals*, 2003-SOX-32 (DOL ALJ Order under Sarbanes-Oxley Act) (February 11, 2005) (managers "hid the existence" of suspect contract from vice president of investor relations).
Ignoring employee's safety concerns.	*Evans v. Miami Valley Hospital*, 2006-AIR-22 (DOL ARB) (June 30, 2009).
Instructing employee not to file safety concern/backdating response to safety filing.	*Lawson v. United Airlines*, 2002-AIR-6 (DOL judge) (December 20, 2002).
Pressure on employee to work in unsafe conditions.	*Ferguson v. New Prime*, 2009-STA-47 (DOL judge) (March 15, 2010) (pressure to operate truck in unsafe conditions).
Whistleblower allegations of wrongdoing found to be correct.	*Seater v. Southern California Edison.*, 95-ERA-13 (DOL ARB) (September 27, 1996). *Dilback v. General Electric Company*, 2008 WL 4372901 (W.D. Ky. Sept, 22, 2008 ("existence of false claims . . . may be probative of the Defendant's motivation.")
Evidence that the company permitted safety violations.	*Khandelwal v. Southern California Edison*, 97-ERA-6 (DOL ARB) (March 31, 1998).

Statements of decision maker.	*Patane v. Clark*, 508 F.3d 106, 117 (2nd Cir. 2007) (overhearing conversation between supervisors to "drive" employee "out of her job"). *Doe v. C.A.R.S. Protection Plus, Inc.* 527 F.3d 358 (3rd Cir. 2008) ("stray remarks" demonstrating hostility toward protected conduct). *Santiago-Ramos v. Centennial P.R. Wireless Corp.,* 217 F.3d 46 (1st Cir. 2000) (comments made by key decision maker or those in position to influence decision). *Bess v. J.D. Hunt Transport,* 2007-STA-34 (decision of DOL judge) (January 7, 2008) (manager's statement that if he believed employee's concern was legitimate, he would not have fired him). *Carter v. Marten Transport,* 2005-STA-63 (DOL ARB) (June 30, 2008) (statement by deciding official that employee raised "excessive complaints").
Evidence that company violated rules/failed to discipline employees who violated rules.	*Assistant Secretary v. R&B Transportation,* 2006-STA-12 (DOL ARB) (June 26, 2009) (government report demonstrating that company was "cited for violations" was introduced into evidence).

I. Knowledge of Protected Activity

Employer knowledge required to demonstrate retaliation.	*Staub v. Proctor Hospital,* 131 S.Ct. 1186 (2011) (upholding "cat's paw" theory of liability) ("if supervisor performs an act" that is "motivated by animus" that is part of the "proximate cause" for an adverse action, the company is liable, even if the final decision maker was unaware of the protected activity).
	Bobreski v. J. Givoo Consultants, 2008-ERA-3 (DOL ARB, June 24, 2011) (citing cases) (rubber stamp approval of discharge by "neutral" decision maker can be tainted with bias).
	Gordon v. New York City Board of Education, 232 F.3d 111 (2nd Cir. 2000) (general corporate knowledge of complaints satisfied this requirement) (jury can find knowledge of retaliation even if company agent denies knowing that employee filed a complaint).
	Patane v. Clark, 508 F.3d 106, 115 (2nd Cir. 2007) (general corporate knowledge sufficient/complaint to company employee whose job required investigation into discrimination sufficient).
	Stegall v. Citadel Broadcasting Company, 350 F.3d 1061 (9th Cir. 2003) (employer denial of knowledge of protected activity found not credible).
	Donovan v. Peter Zimmer America, Inc., 557 F. Supp. 642 (D.S.C. 1982) (firing "innocent" employees merely suspected of contacting government is retaliatory).
	Reich v. Hoy Shoe Co., 32 F.3d 361 (8th Cir. 1994) (termination of employee "suspected" of blowing whistle constituted retaliatory action).

J. Outside Chain of Command/Failure to Follow Chain of Command

"An employer may not, with impunity, discipline an employee for failing to follow the chain of command, failing to conform to established channels, or circumventing a superior, when the employee raises a health or safety issue."	*Talbert v. WPPSS*, 93-ERA-35 (Labor Department Administrative Review Board) (Sept. 27, 1996) (nuclear safety case). *Leveille v. New York Air National Guard*, 94-TSC-3/4 (Secretary of Labor) (December 11, 1995) (environmental whistleblower case). *Anthoine v. North Central Counties*, 605 F.3d 740 (9th Cir. 2010) ("low-level employee" "jumping chain of command to report directly to the governing board).
Upset that employee filed complaint to manager above employee's immediate supervisor.	*Wallace v. DTG Operations*, 442 F.3d 1112 (8th Cir. 2006) ("displeased" that employee "had gone over" supervisor's "head").
Policy mandating "chain of command" reporting.	*Robinson v. York*, 566 F.3d 817 (9th Cir. 2009) ("An employer's written policy requiring speech to occur through specific 'channels' cannot serve as pretext for stifling legitimate speech.") *Brockell v. Norton*, 732 F.2d 664 (8th Cir. 1984) (chain of command requirements in local police department).
Increasing restrictions against "outside" speech.	*Brammer-Hoelter v. Twin Peaks*, 492 F.3d 1192 (10th Cir. 2007) (imposing "strict prohibitions on speaking outside of school as a result of plaintiff's speech").
Direct evidence of pretext.	*Anderson v. All Flex*, 2003-WPC-6 (Decision of Labor Department Administrative Law Judge) (March 3, 2004).

K. Pretextual Justification for Termination/Adverse Action

Unworthy credence of proposed reason.	*Smith v. Xerox Corp.,* 584 F. Supp. 2d 905 (N.D. Texas 2008); *Clemmons v. Ameristar,* 2004-AIR-11 (DOL Airline Whistleblower Case, 2010).
Proof that reason given for adverse action is "unworthy of credence" is evidence of discrimination.	*Reeves v. Sanderson Plumbing Products, Inc.* 530 U.S. 133 (2000) ("trier of fact can reasonably infer from falsity of the explanation that the employer is dissembling to cover up a discriminatory purpose. . . . factfinder is entitled to consider a party's dishonesty about a material fact as 'affirmative evidence of guilt.'"). *Desert Palace v. Costa,* 539 U.S. 90 (2003) ("evidence that a defendant's explanation for an employment practice is unworthy of credence is one form of circumstantial evidence that is probative of intentional discrimination"). *Handzlik v. U.S.,* 2004 U.S. App. LEXIS 2493 (5th Cir.) ("trier of fact may infer retaliation . . . from the falsity of the employer's explanation"). *Richardson v. Monitronics,* 434 F.3d 327 (5th Cir. 2005); *Smith v. Xerox Corp.,* 584 F. Supp. 2d 905 (N.D. Tex. 2008). (Desert Palace analysis applies to retaliation cases).
Discrepancies in justification.	*Gordon v. New York City Bd. of Edu.,* 232 F.3d 111 (2nd Cir. 2000) (employee not required to demonstrate pretext to prove retaliation). *Abramson v. William Paterson College,* 260 F.3d 265 (3rd Cir. 2001) ("Revealing discrepancies in the proffered reasons can also constitute evidence of the causal link").
A lie is evidence of consciousness of guilt.	*AKA v. Washington Hospital Center,* 156 F.3d 1284, 1293 (D.C. Cir. 1998); *Salazar v. WMATA,* 401 F.3d 504 (D.C. Cir. 2005) ("jury can conclude that an employer who fabricates a false explanation has something to hide; that 'something' may well be discriminatory intent").
Evidence of pretext also can be used as evidence of causation.	*Wells v. Colorado Dept. of Trans.,* 325 F.3d 1205 (10th Cir. 2003) ("evidence of pretext can be useful in multiple stages" of a "retaliation claim").
Unfounded claims against plaintiff.	*Centeno-Bernuy v. Perry,* 302 F. Supp. 2d 128 (W.D. N.Y. 2003).
Unfavorable attitude toward employees who reported violations first to the government rather than discussing them with company personnel.	*Housing Works, Inc. v. City of New York,* 72 F. Supp. 2d 402, 422, (S.D.N.Y. 1999).

Reference to employee as troublemaker.	*Stone & Webster v. Herman*, 115 F.3d 1568 at 1574 (11th Cir. 1997).
Determination that the employee was not guilty of violating the work rule under which she was charged.	*Lewis Grocer Co. v. Holloway*, 874 F.2d 1008 (5th Cir. 1989).
"After-the-fact justifications" for the adverse action.	*Santiago-Ramos v. Centennial P.R. Wireless Corp.*, 217 F.3d 46 (1st Cir. 2000) (memo justifying termination prepared after company learned employee was filing legal challenge).

L. Temporal Proximity

Timing between a protected disclosure and an adverse action evidence of improper motive.	*Clark County v. Breeden,* 532 U.S. 268, 273–74 (2001) (temporal proximity must be "very close" in time if used, standing alone, to demonstrate causation). *Marra v. Phila. Housing Authority,* 497 F.3d 286, 301 (3rd Cir. 2007). *Mariani-Colon v. Department of Homeland Sec.,* 511 F.3d 216, 224 (1st Cir. 2007) (timing sufficient to establish prima facie burden). *Yartzoff v. Thomas,* 809 F.2d 1371 (9th Cir. 1987) (years of good performance ratings until employee engaged in protected activity, then bad ratings). *Dohner v. Clearfield County,* 2009 U.S. Dist. LEXIS 77121 (W.D. Pa. 2009) (termination within one month of protected disclosure evidence of causation). *Stegall v. Citadel Broadcasting Company,* 350 F.3d 1061 (9th Cir. 2003) ("timing of adverse action can provide strong evidence of retaliation"). *Lindsay v. Yates,* 578 F.3d 407 (6th Cir. 2009) (close temporal proximity circumstantial evidence of causation). *Wallace v. DTG Operations,* 442 F.3d 1112 (8th Cir. 2006) (timing part of overall record justifying finding of retaliation). *Bechtel Construction v. SOL,* 50 F.3d 926, 934 (11th Cir. 1995) (employee "terminated shortly after he complained" raised an "inference of causation"). *Housing Works, Inc v. City of New York,* 72 F. Supp. 2d 402, 422 (S.D.N.Y. 1999). *Ellis Fischel State Cancer Hosp. v. Marshall,* 629 F.2d 563 (8th Cir. 1980). *Moon v. Transportation Drivers, Inc.* 836 F.2d 226, 229 (6th Cir. 1987) (adverse action shortly after the employee engaged in protected activity). *Jim Causley Pontiac v. NLRB,* 620 F.2d 122, 125 (6th Cir. 1980). *Dietz v. Cypress Semiconductor,* 2014-SOX-2 (DOL ARB) (actions taken by employer after protected disclosures).

Temporal proximity meets "Contributing Factor" test.	*Collins v. Beazer Homes,* 334 F. Supp. 2d 1365 (N.D. Ga. 2004) (contributing factor test); *Vieques Air Link v. DOL,* 437 F.3d 102 (1st Cir. 2006) (contributing factor test); *Fato v. Vartan National Bank,* 2009 U.S. Dist. LEXIS 620 (M.D. Pa).
Lack of temporal proximity.	*Farrell v. Planters Lifesavers,* 206 F.3d 271 (3rd Cir. 2000) ("when temporal proximity between protected activity and allegedly retaliatory conduct is missing, courts may look to the intervening period for other evidence of retaliatory animus").
	Mandell v. County of Suffolk, 316 F.3d 368 (2nd Cir. 2003) (long lapse of time between protected disclosures and denial of promotion not, per se, grounds to dismiss plaintiff's case).
	Riess v. Nucor Corp., 2008-STA-11 (DOL ARB, Nov. 30, 2010) (the closer the temporal proximity, stronger the inference).
	Pardo-Kronemann v. Jackson, 541 F.Supp.2d 210 (D.D.C. 2008); *Porter v. Cal. Dept.,* 419 F.3d 885 (9th Cir. 2005) (causal connection found based on "first opportunity" to retaliate).

M. Unfounded Allegations/Lawsuits Against Employees/References Disclosing Protected Activity

Making "baseless allegations" against employees. Accusing employees of being terrorists. Reporting employees to INS to try to have them deported.	*Centeno-Bernuy v. Perry,* 302 F. Supp. 2d 128 (W.D.N.Y. 2003). *Sure-Tan v. NLRB,* 467 U.S. 883 (1984) (reporting employees to INS for deportation in retaliation for asserting workplace rights constitutes an unfair labor practice).
Filing baseless lawsuit against employees in response to protected activities.	*Bill Johnson's Restaurants, Inc. v NLRB,* 461 U.S. 731 (1983); *Martin v. Gingerbread House,* 977 F.2d 1405 (10th Cir. 1992); *EEOC v. Outback Steakhouse,* 75 F. Supp. 2d 756 (N.D. Ohio 1999).
References that inform new employers that employee engaged in protected activity.	*Johnston v. Davis Security,* 217 F. Supp. 2d 1224 (D. Utah 2002) ("calling and telling her new employer that she was suing"). *Gaballa v. Atlantic Group,* 94-ERA-9 (Secretary of Labor, January 18, 1996) (nuclear whistleblower case). *Earwood v. Dart Container,* 93-STA-16 (Secretary of Labor, December 7, 1994) (surface transportation whistleblower case).

N. Warning or Prohibition Against Blowing the Whistle

Warning not to "push" complaints.	*EEOC v. Thomas Dodge Corp.*, 2009 U.S. Dist. LEXIS 24838 (E.D.N.Y.) (warning by direct supervisor "not to push" complaints).
Warning to "keep mouth shut."	*Mandell v. County of Suffolk*, 316 F.3d 368 (2nd Cir. 2003) (supervisor telling plaintiff to "keep his mouth shut").
Warning not to make "unsubstantiated charges" against company.	*Simas v. First Citizen*, 170 F.3d 37 (1st Cir. 1999) (warning not to make "unsubstantiated charges" against company direct evidence of animus).
Requiring employee to sign waiver of rights to sue employers for blacklisting under the ERA as a condition ofn employment constituted discrimination.	*Rudd v. Westinghouse Hanford Co.*, 88-ERA-33, D&O of Remand by ARB, at 8 (November 10, 1997).
Restrictions that interfere with an employee's right to engage in protected activity violate the whistleblower laws.	*CL&P v. DOL*, 85 F.3d 89 (2nd Cir. 1996).
Interrogation of employees regarding protected activity.	*Fasold v. Justice*, 409 F.3d 178 (3rd Cir. 2005) (questioning employee about his complaint).

CHECKLIST 6

Discovery in Whistleblower Cases: Obtaining the Evidence Needed to Win a Case Against an Employer

A. Whistleblowers Have a Right to Broad Discovery in Their Retaliation Cases

Broad right to discovery.	*McDonnell Douglas v. Green*, 411 U.S. 792, 804–05 (1973) (recognizing importance of pretrial discovery to prove pretext in employment cases).
	Hollander v. American Cyanamid Co., 895 F.2d 80, 85 (2nd Cir. 1990) (broad discovery in employment cases).
	Morrison v. City and County of Denver, 80 F.R.D. 289, 292 (D. Col. 1978) ("very broad scope of discovery" because "plaintiffs must rely on circumstantial evidence" to prove case).
	Jones et al. v. Forrest City Grocery Inc., 2007 U.S. Dist. LEXIS 19482 (E.D. Ark. 2007) (scope of discovery broad, not limited to admissible evidence, issues raised in the pleadings or the merits of a case).
	Williams v. the Art Institute of Atlanta, 2006 U.S. Dist. LEXIS 62585 (N.D. Ga. 2006) (permitting discovery into company's affirmative defenses).
	Sallis v. Univ. of Mich., 408 F.3d 470, 478 (8th Cir. 2005) ("the Supreme Court has acknowledged . . . liberal civil discovery rules give plaintiffs broad access to document their claims.").
Basic rules of discovery set forth in Federal Rules of Civil Procedure (FRCP).	General Scope of Discovery, Obtaining Protective Orders and Mandatory Disclosure Rules. FRCP 26.
	Rule permitting employees to obtain documents from employers and other witnesses. FRCP 34.
	Rule permitting employees to depose (question under oath) witnesses. FRCP 30.
	Rules permitting employees to file written questions or requests for admission from their employer. FRCP 33 and 36.
	Rule concerning disclosure of expert witness discovery. FRCP 26(a)(2).

Conducting depositions as an important discovery tool in whistleblower cases.	*Naftchi v. N.Y.U.*, 172 F.R.D. 130 (S.D.N.Y. 1997) ("exceedingly difficult" to justify blocking deposition of witness).
	Alexander v. FBI, 186 F.R.D. 113, 121 (D.D.C. 1998) (depositions "rank high in the hierarchy of pretrial, truth-finding mechanisms").
	Daniels v. AMTRAK, 110 F.R.D. 160 (S.D.N.Y.) (discovery materials may be withheld until after deposition is conducted to preserve the opportunity to impeach witness).
Private confidentiality agreements do not limit discovery.	*Zoom Imaging v. St. Luke's Hospital*, 513 F. Supp. 2d 411 (E.D. Pa. 2007).
	U.S. v. Davis, 702 F.2d 418, 422 (2nd Cir. 1983).
Broad right to obtain computer-related discovery.	*In re: Yasmin*, 2010 U.S. Dist. LEXIS 14092 (S.D. Ill.) (definition of "documents" included "electronically stored information on hard drives, USB or thumb drives, databases, computers, handheld devices, floppy disks, CD-ROM, magnetic tape, optical disks, or other devices for digital data storage or transmittal" and "e-mail, removable computer storage media, document image files, Web pages" and "digital records").
Sanctions against employers for hiding documents requested in discovery.	*Roadway Express v. DOL*, 495 F.3d 477 (7th Cir. 2007); *Dann v. Bechtel*, 2005-SDW-4/5/6 (DOL ALJ Aug. 26, 2005); *Beliveau v. Naval Undersea Warfare Center*, 97-SDW-1 (DOJ ALJ June 29, 2000).

B. Ten Key Areas of Discovery

1. Disparate Treatment: Comparison between How Whistleblower Treated/Disciplined Compared to Other Employees

Employee disciplinary records.	*Morrison v. Philadelphia Housing Authority*, 203 F.R.D. 195, 197 (E.D. Pa. 2001) (disciplinary records of other employees).
	Northern v. City of Phil., 2000 U.S. Dist. LEXIS 4278 (E.D. Pa.) (disciplinary records of employees accused of violating same rule as plaintiff).
Employee performance records.	*Ellison v. Patterson-UTI*, 2009 U.S. Dist. LEXIS 88313 (S.D. Tex. 2009) (upholding request for "any and all documents evaluating the work of plaintiff or comparing his job and work performance to other employees of defendants").

Proof of pretext.	*Onwuka v. Federal Express,* 178 F.R.D. 508 (D. Minn. 1997) ("wide discovery of personnel files" to "demonstrate pretext"). *Coughlin v. Lee,* 946 F.2d 1152, 1159 (5th Cir. 1991) (discovery of personnel files of other employees to demonstrate pretext).
Statistical evidence.	*Lovoi v. Apple One Employment Services,* 2000 U.S. Dist. LEXIS 18811 (E.D. La. 2000); (discovery of list of previous employees).
Documents showing egregious acts of similarly situated employees who were not disciplined.	*Northern v. City of Philadelphia,* 2000 U.S. Dist. LEXIS 4278 (E.D. Pa. 2000) (personnel files of "similarly situated" employees). *Graham v. Long Island Rail Road,* 230 F.3d 34, 39 (2nd Cir. 2000) (records of other employees relevant in case).
Company practices.	*Schreiber v. State of Nebraska and the Nebraska State Patrol,* 2006 U.S. Dist. LEXIS 78211 (D. Neb. 2006). *Williams v. The Art Institute of Atlanta,* 2006 U.S. Dist. LEXIS 62585 (N.D. Ga. 2006) (company handbooks and documents governing corporate policy). *Gutierrez v. Johnson and Johnson, Inc.,* 2002 U.S. Dist. LEXIS 15418 (D. N.J. 2002) (only sought parent's headquarters practices and were therefore not overly broad). *EEOC v. Lockheed,* 2007 U.S. Dist. LEXIS 39342 (D. Haw. 2007) (documents produced for all entities plaintiff worked).
Personnel files.	*Beasley v. First American Real Estate Information Services, Inc.,* 2005 U.S. Dist. LEXIS 34030 (N.D. Tex. 2005) (files containing ratings of employees are discoverable except for Social Security information). *Morrison v. Philadelphia Housing Authority,* 203 F.R.D. 195, 197 (E.D. Pa. 2001) (disciplinary records are clearly relevant to evidence in a disparate treatment claim). *MacIntosh v. Building Owners,* 231 F.R.D. 106, 108–09 (D.D.C. 2005). *Ellison v. Patterson-UTI,* 2009 U.S. Dist. LEXIS 88313 (S.D. Tex. 2009) (upholding document request for personnel files of employees who replaced discharged plaintiff) (upholding interrogatory question to identify other employees, including names, addresses, dates of hire, dates of separation, and job position). *Duke v. University of Texas,* 729 F.2d 994 (5th Cir. 1984) (companywide discovery on information concerning employees).

Past practice of employer in similar situations.	*Timmons v. Mattingly Testing*, 95 ERA-40 (DOL ARB, June 21, 1996) (past practices "relevant to determining . . . disparate treatment, which may provide highly probative evidence of retaliatory intent").
Time frame.	*Briddel v. Saint Gobain*, 233 F.R.D. 57, 60 (D. Mass. 2005) (employee files discoverable for time periods ranging from three to ten years).

2. Use Discovery to Obtain Information on Investigations

Investigative reports.	*St. Paul Fire and Marine Ins. Co. v. SSA Gulf Terminals, Inc.*, 2002 U.S. Dist. LEXIS 11776 (E.D. La. 2002) (in-house insurance documents are not protected by the work product privilege). *Fernandez v. Navistar International Corp. et al.*, 2009 SOX-43 (DOL ALJ, October 16, 2009) (reports from investigation conducted by a law firm and distributed to third party).
Self-critical analysis (discovery into internal corporate reviews of employee concerns or internal peer reviews).	*Univ. of Pa. v. EEOC*, 493 U.S. 182 (1990) (declining to permit a company's assertion of a so-called "self-critical analysis privilege" to block discovery). *Zoom Imaging, L.P. v. St. Luke's Hospital and Health Network*, 513 F. Supp. 2d 411, 413 (E.D. Pa. 2007).
Attorney-client documents provided to the FBI during investigation ordered produced.	*Beliveau v. Naval Warfare Center*, 1997-SDW-6 (DOL ALJ, May 31, 2000.) *U.S. v. Quest Diagnostics*, 734 F.3d 154 (2nd Cir. 2013) (restrictions on attorney whistleblowers using privileged information).
Work product doctrine not applicable.	*St. Paul Fire v. SSA Gulf Terminals*, 2002 LEXIS 11776 (E.D. La.) (work product doctrine not applicable to in-house investigative report).
"Hotline Reports" discoverable.	*McDougal-Wilson v. Goodyear*, 232 F.R.D. 246 (E.D.N.C. 2005) (compelling production of "reports on concerns" made on the company "hotline").
Corporate communications with government regulators.	*Winstanley v. Royal Consumer Information*, 2006 U.S. Dist. LEXIS 44702 (D. Ariz).

3. Try to Obtain Access to Information on Investigations Conducted by Corporate Attorneys

Investigative report prepared by attorney.	*Walker v. County of Contra Costa, et al.,* 227 F.R.D. 529, 534 (N.D.Cal. 2005) (discoverable when company asserted affirmative defense based on internal investigative findings). *Matter of the Application of Vincenzo Nieri, for subpoenas pursuant to 28 USC 1782,* 2000 U.S. Dist. LEXIS 540 (S.D.N.Y. 2000) (attorney-client privilege did not per se protect in-house investigative reports). But see *In re KBR,* 796 F.3d 137 (D.C. Cir. 2015) (prohibiting disclosure of investigatory reports prepared for an attorney).
Memoranda of interviews conducted by attorney for city employees.	*Reitz v. Mt. Juliet,* 680 F.Supp.2d 888 (M.D. Tenn. 2010) (use of attorney report to justify defense results in waiver of "work product" privilege).
Correspondence to general counsel.	*Ovesen v. Mitsubishi Heavy Industries of America Inc.,* 2009 U.S. Dist. LEXIS 9762 (S.D. N.Y. 2009) (the general counsel served as vice president of the defendant's predecessor company as well). *Sokol v. Wyeth, Inc.,* 2008 U.S. Dist. LEXIS 60976 (S.D. N.Y. 2008) (communications between attorney and third parties not represented by counsel).
Information compiled for federal investigators or pursuant to law.	*Georgia Power Co. v. EEOC,* 412 F.2d 462, 468 (5th Cir. 1969).

4. Obtain Discovery from Government Regulators

Correspondence between agencies/with agencies.	*Winstanley v. Royal Consumer Information Products, Inc., et al.,* 2006 U.S. Dist. LEXIS 44702 (D. Ariz. 2006). *Winstanley v. Royal Consumer,* 2006 U.S. Dist. LEXIS 44702 (D.C. Ariz. 2006).
Copies of complaints filed by employees with state or federal regulatory agency.	*Owens v. Sprint/United Management Company,* 221 F.R.D. 649, 653 (D. Kan. 2004) (other employee complaints filed with state or federal regulatory bodies).
Statements of employees gathered by government agency.	*Chao v. General Interior System, Inc.,* 2009 U.S. Dist. LEXIS 90066 (N.D. N.Y. 2009) (rejecting informant's privilege).
Compelling testimony of public officials.	*United States v. Lake County Board of Commissioners,* 233 F.R.D. 523, 528 (N.D. Ind. 2005). *Chaplaincy of Full Gospel Churches v. Johnson,* 217 F.R.D. 250, 256 (D.D.C. 2003).

Discovery into government's decision-making process.	*Jones v. the City of College Park, Georgia*, 237 F.R.D. 517, 520-521 (N.D. Ga. 2006) (the government's interest in protecting these communications is outweighed by the plaintiff's interest in disclosure). *Tri-State Hospital Supply Corporation v. United States of America*, 226 F.R.D. 118, 130 (D.D.C. 2005). *Anderson v. Cornejo*, 2001 U.S. Dist. LEXIS 10312 (N.D. Ill. 2001).
Government's deliberative process privilege waived if evidence of misconduct.	*Alexander v. FBI*, 186 F.R.D. 154, 164 (D.D.C. 1999). *In re Sealed Case*, 121 F.3d 729, 746 (D.C. Cir. 1997).
Deliberative process privilege waived if government's intent at issue.	*Tri-State Hosp. v. U.S.*, 226 F.R.D. 118, 134-35 (D.D.C. 2005); *U.S. v. Lake County*, 233 F.R.D. 523 (N.D. Ind. 2005). *Jones v. City of College Park*, 237 F.R.D. 517 (N.D. Ga. 2006).
Law enforcement privilege may be waived.	*Tri-State Hosp. v. U.S.*, 226 F.R.D. 118 (D.D.C. 2005) (citing the Rizzo factors).
Government employee interview statements.	*Reitz v. City of Mt. Juliet*, 680 F.Supp.2d 888 (M.D. Tenn. 2010).
Information may be obtained from federal government agencies under Freedom of Information Act.	Freedom of Information Act, 5 U.S.C. 552.
Government agencies must produce records on individuals maintained in a "system of records."	Privacy Act, 5 U.S.C. 552a.

5. Use Discovery to Prove That the Employer Engaged in Misconduct or Disregarded the Law

Discovery into company wrongdoing.	*In the Matter of the Application of Vincenzo Nieri, for subpoenas pursuant to 28 USC 1782,* 2000 U.S. Dist. LEXIS 540 (S.D.N.Y. 2000) ("the extent and circumstances of any wrongdoing . . . might help to explain why the company fired [the whistleblower]").
Hostility toward regulations/ deliberate violations of law or safety rules.	*Timmons v. Mattingly Testing Services,* 95-ERA-40 (DOL ARB, June 21, 1996) (opportunity for broad discovery critical for achieving the safety purposes behind the nuclear whistle-blower law) (evidence of "deliberate violations" of government regulations relevant). *Khandelwal v. Southern California Edison,* 97-ERA-6 (DOL ARB) (March 31, 1998) ("discovery in a whistleblower proceeding may well uncover questionable employment practices and nuclear safety deficiencies about which the government should know"). *Tipton v. Indiana Michigan Power Co.,* 2002-ERA-30 (ALJ June 29, 2004). *McNeil v. Crane Nuclear, Inc.,* 2001-ERA-3 (ALJ Oct. 4, 2001). *James v. Pritts McEnany Roofing, Inc.,* 96-ERA-5 (ALJ Aug. 22, 1996).
Manager failed to follow findings of government investigation.	*Northern v. City of Philadelphia,* 2000 U.S. Dist. LEXIS 4278 (E.D. Pa. 2000).

6. Get Every Document the Company Has About the Whistleblower

Court upheld this document request filed by employee: "Any and all documents evaluating the work of plaintiff or comparing his job and work performance to other employees of defendants."	*Ellison v. Patterson-UTI,* 2009 U.S. Dist. LEXIS 88313 (S.D. Tex. 2009).
Information on employee's pay and benefits.	*McDougal-Wilson v. Goodyear,* 232 F.R.D. 246 (E.D. N.C. 2005).
Employee's own personnel file.	*Milner v. National School,* 73 F.R.D. 628, 633 (E.D. Pa. 1977).

7. Learn About Witnesses and Obtain the Personnel Files on
   Supervisors Who Engaged in Retaliation

Personnel files on managers and employee's supervisor.	*Williams v. The Art Institute of Atlanta,* 2006 U.S. Dist. LEXIS 62585 (N.D. Ga. 2006) (supervisor's file); *Owens v. Sprint,* 221 F.R.D. 649 (D. Kan. 2004) (supervisor's file); *Phillips v. Berlex Laboratories, Inc.,* 2006 U.S. Dist. LEXIS 27389 (D. Conn.) (supervisor's file). *Cardenas v. The Prudential Insurance Co. of America,* 2003 U.S. Dist. LEXIS 1825 (D. Minn. 2003) (personnel files of company CEO and other top managers).
Deposition of high-ranking executives.	*Blanton v. Biogen IDEC, Inc.,* 2006-SOX-4 (DOL ALJ, April 18, 2006) (allowed because inquiry might lead to admissible evidence, despite the executive seemingly had no "superior and unique" knowledge).
Personnel files on employees who engaged in harassment.	*Cason v. Builders,* 159 F. Supp. 2d 242, 247 (W.D.N.C. 2001) (personnel files of "harassers" discoverable).
Information on conduct and character of witness.	*Phillips v. Berlex Laboratories, Inc.,* 2006 U.S. Dist. LEXIS 27389 (D. Conn. 2006) (evidence of the conduct or character of witness that suggests testimony may be untruthful).
Home addresses and phone numbers of witnesses.	*Phillips v. Berlex Laboratories, Inc.,* 2006 U.S. Dist. LEXIS 27389 (D. Conn. 2006).
The "thoughts" and "mental impressions" of decision makers are discoverable.	*U.S. v. Lake County,* 233 F.R.D. 523 (N.D. Ind. 2005); *RECAP v. Middletown,* 294 F.3d 35, 49–53 (2nd Cir. 2002).

8. Obtain Documents on the Prior Discrimination Complaints Filed Against the Company

Evidence that company or manager discriminated or retaliated against other similarly situated employees.	*Sprint v. Mendelson,* 552 U.S. 379 (2008) (standard for discovery regarding discrimination or retaliation against other employees). *Cardenas, Muldoon, Struzyk v. The Prudential Insurance Co. of America;* 2003 U.S. Dist. LEXIS 1825 (D. Minn. 2003) (company-wide information concerning past history of employees is relevant to discrimination cases and is therefore discoverable). *Williams v. The Art Institute of Atlanta,* 2006 U.S. Dist. LEXIS 62585 (N.D. Ga. 2006). *Jones et. al v. Forrest City Grocery Inc.,* 2007 U.S. Dist. LEXIS 19482 (E.D. Ark. 2007). *Equal Employment Opportunity Commission v. Lockheed Martin,* 2007 U.S. Dist. LEXIS 39342 (D. Haw. 2007) (documents are relevant to case and had to be produced despite the burden of producing such large amounts of documents, discovery limited to a reasonable number of years prior to discrimination).

9. Beware of Employer's Efforts to Abuse Discovery or Obtain Damaging Information on Whistleblower

Limits on employer's use of discovery to obtain psychological or medical information on employee.	*Fox v. Gates Corp.,* 179 F.R.D. 303, 307 (D. Col. 1998) (setting forth conditions in which an employee would not be required to submit to an independent medical examination conducted by doctor for employer) (majority rule).
	Vanderbilt v. Town of Chilmark, 174 F.R.D. 225 (D. Mass. 1997) (narrow view of waiver; rejecting discovery and finding no waiver of patient privilege simply for seeking emotional distress damages).
	Jackson v. Chubb Corporation, 193 F.R.D. 216, 225 (D. N.J. 2000); (records not privileged because plaintiff placed her current medical condition at issue) (rejecting holding in *Vanderbilt*).
	Williams v. the Art Institute of Atlanta, 2006 U.S. Dist. LEXIS 62585 (N.D. Ga. 2006) (medical records discoverable, provided proper protective order issued).
Blocking discovery against journalist who obtained information from whistleblower.	*Management Information Technologies v. Alyeska Pipeline,* 151 F.R.D. 471 (D.D.C. 1993).
Denying request for protective order shielding information produced in discovery from public access.	*Avirgan v. Hull,* 154 F.R.D. 252 (D.D.C. 1987); *Alexander v. FBI,* 186 F.R.D. 60, 65-66 (D.D.C. 1998).
Shielding whistleblowers from identifying their confidential sources that are employed by the company.	*Management Information Technologies v. Alyeska Pipeline,* 151 F.R.D. 478 (D.D.C. 1993).

10. Beware of Employers Using Discovery to Try to Obtain Evidence that the Whistleblower Engaged in Misconduct Such as Lying on a Résumé or Stealing Company Documents

	McKennon v. Nashville Banner, 513 U.S. 352 (1995) (no fishing expeditions into employee misconduct under the "after-acquired evidence" doctrine permitted).
	Nesselrotte v. Allegheny Energy, Inc., 2007 U.S. Dist. LEXIS 79147 (W.D. Pa. 2007) (plaintiff's removal of documents from work could give rise to an employer defense).

CHECKLIST 7

Dodd-Frank Act, Securities Fraud, and FCPA "Q&As"

Procedures for Obtaining Rewards from the Securities and Exchange Commission

(Some of the following "Q&A's" were taken directly from the "Q&A" fact sheet published in August 2011 by the SEC's Whistleblower Office, www.sec.gov/whistleblower)

What is the SEC Whistleblower Program?	The Whistleblower Program was created by Congress to provide monetary incentives for individuals to come forward and report possible violations of the federal securities laws to the SEC. Under the program eligible whistleblowers (defined below) are entitled to an award of between 10% and 30% of the monetary sanctions collected in actions brought by the SEC and related actions brought by other regulatory and law enforcement authorities. The Program also prohibits retaliation by employers against employees who provide the SEC with information about possible securities violations. (This Q&A taken from SEC Fact Sheet.)

Who is an eligible whistleblower?	An "eligible whistleblower" entitled to collect a reward is a person who voluntarily provides the SEC with original information about a possible violation of the federal securities laws that has occurred, is ongoing, or is about to occur. The information provided must lead to a successful SEC action resulting in an order of monetary sanctions exceeding $1 million. One or more people are allowed to act as a whistleblower, but companies or organizations cannot qualify as whistleblowers. You are not required to be an employee of the company to submit information about that company.
	See SEC Rule 17 C.F.R. § 240.21F-2. (This portion of the Q&A taken from SEC Fact Sheet.)
	Under the Dodd-Frank Act and SEC rules, "any individual" or group of individuals may qualify as a whistleblower. This includes persons who are not employees and persons who obtain their information on the basis of conducting an "independent analysis" of public information. See SEC Rule 17 C.F.R. § 240.21F-2(a) and F-4(b)(3).
	The total "sanction" collected by the SEC must total more than $1 million dollars. The term "sanction" is a broad definition and includes all monies obtained by the SEC in response to any enforcement action or multiple actions taken against the wrongdoer. 17 C.F.R. § 240.21F-4(d) and (e). The SEC rules define sanction as: "any money, including penalties, disgorgement, and interest, ordered to be paid or any money deposited into a disgorgement fund . . . as a result of a Commission action or a related action." 17 C.F.R. § 240.21F-4(e).
	To qualify as a whistleblower entitled to a reward you must submit your application for a reward "in accordance with the procedures and conditions" published by the SEC in Rules 17 C.F.R. § 240.21F-4, F-8 and F-9.
	See SEC Rule 17 C.F.R. § 240.21F-2(a)(2).
What does it mean to "voluntarily" provide information?	Your information is provided "voluntarily" if you provide it to the SEC or another regulatory or law enforcement authority before (i) the SEC requests it from you or your lawyer or (ii) Congress, another regulatory or enforcement agency, or self-regulatory organization (such as FINRA) asks you to provide the information in connection with an investigation or certain examinations or inspections.
	See SEC Rule 17 C.F.R. 240.21F-4(a). (This Q&A taken from SEC Fact Sheet)

What is "original information?"	"Original information" is information derived from your independent knowledge (facts known to you that are not derived from publicly available sources) or independent analysis (evaluation of information that may be publicly available but that reveals information that is not generally known) that is not already known by the SEC. So if the SEC received your information previously from another person, that information will not be original information unless you were the original source of the information that the other person submitted. *See* SEC Rule 17 C.F.R. § 240.21F-4(b)(1). (This Q&A taken from SEC Fact Sheet.)
How might my information "lead to" a successful SEC action?	Your information satisfies the "led to" criterion if your information causes the SEC to open a new investigation, re-open a previously closed investigation, or pursue a new line of inquiry in connection with an ongoing investigation, and the SEC brings a successful enforcement action based at least in part on the information you provided. Additionally, you may still be eligible if your information relates to an ongoing examination or investigation, if the information you provide significantly contributes to the success of the SEC's resulting enforcement action. You may also be eligible if you report your information internally first to your company, and the company later reports your information to the SEC, or reports the results of an internal investigation that was prompted by your information, as long as you also report directly to the SEC within 120 days. *See* SEC Rule 17 C.F.R. § 240.21F-4(c). (This Q&A taken from SEC Fact Sheet.)

I work at a company with an internal compliance process. Can I report internally and still be eligible for a whistle-blower award?	Although internal reporting is not required to be considered for an award, you may be eligible for an award for information you reported internally if you also report the information to the SEC within 120 days of reporting it internally. Under these circumstances, the SEC will consider your place in line for determining whether your information is "original information" to be the date you reported it internally. In addition, if the company to which you reported conducts an investigation and reports the results to the SEC, you will benefit from all the information the company's investigation turns up when the SEC is considering whether you should receive an award and if so where the award should fall in the 10% to 30% range. *See* SEC Rules 17 C.F.R. § 240.21F-4(b)(7) and F-4(c)(3). (This portion of the Q&A taken from SEC Fact Sheet.) *Best Practice:* If you report your allegations through a company's internal legal or compliance program, you should file your SEC Reward application no later then 120 days after making the internal disclosure. In this manner, you are covered if either the company self-reports the violation to the SEC or if the company takes no action, and the SEC independently finds the violation. The 120-day rule is described by the SEC as follows: "(If you initially file a concern internally with the company) you must also submit the same information to the Commission in accordance with the procedures set forth in § 240.21F-9 within 120 days of providing it to the entity." 17 C.F.R. § 240.21F-4(c)(3). Additionally, you must be able to fully document the fact that you made the internal disclosure and the information provided to corporate compliance. 17 C.F.R. § 240.21F-4(b)(7) ("You must establish the effective date of any prior disclosure . . . to the Commission's satisfaction.")
Can I report violations directly to the SEC, even if my company has an internal corporate compliance program?	Yes. The Dodd-Frank Act and the SEC rules permit you to report violations directly to the SEC or other appropriate law enforcement entities, without first reporting the violations to your supervisor or to your company's compliance department. SEC Commentary on Final Rule, 76 *Federal Register* 34300, 34301 (no requirement that whistleblowers report violations internally) (June 13, 2011); 17 C.F.R. § 240.21F-2 (retaliation prohibited if employee has a "reasonable belief" related to a "possible securities law violation" and reports this information to the SEC).

Are there any advantages to reporting violations internally to my company's audit committee or compliance department?	Yes. The SEC wanted to create a "clear alternative path" giving employees a choice between filing their complaints directly with the SEC or with their company's internal compliance program. To make this choice real, the SEC authorized the payment of rewards to employees regardless of whether the employee made his or her initial disclosure to a compliance department or the SEC. The Commission also created "incentives for employees to utilize their company's internal compliance systems." SEC Commentary on Final Rule, 76 *Federal Register* 34300, 34322 (June 13, 2011).
	These incentives are as follows: (1) If you report a violation internally to the company's compliance program and the company investigates the allegation and self-reports the violation to the SEC, you can qualify for a reward based on the self-reported violations, even if your initial allegation resulted in the company discovering larger violations; (2) Provided you report your allegations to the SEC within 120 days of your internal report, you are entitled to a full reward based on your disclosures to internal compliance; (3) The SEC will take such reports into consideration when evaluating how large of a reward you should be granted; (4) Although not discussed in the SEC rules, if a company attempts to cover up your allegations, the ultimate sanctions issued by the SEC could be much larger than if the company was not caught trying to hide problems.
	The largest downside to making an internal report is an employee's loss of anonymity. Even if a company promises to keep a whistleblower's identity strictly confidential, there is still a significant risk that you will be identified by your employer/supervisor if you file an internal complaint.
	The SEC rules encouraging employees' utilization of internal compliance programs (and permitting employees to qualify for rewards based on those internal complaints) are set forth as follows:
	17 C.F.R. § 240.21F-4(b)(5), fully discussed in 76 *Federal Register* 3400, 34365 (whistleblower an "original source" entitled to a reward if his or her employer "self-reports" information to the SEC that the whistleblower initially reported to the company);
	17 C.F.R. § 240.21F-4(b)(7) (whistleblower who provided information to internal compliance program is considered an "original source" for qualifying for a reward);

	17 C.F.R. § 240.21F-4(c)(3) (information provided to a company's internal compliance program that results in a company self-reporting a violation will be credited to the whistleblower as constituting "information that leads to successful enforcement" of the law);
	17 C.F.R. § 240.21F-6(a)(4) (reward can be increased if employee first reported to internal compliance).

Can I blow the whistle if I work for a company's compliance department or if I have official responsibility for identifying violations?	Yes, provided that you meet any one of four requirements.
	The SEC rules have an initial disqualification for employees who perform compliance or audit-related functions. But this disqualification has four major exceptions. Based on these exceptions, most compliance-related employees should still be able to qualify for a reward. *See* SEC Rules 17 C.F.R. § 240.21F-4(b)(4)(iii) and (b)(4)(v).
	As a threshold matter, employees who "learn" of violations "in connection with" a company's internal compliance program are disqualified from obtaining whistleblower rewards. This disqualification includes directors and partners who learn about violations in "connection with the entity's processes for identifying, reporting, and addressing possible violations of law." Likewise, employees from outside firms hired to perform compliance or audit functions, employees from public accounting firms, and other compliance-related employees are all subject to the initial disqualification. SEC Rule 17 C.F.R. § 240.21F-4(b)(iii)(A)-(C).
	However, this disqualification terminates, and these compliance-related employees become completely eligible to file whistleblower claims and obtain large rewards, if any one of the following four exceptions is met. The four exceptions are:
	(1) The employee has a "reasonable basis" to believe that providing the information immediately to the SEC is "necessary to prevent" the company "from engaging in conduct that is likely to cause substantial injury to the financial interest" of the corporation or investors;
	(2) The employee has a "reasonable basis" to believe that the company is engaging in conduct "that will impede an investigation of the misconduct";
	(3) At least 120 days has elapsed since you provided the information to the relevant entity's audit committee, chief legal officer, chief compliance officer (or their equivalents), or your supervisor; or
	(4) At least 120 days has elapsed since you have personal awareness that your company's audit committee, chief legal officer, chief compliance officer (or their equivalents), or your supervisor were made aware of the information.
	See SEC Rules 17 C.F.R. § 240.21F-4(b)(4)(v)(A)-(C).

What if I blew the whistle to Congress or another government agency before I contacted the SEC?	You can still qualify for a full reward even if you initially provided your allegations to another government agency. If you provided information to another government agency before contacting the SEC, you should file your SEC reward application within 120 days of that communication. Under the SEC rules, you will be given full credit toward your reward for all the information you provided to "Congress, any other authority of the Federal government, a state Attorney General or securities regulatory authority, any self-regulatory organization, or the Public Company Accounting Oversight Board" provided you also file a formal request for a reward pursuant to SEC Rule 17 C.F.R. § 240.21F-9 within 120 days of the initial whistleblower disclosure. *See* SEC Rule 17 C.F.R. § 240.21F-4(b)(7).
How do I submit information under the SEC whistleblower program?	In order to qualify for an award under the whistleblower program, you must submit your information either through the SEC's online Tips, Complaints, and Referrals questionnaire or by completing the hardcopy Form TCR and mailing or faxing it to the SEC Office of the Whistleblower, 100 F Street NE, Mail Stop 5971, Washington, DC 20549, Fax (703) 813-9322. *See* SEC Rule 17 C.F.R. § 240.21F-9. (This Q&A taken from SEC Fact Sheet.)
Can I submit my information anonymously?	Yes, you may submit anonymously. To do so, you must have an attorney represent you in connection with your submission. You must also provide the attorney with a completed Form TCR signed under penalty of perjury at the time you make your anonymous submission. *See* SEC Rule 17 C.F.R. § 240.21F-7. (This Q&A taken from SEC Fact Sheet.)
Can I still provide the SEC with information even if I signed a confidentiality agreement with my employer?	Yes. It is illegal for any person or company to interfere with a whistleblower's right to lawfully provide information to the SEC. The SEC rule on this matter is very clear: "No person may take any action to impede an individual from communicating directly with the Commission staff about a possible securities law violation, including enforcing, or threatening to enforce, a confidentiality agreement . . . ." *See* SEC Rule 17 C.F.R. § 240.21F-17. Such restrictions also would violate the federal obstruction of justice statute. 18 U.S.C. § 1513(e).

Will the SEC keep my identity confidential?	Whether or not you seek anonymity, the SEC has stated that it is committed to protecting your identity to the fullest extent possible. For example, the SEC maintains that it will not disclose your identity in response to requests under the Freedom of Information Act. However, there are limits to the SEC's ability to shield your identity and in certain circumstances the SEC must disclose it to outside entities. For example, in an administrative or court proceeding, the SEC may be required to produce documents or other information that would reveal your identity. In addition, as part of the SEC's ongoing investigatory responsibilities, the SEC may use information you have provided during the course of the investigation. In appropriate circumstances, the SEC may also provide information, subject to confidentiality requirements, to other governmental or regulatory entities. *See* SEC Rule 17 C.F.R. § 240.21F-7. (This Q&A taken from SEC Fact Sheet.) *Best Practice:* If you do not want your employer to learn your identity, file the claim anonymously. During the investigation of your claim, you can always make the decision to tell the SEC who you are, but if you do not file anonymously, there is a risk that the SEC may expose your identity.
How will I learn about the opportunity to apply for an award?	The SEC will post on its website notices of actions exceeding $1 million in sanctions so that anyone who believes they may be eligible will have an opportunity to apply for a whistleblower award. In addition, if the SEC has been working with you and believes you may be eligible, the SEC has committed to contacting you or your attorney directly to alert you to the opportunity to apply for an award. This posting triggers a requirement that the whistleblower file a new Form WB-APP with the SEC within 90 days. *See* SEC Rule 17 C.F.R. § 240.21F-10. (This Q&A taken from SEC Fact Sheet.)
How do I apply for an award?	Once the SEC posts on its website confirmation that a sanction was obtained against the company you blew the whistle on, you must complete and return Form WB-APP within 90 calendar days to the Office of the Whistleblower via mail to 100 F Street NE, Mail Stop 5971, Washington DC 20549, or by fax (703) 813-9322. *See* SEC Rule 17 C.F.R. § 240.21F-10. (This Q&A taken from SEC Fact Sheet.)

What factors does the SEC consider in determining the amount of the award?	The Rules require that the SEC consider many factors in determining the amount of an award based on the unique facts and circumstances of each case.
	The SEC may *increase* the award percentage based on the existence of these factors: (1) The significance of the information you provided the SEC to the success of any proceeding brought against wrongdoers; (2) The extent of the assistance you provide to the SEC investigation and any successful proceeding; (3) The SEC's law enforcement interest in deterring violations of the securities laws by making awards to whistleblowers who provide information that leads to the successful enforcement of these laws; (4) Whether, and the extent to which, you participated in your company's internal compliance systems, such as, for example, reporting the possible securities violations through internal whistleblower, legal, or compliance procedures before, or at the same time, you reported them to the SEC.
	The SEC may *decrease* the award percentage based on the existence of these factors: (1) If you were a participant in, or culpable for the securities law violation(s) you reported; (2) If you unreasonably delayed reporting the violation(s) to the SEC; (3) If you interfered with your company's internal compliance and reporting systems, such as, for example, making false statements to your compliance department that hindered its efforts to investigate possible wrongdoing.
	See SEC Rule 17 C.F.R. § 240.21F-6. (This Q&A taken from SEC Fact Sheet.)
Can I qualify for a reward if I participated in the violations at issue?	Yes. One of the central premises of the rewards law is its intent to induce insiders with direct knowledge of fraud to report these violations. The Dodd-Frank Act does not include any provision for disqualifying a whistleblower from obtaining rewards because the whistleblower participated in the underlying violations.
	The SEC Commission, in enacting its final rules, cited with approval from the original 1863 legislative history of the False Claims Act (the first whistleblower rewards law), where the principle Senate sponsor of the bill stated: "I have based (the first whistleblower rewards law) on the old-fashioned idea of holding out a temptation and 'setting a rogue to catch a rogue,' which is the safest and most expeditious way to bring rogues to justice." *See* SEC Final Rule Commentary, 76 *Federal Register* 34200, 34350 (June 13, 2011).
	See SEC Rule 17 C.F.R. § 240.21F-6(b)(1).

Can I qualify for a reward if I am convicted of a criminal violation or if I directed, planned, or initiated the violations in question?	It depends. If you are convicted of a crime related to the violations you have reported, you may be disqualified completely from obtaining any reward. *See* SEC Rule 17 C.F.R. § 240.21F-8(c)(3).
	Even if you are not convicted of a crime, the SEC may reduce the amount of a reward for which you would otherwise have been entitled if the money it obtained was based on violations that you "substantially" caused and you "directed, planned, or initiated." *See* SEC Rule 17 C.F.R. § 240.21F-16.
	However, the SEC rules make it very clear that whistleblowers who engaged in misconduct could still be eligible for rewards: "(W)e do not believe that a per se exclusion for culpable whistleblowers is consistent with Section 21F of the Exchange Act." *See* SEC Final Rule Commentary, 76 *Federal Register* 34200, 34350 (June 13, 2011).
	Blowing the whistle to the SEC does not entitle you to amnesty from criminal prosecution or immunity from other enforcement actions. The SEC has, however, committed itself to considering the level of cooperation provided by a whistleblower in weighing whether or not to prosecute an individual. The rules the Commission will apply in these circumstances are set forth in its "Policy Statement Concerning Cooperation by Individuals in Investigations and Related Enforcement Actions," 17 C.F.R. § 202.12.
	See SEC Rule 17 C.F.R. § 240.21F-15 and F-16.
If my information leads to a monetary sanction issued by another federal agency, can I still obtain a reward?	The SEC rules permit whistleblowers to obtain rewards based on monies obtained by the government in a "related action." SEC Rule 17 C.F.R. § 240.21F-3(b).
	A qualified "related action" is a "judicial or administrative action that is brought by" the U.S. Attorney General, an "appropriate regulatory agency," a "self-regulatory organization, or a state Attorney General in a criminal case."
	A "related action" must be "based on the same original information that the whistleblower voluntarily provided" to the SEC, and also must have resulted in the SEC's issuance of monetary sanctions of over $1,000,000.
	The filing procedures for obtaining a reward based on a "related action" are complex.
	First, in order to qualify for a reward based on a "related action," the whistleblower must file SEC Form WB-APP seeking a reward flowing for the "related action."

Second, if a final order was issued awarding sanctions in the related action *before* you filed your initial WB-APP application with the Commission, you are required to include both your request for a Commission reward and a "related action" reward in the same initial WB-APP application.

However, if a final order awarding sanctions in a "related action" is issued *after* you filed your initial WB-APP application, you must file a *new* WB-APP application "within 90 days" of the award of sanctions in the related action.

Best Practice: The rules for filing a reward application for a "related action" are unnecessarily burdensome. The SEC rules do not explain how a whistleblower learns that his or her information resulted in sanctions being awarded in a "related action." Thus, it is imperative for the whistleblower to carefully monitor all judicial or regulatory actions taken that may have resulted from the information provided by the whistleblower to various regulatory or law enforcement authorities.

A whistleblower should file WB-APP applications in any case in which he or she believes the United States, an "appropriate regulatory agency," a "self-regulatory organization," or a State Attorney General issues any form of fine or sanction directly or indirectly related to the information provided by the whistleblower to the SEC.

A whistleblower should, unless there is a good reason not to, cooperate with these other agencies in order to maximize the number of sanctions obtained through various "related actions" and to ensure that the whistleblower has a firm factual basis to demonstrate that his or her information resulted in the "related action" sanctions.

See SEC Rule 17 C.F.R. § 240.21F-3(b) (substantive rule governing related actions) and 17 C.F.R. § 240.21F-11 (procedural rule for applying for a "related action" reward).

Can I appeal the SEC's award decision?	It depends. If the Commission follows the factors described above, authorizes an award, and the amount awarded is between 10% and 30% of the monetary sanctions collected in the Commission or related action, then the Commission's determination of the amount of the award is not appealable. If the Commission denies your application for an award, you may file an appeal in an appropriate United States Court of Appeals within 30 days of the decision being issued.
	See SEC Rule 17 C.F.R. § 240.21F-13. (This portion of the Q&A taken from SEC Fact Sheet.)
	However, in order to file a judicial appeal of an SEC ruling denying your whistleblower rewards case, you must "exhaust" your administrative remedies. Under the SEC rules, the Commission's "Claims Review Staff" will issue a Preliminary Determination concerning your reward claim. If you object to that Preliminary Determination, you *must* file a written response to the SEC's Office of the Whistleblower, setting forth the grounds for your objection.
	The failure to file this written response objecting to the denial will negate your right to file a judicial appeal of a final order denying your reward. The Final Rule clearly sets forth this requirement: "Your failure to submit a timely response contesting a Preliminary Determination will constitute a failure to exhaust administrative remedies, and you will be prohibited from pursuing your appeal" in court.
	See SEC Rule 17 C.F.R. § 240.21F-10(d)-(i).

What rights do I have if my employer retaliates against me for submitting information to the SEC?	Employers may not discharge, demote, suspend, harass, or in any way discriminate against you because of any lawful act done by you in providing information to the SEC under the whistleblower program or assisting the SEC in any investigation or proceeding based on the information submitted. If you believe that your employer has wrongfully retaliated against you, you may bring a private action in federal court against your employer. If you prevail, you may be entitled to reinstatement, double back pay, litigation costs, expert witness fees, and attorneys' fees. The Commission can also take legal action in an enforcement proceeding against any employer who retaliates against a whistleblower for reporting information to the SEC. *See* SEC Rule 17 C.F.R. § 240.21F-2. (This portion of the Q&A taken from SEC Fact Sheet.) There is a second law that may also prohibit an employer from firing you. Under the Sarbanes-Oxley Act (SOX), you may be entitled to file a complaint with the Department of Labor if you are retaliated against for reporting possible securities law violations, including making internal reports to your company. If you prevail in an SOX case, you may be entitled to reinstatement, back pay, special damages, litigation costs, expert witness fees, and attorneys' fees. There is a 180-day filing deadline for SOX claims. 18 U.S.C. § 1514A.

If I am retaliated against, should I file a case under the Sarbanes-Oxley Act or under the Dodd-Frank Act?	Because two federal laws will provide protection for most corporate whistleblowers who expose violations of securities laws or fraud against shareholders, you have a choice of remedy. You can file under the Dodd-Frank Act law or the Sarbanes-Oxley Act (SOX) law. These two laws are nonexclusive, and you may be able to file claims under both laws.

There are pros and cons to each approach. The Dodd-Frank Act has a stronger definition of protected activity, a longer statute of limitations, provides direct access to federal court and jury trials, and permits a wrongfully discharged employee to obtain double back pay.

The SOX law provides for an OSHA investigation (that can lead to a preliminary reinstatement order), permits employees a choice of forum (either the Labor Department or federal court) to adjudicate their claims, and provides for "special damages," which include compensatory damages.

If you have signed a mandatory arbitration agreement with your employer, you should file a SOX complaint. The SOX law explicitly prohibits employers from forcing employees to arbitrate their cases. Under SOX, even if you agreed to arbitrate your disputes with the company, you still can have your whistleblower retaliation case heard by independent Department of Labor judges or by a jury of your peers. 18 U.S.C. § 1514A.

Best Practice: File a claim under SOX. If the Department of Labor investigators and judges fairly adjudicate your case, you may decide to rely completely on the DOL remedy. However, after exhausting administrative remedies (i.e., waiting 180 days) you can remove your case to federal court prior to the Labor Department issuing a final decision.

The benefits to federal court removal are: (a) right to a jury trial; (b) ability to subpoena third-party witnesses; and (c) you may join your case with other applicable federal or state actions, including a Dodd-Frank Act wrongful discharge claim that may entitle you to double back pay. However, before you remove your case from the DOL, you should research to ensure that the federal court that will hear your case provides protections equal to those afforded by the DOL. Sometimes an administrative proceeding can be less costly, more expeditious, and more protective than a federal court proceeding.

If you miss the 180-day statute of limitations for filing a SOX case, then you should file a claim under the Dodd-Frank anti-retaliation statute, which has a minimum 3-year statute of limitations. |

	The two antiretaliation laws are codified as follows:
	Sarbanes-Oxley Act, 18 U.S.C. § 1514A;
	Dodd-Frank Act, 15 U.S.C. § 78u-6.

What types of misconduct can I report to qualify for a reward?	Rewards can be based on sanctions obtained by the SEC for any violation of the securities laws and for sanctions obtained as a result of other "related actions" prosecuted by other government entities. There is no finite list of actions that can constitute a violation covered under Dodd-Frank. Each whistleblower must determine the nature and scope of any potential violation and present the case to the SEC.
	In its final rules, the SEC summarized some of the violations for which a sanction could be imposed, including:
	Abuse of authority in discretionary trading;
	Advance fee fraud;
	Breach of fiduciary duty;
	Churning/excessive trading;
	Cold calling;
	Conflicts of interest by management;
	Corporate disclosure and reporting violations;
	Customer account violations;
	Excessive or unearned fees, mark-ups, or commissions;
	Executive compensation violations;
	Failure to disclose break-points;
	Failure to disclose fees/insufficient notice of change in fees;
	Failure to file reports;
	Failure to follow client instructions;
	Failure to notify shareholders of corporate events;
	False/material misstatements in firm research that were basis for transactions;
	False or misleading financial statements, offering documents, press releases or proxy materials;
	False or misleading marketing or sales information;
	Financial fraud;
	Foreign Corrupt Practices Act violations;

	Going private transactions;
	Guarantee against loss/promise to buy back shares;
	High-pressure sales techniques;
	Illegal extension of margin credit;
	Inaccurate or misleading statements or nondisclosure by a broker-dealer, investment advisor, and associated persons;
	Inaccurate valuation of Net Asset Value;
	IPO eligibility or allocation violations;
	Misconduct in mergers and acquisitions;
	Offering fraud;
	Operational violations;
	Ponzi schemes;
	Registration violations;
	Regulation T restrictions;
	Restrictive legends;
	Reverse stock splits;
	Sales and advisory practice violations;
	Selective disclosure;
	Tax reporting problems;
	Theft and misappropriations;
	Trading violations (including after-hours trading, algorithmic trading, manipulation of securities/prices, insider trading, front running, inaccurate quotes/pricing information, and market timing;
	Unauthorized transactions;
	Unregistered securities offering; and
	Any other violation of securities law.
	See Example of violations listed at 76 *Federal Register* 34373 (June 13, 2011).

Can I report violations of the Foreign Corrupt Practices Act that occur in foreign countries and still obtain a reward?	Yes. Violations of the Foreign Corrupt Practices Act (FCPA) are also violations of the Security Exchange Act and are within the jurisdiction of the Dodd-Frank Act's whistleblower reward program. This includes bribes paid in foreign countries to foreign government officials. *See* 15 U.S.C. § 78dd-1, *et seq.* The FCPA is part of our nation's securities laws and is enforced by the SEC and Department of Justice. The law applies to bribes paid to foreign officials by U.S. citizens or foreign nationals in order to obtain favorable business deals. The law covers corporations "traded" in the United States, regardless of whether the company is a U.S.-based company, a domestic or foreign subsidiary, or a foreign corporation. On the day the Dodd-Frank Act was signed into law, a leading corporate defense firm warned that the whistleblower reward provisions "are likely to have a particularly significant impact on enforcement of the Foreign Corrupt Practices Act." (Morrison & Foerster, LLP, published by the *Association of Corporate Counsel/Lexology* [July 21, 2010].) This is based on the recognition by corporate spokesmen that employee-insiders are well placed to obtain information on bribes paid by large multinational corporations in order to obtain business in markets such as China, Russia, Latin America, Africa, and Eastern Europe. The following are examples of recent successful prosecutions under the FCPA: *Alcalel-Lucent:* $137 million for bribing Latin American officials; *Armor Holdings:* $10.29 million for bribes paid to induce UN official to buy their body armor; *BAE Systems:* $400 million for bribes and illegal payments made through offshore shell companies; *Chevron Corp.:* $30 million for illegal payments made as part of the Oil for Food program in Iraq; *Daimler, AG:* $185 million for bribes paid in China, Russia, and 20 other countries; *ENI, S.p.A/Snamprogetti Netherlands:* $125 million disgorgement to the SEC for bribing foreign officials to obtain construction contracts; *Kellog Brown & Root* and three other companies: $1.28 billion for paying bribes;

	Monsanto Corp.: $1 million for bribes paid to Indonesian environmental official;
	Siemens: $800 million for paying bribes;
	SSI International: $7.5 million in fines for bribing officials in China;
	Transocean, Inc. and five other oil and gas services companies: $156 million for bribes paid in seven countries;
	Tyson Foods: $4 million for bribes paid to veterinarians working for the Mexican government.
	The SEC's final rule excluded employees who work for foreign governments for eligibility for a reward. *See* SEC Rule 17 C.F.R. § 240.21F-8(c)(2). However, this exclusion is not found in the actual text of the Dodd-Frank Act, and could be judicially challenged by an otherwise qualified whistleblower who worked for a foreign government.
	The U.S. Department of Justice Fraud Division published *The Lay-Persons Guide to the FCPA* online at: www.justice.gov/criminal/fraud/fcpa/docs/lay-persons-guide.pdf.
What if I witness violations of the Commodity Exchange Act?	The Commodity Exchange Act contains a whistleblower reward provision nearly identical to the SEC's law. On August 25, 2011, the Commodity Futures Trading Commission (CFTC) published regulations implementing the whistleblower section. 76 *Federal Register* 53172. In order to qualify for a reward, whistleblowers must follow the procedures set forth in these regulations. The CFTC regulations are nearly identical to the SEC's rules and are published at 17 C.F.R. Part 165. Under the CFTC rules, reward applications must be filed with CFTC using a "Form TCR." 17 C.F.R. § 165.3(a).
	The Form TCR can be completed online and submitted electronically at the following website: http://www.cftc.gov or by mailing or faxing the form to: The CFTC, Three Lafayette Centre, 1155 21st Street NW, Washington, DC, 20581, Fax (202) 418-5975.
	The Commodity Exchange Act also includes a provision prohibiting employers from retaliating against employees who file reward claims under that Act. 7 U.S.C.§ 26.

What long-term impact will the enhanced SEC whistle-blower protection program have on financial markets?	In approving its final rules, the Securities and Exchange Commission recognized the positive impact whistleblower protections bring to financial markets. Far from imposing "undue burdens on competition," the Commission concluded that whistleblowers will have a significant positive impact on the market and an overall "pro-competitive effect." The Commission explained the basis for these findings: "We do not believe the final rules will impose undue burdens on competition and, indeed, we believe the rules may have a potential pro-competitive effect. Specifically, by increasing the likelihood that misconduct will be detected . . . the rules should reduce the unfair competitive advantage that some companies can achieve by engaging in undetected violations." The Commission also explained how its whistleblower program will result in strengthening voluntary corporate efforts to detect and report fraud: "(I)ssuers who previously may have underinvested in internal compliance programs may respond to our rules by making improvements in corporate governance generally, and strengthening their internal compliance programs in particular." SEC Final Rule Commentary, 76 *Federal Register* 34300, 34362 (June 13, 2011).

CHECKLIST 8

Foreign Corrupt Practices Act Recoveries 2015–2016

GlaxoSmithKline	The U.K.-based pharmaceutical company agreed to pay a $20 million penalty to settle charges that it violated the FCPA when its China-based subsidiaries engaged in pay-to-prescribe schemes to increase sales. (9/30/16)
Och-Ziff Capital Management Group	The hedge fund and two executives settled charges related to the use of intermediaries, agents, and business partners to pay bribes to high-level government officials in Africa. Och-Ziff agreed to pay $412 million in civil and criminal matters, and CEO Daniel Och agreed to pay $2.2 million to settle charges against him. (9/29/16)
Anheuser-Busch InBev	The Belgium-based global brewery agreed to pay $6 million to settle charges that it violated the FCPA by using third-party sales promoters to make improper payments to government officials in India and chilled a whistleblower who reported the misconduct. (9/28/16)
Nu Skin Enterprises	The Provo, Utah-based skin care products company agreed to pay more than $765,000 for an improper payment made to a charity related to a high-ranking member of China's Communist Party in order to influence the outcome of a pending provincial regulatory investigation in China. (9/20/16)
AstraZeneca	The U.K.-based biopharmaceutical company agreed to pay more than $5 million to settle FCPA violations resulting from improper payments made by subsidiaries in China and Russia to foreign officials. (8/30/16)
Key Energy Services	The Houston-based oil field services company agreed to pay $5 million to settle charges that it violated the FCPA as a result of payments made by its Mexican subsidiary to an official responsible for negotiating contracts at Mexico's state-owned oil company. (8/11/16)
LAN Airlines	The South American–based airline agreed to pay more than $22 million to settle parallel civil and criminal cases related to improper payments authorized during a dispute between the company and union employees in Argentina. (7/25/16)
Johnson Controls	The Wisconsin-based global provider of HVAC systems agreed to pay more than $14 million to settle charges that its Chinese subsidiary used sham vendors to make improper payments to employees of Chinese government–owned shipyards and other officials to win business. (7/11/16)
Analogic Corp. and Lars Frost	The Massachusetts-based medical device manufacturer agreed to pay nearly $15 million to settle parallel SEC and DOJ actions after its Danish subsidiary acted as a conduit for distributors to funnel money to third parties in hundreds of highly suspicious transactions. Frost, the subsidiary's CFO at the time, agreed to settle SEC charges and pay a penalty. (6/21/16)

Las Vegas Sands	The casino and resort company agreed to pay $9 million to settle charges that it failed to properly authorize or document millions of dollars in payments to a consultant facilitating business activities in China and Macao. (4/7/16)
Novartis International AG	The Swiss-based pharmaceutical company agreed to pay $25 million to settle charges that it violated the FCPA when its China-based subsidiaries engaged in pay-to-prescribe schemes to increase sales. (3/23/16)
Nordion (Canada) Inc. and employee	The Canadian-based health science company and a former employee agreed to collectively pay more than $500,000 to settle FCPA charges. Mikhail Gourevitch, an engineer, arranged bribes to Russian officials for drug approvals and received kickbacks in return. Nordion lacked sufficient internal controls to detect and prevent the scheme. (3/3/16)
Qualcomm	The San Diego–based company agreed to pay $7.5 million to settle charges that it violated the FCPA when it hired relatives of Chinese officials deciding whether to select company's products. (3/1/16)
VimpelCom Ltd.	The Dutch-based telecommunications provider agreed to a $795 million global settlement to resolve its violations of the FCPA to win business in Uzbekistan. (2/18/16)
PTC	The Massachusetts-based tech company and its Chinese subsidiaries agreed to pay more than $28 million to settle FCPA cases involving bribery of Chinese government officials to win business. (2/16/16)
SciClone Pharmaceuticals, Inc.	The California-based pharmaceutical firm agreed to pay $12 million to settle SEC charges that it violated the FCPA when international subsidiaries increased sales by making improper payments to health care professionals employed at state health institutions in China. (2/4/16)
SAP SE	The software manufacturer agreed to forfeit $3.7 million in sales profits to settle SEC charges that it violated the FCPA when its deficient internal controls enabled an executive to pay bribes to procure business in Panama. (2/1/16)
Bristol-Myers Squibb	SEC charged the New York–based pharmaceutical company with violating the FCPA when employees of its China-based joint venture made improper payments to obtain sales. Bristol-Myers Squibb agreed to pay more than $14 million to settle charges. (10/5/15)
Hitachi	SEC charged the Tokyo-based conglomerate with violating the FCPA by inaccurately recording improper payments to South Africa's ruling political party in connection with contracts to build power plants. Hitachi agreed to pay $19 million to settle charges. (9/28/15)
BNY Mellon	SEC charged the global investment company with violating the FCPA by providing valuable student internships to family members of foreign government officials affiliated with a Middle East sovereign wealth fund. BNY Mellon agreed to pay $14.8 million to settle charges. (8/18/15)

Mead Johnson Nutrition	SEC charged the infant formula manufacturer with violating the FCPA when its Chinese subsidiary made improper payments to health care professionals to recommend the company's product to new and expectant mothers. Mead Johnson Nutrition agreed to pay $12 million to settle the case. (7/28/15)
BHP Billiton	SEC charged the global resources company with violating the FCPA when it sponsored the attendance of foreign government officials at the Summer Olympics. BHP Billiton agreed to pay a $25 million penalty to settle the case. (5/20/15)
FLIR Systems	SEC charged Oregon-based FLIR Systems with violating the FCPA by financing a "world tour" of personal travel for Middle East government officials who played key roles in decisions to purchase FLIR products. FLIR, which earned more than $7 million in profits from such sales, agreed to pay $9.5 million to settle the charges. (4/8/15)
Goodyear Tire & Rubber Company	SEC charged Goodyear with violating the FCPA when its subsidiaries paid bribes to land tire sales in Kenya and Angola. The company agreed to pay $16 million to settle the charges. (2/24/15)
Walid Hatoum / PBSJ Corporation	SEC charged a former officer at a Tampa, Florida–based engineering firm with violating the FCPA by offering and authorizing bribes and employment to foreign officials to secure Qatari government contracts. Hatoum agreed to settle the charges; PBSJ entered into a deferred prosecution agreement and must pay $3.4 million. (1/22/15)

ANNOTATED CHAPTER SOURCES

Introduction: What to Do if the Boss Is a Crook?

Studies that document the importance of whistleblowing in the detection of fraud and misconduct: Association of Certified Fraud Examiners, "Report to the Nations on Occupational Fraud and Abuse: 2016 Global Fraud Study"; Alexander Dyck, et al., "Who Blows the Whistle on Corporate Fraud," *The Initiative on Global Market's Working Paper No. 3,* University of Chicago Booth School of Business (Oct. 2008); Corporate Crime Reporter, "Twenty Things You Should Know about Corporate Crime," *Corporate Crime Reporter* (June 12, 2007); Ethics Resource Center, "The Ethics Resource Center's 2011 National Government Ethics Survey: Workplace Ethics in Transition"; Julie Goldberg, "Compliance Officers Take Their Own Path," *New York Law Journal* (April 19, 2007); PricewaterhouseCoopers, Investigations and Forensic Services, "Economic Crime: People, Culture, and Controls; Geoffrey Rapp, "Beyond Protection: Invigorating Incentives for Sarbanes-Oxley Corporate and Securities Fraud Whistleblowers, 87 *Boston University Law Review* 91 (2007). Andrew C. Call, et al., "Whistleblowers and Outcomes of Financial Misrepresentation Enforcement Actions," *papers.ssrn.com* (last revised on January 24, 2017); Ernesto Reuben, "Nobody likes a rat: On the willingness to report lies and the consequences thereof," Vol. 93 *Journal of Economic Behavior & Organization* 384 (Sept. 2013)

The National Business Ethics Survey is published by the Ethics Resource Center (Arlington, VA, 2007): *see* "An Inside View of Private Sector Ethics," p. 1. A wide range of major corporations, such as Northrop Grumman, Shell Oil, Raytheon, and BAE Systems sponsored the 2007 ethics survey. The center has conducted five ethics surveys since 2000. Over the approximately ten-year time span covering these surveys, the center found an average of 51.6 percent of the workforce witnessed misconduct. *See* "2009 Ethics Survey: Ethics in the Recession," p. 16. In its 2009 survey the center reported that 15 percent of employees reporting misconduct stated that they suffered some form of retaliation. Ibid. p. 36. In 2012 a survey was conducted limited to employees who work for the "Fortune 500" corporations. This survey found that 52 percent of workers in those companies admitted to observing "misconduct" at work.

Statistics documenting the successful monetary recoveries obtained by the United States under the False Claims Act are available online at: U.S. Department of Justice, Civil Division, Commercial Litigation Branch, Civil Fraud Division: *Fraud Statistics—Overview: Oct. 1, 1987–Sept. 30, 2016*, www.doj .gov/civil/frauds.

Greenberg Quinlan Rosner Research, "Democracy Corps Frequency Questionnaire" (Feb. 14-19, 2007) (79 percent support for "strong whistle-blower law").

The hardships and emotional distress facing whistleblowers, even those who prevailed and obtained large monetary recoveries, are set forth in "Special Report" published by the *New England Journal of Medicine*: Aaron Kesselheim, et al., "Whistle-Blowers' Experiences in Fraud Litigation against Pharmaceutical Companies," *N. Engl. J. Med.* 362:19 (May 13, 2010). Institute of Internal Auditors, "Political Pressure Intense on Internal Audit: IIA Research Report Reveals Pervasive Efforts to Influence Internal Audit Findings," press release (March 10, 2015).

Early whistleblower cases: Daniel Ellsberg, "Secrets: A Memoir of Vietnam and the Pentagon Papers" (Viking Press, NY: 2002); *Nixon v. Fitzgerald*, 457 U.S. 731 (1982); Romesh Ratnesar and Michael Weissakopf, "How the FBI Blew the Case: The Inside Story of the FBI Whistle-blower Who Accused her Bosses of Ignoring Warnings of 9/11," CNN.com/Inside Politics (May 27, 2002); *Silkwood v. Kerr-McGee Corp.*, 667 F.2d 908 (10th Cir. 1981), *reversed at* 464 U.S. 238 (1984); Bob Woodward, "The Secret Man: The Story of Watergate's Deep Throat" (NY: Simon & Schuster, 2005).

The Pen Center USA selected the "Top Ten Books About Whistleblowers," listed at https://penusa.org/blogs/mark-program/top-ten-books-about-whistleblowers. The books include *No Place to Hide: Edward Snowden, the NSA, and the U.S. Surveillance State* by Glenn Greenwald, *State of War: The Secret History of the CIA and the Bush Administration* by James Risen, *All the President's Men* by Carl Bernstein and Bob Woodward, *The Pentagon Papers* leaked by Daniel Ellsberg, *Power Failure: The Inside Story of the Collapse of Enron* by Mimi Swartz with Sherron Watkins, *No One Would Listen: A True Financial Thriller* by Harry Markopolos, *The Whistleblower: Sex Trafficking, Military Contractors, and One Woman's Fight for Justice* by Kathryn Bolkovac and Cari Lynn, *Bad Blood: The Tuskegee Syphilis Experiment* by James H. Jones, and *The Whistleblowers: Exposing Corruption in Government & Industry* by Myron Peretz Glazer and Penina Migdal Glazer.

Early books by and about whistleblowers include Clark R. Mollenhoff, *Washington Cover-Up* (New York: Doubleday, 1962); A. Ernest Fitzgerald, *The High Priests of Waste* (New York: W.W. Norton, 1972); and Ralph Nader, et al., *Whistle Blowing* (New York: Grossman Publishers, 1972).

Richard Lacayo and Amanda Ripley, "The Whistleblowers: Persons of the Year," *Time* (Dec. 22, 2002).

Tom Herman, "Whistleblower Law Scores Early Success," *Wall Street Journal* (May 16, 2007), quoting Senator Grassley plea that whistleblowers "not be treated like skunks at the picnic."

The international conventions requiring the protection of employees who blow the whistle on fraud include: Council of Europe, *Civil Law Convention on Corruption*, Article 9 (Strasbourg, 1999); Organization of American States, Department of International Law, *Inter-American Convention Against Corruption*, Article III (8), ratified by the United States Senate on July 27, 2000, available at www.oas.org; United Nations, *Convention Against Corruption*, Article 33 (Vienna: UN Office on Drugs and Crime, 2004).

An increasing number of international organizations are advocating for international whistleblower protections. *See* Transparency International, "Whistleblowing: an effective tool in the fight against corruption," Policy Position #01-2010.

Rule 1: Use the New Legal Tools

The Chair of the SEC's statement on the effectiveness of whistleblower reward laws is found at: Mary Jo White, "Remarks at the Securities Forum" (Oct. 9, 2013), located at https://www.sec.gov/News/Speech/Detail/Speech/1370539872100.

Statement of Attorney General on the False Claims Act: Eric Holder, U.S. Department of Justice, "Attorney General Eric Holder Speaks at the 25th Anniversary of the False Claims Act Amendments of 1986" (Jan. 31, 2012).

Statement of the Assistant Attorney General on the False Claims Act: Assistant Attorney General, U.S. Department of Justice, "Remarks at American Bar Association's 10th National Institute on the Civil False Claims Act and Qui Tam Enforcement," (June 5, 2014).

Motion by U.S. Attorney Christopher Christie on whistleblower rewards in ocean pollution cases: *United States v. Sun Ace Shipping Company*, 2:06-cr-00705, "Motion and Memorandum in Support of Award" (D. N.J. Nov. 15, 2006).

The testimony of the Senate Judiciary Chair in support of the False Claims Act: "Statement for the Record by Senator Chuck Grassley of Iowa Chairman, Senate Judiciary Committee at a House Judiciary Subcommittee on the constitution and Civil Justice Hearing on 'Oversight of the False Claims Act' April 28, 2016."

Overview of effectiveness of reward laws: Testimony of Stephen Kohn, House Committee on Government Oversight and Reform: https://oversight.house.gov/wp-content/uploads/2016/12/2016-12-01-NWC-Kohn-Testimony.pdf

Decisions that whistleblower allegations need not be proven true, but only made in good faith: *Passaic Valley Sewerage v. Department of Labor*, 992 F.2d 474, 478-79 (3rd. Cir. 1993); *DeKalb County v. Department of Labor*, 813 F.3d 1015 (11th Cir. 2016).

Association of Certified Fraud Examiners, *Report to the Nations on Occupational Fraud and Abuse* (2016) (excellent source for statistics on fraud detection). The Department of Justice publishes annual statistics on civil fraud recoveries, as well as rewards paid under the False Claims Act. *See* Civil Division, US Department of Justice, "Fraud Statistics—Overview" (Oct. 1, 1987–Sept. 30, 2016).

The Ethics Resource Center conducted numerous studies on employee reporting behavior. The study that focused on whistleblowers was *Blowing the Whistle on Workplace Misconduct*, published by the ERC in December 2010; available at www.whistleblowers.org/storage/documents/DoddFrank/ercwhistleblower wp.pdf.

Alexander Dyck, Adair Morse, and Luigi Zingales, *Who Blows the Whistle on Corporate Fraud?* The University of Chicago Booth School of Business Working Paper No 08-22 (2009); http://faculty.chicagobooth.edu/luigi.zingales/papers/research/whistle.pdf.

Citations to the relevant reward laws, and supporting materials, are contained in the Practice Tips and Sources for the following rules: 3, 6–12, 30 and Checklists 1 and 4.

Rule 2: Navigate the Maze

William J. Broad, "The Shuttle Explodes; 6 in Crew and High School Teacher are Killed 74 Seconds after Liftoff," *New York Times* (Jan. 28, 1986); Roger M. Boisjoly, "Ethical Decisions—Morton Thiokol and the Space Shuttle *Challenger* Disaster," http://onlineethics.org/essays/shuttle (Last modified on Oct. 18, 2005).

Checklists 1–3 cite the numerous federal and state laws that protect whistle-blowers. In addition to these laws, traditional common law remedies such as breach of contract, libel, and intentional interference tort claims may also be applicable in a whistleblower case. *See Empiregas v. Hardy*, 487 So.2d 244 (Ala. 1985) (intentional interference with contract); *Bass v. Happy Rest, Inc.*, 507 N.W.2d 317 (S.D. 1993) (intentional infliction of emotional distress). It is important to remember that laws are constantly being amended and reinterpreted by court rulings. Additionally, Congress and various state legislatures are still enacting whistleblower protection laws to fill in the numerous loopholes in protection.

University of Nebraska College of Law Professor Richard Moberly explained the maze confronting most whistleblowers as follows: "The complex com-bination of federal and state statutory protection and the tort of wrongful discharge provide inconsistent antiretaliation protection that depends sub-stantially on whether the whistleblower is the 'right' type of employee who works for the 'right' type of employer in the 'right' type of industry. Protection also depends upon whether the employee reported the 'right' type of mis-conduct in the 'right' way." Richard Moberly, "Protecting Whistleblowers by Contract," 79 *University of Colorado Law Review* 975 (2008). *See also* Stephen Kohn, *Concepts and Procedures in Whistleblower Law* (Westport, CT: Quorum Books, 2001) and *Federal Whistleblower Laws and Regulations* (Washington, DC: National Whistleblower Center, 2009).

The loopholes that face many employees was well stated in *Bricker v. Rockwell*, 1991 U.S. Dist. LEXIS 18965 (E.D. Wash.), where he noted that a "gap in cover-age" had "caught" a well-deserving whistleblower in "limbo." After highlight-ing the credibility of the whistleblower and his "compelling evidence of health and safety problems," the court found that the "system" "failed him miser-ably." The whistleblower's case was thrown out of court.

Rule 3: Follow the Money

Checklist 1 lists the major state and federal *qui tam* or rewards-based whistle-blower laws. Rules 6–12 set forth details on how to utilize the major *qui tam* and rewards laws available to whistleblowers.

Currently twenty-nine states, the District of Columbia, and several major cities have local versions of the False Claims Act. Because of the effectiveness of these laws and federal incentives encouraging states to enact FCAs modeled on the federal law, the number of local FCAs is growing.

The legislative history of the FCA is set forth in three critically important Senate reports. The first explains in detail the history of the FCA and the impact of the 1986 amendments that revived the law. *See* S. Rep. 99-345, 99th Cong., 2nd Sess. (1986). This Senate Report remains the most authoritative source for interpreting the FCA.

A second major source of information is the legislative history of the False Claims Act Correction Act of 2008. *See* S. Rep. 99-345, 99th Cong., 2nd Sess. (1986); S. Rep. 110-507, 110th Cong., 2nd Sess. (2008). Although this law did not pass, many of its provisions were approved (either in whole, in part, or in a modified form) by Congress in three separate laws. *See* the Fraud Enforcement and Recovery Act, Public Law No. 111-21, § 4 (May 20, 2009); the Patient Protection and Affordable Care Act, Public Law No. 111-148, § 10104(j)(2) (March 23, 2010); and the Dodd-Frank Act, Public Law No. 111-203, § 1079A (July 21, 2010).

The third report explains the meaning of the FCA amendments included in the Fraud Enforcement and Recovery Act of 2009. *See* S. Rep. No. 111-10, 111th Cong., 1st Session (2009).

U.S. Department of Justice, Civil Division, *Fraud Statistics—Overview: Oct. 1, 1987 –Sept. 30, 2016*, These statistics are updated annually. Published at www.doj .gov/civil/frauds (FCA statistics).

The early legislative history of the FCA can be found at: Cong. Globe, 37th Cong., 3d Sess., 952-958 (1863); "Report of the House Committee on Government Contracts," March 3, 1863; H. R. Rep. No. 2, 37th Cong., 2d Sess., pt. ii–a, pp. xxxviii–xxxix (1862). President Lincoln signed the original FCA into law on March 2, 1863. *See* Statutes at Large, 37th Congress, Sess. II, Chapter LXVII (March 2, 1863).

On April 1, 1943, the House voted to repeal the FCA. The repeal would have been readily approved, but for a prolonged filibuster by Senator William Langer (Rep., N. Dak.). During the filibuster Senator Langer put into the Congressional record information on the legislative purposes and cases pending under the FCA. *See* Volume 89 of the *Congressional Record*, Senate debates between July 8 and Dec. 17, 1943. Langer's central arguments in opposition to repealing or gutting the FCA are set forth in his "Minority Views" to Senate Report 291, Part 2, 78th Cong. 1st Session (June 25, 1943) and in the *Congressional Record* on pp. 7437–45 (July 8, 1943), pp. 7576–79 (Sept. 15, 1943), pp. 7601-7 (September 17, 1943). Senator James Murray (Montana) also spoke out against the repeal. *Congressional Record* pp. 7575–76 (Sept. 15, 1943), pp. 7609-10 (Sept. 17, 1943). Senator Joel Bennett Clark (Missouri) also condemned the repeal. *See Congressional Record* pp. 7611–14 (Sept. 17, 1943). In the House of Representatives, Congressman Vito Marcantonio (New York) and Louis Miller (Missouri) opposed the repeal. *See Congressional Record* pp. 10846–49 (Dec. 17, 1943).

Based on Langer's actions the FCA was not repealed, but instead severely weakened. The amendments gutting the law were approved by Congress and signed into law by President Roosevelt on Dec. 23, 1943. *See* 57 Stat. 608.

The Bradley Birkenfeld story has been widely reported in the international press. *See* Michael Bronner, "Telling Swiss Secrets: A Banker's Betrayal," *Global Post* (Aug. 5, 2010); Juan Gonzales, "UBS Whistleblower Bradley Birkenfeld Deserves a Statue on Wall Street, Not Prison Sentence," *New York Daily News* (Jan. 6, 2010); David Hilzenrath, "Beware the Whistle: A Swiss Banker's Saga Offers a Cautionary Tale," *Washington Post* (May 16, 2010). The exchange between the court and the federal prosecutor is contained in the Sentencing Transcript, *U.S. v. Birkenfeld*, 08-60099-CR-Zloch (U.S. Dist. Court, S.D. Florida) (Aug. 21, 2009).

Rule 4: Find the Best Federal Law

The federal whistleblower laws, along with citations to major cases interpreting these laws, are set forth in Checklist 2.

Congress periodically amends these laws, and the most recent version of the law should always be checked. Furthermore, courts are continuously interpreting statutes, and the most recent judicial interpretations must also always be checked. Lower courts often disagree over the interpretation of a law, and it is also important to check the specific judicial rulings relevant in the judicial district or court for which you may file a claim.

AIRLINE SAFETY

Aviation Investment and Reform Act, 49 U.S.C. § 42121. Department of Labor rules implementing this law are codified at 29 C.F.R. Part 1979. "Memorandum of Understanding between the Department of Labor and the FAA," 67 *Federal Register* 55883 (2002). The rules governing administrative hearings are located at 29 C.F.R. Part 18.

Clemmons v. Ameristar, 2004-AIR-11 (Dept. of Labor Administrative Review Board, May 26, 2010); *Evans v. Miami Valley Hospital*, 2006-AIR-22 (Dept. of Labor Administrative Review Board, June 30, 2009) (cases setting forth elements of airline whistleblower case).

The U.S. Department of Labor Office of Administrative Law Judges compiles a comprehensive listing of whistleblower decisions under airline safety law. *See* www.oalj.dol.gov.

BANKING AND FINANCIAL INSTITUTIONS

12 U.S.C. § 1790b (credit unions); 12 U.S.C. 1831j (FDIC); 31 U.S.C. § 5228 (monetary transactions).

CONSUMER FINANCIAL PROTECTION ACT OF 2012

The Dodd-Frank Act created a new Bureau of Consumer Financial Protections. This bureau has jurisdiction over a wide range of consumer protection laws. *See* Martin Bishop, "Meet the New Boss: The Bureau of Consumer Financial Protection," *The CFSL Bulletin* (July 23, 2010).

The whistleblower protection provision for employees who make protected disclosures to the bureau, or concerning matters within the jurisdiction of the bureau, are set forth in Section 1507 of the Dodd-Frank Act, codified at 12 U.S.C. § 5567.

The U.S. Department of Labor Office of Administrative Law Judges compiles a comprehensive listing of whistleblower decisions and will publish administrative rulings under this law. *See* www.oalj.dol.gov.

CONSUMER PRODUCT SAFETY

15 U.S.C. § 2051. The Department of Labor rules implementing this law are published at 29 C.F.R. Part 1983.

The U.S. Department of Labor Office of Administrative Law Judges compiles a comprehensive listing of whistleblower decisions and will publish administrative rulings under this law. *See* www.oalj.dol.gov.

CORRUPTION IN FEDERAL SPENDING/ENHANCEMENT OF CONTRACTOR PROTECTION ACT OF 2016

Public Law No. 111-5, § 1553 (2009). On January 3, 2013 Congress enacted a four-year "pilot program" and expanded the scope of this law to cover nearly all federal contracting. 47 U.S. § 4712. This law was made permanent on December 14, 2016, and is codified at 47 U.S.C. § 4712.

CRIMINAL OBSTRUCTION OF JUSTICE/RICO

18 U.S.C. § 1513(e) (criminal obstruction of justice law applicable to whistleblowers).

Civil RICO, 18 U.S.C. § 1961–62 and 64. *See Beck v. Prupis*, 529 U.S. 494 (2000). In *DeGuelle v. Camilli*, 664 F.3d 192 (7th Cir. 2011) the Court permitted a whistleblower to file a Civil RICO case based on violations of § 1514(e).

Dodd-Frank Act antiretaliation provision, 15 U.S.C. § 78u-6(h)(1).

DISCRIMINATION LAWS

All of the major antidiscrimination laws (i.e., laws that prohibit discrimination based on race, sex, religion, age, disability, national origin, labor union activities, minimum wage violations, etc.) contain antiretaliation provisions that protect employees who "blow the whistle" on discriminatory practices, testify in discrimination cases, or file complaints protected under law. Citations to the antiretaliation provisions of these laws are set forth in Checklist 2. Because of the large number of cases filed under these laws, courts often rely upon case precedent decided under laws such as Title VII of the Civil Rights Act or the National Labor Relations Act as authority in whistleblower cases.

DODD-FRANK WALL STREET REFORM AND CONSUMER PROTECTION ACT

See Handbook Rule 8 and Checklist 7 ("Dodd-Frank, Wall Street, and FCPA 'Q&As'").

Public Law No. 111-203 (2010) is the entire Dodd-Frank Act, including all whistleblower protection and enhanced antifraud provisions. The legislative history of Dodd-Frank is set forth in S. Rep. 111-176, 2nd Session 111th Congress (2010). The securities whistleblower provisions are codified at 15 U.S.C. § 78u-6. The commodities whistleblower provisions are codified at 7

U.S.C. § 26. The SEC's rules on filing securities *qui tam* claims are codified at 17 C.F.R. Parts 240 and 249.

The Dodd-Frank Act contained two provisions designed to protect employees who exposed potential securities law violations from retaliation or wrongful discharge. The two laws overlap. First, Dodd-Frank amended the existing corporate whistleblower protection law, the Sarbanes-Oxley Act, better know as the "SOX." SOX remains the cornerstone for protecting most corporate whistleblowers. It explicitly prohibits mandatory arbitration, provides a strong administrative remedy, and permits employees to remove their cases to federal court and obtain a jury trial. The law has a 180-day statute of limitations. Some courts have given the SOX enhancements contained in the Dodd-Frank Act retroactive effect. *Leshinsky v. Telvent GIT, S.A.,* 873 F.Supp.2d 582 (S.D.N.Y. 2012).

Dodd-Frank included a second new law protecting corporate employees who provided information to the Securities and Exchange Commission and/or engaged in other protected activities. This law has a broader definition of protected disclosure and permits employees to directly file claims in federal court. It has a two-year statute of limitations and provides for double back pay. However, it is not clear whether or not this law also prohibits mandatory arbitration. Consequently, employees who have signed arbitration agreements should initially use the SOX remedy. Both the SOX law and the new Dodd-Frank law are nonexclusive, and can potentially be joined into one lawsuit. But before they are joined it is absolutely necessary for an employee to initially file the SOX case before the Department of Labor and exhaust administrative remedies.

The SEC has sanctioned companies for retaliating against whistleblowers or requiring employees to sign nondisclosure agreements that interfere with an employee's right to communicate with government investigators. See, *In the Matter of BlackRock, Inc.,* SEC Administrative Filing 3-17786 (January 17, 2017) ($340,000 sanction for restrictive language in severance agreements); *In the Matter of SandRidge Energy,* Administrative Proceeding No. 3-17739 (December 20, 2016) ($1.4 million penalty for retaliating against whistleblower); *In the Matter of KBR,* Administrative File No. 3-16466 (April 1, 2015) ($130,000 sanction for requiring employees to sign restrictive nondisclosure agreements as part of the company's compliance program). The SEC has also filed amicus briefs supporting whistleblowers in retaliation cases. These include *Verble v. Morgan Stanley,* No. 15-6397 (6th Cir., Feb. 4, 2016); *Berman v. Neo@Ogilvy LLC,* 14-4626 (2nd. Cir., Feb. 6, 2015); *Liu Meng-Lin v. Siemens AG,* No. 13-4385 (2nd Cir., Feb. 20, 2014).

EMPLOYMENT CONTRACTS/UNION GRIEVANCE PROCEDURES

Wright v. Universal Maritime Service, 525 U.S. 70 (1998) and *Lingle v. Norge Division of Magic Chef*, 486 U.S. 399 (arbitration of claims covered under a union contract).

The National Labor Relations Board and the Department of Labor OSHA division entered into a Memorandum of Understanding concerning retaliation cases for employees who raise workplace safety concerns on January 12, 2017.

ENVIRONMENTAL LAWS

Clean Air Act, 42 U.S.C. § 7622.
Comprehensive Environmental Response (Superfund), 42 U.S.C. § 9610.
Pipeline Safety Improvement Act, 49 U.S.C. § 60129.
Safe Drinking Water Act, 42 U.S.C. 300j-9(i).
Solid Waste Disposal Act, 42 U.S.C. § 6971.
Surface Mining Act, 30 U.S.C. § 1293.
Toxic Substances Control Act, 15 U.S.C. § 2622.
Water Pollution Control Act, 33 U.S.C. § 1367.

The environmental whistleblower laws are all administered by the Department of Labor. The discussion of DOL procedures at the beginning of Rule 4 is applicable to these cases.

The Department of Labor rules implementing these laws are codified at: 29 C.F.R. Part 24 (environmental); 29 C.F.R. Part 1981 (pipeline). The rules governing Department of Labor adjudications are codified at 29 C.F.R. Part 18. The Interior Department has jurisdiction over the Surface Mining Act, 30 C.F.R. § 865.

Collins v. Village of Lynchburg, 2006-SDW-3 (Dept. of Labor Administrative Review Board, March 30, 2009) (elements of proof Safe Drinking Water case); *Hamilton v. PBS Environmental*, 2009-CER-3 (Dept. of Labor Administrative Review Board, Oct. 19, 2010) (elements of proof Superfund case).
The U.S. Department of Labor Office of Administrative Law Judges compiles a comprehensive listing of whistleblower decisions under the environmental whistleblower laws. *See* www.oalj.dol.gov.

FIRST AMENDMENT PROTECTIONS FOR PUBLIC EMPLOYEES

See Handbook Rule 13.

Most states have also enacted specific laws protecting state and local government employees, and some states include government workers under their Whistleblower Protection Act statutes. State legal protections for government workers should always be considered as an alternative or supplement to a government whistleblower claim, especially after the U.S. Supreme Court's decision in *Garcetti v. Ceballos*, 547 U.S. 410 (2006) (a 5-4 ruling that limited the scope of protected activity in First Amendment employment cases).

FINANCIAL INSTITUTIONS ANTI-FRAUD ENFORCEMENT ACT (FIRREA)

The FIRREA whistleblower provision is codified at 12 U.S.C. §§ 4201–23.

Major federal lawsuits under FIRREA: *United States of America vs. The Bank of New York Mellon Corporation*, 941 F. Supp. 2d 438, 451 (S.D.N.Y. 2013); *United States ex rel. O'Donnell v. Bank of America*, No. 12-01422 (S.D.N.Y. filed Oct. 24, 2012); *United States v. Wells Fargo*, No. 12-7527 (S.D.N.Y. filed Oct. 9 2012).

Nan S. Ellis, et al., "Use of FIRREA to Impose Liability in the Wake of the Global Financial Crisis: A New Weapon in the Arsenal to Prevent Financial Fraud," Vol. 18 *University of Pennsylvania Journal of Business Law* 119 (2016).

FOOD SAFETY

Hearings before the U.S. House of Representatives, Committee on Energy and Commerce, Subcommittee on Oversight and Investigations, "The Salmonella Outbreak: The Continued Failure to Protect the Food Supply" (February 11, 2009). The hearing record includes extensive testimony and documentation regarding the Peanut Corporation of America's handling of the contaminated peanut butter scandal.

News articles on the peanut butter contamination scandal: *ABC News*, "Former Manager Says Peanut Plant Complaints Ignored" (February 17, 2009), abcnews.go.com; Michael Moss, "Peanut Case Shows Holes in Safety Net," *New York Times* (February 9, 2009); Darren Perron, WCAX-TV, "Vt. Family Sues Over Salmonella" (February 9, 2009); Corky Siemaszko, "Peanut Corporation Whistleblower: Rates, Cockroaches Roasted with Peanut Butter," *New York Daily News* (February 9, 2009); Around the Nation, "Peanut Recall Prompts FEMA to Replace Meals," *Washington Post* (February 7, 2009); Associated Press, "FDA: Georgia Plant Knowingly Sold Peanut Butter Tainted with Salmonella" (February 6, 2009); Times Wire Services, "Schools, Disaster Victims May Have

Gotten Tainted Peanut Butter," *Los Angeles Times* (February 5, 2009); AFP, "U.S. Launches Criminal Probe in Peanut Better Health Scandal" (January 30, 2009).

Although too late for the victims of the Peanut Corporation of America's misconduct, the peanut butter scandal, along with a series of other food contamination incidents, resulted in Congress passing the Food Safety Modernization Act during the last days of the lame duck session in December 2010. After more than twenty years of missed opportunities, employees who blew the whistle on food safety violations on FDA-regulated foods finally obtained protection. *See* Renee Johnson, *Food Safety in the 111th Congress: H.R. 2749 and S.510,* Congressional Research Service (October 7, 2010). The official bill, H.R. 2751, passed on December 21, 2010, and is codified at 21 U.S.C. § 399d.

On December 21, 2010, Congress enacted the FDA Food Safety Modernization Act. This law contained a strong whistleblower antiretaliation provision modeled on the Sarbanes-Oxley and Airline Safety whistleblower laws. *See* H.R. 2751. The whistleblower provision is codified at 21 U.S.C. § 399d.

Committee on Energy and Commerce, "Food Safety Enhancement Act of 2009," House Report No. 111-234 (July 29, 2009).

Regulations implementing the food safety whistleblower law are published by the Department of Labor at 29 C.F.R. Part 1987.

The FDA and Department of Labor entered into a Memorandum of Understanding to implement the law on June 20, 2011.

FOREIGN CORRUPT PRACTICES ACT

See Handbook Rules 8 and 9 and Checklists 7 and 8.

FRAUD AGAINST SHAREHOLDERS

Sarbanes-Oxley Act: 18 U.S.C. § 1514A (antiretaliation); 15 U.S.C. § 78j-1-4 (confidential employee concerns program); 15 U.S.C. § 7245 (attorney whistleblower rules); 29 C.F.R. Part 1980 (Department of Labor regulations implementing SOX whistleblower law). Two critically important Department of Labor decisions interpreting the scope of protected activity, employer coverage, and the requirements needed for filing a complaint are: *Sylvester v. Parexel International,* 2007-SOX-39/42 (DOL ARB 2011); and *Johnson v. Siemens,* 2005-SOX-15 (DOL ARB 2011). Both cases provide broad protections for employees.

Funke v. Federal Express Corp., 2007-SOX-43 (DOL ARB, July 8, 2011) (broad definition of protected activity covering third party fraud) (disclosures to local law enforcement protected).

Lawson v. FMR LLC, 134 S.Ct. 1158 (2014) (independent contractors working for mutal funds are protected under SOX).

Kohn, et al., "Whistleblower Law: A Guide to Legal Protections for Corporate Employees" (Westport, CT: Praeger, 2004) (comprehensive guide to the Sarbanes-Oxley Act's whistleblower protections prior to Dodd-Frank amendments).

S. Rep. No. 107-146, 2nd Session, 107th Congress (2002) (legislative history of SOX whistleblower law prior to the Dodd-Frank amendments).

The U.S. Department of Labor Office of Administrative Law Judges compiles a comprehensive listing of whistleblower decisions under SOX. *See* www.oalj.dol.gov.

The Sarbanes-Oxley Act is the key federal corporate whistleblower protection law. Under its provisions OSHA conducts a preliminary investigation that can result in the preliminary reinstatement of the whistleblower. The OSHA determination can be appealed, and employees are entitled to either a full hearing before a Department of Labor judge or a jury trial in federal court. The law prohibits mandatory arbitration. The applicability of the nonarbitration provision has been held to be retroactive. *Wong v. CKK,* 2012 WL 3893609 (S.D.N.Y. 2012). SOX claims may be filed in conjunction with reward claims under the Dodd-Frank Act.

HEALTH CARE ENTITLEMENT
Affordable Care Act, Public Law 111-148, §1558, codified at 29 U.S.C. § 218C (reporting violations of the Public Health Service Act). When blowing the whistle on abusive patient care, whistleblowers should also review applicable state laws for potential coverage.

The Affordable Health Care Act's Whistleblower provision primarily covers employers who may seek to retaliate against employees for asserting their rights under "Obamacare" or for reporting infractions of the law's accountability provisions.

IRS WHISTLEBLOWER REWARDS
See Handbook Rule 7.

MILITARY/ARMED SERVICES

Protected Communications, 10 U.S.C. § 1034(a) ("No person may restrict a member of the armed forces in communicating with a member of Congress or an Inspector General"). In addition to permitting members of the armed forces to communicate with Congress and an Inspector General, the statute also permits members of the armed services to blow the whistle to their supervisors, DoD, auditors, or law enforcement officers and other persons designated by rule or regulation. The Inspector General regulation implementing this law is set forth in DoD Directive 7050.06 (July 23, 2007).

A comprehensive paper on the armed services whistleblower law was published online at http://thomasjfiscus.net/files/Whistleblower_Paper_JM.pdf. The paper is entitled "Whistleblowers and the Law; An Analysis of 10 U.S.C. § 1034: The Military Whistleblower Protection Act," and is dated April 30, 2005. No author is listed.

Additional laws and regulations provide protection for members of the Coast Guard (33 C.F.R. Part 53), employees of DoD "non-appropriated fund instrumentalities" (10 U.S.C. § 1587), and former members of the armed services who file complaints concerning the failure of an employer to comply with re-employment rights (38 U.S.C. §§ 4311, 4322-24).

MINE HEALTH AND SAFETY

Mine Health and Safety Act (antiretaliation), 30 U.S.C. § 815(c).
James A. Broderick and Daniel Minaham, "Employment Discrimination under the Federal Mine Safety and Health Act," 84 *West Virginia Law Review* 1023 (1982).

NUCLEAR SAFETY

Silkwood v. Kerr-McGee Corp., 667 F.2d 908 (10th Cir. 1981), *reversed at* 464 U.S. 238 (1984).

Section 211 of the Energy Reorganization Act, 42 U.S.C. § 5851 (nuclear safety whistleblower law). Implemented by the Department of Labor pursuant to 29 C.F.R. Part 24 and 29 C.F.R. Part 18.

The Nuclear Regulatory Commission considers the harassment and intimidation of whistleblowers as a serious safety matter and has implemented regulations that sanction companies that engage in retaliation. 10 C.F.R. § 50.7. *See In re Five Star Products*, 38 NRC 169 (1993); "Freedom of Employees in the Nuclear Industry to Raise Concerns without Fear of Retaliation"; Policy Statement, 61

Federal Register 24336 (1996); "Memorandum of Understanding between NRC and Department of Labor, Employee Protection," 47 *Federal Register* 54585 (1982).

Vinnett v. Mitsubishi, 2006-ERA-29 (Dept. of Labor ARB, July 27, 2010) and *Speegle v. Stone & Webster*, 2005-ERA-6 (Dept. of Labor ARB, Sept. 24, 2009) (cases setting forth elements of nuclear safety claims and proof of discrimination).

The U.S. Department of Labor Office of Administrative Law Judges compiles a comprehensive listing of whistleblower decisions under nuclear safety law. *See* www.oalj.dol.gov.

OSHA/WORKPLACE SAFETY
OSHA section 11(c) is codified at 29 U.S.C. § 660(c). The Labor Department regulations are located at 29 C.F.R. Part 1977.

Government Accountability Office, *Whistleblower Protection Program: Better Data and Improved Oversight Would Help Ensure Program Quality and Consistency*, GAO 09-106 (Jan., 2009).

Reich v. Cambridgeport Air Systems, 26 F.3d 1187 (1st Cir. 1994) (permitting compensatory and punitive damages to be awarded under OSHA).

U.S. House of Representatives, Hearing Before the Subcommittee on Workforce Protections (April 28, 2010) (Testimony of Lynn Rhinechart, General Counsel, AFL-CIO).

Wood v. Department of Labor, 275 F.3d 107 (D.C. Cir. 2001). During the April 28, 2010 hearing before the House Subcommittee, Mr. Neal Jorgensen testified about a similar incident in Preston, Idaho, in which he was fired by Plastics Industries. Again, the OSHA investigators determined that he was illegally fired, but the OSHA attorneys decided that they would not file a lawsuit in court. *See* Statement of Neal Jorgensen.

States court rulings protecting OSHA whistleblowers under state law: *Kinzel v. Discovery Drilling*, 93 P.3d 427 (Alaska 2004); *Boston v. Penny Lane Centers*, 170 Cal. App. 4th 936 (2009); *Fragassi v. Neiburger*, 646 N.E.2d 315 (Ill. App. 1995); *George v. D.W. Zinser Co.*, 762 N.W.2d 865 (Iowa 2009); *Hysten v. Burlington Northern*, 108 P.3d 437 (Kan. 2004); *Abraham v. County of Hennepin*, 639 N.W. 342 (Minn. 2002); *Cerracchio v. Alden Leeds, Inc.*, 538 A.2d 1292 (N.J. Superior 1988); *Gutierrez v. Sundance*, 868 P.2d 1266 (N.Mex. App. 1993); *D'Angelo v. Gardner*, 819 P2d 206 (Nev. 1991); *Jenkins v. Central Transport*, 2010 U.S. Dist. LEXIS 7739

(N.D. Ohio); *Vasek v. Board of County*, 186 P.3d 928 (Okla. 2008); *Walters v. Boll'n Oilfield*, 2008 U.S. Dist. LEXIS 12931 (D. Oreg. 2008). *Contra., Burham v. Karl and Geld*, 745 A.2d 178 (Conn. 2000). *See also* Maine Whistleblower Protection Act, 26 M.R.S. §§ 831-833.

PIPELINE SAFETY ACT

Pipeline Safety Improvement Act, 49 U.S.C. § 60129, implemented by the U.S. Department of Labor under 29 C.F.R. Part 1981. The rules governing administrative hearings are codified at 29 C.F.R. Part 18.

The U.S. Department of Labor Office of Administrative Law Judges compiles a comprehensive listing of whistleblower decisions under pipeline safety law. *See* www.oalj.dol.gov.

RIPPING OFF THE TAXPAYER/FALSE CLAIMS ACT

Rule 6 sets forth a detailed analysis of the False Claims Act.

The False Claims Act is codified at 31 U.S.C. § 3729-32 and the Major Frauds Act is codified at 18 U.S.C. § 1031. Additional antiretaliation provisions protecting employees who work on government contracts are contained in the American Recovery Reinvestment Act, P.L. 111-5 (antiretaliation in stimulus), and at 10 U.S.C. § 2409 and 41 U.S.C. § 265 (federal contractors and defense contractors). An overview of the FCA, written from a defense perspective, was prepared by John T. Boese, "Recent Developments under the Federal False Claims Act," Health Care Compliance Association (April 2016), at www .hccainfo.org/Portals/O/PDFs/Resources/Conference_Handouts/Compliance _Institute/2016/P6handout2.pdf.

SARBANES-OXLEY ACT ("SOX")

See sources listed under "Fraud Against Shareholders" and cases referenced in Checklist 2, "Whistleblower Protection Under Federal Law."

SEAMAN WHISTLEBLOWER PROTECTION

Protection of Seaman against Discrimination, 42 U.S.C. § 2114.

Protection for Members of Coast Guard, 33 C.F.R. Part 53.

The U.S. Department of Labor Office of Administrative Law Judges compiles a comprehensive listing of whistleblower decisions and will publish administrative rulings under this law. *See* www.oalj.dol.gov.

TRADE SECRETS
Defend Trade Secrets Act, 18 U.S.C. § 1833(b).

Senate Committee on the Judiciary, *Defend Trade Secrets Act of 2016*, Report No. 114-220 (March 7, 2016).

TRANSPORTATION (TRUCKING, RAILROADS, AND PUBLIC TRANSPORTATION)
National Transit Systems Security Act, 6 U.S.C. § 1142.

Railway Safety Labor Act, 49 U.S.C. § 20109.

Surface Transportation Act, 49 U.S.C. §§ 31101, 31105.

U.S. Department of Labor rules implementing the transportation whistle-blower laws: 29 C.F.R. Part 1978 (surface transportation); 29 C.F.R. Part 1982 (national transit and railroad safety). The rules governing the administrative hearings are located at 29 C.F.R. Part 18.

Department of Labor cases setting forth elements of railroad and trucking safety laws, damages, and how to calculate statute of limitations: *Anderson v. Amtrak*, 2009-FRS-3 (Dept. of Labor ALJ, Aug. 26, 2010) and *Canter v. Maverick Transportation*, 2009-STA-54 (Dept. of Labor ALJ, Oct. 28, 2010).

The U.S. Department of Labor Office of Administrative Law Judges compiles a comprehensive listing of whistleblower decisions under transportation safety laws. *See* www.oalj.dol.gov.

WITNESSES IN FEDERAL COURT PROCEEDINGS
Civil Rights Act of 1871, 42 U.S.C. § 1985.

The Supreme Court upheld federal claims under this Reconstruction Era statute in *Haddle v. Garrison*, 525 U.S. 121 (1998). Unlike most employment laws, this was enacted in 1871 when the current employee-employer relationships did not exist. Instead of prohibiting wrongful discharge, this statute prohibits "conspiracies" to interfere with witnesses at federal court proceedings. Victims of such conspiracies can obtain full tort remedies, including damages for economic harm, compensatory damages, and punitive damages. An issue critical to the future effectiveness of this law is known as the "intracorporate conspiracy doctrine." Under this doctrine persons employed within one corporation cannot "conspire" with each other. If the courts accept this rule, retaliation cases based on the *Haddle* precedent would be nearly impossible to establish in the modern work environment. However, a number of courts have rejected this doctrine and permitted *Haddle*-based claims to go forward. *See McAndrew v. Lockheed Martin*, 206 F.3d 1031 (11th Cir. 2000) (*en banc*).

Rule 5: Don't Forget State Laws

State "public policy" common law and statutory remedies for whistleblowers, along with citations to major cases, are set forth in Checklist 3.

Lawrence Blades, "Employment at Will v. Individual Freedom: On Limiting the Abusive Exercise of Employer Power," 67 *Columbia Law Review* 1404 (Dec. 1967). This ground-breaking law journal article was relied upon in numerous court decisions as providing a legal justification for changing the "at-will" doctrine.

Petermann v. International Brotherhood of Teamsters, 344 P.2d 25 (Cal. App. 1959). Stephen Kohn, "Concepts and Procedures in Whistleblower Law," Quorum Press 2000 (Chapter 2) (setting forth state-by-state analysis).

Robert G. Vaughn, "State Whistleblower Statutes and the Future of Whistleblower Protection," 51 *Administrative Law Review* 581 (1999).

Workplace Fairness publishes an online, state-by-state guide to local whistle-blower laws. *See* www.workplacefairness.org/whistleblowerclaim.

Wendeln v. Beatrice Manor, 712 N.W.2d 226 (Neb. 2006) (discussing difference in damages available to whistleblower under tort versus contract theories of recovery under state law).

Cases rejecting federal preemption of state whistleblower/employment claims: *English v. General Electric*, 496 U.S. 72 (1990) (state common law not preempted despite existence of federal safety-related whistleblower law); *Gervasio v. Continental Airlines*, 2008 U.S. Dist. LEXIS 58767 (N.J. 2008) (no federal pre-emption under Airline Deregulation Act); *Hawaiian Airlines v. Norris*, 512 U.S. 246 (1994) (no preemption under federal Railroad Safety Act); *Lingle v. Norge Division*, 486 U.S. 399 (1988) (state retaliatory discharge law not preempted by collective bargaining agreement). In addition, many whistleblower statutes, including those in the Dodd-Frank Act and the Sarbanes-Oxley Act, contain an explicit "savings clause" that preserves an employee's right to file state lawsuits based on the same underlying facts as those set forth in the federal lawsuit. *See,* e.g., 18 U.S.C. § 1514A(d) (SOX).

Rule 6: Get a Reward! False Claims Act/*Qui Tam*

The False Claims Act (FCA), 31 U.S.C. §§ 3729-32.

Modern Legislative History of the FCA: Committee on the Judiciary, "The False Claims Act of 1985," S. Rep. 99-345, 99th Cong., 2nd Sess. (1986). The major interpretative tool for understanding the 1986 amendments to the FCA that revitalized the law.

Committee on the Judiciary, "The False Claims Act Correction Act of 2008," S. Rep. 110-507, 110th Cong., 2nd Sess. (2008). Although the 2008 Senate report concerns the False Claims Act Corrections Act, a law that was never passed by Congress, in 2009–10 many of its provisions were approved (either in whole, in part, or in a modified form) and signed into law. *See* the Fraud Enforcement and Recovery Act, Public Law No. 111-21, § 4 (May 20, 2009); the Patient Protection and Affordable Care Act, Public Law No. 111-148, § 10104(j)(2) (March 23, 2010); and the Dodd-Frank Act, Public Law No. 111-203, § 1079A (July 21, 2010). The 2008 Senate Report is an excellent starting point for understanding these three amendments.

Committee on the Judiciary, "Fraud Enforcement and Recovery Act of 2009," S. Rep. 111-10, 111th Cong. 1st Sess. (2009) (legislative history for the 2009 FCA amendments). *See also* Extension Remarks by Congressman Berman, *Congressional Record,* pp, E1296–97 (June 3, 2009).

Decisions interpreting the original intent of the FCA: *U.S. ex rel. Marcus v. Hess,* 317 U.S. 537 (1943); *United States v. Griswold,* 24 F. 361 (D. Ore. 1885).

Decisions interpreting the 1986 amendments: *Vermont Agency of Natural Resources v. U.S. ex rel. Stevens,* 529 U.S. 765 (2000) (FCA is constitutional); *Rockwell International Corp. v. U.S. ex rel. Stone,* 549 U.S. 457 (2007) (limiting recoveries by relators; partially reversed by 2010 amendment to FCA); *Cook County v. U.S. ex rel. Chandler,* 538 U.S. 119 (2003) (municipal corporations covered under FCA); *KBR v. U.S. ex rel. Carter,* 135 S.Ct. 1970 (2015)(clarifying statute of limitations and original source standards); *Universal Health Services v. U.S. ex rel. Escobar,* 136 S.Ct. 1989 (2016) *State Farm v. U.S. ex rel. Rigsby,* 137 S.Ct. 436 (2016) (sanctions for violating seal).

The broad coverage of employers and contractors under the FCA's anti-retaliation provision was explained in *U.S. ex rel. Bias,* 816 F.3d 315 (5th Cir. 2016).

Claire Sylvia, "The False Claims Act: Fraud against the Government," *Thomson/West* (Danvers, Mass: 2004).

Note, "The History and Development of Qui Tam," *Wash. U. L. Q.* 81 (1972).

Joel Hesch, "Understanding the 'Original Source Exception' to the False Claims Act's 'Public Disclosure Bar' in Light of the Supreme Court's Ruling in *Rockwell v. United States*," 7 *DePaul Bus. & Com. Law Journal* 1 (Fall 2008).

Elleta Callahan and Terry Dworkin, "Do Good and Get Rich: Financial Incentives for Whistleblowing and the False Claims Act," 37 *Vill. L. Rev.* 273 (1992).

Thomas Harris, "Alternative Remedies & The False Claims Act: Protecting *Qui Tam* Relators in Light of Government Intervention and Criminal Prosecution Decisions," 94 *Cornell Law Review* 1293 (2009).

The U.S. Department of Justice discloses information on FCA recoveries on the webpage for the site Civil Division, Commercial Litigation Branch, Civil Frauds. *See* DOJ Civil Fraud press releases regarding FCA settlements and judgments, http://www.justice.gov/civil/frauds/Civil%20Fraud.htm. The Civil Frauds web page also has statistics on FCA recoveries and a "primer" outlining basic tenants of the FCA.

As of Sept. 30, 2016, the total recoveries under the whistleblower *qui tam* provisions of the FCA were $37.685 billion.

Some of the 2010 rewards were: Allegan, Inc. paid $600 million for improper "off-label" marketing of Botox; Teva Pharmaceuticals paid $169 million for inflating prices for medications sold under state Medicaid programs; Hewlett-Packard paid $55 million for paying kickbacks to obtain recommendations for agency purchases of its products; Chevron and Mobil paid $45.5 million and $32.2 million, respectfully, for underpaying royalties on natural gas production on federal lands; Tyco International and three other companies paid $39 million for providing substandard parts for water supply systems. *See* Taxpayers against Fraud Education Fund, "False Claims Act Update & Alert," *Press Release* (Oct. 1, 2010).

On December 14, 2016, the Department of Justice issued a statement from Benjamin Mizer, the Principal Deputy Assistant General for the Civil Division, praising the whistleblower provisions of the False Claims Act. He explained that the "beneficiaries" of FCA litigation include "veterans, the elderly, and low-income families who are insured by federal health care programs; families and students who are unable to afford homes and go to college thanks to federally insured loans; and all of us who are protected by the government's investment in national security and defense. In short, Americans across the country are healthier, enjoy a better quality of life, and are safer because of our continuing success in protecting taxpayer funds from misuse."

The types of cases whistleblowers successfully filed has remained remarkably consistent. For example in 2016 taxpayers recovered $2.9 billion from cases filed by whistleblowers, including a $67 million recovery against Genetech Inc. for providing false information about a cancer drug; M&T Bank had to pay $64 million for issuing improper mortgages; Z. Gallerie had to pay $15 million for evasion of customs duties; 21st Century Oncology paid $37.7 million for performing unnecessary procedures; ArmorSource paid $3 million due to illegal manufacturing and testing methods used to produce military helmets; Lockheed Martin paid $5 million for failing to properly dispose of dangerous waste; Centerra Services paid $7.4 million for double billing on wartime security contracts; RehabdCare and Kindred Health Care paid $125 million for performing unnecessary rehabilitation services.

Rule 7: Get a Reward! Tax Cheats and the IRS *Qui Tam*

The IRS rewards law is codified at 26 U.S.C. § 7623. IRS Notice 2008-4, 2008-1 C.B. sets forth procedures for submitting claims to the IRS Whistleblower Office. *See also* Internal Revenue Manual, Part 25.2.2 (updated June 18, 2010). The IRS is in the process of publishing final rules for its whistleblower program at 26 C.F.R. § 301. The IRS Whistleblower Office website: *www.irs.gov/ uac/whistleblower-informant-award*.

The Tax Court can hear appeals filed by whistleblowers that challenge both the amount of an award or the denial of an award. *Cooper v. Commissioner*, 2010 Tax Court LEXIS 20, 135 T.C. No. 4 (July 8, 2010).

Whistleblower 21276-13W v. Commissioner of IRS, 147 Tax Court 4 (Aug. 3, 2016) (Tax Court expands scope of "alternative remedy" provision). (Note: The commission does not approve of this ruling.)

Whistleblower 21276-13W v. Commissioner of IRS, 144 Tax Court 290 (2015) (Form 211 need not be filed before whistleblower provides information to other parts of the IRS).

IRS Whistleblower Office, Annual Report to Congress on the Use of Section 7623 (2009).

Department of Treasury Inspector General for Tax Administration, "Deficiencies Exist in the Control and Timely Resolution of Whistleblower Claims" (Aug. 20, 2009).

Alexander Dyck, et al., "Who Blows the Whistle on Corporate Fraud?" University of Chicago Booth School of Business (Working Paper No. 08-22).

U.S. Tax Court, Title XXXIII, "Whistleblower Actions," Rules 340-344 (tax court rules for whistleblower appeals).

Dennis Ventry, Jr., "Whistleblowers and *Qui Tam* for Tax," Vol. 61 *Tax Lawyer* 357 (2007).

Karie Davis-Nozemack, et al., "Lost Opportunities: The Underuse of Tax Whistleblowers," 67 *Administrative Law Review* 321 (2015).

Government Accountability Office, *IRS Whistleblower Program: Billions Collected, but Timeliness and Communication Concerns May Discourage Whistleblowers*, GAO-16-20 (October 2015).

Government Accountability Office, *Offshore Tax Evasion: IRS has Collected Billions of Dollars, but May be Missing Continued Evasion*, GAO-13-318 (March 2013).

Stephen Ohlemacher, "Tips on tax cheats skyrocket with bigger rewards," Associated Press (Oct. 1, 2009); Barry Shlachter, "Tax Whistleblowers Stand to Reap Bigger IRS Rewards," Star-Telegram.com (April 14, 2010).

John Koskinen, Commissioner, IRS, Prepared Remarks Before the U.S. Council for International Business-OECD, International Tax Conference (Washington, D.C., June 3, 2014).

Bradley Birkenfeld, the most famous tax whistleblower, told his story in his book *Lucifer's Banker: The Untold Story of How I Destroyed Swiss Bank Secrecy* (Greenleaf Book Group Press, Austin TX, 2016).

Rule 8: Get a Reward! Securities and Commodities Fraud

The three main whistleblower protection provisions in Dodd-Frank are codified at 7 U.S.C. § 26 (commodities); 15 U.S.C. § 78u-6 (securities); and 12 U.S.C. § 5567 (consumer protection).

Dodd-Frank Act, Public Law No. 111-203, 124 Statutes at Large 1376 (July 21, 2010). The following sections enhance whistleblower rights: § 748 creates a new section 23 of the Commodities Exchange Act that provides for mandatory whistleblower rewards and prohibits retaliation; § 922 creates a new 21F of the Securities Exchange Act that provides for mandatory whistleblower rewards and prohibits retaliation; §§ 922 and 929A contain the provisions that amended and improved the Sarbanes-Oxley whistleblower protections; § 924 requires the SEC to establish a special whistleblower office and enact regulations enforcing whistleblower rules; § 1507 establishes new whistleblower protections for employees who make protected disclosures related to the enforcement of the Bureau of Consumer Financial Protection; § 1079B(c) amended the False Claims Act antiretaliation law to provide for universal national three-year statute of limitations to file wrongful discharge/retaliation claims under the FCA.

The Securities and Exchange Commission (SEC) and the Commodities Futures Trading Commission (CFTC) will publish rules governing the whistleblower rewards provisions of Dodd-Frank. The SEC's rules are codified at 17 C.F.R. Parts 240 and 249. The CFTC rules are codified at 17 C.F.R. Part 165.

Reward claims must be filed as mandated under the rules of the SEC or CFTC. The failure to follow these procedures can result in the denial of a reward.

On June 13, 2011, the SEC published its final version of these rules, along with an extensive analysis of each requirement. A similar publication by the CFTC was published shortly thereafter, on August 25, 2011. The actual regulations, and the detailed explanation of these rules, are available at: 76 *Federal Register* 34300 (SEC) and 76 *Federal Register* 53172 (CFTC).

U.S. Senate Committee on Banking, Housing, and Urban Affairs, "The Restoring American Financial Stability Act of 2010," *Senate Report No. 111-176*, 111th Cong. 2nd Session (April 30, 2010) (the final Senate report containing the legislative history/analysis of the Dodd-Frank Act).

U.S. Senate Committee on Banking, Housing, and Urban Affairs, "Dodd-Frank Wall Street Reform and Consumer Protection Act: Conference Report," *Senate Report No. 111-517*, 111th Cong. 2nd Session (June 29, 2010) (containing the final text of the Dodd-Frank Act).

The SEC's policy and practices on "disgorgement" in *Janigan v. Taylor*, 344 F.2d 781 (1st Cir. 1978); Elaine Buckberg and Frederick Dunbar, "Disgorgement: Punitive Damages and Remedial Offers," 63 *Bus. Law.* 347 (2008).

Prior to the passage of the Dodd-Frank Act, the Inspector General for the SEC concluded that the existing voluntary bounty program was gravely deficient. Securities and Exchange Commission, Office of Inspector General, Office of Audit, "Assessment of the SEC's Bounty Program," *Report No. 474* (March 29, 2010). The Office of Inspector General was also very critical of the SEC's handling of the Madoff scandal and the whistleblowers who had stepped forward. *See* SEC, Office of Inspector General, Office of Investigations, "Investigation of Failure of the SEC to Uncover Bernard Madoff's Ponzi Scheme," OIG Report No. OIG-509 (Aug. 31, 2009).

Testimony of Harry Markopolos before the House Committee on Financial Services (Feb. 4, 2009); Senate Banking, Housing, and Urban Affairs Committee (Sept. 10, 2009) (Markopolos provided testimony in support of the new *qui tam* provisions contained in Dodd-Frank). *See* Suzy Jagger, "Madoff Warnings 'Ignored for 10 Years,'" *TimesOnline* (Dec. 17, 2008).

U.S. Senate Committee on Banking, Housing, and Urban Affairs, "Dodd-Frank Wall Street Reform: Conference Report Summary" (Committee website, 2010).

U.S. Senate Committee on Banking, Housing, and Urban Affairs, "Dodd Statement on Wall Street Reform Conference" (June 25, 2010).

Congressional Record, S. 4066 (May 20, 2010) (Statement by Senator Feingold).

Geoffrey Rapp, "Beyond Protection: Invigorating Incentives for Sarbanes-Oxley Corporate and Securities Fraud Whistleblowers," Vol. 87 *Boston University Law Review* 91 (2007).

Rule 9: Get a Reward! Report Foreign Corrupt Practices Worldwide

The Foreign Corrupt Practices Act, 15 U.S.C. § 78m and § 78dd-1, et seq.

The Department of Justice (DOJ) resource page on the FCPA is located at www .justice.gov/criminal-fraud/foreign-corrupt-practices-act.

The legislative history of the FCPA is published by the DOJ at www.justice.gov/ criminal-fraud/legislative-history.

The best source of information explaining the requirements of the FCPA is the *Resource Guide to the U.S. Foreign Corrupt Practices Act*, published by the Criminal Division of the DOJ and the Enforcement Division of the Securities and Exchange Commission (SEC). A copy of this guide is available at www.whistle blowers.org.

Resources for understanding the FCPA, including translations of how the law works in more than ten languages, are published at www.kkc.com/Handbook and www.globalwhistleblower.org.

The FCPA statute is translated into fifty languages at www.justice.gov/ criminal-fraud/statutes-regulations.

The SEC publishes a list of FCPA prosecutions at www.sec.gov/spotlight/fcpa/ fcpa-cases.shtml.

The following articles provide additional information and perspectives on FCPA.

Bryan Cave, "Alert: The Implications for FCPA Enforcement of the SEC's New Whistleblower Rules" (June 22, 2011); available at www.bryancave.com.

Philip M. Nichols, "The Neomercantilist Fallacy and the Contextual Reality of the Foreign Corrupt Practices Act," 53 *Harvard Journal on Legislation* 203 (Winter 2016) (broad scope of FCPA).

Daniel Grimm, "Traversing the Minefield: Joint Ventures and the Foreign Corrupt Practices Act," 9 *Virginia Law and Business Review* 91 (2014) (broad reach of FCPA).

The SEC has a web page, "FCPA Spotlight," located at www.sec.gov/spotlight/fcpa.shtml. The SEC's website also contains a list of every foreign company that sells stocks to Americans under the American Depository Receipt program.

An FCPA violation also implicates the following laws, which can give rise to additional penalties: Sarbanes-Oxley Act, Section 302 (15 U.S.C. § 7241) (accuracy of financial reports); Section 404 (15 U.S.C. § 7262) (internal controls over financial reporting); Travel Act (18 U.S.C. § 1952); as well as laws covering money laundering, mail and wire fraud, false certifications, and violations of the Internal Revenue Code.

Rule 10: Get a Reward!: Make Sure Automobiles Are Safe

The antiretaliation law: 49 U.S.C. § 30171.

The Department of Labor regulations implementing the law: 29 C.F.R. § 1988. Statute setting forth entitlement to rewards: 49 U.S. Code § 30172.

Legislative history of the reward statute: Senate Report 114-13, "Motor Vehicle Safety Whistleblower Act, Report of the Committee on Commerce, Science, and Transportation on S. 304" (April 13, 2015).

"Examining S. 3302, The Motor Vehicle Safety Act of 2010," hearing before the Committee on Commerce, Science, and Transportation, U.S. Senate (Senate Hearing 111-991) (May 19, 2010).

Statement of Senator Jay Rockefeller IV, press release (May 4, 2010).

ABC Prime Time Live, "Mini Van Danger" (May 3, 2008).

Bill Vlasic, "Fired Employee Battles Chrysler in Courtroom," the *Detroit News* (July 2003).

Chrysler Corp. v. Sheridan, No. 227757 (Mich. Court of Appeals, 2003) (unpublished) (dismissing whistleblower's lawsuit).

Office of John Thune press statement on reward law: "Thune, Nelson Introduce Legislation to Help Prevent Auto Injuries, Deaths from Faulty Parts by Incentivizing Whistleblowers" (November 20, 2014); www.thune.senate

.gov/public/index.cfm/2014/11/thune-nelson-introduce-legislation-to-help
-prevent-auto-injuries-deaths-from-faulty-parts-by-incentivizing-whistle-
blowers.

Rule 11: Get a Reward!: Stop the Pollution of the Oceans

The APPS whistleblower reward provision is codified at 33 U.S.C. § 1908(a).

The International Convention for the Prevention of Pollution from Ships (MARPOL 73/78) is available at http://library.arcticportal.org/1699/1/marpol .pdf.

A practical guide to the MARPOL convention is available at https://madden maritime.files.wordpress.com/2015/08/marpol-practical-guide.pdf.

U.S. DOJ, Environment and Natural Resources Division. A motion request- ing 50 percent whistleblower reward in *U.S. v. Overseas Shipholding Group, Inc.*, 06-CR-10408 (D. Mass, March 15, 2007) is available at www.globalwhistle blower.org.

Michael G. Chalos and Wayne Parker, "The Criminalization of MARPOL Violations and Maritime Accidents in the United States," 23 *University of San Francisco Maritime Law Journal* 206 (Fall 2011). Although antiwhistleblower in tone and content, this article sets forth the various laws and legal standards applicable to APPS prosecutions.

"Avoiding the APPS Magic Pipe Trap," Officer of the Watch website (November 14, 2012), offers another antiwhistleblower position; https://officerofthewatch .com/2012/11/14/avoiding-the-apps-magic-pipe-trap/.

A detailed listing of APPS cases for which rewards were paid (including cop- ies of the indictments, plea agreements, and whistleblower reward filings) is posted at www.kkc.com/resources/APPS.

The Marine Defenders organization publishes information on APPS whis- tleblower rules, and also has a handbook designed to help seamen involved in government investigations. *See* www.marinedefenders.com/commercial/ rewards.php.

U.S. v. Efploia Shipping Co. S.A., Case 1:11-cr-00652-MJG, Bench Decision *Re: Whistleblower Award* (ECF Doc. 80) (D. Maryland) (April 25, 2016). The Court discussed congressional intent behind the APPS whistleblower provision and the fact that most, if not all, APPS prosecutions come from evidence provided by whistleblowers.

DOJ press release regarding the Efploia Shipping Company and Aquarosa Shipping case is available at www.justice.gov/opa/pr/two-shipping-corporations-plead-guilty-and-are-sentenced-maryland-obstruction-justice.

Rule 12: Get a Reward!: End Wildlife Trafficking

The main wildlife whistleblower reward laws are codified as follows: Lacey Act, 16 U.S.C. §3375(d); Endangered Species Act, 16 U.S.C. §1540(d); Rhinoceros and Tiger Conservation Act, 16 U.S.C. §5305a(f); Antarctic Conservation Act, 16 U.S.C. §§2409 & 2439; Fish and Wildlife Improvement Act, 16 U.S.C. §742l(c)(3); and Wild Bird Conservation Act, 16 U.S.C. §§4912(c) & 4913(b). All of these laws are substaintally identical.

The sweeping authority granted the Fish and Wildlife Service and the National Marine Fisheries Service to award whistleblowers under any wildlife protection laws administered by these agencies for reporting violations was enacted as part of the Fish and Wildlife Improvement Act, Pub. L. No. 97-396, 96 Stat. 2005, 16 U.S.C. §742l(k)(2).

The Congressional history behind the original 1981 amendments to the Lacey Act, which included the whistleblower reward laws, is located in House Report No. 97-276 (Oct. 19, 1981).

The legislative history of the 1982 Fish and Wildlife Improvement Act which empowered the Fish and Wildlife Service and the National Marine Fisheries Service to pay rewards under all wildlife laws administered by these agencies is set forth in 128 CONG. REC. H10207 and H31972 (Dec. 17, 1982).

For a complete understanding of the wildlife whistleblower laws and the scope of their coverage *see* Kohn, *Monetary Rewards for Wildlife Whistleblowers: A Game-Changer in Wildlife Trafficking Detection and Deterence*, 46 Environmental Law Reporter 10054 (January 2016).

President Obama's Exec. Order on wildlife trafficking is codifed as E.O. No. 13,648 (July 1, 2013).

The testimony of Assistant Attorney General John Cruden was submitted to the House Committee on Foreign Affairs, Subcommittee on Terrorism, Nonproliferation and Trade (April 22, 2015), www.justice.gov/opa/speech/poaching-terrorism-national-security-challenge-statement-assistant-attorney -general.

For information on the Lacey Act *see* Association of Fish & Wildlife Agencies, *The Importance of the Lacey Act: The Nation's Champion Legislation Against Wildlife Crime & Illegal Wildlife Trade* 2 (2014) ("The Lacey Act remains one of the nation's most important conservation statutes and a powerful tool for protecting fish and wildlife in the U.S. and supporting conservation worldwide."), available at http://www.fishwildlife.org/files/LaceyAct_FactSheet.pdf.

The Lacey Act is codified at 16 U.S.C. §3372, et seq.

The Convention on International Trade in Endangered Species of Wild Fauna and Flora (CITES), 27 UST 1087; TIAS 8249; 993 UNTS 243. *See* https://www.cites.org/eng.

1 *Id.* at 19. This is the international convention signed by over 150 countries, including the United States, prohibiting trafficking in protected plants, fish and animals. The Lacey Act implements this treaty.

The END Wildlife Trafficking Act, Public Law 114-231 (October 7, 2016).

For information on the wildlife whistleblower reward laws and how to file a claim see www.whistleblowers.org/wildlife.

Rule 13: If Working for the Government, Use the First Amendment

Pickering v. Board of Education, 391 U.S. 563 (1968) (government employee speech on matters of "public concern" protected under the First Amendment) (holding applies to all employees who work in the public sector).

Civil Rights Act of 1871, 42 U.S.C. § 1983 (federal civil rights law that permits state and local employees to file *Pickering* claims in whistleblower retaliation cases). When seeking damages under § 1983 it is advisable to always name the government employees and managers responsible for the retaliation in the lawsuit, as there are strict limits on the ability to directly sue a state or municipality under that law. *See Monell v. New York City*, 436 U.S. 658 (1978) (setting forth rule on suing municipalities); *Will v. Michigan*, 491 U.S. 58 (1989) (states and state employees acting in an "official capacity" immune from lawsuits under § 1983); *Harlow v. Fitzgerald*, 457 U.S. 800 (1982) (setting forth standards necessary to sue individual government managers and supervisors in their "personal capacity" under the "qualified immunity" standard).

Legal standards governing *Pickering* causes of action: *Mt. Healthy v. Doyle*, 429 U.S. 274 (1977) (standard of proof); *Givhan v. Western Line*, 439 U.S. 410 (1979) (complaints raised internally may still be protected, even if no public disclosure); *Connick v. Myers*, 461 U.S. 138 (1983) (First Amendment protections only apply on issues of "public concern," private workplace grievances not covered under *Pickering*); *Rankin v. McPherson*, 483 U.S. 378 (1987) (broad definition of protected activity); *Bush v. Lucas*, 462 U.S. 367 (1983) (when seeking damages, federal employees must exhaust administrative remedies); *Garcetti v. Ceballos*, 547 U.S. 410 (2006) (narrowed definition of protected activity to exclude disclosures made pursuant to "official duties"); *U.S. v. NTEU*, 513 U.S. 454 (1995) and *Sanjour v. EPA*, 56 F.3d 85 (DC Cir. 1995) (*en banc*) (injunctive relief available to prevent chilling effect on First Amendment); *Swartzwelder v. McNeilly*, 297 F.3d 228 (3rd. Cir. 2002) (Circuit Judge—now Supreme Court Justice—Samuel Alito upholding preliminary injunction concerning police department rule that limited employee rights to make protected disclosures).

In *Borough of Duryea v. Guarnieri*, 131 S.Ct. 2488 (2011), the Supreme Court held that petitions to government bodies filed by public employees (including lawsuits filed in court) are protected under the First Amendment if they address matters of "public concern."

Richard Whitmore and David Urban, "Public Employees and Free Speech," www.Dailyjournal.com/cle.cfm.

The laws protecting federal employees are set forth in Rule 4.

Rule 14: Federal Employees—Defend Your Jobs!

The major law covering federal employee whistleblowers is the Civil Service Reform Act, 5 U.S.C. § 2302, and the Whistleblower Protection Act of 1989, *as amended*, 5 U.S.C. §§ 1211–15, 1218–19, and 1221–22. *See* Passman and Kaplan, P. C., *Federal Employees Legal Survival Guide* (Cincinnati, OH: National Employee Rights Institute, 1999); Robert Vaughn, *Merit Systems Protection Board: Rights and Remedies* (New York: Law Journal Press, 1984); and Peter Broida, *A Guide to Merit Systems Protection Board Law and Practice* (Dewey Publications, 1998).

The U.S. Merit Systems Protection Board published a case-law guide for the Whistleblower Protection Act. The guidebook was published before the law was amended in 2012 and is out of date on various issues. *See* MSPB, *Whistleblower Protections for Federal Employees* (September 2010); published at www.mspb.gov/.

The MSBP also publishes a Q&A on filing whistleblower cases: www.mspb.gov/appeals/whistleblower.htm.

An excellent decision outlining the proof employers need to prevail in a WPA action is *Chambers v. Department of Interior*, 2011, MSPB 7 (January 11, 2011) (ordering the Chief of U.S. Park Police reinstated to her position). This decision was issued before the 2012 amendments that significantly strengthened the WPA.

On November 27, 2012, President Obama signed the Whistleblower Protection Enhancement Act (Public Law 112-199) into law. The act improved the legal protections afforded federal workers under the WPA. The legislative history of the Enhancement Act contained in Senate Report 112-155, published by the U.S. Senate Committee on Homeland Security and Government Affairs, "Whistleblower Protection Enhancement Act of 2012) (April 19, 2012).

The Whistleblower Protection Enhancement Act of 2012 prohibited government agencies from using restrictive nondisclosure forms that would prohibit an employee's ability to file complaints with various government agencies, including the Office of Special Counsel or to communicate with Congress. *See* Public Law 112-199 § 115(a). Additionally, Congress uses the Appropriations Act process to prohibit the use of any government funds to pay the salary of any government employee who is responsible for having employees execute nondisclosure forms that restrict an employee's ability to file complaints or blow the whistle to Congress. *See* Consolidated Appropriations Act of 2016, Public Law 114-113 § 713.

Executive Order 12731, § 101(k) (October 17, 1990), mandates that all federal employees "shall disclose waste, fraud, abuse, and corruption to appropriate authorities." The Office of Government Ethics interpreted this mandate broadly and intended that the executive order encourage the "over reporting" of potential abuses. Office of Government Ethics, "Standards of Ethical Conduct for Employees of the Executive Branch, Final Rule," 57 *Federal Register* 35006 (August 7, 1992).

Mixed Cases. If an employee alleges retaliation based on both discrimination (i.e., a sex or race discrimination claim) and whistleblowing, the two cases can be joined and litigated in U.S. District Court: 5 U.S.C. § 7702; *Ikossi v. Navy*, 516 F.3d 1037 (D.C. Cir. 2008); *Bonds v. Leavitt*, 629 F.3d 369 (4th Cir. 2011).

Federal employees are also protected under some specific federal laws that govern limited areas of the government. For example, federal employees of the Nuclear Regulatory Commission and the Department of Energy are protected under Section 211 of the Energy Reorganization Act, 42 U.S.C. § 5851, if they make disclosures related to nuclear safety. Similarly, a number of the environmental whistleblower laws also cover federal employees. In *Erickson v. U.S. EPA*, 1999-CAA-2 (consolidated case; ARB, May 31, 2006) (available online at http://www.oalj.dol.gov/PUBLIC/ARB/DECISIONS/ARB_DECISIONS/CAA/03_002A.CAAP.PDF.), the Department of Labor, after briefings from the Solicitor of Labor, held that federal employees were protected under the Clean Air Act, 42 U.S.C. § 7622, and the Solid Waste Disposal Act, 42 U.S.C. § 6971. The Solicitor of Labor argued that federal employees were also covered under the Comprehensive Environmental Response (Superfund), 42 U.S.C. § 9610 and the Safe Drinking Water Act, 42 U.S.C. § 300j-9(i). The Department indicated that they would follow that guidance, but did not formally decide the issue.

The case law under the federal environmental whistleblower statutes which provide protection for federal employees is located at http://www.oalj.dol.gov/LIBWHIST.HTM.

Employees of the Federal Reserve, the Federal Housing Finance Board, the Comptroller of the Currency, and the Office of Thrift Supervision are covered under the Depository Institution Employee Protection law, 12 U.S.C. § 1831j. Under the Credit Union Act, 12 U.S.C. § 1790b, federal employees of the National Credit Union Administration have whistleblower protections independent of the weaker WPA.

The Privacy Act is codified at 5 U.S.C. § 552a.

Federal employees must first exhaust administrative remedies before they can file a First Amendment retaliation claim (*Bush v. Lucas*, 462 U.S. 367 [1983]). However, pre-enforcement challenges to rules, policies, or practices of federal agencies that violate the First Amendment may be directly challenged in federal court (*Weaver v. USIA*, 87 F.3d 1429 [D.C. Cir. 1996]).

Federal employees who suffer adverse employment actions based on an unconstitutional law cannot challenge that law directly in federal court. They must first exhaust their administrative remedies before the MSBP before being able to raise a challenge in federal court. Moreover, that challenge may have to be raised as part of the appeal of a final decision of the MSPB, which presumably (as a federal administrative agency) will have to uphold the constitutionality of the challenged statute (*Elgin v. Department of Treasury*, 132 S.Ct. 2126 [2012]).

The administrative processes open to federal employees under the Whistleblower Protection Act, and the exclusion of federal employees who perform work for intelligence agencies from protection under the law, have been severely criticized: Senate Committee on Homeland Security and Government Affairs, "The Federal Employee Protection of Disclosures Act: Amendment to the Whistleblower Protection Act," hearing (November 12, 2003); House Committee on Oversight and Government Reform, "Protecting the Public from Waste, Fraud, and Abuse: H.R. 1507, The Whistleblower Enhancement Act," hearing (May 14, 2009).

National Security and Intelligence Agency Whistleblowers. The full public law enacting protections for intelligence agency whistleblowers is located at Pub. L. 113–126, title VI, § 604, July 7, 2014, 128 Stat. 1421.

Rodney Perry, *Intelligence Whistleblower Protection: In Brief*, Congressional Research Service (October 23, 2014), is an excellent overview of the laws covering intelligence agency whistleblowers.

Office of the Director of National Intelligence web pages explaining the Intelligence Community Whistleblower Protection Act are located at www.dni.gov/files/documents/ICD/ICD%20120.pdf and www.dni.gov/index.php/about-this-site/contact-the-ig/making-lawful-disclosures.

U.S. Department of Defense Office of Inspector General, *Guide to Investigating Military Whistleblower Reprisal and Restriction Complaints*: www.dodig.mil/Programs/Whistleblower/ioguide.html.

Presidential Policy Directive 19 (PPD-19) (October 10, 2012), *Protecting Whistleblowers with Access to Classified Information*, provides some protection for intelligence community employees against retaliation for lawfully blowing the whistle. In addition, employees and contractors are protected from reprisals in the security clearance adjudication process. PPD-19 requires that the inspector general review whistleblower reprisal allegations in violation of PPD-19. *See* www.whitehouse.gov/sites/default/files/image/ppd-19.pdf.

The Intelligence Community Whistleblower Protection Act is an early law that sets forth procedures for intelligence agency employees to report information to Congress. It is limited to reporting "urgent concerns." The Act may protect employees from criminal prosecution, but it does not prohibit retaliation. The Act is deficient. *See*, Public Law 105-272.

Dan Meyer and David Berenbaum, "The WASP's Nest: Intelligence Community Whistleblowing and Source Protection, vol. 8, *Journal of National Security Law and Policy* (May 8, 2015).

New York Times Co. v. United States, 403 U.S. 713 (1971) (Pentagon Papers case).

Snepp v. U.S., 444 U.S. 507 (1980); *U.S. v. Marchetti*, 466 F.2d 1309 (4th Cir. 1972) (cases discussing the pre-publication review process).

The FBI Whistleblower Protection Act is codified at 5 U.S.C. § 2303. In 2016 the Senate Judiciary Committee issued a report critical of this Act and proposed reforms. *See* S. Rep. 114-261: www.congress.gov/congressional-report/114th-congress/senate-report/261/1.

In 2015–16 the FBI whistleblower program was studied by both Congress and the Government Accountability Office (GAO). *See* U.S. Government Accountability Office, *Whistleblower Protection: Additional Actions Needed to Improve DOJ's Handling of FBI Retaliation Complaints* (GAO-15-112; January 2015); Senate Judiciary Committee, *FBI Whistleblower Protection Enhancement Act of 2016*, Senate Report No. 114-261 (May 25, 2016), located at https://www.congress.gov/114/crpt/srpt261/CRPT-114srpt261.pdf.

Rule 15: Make Sure Disclosures Are Protected

James Madison floor speech introducing the Bill of Rights in Congress is found in *The Annals of Congress*, 1st Congress, 1st Session (June 8, 1789), p. 451, and is posted on the Library of Congress website at: http://memory.loc.gov/ammem/amlaw/lwac.html.

The following list is a nonexhaustive summary of cases that define the scope of protected activity under various state and federal laws. The whistleblower protection laws themselves also contain explicit statutory provisions defining various protected disclosures. Always double-check the specific law to ensure that your whistleblower disclosures are protected. Not all federal laws protect the same activities. Each state has its own definition of a protected disclosure.

EXAMPLES UNDER STATE LAW

Disclosing a "statutory violation for the public's benefit": *Gantt v. Sentry*, 824 P.2d 680 (Calif. 1992) (cases interpreting state public policy exception).

Exercising statutory or constitutional right: *Gantt v. Sentry*, 824 P.2d 680 (Calif. 1992); *Thompson v. St. Regis Paper Co.*, 685 P.2d 1081 (Wash. 1984) (cases interpreting state public policy exception).

General Common Law/Disclosures protected under "public policy": *Tameny v. Atlantic Richfield*, 610 P.2d 1330 (Calif. 1980); *Carl v. Children's Hospital*, 702 A.2d 159 (D.C. App. 1997) (*en banc*) (see analysis contained in various concurring and dissenting opinions); *Kelsay v. Motorola, Inc.*, 384 N.E.2d 353 (Ill. 1978); *Pierce v. Ortho Pharmaceutical Corp.*, 417 A.2d 505 (N.J. 1980); *Payne v. Rozendaal*, 520 A.2d 586 (Vt. 1986) (cases interpreting state tort laws).

Internal disclosure to upper management: *Tartaglia v. UBS PaineWebber*, 961 A.2d 1167 (N.J. 2008).

Internal Quality Assurance complaint concerning patient safety: *Darrow v. Integris Health, Inc.*, 176 P.3d 1204 (Okla. 2008).

Performing a duty required under law: *Gantt v. Sentry*, 824 P.2d 680 (Calif. 1992) (cases interpreting state public policy exception).

Refusal to commit an act in violation of clear mandate of public policy: *D'Agostino v. Johnson & Johnson*, 628 A.2d 305 (N.J. 1993).

Refusal to violate a law: *Gantt v. Sentry*, 824 P.2d 680 (Calif. 1992) (cases interpreting state public policy); *Thompson v. St. Regis Paper Co.*, 685 P.2d 1081 (Wash. 1984).

Refusal to commit perjury: *Petermann v. International Brotherhood of Teamsters*, 344 P.2d 25 (Calif. App. 1959).

Report to government agency: *Wendeln v. The Beatrice Manor, Inc.*, 712 N.W.2d 226 (Neb. 2006).

Testimony before City Council: *Carl v. Children's Hospital*, 702 A.2d 159 (D.C. App. 1997) (*en banc*); *Williams v. Johnson*, 597 F.Supp.2d 107 (D.D.C. 2009).

Threat to Make Protected Disclosure: *Shallal v. Catholic Social Services*, 566 N.W.2d 571 (Mich. 1997); *Tartaglia v. UBS PaineWebber*, 961 A.2d 1167 (N.J. 2008).

Unsafe employer practices: *Palmateer v. International Harvester*, 421 N.E.2d 876 (Ill. 1981); *Wheeler v. Caterpillar Tractor*, 485 N.E.2d 2d 372 (Ill. 1985) (cases interpreting state public policy exception).

Violation of criminal laws: *Palmateer v. International Harvester*, 421 N.E.2d 876 (Ill. 1981); *Hodges v. Gibson Products*, 811 P.2d 151 (Utah 1991); *Thompson v. St. Regis Paper Co.*, 685 P.2d 1081 (Wash. 1984) (cases interpreting state public policy exception).

EXAMPLES UNDER FEDERAL LAW

Broad Interpretation of Scope of Protected Activity under Federal Laws: *NLRB v. Scrivener*, 405 U.S. 117 (1972) (National Labor Relations Act); *Clean Harbors v. Herman*, 146 F.3d 12 (1st Cir. 1998) (Surface Transportation Act); *U.S. ex rel. Yesudian v. Howard University*, 153 F.3d 731 (D.C. Cir. 1998) (False Claims Act). *See also* definition of protected activity in the EEOC Compliance Manual, § 8-II(B)(2), available at http://www.eeoc.gov/policy/docs/retal.html#IIpartB.

Congress: *Richards v. Mileski*, 662 F.2d 65 (D.C. Cir. 1981); *Tremblay v. Marsh*, 750 F.2d 3 (1st Cir. 1984); *Robinson v. Southeastern Pennsylvania Transp.*, 982 F.2d 892 (3rd Cir. 1993); *Chambers v. Department of Interior*, 515 F.3d 1362, 136768 (Fed. Cir. 2008) (claim under Whistleblower Protection Act). The Lloyd-LaFollette Act of 1912 provides that "the right of employees" to "petition Congress or a Member of Congress" and to "furnish information" to Congress "may not be interfered with." H. Rep. 388, 62nd Cong. 2nd Sess. (1912). The Congressional debates on this early whistleblower law are at 48 *Congressional Record* 671–77,

4513, 4654, 10728–10733, 10792–10804 and 10676 (1912). Congress also enacted antigag rules as part of the appropriations process (i.e., prohibiting federal agencies from spending any money on gag orders that restrict employee communications with Congress). *See* The Consolidated Appropriations Act of 2010, Public Law 111-117 § 717.

<u>Direct Contact with Federal Law Enforcement or Regulatory Authorities</u>: Most whistleblower statutes explicitly protect these contacts. The federal obstruction of justice statute makes it a criminal offense to harm any person in their livelihood who provides truthful information to federal law enforcement. 18 U.S.C. § 1512(e); *DeFord v. Secretary of Labor*, 700 F.2d 281 (6th Cir. 1983).

Disclosing Allegations though an Attorney: *Eng v. Cooley,* 552 F.3d 1062, 1073 (9th Cir. 2009).

<u>Failure to Raise Concerns through the Chain of Command or by Using Mandatory Procedures</u>: *Fabricius v. Town of Braintree*, 97-CAA-14, Decision and Order of Department of Labor Administrative Review Board (Feb. 9, 1999) (Clean Air Act case); *Pogue v. DOL*, 940 F.2d 1287 (9th Cir. 1991) (environmental laws); *Dutkiewicz v. Clean Harbors Environmental Services*, 95-STA-4, Decision of Department of Labor Administrative Review Board (Aug. 8, 1997), *affirmed* 146 F.3d 12 (1st Cir. 1998) (Surface Transportation Act).

<u>Internal Reports "before Plaintiff Puts Together All the Pieces of the Puzzle"</u>: *Young v. CHS Middle East*, LLC, 2015 U.S. App. LEXIS 8732 (4th Cir. 2015).

<u>Internal Complaints to Supervisors</u>: *Munsey v. Morton*, 507 F.2d 1202 (D.C. Cir. 1974); *Phillips v. Board of Mine Operations Appeals*, 500 F.2d 772 (D.C. Cir. 1974) (Mine Health and Safety Act); *Passaic Valley Sewerage Commissioners v. DOL*, 992 F.2d 474 (3rd Cir. 1993) (Clean Water Act); *Haley v. Retsinas*, 138 F.3d 1245 (8th Cir. 1998) (banking whistleblower laws); *Givhan v. Western Line Consolidated*, 439 U.S. 410 (1979) (First Amendment).

<u>News Media</u>: *Pickering v. Board of Education*, 391 U.S. 563 (1968) and *Andrew v. Clark,* 561 F.3d 261 (4th Cir. 2009) (First Amendment); *Dep't of Homeland Sec. v. MacLean*, 135 S.Ct. 913 (2015) (contacting news media protected); *Donovan v. R.D. Anderson*, 552 F.Supp. 249 (D. Kan. 1982) (under OSHA); *Chambers v. Dept. of Interior*, 602 F.3d 1370, 1379 (Fed. Cir. 2010) (media contacts protected under Whistleblower Protection Act); *Haney v. North American Car Corp.*, 81-SWDA-1, Recommended Decision and Order of Labor Department Administrative Law Judge (Aug. 10, 1981), *affirmed,* Secretary of Labor (June 30 1982) (under

environmental whistleblower laws); *Diaz-Robainas v. Florida Power & Light Co.,* 92-ERA-10, Order of Secretary of Labor (Jan. 10, 1996) (Atomic Energy Act); *Wrighten v. Metropolitan Hosp., Inc.,* 726 F.2d 1346, 1355 (9th Cir. 1984) (holding a press conference is protected under Title VII); *Huffman v. Office of Personnel Management,* 263 F.3d 1341, 1351 (Fed. Cir. 2001) (citing *Horton,* 66 F.3d at 282, holding that media disclosures are an indirect way of disclosing information of wrongdoing to a person in a position to provide a remedy) (Whistleblower Protection Act case). In a 2011 decision, a three-judge panel of the U.S. Court of Appeals for the Ninth Circuit broke with most precedent and found that employee contacts with the press were not protected under 18 U.S.C. section 1514A(a)(1) of the Sarbanes-Oxley Act. However, the court left open the issue as to whether contacts with the press were protected under another clause of the Act, section 1514A(a)(2). *Tides v. Boeing,* 644F.3d 809 (9th Cir. 2011). Even if a contact with the news media is protected under federal law, whistleblowers who use a state law as the basis for a complaint risk losing their case. *Pacheco v. Waldrop,* 84 F.3d 606 (W.D. Ky. 2015) (media disclosure not protected under state whistleblower statute).

The significant impact of whistleblower disclosures to the news media is well documented in U.S. history. *See* Carl Bernstein and Bob Woodward, *All the President's Men,* NY: Simon & Schuster, 1974.

Opposing Conduct Made Illegal Under Federal Law: *Learned v. City of Bellevue,* 860 F.2d 928 (9th Cir. 1988) (Title VII).

Participating in Legal or Administrative Proceedings: *Pettway v. American Cast Iron,* 411 F.2d 998 (5th Cir. 1969) (Title VII); *Merritt v. Dillard Paper Co.,* 120 F.3d 1181 (11th Cir. 1999) (Title VII).

Public Interest Organization: *Nunn v. Duke Power Co.,* 84-ERA-27, Decision and Order of Deputy Undersecretary of Labor (July 30, 1987) (Atomic Energy Act).

Quality Control Inspectors or Compliance Officials Reporting Violations: *Mackowiak v. University Nuclear Systems,* 735 F.2d 1159 (9th Cir. 1984); *Kansas Gas & Electric v. Brock,* 780 F.2d 1505 (10th Cir. 1985) (Atomic Energy Act); *White v. Osage Tribal,* 1995-SDW-1 (DOL ARB, 1997); *Warren v. Custom Organics,* 2009-STA-30 (DOL ARB, 2012).

Refusing to Accept a "Hush Money" Settlement Agreement: *CL&P v. Secretary of Labor,* 85 F.3d 89 (2nd Cir. 1996).

Refusing to Perform Dangerous Work: *Whirlpool Corp. v. Marshall*, 445 U.S. 1 (1980) (OSHA); *NLRB v. Washington Aluminum Co.*, 370 U.S. 9 (1962) (NLRA); *Gateway Coal Co. v. United Mine Workers*, 414 U.S. 368 (1974).

Statements Made to Employer During Internal Investigation: *Crawford v. Metropolitan Government of Nashville*, 129 S.Ct. 846 (2009).

Taping: Under Department of Labor precedent, one-party taping for the purpose of gathering evidence of retaliation or violations of law (if permitted under state law). *See Benjamin v. Citationshares Management*, 2010-AIR-1 (DOL Administrative Review Board, Nov. 5, 2013) and *Mosbaugh v. Georgia Power Co.*, 91-ERA-1/11 (Secretary of Labor, Nov. 20, 1995).

Testimony in Court or Deposition: *Merritt v. Dillard Paper Co.*, 120 F.3d 1181 (11th Cir. 1997) (protected under Title VII's antiretaliation provision); *Karl v. City of Mountlake*, 678 F.3d 1062 (9th Cir. 2012); *Alpha Energy Savers Inc. v. Hansen*, 381 F.3d 917 (9th Cir. 2004); *Haddle v. Garrison*, 525 U.S. 121 (1998) (under 42 U.S.C. § 1985).

Threat to Make Protected Disclosure: *Macktal v. DOL*, 171 F.3d 323 (5th Cir. 1999) (Atomic Energy Act); *Thomas v. City of Blanchard*, 548 F.3d 1317 (10th Cir. 2008) (First Amendment).

Union Safety Committee: *Cotter v. Consolidated Edison*, 81-ERA-6 (Department of Labor, July 7, 1987, *affirmed*, Consolidated Edison v. Donovan, 673 F.2d 61 (2nd Cir. 1982).

ATTORNEY DISCLOSURES

Attorneys can file retaliation suits under federal law: *Van Asdale v. Int'l Game Tech.*, 577 F.3d 989 (9th Cir. 2009); *Willy v. ARB*, 423 F.3d 483 (5th Cir. 2005); *Kachmar v. SunGard*, 109 F.3d (3rd Cir. 1997).

17 Code of Federal Regulations Part 205 (SEC rules on attorney reporting).

Lawrence West, "Can Attorneys be Award-Seeking SEC Whistleblowers," *Harvard Law School Forum on Corporate Governance and Financial Regulation* (2013); https://corpgov.law.harvard.edu/2013/06/17/can-attorneys-be-award-seeking-sec-whistleblowers/.

INSUBORDINATE CONDUCT/ILLEGAL DISCLOSURES

Protected disclosures can lose their protection and become an independent justification for disciplining an employee if the activities are illegal, insubordinate, or unjustifiable. *Dunham v. Brock*, 794 F.2d 1037 (5th Cir. 1986) ("abusive or profane language coupled with defiant conduct" stripped employee of protection, even though disclosure was safety related); *Pettway v. American Cast Iron*, 411 F.2d 998 (5th Cir. 1969) (libelous complaint filed with EEOC may be protected); *Linn v. United Plant Guard*, 383 U.S. 53 (1966) (applying *New York Times v. Sullivan* standard in evaluating protected speech under NLRA); *O'Day v. McDonnell Douglas*, 79 F.3d 756 (9th Cir. 1996) (engaging in protected activity "is not" a "license to flaunt company rules").

However, courts have recognized that employees filing a protected complaint "may well engender disruption, controversy, and adverse publicity" but "nevertheless" are fully protected because "Congress has elected to protect employees who file such charges from retaliation . . . allegations of disruption and injury to close working relationships become irrelevant." *Curl v. Leroy Reavis and Iredell County*, 740 F.2d 1323 (4th Cir. 1984).

See Rule 20, Cautiously Use "Self-Help" Tactics.

Rule 16: Yes, You Are a "Whistleblower"

The Senate Judiciary Committee. "The Corporate and Criminal Fraud Accountability Act of 2002," S. Rep. No. 107-146 (May 6, 2002), pp. 4–5, 10, 20 (discussing Enron attorneys' advice regarding firing Sherron Watkins after she blew the whistle internally to her management).

Mimi Swartz and Sherron Watkins. *Power Failure: The Inside Story of the Collapse of ENRON.* NY: Doubleday, 2003.

Cases discussing development of internal protection for whistleblowers: *Phillips v. Interior Board of Mine Op.*, 500 F.2d 772 (D.C. Cir. 1974); *Mackowiak v. University Nuclear Systems*, 735 F.2d 1159 (9th Cir. 1984); *Atchison v. Brown & Root*, 82-ERA-9, Decision of Administrative Law Judge (December 1982); approved by Secretary of Labor (June 10, 1983); *Brown & Root v. Donovan*, 747 F.2d 1029 (5th Cir. 1984) (lead case holding internal disclosures not protected, overturned by the Fifth Circuit in *Willy*) (*see* below).

Cases decided after *Brown & Root* that upheld internal whistleblowing: *Kansas Gas & Electric v. Brock*, 780 F.2d 1505 (10th Cir. 1985); *Passaic Valley Sewerage Commissioners v. DOL*, 992 F.2d 474 (3rd Cir. 1993); *U.S. ex rel. Yesudian v. Howard University*, 153 F.3d 731 (D.C. Cir. 1998); *Bechtel v. DOL*, 50 F.3d 926 (11th Cir. 1995).

Secretary of Labor William Brock carefully explained the Department of Labor's position that internal whistleblowing must be protected in *Poulos v. Ambassador Fuel Oil Co.* 86-Clean Air Act Case No. 1 (April 27, 1987), published at http://www.oalj.dol.gov/PUBLIC/WHISTLEBLOWER/DECISIONS/ARB_DECISIONS/CAA/86CAA01B.HTM.

Note: The Department of Labor case law cited herein is published by the DOL Office of Administrative Law Judges at http://www.oalj.dol.gov/LIBWHIST. HTM.

Statutes amended (or initially passed) that explicitly protect internal whistleblowing to supervisors: Atomic Energy Act, 42 U.S.C. § 5851; Sarbanes-Oxley Act, 18 U.S.C. § 1514A; Consumer Product Safety Act, 15 U.S.C. § 2051; Aviation Investment and Reform Act, 49 U.S.C. § 42121; National Transit Systems Security Act, 6 U.S.C. § 1142; Railroad Safety Act, 49 U.S.C. § 20109; Surface Transportation Act, 49 U.S.C. §31105; Mine Health and Safety Act, 30 U.S.C. § 815(c); American Recovery Reinvestment Act, Public Law No. 111-5, §1553; Pipeline Safety Improvement Act, 42 U.S.C. § 60129; Dodd-Frank Act (Consumer Protection Bureau), 12 U.S.C. §5567.

Willy v. Administrative Review Board, 423 F.3d 483 (5th Cir. 2005) (after twenty years even the Fifth Circuit Court reversed itself and overturned its *Brown & Root* decision).

Garcetti v. Ceballos, 547 U.S. 410 (2006) (job duty whistleblowing not protected under First Amendment). After *Garcetti* some courts interpreted state and whistleblower statutes narrowly to exclude coverage for internal whistleblowers. *See Skare v. Extendicare Health Services*, 515 F.3d 836 (8th Cir. 2008); *Talhelm v. ABF Freight Systems*, 2010 U.S. App. LEXIS 1663 (6th Cir. 2010). However, the U.S. Congress strongly repudiated the *Garcetti* line of cases when it enacted the Whistleblower Protection Enhancement Act and explicitly reversed court rulings that were consistent with *Garcetti*. In Public Law 112-199, §§ 101 and 102, Congress used words such as "undermine," "wrongly focused," and "contrary to congressional intent" in describing court cases that failed to fully protect whistleblowers who raised concerns with their supervisors.

Committee on Homeland Security and Governmental Affairs, U.S. Senate. "Whistleblower Protection Enhancement Act of 2012," pp. 4–5 (S. Rep.112-155; April 19, 2012); extensive discussion concerning internal protected activity and rejection of *Garcetti* rule for federal employees.

Kasten v. Saint-Gobain, 131 S. Ct. 1325 (2011); oral complaints covered.

The controversy over internal whistleblowing under the Dodd-Frank Act is explained in *Berman v. Neo@Ogilvy,* 801 F.3d 145 (2nd Cir. 2015) (upholding internal whistleblower protection) and *Asadi v. G.E. Energy (USA), L.L.C.,* 720 F.3d 620, 627-28 (5th Cir. 2013) (finding internal whistleblowers not protected).

The email correspondence between the Senate Banking Committee and the National Whistleblower Center related to the antiretaliation provision of the Securities and Exchange Act is available from the National Whistleblower Center, www.whistleblowers.org.

The Institute for Internal Auditors survey of auditors is known as the Global Internal Audit Common Body of Knowledge. The survey's results were analyzed in *The Politics of Internal Auditing* by Patricia Miller and Larry Rittenberg, published by the IIA Research Foundation, Altamonte Springs, FL (2015). *See also* Rittenberg, Larry. *Ethics and Pressure: Balancing the Internal Audit Profession.* The IIA Research Foundation (2016).

Rule 17: Beware of "Hotlines"

The facts concerning the Quality Technology Company's contract with TVA are set forth in *Hill v. TVA,* 65 F.3d 1331 (6th Cir. 1995).

The Goldstein-SAFETEAM cases are published by the U.S. Department of Labor: *Goldstein v. EBASCO Contractors, Inc.,* 86-ERA-36, Labor Department rulings dated March 3, 1988 (Administrative Law Judge ruling), April 7, 1997 (Secretary of Labor ruling), Aug. 16, 1993 (Secretary of Labor ruling).

Corporate sponsored "think tanks" have carefully evaluated the deficiencies in internal compliance programs and have strong recommendations for improving the current systems. *See* Michael D. Greenberg, *Perspectives of Chief Ethics and Compliance Officers on Detection and Prevention of Corporate Misdeeds: What the Policy Community Should Know* (Rand Center for Corporate Ethics and Governance,

2009). A 2010 report by the corporate sponsored Ethics Resource Center entitled "Too Big to Regulate? Preventing Misconduct in the Private Sector" (ERC 2010), quoting leading complaints that programs were simply "paper tigers" and were plagued by a "lack of action and seriousness."

The Sarbanes-Oxley law requiring publicly traded companies to establish independent employee concerns programs is codified at 15 U.S.C. § 78f(m)(4).

The Federal Sentencing Guidelines provide for sentence reductions for corporations engaged in criminal activities that have instituted an internal compliance program. U.S. Sentencing Commission Guidelines Manual, Section 8B2.1.

The Senate Judiciary Committee report on the Enron/WorldCom scandals and enhancing whistleblower protections is published as "The Corporate and Criminal Fraud Accountability Act of 2002," Senate Report No. 107-146 (May 6, 2002).

Jaclyn Jaeger, "Report Highlights Employee Use of Hotlines," *Compliance Week* (Jan. 23, 2008).

David Hess, et al., "The 2004 Amendments to the Federal Sentencing Guidelines and Their Implicit Call for a Symbiotic Integration of Business Ethics," Vol. XI *The Fordham Journal of Corporate and Financial Law* 725 (2006).

The *Close the Contractors Fraud Loophole Act* is Public Law 110-252, Title VI, Chapter 1. This law mandates stronger controls over compliance departments in companies working under government contracts. It is implemented by Federal Acquisition Regulations, Contractor Business Ethics, Compliance Program and Disclosure Requirements, Final Rule, 73 *Federal Register* 67064 (Nov. 12, 2008).

Joseph D. West, et al., "Contractor Business Ethics Compliance Program & Disclosure Requirements," *West Briefing Papers Second Series* (Thompson Reuters, April 2009).

Whether internal complaints to hotlines are protected is an open question, depending on the laws involved. Some laws, like the Sarbanes-Oxley Act, the Consumer Safety Act, and the Atomic Energy Act clearly protect such complaints. State laws are completely confused. For example, courts have now determined that internal complaints, which would cover complaints to compliance departments, are not protected under the Minnesota and Michigan whistleblowers laws. *See Skare v. Extendicare Health Services,* 515 F.3d 836 (8th Cir. 2008); *Talhelm v. ABF Freight Systems,* 2010 U.S. App. LEXIS 1663 (6th Cir.). As for government workers who seek protection under the First Amendment, the Supreme Court completely confused this issue. In the case of *Garcetti v. Ceballos,* 547 U.S. 410 (2006), the Court held that employees who make disclosures "pursuant to their professional duties" are not protected. Are reports to an internal hotline part of an employee's "professional duties"?

Employers that create compliance programs may be subject to breach of contact lawsuits if they violate their promises to employees. Richard Moberly, "Protecting Whistleblowers by Contract," 79 *University of Colorado Law Review* 975 (Fall 2008).

On June 13, 2011, the Securities and Exchange Commission published final rules implementing the Dodd-Frank whistleblower reward program. SEC Commentary and Final Rule. 76 *Federal Register* 34300 (June 13, 2011). These rules created strong incentives for corporations to develop independent and ethical compliance programs. Id., pp. 34317–19 (circumstances in which compliance officials can file reward claims with the SEC); pp. 34322–27 (employee can qualify for rewards based on information they provided to internal compliance programs). Based on these two rules, employees who blow the whistle on corporate fraud should seriously consider the benefits of reporting their allegations to a corporate compliance program. However, if an employee desires complete confidentiality, the anonymous reporting procedures available under the SEC's whistleblower reward program should be utilized.

For cases protecting employees who disclose violations of corporate "internal control" programs who work in compliance programs, see *Feldman v. Law Enforcement Associates,* 2001 W.L. 891447 (E.D. N.C. 2001); *U.S. ex rel. Schweizer v. Oce N.V.,* 677 F.3d 1228 (D.C. Cir. 2012).

The Foreign Corrupt Practices Act prohibits a range of conduct not directly tied to the payment of bribes to foreign officials. The most important of these concerns the obligation of publicly traded companies or "issuers" to maintain quality "internal controls" and record-keeping systems. 5 U.S.C. § 78m(b)(2). *See,* Jones Day Newsletter, "The Legal Obligation to Maintain Accurate Books and Records in U.S. and Non-U.S. Operations (March 2006) ("The Foreign Corrupt Practices Act is usually associated with its prohibitions against foreign bribery. The provisions of the Act relating to bookkeeping and internal controls receive less publicity but are much more likely to form the basis of a government proceeding against companies subject to the Act.")

Rule 18: Don't Talk to Company Lawyers

Donna Boehme, "DOJ Tells HSBC and Corporate America: Reform Your Compliance Departments," *Corporate Counsel* (December 20, 2012).

_____, "Making the CCO an Independent Voice in the C-Suite," *Corporate Counsel*; www.law.com/corporatecounsel/PubArticleCC.jsp?id=1202592518804 &Making_the_CCO_an_Independent_Voice_in_the_CSuite.

_____, *From Enron to Madoff: Why Many Corporate Compliance and Ethics Programs Are Positioned for Failure*. Rand Center for Corporate Ethics and Governance (2009).

Jeffrey Eglash, et al., "Avoiding the Perils and Pitfalls of Internal Corporate Investigations: Proper Use of *Upjohn* Warnings," ABA Section of Litigation Corporate Counsel CLE Seminar (ethical rules governing attorneys who work on or manage corporate compliance investigations).

Ethics Opinion 269: "Obligation of Lawyer for Corporation to Clarify Role in Internal Corporate Investigation" (DC Bar. January 1997). Available at www. dcbar.org/bar-resources/legal-ethics/opinions/opinion269.cfm.

Michael D. Greenberg, *Transforming Compliance: Emerging Paradigms for Boards, Management, Compliance Officers, and Government*. Rand Center for Corporate Ethics and Governance (2012).

_____, *Culture, Compliance, and the C-Suite: How Executives, Boards, and Policymakers Can Better Safeguard against Misconduct at the Top*. Rand Center for Corporate Ethics and Governance (2013).

_____, *For Whom the Whistle Blows: Advancing Corporate Compliance and Integrity Efforts in the Era of Dodd-Frank*. Rand Center for Corporate Ethics and Governance (2011).

_____, *Directors as Guardians of Compliance and Ethics within the Corporate Citadel: What the Policy Community Should Know*. Rand Center for Corporate Ethics and Governance (2010).

Jacelyn Jaeger, "The Importance of Splitting Legal and Compliance," *Compliance Week* (December 2011).

Stephen M. Kohn. "The SEC's Final Whistleblower Rules & Their Impact on Internal Compliance." West Law Publishing (October 2011).

National Whistleblower Center, *Impact of* Qui Tam *Laws on Internal Compliance: A Report to the Securities and Exchange Commission.* National Whistleblower Center (2010).

New York Rules of Professional Conduct, based on The American Bar Association (ABA) Model Rules of Professional Conduct. The Model Rules have been adopted, in whole or in part, and sometimes in variation, as the rules of professional conduct for attorneys in forty-nine states, the District of Columbia, and four of the five inhabited U.S. territories.

Rule 4.2: "Communication with Person Represented by Counsel."

Rule 4.3: "Dealing with Unrepresented Person." The ABA Model Rules of Professional Conduct are available at www.americanbar.org/groups/ professional_responsibility/publications/model_rules_of_professional _conduct/model_rules_of_professional_conduct_table_of_contents.html.

Society for Corporate Compliance and Ethics and Health Care Compliance Association. "Compliance Professionals Overwhelmingly Reject General Counsel Reporting Structure," *P.R. Newswire* (March 11, 2013); www.prnews wire.com/news-releases/compliance-professionals-overwhelmingly-reject -general-counsel-reporting-structure-196884911.html (survey of compliance professionals finding that 88.5 percent oppose general counsel serving as chief compliance officer).

Michael Volkov, Redefining the Relationship of the General Counsel and Chief Compliance Officer, p. 8. Rand Center for Corporate Ethics and Governance (May 28, 2014); available at www.rand.org/jie/centers/corporate-ethics/ pubs.html (comprehensive article supporting a narrow interpretation of the privilege in compliance investigations).

The Chairman of the Senate Judiciary Committee provided strong testimony opposing efforts to require employees to communicate with corporate compliance programs, and pointed out the conflicts of interest in these proposals; "Statement for the Record by Senator Chuck Grassley of Iowa, Chairman, Senate Judiciary Committee At a House Judiciary Subcommittee on the constitution and Civil Justice Hearing on 'Oversight of the False Claims Act' April 28, 2016."

Rule 19: Auditors and Compliance Officials: Qualify for Rewards

Stephen Kohn, "The SEC's Final Whistleblower Rules and Their Impact on Internal Compliance." West Law Publishing (October 2011) (rights of compliance officials to blow the whistle).

Cases discussing whether compliance officials/auditors/attorneys are covered under antiretaliation laws: *Brown & Root v. Donovan*, 747 F2d 1029 (5th Cir. 1984); auditor not protected, but the case was reversed in *Willy v. ARB*, 423 F.3d 483 (5th Cir.) (an attorney protected in *Willy*); *Kansas Gas & Elec. v. Brock*, 780 F.2d 1505 (10th Cir. 1985) (quality assurance inspector protected); *Mackowiak v. University Nuclear*, 735 F.2d 1159 (9th Cir. 1984) (inspector protected); *Van Asdale v. International Game Tech.*, 577 F.3d 989 (9th Cir.) (attorney protected).

SEC Press Release 2014-180 (August 29, 2014) (first compliance official obtains monetary reward).

SEC Press Release 2015-73 (April 22, 2015) (compliance official awarded $1.5 million); www.sec.gov/news/pressrelease/2015-73.html.

Requirement that publicly traded companies have a program to accept confidential employee concerns regarding questionable accounting and auditing practices is codified at 15 U.S.C. § 78j-1(m); 17 C.F.R. § 2400.10A-3.

Speech by Chairman Mary L. Schapiro, U.S. Securities and Exchange Commission, Washington, DC (May 25, 2011); www.sec.gov/news/speech/2011/spch052511mls-item2.htm (SEC whistleblower program).

The pressures facing auditors was outlined by the Institute of Internal Auditors in "Political Pressure Intense on Internal Audit" (March 10, 2015), news release announcing the release of the IIA Research Foundation report *The Politics of Internal Auditing*.

Rule 20: Cautiously Use "Self-Help" Tactics

Argyropoulos v. City of Alton, 539 F.3d 724 (7th Cir. 2008) (warning that antiretaliation laws do not grant employees right to engage in "dubious self-help tactics").

Jefferies v. Harris County Community Action, 615 F.2d 1025 (5th Cir. 1980) (setting forth the "reasonableness test" for self-help tactics). *See also Hochstadt v. Worcester Foundation*, 545 F.2d 222 (1st Cir. 1976); *Wrighten v. Metropolitan Hospital*, 726 F.2d 1346 (9th Cir. 1984) (setting forth "balancing test").

Taping: *Lopez v. U.S.*, 373 U.S. 427 (1963) (Supreme Court permits one-party taping); Omnibus Crime Control Act, 18 U.S.C. § 2511(2)(d) (federal law permitting one-party taping); Reporters Committee for Freedom of the Press, (online publication) (state-by-state review of one-party taping laws); *Heller v. Champion International*, 891 F.2d 432 (2nd Cir. 1989) (one-party taping permitted for gathering evidence of discrimination).

Cases finding one-party taping potentially protected: *Haney v. North American Car*, 81-SWDA-1 (ALJ Order, Aug. 10, 1981), affirmed by Secretary of Labor (June 30, 1982); *Mosbaugh v. Georgia Power Co.*, 91-ERA-1/11 (Order of Secretary of Labor) (Nov. 20, 1995); *Melendez v. Exxon*, 93-ERA-6 (DOL ARB, July 14, 2000) (one-party taping protected activity); *Deltek v. Department of Labor*, No. 14-2415 (4th Cir. 2015) (affirming DOL decision permitting taping); *Heller v. Champion*, 891 F.2d 432 (2nd Cir. 1989) (taping judged case by case).

Documents (obtaining and preserving): *O'Day v. McDonnell Douglas*, 79 F.3d 756 (9th Cir. 1996) (warning against "rummaging through" the "supervisor's office"); *Hodgson v. Texaco*, 440 F.2d 662 (5th Cir. 1971); *JDS Uniphase Corp. v. Jennings*, 473 F.Supp.2d 697 (E.D. Vir. 2007) (requirement to obtain documents legitimately through civil discovery); *Deltek v. Department of Labor*, No. 14-2415 (4th Cir. 2015) (affirming DOL decision permitting removal of documents); *Kempcke v. Monsanto Company*, 132 F.3d 442 (8th Cir. 1998) (innocent removal of confidential documents permitted); *Westlake Surgical v. Turner*, 2009 Tex. App. LEXIS 6132 (removal of confidential documents permitted); *Leon v. IDX Systems Corp.*, 2:03-cv-01158-MJP (W.D. Wash. 2004) (sanctions for wiping out computer hard-drive); *Webb v. Government for the District of Columbia*, 175 F.R.D. 128 (D.D.C. 1997) (default judgment against employer for destroying documents). Under New Jersey state law, an employer that destroys evidence not only can have an adverse inference drawn against it, but can also be liable for the tort of fraudulent concealment. *Tartaglia v. UBS PaineWebber*, 961 A.2d 1167 (N.J. 2008).

The Court in *Smith v. Chi Transit Auth.*, 2016 U.S. App. LEXIS 11553 (7th Clr. 2016) described what a court should consider when evaluating whether an employee was reasonable in disclosing confidential e-mails: "Reasonableness depends on how [the employee] obtained the e-mails, whom he shared them with, the type of confidences revealed, their relevancy to the discrimination charge, whether [the employee] had a good-faith belief in their relevancy, the scope of the [employer's] confidentiality policy, and whether [the employee] could have sought the evidence in a way that would not have violated the policy."

Privacy Rights Clearinghouse, "Fact Sheet 7: Workplace Privacy and Employee Monitoring" (online publication) (information on management's rights to monitor employees at work).

Government employees have had some success in challenging e-mail monitoring. On June 20, 2012, the Executive Office of Management and Budget issued a government-wide "Memorandum for Chief Information Officers and General Counsels" warning that warrantless searching of public employee e-mails could violate whistleblower disclosure laws.

McKennon v. Nashville Banner Publishing, 513 U.S. 352 (1995) ("after-acquired evidence" standards).

Rule 21: Be Prepared for the Lid to Blow

Greenberg v. Kmetko, 840 F.2d 467, 477 (7th Cir. 1988) (*en banc*) (dissenting opinion of Judge Cudahy) ("Dissenters and whistleblowers rarely win popularity contests or Dale Carnegie awards. They are frequently irritating and unsettling. These qualities, however, do not necessarily make their views wrong or unhelpful. ...").

Management Information v. Alyeska Pipeline Services, 151 F.R.D. 478 (D.D.C. 1993) (problems facing whistleblowers).

Halliburton v. ARB, 771 F.3d 254 (5th Cir. 2014) (explaining adverse consequences that follow an employee being "outed" as a whistleblower).

Myron and Penina Glazer, "The Whistleblowers: Exposing Corruption in Government and Industry" (Basic Books, NY: 1989).

Acknowledging that protected disclosures "may well engender disruption, controversy and adverse publicity." *Curl v. Reavis and Iredell County*, 740 F.2d 1323 (4th Cir. 1984).

Aaron Kesselheim, et al., "Whistle-Blowers' Experiences in Fraud Litigation against Pharmaceutical Companies," *N. Engl. J. Med.* 362:19 (May 13, 2010) (documenting the severe emotional distress and hardships suffered by whistle-blowers, even when they prevail in a major case).

The types of damages and hardships experienced by whistleblowers was the subject of major litigation in the case of *Hobby v. Georgia Power Co.*, 90-ERA-30 (ALJ, Sept. 17, 1998), affirmed, DOL Administrative Review Board (Feb. 9, 2001), affirmed, U.S. Court of Appeals for the 11th Circuit (Sept. 30, 2002). In that case Georgia Power's challenge to the professional damages incurred by a whistleblower, which were the subject of extensive expert testimony, were rejected by the Department of Labor. The record in that case establishes how Georgia Power improperly fought the whistleblower for over ten years, engaging in extensive and relentless litigation in order to defeat the employee. After losing the case, the company engaged in new (and ultimately unsuccessful) litigation trying to limit the employee's damages. The case is a window into the type of aggressive litigation tactics a whistleblower can expect.

The quote from "Deep Throat" comes from Carl Berstein and Bob Woodward, "All the President's Men," (Simon and Schuster, NY: 1974), pp. 268-69.

Rule 22: Delay Is Deadly

English v. General Electric Company, 85-ERA-2, Decision and Order of Administrative Law Judge (Aug. 1, 1985), *reversed* by Final Decision and Order of the Under Secretary of Labor (Jan. 13, 1987).

Delaware State College v. Ricks, 449 U.S. 250 (1980); *Chardon v. Fernandez,* 454 U.S. 6 (1981) (key Supreme Court cases discussing how to calculate running of the statute of limitations).

The doctrines of "equitable tolling" and "equitable estoppel" may provide grounds for an employee to enlarge the filing deadlines based on the actions or statements of an employer: "Equitable tolling focuses on the plaintiff's excusable ignorance of the employer's discriminatory act. Equitable estoppel, in contrast, examines the defendant's conduct and the extent to which the plaintiff has been induced to refrain from exercising his rights." *Rhodes v. Guiberson Oil Tools Div.*, 927 F.2d 876, 878 (5th Cir. 1991), quoting *Felty v. Graves-Humphreys*, 785 F.2d 516, 519 (4th Cir. 1986). *See also Zipes v. Transworld Airlines,*

455 U.S. 385 (1982); *Bonham v. Dresser Industries,* 569 F.2d 187 (3rd Cir. 1977); *School District of Allentown v. Marshall,* 657 F.2d 16 (3rd 1981); *Carlile v. South Routt School Dist.,* 652 F.2d 981 (10th Cir. 1981).

The applicability of the "continuing violation" theory for tolling a statute of limitations was limited by the Supreme Court in *National Railroad v. Morgan,* 536 U.S. 101 (2002).

Whistleblower reward programs all encourage employees to quickly file allegations of fraud with the appropriate authorities. They all have a version of a "first to file" rule that can result in the disqualification of whistleblowers who delay filing a rewards claim, if another whistleblower files a similar or identical claim first. See Handbook Rules 6–12.

The statute of limitations for filing a securities fraud case is generally 5 years. See Gabelli v. SEC, 133 S.Ct. 1216 (2013).

The statute of limitations for filing a False Claims Act reward case is 6 years after the date of the violation *or* within 3 years of the date for which an official of the United States should have been reasonably aware the violation occurred (but in no event greater than ten years from the initial violation). 31 U.S.C. § 3731(b). A wrongful discharge case under the FCA must be filed within 3 years. 31 U.S.C. § 3739(h)(3).

The United States has a catch-all statute of limitations for cases for which a civil fine, penalty or forfeiture may be imposed. See 28 U.S.C. § 2462. Under this law, if a statute does not impose a specific statute of limitations, civil cases that can result in a fine or penalty being imposed must be filed within 5 years of the violation.

Rule 23: Conduct Discovery

Checklist 6 identifies the major cases and precedents applicable to discovery in employment retaliation and whistleblower cases. Rule 20 describes the issues facing whistleblowers who remove documents from their worksite in violation of company rules. The discovery rules for DOL cases are found in 29 C.F.R. Part 18; the rules for federal employee cases before the MSPB are found at 5 C.F.R. Part 1201. Rules for discovery in federal court are located in the Federal Rules of Civil Procedure, starting with Rule 26, which is the overview rule.

Rule 24: Get to the Jury

The basic law setting forth an employee's *prima facie* case necessary to withstand an employer motion to dismiss or for summary judgment is set forth in Kohn, *Concepts and Procedures in Whistleblower Law*, pp. 238–79 (Quorum Books: Westport, CT 2001).

Cases setting forth standard *prima facie* case in whistleblower or retaliation cases: *Aka v. Washington*, 156 F.3d 1284 (D.C. Cir. 1998); *Housing Works v. City of New York*, 73 F.Supp.2d 402 (S.D.N.Y. 1999); *DeFord v. Secretary of Labor*, 700 F.2d 281 (6th Cir. 1983). The Supreme Court uses a similar evaluation process in discrimination cases: *McDonnell Douglas v. Green*, 411 U.S. 792 (1973).

Curl v. Leroy Reavis and Iredell County, 740 F.2d 1323 (4th Cir. 1984) (example of a court review to determine whether the plaintiff qualified as an "employee" under the statute prior to proceeding to review other issues).

Court decisions concerning definition of "employee" under employment law statutes: *Hudgens v. NLRB*, 424 U.S. 507, 510 n. 3 (1976); *Seattle-First National Bank v. NLRB*, 651 F.2d 1272 (9th Cir. 1980); *Sibley Mem. Hosp. v. Wilson*, 488 F.2d 1338 (D.C. Cir. 1973); *Palmer v. Western Trucking*, 85-STA-6, Decision of Secretary of Labor (January 16, 1987); *Hill v. TVA*, 87-ERA-23/24, Decision of Secretary of Labor (May 24, 1989); *Robinson v. Triconex Corp.*, 2006-ERA-31 (DOL ARB, 2012) (broad definition of covered employees under *Labor Department precedent*). But see *Demski v. Department of Labor*, 419 F.3d 488 (6th Cir. 2005) (applying narrow common law definition of "employee").

NLRB v. Schrivener, 405 U.S. 117 (1972); *Pettway v. American Cast Iron Pipe Co.*, 441 F.2d 998 (5th Cir. 1969) (determination of whether employee engaged in protected activity as a threshold legal issue).

Passaic Valley Sewerage Commissioners v. DOL, 992 F.2d 474 (3rd Cir. 1993) (review whether employee's whistleblowing adhered to the "good faith" standard).

Frazier v. MSPB, 672 F.2d 150 (D.C. Cir. 1982) (key case defining proof necessary to demonstrate "knowledge").

Passaic Valley Sewerage Commissioners v. DOL, 992 F.2d 474 (3rd Cir. 1993) (Clean Water Act case on "good faith" whistleblowing referenced in SOX legislative history).

Burlington Northern v. White, 548 U.S. 53 (2006) (landmark case on defining adverse action).

Desert Palace, Inc. v. Costa, 539 U.S. 90 (2003) (key case regarding evidence needed to demonstrate discriminatory motive necessary to survive a motion for summary judgment).

Staub v. Proctor Hospital, 131 S.Ct. 1186 (2011). This case was argued before the Supreme Court on Nov. 2, 2010, and decided the following question: "In what circumstances may an employer be held liable based on the unlawful intent of officials who caused or influenced but did not make the ultimate employment decision." The Court ruled for the employee and held that an employer cannot hide behind a layered decision-making process to escape liability for illegally firing an employee by claiming that the final decision maker was unaware of the protected activity or did not have discriminatory animus.

The exhaustion of administrative remedies doctrine was explained in *Brown v. GSA*, 425 U.S. 820 (1976). The doctrine was applied in Sarbanes-Oxley whistle-blower cases in *Portes v. Wyeth*, 06-cv-2689 (S.D. N.Y. 2007); *Williams v. Boston Scientific*, 08-cv-01437 (N.D. Calif. 2008) and *Curtis v. Century Surety*, 08-16236 (9th Cir. 2009). Under this doctrine, although an employee can eventually have a jury trial, he or she must utilize various administrative remedies in order to file a case in court.

Although this rule is entitled "Getting to the Jury," a large number of whistle-blower laws provide employees with an option of having their case heard before a jury or an administrative judge, specifically, numerous whistleblower laws as administered by the U.S. Department of Labor. The decision as to whether or not to have a case heard before a judge or jury, or whether to have it tried within the U.S. Department of Labor before an Administrative Law Judge is a tactical decision based on numerous factors, including costs, the reputation of the respective judges, and the evidence that will be presented in any given case. The bottom line is to pick the forum that will hear your case with ease, whether that is a state court, a federal court, or an administrative agency.

Rule 25: Win the Case: Prove Motive and Pretext

Rohloff v. Metz Baking Co., L.L.C., 491 F.Supp.2d 840, 848-849 (N.D. Iowa, 2007).

In *Franchini v. Argonne National Laboratory*, 2009-ERA-14 (DOL ARB, 2012) the Labor Department outlined some of the facts that have been used to prove evidence of discriminatory motive, including "temporal proximity, pretext, and material changes in employer practices."

Checklist 4 identifies numerous court precedents regarding the types of proof necessary for an employee to demonstrate improper motive or pretext in a retaliation case.

Rule 26: Get Every Penny Deserved

DAMAGES FOR EMPLOYEES

All state and federal laws contain their own rules governing the types of damages permitted under whistleblower protection laws. The following list spotlights some of the major categories of damages permitted under various laws:

General Damages Available Under Whistleblower Laws: *Reich v. Cambridgeport Air Systems*, 26 F.3d 1187 (1st Cir. 1994); *Nord v. U.S. Steel*, 758 F.2d 1462 (11th Cir. 1985). In *Hobby v. Georgia Power Co.*, 90-ERA-30 (ALJ, Sept. 17, 1998), affirmed DOL Administrative Review Board (Feb. 9, 2001) and the U.S. Court of Appeals for the 11th Circuit (Sept. 30, 2002) carefully reviewed the full range of damages available to employees under the Department of Labor administered whistleblower laws.

"Affirmative Relief," Equitable or Preliminary Relief: *NLRB v. Gissel Packing*, 395 U.S. 575 (1969); *Florida Steel Corp. v. NLRB*, 620 F.2d 79 (5th Cir. 1980); *Donovan v. Freeway Constr. Co.*, 551 F.Supp. 869 (D.R.I. 1982); *U.S. v. Montgomery*, 744 F.Supp. 1074 (M.D. Ala. 1989).

Back Pay: *NLRB v. J.H. Rutter-Rex*, 396 U.S. 258 (1969).

Compensatory Damages: *Walters v. City of Atlanta*, 803 F.2d 1135 (11th Cir. 1986); *Neal v. Honeywell*, 995 F.Supp. 889 (N.D. Ill. 1998); *Smith v. Atlas Off-Shore Boat Service*, 653 F.2d 1057 (5th Cir. 1981); *Heaton v. Weitz Co.*, 534 F.3d 882 (8th Cir. 2008).

Front Pay: *McNight v. General Motors*, 908 F.2d 104 (7th Cir. 1990); *U.S. v. Burke*, 504 U.S. 229, footnote 9 (1992).

Interest: *Parexel International v. Feliciano*, 2008 U.S. Dist. LEXIS 99348 (E.D. Pa. 2008); *Donovan v. Freeway Constr.*, 551 F.Supp. 869 (D.R.I. 1982); *Clinchfield Coal v. Federal Mine Safety and Health Comm.*, 895 F.2d 773 (D.C. Cir. 1990).

Lost Overtime Pay: *Blackburn v. Martin*, 982 F.2d 125 (4th Cir. 1992).

"Make Whole" Remedy: Most laws mandate that an employee who prevails in a retaliation case be made fully "whole." Under this remedy, "compensation shall be equal to the injury" and the "injured party is to be placed, as near as may be, in the situation he would have occupied if the wrong had not been committed." *Albemarle Paper Co. v. Moody*, 422 U.S. 405, 418–19 (1975), quoting from *Wicker v. Hoppock*, 6 Wall. 94 (1867).

Promotions: *Edwards v. Hodel*, 738 F.Supp. 426 (D. Col. 1990).

Punitive Damages: *Smith v. Wade*, 461 U.S. 30 (1983); *BMW v. Gore*, 517 U.S. 559 (1996) (explaining constitutional standards for calculating); *Parexel International v. Feliciano*, 2008 U.S. Dist. LEXIS 98195 (E.D. Pa. 2008); *Weidler v. Big J. Enterprises*, 953 P2d 1089 (N.M. App. 1997); *Howard v. Zack*, 637 N.E.2d 1183 (Ill. App. 1994); *Anderson v. Amtrak*, 2009-FRS-3 (Dept. of Labor ALJ, Aug. 26, 2010).

Reinstatement: *Reeves v. Claiborne County*, 828 F.2d 1096 (5th Cir. 1987).

Restoration of Pension: *Blum v. Witco Chemical Corp.*, 829 F.2d 367 (3rd Cir. 1987).

Restoration of Seniority: *Sands v. Runyon*, 28 F.3d 1323 (2nd Cir. 1994).

Special Damages: *Neal v. Honeywell*, 191 F.3d 827 (7th Cir. 1999).

Stock Options: *Hobby v. Georgia Power Co.*, Civil Action No. 1:01-cv-1407 (N.D. Georgia, Feb. 15, 2006).

"Tort Liability" for First Amendment Claims filed under 42 U.S.C. § 1983: *Carey v. Piphus*, 435 U.S. 247 (1978).

REDUCTION IN AMOUNT OF DAMAGES

Mitigation and Reduction of Damages: Damages can be reduced if an employee fails to "mitigate" the harm caused by the retaliatory discharge. For example, courts have reduced awards where an employee failed to seek other comparable employment after being fired. Similarly, an unconditional offer of reinstatement can act to cut off back pay liability. If an employee obtains a new job after being fired, wages from that new job can be deducted from a back pay award. *Phelps Dodge Corp. v. NLRB*, 313 U.S. 177 (1941); *Tubari Ltd. v. NLRB*, 959 F.2d 451 (3rd Cir. 1992) (explaining the mitigation rule); *Grocer Co. v. Holloway*, 874 F.2d 1008 (5th Cir. 1989); *Donovan v. Commercial Sewing, Inc.*, 562 F.Supp. 548 (D. Conn. 1982) (offers of reinstatement).

Taxes: Under current law back pay, punitive damages, and compensatory damages may be subject to taxation. The Attorney Fee Civil Rights Act exempts employees from being taxed on the attorney fees awarded to their counsel. 26 U.S.C. § 62(a) (20) and (e). As part of the settlement process, employees can have their companies establish tax deferred compensation or annuity plans that help reduce the amount of tax. These plans were approved in the Tax Court case of *Childs v. Commissioner of Internal Revenue*, 103 T.C. 634 (1994).

Rule 27: Make the Boss Pay Attorney Fees

The major cases interpreting the statutory fee provisions contained in most whistleblower protection laws are set forth in the practice tips cited at the end of Rule 27. The best single source of information on how to prepare a fee petition to ensure that attorneys are paid at a fair market value and compensated for all reasonable time are set forth in the numerous rulings decided under the Civil Rights Attorney Fee Act, 42 U.S.C. § 1988. Precedents decided under this act are regularly applied to other civil rights, employment, and whistleblower laws that also contain statutory fee provisions. *Perdue v. Kenny*, 130 S.Ct. 1662 (2010) ("virtually identical language appears in many fee shifting statutes"). Attorney fees are generally not available under state common law remedies. If filing a claim under a statute, review the specific language and ensure that there is a fee provision.

Rule 28: Hold Companies Accountable for Paying Hush Money

The case record for the *Macktal* case is docketed at the U.S. Department of Labor Office of Administrative Law Judges, Case Number 86-ERA-26. The appeals court case is *Macktal v. Secretary of Labor*, 923 F.2d 1150 (5th Cir. 1991). The hearings on the *Macktal* were published by the U.S. Senate Subcommittee on Nuclear Regulation, *Hearings on Secret Settlement Agreements Restricting Testimony at Comanche Peak Nuclear Power Plant*, Senate Hearing No. 101-90 (May 4, 1989).

Connecticut Light & Power v. Secretary of Labor, 85 F.3d 89 (2nd Cir. 1996) (upholding cause of action based on illegal hush money settlement).

Jon Bauer, "Buying Witness Silence: Evidence-Suppressing Settlements and Lawyers' Ethics," 87 *Oregon Law Review* 481, 493 (2008) (listing examples of restrictive settlements that interfered with the public's ability to learn about serious safety issues).

Town of Newton v. Rumery, 480 U.S. 386 (1987) (Supreme Court case on public policy under contract law).

EEOC v. Astra USA, 94 F.3d 738 (1st Cir. 1996); *EEOC v. Cosmair*, 821 F.2d 1085 (5th Cir. 1987) (enjoining corporation from using settlement agreements to prevent employees from disclosing information to the EEOC); *In re JDS Uniphase Corp. Securities Litigation*, 238 F.Supp.2d 1127 (N.D. Calif. 2002) (enjoining use of "confidentiality agreements to chill former employees from voluntarily participating in legitimate investigations into alleged wrongdoing"); *U.S. ex rel Longhi v. Lithium Power*, 575 F.3d 458 (5th Cir. 2009) (refusing to enforce employee release of FCA claims). *U.S. v. Purdue Pharma*, 600 F.3d 319 (4th Cir. 2010) (upholding release of FCA claims when government had prior knowledge of the frauds disclosed by employee).

Gilmer v. Interstate, 500 U.S. 20 (1991) (leading case upholding enforcement of mandatory arbitration of employment disputes); *EEOC v. Waffle House*, 534 U.S. 279 (2002) (arbitration agreement did not prevent federal agencies from filing lawsuits to defend employees); *Doyle v. DOL*, 285 F.3d 243 (3rd Cir. 2002) (waiver of rights to file nuclear whistleblower claim unenforceable).

The Securities and Exchange Commission has enforced strict rules prohibiting restrictions on employee whistleblowing. See Office of Compliance Inspections and Examinations, "Examining Whistleblower Rule Compliance, Vol. VI *National Examination Risk Alert* Issue 1 (October 24, 2016) (explaining Commission decisions on restrictive agreements and warning companies of various improper contractual methods being employed to prevent or intimidate employees from contacting SEC or applying for rewards), posted at www.sec.gov/ocie/announcement/ocie-2016-risk-alert-examining-whistleblower-rule-compliance.pdf.

The SEC has sanctioned companies for having employees sign restrictive non-disclosure agreements. *See e.g., In the Matter of KBR, Inc.*, SEC File No. 3-16466 (April 1, 2015); *In the Matter of NeuStar*, SEC FIle No. 3-17736 (Dec. 19, 2016); *In the Matter of BlueLinx Holding*, SEC File No. 3-17371 (Aug. 10, 2016); *In the Matter of SandRidge Energy*, SEC File No. 3-17739 (Dec. 20, 2016).

Rule 29: Politics Is Poisonous

The Department of Labor–administered laws (including OSHA and the whistleblower laws that permit employees to file in federal court) are discussed in Rule 4.

The laws covering federal employees (including the Office of Special Counsel and the Merit Systems Protection Board) and the laws governing national security whistleblowers are discussed in Rule 14. The Inspector General of the Intelligence Community's procedural rules for reviewing whistleblower cases are available online at www.dni.gov/files/documents/ICIG/C_Employee_ERP_Regs.pdf.

The case of Dr. Marcus is contained in the decisions of the Department of Labor and the case file of the DOL Office of Administrative Law Judges in Case Number 1992–Toxic Substances Control Act Case No. 5. The Inspector General Act that sets forth the authority of the IGs is Title 5 U.S.C. Appendices §§ 3 and 7.

The whistleblower reward laws are discussed in Rules 1–3 (general); Rule 4 (FIRREA); Rule 6 (False Claims Act); Rule 7 (IRS/Tax); Rule 8 (securities, commodities); Rule 9 (Foreign Corrupt Practices); Rule 10 (Auto safety); Rule 11 (Act to Prevent Pollution from Ships/ocean pollution); Rule 12 (wildlife trafficking).

Other independent remedies are discussed in Rule 4 (covering all major federal laws); Rule 5 (state protections); and Rule 13 (First Amendment).

Rule 30: Never Forget: Whistleblowing Works

The statistical studies that scientifically document the effectiveness of whistleblowing as a means of uncovering fraud or misconduct are identified in the references for the handbook's introduction. In addition to these, *see Winters v. Houston Chronicle*, 795 S.W.2d 723, 727–33 (Tex. 1990) (concurring opinion of Justice Lloyd Doggett); Charles S. Clarke, "Whistleblowers," 7 *The CQ Researcher* 1059 (Congressional Quarterly, Inc. 1997). Transparency International, "Whistleblowing: An Effective Tool in the Fight against Corruption," *Policy Position # 01/2010* (Berlin 2010) (available online at www.transparency.org).

The Department of Justice publishes its press releases, which extensively document the amount of money the United States recovers as a result of whistleblower disclosures under the False Claims Act. The recoveries cited in this Rule are derived from these releases. *See* U.S. Department of Justice, Civil Division, Commercial Litigation Branch, *Press Releases,* published at: www.doj.gov/civil/press/index.

The case record for the Jane Turner case is found at: *Turner v. Gonzales,* 421 F.3d 688 (8th Cir. 2005) and the case file in the United States District Court for the District of Minnesota (Minneapolis Division). Dan Browning, "Ex-Agent Wins Lawsuit Against FBI," *Minneapolis Star Tribune* (Feb. 5, 2007); Tad Vezner, "Former FBI Agent Wins Suit," *Pioneer Press* (Feb. 6, 2007).

The Final Rule: Remember July 30, 1778

Letters of Delegates to Congress, 1774-1789, Paul H. Smith, editor (Washington: Library of Congress/Government Printing Office, 1976-2000): Examination of John Grannis by subcommittee of the Marine Committee (March 25, 1777); Letter from Congress to Marven and Shaw (July 31, 1778) (transmitting resolution from Congress).

Journals of the Continental Congress (Washington: Government Printing Office, 1908): Vol. VII, p. 202 (report from Marine Committee after examination of Grannis), p. 204 (suspension of Hopkins); Vol. X, p. 13 (dismissal of Hopkins); Vol. XI, p. 713, p. 732 (first resolution of the United States declaring "duty of all persons" to disclose "earliest information" of "misconduct" to "proper authority;" pp. 732–33 (vote to pay Warren whistleblowers' "reasonable expenses" and to release documents concerning Hopkins to the whistleblowers); Vol. XIV, p. 627 (approved payment of "fourteen hundred and eighteen dollars and 9/90" for the defense of whistleblowers Shaw and Marven. Monies paid to Sam Adams, which included the fees owed to William Channing).

The Warren sailors originally approached a member of the Continental Congress, Robert Treat Paine, a signer of the Declaration of Independence and a delegate from Taunton, Mass. Paine apparently advised the whistleblowers to file their concerns directly with Congress. *See Grannis to Paine* (Feb. 11, 1777). *See Letters of Delegates to Congress,* explanatory note to *Letter from Grannis to Marine Committee* dated March 25, 1777.

John G. Coyle, "The Suspension of Esek Hopkins, Commander of the Revolutionary Navy, Vol. XXI, *The Journal of the American Irish Historical Society* 193 (1922) (reprints original petition from the Warren sailors and the individual statements each of the sailors had delivered to Congress).

Edward Field, *Esek Hopkins, Commander-in-chief of the Continental Navy during the American Revolution, 1775–1778, Master Mariner, Politician, Brigadier-General, Naval Officer and Philanthropist* (Preston & Rounds: Providence, 1898).

A full list of the *qui tam* reward laws enacted by the First Congress of the United States are listed in the Testimony of Stephen M. Kohn before the House of Representatives Committee on Oversight and Government Reform, hearing on "Restoring the Power of the Purse: Legislative Options" (December 1, 2016), available at https://oversight.house.gov/wp-content/uploads/2016-12-01-NWC-Kohn-Testimony.pdf.

Whitney v. California, 274 U.S. 357 (1927) (concurring opinion of Justice Brandeis).

International Toolkit: Taking the Profits out of Corruption

INTRODUCTION TO STATUS OF WHISTLEBLOWERS WORLDWIDE

The United States and more than 140 other nations have approved the United Nations Convention against Corruption, which contains two mandates for the protection of whistleblowers. Article 32 prohibits retaliation against witnesses. Article 33 urges nations to enact "domestic" legislation to "provide protection" against "unjust treatment" for any person who reports evidence of corruption to "competent authorities." The convention is available at www.unodc.org/unodc/en/treaties/CAC/index.html.

Council of Europe, Civil Law Convention on Corruption. Article 9 requires European countries to protect whistleblowers. The text of the convention is published (in multiple languages) at www.coe.int/en/web/conventions/full-list/-/conventions/treaty/174.

The council has approved general protections for whistleblowers as part of its anti-corruption convention and has a web page setting forth its position on whistle-blowing: www.coe.int/t/dghl/standardsetting/cdcj/Whistleblowers/protecting_whistleblowers_en.asp.

Based on input from numerous anticorruption and whistleblower advocacy groups, Transparency International created a set of principles recommended for effective whistleblower laws. These recommendations are posted at www.transparency.org/files/content/activity/2009_PrinciplesFor WhistleblowingLegislation_EN.pdf.

The Centre for Media Pluralism and Media Freedom publishes an online overview of whistleblower protections in all European Union countries at http://journalism.cmpf.eui.eu/maps/whistleblowing.

The Council of Europe has approved general protections for whistleblowers as part of its anticorruption convention and has a web page setting forth its position on whistleblowing: www.coe.int/t/dghl/standardsetting/cdcj/Whistleblowers/protecting_whistleblowers_en.asp.

The Organisation for Economic Co-Operation and Development (OECD) published "Whistleblower Protection: Encouraging Reporting," an overview of international whistleblower laws in its publication *CleanGovBiz* (July 2012). The article is available at www.oecd.org/cleangovbiz/toolkit/50042935.pdf.

Simon Wolfe, et al., *Not Measuring Up: PIDA Now Rates Poorly against International Standard*. Thompson Reuters Foundation (2016). This detailed report is critical of the British whistleblower protection law. It reviews how the law works in practice and compares it with various international standards viewed as necessary for whistleblower protection.

"America Pays Millions to Whistleblower at BHP; We Hound Them from Their Jobs," *Sydney Morning Herald* (August 29, 2016). The article describes problems facing Australian whistleblowers.

Information on the murder of South African whistleblower Jimmy Mohlala is available at www.dailymail.co.uk/news/article-3121989/Widow-murdered-2010-South-Africa-Fifa-World-Cup-whistle-blower-Jimmy-Mohlala-says-husband-alive-today-hadn-t-exposed-multimillion-dollar-stadium-fraud.html#ixzz4MK4PIoyh.

Articles discussing the status of international whistleblower protections are available at https://euobserver.com/justice/121873 (European Union rejects whistleblower protections); http://knowledgeofindia.com/list-of-whistleblowers-in -india/ (whistleblower from India killed); http://mg.co.za/article/2009-01-05 -anc-whistleblower-killed (South African whistleblower killed); www.ifex.org/

philippines/2005/03/30/whistleblower_murdered/ (whistleblower in Philippines killed).

Public Law 112-208 (December 14, 2012) is a U.S. law imposing sanctions on Russia due to the death of whistleblower Sergei Leonidovich Magnitsky.

On July 27, 2000, the U.S. Senate ratified the Inter-American Convention against Corruption. Article III (8) of that Convention stipulates that the United States, and other countries that ratified the agreement, create "Systems for protecting public servants and private citizens who, in good faith, report acts of corruption, including protection of their identities, in accordance with their Constitutions and the basic principles of their domestic legal systems" (www.oas.org).

The following cases hold that international whistleblowers cannot obtain on-the-job protection under U.S. whistleblower laws: *Carnero v. Boston Scientific Corp.*, 433 F.3d 1 (1st Cir. 2006) (international employee not covered under Sarbanes-Oxley Act wrongful discharge law); *Liu Meng-Lin v. Siemens AG*, 763 F.3d 175 (2nd Cir. 2014) (international employee not covered under Dodd-Frank Act antiretaliation law).

FOREIGN CORRUPT PRACTICES ACT

The Foreign Corrupt Practices Act, 15 U.S.C. § 78m and § 78dd-1, et seq.

The Department of Justice (DOJ) resource page on the FCPA is located at www.justice.gov/criminal-fraud/foreign-corrupt-practices-act.

The legislative history of the FCPA is published by the DOJ at www.justice.gov/criminal-fraud/legislative-history.

The best source of information explaining the requirements of the FCPA is the *Resource Guide to the U.S. Foreign Corrupt Practices Act*, published by the Criminal Division of the DOJ and the Enforcement Division of the Securities and Exchange Commission (SEC). A copy of this guide is available at www.whistleblowers.org.

Resources for understanding the FCPA, including translations of how the law works in more than ten languages, are published at www.kkc.com/laws%2c-statues-and-regulations/foreign-corrupt-practices-act and www.globalwhistleblower.org.

The FCPA statute is translated into fifty languages at www.justice.gov/criminal-fraud/statutes-regulations.

The SEC publishes a list of FCPA prosecutions at www.sec.gov/spotlight/fcpa/fcpa-cases.shtml.

The following articles provide additional information and perspectives on FCPA.

Bryan Cave, "Alert: The Implications for FCPA Enforcement of the SEC's New Whistleblower Rules" (June 22, 2011); available at www.bryancave.com.

Philip M. Nichols, "The Neomercantilist Fallacy and the Contextual Reality of the Foreign Corrupt Practices Act," 53 *Harvard Journal on Legislation* 203 (Winter 2016) (broad scope of FCPA).

Daniel Grimm, "Traversing the Minefield: Joint Ventures and the Foreign Corrupt Practices Act," 9 *Virginia Law and Business Review* 91 (2014) (broad reach of FCPA).

The SEC has a web page, "FCPA Spotlight," located at www.sec.gov/spotlight/fcpa.shtml. The SEC's website also contains a list of every foreign company that sells stocks to Americans under the American Depository Receipt program.

An FCPA violation also implicates the following laws, which can give rise to additional penalties: Sarbanes-Oxley Act, Section 302 (15 U.S.C. § 7241) (accuracy of financial reports); Section 404 (15 U.S.C. § 7262) (internal controls over financial reporting); Travel Act (18 U.S.C. § 1952); as well as laws covering money laundering, mail and wire fraud, false certifications, and violations of the Internal Revenue Code.

INTERNATIONAL BANKERS/ILLEGAL U.S. ACCOUNTS

John A. Koskinen, Commissioner, Internal Revenue Service, Remarks at the U.S. Council for International Business–OECD International Tax Conference (June 3, 2014); available at www.irs.gov/PUP/irs/Commissioner%20Koskinen's%20Remarks%20at%20US%20CIB%20and%20OECD%20Int%20Tax%20Conf%20June%202014.pdf.

Matthew Allen, "Swiss-U.S. Tax Evasion Saga: Where Are We Now?" (January 2016); www.swissinfo.ch/eng/business/unfinished-business_swiss-us-tax-evasion-saga--where-are-we-now-/41924910.

IRS Press Release, "Offshore Compliance Programs Generate $8 Billion."

Documentation regarding the impact of Bradley Birkenfeld's whistleblowing is set forth in Stephen Kohn's article "$13.769 Billion Reasons to Thank Whistleblowers on Tax Day" (April 18, 2016); www.whistleblowersblog.org/2016/04/articles/news/13-769-billion-reasons-to-thank-whistleblowers-on-tax-day/.

OCEAN POLLUTION/ACT TO PREVENT POLLUTION FROM SHIPS (APPS)

The APPS whistleblower reward provision is codified at 33 U.S.C. § 1908(a).

The International Convention for the Prevention of Pollution from Ships (MARPOL 73/78) is available at http://library.arcticportal.org/1699/1/marpol.pdf.

A practical guide to the MARPOL convention is available at https://madden-maritime.files.wordpress.com/2015/08/marpol-practical-guide.pdf.

U.S. DOJ, Environment and Natural Resources Division. A motion requesting 50 percent whistleblower reward in *U.S. v. Overseas Shipholding Group, Inc.*, 06-CR-10408 (D. Mass, March 15, 2007) is available at www.globalwhistleblower.org.

Michael G. Chalos and Wayne Parker, "The Criminalization of MARPOL Violations and Maritime Accidents in the United States," 23 *University of San Francisco Maritime Law Journal* 206 (Fall 2011). Although antiwhistleblower in tone and content, this article sets forth the various laws and legal standards applicable to APPS prosecutions.

"Avoiding the APPS Magic Pipe Trap," Officer of the Watch website (November 14, 2012), offers another antiwhistleblower position; https://officerofthewatch.com/2012/11/14/avoiding-the-apps-magic-pipe-trap/.

A detailed listing of APPS cases for which rewards were paid (including copies of the indictments, plea agreements, and whistleblower reward filings) is posted at https://www.kkc.com/laws%2c-statues-and-regulations/ocean-pollution-%28apps002fmarpol%29.pdf

The Marine Defenders organization publishes information on APPS whistleblower rules, and also has a handbook designed to help seamen involved in government investigations. *See* www.marinedefenders.com/commercial/rewards.php.

U.S. v. Efploia Shipping Co. S.A., Case 1:11-cr-00652-MJG, Bench Decision *Re: Whistleblower Award* (ECF Doc. 80) (D. Maryland) (April 25, 2016). The Court discussed congressional intent behind the APPS whistleblower provision and the fact that most, if not all, APPS prosecutions come from evidence provided by whistleblowers.

DOJ press release regarding the Efploia Shipping Company and Aquarosa Shipping case is available at www.justice.gov/opa/pr/two-shipping-corpora tions-plead-guilty-and-are-sentenced-maryland-obstruction-justice-and.

POLITICAL ASYLUM
In interpreting the U.S. immigration laws, numerous courts have recognized that persons who blow the whistle in their foreign countries can, under certain circumstances, obtain political asylum in the United States. The first case to recognize whistleblowing as a potential justification for political asylum was *Grava v. INS*, 205 F.3d 1177 (9th Cir. 2000). *Antonyan v. Holder*, 642 F.3d 1250 (9th Cir. 2011) broadened the scope of the *Grava* holding.

Since 2000 the *Grava* case has been followed in other federal court jurisdictions that considered this issue. *See*, for example, *Bu v. Gonzales*, 490 F.3d 424 (6th Cir. 2007); *Cao v. Attorney General*, 407 F.3d 146 (3rd. Cir. 2005); *Rodas Castro v. Holder*, 597 F.3d 93 (2nd Cir. 2010); *Haxhiu v. Mukasey*, 519 F.3d 685 (7th Cir. 2008); *Hayrapetyan v. Mukasey*, 534F.3d 1330 (10th Cir. 2008); *Zhu v. Mukasey*, 537 F.3d 1034 (9th Cir. 2008).

Aimee L. Mayer-Salins, "Asylum and Withholding of Removal Claims Involving Corruption and Whistleblowing," published in DOJ newsletter Immigration Law Advisor; available at www.justice.gov/sites/default/files/eoir/pages/attachments/2015/02/26/vol9no2ed.pdf.

Information on the Canadian offshore tax reward program is published online by the Canadian Revenue Agency, at http://www.cra-arc.gc.ca/gncy/cmplnc/otip-pdife/menu-eng.html.

Information on the Ontario Securities Commission's whistleblower program is located online at http://www.osc.gov.on.ca/en/whistleblower.htm.

RESOURCES FOR WHISTLEBLOWERS

The author has created an online resource that links to the key statutes, cases and supporting materials cited to in the Handbook. To obtain access to this on-line library go to www.kkc.com/Handbook.

Commodity Futures Trading Commission
Three Lafayette Centre
1155 21st St. NW
Washington, DC 20581
www.cftc.gov
www.whistleblower.gov (website for Office of the Whistleblower)

Website of information on filing claims for rewards under the Dodd-Frank Act. Rewards claims related to fraud in the commodities markets. Rewards must be filed in accordance with the rules published by this Commission.

Department of Defense
Office of Inspector General
Defense Hotline Compliance Complaints
www.dodig.mil/HOTLINE

Information on filing a DoD-related whistleblower complaint, including complaints related to national security issues.

Department of Justice
Civil Division
Commercial Litigation Branch
Civil Fraud Section
www.justice.gov/civil/frauds

Information on the False Claims Act, including an online primer outlining the law and press releases on DOJ cases.

Equal Employment Opportunity Commission (EEOC)
1801 L St. NW
Washington, DC 20507
www.eeoc.gov

The EEOC has jurisdiction over the antiretaliation laws governing traditional employment discrimination matters such as race, sex, or age. The website provides detailed instructions on filing complaints, analysis of legal rights, and reprint copies of major employee protection laws.

Federal Aviation Administration (FAA)
800 Independence Ave. SW
Washington, DC 20591
www.faa.gov.gov/about/initiatives/whistleblower

The FAA website on the airline whistleblower law includes a page entitled "How do I file a whistleblower complaint?"

Inspectors General
Ignet/Federal Inspectors General Web Page
www.ignet.gov

This website contains a central point of contact for all fifty-seven Offices of Inspector General and contact points for OIG oversight bodies. The Inspectors General have responsibility for investigating waste, fraud, and abuse in federal programs.

Internal Revenue Service
Whistleblower Office
SE: WO 1111
Constitution Ave. NW
Washington, DC 20224
http://irs.gov/compliance
www.irs.gov/uac/whistleblower-informant-award (Office of the Whistleblower web page)

The IRS Whistleblower Office's website has information on informant awards and useful links, including links to the tax whistleblower statute and the official government forms used for filing IRS whistleblower reward claims.

Merit Systems Protection Board
1615 M Street, N.W.
Washington, D.C. 20419
(202) 653-7200
(202) 653-7130 (Fax)
email: mspb@mspb.gov
website: www.mspb.gov

The MSPB has jurisdiction over all Whistleblower Protection Act cases filed by federal employees.

National Whistleblower Legal Defense
and Education Fund/National Whistleblower Center
3238 P St. NW
Washington, DC 20007-2756
Phone: 202-342-1902
www.whistleblowers.org

The National Whistleblower Legal Defense and Education Fund and the National Whistleblower Center (NWC) work together to promote stronger legal protections for whistleblowers. Their website provides information on legislative updates, advocacy alerts, publications, attorney referrals, and employee rights.

U.S. Department of Justice
Freedom of Information Act Homepage
www.usdoj.gov/04foia

The Department of Justice web page on the Freedom of Information Act (FOIA) lists FOIA contact personnel at every federal agency and provides detailed information on filing FOIA requests.

U.S. Department of Labor
Occupational Safety and Health Administration (OSHA)
200 Connecticut Ave. NW
Washington, DC 20210
www.osha.gov
www.whistleblowers.gov (OSHA Whistleblower Programs web page)

The OSHA website contains information regarding worker complaints and resources under DOL-administered whistleblower statutes. OSHA has a special whistleblower rights web page published by the Office of Whistleblower Protection Program. The page links to the nineteen federal whistleblower laws for which OSHA is responsible, along with controlling regulations.

U.S. Department of Labor
Office of Administrative Law Judges (OALJ)
800 K St. NW, Ste. 400N
Washington, DC 20210
www.oalj.dol.gov

The OALJ conducts administrative adjudications under numerous federal whistleblower laws (including corporate and environmental). This site contains copies of DOL OALJ rulings, administrative procedures, and a periodic newsletter highlighting DOL whistleblower decisions. It is a key online resource for all whistleblower laws administered by the Department of Labor.

U.S. Military
Office of Naval Inspector General
Building 172
1254 Ninth St. SE
Washington DC Naval Yard, 20374
www.ig.navy.mil/complaints

The Navy's Office of Inspector General publishes information on military whistleblowing, including links to the military whistleblower law and regulations and a link to the Department of Defense Inspector General.

U.S. Office of Special Counsel
1730 M St. NW, Ste. 201
Washington, DC 20036-4505
www.osc.gov

The Office of Special Counsel (OSC) website contains information on the Whistleblower Protection Act (WPA), the law that covers most federal employee whistleblowers The site contains the OSC Form 11, which federal employees must use to file WPA claims with OSC.

U.S. Securities and Exchange Commission
SEC Office of the Whistleblower
100 F St. NE
Mail Stop 5971
Washington, DC 20549
Fax number: 703-813-9322
www.sec.gov/whistleblower

The SEC's Whistleblower Office has an online process for filing complaints with the SEC and also contains information and links related to the Dodd-Frank whistleblower provisions. The website contains information on how to file whistleblower reward claims in accordance with SEC rules.

INDEX

A

Abbott Labs, 318

Abu-Ghraib prison, 320

   See also Manning, Chelsea

Act to Prevent Pollution from Ships (APPS),
137, 138, 139–44, 320,
336, 369

   impact of, 144

   international applications of, 341, 347

   reward law in, 17, 20, 61, 140–41, 147,
309, 358

Affordable Care Act, 282, 307

Age Discrimination in Employment Act,
41, 389

Airline Safety Act, 53, 54, 282, 307, 386

   statute of limitations on, 259

   See also Aviation Investment and
Reform Act

Alabama, whistleblower protections, 67, 393

Alaska, whistleblower protections, 67, 393

Alaska Sea Life Center, 142

Alcalel-Lucent, fine of, 122, 458

Alcatl Lucent, 347

Alito, Justice Samuel, 153, 200, 290

Allegheny Co. (PA), whistleblower
protection in, 68, 84

Alternative Fines Act, 127

   See also Foreign Corrupt Practices Act
(FCPA)

American Depository Receipts (ADRs),
123, 124

   See also Foreign Corrupt Practices Act
(FCPA)

American Recovery and Reinvestment Act,
2007, 370

Americans with Disabilities Act, 41, 389

Amerigroup Insurance, 316

Anaconda Wire & Cable Co., 24

Analogic Corp., 461

Andrew, Michael, 184

Anheuser-Busch InBev, 123, 461

Antarctic Conservation Act, 147

Anti-Bribery Convention, 119

Aquarosa shipping company, 138, 140

arbitration agreements, 298–99

   See also employees

Arizona, whistleblower protection, 67, 393

Arkansas, whistleblower protection, 67, 394

armed forces. *See* Military Whistleblower
Protection Act

Armor Holdings, 316

   fine of, 458

Association of Certified Fraud Examiners,
116, 193

AstraZeneca, 461

Atchison, Chuck, 198–99

Atomic Energy Act, 53, 54, 187, 282, 383

   filing cases with DOL, 275

attorneys

   fees of, 86, 289–92

   and protected disclosures, 188–90

"at will" doctrine, 65, 67, 313

   See also employees

auditors, 227–31

Automobile Safety Whistleblower Act,
282, 386

Auto Safety Act, 310

auto workers

   protections for, 17, 129, 130–31

   rewards for whistleblowing, 131–35

   See also Auto Safety Act

Aviation Investment and Reform Act, 33

   See also Airline Safety Act

B

B. Braun Melsungen AG, 346

Baer, Bill, 75

BAE Systems, fine of, 122, 458

bank fraud

   stature of limitations on, 258

   UBS scandal, 29–30, 89–90, 343, 344

   and whistleblower protection, 34, 367

   See also financial fraud; tax fraud;
specific laws

Bank Leumin, 344
Bank of America, 316, 318
Bank of New York (BNY) Mellon, 48–49, 51
Barko, Harry, 219, 221, 222
Barrday, 346
Bayer Corp., 318
Berman, Howard, 25, 73
Beverly Enterprises, Inc., 316
BHP Billiton, 463
Bill of Rights, 174, 179, 333, 335
    See also First Amendment
Birkenfeld, Bradley, 29–30, 89–90, 91,
    320, 343
Bituminous Coal Operators Assoc., 196
Bloch, Peter, 304
BNP Paribas, 346
BNY Mellon, 462
Boehme, Donna, 214
Boeing, 318
Boese, John T., 76
BP/Amoco, 318
Brandeis, Justice Louis, 335
Breaux, Sen. John, 148, 294
Brewer, James, 327
bribery, international. *See* Foreign Corrupt
    Practices Act (FCPA)
Bristol-Myers Squibb, 316, 462
Brown & Root. *See* Kellogg Brown & Root
    (KBR)
Brown & Williamson Tobacco Corp., 297
Bucy, Pamela, 21
Bureau of Consumer Financial Protection,
    34–35
Bush, Pres. George W., 304

C

California
    and "at will" doctrine, 65
    judgment against, 318
    recording of conversations in, 240
    whistleblower protections, 67, 68, 84,
        359, 394
Canada, whistleblower laws in, 352–55
Carnegie-Illinois Steel Corp., 24
Carnival Corporation, 144
Carter, Pres. Jimmy, 169
Ceballos, Richard, 199–201, 205

Central Intelligence Agency (CIA), 311, 382
    employees of and Civil Reform Act, 169
    Inspector General Act, 381
Ceresney, Andrew, 121
Challenger disaster, 15, 320
Channing, William, 332
Chevron Corp., 122, 318, 458
Chicago (IL), whistleblower protection
    in, 68, 84
Chrysler Corporation, 129
Ciena Capital, LLC., 316
Cisco Systems, 316
Citigroup, 316
Civil Rights Act, 1871, 47, 153, 289, 310,
    362, 376, 390
    protected disclosure under, 182, 185
    witness protection under, 64
Civil Rights Act, 1964
    anti-retaliation provisions in, 41
    Title VII, 155, 168, 176, 275, 289,
        312, 389
Civil Rights Attorney Fee Act, 289, 363
Civil Service Reform Act, 1978, 154, 155,
    169, 303
    and FBI agents, 175
    and WPA, 155
claims
    attorney's fees for, 289–92
    filing False Claims Act claim, 77–87
    filing SEA or CEA, 106–14
    statute of limitations on, 257–61
    See also employees; whistleblowers
Clean Air Act, 46, 169, 275, 307, 369
Clean Water Act, 242, 307
Clinton, Pres. Bill, 175, 320
"Close the Contractor Fraud Loophole
    Act," 213
Coast Guard. *See* seamen, protection for;
    U.S. Coast Guard
Colorado, whistleblower protection in, 67,
    68, 84, 359, 394
Columbia River Conservations Fund, 142
Comanche Peak nuclear power plant, 198
Commodity Exchange Act (CEA), 2, 42, 50,
    104, 147
    anti-retaliation provisions in, 312
    Dodd-Frank's amendments to, 8

international applications of, 341–42
protected disclosures under, 180, 183
qui tam (reward) law in, 10, 19–20, 43–44, 103, 104, 105, 310, 320, 357, 375
stature of limitations on, 258
steps for filing *qui tam,* 106–14
Commodity Futures Trading Commission, 8, 106, 107, 229, 235
whistleblower rules of, 113, 114
companies
and "after-acquired evidence" rule, 246–47
and "at-will" doctrine, 65
and "deliberate ignorance" standard, 27
detecting fraud in, 5–6, 193
and "exhaustion" doctrine, 274–75
and FCPA, 119–20, 122–23, 126
"hotlines" and compliance programs of, 207–18, 222–29
internal compliance programs in, 133–34
interrogatories of, 266
list of fines paid by, 316–18
privacy rules of, 237
reaction to disclosures, 251–55
rewards for auditors/compliance officials of, 227–31
and settlement agreements, 293–302
and whistleblower laws, 68
See also compliance programs; employees; *specific companies*
compliance programs
auditors and compliance officials of, 227–31
effectiveness of, 211–17
KBR's, 219–21
lawyer-run, 222–26
See also companies
Comprehensive Environmental Response, Compensation and Liability Act, 46
See also Superfund Act
Comptroller of the Currency, 168
Connecticut
recording of conversations in, 240
whistleblower protections, 67, 68, 84, 359, 395
Conoco Phillips, 317, 318
Consumer Financial Protection Act, 2010, 282, 307, 365

Consumer Financial Protection Bureau, 44
Consumer Leasing Act, 35
Consumer Product Safety Act, 1972, 35, 52, 282, 307
attorney fee provision in, 290
filing cases with DOL, 275
statute of limitations on, 259
Consumer Product Safety Act, 2008, 16, 37–38, 53, 55, 363
Contractor Protection Act of 2016, 38–39
Contractor Whistleblower Act, 282
Convention on Combating Bribery of Foreign Public Officials in International Transactions, 119
Convention on International Trade in Endangered Species of Wild Flora and Fauna (CITES), 146
conversations, taping, 238–42
See also employees
Cooper, Cynthia, 212
Corporate and Criminal Fraud Accountability Act, 53–54
See also Sarbanes-Oxley Act (SOX)
corporations. *See* companies; specific corporations
Council of Europe, 339
courts. *See* U.S. Court of Appeals; U.S. Supreme Court; federal laws; state laws
Credit Suisse bank, 344
Cruden, John, 146
CVS Corp., 317

D
Daimler, AG, 458
damages. *See* employees
Davis, Roger S., 238–39
Defend Trade Secrets Act, 61–62, 368
Defense Authorization Act, 2013, 39
Defense Intelligence Agency (DIA), 169, 382
DeGuelle, Michael J., 40
Delaware, whistleblower protections in, 67, 68, 84, 359, 395
Delery, Stuart, 80
"deliberate ignorance" standard, 27
See also False Claims Act
departments, government. *See specific U.S. departments*

Deutsche Bank, 317
disclosures, protected, 179–91, 270–71
  to Congress, 181–82
  to federal law enforcement, 181
  to news media, 184–85
  statutory mandates for, 180
  See also employees; whistleblowers
discovery process, 263–68
  checklist for, 431–39
  See also employees; whistleblowers
District of Columbia
  recording of conversations in, 240
  whistleblower protections, 67, 68, 84,
    282, 359, 396
documentation, 265–66
  See also employees; whistleblowers
Dodd, Sen. Christopher, 41
Dodd-Frank Wall Street Reform and
    Consumer Protection Act, 7, 8, 16–17,
    19, 34–37, 41–44, 336
  anti-retaliation provisions, 290
  on arbitration agreements, 299
  checklist for SEC rewards, 440–60
  confidentiality of claims, 272
  Consumer Financial Protection Act, 34
  "first to file" rule, 259
  protected disclosures under, 181, 185
  qui tam (reward) laws in, 45, 103–5, 109,
    217, 218
  and Sarbanes-Oxley Act, 53
  steps for filing claims, 106–14
  whistleblower protection in, 40, 41–44,
    202–4, 206, 364–65, 368
  See also Consumer Financial
    Protection Act
Douglas, Justice William, 171
Drake, Thomas, 171

E

EBASCO Constructors, Inc., 208–9
Efploia shipping company, 138, 140
Eli Lilly and Company, 22, 85, 317
Ellery, William, 332
Ellsberg, Daniel, 170–71, 176
Employee Polygraph Protection Act, 41
Employee Retirement Income Security
    Act, 41

employees, 193–206
  adverse actions to, 273–74
  "after-acquired evidence" rule, 246–47
  arbitration agreements and settlements
    by, 293–302
  and attorney fees, 289–92
  and "at will" doctrine, 65–66
  checklist for rewards from SEC, 440–60
  checklist of legal requirements, 269–70
  and Civil Rights Act claims, 64
  company's reaction to disclosures, 251–55
  confidentiality for, 7–9
  and "contributing factor" test, 281–83
  damages for, 285–88
  discovery process by, 263–68, 431–39
  documentary evidence for, 244–45,
    247–49, 265–66
  and employment contracts/waivers,
    300–302
  and environmental laws, 45–46
  and "exhaustion" doctrine, 274–75
  foreign workers, 17
  "good faith" standard, 272–73
  impact of fraud detection by, 5–7
  laws for protection, 17–18
  and news media, 184–85
  on-the-job safety of, 57–60
  preserving evidence, 245
  proof of retaliation checklist, 416–30
  protected disclosures/activity of, 179–91,
    270–71
  protecting e-mails and computers, 243–44
  proving causation, 277–81
  reinstatement provisions for, 62–63
  removing documents, 242–43, 248
  reporting fraud to SEC, 232–35
  and retaliation cases, 271–72, 364
  reward laws for, 10, 11–14, 19, 21–22, 45
  and settlement agreements, 293–302
  sharing concerns with supervisors, 179,
    186, 193–202
  and "stimulus" claims, 38–39
  taping conversations, 238–42
  and "trade secrets," 61–62
  unions and lawful disclosures, 45
  using "hotlines" and compliance
    programs, 207–18, 222–26

and workplace discrimination, 389-92
  See also federal employees; whistleblowers;
    specific laws
employers. *See* companies
Endangered Species Act, 3, 20, 145, 147,
    149, 310, 320
  international applications of, 341
  reward laws in, 145-49, 345, 358
Energy Reorganization Act, 60, 68, 307
English, Vera, 68-69, 258-60
Enhancement Act, 39, 201-2
ENI, fine of, 122, 458
Enron, 53, 54, 194, 211-12, 320
  collapse of, 6
Environmental Law Reporter, article in, 148
environmental laws, 45-46, 168, 303, 307
  attorney fee provision in, 290
  statute of limitation on claims, 259
  and whistleblower protections, 369-70
  See also Environmental Protection Agency
    (EPA); *specific laws*
Environmental Protection Agency (EPA), 45
  IG and Dr. Marcus, 305
  and Sanjour, 153, 154, 165, 167
  and whistleblowers, 168-69
Equal Credit Opportunity Act, 35
Equal Opportunity Employment
    Commission, 6
Ethics and the Health Care Compliance
    Assoc., 223
Ethics Resource Center, 5
European Union, report on whistleblowers
    in, 351

F
Fair Credit Billing Act, 35
Fair Debt Collection Practices Act, 35
Fair Labor Standards Act, 41, 391
False Claims Act (FCA), 2, 7, 19, 21-30,
    71-87, 104, 336
  amendments to, 15, 17, 25-27, 28, 60-61
  attorney fee provision in, 290
  cap on rewards, 147
  Chamber of Commerce challenge
    to, 334
  confidentiality provision, 7-8, 272
  definition of "false claim," 71-73

and Eli Lilly and Co., 22
examples of frauds covered under, 410-15
and federal contractors, 39
filing evidence under, 253
fines collected under, 12-13
and FIRREA case, 50
"first to file" rule of, 257-58, 260
and health care fraud, 55
and hotline allegations, 217
international applications of, 341, 346-47
modernization of, 3-5, 7
original source requirement in, 108
protected disclosures under, 180, 182,
    183, 185, 371
qui tam (reward) laws in, 10-12, 14, 211,
    215, 283, 288, 308-9, 334, 357, 374
and Rivera case, 73-74
on settlement agreements, 297-98
state and municipal, 66, 68, 359-60
stature of limitations on, 258
steps for filing, 77-87
success of, 28-30, 315-20
and tax fraud, 91-92, 98
False Claims Correction Act, 28
False Claims Reform Act, 25-27
Family and Medical leave Act, 41, 390
FBI Whistleblower Protection Act, 312
Federal Acquisitions Regulations
    (FAR), 213, 216
Federal Acquisitions Regulatory Council, 213
federal agencies. *See* United States;
    specific agencies
Federal Bureau of Investigation (FBI), 17
  employees of and Civil Reform Act, 169
  and Turner, 322-25
  whistleblower protection, 175, 382
federal contractors, regulations for, 370-71
Federal Deposit Insurance Act, 35
federal employees, 155-77
  Ceballos' case, 199-202
  contacting Congress, 163
  and environmental cases, 168-69
  FBI whistleblower protection, 175
  First Amendment protection for, 47,
    151-54, 163-67
  in intelligence agencies, 169-75
  options beyond WPA, 167-69

and protected disclosures, 181–82, 185
Title VII, Civil Rights Act and Privacy Act protections, 176
and WPA, 155–63, 311–13
See also whistleblowers; employees
federal laws, 33–64
  airline safety, 33, 53, 54, 259, 282
  banking and financial institutions, 34, 47–51
  Contractor Protection Act, 38–39
  and "contributing factor" test, 282
  covering whistleblowers, 308–13
  discrimination law, 40–41
  Dodd-Frank Act, 34–37, 41–45
  environmental, 45–47
  False Claims Act, 60–61
  food safety, 51–52
  Foreign Corrupt Practices Act, 52–54
  "good faith" standard, 272–73
  health care, 55
  immigration and asylum, 350, 355
  military/armed services, 55–56
  mine safety, 56
  nuclear safety, 57
  obstruction of justice, 39–40, 301
  pipeline safety, 60
  product safety, 37–38
  protecting whistleblowers, 303–13, 361–92
  for seamen, 61
  trade secrets, 61–62
  transportation, 62–64
  witness protection, 64
  workplace safety, 57–60
  See also specific laws; First Amendment
Federal Mine and Health and Safety Act, 1969, 195–97
Federal Reserve, 168
  Bureau of Consumer Financial Protection, 34–35
financial commodities. *See* Commodity Exchange Act (CEA)
financial fraud, 103–5
  and Dodd-Frank Act, 16–17, 41–44, 103–5
  and federal employees, 168
  and FIRREA, 47–51
  Madoff's case, 16, 103
  against shareholders, 53–54
  statutes of limitations on, 259
  steps for filing *qui tam*, 106–14
  See also bank fraud; tax fraud
Financial Institutions Reform, Recovery and Enforcement Act (FIRREA), 3, 34, 47–51
  reward law in, 310, 358
First Amendment, 47, 151–54, 175, 179, 181, 310–11
  and public employees, 163, 164, 174, 185
  stature of limitations on cases, 258
  whistleblower protection under, 184, 199–202, 334–35, 361–62
Fish and Wildlife Improvement Act, 3, 147–48, 310
  reward laws in, 345, 358, 369
Fish and Wildlife Service. *See* Lacey Act
FLIR Systems, 463
Florida
  recording of conversations in, 240
  whistleblower protections, 67, 68, 84, 359, 396
Florida National Keys Marine Sanctuary, 142
food safety, 51–52
Food Safety Act, 259, 307
Food Safety Modernization Act, 52, 282, 379
Foreign Corrupt Practices Act (FCPA), 2, 14, 20, 119–28, 225
  international applications of, 340, 341, 342
  provisions of, 123–28
  2015-2016 recoveries under, 461–63
  reporting violations of, 8
  reward law in, 10, 17, 43, 52, 104, 147, 309, 348, 358
foreign currency. *See* Commodity Exchange Act (CEA)
foreign workers, protection for, 17
Freedom of Information Act, 112
Frost, Lars. *See* Analogic Corp.

G

General Account Office, on government fraud, 25
General Electric Co., 318
  See also English, Vera
Georgia
  "at-will" law, 17

whistleblower protections, 67, 84, 359, 396
Georgia Power Company, 194
Gerry, Elbridge, 334
GlaxoSmithKline, 122, 317, 461
Glazer, Myron, 255
Glazer, Penina, 255
Goldstein, Ronald J., 208–10, 212, 213
Goodyear Tire & Rubber Co., 463
government workers. *See* federal employees
Grannis, Capt. John, 327, 328–29, 332
Grassley, Sen. Charles, 25, 28
  on lawyers and compliance programs, 222, 223
  tax fraud amendment by, 91, 92, 97, 99
Grava, Dionesio, 350
Grimm, Daniel, 124
Guam, whistleblower protection in, 408
Gunther, Dinah, 247–49

H
Haddock, Roger, 327
Hague Machine, 24
Hancock, John, 329, 332
Harlan, Justice John, 239
Harvard University, 318
Hawaii, whistleblower protections, 67, 68, 84, 359, 396
health care industry, whistleblowers in, 55
Helme, Rouse J., 330
Hercules, Inc., 318
Hesco Bastion Limited, 347
Hitachi, 462
Holder, Eric, 22, 24
Holland America, 144
Homeland Security Act, 2002, 381
Hopkins, Esek, 327, 328, 329–30, 332
Hospital Corporation of America, 317
hotlines, use of, 207–18
Houston Lighting and Power C., 208–9
Howard, Sen. Jacob, 23, 71
Hurley, Jacob, 51

I
Idaho, whistleblower protections, 67, 397
Illinois
  recording of conversations in, 240

whistleblower protections, 67, 68, 84, 359, 397
Indiana, whistleblower protections, 67, 68, 84, 359, 397
Infosys Technologies, 346
Ingersoll-Rand, 318
Inspector General Act, 378, 381
Institute of Internal Auditors, 204, 227
Intelligence Community Whistleblower Protection Act, 172–74, 175, 311–12, 382
Internal Revenue Act, 147, 341
Internal Revenue Code
  protected disclosures under, 180, 183
  reward law in, 55, 319–20, 357
Internal Revenue Service (IRS)
  confidentiality of claims, 272
  and Grassley Amendment, 91–92
  reward law of, 10, 19, 92–93, 309, 375, 380
  rules on whistleblower law of, 94–100
  and UBS fraud, 29–30, 89–90, 342–45
  Whistleblower Office of, 9
International Convention for Prevention of Pollution from Ships, 137
INTERPOL, on wildlife trafficking, 145–46
Iowa, whistleblower protections, 67, 68, 359, 397
Itochu, 346

J
Johnson Atoll Chemical Agent Disposal System, 58
Johnson Controls, 461
Julius Baer Group, LTD., 344

K
Kansas, whistleblower protections, 67, 398
Kansas Supreme Court, and OSHA, 59, 60
Kaplan, Lewis A., 48
Kellogg Brown & Root (KBR), 57, 198, 199, 219–21, 296–97
  fine of, 122, 458
  and Macktal's case, 293–94
Kencar Mine, 195–97
Kennedy, Justice Anthony, 165, 200
Kentucky, whistleblower protections, 67, 398
Kerr-McGee nuclear plant, 57

Key Energy Services, 461
King, Rufus, 334
Kiriakou, John, 171
Koskinen, John, 90
Kotz, Insp. Gen. David, 103

L
Lacey Act, 3, 20, 145, 146–50, 320, 336
  international applications of, 341
  reward law in, 310, 345, 348, 358
LAN Airlines, 123, 461
Langer, Sen. William, 24–25, 76–77
Las Vegas Sands, 462
laws. *See* federal laws; state laws; *specific laws*
Lawyers Comm. for Freedom of the Press,
  booklet by, 240
Lay, Kenneth, 194
Lewis, David, 320
Lincoln, Pres. Abraham, 23, 60
  and False Claims Act, 99–100
Lincoln Fabrics, 346
Lloyd-LaFollette Act, 163, 181–82, 378
Lockheed Martin, 317
logging, illegal. See Lacey Act
Longshore & Harbor Workers'
  Compensation Act, 391
Lopez, German, 238
Lopez, Salvador, 139
Los Angeles Dept. of Water and Power, 317
Lothrop, Barnabas, 327
Louis Dreyfus Group, 346
Louisiana, whistleblower protection in,
  84, 359, 398

M
Mackowiak, Robert, 197–98
Macktal, Joseph J., Jr., 293–96
MacLean, Robert J., 165–66, 167
Madison, James, 179, 334
Madoff, Bernard, 16, 103
Magnitsky, Sergei, 339–40
Maine, whistleblower protections, 60, 67, 399
Major Frauds Act, 61, 372, 375
Manning, Chelsea, 186
MAP-21 (auto safety), 307
Marcus, Dr. William, 305
Markopolos, Harry, 13, 16

Marshall, Justice Thurgood, 151–52, 165, 174
Martin, Lynn, 209
Marvin, Richard, 327, 329–30, 331, 332
Maryland
  recording of conversations in, 240
  whistleblower protections, 67, 68, 84,
    359, 399
Masood, Shehla, 339
Massachusetts
  recording of conversations in, 240
  whistleblower protections, 67, 68, 84,
    359, 399
McAuliffe, Christa, 15
MCI/WorldCom, 318
Mead Johnson Nutrition, 463
Medco Health Solutions, 319
Medicare fraud, and reward laws, 14
Mellon Bank, 318
Merck, 317
Merit Systems Protection Board (MSPB),
    47, 156, 158, 159, 304
  filing case with, 160–62, 163
  See also Whistleblower Protection Act
    (WPA)
Michigan
  recording of conversations in, 240
  whistleblower protections, 67, 68, 84,
    359, 400
Migrant and Seasonal Agricultural Workers
    Act, 41, 391
Military Whistleblower Protection Act, 55–56
Mine Health and Safety Act, 56, 202, 275, 384
  and *Phillips* decision, 195, 196, 197
Minnesota, whistleblower protections, 67,
    68, 359, 400
Mississippi, whistleblower protections,
    67, 400
Missouri, whistleblower protections, 67, 401
Mohlala, Jimmy, 339
"Monetary Rewards for Wildlife Whistleblowers"
    (article), 148
Monsanto Corp., fine of, 459
Montana
  recording of conversations in, 240
  whistleblower protections, 67, 84, 359, 401
Morris, Robert, 334
Morton-Thiokol, 15

Motor Vehicle Safety Whistleblower Act,
    2, 386
    international application of, 348
    reward law in, 20, 358
Moving Ahead for Progress in the 21st
    Century Act, 130–31

N

NASA (National Aeronautics Space
    Administration), 15
National Assoc. of Manufacturers, 37
National Geographic Society, 148
National Geospatial Intelligence Agency, 169
National Highway Transportation Safety
    Administration (NHTSA)
    2014 recalls, 131
    and Sheridan, 129
National Labor Relations Act, 41, 188, 392
National Marine Fisheries Service, 148
National Reconnaissance Office, 169
National Security Agency (NSA), 311, 382
    employees of and Civil Reform Act, 169
    and Snowden, 172
National Transit Systems Security Act, 63,
    307, 387
National Whistleblower Appreciation Day,
    333–34
National Whistleblower Center (NWC),
    148, 202–3, 296
Natural Resources Defense Council, 348
Nebraska, whistleblower protections,
    67, 401
Neustar, Inc., 116
Nevada
    recording of conversations in, 240
    whistleblower protections, 67, 68, 84,
    359, 401
New Hampshire
    recording of conversations in, 240
    whistleblower protections, 67, 68, 84,
    359, 402
New Jersey, whistleblower protections, 17,
    67, 68, 84, 360, 402
New Mexico, whistleblower protections, 67,
    68, 84, 360, 402
New York, whistleblower protections, 67,
    68, 84, 360, 403

New York City (NY), False Claims Act in, 84
New York Times, 170, 171
Nichols, Philip M., 120
Nixon, Pres. Richard, 320
    and Watergate scandal, 170
No Fear Act, 378
Nordion Inc., 462
North Carolina, whistleblower protections,
    67, 68, 84, 360, 403
North Dakota, whistleblower protections,
    67, 403
Northrop Grumman, 317
Norwegian Cruise Lines, 144
Novartis International AG, 123, 462
nuclear power plants
    Kerr-McGee, 57
    South Texas Project, 208–10
Nuclear Regulatory Commission (NRC),
    57, 167
    English's case, 258
    Macktal's case, 293, 294
Nuclear Safety Act, 307
nuclear safety laws, 57, 307
    attorney fee provision in, 290
    cases involving, 197–99
    statute of limitation on, 259
    and whistleblower protection, 383
Nu Skin Enterprises, 461

O

Obama, Pres. Barack, 304
    health care program of, 55
    stimulus package of, 16, 38–39
    and Trade Secrets Act, 61
    and whistleblower protection, 311, 382
    on wildlife trafficking, 146
Occupational Safety and Health Act
    (OSHA), 57, 303, 306, 384
Occupational Safety and Health
    Administration (OSHA), 6, 57–60,
    183, 185
    and DOL-adminstered laws, 46
    and MAP-21, 130
    review of settlement agreements, 295–96
    statute of limitation on, 259
Ocean Pollution Act, 3
oceans, pollution of, 3, 137–44

See also Act to Prevent Pollution from
  Ships (APPS)
Och-Ziff Capital Management Group,
  122, 461
O'Conner, Justice Sandra Day, 278–79
Office Depot, 318
OfficeMax, 318
Office of Inspector General, 80, 304–5
  and military whistleblowers, 56
Office of Special Counsel (OSC), 47, 158–59,
  160, 162, 303–4
  See also Whistleblower Protection Act
  (WPA)
Office of the Director of National
  Intelligence, 169
Officer of the Watch, 137
Ohio, whistleblower protections, 67, 404
Oklahoma, whistleblower protection in, 68,
  84, 360, 404
Oracle, 317
Oregon
  FCA case in, 76
  whistleblower protections, 67, 405
Organon International, 346

P
Patient Protection and Affordable Care Act,
  55, 379
PBSJ Corp., 463
Peanut Corporation of America, 51–52
Pennsylvania
  recording of conversations in, 240
  whistleblower protections, 67, 405
Pentagon Papers. *See* Ellsberg, Daniel
Petermann, Peter, 65
Pfizer, Inc., 317
Philadelphia (PA), whistleblower protection
  in, 68, 84
Phillips, Frank, 195–97, 205
Pickering, Marvin, 151–52, 167
Pilot Program for Enhancement of
  Contractor Protections, 39
Pipeline Safety Improvement Act, 60, 282,
  307, 369
"Practical Guide to Taping Phone Calls
  and In-Person Conversations in the 50
  States and D.C.," 240

Pratt & Whitney, 317
Prendergast, Tom, 24
PricewaterhouseCoopers, 116, 198
  study by, 193, 194
Princess Cruise Lines, 144
Princeton Review, 318
Privacy Act, 134, 155, 245, 385, 436
  and access to federal court, 312
  and Ellsberg, 176
Privacy Rights Clearinghouse, 244
Protection of Seaman Against
  Discrimination law, 61
PTC, 462
Public Contractor Employee Protection, 61
public employees. *See* federal employees
public transportation. *See* National Transit
  Systems Security Act
Puerto Rico, whistleblower protection
  in, 409
Puget Sound Marine Conservations
  Fund, 142
Purdue Frederick Co., 317

Q
Qualcomm, 462
Quality Technology Co. *See* Tennessee
  Valley Authority (TVA)
qui tam laws, 19–21, 29, 33, 60, 283, 357–60
  and arbitration agreements, 299
  and Birkenfeld, 30
  damages under, 287
  in Dodd-Frank Act, 42–44, 103–5
  and IRS employees, 55
  and protected disclosures, 180–81,
  182, 183
  steps for filing financial fraud claims,
  106–14, 117
  and tax fraud, 91–101
  See also False Claims Act (FCA);
  specific laws

R
Racketeer Influenced and Corrupt
  Organizations Act (RICO), 40
Railroad Safety Act, 282, 307, 388
Railroad Safety Labor Act, 63
Ranbaxy Laboratories, 347

Reagan, Pres. Ronald, 25
Reed, John, 327
regulatory agents, disclosures to, 184
retaliation cases, 85, 111
   and federal employees, 156, 168
   right to discovery in, 431–39
   by service members, 56
   statute of limitations on, 258–59
   See also employees; whistleblowers
reward laws, 10, 11–14, 308–10
   and non-government organizations
     (NGOs), 348, 349
   See also qui tam laws; *specific laws*
Reyl, Francois, 89
Rhinoceros and Tiger Conservation Act, 147
Rhode Island, whistleblower protection in,
   67, 68, 84, 360, 405
Rivera, Yarushka, 73–74
Roberts, Justice John, 166, 200
Roche Biomedical Laboratories, 318
Rockwell International, 83, 318, 374
Roosevelt, Pres. Theodore, 163, 181
Royal Caribbean, 144
Royal Dutch Shell, 346

S
Safe Containers for International Cargo
   Act, 388
Safe Drinking Water Act, 46, 169, 307, 369
safety, workplace. *See* Occupational Safety
   and Health Act (OSHA)
salmonella outbreak. *See* food safety
SandRidge Energy case, 111
Sanjour, William, 165, 167
Sap SE, 462
Sarbanes-Oxley Act (SOX), 34, 35, 38, 182,
   282, 293, 306
   access to federal court under, 307
   amendments to, 17, 44–45
   on arbitration agreements, 299
   Corporate and Criminal Fraud
     Accountability Act in, 53–54
   deadlines for filing claims under, 257
   Dodd-Frank amendments to, 112, 113
   and "exhaustion" doctrine, 274
   filing cases with DOL, 275
   and Gunther's case, 248

internal compliance programs in, 212, 213
   protected disclosure under, 188, 189
   statute of limitation on, 259
   whistleblower protection in, 39–40, 111,
     199, 203, 216, 217, 218, 366–67
Scalia, Justice Antonin, 200, 334
Schering Plough, 318
Schneiderman, Eric, 49
SciClone Pharmaceuticals, Inc., 462
Science Applications International
   Corp., 318
Scooter Store, 318
Seaman's Protection Act, 307
seamen
   counsel for, 143
   and ocean pollution, 137, 138, 139, 141
   protection for, 61, 388
   See also Act to Prevent Pollution from
     Ships (APPS)
Seamen Whistleblower Protection Act,
   282, 388
Secretary of Transportation. *See* U.S. Dept.
   of Transportation
Securitas Gmblt Werkschutz, 347
Securities and Exchange Commission
   (SEC), 8, 103, 104, 106, 107
   anti-retaliation provision of, 111, 112
   on attorneys and protected disclosure,
     189–90
   and FCPA, 52, 120, 122, 124, 125, 126–27
   "first to file" rule, 259
   international rewards by, 17, 340–41, 349
   and Macktal ruling, 296, 297
   on NDAs, 112–13
   and *qui tam* provision, 13
   on rewards for compliance officers/
     auditors, 228–29, 230
   on rewards for employees, 206, 232–35
   rewards paid, 10, 114–16
   whistleblower checklist from, 440–60
   whistleblower rules of, 44, 113–14,
     120–21
Securities Exchange Act (SEA), 2, 104, 147
   amendment to, 202
   antiretaliation law in, 40, 41, 312
   Dodd-Frank's amendments to, 8
   and FIRREA, 50

international applications of, 341
protected disclosures under, 180, 183
reward law in, 10, 19, 43–44, 103, 104,
    105, 309, 320, 357, 375
stature of limitations on, 258
steps for filing *qui tam,* 106–14
Sellers, James, 327
Senate Banking Committee, and 2008
    recession, 103
Serono, 346
service members. *See* Military Whistleblower
    Protection Act
settlements, 293–302
    arbitration agreements, 298–99
    Macktal case, 294–95
    restrictive, 297–98
Shaw, Samuel, 327, 330, 331, 332
Shell Oil Co., 318
Sheridan, Paul, 129–30, 131
shipowners. *See* oceans, pollution of; Act to
    Prevent Pollution from Ships (APPS)
Siemens, fine of, 122, 459
Silkwood, Karen, 57
Simpson, Sen. Alan K., 294
Smithkline Beecham Clinical
    Laboratories, 318
Smithsonian Environmental Research, 142
Smithsonian Institution, 148
Snamprogetti Netherlands. *See* ENI, fine of
Snepp, Frank W., III, 174
Snowden, Edward, 171, 172, 311
Society of Corporate Compliance, 223
Solid Waste Disposal Act, 1976, 46, 169,
    307, 369
South Carolina, whistleblower protections,
    67, 406
South Dakota, whistleblower protections,
    67, 406
state laws, 65–69
    "at will" doctrine in, 65
    covering whistleblowers, 62, 66, 67–68,
        312–13
    and documentary evidence, 265
    and OSHA, 59–60, 384
    and punitive damages, 45
    qui tam laws, 45, 312–13, 336
    State False Claims Acts, 2

on taping conversations, 240
    See also specific states
Stevens, Justice John Paul, 201
Stewart, Justice Potter, 171
Stillman, George, 327
Stimulus Spending Act, 282
stock market, scandals in, 5
subpoenas, 265, 266
Superfund Act, 46, 169, 259, 307, 369
Supreme Foodservice FZE, 346
Surface Mining Act, 46, 369
Surface Transportation Act, 33, 53, 282, 307
    appeals in, 62, 63

T

Taft, Pres. William, 18, 163
tax fraud, 91–101
    factors for awards, 92–93
    rules on reporting, 94–101
    UBS case, 89–90
    See also financial fraud
Tax Relief and Health Care Act, 91
Tenet Healthcare, 318
Tennessee, whistleblower protections, 67,
    68, 84, 360, 406
Tennessee Valley Authority (TVA), 210
Texaco Oil, 318
Texas, whistleblower protections, 67, 68, 84,
    360, 407
Thomas, Justice Clarence, 74, 279
    and Ceballos' case, 200
Thune, Sen. John, 131
toothpaste, contaminated, 37
Tousignant, Clifford, 51, 52
Toxic Substances Control Act, 1976, 46,
    307, 369
Toyo, Inc., 346
toys, toxic, 16, 37
TRAFFIC (wildlife trade monitoring
    network), 148
Transocean, Inc., fine of, 459
transportation safety laws, 62–64
    filing case with DOL, 275
    statute of limitation on, 259
    truck safety, 387
Tripp, Linda, 238, 320
Truman, John, 327

Trump, Pres. Donald, 156, 304
Truth in Lending Act, 35
Turner, Jane, 322–25
Tyson Foods, fine of, 459

U

U. S. Dept. of Homeland Security, and MacLean, 165–66
U. S. Dept. of Labor, statues of limitations of, 259
U. S. Dept. of Transportation, 134–35
UBS bank fraud, 29–30, 89–90, 343, 344
United Kingdom, whistleblower laws in, 340, 351
United Nations Convention against Corruption, 339
United Nations Environmental Program, 145–46
United States
  agencies protecting whistleblowers in, 303–8
  airline safety laws, 33
  banking and financial laws, 16, 34
  Convention against International Corruption, 339
  federal agencies protecting whistleblowers, 303–8
  First Congress of, 334
  first whistleblowers in, 327–32, 334
  Great Recession, 2008-09, 103
  impact of SEA and CEA, 104
  intervention in FCA case, 85–87
  and MARPOL Protocol, 137, 138, 139
  Office of Inspector General, 80
  passage of First Amendment, 334–35, 336
  reward laws in, 4, 12–14, 19–21
  suit again Bank of New York, 48–49
  tax fraud in, 91–92
  See also U.S. Congress; federal laws; *specific departments, states of*
United States Fish and Wildlife Service, 148
United Technologies, 318
Universal Health Services, Inc., 74
University of Chicago
  Booth School of Business, 6
  study by, 116–17
University of Pensylvania, 318

University of Phoenix, 318
University of Toronto, 6
U.S. Agency for International Development, 148
U.S. Chamber of Commerce, 232
  and auditors and compliance officers, 228
  on False Claims Act, 13, 334
U.S. Coast Guard
  and APPS, 138, 143
  National Response Center, 143
  whistleblower protection in, 380, 388
U.S. Congress
  auto safety rewards law, 131–33
  Civil Rights Act of 1871, 64, 153, 182, 185
  Civil Rights Attorney Fee Awards Act, 1976, 289
  and compliance programs/antiretaliation law, 212–13
  Deficit Reduction Act, 2005, 360
  and False Claims Act, 3–5, 7
  and Foreign Corrupt Practices Act, 119, 120, 126, 127
  MAP-21 (autoworkers protections), 130–31
  nuclear whistleblower laws, 57
  OSHA Act of 1970, 57, 59
  and pipeline safety, 60
  and transportation safety, 62–64
  whistleblower reward laws in, 6–7
  and wildlife protection, 145, 147
  See also federal laws
U.S. Constitution
  Bill of Rights, 179
  First Amendment, 47, 151–54, 181, 185, 310–11
U.S. Court of Appeals
  Atchison's case, 198
  on employee's conduct, 237
  Grava's case, 350
  KBR ruling, 221
  Mackowiak's case, 197–98
  Macktal's case, 294–95
  Phillips' case, 196
  protected disclosures for attorneys, 188–89
  on whistleblower protection, 204
  whistleblower reward decisions, 135
U.S. Dept. of Agriculture, and Lacey Act, 147

U.S. Dept. of Commerce, 147
U.S. Dept. of Defense, 370, 380
  and contractor fraud, 370
U.S. Dept. of Energy, 57
  and nuclear whistleblower laws, 167, 383
U.S. Dept. of Interior, 147
  on Phillips' case, 196
U.S. Dept. of Justice
  APPS cases (Environment & Natural
    Resources Div.), 138–44
  and Birkenfeld, 90
  and FCPA, 120, 121, 122, 124, 125, 126–27
  on Phillips' case, 196
  2016 rewards claims, 10
  and Swiss bank fraud, 344, 345
  and whistleblower recoveries, 12–13
U.S. Dept. of Labor, 168, 306–8
  and airline safety, 33
  and anti-retaliation law, 1
  on asbestos claims, 384
  Atchison's case, 198–99
  and Consumer Products Safety Act, 38
  environmental laws under, 46
  filing whistleblower cases with, 275
  Macktal's case, 294, 295
  and MAP21, 130
  and Mine Health and Safety Act, 56
  and protected disclosures, 185, 187, 188
  statute of limitations for claims
    under, 259
U.S. Dept. of Transportation, 132–33,
  134–35
U.S. Dept. of Treasury, and Grassley
  Amendment, 92
U.S. Patriot Act, 186
U.S. Senate
  and National Whistleblower
    Appreciation Day, 333–34
  Subcommittee on Nuclear
    Regulation, 294
U.S. Supreme Court
  attorney fees in whistleblower cases,
    290, 291
  Ceballos' case, 200
  1867 damages case, 285
  on employer's whistleblower
    harassment, 274

English's case, 69–69
First Amendment rulings, 151–52,
  153, 154
Lawson v. FMR, LLC, 54
McKennon v. Nashville Banner Publishing,
  246–47
  on Pentagon Papers, 170–71
  and protected disclosure, 182
  on public employees' free speech, 163,
    164–66
  on punitive damages, 286
  and reinstatement provisions, 63
  Rivera case, 73, 74
  Rockwell International case, 83
  on settlement agreements, 297, 299
  Snepp case, 174–75
Utah, whistleblower protections, 67, 407

V

Valeant Pharmaceuticals, 346
Van Asdale, Lena, 189
Van Asdale, Shawn, 189
Vermont, whistleblower protections, 67, 68,
  84, 360, 407
VimpelCom Ltd., 122, 461, 462
Virginia, whistleblower protections, 84,
  360, 407
Virgin Islands, whistleblower protection
  in, 409

W

Walgreens, 318
Walid Hatoum, 463
Wall Street. *See* financial fraud
Walter, Frances, 24
Warren, Justice Earl, 239
Warren (ship), 327, 328
Washington Post, 170
Washington Public Power Supply System
  (WPPS), 197
Washington State
  nuclear safety case involving, 197
  recording of conversations in, 240
  whistleblower protections, 67, 68, 84,
    360, 408
Water Pollution Control Act, 1972, 46, 369
Watkins, Sherron, 194, 212

websites, "whistleblower," 186, 187

Wegelin & Co., 344

West Virginia, whistleblower protections, 67, 408

Whistleblower: Exposing Corruption in Government and Industry (Glazer), 255

Whistleblower Protection Act (WPA), 66, 67, 154, 155–63, 282
  burdens of proof under, 162–63
  and "contributing factor" test, 281–82
  and environmental laws, 168
  and federal employees, 167–69
  filing retaliation complaint, 158–60
  filing with MSPB, 160–62
  and MacLean, 163–66
  protected conduct under, 156–57
  protected disclosure under, 166

Whistleblower Protection Enhancement Act (2012), 155

whistleblowers
  and airline safety, 33
  anonymity of, 105
  and "at will" doctrine, 65–66
  and banking industry laws, 34
  and Bureau of Consumer Financial Protection, 35
  check list for retaliation cases, 431–39
  confidentiality of, 1, 7–9
  court testimony of, 182
  damages for, 285–88
  day honoring, 333–34
  "deliberate ignorance" standard, 27
  federal agencies for, 303–8
  federal laws protecting, 361–92
  filing financial fraud claims, 106–14, 117
  and FIRREA, 49–51
  first U.S. example of, 327–32
  impact of, 193–94, 315–22
  international, 121–23, 128, 339–45, 346–55
  and national security, 169–76, 381–82
  and ocean pollution, 137, 138, 140–44
  and protected disclosures, 179–91
  protections for, 39–41, 42–45, 68–69, 195–96, 202–4, 310–13
  reporting tax fraud, 90, 91, 92–101
  reward laws for, 10, 308–10, 357–60
  rewards for auditors/compliance officers, 228–31
  state laws protecting, 393–409
  statute of limitations on claims, 257–61
  study on, 6–7
  systems governing, 1–3
  websites, 186, 187
  and wildlife trafficking, 145, 146–50, 345
  See also employees; federal employees; False Claims Act (FCA)

White, Mary Jo, 104, 111

Whitehurst, Frederic, 175, 320

"Who Blows the Whistle on Corporate Fraud" (article), 6

Wigand, Jeffrey, 297

Wild Bird Conservation Act, 147

wildlife, trafficking in, 145–50, 369

Wilkey, Malcolm, 196–97, 199

Wilkinson, J. Harvie, 184

Wisconsin, whistleblower protections, 67, 408

Wood, Roger, 58–59

Woodward, Bob, 184, 251

WorldCom, 53, 211–12

Wyoming, whistleblower protections, 67, 408

Z

Zyprexa. *See* Eli Lilly and Company